A HISTORY OF ONLINE INFORMATION SERVICES, 1963–1976

A HISTORY OF ONLINE INFORMATION SERVICES, 1963–1976

Charles P. Bourne
and
Trudi Bellardo Hahn

The MIT Press
Cambridge, Massachusetts
London, England

©2003 Massachusetts Institute of Technology

All rights reserved. No part of this book may be reproduced in any form by any electronic or mechanical means (including photocopying, recording, or information storage and retrieval) without permission in writing from the publisher.

This book was set in Times Roman by SNP Best-set Typesetter Ltd., Hong Kong.

Printed and bound in the United States of America.

Library of Congress Cataloging-in-Publication Data

Bourne, Charles P.
 A history of online information services, 1963–1976 / Charles P. Bourne and Trudi Bellardo Hahn.
  p. cm.
 Includes bibliographical references and index.
 ISBN 0-262-02538-8 (alk. paper)
 1. Information storage and retrieval systems—History. 2. Information retrieval—History. 3. Online bibliographical searching—History. 4. Online information services—History. 5. Online information services industry—History. 6. Information scientists—Biography. I. Hahn, Trudi Bellardo. II. Title.

Z699 .B647 2003
025.04′09—dc21

2002040789

10 9 8 7 6 5 4 3 2 1

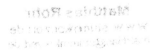

Contents

Acknowledgments		vii
Foreword		ix
Acronyms and Abbreviations		xi
Prologue		xv
1	Introduction	1
2	Early Research and Development Activities	11
3	Further Experimentation and Prototypes in Universities, Mid-1960s to Early 1970s	61
4	Experimental Systems Developed in Nonacademic Laboratories, Mid-1960s to Early 1970s	101
5	Lockheed DIALOG and Related Systems, 1961–1972	141
6	SDC ORBIT and Related Systems, 1963–1972	185
7	Computer Searching for the Legal Profession: Data Corporation, OBAR, Mead Data Central, 1964–1972	229
8	State University of New York Biomedical Communication Network, 1965–1976	259
9	The Online Industry: The Public View	279
10	Building the Online Industry: Behind the Scenes	353
11	Summing Up the Story	405
Notes		411
Summary of Online Milestones		415
Bibliography		419
Index		469

Acknowledgments

Many people gave their time and effort to this work and must be recognized. Some contributed by participating in face-to-face recorded interviews. They were: Mark Bayer, Joe Becker, Don Black, Hal Borko, Anne Caputo, Tom Crawford, Carlos Cuadra, Mike Koenig, Bob Landau, Barbara Lawrence, Dave McCarn, John Murdock, Ed Parker, Fran Spigai, Roger Summit, and Van Wente.

Other individuals were interviewed, but the comments were captured only in our notes, not on tape. These included: Pauline Angione, Bob Asleson, Pauline Atherton Cochrane, Bob Donati, Dick Giering, and Jerry Rubin.

In an effort to ensure an accurate and balanced story, relevant portions of the book draft were sent to many of the people named, or whose work was described in this text, in the hope that they would identify errors or other problems that needed fixing before publication. Thus many helpful folks reviewed a large amount of text for areas relevant to their own professional experience, and in several cases, even did additional background work to locate missing documents, help sort out conflicting claims, or answer unresolved questions. Text reviewers included: Pauline Angione, Stanley Backer, Phil Bagley, Mark Bayer, Don Black, Ted Brandhorst, Bob Burket, Dave Chafe, Bob Chartrand, Pauline Atherton Cochrane, Carlos Cuadra, Jay Cunningham, Al De Lucia, Dan Drew, Jake Feinler, Oscar Firschein, Peggy Fischer, Carl Fisher, Bob and Janice Freeman, Dick Giering, Dake Gull, Bob Hayes, Don Hillman, Allen Humphrey, Marjorie Hyslop, Larry Jenkins, Bob Katter, Sam Kaufman, Henry Kissman, Mike Koenig, Barbara Lawrence, Joe Magnino, Dick Marcus, Bill Mathews, Dave McCarn, Lucretia McClure, Linda McGinnis, Charlie Meadow, William Mitchell, Herb Ohlman, Bill Paisley, Jeff Pemberton, Dave Penniman, Mark Radwin, Roger Roach, Jerry Rubin, Claire Schultz, Win Sewell, Bob Sheldon, Roy Tally, Bill Vaden, Ann Van Camp, Van Wente, Herb White, Dan Wilde, Martha Williams, and Rose Marie Woodsmall.

Other helpful reviewers and contributors included: James Aagaard, Harry Allcock, Bob Bennett, Irene Bogolubsky, Hal Borko, Lee Burchinal, Fernando Corbató, John Crossin, Marty Cummings, Fred Damerau, Bernie Dennis, Bernie DiTano, Jan Egeland, Bahaa and Lily El-Hadidy, Art Elias, Gene Garfield, Bill Gorog, Madeline Henderson, Olaf Kays, Dave Kenton, Minuetta Kessler, Fred Kilgour, Dick Kollin, Bob Landau, Ben Lipetz, Harvey Marron, Bill Mathews, Jo Maxon-Dadd, Kurt Molholm, Alan Negus, Jessica Perry, Jane Riddle, Vic Rosenberg, Mary Jane Ruhl, Ev Wallace, Judith Wanger, Bob Wedgeworth, and Hal Wooster.

Trudi Bellardo Hahn received grants from the Council on Library Resources and Catholic University of America to support her research and writing.

Last, in addition to all the individuals named above, we want to acknowledge the reference and interlibrary loan librarians who assisted in the taxing tasks of tracking down elusive bits of documentation, as well as the extremely supportive and responsive staff at The MIT Press. Our deepest appreciation goes to our families, friends, and colleagues who abetted, or at least tolerated, our obsession with this project for so many years.

Foreword

There are many different kinds of history book: biographies, textbooks, memoirs, highly specialized monographs, and so on. Some are speculative, others less so. These different genres serve different purposes. The most basic need, however, in any field is for a basic chronology of what happened: who did what and when. In the absence of such a narrative, mythic accounts flourish. It is for this reason that the very detailed, factual narrative of the early development of online information retrieval services from 1963 to 1976 presented here is so welcome. It is the first such history, and it is very thorough. Although additions and expansions will be made, we can expect it to remain the generally accepted account. And it provides a framework for the work of others.

What follow reflects both Trudi Bellardo Hahn's detailed knowledge of online services and also Charles Bourne's personal career, during which he was personally involved in the developments chronicled in this book to a remarkable extent. Their work was very timely. As each year goes by, a few more of the pioneers whose activities are recorded pass on and their papers are lost or become difficult to understand without their help.

There has been increasing interest, in recent years, in the history of information science and information services, as distinct from the history of science or the history of computing. This work adds substantially to the resources available to us and for that we are grateful.

Michael Buckland
Berkeley, California
January 23, 2002

Acronyms and Abbreviations

For associations, organizations, government agencies, and specialized terminology. Does not include online systems, databases, or publications.

3i Co.	Information Intersciences, Inc.	BIOSIS	BioSciences Information Service
ABA	American Bar Association	BMI	Battelle Memorial Institute
ABF	American Bar Foundation	CAS	Chemical Abstracts Service
ACM	Association for Computing Machinery	CASI	Center for Aerospace Information
ACS	American Chemical Society	CBC	Center for Biomedical Communications
ADI	American Documentation Institute	CCA	Computer Corporation of America
ADL	Arthur D. Little	CCCC	Computer Command and Control Company
AEC	U.S. Atomic Energy Commission		
AEWIS	Army Electronic Welfare Information System	CCI	Computer Communications, Inc.
		CDA	Copper Development Association
AFAFC	Air Force Accounting and Finance Center	CFSTI	Clearinghouse for Scientific and Technical Information
AFCIN	Air Force Chief of Intelligence	CIA	U.S. Central Intelligence Agency
AF-ESD	Air Force Electronic Systems Division	CIS	Current Information Selection
AFIPS	American Federation of Information Processing Societies	CISTI	Canada Institute for Scientific and Technical Information
AFOSR	Air Force Office of Scientific Research	CLR	Council on Library Resources
AHI	Augmented Human Intellect	COM	computer output microfilm
AIAA	American Institute of Aeronautics and Astronautics	COMNET	Computer Network Corporation
		COSATI	Committee on Scientific and Technical Information
AICPA	American Institute for Certified Public Accountants	COSMIC	Computer Software Management and Information Center
AIP	American Institute of Physics		
ALA	American Library Association	CRC	Chemical Rubber Company
APA	American Psychological Association	CRS	Congressional Research Service
ARL	Association of Research Libraries	CSC	Computer Sciences Corporation
ARPA	Advanced Research Projects Agency	CS&M	Craveth, Swain and Moore
ASIDIC	Association for Information Dissemination Centers	CSUC	California State University and College
ASIS	American Society for Information Science	CTC	Computer Technology Center (Union Carbide)
ASIST	American Society for Information Science & Technology	DIA	U.S. Defense Intelligence Agency
		DDC	Defense Documentation Center
ASM	American Society for Metals	DIMDI	Deutsche Institute für Medizinische Dokumentation und Information
ASTIA	Armed Services Technical Information Agency		
		DMIC	Defense Metals Information Center
BCL	Battelle Columbus Laboratories	DOD	U.S. Department of Defense
BCN	Biomedical Communications Network (NLM)	DOE	U.S. Department of Energy
		DOJ	U.S. Department of Justice
BEL	James M. Barker Engineering Library (MIT)	DPF&G	Data Processing Financial and General

DRB	Canadian Defence Research Board	ICSU/AB	International Conference on Scientific Unions/Abstracting Board
DSIS	Defence Scientific Information Service	IDA	Institute for Defense Analysis
DTI	Division of Technical Information (AEC)	IEEE	Institute of Electrical and Electronic Engineers
DTIC	Defense Technical Information Center	IIA	Information Industry Association
		IDC	Information Dynamics Corporation
DTIE	Division of Technical Information Extension (AEC)	IDRC	International Development Research Centre
EMF	Excerpta Medica Foundation	IGC	Information General Corporation
EPA	U.S. Environmental Protection Agency	ILO	International Labour Office
		ILR	Institute of Library Research
ELDO	European Launcher Development Organization	INWATS	Inward Wide Area Telephone Service
ERDA	U.S. Energy Research and Development Administration	I/O	input/output
		IPC	Information Products Corporation
ERIC	Educational Research Information Center, Educational Resources Information Center	IR	information retrieval
		IRS	Information Retrieval Service (ESA)
		ISD	Information Systems Division (Data Corporation)
ESA	European Space Agency		
ESD	Electronic Systems Division (U.S. Air Force)	ISI	Institute for Scientific Information
		IST	Information Sciences Technology (COSATI panel)
ESL	Electronic Sciences Laboratory (Lockheed)		
		ITIRC	IBM Technical Information Retrieval Center
ESRIN	European Space Research Institute		
ESRO	European Space Research Organization	IUCOM	Interuniversity Communications Council
EUDISIC	European Association of Scientific Information Dissemination Centers	JICST	Japan Information Center of Science and Technology
		KASC	Knowledge Availability Systems Center
FAO	Food and Agricultural Organization		
FBC	Federal Broadcasting Corporation	KWIC	keyword-in-context
FEDLINK	Federal Library and Information Network	KWOC	keyword-out-of-context
		LAPD	Los Angeles Police Department
FID	International Federation for Documentation	LC	Library of Congress
		LCCN	Library of Congress Card Number
FOIA	Freedom of Information Act	LCELR	Lawyers' Center for Electronic Legal Research
FTD	Foreign Technology Division		
GE	General Electric	LLL	Lawrence Livermore Laboratory
HEW	U.S. Department of Health, Education, and Welfare	LMSC	Lockheed Missiles and Space Company
IAC	information analysis center	MARC	Machine-Readable Cataloging
IAEA	International Atomic Energy Authority	MCIC	Materials and Ceramics Information Center
IBM	International Business Machines	MDC	Mead Data Central

Acronyms and Abbreviations

MIT	Massachusetts Institute of Technology	ODDR&E	Office of the Director of Defense Research and Engineering
MLA	Medical Library Association	ONR	Office of Naval Research
MTL	Mead Technology Laboratories	ONULP	Ontario New Universities Library Project
NAL	National Agricultural Library	OPAC	online public access catalog
NALNET	NASA Library Network	ORNL	Oak Ridge National Laboratory
NAS	National Academy of Sciences	OSTI	Office of Science and Technical Information
NASA	National Aeronautics and Space Administration	OSU	Ohio State University
NBS	National Bureau of Standards	OTS	Office of Technical Services
NCAIR	National Center for Automated Information Retrieval	PCIC	Pittsburgh Chemical Information Center
NCCD	National Council on Crime and Delinquency	PLAN	Public Library Automation Network
NCLIS	National Commission on Libraries and Information Services	PMA	Pharmaceutical Manufacturers Association
NCR	National Cash Register	POLLS	Parliamentary On-Line Library Study
NC/STRC	North Carolina Science and Technology Research Center	PRC	Planning Research Corporation
NELINET	New England Library Information Network	PSEF	Pennsylvania Science and Engineering Foundation
NFAIS	National Federation for Abstracting and Indexing Services	PTT	Postal Telephone and Telegraph
NHI	National Heart Institute	R&D	research and development
NIH	National Institutes of Health	RADC	Rome Air Development Center
NINDB	National Institute of Neurological Diseases and Blindness	RDT&E	research, development, test, and evaluation
NINDS	National Institute of Neurological Diseases and Stroke	RFP	request for proposals
NLL	National Lending Library for Science and Technology	RISC	Remote Information Systems Center
		RISE	Research & Information Service for Education
NLM	National Library of Medicine	RLG	Research Libraries Group
NOAA	National Oceanic and Atmospheric Administration	RLIN	Research Libraries Information Network
NRC	National Research Council	SACCS	Strategic Air Command Control System
NSA	National Security Agency	sci-tech	scientific and technical
NSF	National Science Foundation	SDC	System Development Corporation
NSL	National Science Library (Canada)	SDI	Selective Dissemination of Information
NSR&DC	Naval Ship Research and Development Center	SDS	Space Documentation Service
		SIA	Science Information Association
NTIS	National Technical Information Service	SLA	Special Libraries Association
		SLAC	Stanford Linear Accelerator Center
NYSBA	New York State Bar Association	SMERC	San Mateo County Educational Reference Center
OBAR	Ohio Bar Automated Research	SOLINET	Southeastern Library Network

Acronyms and Abbreviations

SRI	Stanford Research Institute
SSIE	Smithsonian Science Information Exchange
STEP	Science and Technology Exploitation Program
STIF	Scientific and Technical Information Facility
SUNY	State University of New York
SUNY BCN	Biomedical Communication Network of the State University of New York
SURC	Syracuse University Research Corporation
TI	Texas Instruments
TIC	Technical Information Center (Lockheed)
TRIS	Transportation Research Information Service
TRW	Thompson Ramo Wooldridge, Inc.
TWX	TeleypeWriter Exchange Network
UC	University of California
UCLA	University of California-Los Angeles
UDC	Universal Decimal Classification
UKCIS	United Kingdom Chemical Information Service
UKAEA	United Kingdom Atomic Energy Authority
UMI	University Microfilms Inc.; University Microfilms International
UN	United Nations
USAF	U.S. Air Force
USC	University of Southern California
USGS	U.S. Geological Survey
USOE	U.S. Office of Education
USPHS	U.S. Public Health Service
WESRAC	Western Research Application Center
WLN	Washington Library Network
WPAFB	Wright-Patterson Air Force Base
WRISC	Western Regional Information Service Center
WRU	Western Reserve University
WSU	Washington State University

Prologue

In 1957, IBM, already a giant in the computer hardware industry, provided technical assistance and advice to Henry Ephron and 20th Century Fox to produce a movie titled *Desk Set*. Billed as a love story starring Katharine Hepburn and Spencer Tracy, it is set in the New York City headquarters of the fictional Federal Broadcasting Corporation (FBC). Most of the action takes place in the corporate library, called the "Research and Reference Department." The head librarian is Bunny Watson (played by Hepburn), a graduate of the Columbia University School of Library Service and a whiz-bang librarian with a prodigious memory and exceptional analytical abilities.

Prologue

As the story unfolds, Miss Watson's wits are pitted against Richard Sumner (played by Tracy), an IBM Methods Engineer, or, more accurately, against Mr. Sumner's invention: an Electronic Brain Machine called EMERAC (Electro-Magnetic Memory and Research Arithmetic Calculator). Mr. Sumner describes the operation of EMERAC thus: "Visual readoffs are all centralized, miniaturized, and set on schematic panels now, and then the data compiled are all automatically computed, and there's an automatic typewriter panel on it...." Mr. Asae, the president of the FBC, interrupts at this point: "I don't understand one word!" Sumner continues to describe how the computer will be used in the library to answer reference questions: "The nature of the activity is such that the operation will be different than anything that has ever been designed. It's a fascinating problem."

From the point of view of the library staff, having a computer installed in their department means that they will get air conditioning. However, Mr. Sumner predicts that EMERAC will save 6,240 man hours a year; the staff are worried, therefore, that the machine will replace them and they will be fired. Miss Watson tries to reassure them: "No machine can do our job!"

After the computer is installed, the library staff spend two weeks to feed into it all the facts stored in the library's books. An IBM (International Business Machines) programmer, Miss Warner, arrives to operate the machine. She waves a pack of punched cards in the air before she crisply types a demonstration question into the console: "How much damage is done annually to American forests by the spruce bud worm?" Then Miss Warner smartly taps a few buttons in various places on the room-sized machine, which she affectionately calls "Emmy." Within a few seconds, the "answer" comes chugging out and Miss Warner proudly peels off the printout. The library staff, who had spent several weeks digging to find the same answer, are daunted by this impressive show, and openly hostile when Miss Warner insists that no smoking is allowed in the room and the outside door has to be kept closed: "You know how sensitive EMERAC is to changes in temperature! One thing we don't like, don't like it at all, is a speck of dust." The assistant librarian adds drily: "Emmy gets pneumonia if she gets caught in a draft."

While this demonstration is going on, Mr. Sumner is explaining to FBC executives: "The purpose of this machine, of course, is to free the worker from the routine and repetitive tasks, and liberate his time for more important ones." Mr. Asae gushes: "And it never makes mistakes!" Mr. Sumner: "Well, that's not entirely accurate; Emmy *can* make a mistake, but only if the human element makes a mistake first."

An opportunity for the library staff to expose the weakness of EMERAC comes quickly. In attempting to respond to a telephone reference question, Miss Warner, who lacks sufficient background knowledge as well as training in reference librarianship, misunderstands the client, hearing the word "curfew" instead of "Corfu." Bunny Watson knows that the IBM programmer has not understood the question, but she smugly stands by while Miss Warner struggles with the client and the machine. In her confusion, she panics and hits a wrong button on the machine, which causes it to screech and flash crazily, further unnerving her. She loses her temper and stomps out. Mr. Sumner reacts more philosophically: "Human element—entirely unpredictable."

The issue of the computer's role in the library is resolved when Bunny Watson asks, "What's going to happen when EMERAC takes over?" Mr. Sumner replies, "EMERAC is not going to take over. It was never intended to take over. It was never intended to replace you. It is here merely to free your time for research. It is just here to help you." Appeased, the librarian types into the console a test question of her own: "What is the total weight of the earth?" Mr. Sumner shows her how to hit the Turing Key. EMERAC responds: "With or without people?" Impressed at this display of artificial intelligence, Miss Watson exclaims, "Good girl, Emmy, good girl!" She is falling in love with the machine and, of course, with Richard, Sumner, too.

1 Introduction

The Online Retrieval Story

Historians of the 1960s and 1970s recall a turbulent and exciting era. It was the time of the Vietnam War and antiwar protests, shocking political assassinations, the Watergate scandal, social activism in the form of the civil rights movements, and political action for the rights of women, gays, Native Americans, and new concern for protecting the environment. Invasions, warfare, and coups in Cuba, the Middle East, Czechoslovakia, Northern Ireland, and Chile dominated the headlines. Startling developments in science and technology captured the public's attention, such as Christiaan Barnard performing the first successful heart transplant operation in 1967 and astronaut Neil Armstrong becoming the first human to set foot on the moon in 1969. Computers expanded enormously in speed and capacity even as their physical size and costs shrank.

Set in this context of social, political, and technological upheaval, our story, which covers roughly the period 1963–1976, unfolded quietly. Not only the general public was unaware of online retrieval research and development; most information practitioners were uninformed until the late 1970s or early 1980s when the major systems were already well-established operations. Nonetheless, the story of the early developmental period in online information retrieval is not insignificant. As Lauren Doyle asserted in 1975, "We regard the advent of online retrieval as the foremost development so far in the era of information storage and retrieval" (281). The world, including the online retrieval world, has changed, but Doyle's words are still defensible. Even though many new databases, services, and technologies have since come on the scene, none has represented as striking a demarcation between the old and new ways of searching for information.

The shift to the online era was marked with striking emotional responses. In the early training sessions, the hands of first-time searchers trembled as they touched the keyboard. A few were immobilized with fear. Others laughed out loud when the terminal came to life with messages and answers from a computer located far away. For information searchers, the introduction to online retrieval systems was like the discovery of DNA, the moon landing, or the first heart transplant.

Not only did online represent a remarkable break with the past and open new avenues of progress, the story of its development is extraordinary in that many diverse elements had to come together for it to happen. The development of third-generation computers, machine-readable databases, and long-distance telecommunications networks, and experimentation with batch-mode serial searching of databases of bibliographic records on magnetic tapes and current awareness services (SDI, or Selective Dissemination of Information) are for the most part outside the scope of this book. Nonetheless, we should not forget that these and other developments in the decades just before we begin the online story were necessary precursors. In fact, some important computer advancements and database developments that shaped the evolution of retrieval systems continued well into the online era covered in this book. Jules Schwartz (1968) described very well the progress in the 1950s and 1960s in regard to time-sharing and interactive systems.

The online story is not just a description of tapes and disks, terminals and telephones, and search algorithms. A critical element was the main actors, the online pioneers. This history is both an homage to their foresight, determination, and diligence, as well as a reminder of the foibles, mistakes, and random turns that are associated with any human endeavor. Thus, some biography is woven into the historical narrative, in an effort to understand a bit about the backgrounds and personalities of the pioneers. What motivated them? How did they communicate and compete with each other? We will see how they struggled to keep their dreams alive in the face of technological impediments, organizational obstacles, and funding and market competition.

We believe that the first online information retrieval system appeared in 1963—although a few prototypes had appeared before that had some of the characteristics of online, so an exact date of the "invention" of online is hard to pinpoint. Online systems and databases are continuing to evolve even as we write this text, and now a large number have become available on the World Wide Web. At what point in the developmental cycle of a technology, an organization, a service, is it appropriate to review its origins, its goals, its accomplishments, and to write its history? Has enough time elapsed to digest the whole story, and to obtain access to proprietary records and private reminiscences of the industry pioneers? In most cases, the answer is yes, but in some, it is still no. On the other hand, have some important documents that were never published already been lost or destroyed? Have personal memories already faded or been tainted by intervening events? Have some key players already left the field? Unfortunately, the answer to all of these is yes. Enough was still intact, however, as we conducted our research (a process that has taken about 15 years) to reveal many aspects of the story. We hope that this work is timed about right—not too soon and not too late.

Existing Histories of Online

A major milestone in the literature of online systems was Wilfrid Lancaster and Emily Fayen's book (1973), which earned the ASIS (American Society for Information Science) Best Information Science Book Award in 1974. More than just a narrative, it functioned for years as a textbook, handbook, and encyclopedia on all aspects of online retrieval systems. Lancaster and Fayen's descriptions of systems existing at the time they were writing helped us to trace some developmental activities.

In the following year two retrospective reviews of developments leading up to online retrieval systems appeared. One was Frank Rogers's paper in *Library Trends* in July 1974. Rogers reviewed the need for online, and suggested such factors as the limitations and frustrations of batch searching. He also identified briefly the advances that made online systems feasible, both technologically and economically. These included third-generation computers, fast disk drives with large storage capacity, cheap terminals and printers, and reliable, reasonably priced long-distance data communication networks.

Joseph Becker (1975) presented the other retrospective at a symposium in March 1974. Like Rogers, Becker devoted most of his story to the background factors that set the stage for online developments. He gave more emphasis, however, to the role of large machine-readable databases and research on natural language interfaces.

In a textbook on information retrieval, Lauren Doyle (1975) reviewed the developments of the previous twenty years. Doyle recalled that Calvin Mooers coined the term "information retrieval" in 1950, and that Philip Bagley conducted the earliest experiment in computerized document retrieval and documented it in 1951 in his MIT master's thesis.

Continuing in his role as the chief historian of the online era up to this point, Lancaster, with Jeanne Owen, published in 1976 a chapter in a book titled *The Information Age; Its Development and Impact*. They painted a broad picture of the major milestones in modern information retrieval systems, beginning with the paper-based systems of the 1940s and 1950s, championed by W. E. Batten, Calvin Mooers, Mortimer Taube, and others. From these primitive peek-a-boo and edge-notched card systems, they traced the rapid evolution to punched cards and batch processed computer-based retrieval systems of the 1960s. They discussed batch processing advantages and disadvantages (mostly the latter). By comparison, in Lancaster and Owen's view, online retrieval systems had all the same advantages and none of the disadvantages. In spite of the use statistics being reported throughout the first decade of development, Lancaster adhered to his often repeated belief that users could search online retrieval systems directly for their own information needs. Lancaster and Owen credited M. M. Kessler at MIT with creating TIP, "one of the earliest, if not the earliest, experimental on-line" systems (15), and identified BOLD as another. They asserted, however, that although TIP and BOLD were ahead of their time, they had little direct influence on the design of later online systems. In regard to TIP, we challenge this statement. Three other important early developments that they felt did have long-lasting influence were COLEX, forerunner of ORBIT; RECON, a version of DIALOG developed by Lockheed Missiles and Space Company; and Data Central's OBAR, the forerunner of LEXIS. We agree with their assessment, and accordingly trace these three developments in detail in chapters 5, 6, and 7. Lancaster and Owen gave special attention to the Biomedical Communication Network of the State University of New York (SUNY BCN), because it existed in the "library sphere" and was a notable example of a "well-developed on-line bibliographic network" (17). They could not have known, of course, that within a year, SUNY BCN would cease to exist, and BRS would rise out of its ashes. We devote all of chapter 8 and parts of 9 and 10 to this remarkable story. Lancaster and Owen either were unaware of or ignored the other systems developed in the late 1960s and 1970s.

Our quest for documentation was facilitated greatly by three significant bibliographies. The first was published after a workshop, whose proceedings and bibliography were prepared by Donald Walker (1971a,b). Jim Hall (1977) offered a bibliography on online information retrieval covering 1965–1976, with brief descriptions of databases and systems. Donald Hawkins (1980) used a computer to prepare a bibliography covering 1964–1979.

Bernard Houghton and John Convey (1977) wrote perhaps the first textbook on online searching. Typical of the online textbooks that followed, theirs scanned only the highlights of development without citing any sources or interpreting any events. According to Houghton and Convey, System Development Corporation (SDC) in 1965 and Lockheed in 1966 developed the earliest online systems. Next, the National Library of Medicine (NLM) in 1967 experimented with a small bibliographic database of neurology references, followed by the AIM-TWX pilot service in 1970. Suddenly from that point, the online industry was launched and grew rapidly. By overlooking about 75 percent of the developmental activity, Houghton and Convey, as did later textbook writers, kept their history simple, if somewhat implausible.

At the Aslib annual conference in 1977, Carlos Cuadra, by that time a major figure in the online industry, traced the genesis of online retrieval back to the first online computers in the late 1950s, and to prototype systems developed in the 1960s. Ignoring the work done in universities, he asserted that the earliest prototypes of online retrieval systems "were developed by organizations in the private or commercial sector" (1978, 8). Cuadra acknowledged that the work was accomplished "sometimes with government funding contributions either to the initial development or to some of the subsequent improvements." Other than this brief observation, however, he did not give credit to the U.S. government agencies that funded and participated in the developmental activities. Cuadra (1978, 8) counted in 1977 at least fifteen online retrieval services of international scope in operation, about twelve of which were based in the United States: "Most of the on-line retrieval services that are operating or are about to begin operating in Europe are government-sponsored, in whole or in part. In contrast, most of the major on-line systems based in the United States are commercially supported. This difference is a function of the American tradition of free enterprise which, in the field of on-line retrieval services, has proved to be very beneficial to users." We hope to demonstrate how critical funding from the United States federal government was to the development of nearly all of the online retrieval systems in the 1960s.

In his 1979 textbook on retrieval systems, Lancaster reported a few developmental highlights, but ignored others. Lancaster claimed that the first (and only) experimental system was TIP at MIT. In 1969, NASA-RECON became the first large-scale operational online system. The ORBIT software, used by the NLM in the MEDLINE service in 1971, was the next development. Lancaster briefly mentioned Data Central and the *New York Times* Information Bank. Lancaster, as an author and principal investigator of significant evaluation studies in the 1960s and 1970s, was well aware of other historic developments. He drew a simple picture, however, without a hint of the complexity of the reality.

In 1979, Alex Tomberg, the European editor of *Online Review*, compared developments in databases and database access in Europe with those in the United States. In Tomberg's view, the freedom in the United States to build multihost communications networks fostered rapid growth of the online industry there. Also, the support of the U.S. government for both system development and the construction of large databases in education, medicine, the environment, aerospace technology, agriculture, and energy contributed greatly to the industry's success.

Charles Bourne (1980a) outlined a chronology of firsts: for example, the first investigation into the feasibility of online retrieval (1951), the first public demonstration of what appeared then to be online retrieval (1960), and the first online network on a national scale (1965), including some developments that had not been identified previously in the literature. This brief, but orderly, overview provided a framework for our chronology of major milestones. However, after his much deeper research for this text, Bourne recants some of the firsts that he described in 1980; that paper has been made obsolete by this book. Sara Knapp (1983) cited Bourne's overview, in her reflections on how online databases can be traced to the computer-assisted typesetting developments of the 1960s, as well as batch searching services such as NLM's MEDLARS.

In his 1981 book on the history of SDC, Claude Baum gave an unusual perspective on the ORBIT Search Service. Although well-known in the field of library and information science, ORBIT was but a tiny part of the activities of a giant computer research and development organization.

In 1983, as editor of *Online*, Jeffrey Pemberton wrote a lengthy piece that gave an extremely rare and candid insider's view of the management and mismanagement of the *New York Times* Information Bank. Although we could not confirm his allegations about Information Bank administrative decisions, we found the piece useful for Pemberton's own experiences as an online marketing representative. His narrative supplemented and confirmed stories we heard in the interviews.

In 1984, Irwin Pizer, the major driving force behind SUNY BCN, reviewed his personal view of how it fit into the progress of automated medical information. From Pizer's memoirs, we get a sense of the "electric" atmosphere in the 1960s at the NLM, sparked by librarians who were innovative, imaginative, and resourceful. William Harrington (1984–1985) similarly chronicled the various technical, political, and personal developments that contributed to the history of computer-assisted legal research. Frederick Kilgour (1987) did the same for the history of OCLC. We encountered similar environments in other organizations in this period, where the fortunate combination of energetic employees, emerging technologies, and a healthy dose of funds set the stage for a seminal period in library automation and information retrieval.

In 1986, Lynne Neufeld and Martha Cornog reviewed twenty years of database development. Although not the focus of this book, the evolution of large machine-readable databases complements the growth of online system capacity and retrieval speed. Neufeld and Cornog also generated a timeline of major events that, while oriented toward databases, illustrated how interrelated were database and online system developments.

On the occasion of the tenth anniversary of the debut of *Online* magazine, Dominic Provenzano in 1987 traced the personal histories of eleven "leading lights of the information industry." In 1988, to commemorate the tenth anniversary of the journal *Database*, Richard Harris, James Kollegger, and Ann Van Camp reminisced in separate articles about their careers as database manager (Harris), database developer (Kollegger), and online system user (Van Camp). As a complement to our interviews, we found these articles useful for better understanding how certain individuals came to be involved in online and what that involvement meant to their careers.

In the same issue of *Database*, Charles Meadow (1988a,b) wrote what might be construed as the first complete history of online. It is complete, however, only in the sense that his perspective was broad chronologically, beginning with the first alphabet and the first libraries 5,000 years ago, and including the inventions through the centuries (such as printing press, abacus, telephone, computer, and punched card) as well as scientific achievements (zero, algebra, logarithms, and accounting systems), that were necessary antecedents to modern information technology. After an entertaining narrative of these and other scientific and technological contributions up to the middle of the twentieth century, Meadow then constructed an online industry timeline, beginning in 1945 with publication of Vannevar Bush's article, "As We May Think." Not all of the entries are dated accurately or are related directly to the advancement of online searching or the online industry. Nonetheless, this timeline was another existing framework upon which we could build.

Pemberton (1994, 1996, 1997) and Van Camp (1994) wrote other personal or "insider's" reminiscences. Colin Burke (1996) wrote a retrospective analysis of Intrex, and Richard Marcus (1997) offered a refutation. In the 1990s also appeared obituaries of important figures in the online story, which had useful historical perspectives: J. C. R. Licklider (Taylor 1990) Irwin Pizer ("Irwin Howard Pizer," 1992), Joseph Becker (Hayes 1995), and Gerard Salton (Lesk 1996).

As a spin-off of the work in progress on this book, or at least inspired by it, we ourselves have published brief histories of aspects of the period: Bourne (1999) and Hahn (1994, 1996, 1997, 1998, 1999).

Research Methodology

Given the paucity of archival sources and secondary historical analysis in this area, we resorted to oral history techniques and a lengthy search for written documentation. We learned quickly how difficult it is to conduct historical research on a part-time basis, fitting the tasks around our usual jobs.

We have tried to avoid a narcotic recital of events. However, we felt an obligation to set some facts straight, to the extent that we could. We discovered that many of the historical overviews up to now played loose with dates, names, and key developmental milestones. Some seem to have borrowed the "facts" from each other, without apparent concern for verifying them.

Interviews

Fortunately, part of our regular jobs was to travel and attend conferences, which provided convenient opportunities to rendezvous with the interview subjects. Some interviews took place in restaurants and hotel lobbies; others were held in offices and in homes of those who have retired. We were initiated rapidly into the large amount of work involved in preparing for interviews, and in transcribing and analyzing the contents. Several texts on oral history interviewing were helpful, including those by Brady (1976) Gordon (1969), Hoopes (1979), and Ives (1980).

The interviews themselves were enjoyable. The subjects were cooperative, forthcoming, and expansive, and seemed delighted to discuss their own achievements or the contributions of their own systems. All conveyed the sense of a significant era and a vital, exciting time in their professional lives. In addition to the formal interviews, we raised questions and discussed issues with many other colleagues.

Pitfalls exist, however, in trusting the recollections of those whose memories have faded. We swiftly became aware of the problems in dealing with those who are reluctant to discuss all aspects of the operation or system, including the setbacks, failures, and frustrations. Whenever possible, therefore, we obtained verification of stories from other sources. We exploited the interviews primarily for personal impressions, interpretations, and undocumented anecdotes, rather than for historical facts. The interview subjects are listed in the acknowledgments.

Documentation

In gathering documents, we attempted to gain as complete a picture as possible of the design, development, and evaluation of the first online systems. The process of combing the published monographic and journal literature also unearthed grant reports to funding agencies and technical reports from commercial and nonacademic organizations, academic institutions, and government agencies. Fortunately, an ERIC (Educational Research/Resources Information Center) Clearinghouse or the National Technical Information Service (NTIS) had archived most of these reports, which thus had an AD, PB, or ERIC number that made it relatively easy to find copies. We also found newsletters and annual reports from Lockheed, SDC, and the NLM; manuals for system design specifications and for system users; proceedings of special conferences, institutes, colloquia, workshops, and forums, as well as for the regular annual conferences of the American Federation of Information Processing Societies (AFIPS), the American Society for Information Science (ASIS) (earlier known as ADI, or the American Documentation Institute; now known as ASIST, or the American Society for Information Science & Technology), the Association for Information Dissemination Centers (ASIDIC), the European Association of Scientific Information Dissemination Centers (EUSIDIC), and the National Federation for Abstracting and Information Services (NFAIS). Other document sources included master's theses and doctoral dissertations, intradepartmental reports and memos from various search services, and articles in journals from outside the field of information science and systems. Chapters of the *Annual Review of Information Science and Technology* yielded many leads to this cross-disciplinary literature.

This list of documents demonstrates how scattered the literature of online systems was during the period, which is yet another rationale for this book; at that time, no focus for articles or for announcements of events existed such as we have today in the journals and newsletters devoted to databases and online searching.

"Pas de documents, pas d'histoire"—no documents, no history—declared French historians Charles Langlois and Charles Seignobos at the turn of the twentieth century. Despite the exhaustive search for records to support the history, there is undoubtedly more to the story. Pieces of the tale remain unknown, either because they were not documented or because the records were not known or available to us. Some unpublished documents that served as the first user manuals or system guidelines apparently were discarded, as their owners changed jobs or retired, companies moved or folded. Some are available now only because they were reprinted in journals or textbooks. We talked to many pioneers who had just discarded old papers and photographs that they had saved and stored for many years. Perhaps this book will spur individuals who have retained copies of unpublished materials to contribute them to the appropriate libraries or archives where they will become part of the public record.

Dating the Milestones, the "Firsts"

To give proper credit to the genuine trailblazers, it was imperative to describe and date as accurately as possible what we judged to be the major milestones. Verifying dates proved to be more difficult than anticipated. As Kuhn (1970) described the dating of first discoveries (his examples were oxygen, X rays, and the Leyden jar), the task of establishing scientific priority is compounded in several ways. First, ordering sequences of events by dates of publication (which are in the public record) rather than by dates of actual activity (which are often unknown), may result in credit being misplaced. Another problem is terminological inconsistencies; in a new specialty lacking standard nomenclature, it may be difficult to determine whether two authors are describing the same or different concepts. Kuhn emphasized that dating a scientific discovery to a single individual and a single moment in time is often impossible; discovery involves an extended process of conceptual assimilation.

Dating inventions perhaps is not as problematic as dating scientific discoveries, but other problems confound the process of crediting priority. For example, the documentation often fails to make clear which stage of development is being described. Is the system completed and working satisfactorily? Is it in development, but not quite finished? Or, is it merely anticipated or intended? Some reports were maddeningly vague on this score. It is possible that some publications were intentionally vague or suggestive, in order to support a marketing or funding objective. We examined alternative sources, double-checking dates, sizes of databases, numbers of users, capacities, and features. Usually we presumed that the source created closest to an event in time and geography was the most authoritative.

The interviews did not prove that helpful in clarifying precedents. Not only were subjects' memories unreliable for dates and sequences of events, the subjects were vague about progress at institutions other than their own. They sometimes did not know the true innovator and thus assumed credit for something that had been developed elsewhere first. Schooled in scientific investigation and hypothesis testing, where it is important to corroborate data from several different instruments or sources before claiming that a fact or relationship has been proven, we learned that the same skepticism and deferment in reaching conclusions is necessary in historical research.

We have woven into the narrative only the milestones that we were able to confirm with reasonable certainty. We have highlighted these firsts using boxes labeled milestones, in order to call the reader's attention to these significant events. These same milestones are also summarized at the end.

This book was written and edited over a period of more than a decade, and the background research extended to nearly two decades. As we wrote and revised, we realized that the concept of "now" and "at this time" was continually shifting. Therefore, when we tried to bring the story up to date on what was happening now with individual pioneers, organizations, systems, or databases, our information was likely to be out of date by the time a reader cracked open this book. So we shifted the language to "as of this writing," which could mean "as of 1990," or "as of 2001," or any date in between. This increasingly sounded ludicrous, given the phenomenal speed of IT developments in the 1990s. Consequently, we eliminated many of those statements, and for those that we left, we hope our readers will tolerate the ambiguity of the statement "as of this writing."

In any case, this book is not mainly about what is current as of this writing. Descriptions of what is happening now belong in newspapers and magazines, broadcast media, at conferences, on Web sites, and other communication channels of the moment. This book is intended as a record of what was "then," to the best of our ability to capture all the relevant facts, interpret and synthesize them, and mold them into a coherent story.

In spite of the fact that many online pioneers read and commented on sections of the text—adding additional material and correcting misstatements, we know that we can be challenged by someone else's viewpoint, documentation, interpretation, or recollection. In spite of the huge number and variety of documents that we assembled for the research, others may yet produce more key material. In spite of our efforts to tackle a wide scope for the story, we have, either intentionally or inadvertently, left out some aspects. The sheer size of the growing manuscript dictated that we had to eliminate certain sections that were peripheral to our main scope. We look forward to more research and writing about information technologies by historians of our field.

Organization and Themes

This book is organized roughly by chronology. Chapter 2 covers the prototypes and experiments of the early 1960s. Chapters 3 and 4 carry the story through the late 1960s and early 1970s. Chapters 5 through 8 focus on four major systems individually and trace their convoluted development throughout the 1960s and early 1970s. Chapters 9 and 10 describe the operational systems of the 1970s and expansion of the online industry. Finally, chapter 11 summarizes our interpretation of what we learned from the investigation.

Although actual developments do not always follow neat time frames, the order of the chapters is meant to convey a sense of progression, and the maturation of the industry through time. Throughout the book, certain themes or motifs keep reappearing. They represent the research questions that guided our investigation:

What role did hardware, software, telecommunications, and database developments play in driving the progress of online systems?

The computers and terminals used in each prototype, experimental system, or fully implemented system were tracked carefully. We hoped to reveal that the storage and processing capacities of the hardware, whether the machines were general or special purpose, and whether they were dedicated or shared, made a difference in how the interface was designed and how services were enhanced or constrained.

The software interface programs likewise were examined in some detail. We sought to determine how they were structured, how complex or sophisticated they were, how easy they were to use by intermediaries or end-users, and what specific features were available to enhance the power and control of users in devising search strategies.

Even the earliest online retrieval systems needed some sort of database in order to function. When no machine-readable files were available, the developers had to create their own. These small files were examined as integral, critical components in the total systems. Later, as full-scale operating online systems began operations, the databases were analyzed as key factors in the acceptance and appeal of online systems. Specifically, the databases of the 1960s and early 1970s were examined to find out what topics or disciplines were covered. Also, how large were the databases and how rapidly did they grow? Which of them contained bibliographic references, abstracts, the full text of documents, or other types of data? How were they structured and which fields in the records were searchable? What types of subject access were possible (controlled vocabulary terms, natural language terms, or classification codes)? Who was producing the early databases and what was the relationship of the producers to the online system builders?

What were the characteristics of the early online services? What were their purposes and functions, and how well did they accomplish them? What role did formal evaluation play in the progress of online systems and services?

What were the purposes and goals of the first online retrieval projects? What research questions were being addressed? What problems were the developers trying to solve? To what extent were the goals accomplished and how did the goals change over time? When the first full-scale operational systems appeared in the late 1960s, how well did they serve their intended users? What operational problems did users experience and how were they solved? What service limitations existed and what were the obstacles to satisfactory performance? How did the first users perceive the performance of the systems? What role did the users play in providing evaluative feedback? How did the developers elicit this feedback and use it for system modification?

What was the role of government and private funding?

Some research and development activities took place in private organizations and some in university-based laboratories. Who paid for this work? How dependent were the research and development projects on outside funding? What percentage of the support can be attributed to the U.S. federal government and what percentage to other sources? To what extent did the missions of the various funding sources influence the goals of the researchers? How and when did any of the online systems become self-sustaining?

What were the characteristics, behavior, and attitudes of the online pioneers?

Three groups of pioneers appear throughout the story. Chronologically, the first group was the programmers, system designers, and researchers. This group was diverse in their geographic and disciplinary backgrounds. We find also, however, a great deal of similarity in their aggressiveness in competing for research funds, in vying for priority of discovery and invention, and in exploiting the opportunities to make use of state-of-the-art hardware and software programs. They also monitored one another's progress by visiting laboratories and attending conferences and seminars. For example, in attendance at a workshop on "The User Interface for Interactive Search of Bibliographic Data Bases," held in Palo Alto, California, in January 1971, were Pauline Atherton (Syracuse University), John Bennett (IBM Research Laboratory), James Carlisle (Yale University), John Fried (Battelle Memorial Institute), Viktor Hampel (Lawrence Radiation Lab), Robert Katter (SDC), Richard Marcus (MIT), William Mathews (MIT), Davis McCarn (NLM), Benjamin Mittman (Northwestern University), Edwin Parker (Stanford University), Roger Summit (Lockheed), David Thompson (Stanford University), and Van Wente (NASA). All were key players in the online story and each will be introduced individually at the appropriate time in the narrative.

The second group of pioneers included the managers, promoters, trainers, and customer service representatives. Their job was to sell potential users on the idea of online searching and to convince them to change their ingrained information-seeking habits. They set pricing and service policies. They wrote newsletters, manuals, advertisements, and promotional brochures. They traveled, lectured, and gave countless demonstrations and training sessions in order to convince librarians, scientists, lawyers, and others to adopt these marvelous but unknown services. They resorted to conniving with the computer operators to create an impression of reliable, responsive online service that was quite disparate with the reality of the time. The personal qualities—zeal, perseverance, and charm—of members of this group seemed to be a critical factor in the success of the major online systems. We examine the development of the industry through their eyes. In the 1970s, they were not in a position to reveal publicly their personal views about their own activities, their opinions of the industry, the users, or the systems. Enough time has passed, however, that many of them could speak candidly in the interviews. Their insider perspective is exposed in chapter 10.

The users themselves constituted the third group. Their perspective provides yet another angle from which to assess the successes and failures and measure the rate of development. We elicited their views from self-authored published reports, from evaluation studies that the system developers conducted, and from our interviews. We scrutinized users to discover whether they were direct "end-users"—that is, whether they used the online systems to do their own searches, devising their own search strategies and keying in their own search terms, or whether they were intermediaries conducting searches on behalf of others. Most of the early systems were designed for the former group; our goal was to discover who were the actual users.

The struggle to develop and implement a major technological innovation inevitably generated some amusing or surprising incidents. Our story accordingly includes some anecdotes that convey a sense of the novelty and excitement that the developers, marketers, and users experienced, as well as how some developmental stages unfolded through uncontrolled, fortuitous circumstances. The online pioneers faced workers' strikes, they removed outside building walls in order to bring in a *terminal* (not a computer), they "lost" huge terminals among boxes of books in the library, they endured interruptions of online service as a computer was preempted for a space launch, and more. We see how a copy of a questionnaire sent to potential customers found its way to a competitor and helped to launch a new online service. We meet some striking personalities such as the "rat psychologist and piano player" who declined to brave the North Dakota climate to train radar personnel. By staying home in Southern California, he was on the spot to manage his corporate library division when it launched an online searching service. Another important online industry figure was so attached to his boat and Northern California house that he declined a good job offer on the East Coast. Instead, he remained in his position and launched another major online service. One of the service representatives, who set a high standard in the fledgling industry of friendly and supportive customer assistance, had been hired initially because she had been a high school debating champion. These and other anecdotes illustrate how the historical events sometimes hinged on unexpected outside influences and the very personal needs, choices, and styles of individuals involved.

In summary, this book is about four themes: systems, service, funding, and pioneers. These themes are woven together, we hope, in such a way that a well-rounded picture emerges of an exciting, significant, and seminal era in the history of the delivery of modern information services. In recalling in detail, step by step, the rapid evolution of the technology and growth of the industry, we hope to shed light on why the successful online retrieval systems have evolved to their current forms and why the information industry is structured today the way it is. If the past *is* prologue, this history may suggest the shape of future developments. Even though the world of information technology is changing at lightening speed today, we hope that certain fundamental truths will emerge about user-oriented systems and services, dependence on sources of funding, and people who are innovators and risk takers.

2 Early Research and Development Activities

Introduction

The serious application of computers to document reference retrieval began in the late 1950s, with slow serial searches of small files of bibliographic records on magnetic tapes. A precursor of effective, large-scale online information retrieval (IR) systems was an experiment in searching bibliographic records on an IBM disk memory system called RAMAC (Random Access Method of Accounting and Control). Nolan (1958) and Firth (1958a,b) demonstrated how search procedures could be made more efficient, with shorter elapsed times, by searching only those records on a disk corresponding to the index terms specified in a given batch of requests. Their demonstration showed the benefits that could be achieved with random access (also referred to as "direct access") storage devices instead of traditional serial access storage media (tapes). Although their technique might be thought of as "online" in a way, search questions still had to be batched for processing.

Doyle (1975) portrayed the earliest retrieval experiments more as diversions than as purposeful R&D. They were conducted at a time when all the computers in the world numbered only a few hundred and were located mainly in U.S. aerospace firms or defense installations:

> Such organizations typically had documentation sections, with growing stores of documents and inadequate staffs for indexing and abstracting. The idea of making use of computers for document processing, in some way, was inevitable, for although these instruments were very expensive... there was often idle time during which needs of a marginal nature (and documentation was usually so regarded) could be serviced. Early experiments in computerized document retrieval often represented joint efforts by one or two programmers with the assistance (sometimes reluctant) of one or two documentation personnel. (P. 262)

Since literature searches had low priority relative to solving problems in defense and space technology, even a well-designed system could not guarantee rapid retrieval if queries were being bumped to make way for more important uses of the computer. Doyle himself participated in two of the earliest online experiments, Protosynthex and BOLD, as well as concurrent projects on retrieval system evaluation, associative indexing, and automatic generation of association maps. His parenthetical comment about the reluctant participation of documentation personnel probably came from personal experience.

The genesis of online retrieval systems can be traced to the first half of the 1960s. Within a few years, the prototypes of several innovative systems were developed and used for experimentation. Not surprisingly, the prototypes had many limitations. Most operated with only one terminal and one database. Some used equipment that was extremely primitive by our standards—for example, searcher input was via a stack of cards or a roll of punched paper tape. Search output was often cryptic data on teletypewriter printers. The most powerful mainframe computers had no more than 64K of core memory, far less than would be considered adequate for a personal computer today. They took up a lot of floor space and required massive electrical support systems for their operation and air conditioning to keep them working. For example, the AN/FSQ-7 computer systems of the SAGE (Semi-Automated Ground Environment) system direction centers had "almost 60,000 vacuum tubes, weighing 250 tons, occupying an acre of floor space, and using up to 3 million watts of electric power" (Pugh 1995, 215). By 1965, only about thirty time-shared systems were operating, many in university computing centers. The experimental search systems usually shared these mainframe computers and therefore could run only a few hours a day at most. In one system, because of resource constraints, the program limited output to no more than three records per query.

While none of the earliest systems had all the characteristics we might associate with the powerful online systems of the 1970s or later, each one made or confirmed at least one important contribution that others incorporated later. We find remarkably advanced features such as online thesauri, ranked output, automatic inclusion of synonyms in the search formulation, Boolean logic, left- and right-hand truncation, cited-reference searching, and natural language searching. The hardware featured such technological wonders as sophisticated light pens, interactive large-screen visual displays, and long-distance data transmission through teletypewriters and telephone lines. Some systems had elaborate automatic data collection programs to monitor use and satisfaction.

Most of the earliest systems provided access to a bibliographic database and the rest used a file containing another sort of information—encyclopedia articles, inventory data, or chemical compounds. Another notable distinction among them was their underlying goal. For some developers, the main point was to conduct basic research on linguistic and artificial intelligence phenomena and human-computer interfaces. Others had practical goals of providing better, cheaper, and faster access to library records. Some developers used their systems to study searching behavior or to explore how scientists used the literature. Others used theirs for testing programming and text storage innovations, facilitating data entry and manipulation from online terminals, or enhancing human control over human-computer interactions.

The pioneers worked in teams within their own organizations. The teams focused on their own projects, with their own vision and goals to energize their creative genius and their own technological and economic limitations to temper their dreams. They all enjoyed enlightened sponsors who provided freedom and financial and other resources to support their work. Anecdotal evidence from interviews and personal communications, however, suggests that the pioneers tried to keep up with what others were doing, and they were driven to an extent by a desire to compete—to build a retrieval system better than anyone else's.

The amount of R&D work done in the early years was constrained by the limited number of computer installations available for researchers, and an even smaller number of operating time-shared systems that would permit *practical* use of a computer for such experimentation. The scarcity and accessibility of data transmission equipment and facilities for remote terminal operations further restricted the number of sites where this type of work could be done. Only a small number of primarily federally funded time-shared computer facilities were available that permitted a few fortunate researchers to have access. This is analogous to other situations where researchers worldwide had limited access to scarce tools such as linear accelerators, large telescopes, or satellite payloads.

Major contributors to development of online systems and techniques were the project monitors of various funding agencies who promoted information exchanges between their grantees and contractors. Some funding agencies held conferences to facilitate such information exchanges, and several events were held during this period to permit developers to meet and exchange news about their work. IBM and SDC were major players in these conferences, as arrangers and participants.

Where do we start the online story? It makes sense to begin at the beginning, with the very first online retrieval system. Our research, however, unearthed several candidates for "first." In fact, nearly all of the earliest systems pioneered at least one new feature or capability that we have recorded as a "milestone." Another difficulty in awarding a medal for first is vague and varying definitions of "interactive" and "online" as used by the earliest prototypes. Thus it is difficult to make an absolute claim for which was the very first. The evidence suggests, nevertheless, that the claim for first goes to a tiny unnamed online system from Stanford Research Institute (SRI). So that is where we will begin. This was followed closely by two systems (SATIRE, which probably was never actually online, and Protosynthex), as well as a system at MIT called TIP. SATIRE and Protosynthex were products of SDC, an organization that was responsible for a large amount of basic research and development in online. So we shall introduce SDC's earliest online systems with a description of SDC itself, followed by SDC's other early R&D in computerized retrieval.

The challenges in sorting out priority of claims will become more evident as we review details from our research. After the first four, our narrative then addresses other research and demonstrations that began before 1965 at the University of Pennsylvania, the 1962 and 1964 World Fairs, IBM, Bunker-Ramo, and General Electric. Research was also being conducted in this period that would lead to the Lockheed DIALOG and SDC ORBIT systems. Because of their eventual prominence and the complexity of their histories, however, they are examined separately in chapters 5 and 6. Likewise, the research and development on legal information systems that laid the foundation for the LEXIS system will be described in chapter 7, and the deep roots of another system that achieved commercial success many years later, BRS, will be addressed in chapter 8.

Stanford Research Institute

In the late 1950s, a nonprofit R&D organization in Menlo Park, California, called Stanford Research Institute (later renamed SRI International) was among the largest research institutes in the United States and had an engineering group active in information processing using modern technology. This included developing basic technology in character recognition, printing, electronic components, communications, computer development work (e.g., the first banking system for machine reading and handling of traveler's checks, customer bank checks, and deposit slips), and large-scale information handling problems for commercial and government clients.

In 1959, Douglas Engelbart began the Augmented Human Intellect (AHI) Program at SRI, the goal of which was to improve the productivity and effectiveness of individual researchers using emerging computer technology (Engelbart 1962). Several U.S. Department of Defense (DOD) organizations, including Advanced Research Projects Agency (ARPA) and the Air Force Electronic Systems Division (AF-ESD), supported parts of this program. The ARPA support was aimed at computer augmentation of programmers, by developing real-time computer aids for programmers working on a variety of tasks—conception, design, writing, debugging, commentary, and program maintenance. SRI at this time was also a major participant in developing ARPANET, the precursor of what became known as the Internet. SRI had its own computer facility, but ARPA made the Q-32 computer at SDC-Santa Monica (including its time-sharing system) and a data communication link to SRI available to the SRI group for a short period to use with one of its associated projects. The ESD support, starting in May 1963, was aimed at developing a part of the information management subsystem of this project (an SRI-SDC demonstration), described later.

In his capacity as a technical program committee member for the 1968 AFIPS (American Federation of Information Processing Societies) Fall Joint Computer Conference in San Francisco, Charles Bourne invited Engelbart to demonstrate the AHI system that was then operating on a computer system at SRI. Engelbart's online demonstration was a major attraction at the meeting. While Engelbart worked his terminal on the stage before a large plenary session, his CRT display was shown to the audience by means of a projected display. This was the first time that most in the audience had seen a large projection of a simultaneous image from a CRT. This was also the first time that most of them had heard of, or seen a "mouse."[1] In order to be able to offer this demonstration (something that is relatively easy to do nowadays), the conference organizers obtained special grants from several U.S. federal agencies to pay for what was then extremely expensive high-speed leased lines from San Francisco to SRI's Menlo Park computers (40 miles) and for the leasing and installation of special large-screen graphics display equipment. Engelbart also demonstrated his system at the 1969 ASIS meeting in San Francisco, where Bourne organized an "Online Arena," another meeting highlight—besides the local earthquake! Martin (1975) noted that this was the first time that one could compare live demonstrations of a number of different interactive retrieval systems.

Engelbart's work became familiar to most online developers in the 1960s and 1970s because of his publications, his participation in events such as the highly visible 1968 and 1969 demonstrations, the AFIPS Workshop on the User/Computer Interface in 1971, and his extensive ARPA project and workshop activities.

SRI Online System

In 1957, before the AHI project, Engelbart, as a School of Engineering faculty member at the University of California (UC)-Berkeley in 1957, introduced IR to Bourne, who was one his students in electrical engineering. The introduction took the form of an individual study project to organize a collection of several hundred abstracts of electrical engineering articles for rapid and effective searching. The project involved gluing each abstract to a McBee edge-punched card (with a custom-developed subject indexing scheme for the edge-notch coding), with a template to input-mark the card edges, a hog-ear notcher to notch the cards, and a knitting needle to sort the card deck for retrieval. Although it was a far cry from the computer-based systems that Engelbart or Bourne later worked on, it initiated them into the challenges inherent in any retrieval system: subject analysis, authority control, input conversion, and retrieval effectiveness.

1963 Milestones

SRI demonstrated the first online bibliographic search system.

SRI demonstrated the first online full-text search system.

Bourne earned a B.S. degree in electrical engineering from UC-Berkeley, specializing in computers, and then went to work for SRI as a research engineer. He earned an MS in industrial engineering from Stanford in 1962. For the ten years he was at SRI, he was involved in exploring a wide range of problems in information handling. One of his early projects there was the SRI-SDC online demonstration in support of Engelbart's AHI project. ESD supported this eight-month project (May—December 1963); total funding was a modest $39,000. For the project, Bourne studied almost twenty operational batch search systems that had been demonstrated at other organizations. Trying to incorporate everything he had learned and believing that an online approach was a natural and logical extension of what had already been done with batch systems led him in late 1963, along with programmer Len Chaitin, to demonstrate an online bibliographic and full-text search system they had designed and implemented on the Q-32 computer at SDC-Santa Monica (Bourne 1963, 1999). It was intended to be an experiment to demonstrate general concepts, not an operational system. But even as a "proof-of-concept" or demonstration-only system, it was a significant achievement in 1963 to implement such a system seven months after the start of the project. Full-text searching was not demonstrated on another online system until six years later (Data Central system).

The SRI system was planned to operate with the working documentation (internal memos, bibliographies, technical reports, computer programs) generated by the AHI project. Thus it was perhaps the first of the computer-based personal IR support systems developed, such as the SDC-SURF batch system and the many PC-based systems in operation today. The designers did this by developing tagged and formatted record structures for the various types of material, keyboarding these data online or on paper tape typewriters (Friden Flexowriters), and transferring the data onto magnetic tape for transport to SDC to be loaded into the Q-32. The software developed at SRI for this record-handling work included the kind of text processing techniques (insert, delete, move, copy, spell checker, line justification) that eventually became available widely in commercial word processing software.

The initial demonstration was planned for a file of fifty records. Unfortunately, at the last minute 43 records failed to pass the input editing routine (quality control checks on various fields of data) to get onto the test file on the Q-32. Thus the researchers had to proceed with only seven records. Another 115 items were available on punched paper tape for use in later demonstrations as a byproduct of the regular typing work on the project, including the master bibliography of over 1,200 references for the AHI project, but they were not used for this demonstration. All of this project documentation of about 500 typewritten pages of source information was available in machine readable form for later studies. The high-density tapes then in use on the Q-32 (IBM 729-IV tape drives) permitted approximately 1,400 three-page items to be recorded on a single reel of tape.

1963 Milestones

SRI provided the first demonstration of *remote* online bibliographic and full-text searching.

SRI provided the first long-distance demonstration of an online search system.

SRI provided the first demonstration of an online search system with a CRT terminal for interaction between humans and machines.

SRI provided the first demonstration of an online search system with CRT display of search output.

The equipment used consisted of (1) a Control Data CDC-160A computer at SRI (a relatively small computer used for batch processing work, which served mostly as the console or workstation for interaction with the Q-32); (2) a data communication link established in October 1963 to operate at about 350 cps between SRI and SDC, a distance of 400 miles; and (3) SDC's Q-32 computer. The CDC-160A workstation included a keyboard and CRT display, a light pen, and a pair of experimental five-key keysets. This workstation was developed, with ARPA support, primarily for other experimental studies by Engelbart that would use the Q-32 at SDC. The Q-32 had 65,000 48-bit words of core storage, a half million words of drum storage, and eighteen magnetic tape transports; it was considered to be a large high-speed computer with an extensive amount of core and auxiliary memory. However, its total "fast access" storage capacity was far less than would be considered adequate in today's personal computers.

The Q-32 resources were available to SRI at limited intervals on a time-shared basis. SDC's TSS-0 time-sharing system, which had just become operational in June 1963 with a capacity to handle thirty-four simultaneous users, imposed restrictions on the SRI software, such as limiting the total amount of core memory to 16,383 words out of the 65,000 words possible, providing limited drum memory; and limiting the number of tape transports to one in an online mode. This particular time-sharing system had been established just to give SRI online access to the Q-32, and no attempt was made to provide a generalized or universal system. SDC was then working on a newer time-sharing system (TSS-2) that was scheduled to be made available in November 1963. Most of the SRI programming was done for the Q-32 system (i.e., the search software was to be run on the SDC machine, not the SRI machine). Both the SDC and SRI projects had a contract sponsor (J. C. R. Licklider) who wanted to demonstrate the technical feasibility of a computer-to-computer network, and directed that the experiment be done in this way. The SRI system was working with the earliest of the SDC time-sharing systems, before time-sharing was available for BOLD or other SDC projects. SDC schedules permitted SRI to be connected to the Q-32 for about sixteen hours per week before September 30, 1963, and ten hours per week thereafter. Remote Teletypes had previously been connected to the SDC system, but SRI's CDC-160A was the only remote computer that had been hooked up to the SDC time-sharing system by that time, and as such, was among the first geographically separated computer-to-computer networks (a 2-node network) (Schwartz, Coffman, and Weissman 1964).

> **1963 Milestones**
>
> SRI was the first to demonstrate an online search system that retrieved records on the basis of bibliographic citation elements such as author, publication date, title words, or abstracts.
>
> SRI provided the first demonstration of a user-specified output display format option.
>
> SRI provided the first demonstration of online search and output display of abstracts with bibliographic or full-text records.
>
> SRI provided the first demonstration of a stop list in an online search system.

The search software was designed to allow searchers to specify which portions (e.g., title, source, abstract) of each record were to be examined during the search process, and which portions of the retrieved items were to be displayed. A search statement also allowed for the inclusion of a Boolean operator, but Boolean capability was not implemented. Search input could be a continuous symbol string of any length—one or two text words, or a complete sentence—or a particular instruction in a program listing. Because of constraints on the amount of storage space available for the file indexes, a large stop list was used so that the available online storage was reserved for the most meaningful search terms. Stop lists were in common use then for computer-produced indexes, so it was a logical extension to use one. This was the first time, however, that one was used with an online system. For expediency in this demonstration, the search process was implemented as a serial search of all of the records on the Q-32 tape file. After a user initiated a search, the first item that satisfied the search criterion was displayed on the CRT. After viewing it, the searcher could press a button to display the next item retrieved.

Because of the time constraints on the project and the limited Q-32 time and storage capacity available to SRI, the demonstration was restricted to a test file of the full text of seven project memos and reports and their associated indexing and descriptive information. This amounted to roughly 10,000 Q-32 computer words and was contained on a portion of a single reel of tape. A capability to expand the search formulation to incorporate automatically spelling variations (plurals, possessives, word roots, synonyms, and generic relationships) into the search formulation was planned, but not implemented.

Because of funding constraints at ESD, the project did not receive its expected continuation funding. Consequently, the SRI staff moved to other projects and did not follow up on the planned improvements. They generated no follow-up presentations or publications to describe this online demonstration. In the context of the other projects going on at SRI then, the developers were perhaps jaded by their exposure to, and involvement in, so many other exciting, leading-edge developments. This particular demonstration seemed to be merely an extension of work already going on in other application areas. They judged that it did not warrant any further dissemination other than via the technical report literature. Bourne (1999) provided additional reasons why the work was not continued:

The reasons are twofold: (1) As a nonprofit research institute, the projects went where the money was, and we could not find funding agencies that were interested in directly supporting a continuation of this effort; and (2) there *was* SRI and sponsor support for many more interesting and challenging projects associated with Cold War efforts at that time that claimed a higher priority for SRI . . . this work was going on at a time period when SRI staff members and their families had space assigned to them in the basement of SRI's main building for the pre-positioned storage of food, diapers, clothing, and other essentials, for use in the event of their need of a safe assembly and living area upon notice of a possible or actual Soviet nuclear attack on the San Francisco Bay Area.

Even though catchy names and acronyms were in fashion at the time, SRI's system never was named. Though he was the project manager, Bourne in fact had forgotten about this online system until he came across the associated materials during the research phase of this book.

Bourne later became the director of the Institute of Library Research (covered in chapter 3) and professor-in-residence at the UC-Berkeley School of Library Science, and eventually, a vice president at DIALOG Information Services, until his retirement in 1992. He was honored by ADI with the Award of Merit in 1965 and served as president of ASIS in 1970.

System Development Corporation (SDC)

The origins of SDC of Santa Monica, California, were at Rand Corporation. In the early 1950s, a scientific research study was conducted at Rand "to investigate the problems associated with man's information needs in a complex system environment," specifically, "new techniques useful in manual air defense system training" (*System development study*, 1966, 111). Because the work seemed to be leading to an important new technology, Rand's Board of Trustees established a new, independent organization to concentrate on its development. They chartered SDC in 1957 as a not-for-profit organization "to serve the public welfare and security of the United States in its fields of special technical competence—the behavioral and information system sciences" (111). SDC's charter, when it emerged from RAND, was to do system training for the U.S. Air Force (USAF), using its own system training concept and machinery for building nationwide, simulation-based training exercises. Rand was concerned about the possible appearance of a conflict of interest between its role in giving disinterested advice to the USAF and having a division that was selling products and services to the USAF (Cuadra 1997). SDC could assure corporate objectivity by its not-for-profit status and nonparticipation in hardware manufacturing activities. It was able to provide strict security safeguards for sensitive and proprietary information. SDC's scientists represented a diversity of technical backgrounds and were able to apply their special mix of skills to problems and projects in the public interest.

Soon after its establishment, SDC's charter was expanded to help build the SAGE air defense system, the first large-scale command and control system. SAGE required extensive computer programming (a new technical field in the mid-1950s) and use of large interactive CRT consoles. By 1958, SDC was programming and operating a large time-sharing system for this air defense system—one of the first time-sharing systems in operation. "Each day, for 24 hours a day, more than a hundred military personnel in a four-story building would sit at computer display terminals, monitoring and controlling U.S. air space" (Cuadra 1971a, 128). The first president of SDC, Melvin Kappler, while acknowledging that SDC's energies and talents were devoted to problems of air defense, believed that the same specialized skills in computer programming could find applicability in many other military and nonmilitary problems (Baum 1981).

By 1960, SDC had emerged as a major research and development organization specializing in large-scale computer-based information systems. Among the professional contributions it made was to organize and host several major technical conferences for exchanging information among the many people and organizations with a keen interest in developing and testing large computer-based information handling systems.

SDC also made an early contribution to the development of time sharing. In the early 1960s, researchers at MIT, Bolt Beranek and Newman, and IBM had shown the potential utility of time-shared computers and had provided encouragement for other groups to pursue this approach (Corbató, Merwin-Daggett, and Daley 1962; McCarthy et al. 1963). With ARPA support, SDC staff also worked to develop such a system, and by June 1963, they demonstrated their first system, called simply

Time-Sharing System (TSS) Model Zero (Schwartz, Coffman, and Weissman 1964). Initially, it supported only eight Western Union Teletype terminals and, due to its constant modification, was unstable. It was written for IBM's AN/FSQ-32 computer. With continued upgrades, TSS provided the basic platform for most of the SDC systems in this chapter (Schwartz and Weissman 1967; Spierer and Wills 1969). In 1968, TSS on the Q-32 was replaced by the ADEPT Time-Sharing System on an IBM 360 computer (Spierer and Wills 1968).

Another online precursor at SDC was the development of file management systems such as MADAM (Moderately Advanced Data Management) and SURF (Support of User Records and Files). MADAM was developed for the IBM 1401 and 360 computers by William Crossley at the SDC Santa Monica facility in 1964. It operated in batch mode as file builder, manipulator, and report generator and was used with the SURF system. The programs would translate and interpret the specification statements and then perform the required operations. The specs were incorporated in a control card deck that was used in conjunction with punched card or magnetic tape files. In 1965, MADAM was implemented only on an IBM 1401 computer with 8K core storage and four magnetic tape units (Crossley 1965).

Everett Wallace at SDC-Santa Monica developed a batch-mode computer-based service called SURF to assist individuals and groups in organizing, maintaining, and finding the contents of their personal and office files. Wallace had outlined a research project and program design for the system in 1963, intending to use the time-sharing development work being done for the Q-32, but the project was put on hold until the IBM 360 computer was in place. In early 1964, he became aware of Crossley's MADAM work then being tested at SDC. Wallace proposed to his manager, Carlos Cuadra, that a prototype service be developed for use with an IBM 1401. Crossley and Cuadra agreed to support a prototype, to study how professional staff at a place like SDC would use such a tool and service, and to see if they could use that experience to obtain external support for further development work.

In early 1966, SURF was ready for use. It was programmed in SDC's MADAM language. Users indexed their files, filled out and submitted input coding sheets to the service, and regularly received consolidated index listings (Wallace 1966b). In 1966, once the batch-mode system and service were working well on the IBM 1401 at Santa Monica and had several local SDC users, Wallace offered the service to all SDC staff at all locations. In 1967, SURF was transferred to the successor IBM 360/30, operating in 1401 emulation mode. In 1968 plans were made to operate it in an online time-sharing mode, but this goal was never fully implemented (Wallace 1966a; Wallace 1967; Wallace and Park 1968). Wallace's hope of having SURF mounted on SDC's time-sharing system had to be set aside because the programming staff of SDC's Research Division was already fully committed to ORBIT online search system development.

SURF and MADAM never went online as intended, but we mention them here because they were part of the SDC creative working environment that led to the online systems described in this chapter as well as in chapter 6. Wallace also worked on other SDC projects such as their relevance assessment studies, the *Annual Review of Information Sciences and Technology*, and the IBM 360 version of BOLD.

SATIRE

In 1960, in the SACCS (Strategic Air Command Control System) Department at SDC in Paramus, New Jersey, John Roach developed and implemented a punched card system for use with an in-house technical library (Roach 1961). Using available IBM keypunch and accounting machines, Roach converted more than 10,000 document records into machine-readable form, and used the card equipment to produce 3" x 5" catalog cards and printed indexes. He called the system SATIRE (Semi-Automatic Information Retrieval). Roach (1962) described an upgraded system that replaced the EAM equipment with an IBM 1401, operating in batch mode to produce essentially the same printed products. In 1963, he illustrated how input data and information requests could be transmitted from SDC offices throughout the United States to the IBM 1401 computer complex in Paramus to be processed by SATIRE programs. IBM 066 Data Transceivers could be used to read the source cards and convert the information into signals to be sent over leased lines to Paramus. Upon arrival, the signals were received by an IBM 066 and punched into IBM cards. The cards were then used for twice-daily batch runs with the SATIRE software. This was remote retrieval, but the searcher was disconnected from the computer by a card punching step, and so it was not yet an online system (Roach 1963b).

1963 Milestone

SATIRE was the first bibliographic retrieval system (but probably not an online system) in which microform storage at a searcher's workstation provided expanded versions (e.g., abstracts, extracts, tables of contents, source publications) of the information available online. (See parallel milestone for MICRO.)

At the ADI annual meeting in October, Roach (1963a) described a further upgrade of his system. It included an IBM 1407 remote teletypewriter unit cabled directly to the 1401, and it allowed users to search by keying in predetermined search codes. Users received printouts of citations that included microfilm reel and frame numbers. A Kodak Recordak/Lodestar motorized microfilm reader-printer and archive film cartridges were situated next to the terminal so users could look up the record numbers of retrieved citations. A source document could be brought up on the viewer screen in an average of five seconds. An accompanying microform system was perhaps never used with SATIRE, but it was used with later SDC systems (MICRO, COLEX, CIRCOL). The IBM 1401 was limited, with little or no capability for time sharing; computer searching appeared to be done in a fast batch manner. However, the computer was described as under the control of the person at the terminal, so technically it functioned as an online system. SATIRE retrieved and typed out the selected records, and provided bibliographic references (document number, pagination, author, title, date). It was single-user, noninteractive, nonrecursive, and nonremote, but as described, it could be characterized as an online bibliographic search system. We were unable to find any information regarding SATIRE search features (e.g., Boolean logic, full-text searching).

SATIRE was intended to be used in a self-service, walk-up mode (Roach 1963a). It was expected to provide answers in a fast turnaround time: "an average of a 6-second interval from the time a user formulates his question to the time the 1407 prints out his answers" (Roach 1963a, 166). Roach's presentation was written in a somewhat promissory style, blending descriptions of what the prior batch computer system did, along with statements such as "is designed *to allow*," "*can* provide an average of a 6-second interval," "the complete operational time ... *would be*," and "the SATIRE Display Center *could be used* by Department personnel" [emphases ours]. No statement was made that SATIRE had in fact been demonstrated or put into use, nor claims made about any performance results. It is quite possible that this presentation was in fact a description of extrapolated changes and a proposed future version of the then-functional batch search system. We could not find any evidence that SATIRE actually operated in an online mode.

Roach described SATIRE at an IBM IR workshop in San Jose, California, in March 1963. He was identified as head of SDC Information Services in Paramus, New Jersey. Workshop participants included several IBM representatives active in computerized information processing. A class picture of this interesting and influential group shows several other developers who later demonstrated their systems (Bourne at SRI in September 1963, Summit at Lockheed in 1964–1965, and Freeman at AIP in 1965). They became familiar with Roach's work as a result of attending that workshop.

Healy (1964) provided more background on the history and details of SATIRE. Developed in eight weeks in 1960 by SDC's Command and Control Division, it had been in operation since September 1963. It was installed in a military organization to support use of a collection of 12,000 documents, including 3,000 with security classifications. One of the initial requirements was that it operate on available EAM equipment, and have the potential for conversion to a computer-based system at some future time. The EAM system that was implemented, and was still in use at the time the April 1964 report was published, included a bibliographic description of the reports and numeric codes for subject descriptors, and was used to prepare printed indexes to the report collection.

Healy made no mention of an online system, which supports our suspicion that Roach's discussion of an online system was a proposal for what *could be* done, and not a description of what *had been* done. In spite of its probable limitations, we spotlight SATIRE to show the SDC environment of spawning innovative uses of new technology and to note the first instance in which microform storage at a searcher's workstation provided an expansion of the information available in a computer file.

Protosynthex/Synthex

Two research scientists who had been involved with SAGE, Robert Simmons and Lauren Doyle, worked at SDC in its earliest years. Simmons had earned his doctorate in industrial psychology from the University of Southern California (USC). Before joining Rand in 1955, he worked with USAF pilots on flying safety research. As a visiting scientist at MIT in the summer of 1963, he observed the developments there on TIP (described later). Doyle had earned a B.S. in chemistry from UC-Berkeley. After graduation, he worked as a chemist and then joined RAND to write training documents and teach new programmers. When SDC became an independent operation in 1957, both Simmons and Doyle transferred and joined its research program.

In the spring of 1960, the researchers were on the lookout for new applications of the SAGE technology as well as ways to study conscious processes of thinking, behaving, and other human activities. In May, Simmons, Doyle, and D. P. Estavan (1960) submitted a proposal to ARPA to develop a series of language processors, culminating in a system that would read and understand text, answer English questions, and compose the answers into acceptable English essays. From 1960 through 1966, ARPA funded their project, which was named "Synthex," to represent the Synthesis of Complex Verbal Material. The Synthex project had been organized formally in September 1959 in SDC's Research Directorate and was viewed as an analogy to Memex, the desk-drawer memory machine postulated by Bush (1945). Bush had imagined that Memex would have a capability for microfilm storage of a university library with instant retrieval by index or associated codes. Simmons, however, intended for Synthex to be an information synthesizer (Simmons 1960a). Synthex was the first attempt at SDC to program a computer to do things that, if done by a human, might be regarded as evidence of intelligence. Simmons hoped to learn more about human cognitive functions by synthesizing them on a computer.

The project also aimed to produce a practical system for reading, writing, and answering questions in natural English. Therefore, one Synthex task was to create an experimental question-answering program that accepted questions expressed in natural language. The prototype, called Protosynthex I (prototype Synthex),[2] was a primitive species of Synthex, and was the creation of the psychologist Simmons, programmer analyst Keren McConlogue, and Sheldon Klein, who at the time was working on his doctorate in linguistics. McConlogue was instrumental in developing the indexing and combining-merging-maintenance parts of the system, and Klein contributed to designing the grammatical analysis and logical syntax portions.

In the first months, Protosynthex existed as a "simulated computer in a series of card files" on Simmons's desk (Simmons, Klein, and McConlogue 1962, 402). Question answering could be simulated only manually. Simmons (1962) included an example of how these card files could be used to demonstrate the logic and rules that would need to be programmed. As soon as programmers and linguists became available, the computerized Protosynthex began to take shape, first on an IBM 7090 and later on SDC's IBM AN/FSQ-32V computer—commonly called Q-32 (Simmons 1965b). Since the 7090 had a time-sharing system it was possible to run Protosynthex from a terminal (Cuadra 1997). Data were input via keypunched cards that were read onto magnetic tape. Users communicated with the computer through the large SAGE system circular CRT screens where normally aircraft positions and tracks were plotted, and entered questions from their keyboards directly into core memory. Protosynthex operated on text to reduce it and extract meaning, and then printed out a response (Simmons 1960b). Sentences such as "What are aardvarks?" and "What do aardvarks eat?" did not retrieve bibliographic references, but "answers" that were actually a small selection of sentences from the article on aardvarks in the *Golden Book Encyclopedia* (Borko 1985).

McConlogue wrote the Protosynthex program in a language called JOVIAL, which senior programmer Jules Schwartz had developed in 1959 when SDC won a contract to develop the software for SACCS. Schwartz had also participated in developing the TSS, described earlier. Schwartz's assignment for the contract had been to develop "a 'higher-order' programming language that would permit writing of programs in 'near-English,' in code that was independent of a particular machine, and in statements that were expanded automatically to a number of machine instructions" (Baum 1981, 55). The time pressure, the particular requirements of the application, and the fact that no major information system had ever been coded in other than machine or assembly language were all huge challenges for Schwartz and his twelve-member programming team. Nonetheless, they developed the first version in only four months. In fact, the team developed the data-definition capability, "the original heart of JOVIAL" in about thirty minutes, "when we realized we couldn"t postpone it any longer" (Baum 1981, 56). The language received its distinctive name from Schwartz's staff while he was away on a trip. They first proposed "Our Version of the International Algebraic Language" with the resultant acronym "OVIAL." They did not deem "OVIAL" appropriate, however, for the virile SAC system. By adding a "J" for Schwartz's first name, the name became JOVIAL, or "Jules' Own Version of the International Algebraic Language." JOVIAL became a standard language for SDC programmers who used it for many of the online IR prototypes developed in the sixties.

Protosynthex supported only a single file, and a single terminal hard-wired to the Q-32 computer. This military computer had a 64K word core memory and auxiliary storage on magnetic drums and disk, and "possessed attributes of third generation machines long before they were publicly available" (Becker 1975, 9). The Q-32 had arrived at SDC in Santa Monica in July 1961 aboard twelve flatbed trucks (Baum 1981). The system was time-shared, which meant that the machine could switch from one job to another within milliseconds, giving the appearance to each of the simultaneous users that each had sole use of the computer. Through 1963, the response time was from five to ten minutes; in 1964 it improved to ten to ninety seconds per question. In the 1964 annual report, Simmons and Borko (1965) observed, "The time required per question is a function of the number of words in the question, the number of disk users, and the total number of users of the time-sharing systems" (58).

The index-building programs could combine automatically words that had the same root—in effect providing almost the same capability as right-truncation at search time (Simmons and

McConlogue 1963). It is not clear, however, when this capability was first demonstrated as online right-truncation searching. Simmons (1964, 13) noted:

A query system that accepted English questions not exceeding 20–25 words in length was written. Several versions of this system finally evolved into one which used a synonym dictionary, a root-form logic, and a sophisticated technique for scoring the relevance of potential answering sentences and paragraphs. Although a great many interesting improvements on this query system could be introduced to make it a truly efficient information retrieval vehicle, our decision was that these improvements were of less importance to an understanding of language processing than was the more direct study of what constitutes an answer to a question.

In 1963, Protosynthex used Volume, Article, Paragraph, and Sentence (VAPS) data for each word in the database text material. This, in principle, gave it a capability to look for two or more terms that occurred in the same sentence. However, without also recording information about word location in a sentence, it would not be possible to do word proximity searching (McConlogue and Simmons 1965). It is not clear when, or if Protosynthex ever did word proximity searching, or did it online.

Simmons and staff linguist John Olney first demonstrated the computerized Protosynthex I sometime in 1963 or 1964 (the event was not documented in the literature). Also, it is not clear whether or not this was an online system. Most of the reports suggest that it was not online in 1963. For example, the *Research Directorate Report* for 1963 described how much progress had been made with Synthex in increasing understanding of natural language processing, but made no mention of online. According to the report, Protosynthex was "nearing completion," and further, "This protosynthex uses the learning parser . . . as a basis for obtaining the dependencies used for matching the structure of questions and of proposed answers" (Simmons et al. 1964, 7). The 1964 annual report noted the installation of the first disk file in 1964; thus, Synthex could not have been on disk files before 1964. The report also said that plans for online retrieval of facts about the time-sharing system were being formulated. In May, Simmons (1964, 11) described the system as online only in the context of an online parser; he gave no evidence of online searching. He noted:

The McConlogue dependency parser is the current version. It is an on-line system that attempts to parse a sentence, submit the result to a human, and only after the human accepts or corrects the analysis adds the newly computed word classes to its dictionary. This system, in conjunction with the on-line operating capability offered by the ARPA/SDC time-sharing system, for the first time allows a protosynthex to bypass (and eventually to solve) the problems raised by ambiguous syntactic analyses.

This hints at an online aspect to the parsing program, but perhaps only as a research tool for building the language analysis tools, not for retrieving relevant text, which would have been a more complex retrieval process than Boolean term matching. This report thus confirmed that Protosynthex was online in 1964, but did not make clear which parts (parser, question-answer) were online. In concluding sections where he talked about his immediate and future plans for Protosynthex, Simmons made no mention of online activities. One could infer from this that Protosynthex had no online query and retrieval capability before 1965. In another paper written originally as an in-house technical report in April 1964, Simmons (1965a, 60) said that the most relevant sentences were "then retrieved from tape on which the original text was stored." That suggests that Protosynthex did not have access to disk storage before 1965, searching was not interactive before 1965, and probably was not online before 1965.

In May, Farell (1965, 17) stated that the output of the Synthex indexing program "could be stored on the disk for quick random access during Time-Sharing operations." This statement, along with later confirmation by staff who were there at the time, sets early 1965 as the time by when we can be fairly certain that Protosynthex was an online retrieval system. We have to be careful about inferring too much from these early reports regarding the state of the online technology being used or not used. Probably because the developers were most focused on building a question-answering system with sophisticated language processing capabilities, the issue of whether or not parts or the entire program were online is not documented clearly.

Harold ("Hal") Borko was an attentive observer and admitted kibitzer of the Protosynthex project. He recalled (1985) that in an early version the questions were keypunched into IBM punched cards, read into the computer, and then, less than fifteen seconds later, the system generated large stacks of cards and huge printouts. As no intermediate set numbers were generated to facilitate later processing, modifying the question required that a new query be keypunched. Thus the system was online query and retrieval, but it was not interactive or recursive; a searcher could not modify and continue a search on the basis of intermediate search results. The program did not have a Boolean search capability and was cumbersome in input-output communication. It was, nevertheless, an operating online system (Simmons and Borko 1965).

The earliest demonstration of Protosynthex illustrated the concepts, but the system was not ready for users. Only a few pages of the encyclopedia were in the file, entered by keypunching (expensive and slow), and according to Parker (1988), who witnessed a demonstration, only a small portion of the branching tree menu was implemented at this time. Searchers had in reality only one "choice" or path at each branch of the tree; everything else was blank. Protosynthex used a synonym dictionary, a complex intersection logic, and a simple information scoring function to select those sentences, paragraphs, or encyclopedia articles that most resembled the question. Both the question and the retrieved text were parsed and compared. Matching was accomplished by a complex set of programs that built a matrix of all the words from the question and from the possible answers. Users could interact with the parser to correct errors and clarify ambiguities and thus filter out irrelevant data and gradually arrive at the answer to the question (Simmons, Klein, and McConlogue 1964). Simmons (1967, 270) called it "a symbiotic system in which man works with the computer to help resolve both syntactic and semantic ambiguities. Only in this fashion is the program able to overcome the problems associated with multiple, apparently valid interpretations of the same sentence or question."

During 1965 the indexer and query system of Protosynthex I were rewritten to take advantage of more detailed information, including sequence numbers for each text word. The new query system allowed a user to select and change the set of function words to be ignored, since the indexing program indexed all words. The algorithm used to score the relevance of retrieval strings was also modified to improve its performance.

McConlogue and Simmons (1965) reported the results of empirical tests with a Pattern Learning Parser that could parse correctly a sample of 400 sentences in "basic English," but needed further development for its use on "ordinary English." Protosynthex II, a question-answering system based on a specialized conceptual dictionary, was also developed during 1965. It was programmed under LISP 1.5 and used experimentally under the name LEARN (Simmons and Borko 1966). "It successfully answered a limited range of English questions and offered an extremely limited capability to generate childish essays in response to a 'describe' command" (Simmons et al. 1967, 5–9). In an August 1965 presentation published in March 1966, Simmons (1966c) reported that their conceptual dictionary existed as an experimental program in 47K of Q-32 core memory, limiting them to a dictionary of from 200 to 300 words and a small set of program functions. Experiments were run with both Protosynthex I and II in 1965, using 600 sentences from the *Golden Book Encyclopedia*. Protosynthex II could parse and store sentences as subsets of a database, and respond to queries such as "What do policemen do?" "What do horses eat?" "What do baby octopi eat?" "Describe a cat" "Name four small animals with long tails" (Simmons 1966a, 5–6).

Plans at the end of 1965 were to translate Protosynthex I from the Q-32 time-sharing system to the

IBM 360 system and also to continue further developments of Protosynthex II (Simmons, Burger, and Long 1966). According to the annual report for 1965 (Simmons and Borko 1966, 5-2), Protosynthex I and II were both online in 1965: "Mainly as the result of last year's efforts several interesting and at least moderately useful systems have come into existence. These include the document retrieval system, BOLD; the question answering systems, Protosynthex I and II; the McConlogue Pattern Learning Parser; and a group of automatic indexing and classification tools useful at both the language and library analysis levels."

As of January 1967, Protosynthex I had been translated to SDC's IBM 360 time-sharing system. Final checkout as an effective retrieval tool, however, was still waiting for further development of IBM 360 software. After checkout, it was expected to become a shelf product for use in demonstrations and selected text retrieval applications, with no further modification.

Based on the experience with Protosynthex II, Protosynthex III was designed as the first breadboard model of a complete-language processing system, including question-answering. Protosynthex III was implemented in 1966 on the Q-32 time-sharing system. Although a major effort was made in 1967 to further develop it, Simmons, Burger, and Schwarcz (1968, 454) portrayed Protosynthex III as slow and cumbersome, and sharply limited in its storage capacity: " 'Slow' means concretely that a typical sentence requires 90 seconds of compute time to analyze while an equivalent question requiring no great amount of inference may compute for three to four minutes. When these compute times are translated to wait-times on the time-shared system, analyzing and answering a question may take from fifteen to thirty minutes." A JOVIAL version of Protosynthex III, also for the Q-32 time-shared system, had been designed and already partly programmed by William Schoene. This JOVIAL version was to have access to eight million words of disk storage and expected turnaround times of from five to fifteen seconds.

Schwarcz, Burger, and Simmons (1970) provided a further description of Protosynthex III. The capabilities for sentence analysis and generation, lexical and syntactic paraphrase, and deductive question answering were combined for the first time in a single system. The researchers concluded that developing Protosynthex III into a practical system to work with large files was possible, but would require changes in both the data structures and algorithms used for question answering.

The emphasis of Protosynthex was more on linguistic research than on retrieval, with the goal being to create useful and practical automated language processors. The project was part of a general series of studies on linguistics and artificial intelligence and of all of the studies at that time, provided the richest source of insights and technology. It was also the first of a series of natural language query systems that scientists at SDC developed over many years (Baum 1981). Even though Protosynthex answered questions rather than retrieving bibliographic citations, the technology developed for the question answering systems (syntactic analysis of questions and file text, relevance assessment and ranking, query enhancement by truncation of search terms, prompting, or inclusion of alternate word forms, and search aid displays) was relevant and transferable to bibliographic or text retrieval systems and should be recognized as truly innovative. This early work is also relevant to later efforts to develop "user-friendly" online full-text search systems. Protosynthex was actually used, but reprogrammed and modified to improve operating efficiencies, with 1965 TEXTIR that we examine next.

Simmons continued his work at SDC until the end of 1968 when he left to join the University of Texas at Austin as a professor of psychology and computer science. The Synthex work at SDC stopped at that time. Doyle continued at SDC until 1966 when he left to form a consulting practice and to work for Becker and Hayes, Inc. He contributed to other information processing studies and authored several publications.

TEXTIR

From the domain of a children's encyclopedia to the grownup world of robbery reports was a short step for the next application of Synthex. Since 1963, SDC had been cooperating with the Los Angeles Police Department (LAPD) to explore use of natural language computer processing of crime reports in a time-shared manner and to develop a system to process crime information in natural English language (Herrmann and Isaacs 1964). This was a logical extension of work already done by LAPD to implement a large-scale information system that used punched card tabulating equipment and files of punched cards. For this project SDC expended a great effort on the system's ability to handle the semantic issues (Barden 1965).

1964 Milestones

TEXTIR was the first online search system to accept search questions in natural language form.

TEXTIR was the first online search system to demonstrate a search approach that selected the source text material that most closely represented the question text.

In April 1964, Herbert Isaacs and other SDC and LAPD staff announced a year-long joint program of experimentation in computer processing of crime information in natural English language. They reported that a prototype version of the Synthex software had been successfully demonstrated in March on a database of full-text robbery reports (a structured report form with fixed field formatted data and narrative full-text information). Queries were sent to SDC's Q-32 computer in Santa Monica via telephone from a Teletype Model 35 terminal at LAPD headquarters. In response, the system searched its file and transmitted the texts of retrieved reports back by Teletype in relevance rank order. File conversion work had begun in June 1963 using punched card equipment, but was changed in October 1963 to Model 35 teletypewriters that produced punched paper tape that was later converted to the magnetic tape needed for the Q-32 and Synthex programs.

The March 1964 experiments used a file of unspecified size, but we have surmised that it was less than 200 records. The Synthex QUEST (Question) program was stored in auxiliary memory and available on-demand to operate on the index and source data stored on magnetic tape. No disk storage was used for the file at this time. The indexing program parsed the entire content of the narrative portions of the records, and on request produced the complete records as output. This initial experimentation revealed a need for several modifications to be made to the research-oriented Synthex software to make it more useful for this application. Staff began to make those changes in April 1964.

In May 1965, Isaacs and Jules Farell provided separate update reports on the project (Isaacs 1966; Farell 1965), which now carried the name TEXTIR (Text Indexing and Retrieval, or Textual Information Retrieval). While TEXTIR incorporated the concepts of Synthex, which was still operating in prototype mode at that time, TEXTIR was more suited to applications (Spierer and Wills 1969). Separate programs were written for the TEXTIR project: INDEX to build the file and indexes, and FIND to do the search and output processing. Basic TEXTIR capabilities included automatic indexing of every substantive word in machine-readable documents, and retrieving preselected portions of those indexed reports in response to natural English queries.

Isaacs and Farell, along with LeRoy McCabe and William Crossley, modified the Synthex programs for the experiment in order to improve operating efficiency on the Q-32, and to accommodate the particular data used. Their database contained about 3,000 robbery reports, representing 1.5 million word occurrences with about 20,000 unique content words. The indexing program had a small stop list.

The retrieval program was initiated by a teletyped request from a user; the system responded by asking for the tape reel numbers containing the data to be searched.

> **1965 Milestone**
>
> TEXTIR was the first online search system to incorporate synonyms automatically into the search formulation.

TEXTIR could not perform simultaneous searches, and output was restricted to a single dedicated Teletype terminal. However, searches were made remotely from LAPD terminals, as well as locally at SDC in Santa Monica. A single query was limited to a maximum of six questions of six English words each. Searchers were asked to enter synonyms, although the retrieval program (FIND) did include a capability (adapted from the Synthex offline index-building program) to store a table of common abbreviations and synonyms to be included automatically into the search formulation. This was a change first considered in 1964. Protosynthex in 1964 had a synonym capability, but only in its offline version. It was proposed, but not implemented in the 1963 SRI system for plurals, variant forms, synonyms, and generic relationships. It was done with TEXTIR to address the practical problem of handling nomenclature unique to this particular application, but the principle was the same as that used later (e.g., SUNY BCN in 1971) for handling the most common misspellings and variants in medical terminology, and even later in the 1980s with systems to handle British versus American spellings (e.g., grey gray; honor honour).

Because the search process was slow (the first replies were provided within 5 to 10 minutes of query input), a status report message (n REPORTS SEARCHED) was displayed periodically (after each 1,000 reports had been searched). This was an early attempt to pacify a searcher who was waiting impatiently at a quiet terminal for an answer and wondering whether the system was still working on it. Along with the status report was an interim printout of the best answer (by a relevance-judging algorithm) found up to that point. A variation of the normal TEXTIR operation existed in which the extracts of all reports were stored on the Q-32 disk file instead of magnetic tape; this speeded up the retrieval process considerably, but had to remain an optional feature because the availability of the Q-32 TSS disk space was unknown at any given time.

> **1965 Milestone**
>
> TEXTIR was the first online search system to prompt a searcher for information about search specifications.

TEXTIR also provided searchers with some control over the level of detail and number of documents displayed, by asking whether extracts of retrieved source documents were to be included in the output display (EXTRACTS Y/N), and how many records were to be displayed (HOW MANY REPLIES/QUERY). TEXTIR seems to have been the first of the SDC family of search systems that asked a searcher a variety of YES/NO questions. It was an important and useful option in 1965 because the teletypewriter was such a slow output device.

> **1964 Milestone**
>
> TEXTIR was the first online search system to demonstrate an output relevance ranking algorithm, and the first to provide search output in rank order by a query relevance score.

A "no" answer to the EXTRACTS Y/N prompt produced search output consisting of the document record numbers, the subset of query words that matched words in the source text, and the scores used to rank the degree of match (relative relevance) of each item retrieved. The scores were included primarily as an evaluation aid to the experimenters. The retrieval value of each query word was assessed by the FIND program by the inverse frequency of its use in the total database—the assumption was that less frequent words have greater value. The scores of the words (score values for each word were 1, 2, or 3) that intersected a document were totaled in order to calculate a score for the document's relevance to a query. Scores were computed on a sentence-by-sentence basis. Then the system followed up with a sorting of the output records into rank order by relevance scores. This seems to have been the first instance of a display of a relevance score with the online search output; as we saw earlier, TEXTIR had been computing such a score since 1964 and following up with a sorting of retrieved output records into rank order by relevance scores. Farell (1965, 14) reported that in practice: "The computer would search its alphabetic index, find all the question words and the reports in which they appeared, sort these to choose those reports in which some number of question-words appeared together in sentences, and print out for the user a list of the most relevant reports, in order of relevance, along with automatically produced extracts of each report." Protosynthex used relevance scoring, but it does not appear to have been done in an online manner before the TEXTIR demonstration.

> **1965 Milestone**
>
> TEXTIR was the first online search system to demonstrate search term weighting.

In 1965, TEXTIR permitted users to do some search term weighting. By preceding a term with a plus sign, a searcher could direct TEXTIR to increase the score assigned to that word, and thus raise the score of the source document that contained that word. The score was increased by an absolute fixed amount, so the searcher did not have a fully flexible term weighting system as used at that time in several batch search systems; it was more like major/minor descriptor searching used later in other search systems.

McCabe and Farr (1966) reported on the system design study for Phase I of the LAPD (Los Angeles Police Department) Information System conducted between June 1965 and January 1966 jointly by LAPD and SDC. The major study product was documentation of a concept for the design and operation of an automatic information system for crime and related reports, wanted and warrant information, and field interview information.

As used in this project, TEXTIR operated in a time-shared, remote-access online mode. However, because most of its operation was based on magnetic tape storage instead of direct-access devices (the 1,000 most used terms were stored in core, the remainder were stored on tape), it could not provide truly interactive online searching. It was, nonetheless, another example of an early online search system, further indication of the innovative work environment at SDC, and a demonstration of new features such as system status reports, user prompts, relevance ranking, and automatic inclusion of synonyms, all of which would be used in later online systems.

In 1965 reports appeared of SDC participation in developing a major online system for New York State that would allow law enforcement officers throughout the state to query a computer through remote input and output devices, and to receive facsimiles of important documents and information as well as identifying fingerprints. The proposed system was expected to begin partial operations by April 1967 and to be fully operational by 1969 (Smith 1965). During 1963–1965, New York State provided over $600,000 to SDC for this project.

LUCID

Another SDC development took place in November 1964, also under an ARPA contract. LUCID (Language Used to Communicate Information System Design) Phase I was demonstrated using the Q-32 computer, under the direction of Emory Franks, with the participation of P. A. DeSimone. In June of the previous year, Franks (1963) had described LUCID as providing both a language in which designs of data management systems could be expressed, and a programming system to convert this expression of design automatically into something that could be run on a computer. Ivan Sutherland[3] was the project monitor at ARPA, and he successfully tested LUCID by Teletype from Washington during the last weeks in 1964. LUCID provided all the machinery necessary to describe, load, maintain, and interrogate large files. However, a report of 1964 activities (Franks and DeSimone 1965) gave no indication that LUCID had been used for bibliographic or full-text searching. LUCID was an interactive data management system, performing as a question-answering system, using a structured database (Simmons 1966a). It was impressive at the time for its speed and flexibility. Other existing systems were rigidly preprogrammed, which meant that changing the format or content of a computer response involved weeks or months of reprogramming. "By contrast, the LUCID user could conduct a flexible, instantaneous dialog with a complex data base, browse through data at random, and derive new comparisons and unanticipated relationships" (Baum 1981, 117). Phase I capabilities allowed LUCID to accept user-defined data and processes in symbolic form, to load and organize user data automatically, and to permit users to search the file online.

In 1965, Robert Bleier, the TSS-LUCID project leader, directed the reprogramming to make LUCID-generated files compatible with Q-32 disk storage and to integrate major LUCID subsystems into time sharing. By fall 1965, SDC programmers used LUCID for experiments in design trade-offs in online operations. In September 1965, LUCID was among the systems demonstrated at the SDC second symposium on computer-centered database systems.

In early 1967, work began on a graphical display system for the Q-32, to expand the role of CRT displays and light pens in data management systems. This program was operating in 1968, and was the forerunner of the display components of TDMS. The Q-32 time-sharing system with this software was averaging 25–30 simultaneous users during prime time in 1968. Bowman and Lickhalter (1968) described LUCID as SDC's initial large-scale, time-shared data management system and gave several examples of applications with various databases (none, however, were with bibliographic or full-text). One application to an outside database, when it was used as part of CONVERSE to search the U.S. Census database, will be described later. LUCID was included in an August 1968 report that described the capabilities of five interactive data handling systems that could be used to access online the COSATI inventory of U.S. government–sponsored work in progress in the area of information science and technology (Welch 1968), as well as in a COSATI film, described in chapter 4.

1965 Milestone

LUCID was the first search system to permit a searcher to modify the database online.

Welch's report (1968, 51) provided tantalizingly brief descriptions of LUCID features, including: "Automatic assignment of synonyms-user may use synonyms in place of longer alpha terms. . . . System acknowledges all input as soon as received by typing out 4 dashes. . . . On-line file maintenance is possible-allows user to immediately correct any errors he detects in his data base." The high level of direct interactivity with the database content implied by this last statement suggests that the user group was small and highly selected.

LUCID became obsolete at the end of the sixties when SDC phased out the Q-32 and replaced it with the newest third-generation IBM 360 computer, which had become available for DOD agencies and contractors. LUCID had served well, however, as an important predecessor of SDC's later data management system, TDMS (chapter 6) (Bleier 1967). Even though TDMS was developed as an improvement upon LUCID, LUCID continued to be used extensively. Spierer and Wills (1969) observed that LUCID accounted for 15 percent of total Q-32 processing and console time, and even though it was originally designed in 1962 as a vehicle for research and experimentation in information system design, it had been continually refined since then in response to user demand. This paper made no mention of use of LUCID for bibliographic or full-text files, so we suspect it was never used for that purpose.

BOLD

Another human factors research scientist working at SDC in the 1960s was Hal Borko, who had earned his Ph.D. in clinical psychology from USC in 1952. He served in the U.S. Army as a clinical psychologist until 1956, when he resigned his commission to accept employment with Rand Corporation. He joined SDC in 1957 when it split off from Rand, and gained experience with computers and their application to the behavioral sciences from his involvement with a system training program for the U.S. Air Defense Command in which computers were used to design, produce, and analyze the effectiveness of training exercises. Borko worked on the Cranfield experiments on recall and precision in 1958 and, by the early 1960s, was studying the application of computers to language processing and IR, as well as other IR research projects, including one on abstracting techniques and another on automated document classification. Throughout the 1960s, he worked on methods for developing computer-derived subject classification schemes. In 1964, Borko was associate head of the Language Processing and Retrieval group at SDC. The head was Simmons, the chief in the Synthex and Protosynthex projects. Other staff working with Borko were Doyle (also associated with Protosynthex), Robert Katter, Howard Burnaugh (who did the BOLD programming, particularly the displays), William Moore, and other investigators in linguistics, logic, and library science. They all wanted to understand the concepts underlying retrieval of information from documents, with the practical goal of automating the process. They studied the statistical distribution of words in text, sentence grammar (machine parsing), the strategies employed by humans for abstracting and indexing documents, the conceptual structure of libraries, and the potential of machine-aided document searching. All of this research contributed to Borko's familiarity with a range of IR issues and techniques of that time. Borko reported later that Simmons continually pushed him, however, "to do something practical." The result in 1964 was BOLD.

Becker (1975, 10) referred to BOLD as "Borko's Own Little Demonstrator." Others, including Borko himself, joked that it was "Borko's Old Lousy Display" (Spigai 1986, 75). SDC's 1964 annual report referred to it as "Bibliographic Organization for Library Display." Borko's June 1965 technical memo (Borko 1965a) and a magazine article ("The BOLD Librarian" 1966) defined the acronym as "Bibliographic On-Line Display." Borko (1985) recalled that, in the national economic climate of 1964, BOLD was an expensive research project. Part of its support came from the National Science Foundation (NSF) and Office of Naval Research (ONR), which supplied "all the money we wanted—for any *reasonable* project" (Borko 1985).

The BOLD research team was fortunate also to be situated at SDC, which in the 1960s possessed several state-of-the-art computers and boasted that "these machines unquestionably make SDC's in-house facilities the largest computer complex in the world" (Baum 1981, 92). The BOLD terminal was cabled to the Q-32, which was used heavily for research and development and training systems for real-time processing of early-warning air defense data. The team managed to get time on the machine to develop and test BOLD. Burnaugh wrote the file generation, display and retrieval programs and prepared a technical description of the subsystems (Burnaugh 1966b,c). Borko (1985) considered it a small leap from SAGE online retrieval of resource statements on fighter planes, to BOLD retrieving record numbers associated with specific words.

BOLD was an experimental system for file generation and real-time document retrieval that was part of the larger SDC research effort on machine processing of English text. A goal for BOLD was "the integration of display capabilities to allow browsing through the magnetic tape file as well as for search on-line for specific information" (Carter, Marzocco, and Drukey 1965, 62). Like TIP at MIT, BOLD was intended to be a research tool for studying computer-based document storage and retrieval, and also for comparing retrieval effectiveness of various indexing and classification systems. Burnaugh (1967, 53) described BOLD as "a usable retrieval system, but [it] also affords a means for research on the components of such a system."

The BOLD display program was based on an SDC-developed, ARPA-supported program called VARDIS (Variable Display) and on other SDC work on output display systems, including the General Purpose Display System (GPDS), developed in 1964–1965 (Vorhaus 1965; Bowman 1965). Burnaugh and Moore directed the VARDIS project, which was intended for retrieval and arrangement of specific data needed for an immediate problem. VARDIS was a flexible tool for providing tabular displays for military command post simulations. It operated under the Q-32 time-sharing system and used input-output devices such as teletypewriters, CRT display consoles, and light pens that the staff adopted for BOLD. By late 1964, an initial version had been programmed and was in operation with several sample databases. BOLD can be viewed as an improved version of VARDIS, adapted for retrieval of document references.

By the end of 1964, the system design specified two main functions: to facilitate browsing by displaying document references and abstracts within specified classification categories; and to facilitate retrieval by displaying document references correlated with specified terms. The planners wanted future users to be able to request documents by specifying either broad classification categories (to permit browsing in a manner similar to card catalog use), or a specific classification category with publication date ranges, or one or more authors, or tag terms that could be designated as inclusive or exclusive for the set. As a user defined a set, BOLD was to respond with a tally of the total number of records in that set, before it proceeded with the display of the individual titles or abstracts. Also by the end of 1964, work on the file and index building programs had progressed through design of the tables and coding of the most important subroutines. Available machine-readable texts were examined for use in testing. The system was not yet operational, but it was close.

In March 1965, the first version was just about debugged; and the team was planning and writing programs for BOLD, hoping to have it in operation in the near future (Simmons 1965b). In August, Borko reported that BOLD's main functions had been modified to provide three capabilities: (1) browsing through a tape file by subject category and displaying titles, authors, and abstracts of retrieved documents on a CRT; (2) retrieving documents on given subjects by combining index terms and having a user select relevant items from a CRT display of document references and abstracts; and (3) studying the comparative retrieval effectiveness of various indexing and classification systems (remember that Borko was working at the same time on other funded research projects on automatic classification and subject analysis). At this time, Borko (1965b) said BOLD was an experimental computer-based system for file generation and real-time document retrieval; even though it did use files on magnetic tape (upon initiation of the search process, the tape was transferred to disk memory for faster processing).

In 1965, BOLD was available to Q-32 users and it was SDC's "major line of research in improving query capability" (Simmons and Borko 1966, 5-1). Interaction was accomplished by typing search input on a Teletype. Output was displayed on a CRT console (also called a scope). Users could select options by pointing a light pen at the scope, which also displayed all the essential instructions for using BOLD. Users could obtain permanent copies of the retrieved records on the Teletype. BOLD was planned for eventual incorporation into a total system for automatically indexing, classifying, and abstracting a 1–10 million document library. The designers intended that it would operate in a time-sharing environment that permitted multiple users to do simultaneous real-time retrieval from the same database. Borko recalled later, however, that BOLD was never used by more than one person at a time. The retrieval was online, in real-time, but searchers could not manipulate the sets online—they could only reenter them or further restrict the last answer set. Thus, searching was not recursive, because no set numbers were created to be incorporated into the search process. Borko (1994) commented, "None of the BOLD stuff was really interactive; it was all fast-batch time-shared operation, in which you had to re-run a search with a modified new search, rather than modifying the results of a current search."

Like Protosynthex, BOLD was written in JOVIAL, with some subroutines in machine code (SCAMP). The query language was intended to be a close approximation of natural language and easy to use. Many conventions could be accomplished simply by pointing the light pen to the proper place on the scope. Borko was proud of the BOLD interface, but not optimistic about the long term: "Ideally, the user with only a knowledge of the English language and a skill in typing should be able to establish a rapport with the machine . . . this ideal may never be fully achieved" (Borko 1967, 331). Some commands had to be followed by a slash, and a question mark was used to interrogate the system, but the other interactions did not require any punctuation. Borko (1968, 594) listed the commands:

B = Begin or start over
↑ = Go back to the previous display
□ = Browse
◇ = Search
R = Remove
S = Save on tape
T = Print on teletypewriter
E = Exchange
C = Continue

1965 Milestone

BOLD was the first online search system to use an existing machine-readable file of bibliographic records (a sample from the DDC database) created by another organization.

The records were 6,000 bibliographic citations plus abstracts of technical reports from the Defense Documentation Center (DDC), grouped into subject categories according to the DDC subject classification system. Up to this point, all online system developers had used machine-readable files of library catalog records already existing in-house, or had created their own files, or had used nonbibliographic records. Even though more than 6,000 bibliographic records and their abstracts had been processed, searching was done on a subset of only 534 records, and since the texts of the abstracts were not parsed into the online index, the abstracts were displayable but not searchable.

1965 Milestone

BOLD was the first online search system to demonstrate retrieval by subject classification codes rather than text words.

BOLD was flexible enough to use various classification and indexing systems. BOLD offered two modes of access. The first was the browse mode, in which searchers used a light pen to choose one of thirty-two main classification categories (e.g., Electronics; Fluid Mechanics; Fuels and Combustion). Then a searcher could request a display of full bibliographic information (title, author, date and place of publication, index terms, and abstract) of every document in that subject category. Further subdivisions could be displayed by using the light pen to flash a particular division. The idea was to simulate using a card catalog or wandering through open library stacks, by supplying the same kinds of clues that these familiar information-seeking modes provided.

In 1965 BOLD also permitted an online interrogation of a dictionary for synonyms or for words related either by spelling or hierarchy. After displaying particular subject classification categories selected by a searcher, BOLD could also display any available subcategories and/or synonyms for the one selected. Using Boolean connectors with the retrieval phrases, the searcher then defined a document set for retrieval. The information in the answer set could be provided in several different formats as requested, including display of the abstracts associated with the retrieved bibliographic records. By the end of 1965, the retrieval and display capabilities that were available included dictionary interrogation, abstract browsing, search mode, and creation of synonyms and hierarchies in the dictionary.

Burnaugh (1966c) documented the earliest and most complete description of the BOLD system as it existed in January 1966 (and presumably in late 1965), including search examples and sample displays. He noted that it provided posting counts for individual search terms and sets of search terms. BOLD produced copies of retrieved information on the Teletype or on a magnetic tape for offline listing. Stem searching was done automatically for any search term keyed in; that is, for interrogating the dictionary, the search program stripped the retrieval term of any suffix and searched for the root word. The program responded with all forms of the root word in the dictionary. In September, Burnaugh (1966a) created a user's manual.

1966 Milestone

BOLD may have been the first online bibliographic search system that enabled users to display an online thesaurus as a search aid. (See parallel milestone for TIRP.)

In the commonly used search mode, users specified a combination of descriptors using the Boolean operators OR, AND, and NOT (BOLD interpreted a blank between terms as OR). Since BOLD used a form of coordinate indexing, users were helped to develop a search strategy by being allowed to interrogate the online dictionary for synonyms and related indexing terms (either by spelling or hierarchy). For example, by entering SPACESHIPS? a user received a list of terms associated with that word. BOLD thus may have been the first system to demonstrate the provision of an online search aid such as a thesaurus. The intention was to free users from having to rely on trained information specialists to select appropriate controlled indexing terms.[4]

As a unique feature, the program displayed a matrix on the CRT showing how many search terms were present in each document by means of asterisks to represent the number of occurrences of the terms. From this matrix, a user had a good idea of which documents were likely to be most relevant. This display appears to have been a precursor to later developments in ranking output and providing postings counts for search terms. BOLD also supplied the number of documents matching each search term and the total number of documents in the set. The provision of posting count information, particularly for individual search terms, became an important feature of many later online search systems.

Before printing the output, a user could modify the display by using a light pen to specify display options (titles, authors, abstracts, or index terms), remove references that were not of interest, or reorder the arrangement of the document identification numbers. Then a hard copy of the display could be printed on the teletypewriter or saved on magnetic tape for offline printing.

A February 1966 SDC proposal forecast that, "When the system is complete, it will be possible to use it for on-line information retrieval and for preparing data files for computer-based systems" (*System development study* 1966, 105). Plans for 1966 included development of the dictionary interrogation capability to present better information to a user, refinement of the query process by a Boolean expression in order to provide guidance and more precise query formulation, provision of a capability to accomplish online modifications to the database and the dictionary, and production of a more efficient and compact program. In April, Burnaugh said that BOLD was being checked with a database of 1,121 records from the DDC tape of 6,000 citations and abstracts—an increase from the 534 records used for the initial experimentation.

1965 Milestone

BOLD was the first online search system to provide posting counts of the number of records associated with each search term.

Burnaugh also noted that BOLD was providing posting counts with answer sets. Posting counts had been provided on demand in TIP in 1964, but this appears to be the first instance in which posting counts were provided automatically with each search expression. With a light pen, entries could be removed from the CRT display and/or transferred to a listing tape for hard copy printout. Users had extensive capability at this time for interrogating and modifying the dictionary. BOLD was designed to be operated in a time-shared environment to serve multiple simultaneous users doing real-time retrieval.

BOLD at this time required that a request for dictionary information be preceded by a period. Burnaugh (1966c) illustrated how BOLD responded with all of the entries in the dictionary (index) that had that root, along with their posting counts:

```
.HEAT
  6 entries are ref'd by heat
  1 entries are ref'd by heaters
  2 entries are ref'd by heating
*end.
```

This form of assumed search mode (i.e., a user did not have to enter a command word for searching, but only had to enter a period followed by a search term and the system proceeded directly to an index lookup), entry, and response continued through later systems (e.g., ORBIT, MEDLINE, BRS).

Burnaugh (1967) also described a thesaurus capability. The thesaurus feature was invoked by entering an input phrase followed by a question mark. The program then sent back all dictionary entries (but without posting counts) that had similar spelling or that were defined as synonyms or as superordinate to the input phrase. For example:

```
.HEAT?
The following may be similar to
heat
  heat
  thermodynamics
  enthalpy
  heat exchanges
  heat of formation
  heat of fusion
  heat of sublimation
  heat production
  heat resistant alloys
  heat resistant polymers
  heat transfer
  heat treatment
  heaters
  heating
*end
```

In the previous example, thermodynamics and enthalpy were defined as a superordinate word and synonym, respectively, and the rest qualified because of spelling.

Burnaugh's April 1966 report also described an output relevance ranking feature. Items retrieved were sorted into rank order by relevance (as measured by the sum of hits on the search terms). Relevance was considered to be proportional to the number of matching search terms found in each record. A matrix display was also produced, with search term numbers at the top of the row columns, and report numbers as the lines of the matrix. An X was placed at the intersection of each report number and its matching term, and the lines sorted and displayed in rank order sequence by the number of hits per document. Relevance scoring and output ranking had been demonstrated earlier at SDC with TEXTIR and MICRO.

Borko and Burnaugh (1966) updated the description of BOLD. They expected that the JOVIAL programs for file building, display, and retrieval would be rewritten for an IBM 360/67 when that computer became available later in the fiscal year. The database had now grown in size to be the first 1,745 records from the DDC tape. When a user logged on to BOLD, the system acknowledged that the file and program tapes were loaded, and then the user started the search by entering the B or BEGIN character, followed by a slash. This BEGIN initialization command was later used by DIALOG and all of its derivative systems.

In another report, Borko (1967) gave examples of the utility of online interactive displays, as used with three different SDC systems, the General Purpose Display System (GPDS), the Pattern Learning Parser (PLP-II) described earlier as part of Protosynthex, and BOLD. He stated that BOLD was supported by SDC's independent research funds. This really meant that BOLD was developed with U.S. government support, since SDC's independent research funds were part of the overhead charge included in their billing for their other government projects.

Simmons (1966b, 8) gave credit to both Borko and Burnaugh as the developers of BOLD, observing that "The system works almost instantaneously, even in the time-shared mode with fifteen or more users of the computer." Freeman (1995), then working on a project at the American Institute of Physics (AIP) to develop a computer-based search system for the physics literature, recounted his experience in using BOLD in 1966: "Time-shared systems in those days were often quite slow. However, my time came directly after a demo for an Air Force general and they had kicked all of the other users off the system for him. So I had good, fast response time."

SDC's 1966 annual report (Simmons and Borko 1967, 5-22) summed up the year's progress: "We have completed the programming of BOLD and have been improving the displays and interactive aspects in order to make it more responsive and easier to use. The programs have also been modified so that the system can be used without the scope facilities, thus making the system available to remote users." The report predicted that BOLD would be reprogrammed in 1967 for the IBM 360 system. The reprogramming, however, never happened. Because SDC was planning at that time to change to a for-profit organization, it could not justify that R&D investment. Borko (1994) recalled, "Wes Churchman kept pushing us, asking 'what products can you produce?' ORBIT became that profit-making product, and the recipient of the SDC internal development support."

1967 Milestone

BOLD was the first online search system to be searched from a terminal outside the country in which the computer operated.

Borko demonstrated BOLD in Rome in June 1967. This appears to have been the first overseas demonstration of an American online retrieval system. This was not, however, the first long-distance demonstration; three years earlier, SRI's search system had demonstrated online searching over a distance of about 400 miles. After BOLD, the next international demonstration was done with TIRP in July 1967.

Spierer and Wills (1969) observed that BOLD was intended to have been a research vehicle, but had been used at SDC to retrieve information on document holdings from the U.S. Geologic Survey, DDC, NIH, and the Armed Forces Technical Information Agency (ASTIA). We have no information about these BOLD experiments that used databases other than DDC records. BOLD was designed to deal with up to 100,000 bibliographic records and to be tested in live situations with users (Simmons 1966b). Even though these ambitions were never realized (the database did not appear to grow beyond 1,745 records), BOLD should be recognized for being a pioneering prototype of an online bibliographic search system that employed a simple command language intended for end-users, but also sophisticated equipment, innovative displays, controlled indexing terms, online thesaurus and search aids, a classification system for browsing, and user-specified output. Even though it was never used as a production search service, it demonstrated many approaches and techniques. The developers of later SDC search systems (CIRCOL, ORBIT-1, ELHILL) were familiar with BOLD, but wrote new programs for the new hardware and software of their time instead of modifying existing BOLD programs.

In addition to his work on developing this early, innovative prototype, Borko also served in 1966 as the president of ADI. After leaving SDC in 1967, he joined the faculty of the University of California-Los Angeles (UCLA) School of Library Service, where he used his experiences in research and development to contribute to the design of the information science curriculum and to teach courses in information storage and retrieval, and the design and analysis of information systems. In 1988, ASIS awarded Borko the Outstanding Information Science Teacher Award for these contributions. In 1994 he received the ASIS Annual Award of Merit.

Based on the experience and knowledge gained from BOLD, SDC management decided in 1968 to develop a new reference retrieval system for the IBM 360 that would combine the useful features of BOLD with self-instructional features. The new system would be called General Purpose ORBIT. Black (1987) recalled: "Because SDC had become a profit-seeking organization, we were told to develop something useful. So here we had a time-sharing background and we had these retrieval experiments, including BOLD. We took these ideas and started developing a new version of ORBIT. Since ORBIT was a name that had been developed by SDC, we simply borrowed it from the guys at Wright Patterson who were sort of scattering to the winds anyway. So we were working on a revised version of that system." The ORBIT system, and more about the naming story, is covered in chapter 6.

MICRO

Another SDC project to develop and test an online reference retrieval system began in 1965 and was called MICRO (Multiple Indexing with Console Retrieval Options). James Smith was principal investigator and R. L. Bichel also worked on this SDC-funded project. They based the design of MICRO in large part upon techniques and prototype programs developed in 1964–1965 during SDC's Multilist Techniques Study for RADC (Rome Air Development Center). During the study, SDC-Santa Monica staff tested the use of list processing software for the CIRC system (chapter 6) that was then under development for the USAF Foreign Technology Division (FTD). Several programs were written (IPL-V and SLIP) at SDC for the Philco 2000 computer. The IPL-V program was used in connection with an SDC-Dayton study sponsored by RADC, in which comparison programs were written in both JOVIAL and IPL-V to investigate possible applications of list-processing techniques to a document retrieval system, including the investigation of search techniques using list processing (Shaffer 1965). SDC investigated several list-processing approaches and several list-processing languages, including Multilist, developed at the University of Pennsylvania.

MICRO was operational in 1965, running with a database of 3,000 references to foreign-language science and technology journal articles. The retrieval program operated under the TSS of the Q-32 and PDP-1 computers in Santa Monica, on a system that used drum and disk storage, and sixteen tape drives, with users communicating directly to MICRO via Teletype terminals.

1965 Milestone

MICRO was the first online search system to allow searchers the option to work in either a novice or experienced searcher interface mode.

MICRO instructed users in the sequence of operations, made searches as requested, and printed out relevant references. The retrieval program could be operated in either of two modes, the first of which was the "instructional or self-teaching mode" that displayed to an untrained user all necessary instructions and retrieval options. After becoming experienced, a searcher could use an abbreviated mode, in which all retrieval options were available but instructional material was shortened. In either mode, users were given a brief description of the database content and size (Smith 1966). This approach of allowing users to designate the experience level at which they wanted the interface to work (e.g., New/Experienced User?) was carried on in later systems developed at SDC (COLEX, ORBIT, MEDLINE).

The online database, stored on disks, consisted of bibliographic citations, including accession number, title, authors, journal name, volume, issue, pagination, broad subject codes (33 general subject areas), geographic areas covered by the publication, specific index terms or descriptors (from 2 to 15 multiword descriptors per citation), various dates, and microfilm reel and frame number. Inverted index files were used instead of serial searching of the records. Search options included subject index terms, authors, or general subject areas. A dictionary was available with all index terms and their posting counts. It is not clear, however, whether this user search aid was available online, or whether it was available only in print or microform.

1965 Milestone

MICRO was the first online search system to allow searchers the option of receiving a user-specified number of long or short output records.

MICRO gave users an option of receiving long or short output records. The long form consisted of the full bibliographic citation; the short form provided the document accession number, microfilm reel, and frame number, title, and index terms. The short option was provided as a way to reduce the output time.

1965 Milestone

MICRO was the first online search system to provide at the terminal site microform storage of expanded versions (e.g., abstracts, extracts, tables of contents, source publications) of the information available online. (See parallel milestone for SATIRE.)

The translated abstracts were stored on microfilm, and a microfilm viewer-printer and film collection were located adjacent to the terminal. The developers' rationale for having the microform file available at hand was to allow searchers to use the initial search output with microfilm reel and frame number to reproduce and study abstracts of retrieved references while the search program continued to provide additional output records (Smith 1966). This justification, along with the option of a short output display, implies a relatively long elapsed time for a search to be completed.

The arrangement of close coupling the auxiliary microform storage to the limited amount of online storage was first proposed in 1962 for SATIRE but was not implemented. This approach continued with the SDC-developed systems, COLEX and CIRCOL. A modification of this approach was also used in 1967 in a test system (OSIRIS) at the U.S. Naval Material Command (described later), with remote video display of the microfiche images.

MICRO ranked the output records in order by the total number of matches with the search terms (an implied rank order of relevance). This feature had been demonstrated already with TEXTIR, which provided its output (LAPD full-text robbery reports) in rank order by relevance during its first demonstrations in March 1964, and later by BOLD in 1966 that displayed a matrix of document-term hits, although BOLD did not carry the results to the point of actually sorting the records before output. MICRO was thus the first demonstration of relevance-ranked output of *bibliographic* records.

After MICRO processed a search and provided the posting count for the total number of references along with the output ranking information (e.g., "14 documents exist for this retrieval request. 2 documents contain 3 of the retrieval topic tags, 3 documents contain 2 of the retrieval topic tags . . ."), a searcher could further restrict search output by any one or more of four types of qualifiers: country about which the document was concerned, whether the document was a full or partial translation, subject areas, or publication date. After processing the qualifications, MICRO again notified the searcher of the resulting total document count and output ranking information. Another interactive feature of MICRO was the display of any search term with zero postings, while the search continued with the other terms.

University of Pennsylvania

Multilist

In November 1961, members of a research team at the University of Pennsylvania Moore School of Electrical Engineering unveiled preliminary results (Gray et al. 1961). Noah Prywes and Harry Gray were the team leaders in development work in online retrieval that had been going on for 18 months, which dates the beginning of the project in mid-1960. At the IFIPS Congress in Munich in August 1962, Prywes and Gray described their concept for a system that would search interactively the information and administrative files of a technical library. The system was first called Multi-List, and later shortened to Multilist (Prywes and Gray 1963). It was probably not fully operational in 1962, but the team had given it enough thought by December 31, 1962, to file a seventy-nine-page U.S. patent application on the approach, for which a patent was issued in 1968 (Prywes, Litwin, and Gray 1968). Part of the patent described Multilist's application to reference searching in ASTIA (predecessor to DDC) and NTIS document collections. The ASTIA example is important because it shows that the Moore School team at that early date addressed their attention to real operational problems with bibliographic systems. It also reflects the R&D emphasis at that time on solving national defense-related sci-tech (scientific and technical) problems.

Prywes was a computer scientist and engineer who was born in Warsaw, educated in Israel, and who earned his Ph.D. in applied physics at Harvard University. IR was just one of his several research interests. Gray was an electrical engineer, educated at Penn, whose contributions to the research were more on the technical side. Other active contributors were David Lefkowitz, Samuel Litwin,

W. Landauer, and Barry Zimmerman. ONR and RADC supported the work.

Even though computers of the time could store large amounts of business and scientific data, the team felt that as yet no efficient means existed to mechanize the man-machine conversation so that a computer responded easily and quickly to human inquiries. Therefore their research objective was to increase efficiency, measured by processing speed and cost, by several orders of magnitude and to ease communication with the computer. The Multilist real-time retrieval system ran on available IBM equipment (including the 7040 computer) rather than specially built hardware.

Multilist for Inventory Control

With ONR funding, the first pilot Multilist began operating in October 1962, as a cooperative effort between the Moore School and Zimmerman at the U.S. Naval Aviation Supply Office in Philadelphia (Prywes 1965a). Zimmerman needed a system for handling the records of a half-million supply items, which he presumed were similar to library document records. In at least one way they were; the records contained data of highly variable type and length. On the other hand, they required frequent manipulation daily to add, delete, and revise. These records that required real-time transaction processing were stored in a random access IBM 1405 disk file, along with the trees (hierarchical index files) and various programs for retrieving, storing, and updating the files. The pilot used a database of 4,100 inventory items and various pieces of IBM equipment: a 1401 central processor with an 8,000-character core memory, 1407 console, 1403 printer, and 729-IV tape units, as well as an IPC (Information Products Corporation) remote inquiry station Model 1501 that consisted of a keyboard for inquiries and a CRT display of 100 characters on an area $2'' \times 4\frac{1}{2}''$—about half as large as a postcard (Zimmerman, Lefkowitz, and Prywes 1964). This inventory application did not address online bibliographic searching, but it was a sign of the Moore School's interest in developing technology for application to real problems, and this particular experience was directly transferrable to their later work on library problems. Prywes acknowledged the transferability in a June 1964 conference presentation and that ONR's support had been motivated by the possibility of library applications. He described the approach that could be taken to a million-item library with a system of 100 remote terminals (Prywes 1965a).

Multilist permitted interactive retrieval by logical expressions (AND, OR, NOT) to specify the particular information desired from a large file. It permitted the storing of abbreviated files of variable length records in the form of dynamic trees that translated keys into the addresses of the respective items in the file. The keys were units of descriptive information (e.g., Manufacturer Parts Number) that provided the entry to a tree, and thereby to the file. Prywes prepared two Moore School technical reports to describe more details of Multilist and its application in a research program on military problem solving (Prywes 1964, 1965b).

Multilist for Library and Other Applications

Prywes's June 1964 symposium paper (1965a) offered a long-range vision for a fully automated library, supported by Multilist. His goals included lowering the cost of providing standard library services (mainly through manpower reduction) and providing novel services, including rapid updating of catalogs, publication of bibliographies on request, publication of thesauri, and selective dissemination of information to a sizable community of researchers. His automated library would contain a variety of types of documents, including preprints, reports, and descriptions of research in progress.

Prywes envisioned an ambitious plan for a four-part record for each document. The first part was to consist of the standard bibliographic description (author, title, accession number, volume, and issue for journals; publisher and publication date for monographs; and any of various classification numbers, subject headings, or descriptors). The second part of the record was to include the table of contents and the abstract as well as holdings information (i.e., which libraries store the document). The third part would consist of the references or bibliographic citations and index of each document. The fourth part was to be the document itself. Only the first part would be stored on drum or disk; parts 2 and 3 would be stored on magnetic tape and part 4 would be stored on some sort of "image storage unit." This breakdown of parts 1–4 of the record reflected Prywe's perception that users' needs for accessing speed and storage capacity would vary correspondingly. Only the first three parts were to be searchable; a user would probe these parts of the record in order to make a decision about retrieving the fourth part, the full document. From any of 100 remote consoles, a user would obtain full documents by means of interlibrary loans, provision of reprints, or, eventually, through facsimile transmission to the console.

The consoles available in the early sixties were to be connected through telephone lines to the central computer installation. The transmission rates in June 1964 were approximately twenty characters per second. Prywes imagined that eighty characters a second would be necessary for efficient use of consoles, and for transmission of entire documents. He also imagined that creation of a machine-readable four-part document record would be hampered if it were dependent on key-punching, especially for part 3. He anticipated the need for automatic scanning machines, which were not yet available, but he assumed they were in the developmental stage.

Prywes's vision of the automated library included other applications besides searching and retrieval, such as automated record keeping of acquisitions and expenditures, usage statistics, maintenance of circulation records, union catalogs for cooperating libraries, automatic cataloging and classification of new acquisitions, preparation of accessions lists, automatic records of collection growth rate to permit planning for shelf and floor space requirements, and more. He expected that the mechanization and centralization of technical services would increase speed and efficiency and would lower the total costs to the point where even small research libraries could participate. Although Prywes never achieved this ambitious plan, it was partly accomplished, and even exceeded in part, by the Intrex-augmented catalog at MIT a year or so later.

1966 Milestone

Multilist was the first online search system to permit a searcher to retrieve automatically all the records that were either hierarchically subordinate to or hierarchically superior to a given search term.

Prywes (1966) described a modest library application that served as the basis for experiments conducted at the University of Pennsylvania, as well as two commands that searchers could use. One command retrieved all records that were placed higher in the hierarchy than the records specified by a searcher. The other command went the other way: it retrieved all records that were hierarchically lower than the term specified by a searcher. One of the experiments, the subject of a master's thesis by Philippe Gabrini (1966), used a collection of records for physics articles that had been prepared at MIT for a project called TIP. This appears to have been the first use of Multilist for online bibliographic searching. In 1967, while they were being supported by ONR, Hsiao and Prywes (1968) portrayed their online multifile, multiconsole system as the "Moore School Problem Solving Facility." Lefkowitz (1969) and Prywes continued their work in file organization and online retrieval systems at Penn, including work on U.S. Navy strategic command and control systems with the Computer Command and Control Company (CCCC). CCCC was a commercial venture that was spun off of the original Multilist work, where work continued in computer-based information processing with support from ONR and others. Lefkowitz, who had collaborated with Prywes on the earlier projects, continued on the Moore School faculty while also serving as staff consultant to CCCC.

In summer 1965, the University of Pennsylvania Law School initiated a pilot project on using computers for legal IR, using Multilist and the Moore School Problem Solving Facility. The database was the text of the law relating to U.S. race relations, both from Federal statutes and from cases decided by the U.S. Supreme Court from 1865 to 1965 (249 summaries of opinions, and about 170 sections of Federal statutes). The opinions were keyboarded onto 15,000 IBM cards, and the Federal statutes text was furnished on tape by John Horty at the University of Pittsburgh. A modification was made to the basic Multilist software to provide a more user-friendly interface for use by lawyers instead of programmers, and the resulting program was called LAWSEARCH. LAWSEARCH operated in either batch or online mode. Morris Cohen and Joseph Elmaleh were joint supervisors of this project (Elmaleh 1968).

Multilist was still being used in test and research activities at Penn in 1968 (Prywes 1968). The online storage and retrieval work, and other work at the Moore School on topics related to computer-based information processing, continued into the early 1970s (Prywes and Litofsky 1970; Hsiao and Manola 1972).

CIDS (Chemical Information and Data System)

David Lefkowitz, who worked on earlier Multilist applications, had a particular interest in developing online systems to search chemical information. At a meeting of the American Chemical Society (ACS), Lefkowitz and Clarence Van Meter announced a special application of the Multilist program, the computer searching of chemical compounds (Lefkowitz and Van Meter 1966). Project CIDS used an online system designed specifically to satisfy the U.S. Army need for input, storage, and retrieval of chemical compounds and associated information. Van Meter directed the project and the U.S. Army Edgewood Arsenal supported it. The major participants also included Ruth Powers, Paul Weinberg, Helen Hill, Mary Milne, Bonnie Sherr, Richard Haber, John Leggett, and Thomas Angell. Powers was working on her master's degree and Weinberg was writing his doctoral dissertation, both at the University of Pennsylvania.

Chemical data were entered into the CIDS database using punched paper tape and special typewriters with a chemical type font. An elaborate error checking system and a registry system to avoid duplication of entries helped with the difficult job of maintaining quality control. The file contained the following information about each compound: registry number, molecular formula, structural formula, nomenclature, bibliographic references, references to other data files, and structural screens and compound descriptors. CIDS was run on an IBM 7040 computer. In 1966, users could submit queries in real time from a single remote teletypewriter. Lefkowitz and Van Meter considered the typical reaction times of a few seconds to one minute normal and tolerable.

1965 Milestone

CIDS was the first system to demonstrate online searching of chemical structures.

Work on computer searching of chemical compounds and their structures dates back to the 1950s (Opler and Norton 1966). However, CIDS in 1965 appears to have been the first time this was demonstrated in online mode (Lefkowitz and Van Meter 1966; Lefkowitz and Powers 1967). This experiment with its database of 3,100 compounds was a feasibility model to explore the problem, and was useful in revealing the obstacles to scaling up to a more practical system that would have to handle many millions of compounds, as is done regularly in several online systems today. The U.S. Army section of the COSATI 1967 annual report noted that a CIDS test file of 268,000 organic compounds was established during 1967, and that another 377,000 compounds were on tape awaiting entry into the system. The report also said that federal testing showed the system to be responsive to Army chemists, that six other federal agencies began to participate in the program in 1967, and that NLM's Remote Information Systems Center (RISC) was planning to access CIDS.

In 1970, CIDS was operating in a multiterminal mode with a joint Digital Equipment PDP-8 and IBM 7040 computer at Penn, using a fifty-six-million character IBM 1301 disk and interfacing storage unit, with Teletype machines, a DEC 338 CRT display device, and a remote high-speed chemical font line printer. Two chemical typewriters were used to enter data into the file of over 47,000 unique compounds (Powers and Hill 1971). During 1970, plans were completed to transfer the developmental CIDS file from Penn to the Edgewood Arsenal, where it would be run on the Arsenal's new scientific computer. In 1971, the transfer of this database of over 1.2 million compounds to a UNIVAC 1108 system and Teletype Model 37 terminals with chemical notation fonts for remote access was well underway. By this time, several other organizations had demonstrated online chemical information systems. The Edgewood Arsenal continued to support the project through the early 1970s with the participation of Lefkowitz and Van Meter.

By 1970 CIDS was operating with a file of 70,000 compounds and could be accessed from multiple remote consoles. The time-sharing system was designed for CIDS to ensure rapid and reliable response times. Users could search by any of several keys, including functional groups, hydrocarbon radicals, and cyclic nuclei. Searchers could display output of structural formulas either on a high-speed remote chemical line printer or on punched paper tape that would be used to print later on a chemical typewriter. Powers and Hill (1971) wrote a brief description of the CIDS chemical search keys and the three-level search strategy. In early 1974, a hybrid inverted list approach, based upon the Multilist work, was used to implement a chemical substructure search system at the National Cancer Institute (Lefkowitz 1975).

Massachusetts Institute of Technology

Just as SDC had its early time-sharing system that served as a platform for several online search systems, so did the Massachusetts Institute of Technology (MIT). Staff at the MIT Computation Center, under the leadership of Fernando Corbató, a professor in electrical engineering, developed the Compatible Time-Sharing System (CTSS), a version of which was first demonstrated in November 1961. Actually, two operating systems were known as CTSS. One was installed on campus at the Computation Center to support the general MIT community. The other was installed on the computer of Project MAC (abbreviation for Multiple-Access Computer, or Multiple Access to Computers, or Machine-Aided Cognition, or Mathematics and Computation—readers may choose among the many names we found), and served the more experimental community, especially members of Project MAC. The second system was used to help build its descendant, MULTICS (Multiplexed Information and Computing Service), which was designed to be a computer utility. The MULTICS effort started in 1965, and became a service in 1969. As it became a service, Project MAC phased out their CTSS, leaving the Computation Center's CTSS for running systems like TIP and TIRP. That system ceased operation in July 1973. In this text, CTSS refers to the operating system, and Project MAC refers to the development group and its facility.

The primary MAC terminals were Teletypes and IBM 1050 Selectric teletypewriters (adaptations of the "golfball" office typewriter). Most of these terminals were on the MIT campus and could dial through an MIT private exchange to reach either the IBM 7094 installation of Project MAC or a similar facility at the MIT Computation Center. Access to the Project MAC system could also be gained from any station of the Telex or TWX telegraph networks. The system initially imposed a limit of ten simultaneous terminals, but by 1965 this had grown to twenty-four (Fano 1965a,b). The online projects described later (TIP, TIRP, Intrex) relied upon this time-sharing system.

Another stimulus for the online developments that blossomed at MIT in the sixties can be traced to studies that began at MIT's Lincoln Laboratory around 1958, and continued through at least 1966. With NSF support, Myron Kessler (who published as "M.M." and was known to his colleagues as "Mike") directed a pioneering research team that explored citation coupling relationships between scientific papers and their authors. The researchers worked with batch-mode programs for the IBM 709 computer to process large numbers of citations to determine the nature and extent of their bibliographic coupling. This work with computer processing of bibliographic records, while useful on its own merits, was also good preparation for Kessler's involvement in developing an online search system that used similar kinds of records, and the implementation of other effective means (e.g., online cited reference searching) of looking at bibliographic coupling in the technical literature. As we shall see, TIP was the outgrowth of several years of study led by Kessler of the general properties and requirements of a system to provide better communication between scientists and engineers.

TIP

In a report that summarized two years of work supported by MIT's Lincoln Lab, Kessler (1960) recommended that a pilot model be established for a science information network. The work was supported partly by NSF and Project MAC, which was funded by ARPA. Finally, after a few more years of work, at the annual meeting of ADI in October 1964, Kessler, William Mathews, and Evan Ivie, a doctoral student, reported on the Technical Information Project (TIP), a working model of an online system that had been in development since 1962 on MIT's computer system (Kessler, Ivie, and Mathews 1964). As mentioned earlier, time-sharing had come to MIT in 1961 with CTSS, the predecessor to the MAC, and then with the MAC system itself in 1963. The TIP programs ran in batch mode on CTSS until November 1963 when time sharing was provided by the MAC system (Mathews 1995). Actually, the "Project TIP" name came with the NSF funding and online capability in 1964.

In May 1964, Kessler and Mathews demonstrated TIP to their NSF project sponsors and a site visit committee. This was TIP's first public demonstration, done with multiple terminals simultaneously searching the database (Mathews 1995). This was a few months after the first demonstration of simultaneous multiterminal online searching, which was at the Library/USA exhibit at the New York World's Fair. The next public demonstration of TIP was in the fall at a Project MAC Seminar and then Kessler demonstrated it for the first time to a large public audience at the ADI annual meeting in Philadelphia in October, which was reported in the *Boston Sunday Herald* by Kessler's son (R. Kessler 1964). SRI had demonstrated online bibliographic searching in 1963, but it was not as interactive as TIP was. It could be argued that TIP was interactive for entering search requests, but that it was not *fully* interactive; waiting five minutes for search results was hardly interactive. "Interactive" as a definition is in the eye of the beholder, and depends in large measure on the response time. Therefore we are unlikely to obtain universal agreement on which one was the first truly "interactive" online search system.

Mike Kessler was born in Odessa, Russia, and earned B.S. and M.S. degrees in biophysics at MIT, and a Ph.D. in physics from Duke in 1948. He joined Lincoln Lab as a physicist in 1954, and his interest in the storage and retrieval of information stemmed from his own problems in dealing with growing amounts of sci-tech literature. In 1959, he chaired a committee to look at communication problems within the library, which fed his interests in the larger problems of scientific communication. His experience at Lincoln Lab with large computers such as the SAGE air defense system led him to consider using such equipment for technical information problems. In 1962, Kessler moved to the main campus of MIT at Cambridge to head up TIP within the MIT Libraries, and he became associate director of libraries in 1964. Kessler the librarian wanted to use TIP to explore relationships between scientists and their literature and to study properties of the scientific literature such as interdisciplinary flow, international flow and exchange, and citation patterns.

Just as interesting as looking at what TIP was is recalling what it was *not*. Also at MIT in the sixties was a linguistic researcher named Noam Chomsky, whose novel theories challenged everyone's basic assumptions about language and its structures. Linguists and programmers involved in language-based retrieval systems all around the country, including Simmons's team at SDC, were paying close attention to Chomsky's work and sometimes used Chomsky as a consultant. However, the TIP group at Chomsky's home university were more concerned with issues of scientists' interactions with their own literatures.

TIP was a prototype, used for experimentation, monitoring and evaluation. To accomplish these goals, it had to be able to perform real library functions under realistic conditions. It was to be the first experiment with a large (i.e., more than a few thousand records) and active database operating within a time-sharing environment. Further, it was designed for general application, not for any single type of search scheme or user population. TIP users were scientists, teachers, students, scholars, librarians and others scattered throughout the Boston-Cambridge area.

TIP used the IBM 7094 time-sharing computer of Project MAC, with teletypewriters (IBM 1050 communications terminals) in the MIT library connected to the computer by telephone wires. In 1963, the computer could support twenty-eight simultaneous users without degrading response time, which was not more than a few seconds. In 1964, other users could obtain access through any of the other ninety-six campus stations of the Telex or TWX networks. In 1965, the Project MAC computer facility supported 150 standard Teletype consoles, with the system (including TIP), available to about 500 people with access to the time-sharing system (30 people could use the computer simultaneously). TIP became "publicly available" to the Project MAC community in August 1965. A limit of thirty simultaneous users still applied in 1966.

TIP files and programs were stored on disks and available at all times. However, storage space was at such a premium that code numbers were assigned to the most cited journals, and only the code numbers were stored, not the full names of the journals (e.g., J384 for the *Annals of Physics*); this practice continued at least through 1967. Similarly, the entire citation was stored in very abbreviated form. For example, a short form retrieved record appeared to a requestor as "J001 V034 P0057," which would be interpreted as "*Physical Review* (Journal No. 1), volume 34, article starting on page 57." TIP did not search an inverted file but searched instead in a linear manner, examining 100 to 150 records per second (Mathews 1967). In 1966 a second-phase TIP was planned that would use inverted files but this never happened. Mathews (1995) observed that the emphasis became one of generalizing input data so that users could create any data elements they wished and of simplifying the user interface so that nobody would need a manual until they got "hooked" and wanted to do something sophisticated.

1964 Milestone

TIP was the first online search system to retrieve citations on the basis of cited references or bibliographic coupling.

The most interesting features of TIP, in addition to the searching capabilities on key word from the article title, author, and author affiliation, were three special programs. The first program retrieved records on the basis of bibliographic coupling:

given a known publication, identify all other publications that share one or more cited references with it.[5] The second program prepared a citation index: given a publication, list all later publications that cite it.[6] Online cited reference searching had been described and proposed for the 1963 SRI system, but not implemented; TIP was the first system to implement it. Kessler (1967d) described the operation of a regular SDI service provided to MIT authors to alert them to recently published physics papers that had cited their previous publications. This may have been the first use of cited author searching in a computer-based SDI system. The third program was a KWIC (keyword-in-context) indexing feature that arranged the titles of a group of selected papers according to the occurrence of words within their titles. While KWIC had been in use with batch-processing systems long earlier, TIP adopted it for the online era.

Other special programs in TIP counted the number of papers per author in a given date range, listed the papers that were most or least cited, traced the geographic or institutional mobility of authors, made special lists of authors and institutions. In 1965, Kessler was developing a system in which a search could be started by naming a list of papers, and the result would be a list of similar papers (presumably by using the bibliographic coupling information in the records). Users devised other applications as well; an MIT physics professor reported how he used TIP to update a basic handbook on plasma physics. S. C. Brown (1966) observed that it only took 273 seconds (4.55 min.) of computer time to search the entire file, but it could take hours to print the output records on the slow Teletype machines. For long bibliographies, it was better to use the offline printer at the computer site.

Kessler wrote the *TIP User's Manual* in December 1965 (1965c) and revised it in October 1967 (1967f). Mills (1967, 241) described it as an "extremely well-done example of user-oriented documentation. Through the use of extensive examples, it conveys a great deal of the 'feel' of using the TIP subsystem." Mathews also wrote a primer for TIP in 1968.

1964 Milestones

TIP was the first online search system to allow a searcher to save search output for later searching or use.

TIP was the first online search system to provide a searcher the option of online output or later offline printing.

Kessler (1965b) described additional features not mentioned in the 1964 ADI presentation but which were available in September 1964. One was OUTPUT SAVE, which made a copy of the output so that a user could search or print it. Another was OUTPUT STORE, a print file-to-disk option. Each user was allotted a portion of online disk storage space for use to save retrieved records for future reference or future searching as a private file. These output files were not stored as part of TIP, but could be manipulated by executive commands outside of TIP. A user could designate any arrangement of the five data fields for online or offline printing. Offline printing was done outside of TIP and required a STORE FILE command and a print request (Kessler 1965c; Wolfe 1970).

1964 Milestone

TIP was the first online search system to implement stem searching.

"Stem searching" is searching on the root characters of a family of words (e.g., search on

COMPUT to retrieve all records that have words starting with that stem: COMPUTE, COMPUTER, COMPUTERS, COMPUTED, COMPUTATION). It is also called "prefix searching" or "right-truncation" and is a useful feature for simplifying search formulations. It was a regular feature in computer-based batch searching and SDI systems at this time. It had been proposed, but not implemented for the 1963 SRI online system. TIP appears to have been its first use with an *online* system; it was part of the implementation in 1964. This feature as implemented in most search systems is more properly called "truncation searching" rather than "stem searching." True stem searching, more correctly called "word root" searching, retrieves matches only on words that have the same root. Marcus (1997) supplied this illustration: A truncation search on "hear" will retrieve matches on the words "heart" and "hearse" as well as on the truly associated words "hear," "hears," and "hearing." A true word root search would match on only the last three terms. Word root searching was used in Intrex.

1964 Milestone

TIP was the first online search system to implement left-truncation searching.

Left-truncation searching (looking for terms that *end* in a specified character string) is a feature that is particularly helpful in searching chemical or pharmaceutical information. For example, a search for terms ending *MYCIN will retrieve records with ACROMYCIN, BIOMYCIN, ERYTHROMYCIN, STREPTOMYCIN, and others. A search on *ASE will retrieve records with enzymes such as AMYLASE, GLUCOPONDASE, TYPOSINASE, and others. The term *CHLOROBENZENE would retrieve records that included that character string at the end of any term (e.g., AMINOCHLOROBENZENE, BUTYLCHLOROBENZENE). Left-truncation was available on several batch search systems then, so the concept was well established, and those who used the feature appreciated it. It was available on TIP in September 1964 (Mathews 1995).

1965 Milestone

TIP was the first online search system to implement "wild card" character searching.

A "wild card" character or characters is another handy feature for search formulation (e.g., WOM*N to be interpreted for searching as WOMAN or WOMEN). According to Mathews (1995), this feature, for single or multiple characters, was added to TIP shortly after truncation was made available. Although we found no confirming documentation for the implementation date, it appears to have been 1965.

1965 Milestone

TIP was the first online search system to permit a searcher to store a search formulation to be recalled and incorporated into another query or used for later runs on updated files.

The ability to create and save search formulations (profiles) was available on TIP by early 1965 (Kessler 1965b). This feature was later included in the experimental SOLAR and SUPARS systems in 1970 (SUPARS also allowed searchers to retrieve strategies prepared by others) but was not included in other major online systems until the early 1970s.

> **1964 Milestone**
>
> TIP was among the first online search systems to use Boolean logic to combine terms in searching for bibliographic records. (See parallel milestone for GE-Valley Forge.)

TIP provided a Boolean search capability with AND, OR, and NOT logic. This feature was described in the December 1965 TIP *User's Manual* (Kessler 1965c) and is believed to have been operational as part of the TIP system that was first demonstrated in May 1964. This may have been the first implementation of Boolean logic in an online bibliographic search system. SRI proposed that capability for the system they demonstrated in 1963, but did not implement it. The General Electric Valley Forge Library also implemented this feature in 1964, but we are uncertain which system was the first to do it. We will credit both, and say that it was implemented simultaneously at MIT and GE.

Interaction between users and the TIP program was achieved by a command language. SEARCH allowed users to specify the literature to be searched: "search: all"—all journals in the database; "search: phyrev all"—just a particular journal, in this case, *The Physical Review*. Users could specify search terms using FIND: "find author: Smith"—for authors' names; "find title: cryogenics"—for words in titles; "find location: Massachusetts Institute of Technology"—for author's institutional affiliation. If a user typed two terms on the same FIND line (e.g., cryogenics refrigerants), the system assumed AND logic. The system interpreted two terms of the same type entered on two FIND lines as OR logic. Thus,

```
find author: Smith
find author: Jones
```

would be interpreted as a user wanting papers by Smith or by Jones. All commands could be abbreviated, most to a single character (e.g., S for SEARCH). Retrieved documents could be counted, displayed or stored with an OUTPUT command plus COUNT, PRINT, or STORE (Kessler 1965b).

The OUTPUT COUNT command gave a count of the number of records retrieved by a search expression. Separate counts could be requested for a running count of the number of items searched (Total Input Count) during an interaction, or a running count of the total number of items that have been selected (Total Output Count) by the FIND criterion during an interaction. As such, it was among the earliest online search systems to provide posting counts for a search term. It had to be requested, however, rather than being the default condition. Term postings as a regular default feature for all search terms was first demonstrated in 1965 on BOLD; it was also included in Drew's August 1965 specification for what later became DIALOG. As for TIP, the earliest documented evidence for postings counts was in the 1968 TIP user's manual (Mathews 1968). We could not determine exactly when it was implemented.

> **1964 Milestone**
>
> TIP was the first online search system to use a database of more than 25,000 records.

TIP was based initially on the journal literature of physics, in particular those nineteen to twenty-one titles that were closely interrelated by means of reciprocal citation patterns, dating from 1950. In late 1964, the file contained at least 25,000 citations to journal articles (as reported by one source; another source said 35,000) and was growing at the rate of at least 1,000 a month (another source said 1,500 a month) (R. Kessler 1964; M. M. Kessler 1964). The data for one of the journals, *Physical Review*, was for 1950–1964, because those records were already available from the bibliographic coupling projects. When TIP was demonstrated at the

International Federation for Documentation (FID) Congress in October 1965, it represented the contents of twenty-five physics journals (M. M. Kessler 1965a). In 1965, the file was being updated weekly (Mathews 1966). In 1967, the database consisted of about 60,000 citations from thirty-two physics journals. Because of computer memory constraints, however, only 30,000 were in disk storage for immediate access. The rest were on tape and waiting for the project to acquire additional storage capacity. At this time, TIP was operating on an IBM 7094 computer with access for about thirty simultaneous users from about 150 IBM-1050 terminals distributed around the MIT campus (Kessler 1967a).

The various reports generated by the research team members between 1964 and 1967 gave varying file sizes and numbers of journals indexed. The fluctuations of the TIP file size and coverage reflected the changing file content. The entire MIT computer system only had 600 megabytes of storage, and TIP used about 40 percent of that. The storage space was not enough to continue accumulating a growing volume of machine-readable data. In an attempt to use space effectively, the storage contents were modified to suit the needs of particular searchers at any given time. Mathews (1995) recalled, "We spent hours every weekend loading and unloading data in a rotating scheme that made the least interesting data appear only occasionally."

Only simple bibliographic data that could be keyed by a typist were entered into the records; it was assumed that abstracting and indexing requiring the intellectual efforts of trained librarians would limit the growth and expandability of TIP. Each of the bibliographic records included the following data elements: all authors and their institutional affiliations, title, bibliographic details (journal, volume, starting page), the cited references (journal, volume, page) given in each source article, and the article's location information and subject index information in Physics Abstracts. Kessler (1966, 24, 26) remarked:

An important implication of this requirement [that the model must be capable of being scaled one or two orders of magnitude] is that we decided very early to use only clerical input. This means that no pre-indexing or keyword assignment or anything that requires intellectual judgement was used. Everything that goes into the computer memory has to be capable of purely clerical treatment by persons who know nothing of the subject.... Because we didn't want to tackle the whole universe of literature, we decided to experiment with a specialized subject and chose the journal literature of physics. There are perhaps one to two thousand journals where physics literature may be found, but a very elaborate study showed that about fifty journals account for sixty to seventy percent of the literature ... we chose ... specifically, twenty-seven journals. It is interesting to note that these journals account for some sixty percent of the abstracts that appear in *Physics Abstracts*.

Even with a powerful computer (for that time) being used, considerable computer time (by today's standards) was required. Records were searched at the rate of about 10,000 articles per minute. "This means that to find all the articles that have the word 'plasma' in the title, searching 35,000 articles would take roughly three and one-half to four minutes" (Kessler 1966, 26).

Two researchers from the National Bureau of Standards (NBS), Franz Alt and Russell Kirsch (1968), reported on their experience in using TIP during the their NSF-supported research project in 1964–1967 on bibliographic coupling. In the spring of 1964, when they started their experiment, the TIP file was the only readily available citation index in machine-readable form that matched their interests. Alt and Kirsch observed that in the spring of 1964 long-distance access to the MAC computer was not practical, and so their original plan was to have computer runs carried out by the TIP group. After a time, however, it became clear that this was not feasible. So they looked for ways to get remote access. Because the TIP file was temporarily removed from the MAC computer to allow for system remodeling, it was not until November 1965 that they could run their first trials from remote consoles at NBS in Gaithersburg, Maryland, and then resume the rest of their experiments from those terminals during the summer of 1966. They noted that TIP continued to operate under severe computer memory constraints during all of this time, with constant pressure on the size of the file; it covered three or four years for most of its journals, but some older volumes were kept on magnetic tape because of disk memory limitations. The practice of using a three-digit number to represent individual journal names continued from TIP's beginning through at least 1968. The search time was long, longer than that suggested by the user manuals. Alt and Kirsch reported an average search speed of 100 papers per second. At that rate, they estimated that it would take five to six minutes of mainframe time (and a longer time under the time-sharing system) to search the file for a single query.

TIP involved just a few hard-working researchers at MIT, including Mathews (associate project director), T. F. Dempsey, L. H. Morton, and W. I. Nissen, and a relatively small budget. In sheer numbers of staff and dollars, it was overshadowed by another MIT project called Intrex, which we examine in chapter 3. The large numbers of literature citations and testimonials to TIP, however, testify to the enormous influence that this small-scale project had on the development of later online retrieval systems. TIP started as an experiment, but evolved into a functional working system used by its local constituency into the 1970s. The TIP story continues in the next chapter.

Before we move on, however, we want to reintroduce another person who had an impact on the TIP project: J. C. R. ("Lick") Licklider, whom we met in connection with SRI and SDC projects. Licklider was an MIT professor in computer science with a strong background in psychology. In 1957, he left MIT to join Bolt, Beranek and Newman. His research focused on human-computer interaction, and from 1962 for several years he held concurrent positions as consultant to IBM at the Thomas J. Watson Research Center in Yorktown Heights, New York, and as ARPA's director of Behavioral Science and Information Processing Research. As the head of a major funding agency for advanced information handling techniques, he was the ARPA "angel" who funded many innovative projects. He was known personally to many leading researchers in the field, and in his work and travels he spread the word about what was happening at various labs. He not only fertilized R&D efforts with his ARPA support but cross-pollinated the projects by facilitating exchanges of information among the many participants. He was, to a large extent, a supportive scientific troubadour in addition to his own direct contributions to several areas of research and development (Taylor 1990). Later he returned to MIT and was director of Project MAC after Fano. He had a close collegial influence on all retrieval projects on the MIT campus. A keen observer and futurist, he is known for his insightful writings about information technology (Licklider 1964, 1965a,b). We meet Licklider again in our discussion of Intrex.

American Library Association (ALA)

LIBRARY 21 (Seattle)

In 1958, ALA commissioned Joe Becker to conceptualize a "library of the future" as the centerpiece of an ALA exhibit at the 1962 Seattle World's Fair. Between 1960 and 1962, working with Alphonse Trezza and ALA staff, he planned and installed a fair exhibit known as LIBRARY 21. The exhibit grew out of a feasibility study Becker had prepared for ALA under a grant from the Council on Library Resources (CLR) and out of a contract that RADC awarded to ALA. Gordon Martin served as the local project director (*Library/USA* 1967). The exhibit was cosponsored by ALA and members of the data processing and publishing industries, including IBM, UNIVAC, *Encyclopaedia Britannica,* Xerox Corporation, RCA, NCR, and others. Becker was, among other things, responsible for assembling the team of industrial participants. The exhibit was significant because it was the first integrated presentation of electronic equipment for library applications within a setting not restricted to the clientele of a few special libraries but open to the general public. Wedgeworth (1997) recalled: "It was a major public relations coup for the library community because it demonstrated publicly a whole range of technologies that would become commonplace.... Virtually all of the technologies were in active use by the end of the 1970s."

The exhibit was open in April–October 1962 and was visited by 1.8 million people (American Library Association 1963). It included a UNIVAC Solid State 90 computer, with space for a high-speed printer and desks where visitors could ask for information from the computer. A committee of the ALA Adult Services Division, in cooperation with the UNIVAC Division of Sperry Rand Corporation, prepared three kinds of information for storage on magnetic tape: (1) personalized bibliographies from a store of 8,400 annotated book titles; (2) quotations from seventy-four authors whose work appeared in the Great Books of the Western World Series; and (3) gazetteer information on ninety-two nations of the free world.

People passing through the exhibit filled out a form with information about themselves and indicated a subject in which they were interested (actually, they picked one from a list of possible topics). Each visitor was given a code number (e.g., 206) and the completed forms were passed to a keypunch operator who provided the appropriate cards and then immediately ran the searches in batches. In this fashion the computer was able to provide short annotated bibliographies on the chosen subjects—limited by specified variables such as requestor's age, sex, purpose, education, and reading level. As the bibliographies were printed out, they were rolled up "like diploma scrolls and placed in bin boxes. When visitor number 206 exited the exhibit, he went to box number 206 and pulled out his roll" (Becker 1987). Visitors who desired "an opportunity to converse with the great minds of the Western World" received a list of quotations from the seventy-four authors mentioned earlier. A total of 84,000 personalized printouts were given to visitors during the fair.

The professional library staff for LIBRARY 21 received special training from the University of Washington School of Librarianship, financed by the U.S. Department of Health, Education, and Welfare (HEW) (Martin, Hayes, and Lieberman 1963). Robert Hayes conducted the training sessions. Hayes had earned a Ph.D. in mathematics from UCLA in 1952 and, before the World's Fair activity, had several years experience with Magnavox Research Laboratories, which was a contractor to several of the intelligence agencies, with responsibility for systems work in developing computer-based tools.

The Seattle exhibition was not online searching; it was fast-batch report generation with a restricted set of retrieval possibilities. We describe it here because it set the stage and showed the experience and context of planning for the 1964 fair, which did offer online retrieval.

Computers had been used for online file searching for online passenger seat reservations since 1951 when Teleregister installed a system for American Airlines, serving LaGuardia Airport in New York. In 1958 it installed a much more elaborate system for United Airlines, serving the entire United States including Hawaii. This experience with high-volume searching of large data files in conjunction with a widely dispersed data communications would stay with one of the senior Teleregister engineers, Herbert Mitchell, when he later moved to Bunker-Ramo Corporation and implemented the first NASA/RECON system. That story is in chapter 5.

Library/USA (New York)

The 1964 New York World's Fair was open from April 1964 to October 1965. The children, women, and men who visited the U.S. pavilion were privileged to be the first outside the labs to see an online bibliographic retrieval system in operation. Through a glass wall they could view a large computer, computer technicians, and reference librarians. The Library/USA exhibition was funded by UNIVAC, *Encyclopaedia Britannica*, *World Encyclopedia*, and other organizations. Featured in the exhibit was the American Reference Center, operated by ALA, ADI, and the Special Libraries Association (SLA). "The American Reference Center demonstrated for visitors an actual functioning library staffed with professional librarians who answered any and all reference queries posed and used state-of-the-art computerized retrieval systems" (Schmidt 1994, 470).

> **1964 Milestone**
>
> The Library/USA demonstration was the first time that the general public witnessed and participated in retrieving bibliographic information using online technology.

Again, the producer and chief reporter of this remarkable event was Becker, technical director of computerized library exhibits. With an engineering degree from Brooklyn Polytechnic Institute and an M.A. in library science from Catholic University of America, Becker worked for twenty-five years at the U.S. Central Intelligence Agency (CIA) as an information specialist in electronic data processing. In 1958, the CIA sent Becker to the Western Data Processing Center at UCLA to gain experience and familiarity with current developments in computer-based information processing. Under ALA's institutional direction, Becker designed Library/USA to introduce online retrieval to the general public (Becker 1964, 1984). While a team from IBM worked with Becker to train reference librarians to staff the exhibit, the person with whom Becker worked most closely during both fairs was Trezza, associate executive director of ALA. In 1969, Trezza became state librarian for Illinois and played crucial roles in developing state library networks.

> **1964 Milestone**
>
> The Library/USA demonstration may have been the first online search system to demonstrate inverted file searching.

The demonstration used third-generation computer technology: the UNIVAC 490 Real-Time computer, composed of a console, control unit, four Uniservo tape drives, central processor, UNIVAC 1004 card processor and punch, communications subsystem, and random access Fastrand Drum Memory, which was the key element that made an online approach possible. This equipment was used normally as an online airline reservation system. Instead of flight numbers, dates, and passenger data, however, different labels were assigned to the columns for subjects, titles, and other bibliographic data (Becker 1987). This may have been the first online search system to demonstrate inverted file searching as an alternative to serial searching of all of the records in a file.[7] The UNIVAC Division of Sperry Rand had loaned the system to ALA for the fair, along with technicians to operate it. UNIVAC computers had been operating since 1960 in online mode with over 2 million records available for seat inventory on various airline systems, with Agent Sets communicating online from over fifty U.S. cities, servicing 4,500 requests per hour. It was well within the reach of this equipment and technology to provide this online subject search capability at this exhibit.

> **1964 Milestone**
>
> Library/USA may have been the first demonstration of an online search system providing a searcher with a choice of multiple online databases.

Stored in the computer were three types of information. The first type was essays written by *Encyclopaedia Britannica* research assistants. The seventy-five different topics were ones treated in the U.S. exhibit (e.g., democracy, minorities, and ecology). Each topic was written on an adult's and a child's comprehension level, and twenty of the

Early Research and Development Activities 51

essays were translated into French, German, and Spanish. The second type, prepared by librarians from the ALA Adult Services Division, was annotated reading lists on various topics and each list was on five reading levels.

> **1964 Milestone**
>
> The Library/USA demonstration was the first instance of an update as frequently as weekly to an operational online bibliographic retrieval system.

The third type of information was bibliographic entries from *Reader's Guide to Periodical Literature*. Each week the H. W. Wilson Co. sent carbon copies of slips containing its new, raw-form index entries, on seventy-five subjects (the same 75 subjects used with the encyclopedia database) covered by eighteen periodical journals. The subjects also pertained to exhibit topics. UNIVAC staff keypunched the entries into machine language and then entered them as data into the computer. This extra step of data entry was necessary because H. W. Wilson did not start to put indexing data on tape until years later. Wilson records were chosen for the exhibit rather than other files that were already machine-readable, because Becker's team expected that "the people coming through the exhibit were mommy, daddy and the kids, and we thought that the *Reader's Guide* would have the most popular audience" (Becker 1987). Fair workers updated the file weekly and thus made it available for searching before the printed *Reader's Guide* was sent to libraries. The computer could produce on command a printout of either the most current periodical references on a given subject or, alternatively, the full list of references under a subject heading.[8]

> **1964 Milestone**
>
> Library/USA was the first online search system to demonstrate simultaneous multiple-terminal access to the same database and search software.

The reference librarians were prepared to answer questions about the U.S. pavilion. Each librarian sat at a desk equipped with a Uniset device for keying inquiries directly to the computer. An inquiry consisted of a predefined exhibit topic, reading level, and language. These search terms were entered quickly using code numbers. This was category code searching, not text searching, and it was not interactive (Becker 1987; Hayes 1995). Within easy reach were high-speed (1,200 lines per minute) printers that took less than four seconds to print a 700-word response. Over 800,000 such printouts were generated during the eighteen months of the fair. This appears to have been the first time that an online system was used with multiple terminals simultaneously accessing the same database and search system. TIP had this capability, but its first multiple-terminal demonstration was reportedly in May 1964, shortly after Library/USA was in regular operation.

> **1964 Milestones**
>
> Library/USA provided the first possibility for interactive communication through a computer with reference librarians remotely located from the computer facility and the requesters.
>
> Library/USA provided the first access for the general public to an online retrieval system from long-distance, using teletypewriters or standard telephone lines.

This was technically an online system but not interactive. ALA's demonstration was nonetheless pioneering for its time in that the public was able to access simultaneously the central database either onsite at the fair or from teletypewriter machines via the standard dial-up telephone system at various participating libraries in the United States. From these remote locations, users could ask the same questions and receive the same kind of printout as was provided to fair visitors. The response time, using either teletypewriter or standard telephone lines, was less than twenty seconds.

Librarians who went through the training experience for the world fair exhibits and then continued on in successful library careers included Robert Wedgeworth (executive director, ALA, Dean, Columbia University School of Library Service, president of IFLA, university librarian at University of Illinois at Urbana-Champaign), Clara Jones (director, Detroit Public Library), Louis Vagianos (university librarian, Dalhousie University, and consultant on library technology), and Peggy Barber (director of communications, ALA).

After the fair, from 1966 to 1970, Becker was vice president of the Interuniversity Communications Council (EDUCOM). He served as the 1969 president of ASIS and later was a member of the National Commission on Libraries and Information Services (NCLIS) and the National Archives Advisory Council. In 1984, he received the ASIS Award of Merit. In 1991 he received an honorary membership in SLA. In 1992 he received an achievement award and was made an honorary member of ALA (Hayes 1995).

At the time of the 1962 Seattle World's Fair, Hayes was president of his own consulting company, Advanced Information Systems, and was in the middle of his term as president of ADI. After the 1964 World's Fair, he remained an active researcher and teacher, was the ASIS Distinguished Lecturer from 1968 to 1969, and retired in 1989 after serving fifteen years as Dean of the Graduate School of Library Science at UCLA. He received the ASIS Annual Award of Merit in 1993. Among the many contributions to the field by the Becker and Hayes team were pioneering textbooks in library automation that they coauthored: *Information Storage and Retrieval* (Becker and Hayes 1963) and *Handbook of Data Processing for Libraries* (Hayes and Becker 1970), which won the ASIS Best Information Science Book Award in 1971.

International Business Machines Corporation

The worldwide leadership position of "Big Blue" among computer equipment manufacturers in the second half of the twentieth century has been well documented. What is not so well known is that from the 1960s until the mid-1970s, IBM also held a dominant position within the computer industry in the area of IR. This dominance was based on several factors, including knowledgeable industry specialist-consultants, who wrote and presented papers at relevant conferences and were well known and accessible to the information community. In this section and later chapters, we meet IBM staff members who made notable contributions to the online field. IBM was also notable for research and development in large-scale character-based information storage and processing technology, IBM-developed software for batch and online searching, and contract programming and development projects for specific customers. We examine these influences separately. Oddly, even with its dominance in IR work in general, IBM staff and management were not universally supportive of *online* systems; the concept was new, the system overhead was perceived as being too high, and many staff felt that this was not the right way to run a computer.

IR Equipment

In addition to extensive advanced research and development work on basic storage device technology (e.g., thin films, solid state physics), IBM staff developed major new storage systems. The first of these was a "random access" (or "direct access") disk storage device (IBM 350), first demonstrated with the IBM 305 RAMAC system in 1956 (Lesser and Haanstra 1957; Firth 1958a,b; Nolan 1958). Developed for general data processing applications, this disk storage unit with its large (for that time) amount of rapid access storage capacity (5 million alphanumeric characters) at relatively low cost, removed the previous need to use tape storage for library file applications, and made it feasible to consider making more use of the computer for storage and retrieval applications. This approach was reinforced as the cost of direct access memory continued to decline significantly. The same IBM lab that produced the RAMAC unit in 1956 with a storage capacity of about 20,000 bibliographic records, at a cost of about $1.00 per year per character, later delivered direct access storage devices in 1968 with a capacity of 32 million bibliographic records, at a cost of less than $0.008 per year per character. RAMAC was followed by several disk drive systems for the IBM 360: the IBM 2311, followed by the IBM 2314 in April 1965. The 2314 provided a fourfold increase in capacity per spindle, a twofold improvement in data rate, and the ability to operate online. The 2314 now provided a practical cost for the random access user. IBM badly underestimated the demand for such devices, and was hard-pressed to deliver them as fast as customers demanded. The availability of the 2314 was a catalyst to make many sales for previously undeveloped computer applications (Fisher, McKie, and Manke 1983).

The RAMAC system was an advance in digital storage capability by means of magnetic recording technology. IBM also investigated optical techniques for high-volume digital storage. Based on work at International Telemeter Corporation by Gilbert King and others in the early 1950s (King, Brown, and Ridenour 1953), and with the support of the Intelligence Laboratory at RADC, IBM developed a large-scale photographic memory for use in an experimental language translation computer, the AN/FSQ-16, as well as an experimental Stenotype-to-English translation system (Shiner 1958).

Retrieval Software

PRIME

After serving as a U.S. Army tank commander, Joseph Magnino earned a B.S. in biology-chemistry from Norwich University and then served several years in Air Force assignments involving electronics R&D work. He began his thirty-seven-year career with IBM in 1953 as an electronics engineer in their Poughkeepsie laboratory. In 1956, he joined the office of the vice president of research and engineering in New York City, and in 1957, he moved to corporate headquarters in Armonk, New York. In 1959, he received an MBA in international business from Columbia University. As manager of IBM's Technical Liaison activities in Armonk, he was responsible for developing a batch search system for possible in-house use. He recruited Samuel Kaufman to lead the technical development effort.

Kaufman, a Ph.D. chemist from the University of Michigan in 1952, joined IBM in 1957 as an applied science representative, became project coordinator in 1960 for FORTRAN software for the IBM 7070, and in April 1961 joined the IBM corporate staff office to work for Magnino on full-text processing programs. At that point, they shifted to upgrading the text searching programming from an IBM 650 to an IBM 705 computer. An IBM 650/705 prototype searching system was operating, but it was limited to processing words of five characters or less. Kaufman (1998) recalled the events at that time:

On the basis of modest success, it was decided to have the Service Bureau do a systems analysis and write a program to run on a 704/705. The computers were in the IBM showroom at the old 590 Madison Avenue headquarters. The question of what number of text characters was optimum for searching was raised. There were console switches which made it possible to search on 6, 12, or 18 characters (1, 2, or 3 IBM 704 storage words). Not surprisingly, the tests resulted in choosing 18 characters. From this beginning, the IBM Service Bureau wrote what became the first 7090/1401 PRIME system.

Magnino (1962a) described his new 7090/1401 version of the normal text retrieval program at an internal engineering conference for patent engineering managers, and told of its utility for searching IBM Invention Disclosures. The system he described used a database of words edited from technical reports, project descriptions, and invention descriptions.

The first appearance of a name for the system seems to have been in a presentation at an internal IBM meeting (Magnino 1962b). PRIME (Planning through Retrieval of Information for Management Extrapolation) accepted and stored the text of over 1,000 descriptions of internal IBM Research and Engineering projects, over 5,000 author abstracts for all published IBM Technical Reports, approximately 5,000 abstracts for all IBM Patent Disclosures, and abstracts of experimental activities from *Solid State Abstracts* and *Computer Abstracts*. PRIME could search up to thirty questions (up to 30 question words—up to 18 characters per word—per question) per pass of the tape. The program permitted Boolean logic and adjacent word searching. The first public description of PRIME was a presentation at an ACS meeting (Kaufman, Lindsley, and Magnino 1963). PRIME was operating then in the IBM corporate staff office, available to all IBM librarians, researchers, and engineers.

Magnino (1964) described PRIME as a "normal text" (meaning not indexed, classification coded, or structured in any way) retrieval system that had been developed, tested, and used experimentally since late 1961 within IBM. PRIME was the first of the IBM search systems that could accept upper- and lowercase information, carry it in the records, and print the search results out in upper- and lowercase if the correct IBM 1401 print train were used. However, it was not possible to use upper and lower-case information as part of the search logic on this system; that came later with the IBM TEXT-PAC system (chapter 4).

In 1963, Magnino became manager of the newly established ITIRC (IBM Technical Information Retrieval Center), an internal corporate-wide center for scientific and technical information at the Thomas J. Watson Research Center. ITIRC came into existence as a result of an internal management audit. The overlapping and duplicated retrieval functions within IBM were eliminated and were merged into "the most promising" retrieval system (PRIME). ITIRC was formed to incorporate the PRIME system from corporate headquarters, the Technical Information Center from the Poughkeepsie facility, the SDI system from the Mohansic facility, and the dissemination system from the Data Processing Division in Chicago (Kaufman 1998). ITIRC was formed partly to serve as a useful real-world test facility for many of the new IR techniques developed by IBM (Magnino 1966).

In late 1964, PRIME moved from experimental into regular production use at ITIRC. It was used in 1965 with various text files, including internal research and engineering project file descriptions for each project in the twenty-six IBM labs, and for searching the text of technical publications, invention disclosures, selected U.S. patents, and about 200 new input suggestions daily against an employee Suggestion Plan database of 60,000 records (Magnino 1965a,b).

At the time that the ITIRC organization was created in 1964 by absorbing several other internal operations, including an SDI service operation, PRIME was fully operational as a data processing and retrospective searching system. Kaufman designed an additional set of programs for PRIME to accommodate the SDI service called CIS (Current Information Selection) and its requirements. After this new combined system was established, use of the PRIME name diminished. The PRIME software was released in late 1965 as a Type III program to the SHARE General Program Library (Kaufman and Brooks 1965). Other than its inclusion in CIS, PRIME was not directly related to any other IBM software (Kaufman 1998). Kaufman (1966, 511–512) noted that for some experiments, this improved system had begun to operate in an online mode, both for data input and for searching: "An experiment utilizing remote entry of questions from an IBM 1050 terminal and transmission of answers to the terminal was made, using an experimental IBM 7090 Time Share Monitor.... Future developments in the system will be designed to take full advantage of the features available on the IBM 360, including remote terminal entry of data, remote inquiries, teleprocessing, direct access storage devices, and time sharing."

In mid-1967, ITIRC production was still in batch mode, averaging twenty to forty retrospective questions per day and running 2,500 SDI profile searches weekly. Even with an upgrade to an IBM 360 computer, ITIRC was still not ready to move to online searching. Magnino (1967b, 8) noted: "We cannot yet provide managers with their own terminals to establish their question, key it to the computer directly, and receive back an answer." Magnino confirmed this in an August 1967 presentation in which he repeated that they were developing and testing IBM 360 system software for online searching, but they were not yet operational (Magnino 1967a). Kaufman (1998) observed: "Several problems... prevented us from going into interactive production mode at that time, including difficulty in scheduling TSS time and the inability then for TSS system management to support a large enough number of typewriter terminals as well as the cost of those terminals."

Magnino continued to stay involved with search software and services until his retirement from IBM in 1989. Kaufman, the person most responsible for developing the technical aspects of PRIME and TEXT-PAC, continued his thirty-one-year involvement with IBM search software, particularly TEXT-PAC (chapter 4), until his retirement from IBM in 1988.

After PRIME, ITIRC staff turned to developing TEXT-PAC, STAIRS, and other systems, all described in chapter 4.

QUIKTRAN

In 1964, IBM demonstrated their QUIKTRAN system for remote entry and output of batch programs. This system was not retrieval software, but it facilitated remote searching and was used that way in several demonstrations of remote searching.

Terminals could be used to send programs over a phone line to a computer center, to have those programs executed, and to have the results sent back to a user's terminal. It was recognized that this capability could be used with file searching programs, and experiments were done with that approach at Lehigh University, Lockheed, and the University of Iowa (chapters 3, 5, and 7).

Other Software

A joint American Bar Foundation-IBM study of legal data processing and full-text searching of legal publications used in 1963–1965 computer software developed by IBM. This major study, with support from IBM and CLR, is described further in chapter 7. Additional IBM search software developments such as TEXT-PAC and STAIRS are described in chapter 4.

Contract Programming

Much IBM activity during this time period was done under contract for study and developing programs and systems for specific clients. IBM engineers and programmers were contracted to provide solutions to problems for which general-purpose programs had not yet been written; in that sense they participated in developing new techniques and programs, some of which eventually were available for others to use. An example of an IBM contract IR project was the LITE full-text batch search system, developed during 1963–1964, with contract support from the USAF Accounting and Finance Center (chapter 7). Another example was information handling systems for several U.S. intelligence agencies. IBM Federal Systems Division staff on those projects included Robert Chartrand and Charles Meadow (Meadow 1987). IBM work on text searching for the USAF started in 1959, for intelligence data processing (Damerau 1997). IBM made additional contributions to developing automated IR systems, including a total library system called DOBIS (chapter 9).

TRW and Bunker-Ramo Corporation

Ramo Wooldridge, a division of Thompson Ramo Wooldridge, Inc. (known also as TRW) in Canoga Park, California, was involved in computer-based information retrieval and text processing studies as early as 1959. For example, Donald Swanson worked with support from CLR on automatic indexing studies, and H. P. Edmundson of the Computer Division of TRW worked with RADC support on studies of automatic indexing.

In the early 1960s, ONR gave contracts to the company to develop online information handling techniques for application to military intelligence systems. For example, in 1964 they demonstrated in Washington, D.C., an online system with an interpretive compiler that allowed a user to assemble instructions or queries and a query language of nouns and verbs to describe the data and operations. The computer system consisted of an AN/UYK-3 computer and various pieces of proprietary Bunker-Ramo equipment. The display unit included a CRT that could display line drawings, point plots, or text. The database consisted of information on fifteen ships (name, location, course, speed, supplies) and ten ports (name, location, special problems or functions) in an imaginary area representing the Mediterranean. Special function keys on the keyboard were used to represent directions such as "Find the closest port to a given ship" or "Find the closest port having a repair capability large enough to handle a particular ship" (Wilkinson and Martins 1965).

In July 1964, two aerospace organizations, the Electronics Division of Martin-Marietta and the Computer Division of TRW, merged to form a jointly owned subsidiary called Bunker-Ramo Corporation to exploit new markets in automatic control and computer applications. It was named after George Bunker, president of Martin-Marietta, and Simon Ramo, vice chairman of the board of TRW. Ramo became president and chairman of the board of Bunker-Ramo. The president of Teleregister, John Parker, was a member of the board of directors of Martin-Marietta, and he offered Teleregister as a third constituent of the new organization. TRW's Computer Division, experienced in government contracting, was to be based in Canoga Park, California. It was joined in the new organization with the Teleregister group in Connecticut and the Marietta group in Maryland. Teleregister at that time was a relatively small company that had been founded by Western Union. Its principal business was to provide real-time stock and commodity information to brokers all over North America and to develop and install airline seat reservation systems.

Some of the existing TRW projects were transferred to Bunker-Ramo, and new projects in information processing were brought into the new organization. In November 1964, another project started with RADC support, again to develop online information handling techniques for military intelligence systems, but this time to work with textual information. RADC's project engineer was Richard Rawson. A remote access capability was demonstrated in 1965, using a BR-85 display console at RADC offices in Rome, New York, to access the Canoga Park computer facility through a 201A Dataphone set. The remote terminal capability was used to demonstrate information processing functions then deemed necessary for most intelligence systems: text manipulation, creation of text and formatted files, search and retrieval operations, and creation of graphic displays.

Two files were used for experimentation and demonstration. The first test file, the *New York Times* database, consisted of about 1,400 short articles from the *New York Times* and other newspapers, covering Vietnam during the period from October 1961 to December 1964, with a range of topics such as U.S. military equipment and personnel sent to Vietnam or in use there, incidents of sabotage, terrorist activity, civil disturbances, border violations, tactical military information, and government leaders' attitudes on foreign policy questions. The original data were keyed into punched cards and then transferred to magnetic tape. The second database, "Fort Huachuca," consisted of simulated intelligence reports received during a six-day period in a test scenario, containing tactical information received from patrols, civilians, and prisoners for decision making in a simulated war game scenario.

Testing with the online system included searching on words or terms in the *New York Times* database for information about Viet Cong activities, and using this information to create and store formatted files for an intelligence analyst. In spite of considerable data transmission difficulties, the findings suggested that online techniques would be a valuable mechanism for an intelligence analyst (*On-line intelligence* 1966).

Bunker-Ramo produced an upgraded workstation, the BR-90 Visual Analysis Console, that had an extensive capability to work online with text, graphics, and complex output displays. The equipment was used with the PACER system (chapter 4).

In September 1962, Herbert Mitchell, who had previously worked with Parker at UNIVAC, joined Teleregister as vice president for advanced research. For two years, Mitchell worked there on the design of a high-speed switching computer and proposals for a major upgrade of their airline seat reservation system. Mitchell had been commuting monthly from his home in California to the Teleregister offices in Stamford, Connecticut, so when the Bunker-Ramo organization was formed in 1964, located in Canoga Park (20 miles from his home in North Hollywood), he asked to be transferred to that group. He was charged with developing the commercial side of the division's business. The new company was scrambling for business as the Teleregister division was losing its airline reservations business to IBM. Ramo suggested that Mitchell explore how the company's expertise in online desktop communications could be brought to bear on online information retrieval. That story continues in chapter 5 with Bunker-Ramo's unsolicited proposal to develop the NASA-RECON system.

General Electric Company

DEACON

General Electric (GE) was one of several American companies that worked with the U.S. intelligence and military community in the late 1950s and 1960s to search for ways to introduce new data processing techniques into intelligence systems and military command and control systems. With several years of support from GE and RADC, researchers at the GE TEMPO (Technical Military Planning Operation) research facility in Santa Barbara, California, established the feasibility of using conventional English for input and control. They showed that basic techniques were adequate for developing a system that permitted direct access and control of computers using unconstrained English. They also developed an operational online question-answering system called DEACON (Direct English Access and Control). Intended for application to military command and control systems, the system allowed user-computer interactions in fairly unconstrained English. DEACON used text parsing techniques and a file structure that allowed direct answers to these types of questions:

• Does Parker's date of rank precede Olsen's date of rank?

• Is the 638th scheduled to arrive at Ft. Lewis before the 425th leaves Ft. Lewis?

• What is the distance from the 638th Battalion to San Diego?

In 1964, the first phase of the project proved the feasibility of using interpretation rules for relating English statements to computer-stored data structures (Simmons 1965a). In 1966, an experimental system was operating in an online mode, with a GE-225 computer, disk storage, and Teletype terminal units that provided interactive but not time-shared operation (Craig et al. 1966).

Frederick Thompson was the person most responsible for conceiving and developing the theoretical basis for DEACON (Thompson 1966). His background included studies of methods of using English text with computers. He left the DEACON project in 1965 to join the faculty of California Institute of Technology. Because of its geographic proximity and coincident Air Force funding, some of this work was coupled with the work going on at SDC in Santa Monica (e.g., Synthex, BOLD) described earlier. We are not aware of any bibliographic or full-text applications of DEACON, but it was important as an early attempt to develop a user-friendly interface for online searching.

Valley Forge Library

Separate from the DEACON work taking place on the West Coast, the library staff of GE's Missile & Space Division in Valley Forge, Pennsylvania, were working to find data processing solutions to their practical operating problems. Staff members started with an IBM punched card circulation control system in 1961 for a collection of more than 110,000 documents, then implemented a batch tape searching system for subject heading searching.

1964 Milestone

GE-Valley Forge was among the first online search systems to use Boolean logic to combine terms in searching for bibliographic records. (See parallel milestone for TIP.)

In January 1964, they transferred the tape records to disk storage on a GE-225 computer with a Teletype in the library to perform online searches. This unnamed system provided relatively high-speed (30–45 seconds) Boolean searching on assigned subject headings. The database, however, was primitive, and output was limited to a posting count and document accession numbers (Chasen 1967). This may have been the first implementation of Boolean logic in an online bibliographic search system. SRI staff proposed that capability for the system they demonstrated in 1963, but did not implement it. TIP also implemented this feature in 1964, but it is not known which system was the first to do it. It is probably appropriate to credit both of them, and say that it was implemented simultaneously at MIT and GE.

The system included a GE DATANET-30 communications interface link that permitted up to thirty remote terminals to be used with it. In early 1966, additional terminals were established at other locations within this organization for use directly by engineers or scientists. In late 1966 the database was still primitive, with limited search attributes and the output was still restricted to document accession numbers. "Intrinsic limitations on the disk storage unit make it extremely expensive to add title, author, corporate author, etc." (Chasen 1967, 100).

In 1966, the library also planned to obtain the NASA database and add it to its system, so it could provide online access to that database (they already maintained a NASA microfiche collection on site). At this time (described in chapter 5) NASA was already working with Bunker-Ramo and Lockheed to develop and demonstrate an online search capability. At the time (May 1967) that Chasen was describing his system and plans for a GE in-house NASA (National Aeronautics and Space Administration) online database, Bunker-Ramo had just completed its feasibility demonstration project for NASA with an online database of about 200,000 NASA citations. Lockheed had been busy for a year with a NASA project to demonstrate online searching of the full file of 300,000 citations, and since January 1967 it had been providing online service to NASA Ames Laboratory for a scheduled two hours per day with the NASA database.

Summary

We end this chapter roughly at the midpoint of the 1960s, although, as we have seen, some of the work started before 1965 continued into the late sixties or even beyond. What this exploration of the earliest systems has revealed, nonetheless, is that the concept of online retrieval was firmly rooted by 1965 and several prototypes had sprouted. Even though we might view them as puny little plants, they had established by mid-decade many online milestones, including:

- both full-text and bibliographic systems;
- microform storage of fuller documents near a terminal, to extend the data stored in the computer file;
- system acceptance of search queries in natural language form, and matching of the queries to the source text materials;
- automatic incorporation of synonyms into a search formulation;
- relevance scoring and ranking of output;
- search term weighting;
- retrieval based on bibliographic citation elements, cited references, and classification codes as well as subject headings or text words;
- display of an online thesaurus as a search aid;
- postings counts of the number of records in a file associated with each search term;
- users' ability to modify the database online;
- user's choice of novice or experienced searcher interface mode;
- user's specification of number, content, and format of records in the output;
- system prompting for information about search specifications;
- use of a CRT for search interaction between humans and machines and output display;
- use of a stop list;
- searching of chemical structures;
- user's ability to save output for later searching or use;
- user's ability to save search formulations for use in another formulation, or for later runs on an updated file or another file;
- "stem searching," left-truncation, and "wild card" character searching;
- hierarchical searching;
- Boolean logic to combine terms for searching bibliographic records;
- inverted file searching;
- use of a database created by another organization; user access to multiple databases;
- weekly updates of bibliographic records;
- remote database searching by means of long-distance telecommunications.

Another milestone that was thrilling not just for the IR elite, but the general public as well, was the exhibition of online searching and retrieval at the 1964 World's Fair. Even though the visitors may have had fanciful and unrealistic notions of what was really happening inside the computer, the event foreshadowed by thirty years the advent of the World Wide Web and the explosive growth of online, interactive access to data and documents by people of all ages and walks of life.

This early period also revealed the crucial importance of internal and external funding support for online R&D. The names of several U.S. government agencies and private foundations have popped up repeatedly, and we shall see their acronyms again and again throughout our story. The most notable so far have been ARPA, CLR, ESD, NSF, ONR, and RADC.

It is also apparent that IBM was dominating the world of IR hardware. We can only speculate how different the course of events would have been without IBM computer systems (705, 709, 1401, 7040, 7090, 7094, AN/FSQ-32, and 360), IBM disk storage devices (350, 1301, 1405, 2311, 2314), IBM terminals (1050, 1407), IBM printers (1401, 1403), and related equipment such as the 066 Data Transceiver, 729-IV tape drive, and keypunch and accounting machines. Other companies were in the business of supplying equipment to R&D organizations at this time, but no one even came close to the impact of IBM.

In the next two chapters, we examine activities that flourished in the second half of the decade and in the early 1970s. In chapter 3 we visit universities in the United States and around the world, and in chapter 4 we canvass the concurrent activities in nonacademic labs.

3 Further Experimentation and Prototypes in Universities, Mid-1960s to Early 1970s

Introduction

During the second half of the 1960s, a protracted, agonizing war was raging in Vietnam that troubled many people in the United States, where university campuses simmered and sometimes exploded in dissenter demonstrations. Despite the campus turmoil, however, government and private funding for university research reached an all-time high and many academics with vision and energy took advantage of the opportunities to obtain support for fundamental research, mission-oriented research and development, and evaluation projects. The funding support in the United States came, as earlier, from NSF, CLR, and various DOD research agencies, and now also from the U.S. Office of Education (USOE) and Carnegie Corporation. In Great Britain, the Office of Scientific and Technical Information (OSTI) provided the necessary support. In Canada, the provincial government of Ontario underwrote the development work at the University of Toronto.

Since university researchers had no long-distance access to, or participation in, the few existing online retrieval systems, they constructed their own. Thus many variants materialized at universities in the United States, Canada, Ireland, England, and Japan. Like the projects begun earlier in the decade, these projects had a variety of practical and basic research goals. Most, however, were oriented toward using a computer to accomplish the functions of a library, technical information center, filing cabinet, or reference book. They were specialized forms of data management systems in which the data structure contained document data such as author name, title, publisher name, descriptive keywords, and sometimes an abstract or full text.

Certain common elements distinguish the activities during this rich period of research and development:

• Most projects emphasized planning, testing, and evaluation, both to test system workability and to measure users' reactions and preferences.

• The experimentation and evaluation served to heighten the developers' appreciation of the value of quality subject indexing (including depth, comprehensiveness, and variety) and careful construction of the bibliographic record.

• Carefully designed instruction programs revealed training users to be more difficult than had been imagined, systems were more difficult to learn than had been anticipated, and users have a strong innate resistance to expending time and effort to learn online searching.

• Virtually no university-based projects developed into a commercial search service (with the exception of SUNY BCN, the precursor of BRS, see chapters 8 and 9), but at least one—LEADERMART—tried (chapter 9). Either the developers and sponsors had no interest in selling their services commercially, or they could not muster a strong enough marketing and financial program that would result in earning a profit selling online searching services.

• In spite of strong funding support from outside agencies, and contributions of countless hours of labor from faculty and staff, developers were cost conscious. They endeavored to design software that used computer resources efficiently and still maintained a reasonable performance level and rapid response time. This extraordinary challenge, to run a system efficiently and effectively, particularly with the relatively high costs of computers and communications equipment at that time, deterred most of these developers from considering a commercial venture.

The majority of projects during this time period, and surveyed in this chapter, were based in American universities. Several leading researchers, however, were not native-born Americans. For example, engineering professor Carl Overhage was born in England; Morris Rubinoff, an electrical engineer, came from Canada; Ritvars Bregzis was a Canadian technical services librarian born in Latvia; Donald Hillman, a philosophy professor, came from England; social scientist Ed Parker was Canadian-born; Gerard Salton, an applied mathematician, came from Germany. It is likely that they were attracted by the openness and largesse available at U.S. universities at that time. Their contributions, however, repaid any such compensation.

Our narrative begins with the TIP story continuation and then moves to another MIT initiative, Project Intrex, an endeavor that was typical of this group of projects in its focus on planning, experimentation, and evaluation.

Massachusetts Institute of Technology

TIP

Under Kessler's leadership, the TIP project (chapter 2) continued through the 1960s (Kessler 1967e). During 1965–1966, staffs of TIP, NSF, and AIP held discussions concerning the possible expansion of TIP into a prototype system. They decided that AIP could make better use of TIP data if the number of journals covered and the amount of data recorded from each article were expanded. As a result, TIP increased its journal coverage from twenty to thirty-eight journals. Through 1966, data input was from IBM card punching; in 1967 input processing shifted to Friden Flexowriter (punched paper-tape) equipment, which permitted data to be processed in upper- and lowercase. The file was still limited by the amount of Project MAC disk storage space available for TIP. Consequently, citations older than 1963 were not included, even though data were available in machine-readable form for some journals back to 1960, and in the case of *Physical Review*, back to 1950. In 1966, an evaluation was conducted to measure TIP retrieval performance by comparing TIP searches for articles on lasers in 1964 with a search of a major printed bibliography on that topic (Keenan and Terry 1968).

In 1967, several NSF project reports provided a more complete description of TIP at that time (Kessler 1967b, c, d). TIP was described as still experimental and subject to change. Usage was up to an average of fifteen log-ins per week to the database, which had grown to 30,000 papers. About 1,500 articles were processed per month. However, storage capacity was at such a premium that Kessler (1967f, 11) concluded, "An examination of the technical problems involved in text retrieval convinced us that at this time, it would be quite impractical to store any appreciable amount of text on the disk in digital form. Even limited text, such as abstracts or enriched titles, would unduly load our memory capacity." Nonetheless, a few small systems already had included abstracts online (SRI's system in 1963, BOLD in 1965). TIP's compromise was to provide a microfilm viewing station at terminal locations, along with microfilm copies of source journals. They changed their four-character journal code to the four-character CODEN but were still reluctant to allocate any additional storage capacity to journal titles. However, they did add more detail to the cited reference information. Searching the entire file still took about three minutes. Kessler (1967f, 21) noted: "This is a sizeable work load for MAC and will therefore be given a low priority. Users are advised not to attempt 'search all' in the daytime when the call on MAC is very heavy. Weekends and nights are more suitable. The user must also weigh the time cost of this procedure against his total time allotment."

By 1968, the main file had grown to about 100,000 physics journal papers. Licklider described the development of TIP as a process of evolution, guided by means of data collected and periodically analyzed for the purpose of making continuous modifications and adjustments. Licklider acknowledged, though, that TIP had been hampered by the slow pace of the typewriter output; the MIT researchers looked forward eagerly to CRT displays (Licklider 1968). With NSF funding, TIP experimented in 1969 with the production of library catalog cards using a TIP subsystem (Mattison 1969). TIP continued as part of MIT Libraries technical processing systems through the early 1970s (Sheehan 1971). In 1970 it was operating on MIT's IBM 7090 computer used in Project MAC, with access via IBM Selectric 2741 terminals. Recognition of TIP online system and activities as significant at that time was exemplified by Wolfe (1970, 34) including it in his review: "Because of its prestigious academic setting and extensive review and discussion in professional journal literature, ... TIP ... is probably the most widely known remote access on-line information retrieval system."

Evan Ivie earned his Ph.D. at MIT in 1966, with a dissertation that focused on IR issues (see Ivie 1966). Mike Kessler retired from MIT in 1974. Bill Mathews moved from the TIP project to a position at NELINET, then to NCLIS, then to the Jockey Club in New York. He then became manager of the Computer Services Division of Engineering Information, Inc. until he left in 1991 to join Research Publications, then Derwent (both Thompson companies). NSF and other external funding for TIP programs stopped in mid-1973. The system was unplugged in 1974 when the IBM 7094 computer was turned off (Mathews 1970, 1995). MIT did not support TIP after that.

Intrex

The Independence Foundation of Philadelphia sponsored a month-long planning conference at the National Academy of Sciences facilities at Woods Hole, Massachusetts in fall 1965. The seventy-eight attendees included leading librarians, documentalists, scientists, engineers, educators, and heads of government information agencies. Many distinguished participants and visitors, including Vannevar Bush, J. C. R. Licklider, I. A. Warheit, Herman Fussler, and Ithiel de Sola Pool, delivered formal papers that were published in the conference report. Kessler also attended.

The group brainstormed many wide-ranging suggestions. By selecting from all the ideas, a coherent project plan emerged that was called Intrex (Information Transfer Experiments).[1] The initial proposal was for a four-year program of research and experiments to be conducted in the MIT School of Engineering, in close concert with the MIT libraries (Overhage and Harman 1965; Overhage and Reintjes 1974). Beginning in September 1965, grants and contracts from CLR, Carnegie Corporation, NSF, and ARPA supported the programs (*Project INTREX* 1966).

Intrex was the brainchild of Carl Overhage, professor of engineering and former director of MIT's Lincoln Laboratory. Born in London, England, Overhage had earned a Ph.D. in physics from the California Institute of Technology and his research specialties were photography and electronics. As overall project director, Overhage concentrated on bringing the James M. Barker Engineering Library (BEL) into the experiments; his goal was to exploit technology as a means for increasing the library's effectiveness as a modern information transfer facility (Marcus 1991). Overhage's vision for Intrex, to build an experimental foundation for the design of future libraries, was shared with Frank Reintjes (Overhage and Reintjes 1969). Reintjes provided day-to-day leadership of the MIT Electronic Systems Laboratory research program. Richard Marcus, Robert Kusik, and Peter Kugel were the original design and programming team, with others providing programming support from time to time. Marcus had worked as a systems engineer at Itek from 1962–1966 on a laser disk retrieval system and methods of file conversion applicable to large library collections; he joined MIT in January 1967, after which the software design efforts were initiated in earnest. Alan Benenfeld was responsible for literature selection, cataloging and inputting, and Donald Knudson led the hardware group. Intrex inverted files used sorting and merging software developed for TIP (Mathews 1995).

While a goal of Intrex was to develop an online library system, Intrex was fundamentally a program of experimentation to address the broad problems of physical and intellectual access to information found in bibliographic records, documents, and data banks. Licklider (1968, XIV/3) described the purpose of Intrex as "conduct experiments that will clarify design objectives, methods, and techniques for information-transfer systems of about 1975. Emphasis is placed on the word 'experiments.'" Experiments and observations were to take place under conditions of actual use and real information needs, with the researchers varying parameters and taking measurements of preference and performance. Marcus (1997) recalled:

> While libraries, especially academic, were one focus for Intrex (after all, CLR was a major sponsor), and librarians and libraries played important roles in design, development, and in running the experiments, Intrex always had a larger focus as well: how information centers, wherever located, could best serve users in the forthcoming online age. Thus, we pushed . . . having libraries be central to this new age . . . with new computer tools.

The experimental retrieval system developed for Intrex was used at BEL from the end of 1968 to near end of the project in 1973. Besides the central location at BEL, other satellite sites were used: MIT's Materials Science Center, MIT's Electronics Lab, Harvard University, and Rutgers University. In July 1968, the prototype Intrex, running on MIT's computer, was demonstrated in West Berlin during a conference, using a database of only forty-eight catalog records (*Project Intrex* 1968). This was among the earliest demonstrations of international online access; BOLD had been the first, in Rome in June 1967, and TIRP (described in the next section) had been demonstrated in July 1967 in Manchester, England.

Intrex addressed the problem of quick and easy retrieval of source information in professional journal articles, a class of literature not indexed in library card catalogs. The heart of the system was a catalog of records for twenty thousand journal articles, theses, reports, news articles, and books in materials science and engineering held in the MIT libraries, stored in the MIT computer (an IBM 7094), as well as full-text images of articles stored on microfiche. Each catalog record had potentially fifty data fields, although not all were used for any one entry (Benenfeld 1969). The indexers, who were librarians and MIT undergraduate students, did not use controlled indexing terms, but rather lengthy natural language phrases from the documents. The developers chose this form of indexing to avoid having to wait for a thesaurus to be developed in materials science, and because it seemed amenable to either machine or author indexing, which they thought might "be required if this kind of system is to be economically viable" (Marcus, Benenfeld, and Kugel 1971, 166–167).

An evaluation revealed that users could get started easily with an uncontrolled vocabulary, and those users who wanted only a few documents on a topic were satisfied with their results. Users who wanted all relevant documents, however, did not seem to understand the requirement to generate synonyms and alternatively worded requests, and thus failed to retrieve all that they wanted. Marcus, Benenfeld, and Kugel (1971, 168–169) observed:

> Interviews suggest that a major cause for this is that users think the vocabulary is controlled, primarily because they seldom encounter an uncontrolled vocabulary in the library. Another reason appears to be the feeling that the computer is a giant brain that can (and does) do all their thinking for them. Users may also feel that since they can use the natural expressions in subject searches that they use in casual conversations with their colleagues (who understand them) that the computer can understand them too.

However, Marcus (1997) noted that sometimes even naive users retrieved *more* with the natural vocabulary approach than they would have retrieved with a controlled vocabulary, "especially for users who were not expert in the controlled vocabulary. This was a major result of our experiments."

One experimental goal was to determine which of the fifty fields searchers truly needed when full documents were close at hand and a bibliographic description appeared on the first page of each document. The documents themselves were short (average 6 pages) and were stored on microfiche because of its economy, compactness, and ability to preserve pictorial information. Each sheet of microfiche held about ten documents. Two Compact Automatic Retrieval Device (CARD) units, manufactured by Houston/Fearless Image Systems, Inc., and delivered in 1968–1969, stored the 1,500 sheets of microfiche (750 sheets each) (Overhage 1972). In early 1969, one CARD system was in operation with 350 microfiche. Using the COSATI fiche format, 45,000 pages could be stored on the 750 fiche (Knudson and Teicher 1969). A project objective was to be able to deliver page images of retrieved or requested documents at a viewer's remote terminal location. The first working image display terminal in Intrex was a "standalone" in 1969 that used the Tektronix storage tube and required the user to manually dial in the microfiche locations obtained from a catalog lookup on a separate catalog search terminal (*Project Intrex* 1969b). A goal realized in 1970 was demonstration of a capability to use the same display unit for both computer-generated output and full-text images of stored microfiche (Haring 1968a, b; Haring and Roberge 1969). At their remote terminals, users could now display page images, including graphics, of documents they found from a catalog search.

> **1970 Milestone**
>
> Intrex was the first online search system in which a terminal could display on the same viewing screen input-output communication and microform images of source documents.

Interestingly, however, some users actually preferred *separate* terminals, side by side, for the two functions, because that allowed them "to view catalog output at the same time as viewing document images—namely, an early version of a two-window operation (albeit on separate screens) (Marcus 1997). A document could be retrieved from the mechanized microfiche storage device within a few seconds (actually, seven seconds for the first page and three seconds for each succeeding page), and from the same console used to access the online database (Reintjes 1969). Once retrieved and displayed in a viewing aperture, a flying-spot scanner generated video signals from the image in the aperture for display at the receiving terminal.

Training users to conduct their own searches proved to be more challenging than anticipated.

Marcus, Benenfeld, and Kugel (1971, 190–191) reported their observations:

> To the system designer, the user often seems contrary or slow ... we have observed certain characteristics of user behavior that can cause difficulty in instructing them:
> (1) <u>Failure</u> of users <u>to notice</u> even the most explicit instructions (For example, 'Please don't forget the carriage return').
> (2) The fact that <u>no single instruction method</u> or booklet, no single 'style' of presentation, no single compromise between brevity and completeness, seems to satisfy all, or even a majority of users.
> (3) On the other hand, if there are too many instructional options, users tend to ignore them all. We refer to this as the '<u>clutter effect</u>.' Users seem to prefer to be given instructions only when they need them.
> (4) Users <u>do not like to spend time to prepare</u> themselves for system use.
> (5) Users assume that the given system works like some other system (e.g., the traditional library catalog) that they already know about. Some users seem <u>not to like to learn anything new</u>, or unfamiliar.
> (6) Some users suffer from an extreme case of what we might call 'computer angst' or fear of the machine. Such fear seems to come in two varieties—the fear of the user who is anxious about making a mistake because he will appear foolish, and the fear of the user who is afraid his actions will damage the system.
> (7) Users often assume that the computer is a giant brain that will do all their thinking for them or that it is so complex that they cannot possibly understand it. They therefore <u>assume they need not or cannot understand the system</u> and this impedes learning.

The Intrex designers proposed solutions such as giving users immediate feedback on errors, informing them that they could not possibly break the system, presenting general ideas by means of examples rather general rules, tailoring instruction to whether a user wants to understand the system or simply wants to know what to do, and giving human instruction whenever possible and online instruction when human instruction was not possible; both human and online instruction had proven more effective than printed materials. However, Marcus (1997) recalled: "Even in these early stages the main interesting—and, at least somewhat, novel—

result was that end-users inexperienced in computer searching could get good retrieval results by taking advantage of . . . all-fields keyword-stem searching of natural language input, some improvements over other systems in interface design and operations, deep free-vocabulary indexing, and easy search modification by online interactions."

By mid-March 1969, all the Intrex elements had been completed, all were working individually, and with the exception of the display work station and magnetic driven links, all the elements had been interconnected and made to work as a complete system (*Project Intrex* 1969a). However, the developers' vision for Intrex was more than just an online catalog and document display device. They intended it to be a comprehensive network facility for information transfer, linking the entire academic community. Overhage (1966, 1032) predicted, "Data just obtained in the laboratory and comments made by observers will be as easily available as the texts of books in the library or documents in the departmental files." MIT's time-sharing computer would monitor all the traffic and would connect the MIT community to users and information sources elsewhere. Marcus, Kugel, and Kusik (1969) acknowledged that their work blended various techniques and features developed by numerous preceding systems. They credited BOLD, TIP, Multilist, SPIRES, SMART, and NASA RECON as having the greatest influence on Intrex.

By 1971, Intrex had served hundreds of users, whose system interactions were recorded and studied (Marcus, Benenfeld, and Kugel 1971). Initial findings indicated that users could operate the system with minimal instruction. They were unable, however, to master the more sophisticated features. Users also plainly disliked and were baffled by command mnemonics that were not single English words (e.g., MATCHSUB, which stood for "MATCHing SUBjects," or INFIELD, used for searching a phrase "IN some FIELD").

Funding from CLR, NSF, Carnegie Corporation, and the Independence Foundation allowed the experiments to continue during the original four year program, and beyond. In the 1970s, the system was reprogrammed for an IBM 370/165 computer, and advanced from an experimental to an operational status. Intrex provided support to its users over the four-year period 1969–1973 during which it was operational. It was always intended to be an experiment—not to continue operating beyond that time. Nonetheless, it did provide service to over 2,000 users in the four years of its existence (Marcus, Kugel, and Benenfeld 1978). Intrex was among the online systems whose features were examined at an April 1973 workshop at Stanford University; a summary of its characteristics at that time was given in Martin's (1974) workshop report.

In recent years, historical researchers have revived interest in the Intrex activity and have written critical assessments; Burke (1996) and Marcus (1997) have dueled over this topic.

Marcus continued to work at MIT on development and evaluation projects in online multifile, multisystem searching. Other staff went on to work on other online ventures. For example, Benenfeld went to work for NASIC at MIT and then left in 1975 to take academic librarianship positions at UCLA and Northeastern University. Fran Spigai (who worked there as a staff engineer in 1970–1971, then worked for Becker and Hayes, Richard Abel Co., the Oregon Higher Education Library Council, and DIALOG, and then in 1980 established her own consulting practice. Charles Stevens went on to serve as the first executive director of NCLIS, then executive director of SOLINET (Southeastern Library Network).

TIRP

Another online bibliographic system was developed at MIT during 1966–1967 by a group of faculty and students of the Mechanical Engineering Department's Fibers and Polymers Division that included Stanley Backer, Robert Sheldon, and Roger Roach. Started with U.S. Department of Commerce support, TIRP (Textile Information Retrieval Project) was concerned with the general problem of injecting timely data into the information systems of a professional society (Backer

1967). Working on his master's thesis in mechanical engineering, Sheldon was responsible for the design and development (Sheldon and Backer 1967). Backer was his thesis supervisor. Sheldon acknowledged that the system was the product of a group effort involving himself and a team of nine undergraduate students, each of whom contributed to ideas and applications presented in his thesis. The lead student in the team was Roach, whose role Backer (1997) described as being at the interface between the technology of the fiber/textile/apparel industry and the computer retrieval system, with his primary focus on developing a textile thesaurus. Also working with the MIT team until June 1966 was A. B. McNamara, director of the Textiles Division at the Industrial Research Centre in Dublin, Ireland.

Like TIP and Intrex, TIRP used the CTSS of MIT's Computation Center, operating on the IBM 7094 with its thirteen tape drives, two IBM 2302 disk drives (76 million computer words total capacity) and an IBM 7320 drum storage unit (Sheldon, Roach, and Backer 1968). The drums provided a high-speed data transfer rate, while the disk drives had a much larger storage capacity. Communications lines were provided to the TWX and TELEX networks as well as the MIT private branch exchange. The time-sharing system could accommodate up to thirty independent simultaneous users. Data input was accomplished by typists who keyed online via typewriter terminals, with input editing and checking programs to report problems back immediately as data were being entered. This was among the earliest instances of an online data input and error checking system. The frailties and operation of large computer systems of that time were captured in a recent and light-hearted account by Sheldon (1998):

As I recall, most of my time on the TIRP project was ten percent idea-generation, while the rest was consumed by working with the TIRP team to decipher the numerous CTSS crashes in a most sophisticated manner: by printing out the 80 meg drum dumps in octal, spreading printouts all across the computer room floor, and then crawling around on our hands and knees to figure out how to re-link various printer files together to get system and user files back together. We needed batch processing time to run some heavy-duty TIRP file inversion programs, and the only way we could get affordable time was to agree to operate the MIT Computation Center by ourselves, serving as surrogate staff during the wee hours. This would not have been much fun save for the fact that we had been given the run of the machine room for the third and fourth shifts, since (to us anyway) it seemed that we probably knew as much about running the CTSS system as did the system programmers, and we were young enough to not mind staying up all night. Besides learning how to assign a higher priority to our passwords than any of the other CTSS users, we managed to secrete a case of two of Grand Execheux '64, Reichbourg '64 (my personal favorite) and Chateux Lafitte '57 beneath the Computation Center's floorboards, where the A/C kept everything at an ideal temperature. We also managed to provide late night entertainment to a few of the more gullible MIT and Boston College coeds—high-lighted by our showpiece keyboard artistry on the 7094 II's main console during recovery from the frequent crashes.

The bibliographic data elements used with TIRP included author, title, journal name, location of abstract in an abstract journal, subject keywords, and sometimes lists of cited references. The cost of online storage space precluded the online storage of an abstract. The database contained about eleven thousand citations to journal articles and patents from *Journal of the Textile Institute* and *Journal of the Society of Dyers and Colourists* covering the period 1950–1967.

1966 Milestone

TIRP may have been the first online bibliographic search system that allowed users to display an online thesaurus as a search aid. (See parallel milestone for BOLD.)

Because of the textile industry's long and international history, the descriptive language has considerable diversity: "What to a Yorkshireman is a ginnel, to a Lancastrian is a snicket, and nobody else understands what they mean" (McNamara 1969, 210). This fact needed to be considered as a central part of any textile information system. Backer was interested in this language problem and had participated in developing a thesaurus for the textile field, publishing his first one in 1966, for intended use with TIRP (Backer, Valko, and Liang 1967). He also participated in 1972 in developing a multilingual textile thesaurus, which accelerated information transfer across national boundaries, and was the basis for later controlled vocabulary efforts of the Shirley Institute and the Institute Textile de France for their present World Textile Abstracts and TITUS information systems, respectively. It is not surprising then that TIRP included an online thesaurus capability that allowed searchers to enter a keyword or phrase and receive a list of related terms (with the conventional Narrower Term, Related Term, and Use For relationships displayed. As described earlier, BOLD also provided an online thesaurus display in 1966. However, the TIRP group was unaware of it during their project.

1966 Milestones

TIRP was the first online bibliographic search system to offer a way to distinguish major and minor descriptors in searching.

TIRP was the first online bibliographic search system to display automatically alternate search terms and their posting counts when a query found no records for a term.

TIRP provided for searching by subjects and bibliographic data, as well as cited references, which was an extension of the cited reference searching and bibliographic coupling search techniques that Kessler had demonstrated several years earlier. TIRP allowed searchers to specify the role in which a search term was used—for example, a concept was the primary focus of an article (Roach 1997). The terminology of "major" and "minor" descriptors was not used with TIRP, as it was later with the DDC system in 1969 and in some current systems, but the function was provided. A user-friendly innovation was the response to a search that produced zero hits: The system prompted the searcher to use alternative or additional terms. It did this by displaying several alphabetically adjacent search terms with their posting counts, labeled as "near misses" (Sheldon and Backer 1967).

1966 Milestone

TIRP was the first online bibliographic search system to provide a means of identification and removal of duplicate records from search output.

The search system provided a means to rank and list search output by relevance (i.e., by the closeness of match of a retrieved record to a search statement), or by general subject classification. The output system also offered a user-specified feature to identify and eliminate duplicate records in the search output before printing. TIRP appears to have been the first online search system to incorporate this feature.

An initial version of TIRP was available in late 1966 with an almost complete version by February 1967. It was demonstrated at a Textile Research Institute meeting in New York in April, using a Teletype terminal for communication with the MIT computer in Cambridge (a distance of about 190 miles). TIRP was demonstrated in July at the Textile Research Institute annual meeting in Manchester, England, using TELEX and the Transatlantic cable to connect to the MIT computer. This was only a month after the first demonstration of international access to an online search system (BOLD).

TIRP was not intended to be a production system. It was a proof of concept, used only for demonstrations and testing. Only minor changes were made to the system after 1967. TIRP activities and development were separate from TIP activities and TIRP did not directly use TIP software (Mathews 1995). Backer acknowledged the concurrent Intrex and TIP work at MIT, the cooperation and guidance given by Kessler and Overhage, and Kessler's prior work at MIT in citation and bibliographic coupling searching. Sheldon (1998) commented on the TIRP project's status relative to other concurrent high-profile MIT projects:

Although but a lowly graduate student, I picked up enough about the politics of MIT to discern that our TIRP effort was not in the 'right' department to be considered as part of MIT's 'mainstream' information research. We knew that this bothered Professor Backer, but he never let it show. To his everlasting credit as a teacher, he believed in us when we told him that his bunch of students could develop a system faster that would be more technically robust than the 'mainstreamers'—something that must have seemed a youthful boast at that time. Professor Backer also provided a role model to us on a commitment to research, even if it came down to performing much of the grunt work himself. Many times we would find him and his colleagues working long hours into the night and weekends, indexing extremely technical documents, because that was the only way they could be assured that the system would perform at its best. That personal dedication to technical excellence and commitment to his students, was the best memory that I carry about my MIT experience.

Sheldon also expressed his hope that Backer would be recognized for his accomplishments in IR design:

In hindsight, I now understand that his ideas about information feedback during query formulation was a true advance at the time. His thoughts about concept querying, which is allowed when one has a thesaurus which can expand searches in a pertinent manner, allows one to amass a document set that is in balance, a better response collection than one might get from pure bibliographic coupling. By making authors' names, and places of affiliation keywords in themselves, the advantages of concept coupling with bibliographic coupling can become synergistic.

Syracuse University

AUDACIOUS

High in the sky, flying back to Washington, D.C., from a trip to California in 1966 to view BOLD, Robert Freeman was inspired to develop a system better than BOLD and to give it an equally assertive name: AUDACIOUS (Automatic Direct Access to Information with the On-Line UDC System) (Cochrane 1989). Freeman (1995) admitted that the acronym came first, on the plane ride, but deciding what it stood for took many hours of thought afterward. AUDACIOUS was used in an NSF-funded classification research project at AIP that started in July 1965. The project director was Pauline Atherton (later, Cochrane), whose earlier accomplishments included cross-reference editing of the *World Book Encyclopedia*, several AIP projects from 1961–1966 evaluating the major information systems that covered the physics literature (*Physics Abstracts, Physical Review Letters*), and a study with Borko at SDC to test automatic classification techniques as applied to work descriptions and search requests of nuclear physicists. Freeman, the assistant project director, had been an original member of the R&D staff of Chemical Abstracts Service before moving to Washington.

The project's primary goal was to investigate the feasibility of using the Universal Decimal Classification (UDC) as the indexing language in a mechanized retrieval system (Freeman 1966; Freeman and Atherton 1968a, b). A driving force behind NSF sponsorship was the fact that, in those Cold War days, every abstract in the mammoth Soviet-produced *Referativny Zhurnal* information service included UDC numbers. Numerous European university and special libraries and technical information centers also used UDC. Freeman and Atherton had had a chance to trade notes with European users in the United Kingdom, Netherlands, Germany, Denmark, and Sweden and at a NATO Summer Institute on Information Retrieval held at The Hague in 1965.

Project planning began in 1965 while Atherton was at AIP, but in October 1966 she left to join the School of Library Science faculty at Syracuse University. It was there that the final AUDACIOUS/UDC experiments took place, with cooperation of the Administration, School of Library Science, and Department of Physics, as well as Xerox staff and subcontractors in Rochester, New York, who provided the DATRIX online service. AIP continued to administer the project, even though Atherton was at Syracuse and Freeman was at the Center for Applied Linguistics in Washington. The work was published in a series of AIP reports. For simplicity's sake, we describe this project in this section because of its relationship to Atherton's other work at Syracuse.

Freeman and Malcolm Rigby were the first to apply computers to UDC processing, in their 1964 production of keyword-out-of-context (KWOC) indexes (where UDC numbers took the place of key words) for *Meteorological and Geoastrophysical Abstracts* (Freeman 1964). In late 1966, Freeman and Atherton began experimenting with batch-searching systems to test the use of UDC in computer searching. In their first experiment they posed a set of twenty-five questions to a database of 9,159 bibliographic records on nuclear energy (all the abstracts to periodical articles published in 1965 by the Iron and Steel Institute in London) that had been augmented by UDC codes. The test questions had been processed previously by the American Society for Metals in their search service against a database that contained many of the same documents. An evaluation of system performance and analysis of failures for the test was reported in April 1968 (Freeman 1968). It was after this experience with batch-search systems that they considered running their indexing evaluation studies on online systems instead of batch systems. Freeman (1995) recalled:

Pauline suggested that we use an online retrieval system. I told her that I had read about them, but I thought they were several years from being practical for use at that time. She got on the phone to SDC, and three weeks later, I was sitting at the console in Santa Monica, trying out the BOLD system. Time-shared systems in those days were often quite slow. However, my time came directly after a demo for an Air Force general, and they had kicked all of the other users off the system for him. So I had good, fast response time.

Atherton was already familiar with TIP, BOLD, and the Bunker-Ramo and Lockheed RECON online systems. The search for an online system suitable for their application led the project staff to Noah Prywes and Multilist at the University of Pennsylvania, and then to Xerox. A modified version of Multilist was then being developed by Xerox Corporation's Information Systems Division. In July 1967, Xerox, through its University Microfilms Division, announced a batch-mode computer search service called DATRIX (Direct Access to Reference Information: A Xerox Service) that used its extensive collection of doctoral dissertations (Freeman and Atherton 1968a). Discussions with Xerox staff led Atherton to conclude that demonstrating the feasibility of searching a file of UDC-document references using DATRIX would not be difficult. AUDACIOUS was thus a "grandchild" of Multilist, since it was based directly on DATRIX. AUDACIOUS was not a system per se, but a specially adapted application of DATRIX; it had no software that was independent of DATRIX except some special modules that Xerox programmers wrote to accommodate the needs of the AUDACIOUS application.

By fall 1967, AUDACIOUS was operational, running on an IBM 7044 at the Xerox computer center in Rochester, and queried from a terminal ninety miles away in Syracuse. The computer was not time-shared, so a user had full control of it and thus, response time was more satisfactory and predictable than in contemporaneous time-shared systems. The lack of time sharing was highly advantageous for the experiment but would not have been economically feasible in a real system for public use. The terminal was a Raytheon DIDS-400 that had a CRT for display and editing and a keyboard for user input.

In November 1967, searches were run against the database for about one hour per week to obtain data for the UDC evaluation. The project paid Xerox for this computer time. The AUDACIOUS/UDC test was unique in its subject access via a classification system in addition to controlled vocabulary from the *Euratom Thesaurus of Indexing Terms*. Use of classification for indexing documents in detail was common then throughout the rest of the world. In the United States, however, classification was used only for physical arrangement of documents. Subject retrieval by classification numbers rather than by terms from titles, abstracts, or other text was intended to remove the linguistic barriers that prevented search systems from developing into international information networks. UDC conversion tables permitted speakers of different languages to search the same UDC-indexed file. To use the classification, users could query the UDC authority file with their natural language, retrieve related UDC numbers, make a selection from them, then use the numbers as search terms. The advantage was that UDC numbers were hierarchical concept terms, and using them as truncated search terms retrieved records indexed not only by a number itself but also by broader terms. In theory, it automatically took care of the broader term/narrower term problem of natural language thesauri.

Interestingly, even though the records contained personal and corporate authors, titles, report numbers, or journal references, the sole access point was subjects via the classification numbers or Euratom index terms. This restriction was not so much a system limitation as a deliberate design decision, based on the research objective to emphasize subject searching.

1968 Milestone

AUDACIOUS was the first online search system to demonstrate an online decimal classification authority file as an online search aid.

The database contained 2,330 bibliographic references, without abstracts, from an issue of *Nuclear Science Abstracts* (*NSA*). The issue had Euratom keywords and UDC numbers specially assigned for this project by U.K. Atomic Energy Authority staff. A smaller file of five hundred UDC-indexed references drawn from another collection of about two hundred thousand references also was used. Nuclear science research organizations in North America and Europe contributed sixty search questions. The queries were cast into search statements with UDC numbers and run against the files (Atherton, King, and Freeman 1968). The *Special Subject Edition of UDC for Nuclear Science and Technology* was online to assist users in translating their queries to UDC numbers. Use of an online thesaurus had been demonstrated earlier on BOLD and TIRP, but this was the first time it had been done with a *decimal* classification authority file.

The query language was composed of short commands such as HELP (for instruction in the other commands), PUNT (for instruction in using the terminal), TERM (followed by a natural language search term, used to access the UDC authority file to obtain the proper classification number for a concept), COUNT (to search on a UDC number or Euratom keyword and obtain a posting count), FIND (which caused the first record that satisfied a query to be displayed on the CRT), as well as several others to create temporary, personal files of subsets of terms or document references. Although users could also combine set numbers using logical operators AND, OR, and NOT, the query had to be enclosed in parentheses and the operator had to be surrounded by single quotes, for example, FIND (1 "AND" 2). Freeman and Atherton conceded that correctly entering queries according to these precise syntactical rules was difficult. Searchers also had to be careful to avoid errors in entering the search statement; for example, a request to find "the economics of fluid distribution in nuclear reactor control and operation" had to be entered as: FIND (33 'AND' 621.6 'AND' 621.039.56). Further adding to users' frustration was the error message "BAD EXPRESSION," not accompanied by any diagnostics or suggestions for correcting the error (Freeman and Atherton 1968a, 23–24).

Freeman and Atherton based the 1968 AUDACIOUS evaluation on reactions of about fifty users or observers, including physicists, engineers, graduate library school students and faculty, computer-assisted instruction specialists, and information system designers and managers. The data collected consisted of informal comments as well as reactions tape recorded while users were online. Even though it was informal and based on a small sample, the evaluation revealed that extensive modifications were needed before AUDACIOUS would achieve user acceptance. The findings included the following: (1) Users found AUDACIOUS difficult to use, citing a lack of adequate training, practice exercises, error feedback, or availability of help with a specific command without going through the full set of instructions. (2) During the experiment, users were able to search *NSA* manually as well as online. Retrieving widely differing sets of document references to the same query caused them to question the credibility of AUDACIOUS but not the credibility of the more familiar printed index. (3) The usual response time of ten seconds or less was satisfactory. In the few cases where response time was slower, say, 20–30 seconds, reactions were highly negative, especially since the computer did not acknowledge that a command had been received and was being processed. (4) The small number of commands in the query language were learned easily enough. Users made many errors, however, in placing parentheses and single quotes around the operators AND, OR, and NOT. Every punctuation error resulted in the cryptic message "BAD EXPRESSION." The investigators recommended simplifying input requirements, perhaps with function keys for each command and operator, but not modifying the message. (5) Users were irritated with the system's inflexibility in handling spelling variations and in indexing inconsistencies such as singular and plural forms (Freeman and Atherton 1968a).

Donald King of Westat Research participated in the AUDACIOUS project during the formal evaluation phase to help with the evaluation and to estimate recall performance (Atherton et al. 1970). This was an early evaluation project for King, who continued to work in this area after that, working with Westat Research and then King Research. He also served as president of ASIS in 1984 and received the ASIS Award of Merit in 1987 and ASIS Research Award (with José-Marie Griffiths) in 1990.

Freeman demonstrated the system in Europe at seminars at the Technical Library of Denmark in August 1968, and again at the Zentralstelle für Maschinelle Dokumentation in Frankfurt in June 1970, with the software loaded on computers at those two institutions. Overall, despite technical problems, Freeman and Atherton felt that they had demonstrated the feasibility and desirability of using a subject classification code approach in online subject retrieval. They hoped for further experimentation with other classification schemes such as Dewey Decimal Classification and Library of Congress (LC) Classification. However, NSF funding ended in June 1968 and AUDACIOUS was not further developed.

As a postscript to this story, Freeman and Atherton later noted that the project served as a good example of technology transfer between countries. Translators in Poland were hired to translate parts of the UDC schedule that were not yet in English. Although AUDACIOUS was not further developed, Doreen Heaps (who knew of AUDACIOUS, and had attended the Frankfurt seminar) and her student, Marcel Mercier, at the University of Alberta, took an interest in using UDC for water resources data. Mercier became head of WATDOC, the Canadian water resources information center, and started a project to use UDC as a second indexing language for the WATDOC database. Janice Heyworth (later Freeman) joined WATDOC in 1972 and became head in 1975. Although the WATDOC file went online with QL Systems (as noted in chapter 9), the use of UDC in the record was never implemented because of computer resource constraints. Nowadays, some libraries in Europe and some available on the Internet use UDC as a searchable field (J. Freeman [Heyworth] 1995).

In July 1968, Freeman went to work at NOAA (National Oceanic and Atmospheric Administration) where he later served as deputy director of the

Environmental Science Information Center, until he moved to the United Nations (UN) Food and Agricultural Organization (FAO) in Rome in 1986 and to NTIS in 1990.

Xerox's subsidiary, University Microfilms Inc. (UMI), continued to operate DATRIX in the 1970s for the purpose of storing and retrieving citations to over 150,000 doctoral dissertations. In 1972, DATRIX was still using a multilist file structure (Hsiao and Manola 1972). Batch-mode DATRIX continues to operate and probably holds the record for longest-running commercial computer search service. The UMI database of dissertation citations was among the earliest files to be made available via online services. According to Asleson (1987), who demonstrated DATRIX at the ASIS 1969 annual meeting, UMI had decided to keyboard their bibliographic file of dissertation holdings (about 130,000 records), and Xerox had lots of money and was looking for innovative projects for their programmers. Xerox programmers provided the search software, UMI provided the database, and thus they had the beginnings of DATRIX, a commercial service of UMI. Asleson said that things went well until Xerox had a slight financial decline, at which time Xerox management ordered all programmers back to work on projects directly related to copiers. None of the Xerox programmers wanted to do that, so they all (Harry Kapowitz, Ronald Furman, Robert Schrier, and Robert Loan) quit over a weekend and formed a commercial organization called InfoData Systems, located in Falls Church, Virginia. There they rewrote and improved the search software for the IBM 360 series, and in 1968 marketed it as INQUIRE, a successful IR, reporting, file management and text retrieval system for batch or online applications. INQUIRE is described further in chapter 4.

MOLDS

The story of the use of MOLDS (Managerial On-Line Data System) for both batch and online bibliographic retrieval began in 1965, with a USAF/RADC contract to the Syracuse University Research Corp. (SURC) to plan a general-purpose managerial online system. MOLDS was developed for various projects, as part of a million dollar per year support program to SURC for R & D work in information processing. The operating program was developed by December 1966 and reported in March 1967. The principal investigators and developers were J. M. Allderidge,[2] D. M. LaMar, Franklin Martel, S. M. Stratakos, R. G. Wiley, and P. J. Knoke (Allderidge and Knoke 1966). In April 1968, the Syracuse University School of Library Science applied MOLDS to a demonstration project called MARC ON MOLDS, using about five thousand records of the MARC (Machine-Readable Cataloging) pilot project tapes as a database, donated by the Library of Congress (LC).

The MOLDS program had been written in FORTRAN and the query language was not designed specifically for reference retrieval; the thirty-four distinct commands had to be formulated carefully according to precise syntactical rules. Retrieval depended upon an exact match of punctuation and spelling between users' terms and terms in the database, "a match difficult to achieve" (Atherton and Miller 1970, 162). The MARC records contained a large variety of abbreviations, punctuation, and spelling, and yet MOLDS offered no truncation capability. A special feature of the language, however, was that in addition to retrieval commands, it offered commands for data manipulation, including statistical operations such as median and variance, and the common arithmetic operations, including square root. The intended users were librarians who were expected to become comfortable with the commands after study and mastery of the manual, online practice, and regular use. In theory, the thirty-four commands gave users more power and control than other interactive query languages. In reality, however, the data manipulation commands were not used for bibliographic retrieval, and it was difficult to differentiate among the retrieval commands FIND, EXTRACT, DEFINE, CHAIN, FETCH, SELECT or among the display commands DISPLAY, SHOW, PRINT.

Atherton and Miller (1970, 161) noted that the fact that MOLDS was not "user-friendly" (a term not yet coined in 1968, but a concept that most designers were trying to achieve[3]), was not of great concern:

> A design goal of most other existing interactive retrieval systems seems to be to give the computer certain anthropomorphic qualities and make it into a teacher or a responsive friend. Such systems offer computer-aided query formulation and/or a friendly conversation with the computer. The MOLDS on-line system does not include either of these features . . . Apparently the objective of conversation with the computer . . . is to make it easier for the user to achieve desired results or to make him feel more at ease with the system. The person who plays with an interactive system once or twice probably finds conversations with a computer amusing, novel, and helpful in his first attempts. However, for a serious and steady user, carrying on the same conversation with the computer during each and every session can be tedious, repetitive, time consuming and sometimes circular. The optimum mix of computer-aided and independent user-formulated query is yet to be studied and found. Perhaps MOLDS, because it is a poor conversationalist, could aid in this search.

Perhaps a study of MOLDS use could indeed have aided the design of later retrieval systems. We will never know, since the inefficient FORTRAN program used whole minutes of CPU time to process a single command. Instead of modifying MOLDS to make it more efficient and cheaper to run, the investigators abandoned the project (Cochrane 1990). The short life span of MARC on MOLDS can be attributed probably to the excessive costs involved. Nonetheless, the project appears to be the first case of the LC/MARC records being used in an online interactive retrieval mode (Atherton et al. 1970). The University of Toronto appears to be the first organization to do online searching of a MARC-like database, using records that they produced themselves.

LEEP

Starting in August 1968, a computer-based instructional lab was the focus of the LEEP (Library Education Experimental Project) at Syracuse's School of Library Science. Under Atherton's direction, the project was encouraged and endorsed by Henriette Avram at LC, who wanted a library school to do research with the MARC pilot project records. With USOE support, the project used a batch-oriented search system, the IBM 360/50 Document Processing System (DPS), running on the Syracuse computer. DPS was applied to a file of 50,000 records for books published in 1967.

1969 Milestone

Syracuse University School of Library Science was the first academic institution to introduce and integrate online searching into regular classroom instruction.

As we will see later, DPS was used in several other applications; we mention it here to show the breadth of work going on at Syracuse then and because the project provided a hands-on introduction to computer-based information handling techniques for several hundred library school students. In April 1969, regular batch searching of LC's MARC database was incorporated into the students' course work. This experience served as a preamble to the online searching courses that soon followed at Syracuse and in other library schools (Atherton and Wyman 1969; Hudson 1970; Atherton 1970; Atherton and Tessier 1970).

SUPARS

After LEEP and MOLDS, Atherton and her colleagues next tackled an ambitious project to introduce online searching to a large campus community and to study users' attitudes and search patterns intensively. Called SUPARS (Syracuse University Psychological Abstracts Retrieval Service), the project began in 1969, the same year that Atherton became president-elect of ASIS. Like MOLDS, it was supported by RADC, as part of a university-wide study to investigate free-text automatic indexing in large database systems (Cook 1970). The project was conducted in an unclassified environment to test the approach for use in a classified intelligence community application, another thread of the continuing interplay of R&D for national defense and intelligence with public sector interests (Cook 1971). The RADC project monitor was John McNamara. The other principal investigator besides Atherton was Jeffrey Katzer, a new Ph.D. from Michigan State University, who joined the faculty in 1972. After SUPARS, Katzer continued in an academic career at Syracuse University and received the ASIS Outstanding Information Science Teacher Award in 1992. Sandra Browning and Kenneth Cook were also members of the SUPARS research group and served as searching experts in the evaluation studies. Donald King provided "irreplaceable" help in formulating the evaluation procedures for the cost-benefit analysis (Katzer 1973).

1970 Milestone

SUPARS, with Psychological Abstracts, was the first instance of extensive availability of abstracts online for both searching and output.

SUPARS offered free-text searching, but no vocabulary control, because the subject index field had been deliberately stripped from the records (35,000 bibliographic citations and abstracts from the most recent two to three years of *Psychological Abstracts*). The abstracts were about 200–300 words each and all nontrivial words were fully searchable. This database was the machine-readable equivalent of *Psychological Abstracts* that, starting in 1966, was being prepared under contract for the American Psychological Association (APA) under the direction of Laurence Buckland and Inforonics, Inc. (Smith 1985). The tapes were being used in an APA study of a communication program for a national psychology information system. When Atherton approached APA to see if the tapes could be made available for SUPARS, APA proposed that her project pay the entire cost of developing the database (about $30,000). Atherton argued that the cost was unreasonable; with two customers, APA would have full cost recovery. She countered with a fixed-price offer of $3,000 and a deal was made (Cochrane 1997).

Like LEEPS, the SUPARS search software used a modified version of IBM DPS, as did the CIRCOL (chapter 6) and SUNY BCN (chapter 8) systems and others described in chapter 4. In fact, Atherton and Katzer actually "borrowed" the DPS program from Irwin Pizer at the SUNY BCN office, which was located just off campus, and loaded it on a campus computer (Cochrane 1991). The SUPARS team modified the borrowed DPS software extensively; a major programming effort was required to convert the APA tapes into DPS record format in order to allow it to be used in an online mode with multiple parallel users. The software allowed users to construct search queries using Boolean and positional operators.

1970 Milestone

SUPARS, with Psychological Abstracts, was the first instance of a widely known database made available online on a regular basis to an entire campus community.

SUPARS operated for several hours a day, five days a week, running at Syracuse first on an IBM 360/50 computer and, later, on an IBM 370/155. Access was readily available via one hundred typewriter terminals (IBM 2741) already scattered in various campus buildings. An earlier instance of online access to a database (ERIC) being provided to campus users had been at Stanford University in 1969 during the DIALOG ERIC project, described in chapter 5. However, that experiment used a single terminal and project staff conducted about 75 percent of the searches.

The online service was available free of charge to 17,000 students, staff, and faculty during selected periods in fall 1970 and fall 1971. A two-week pilot program with about fifteen users preceded the full-scale public service start-up, in order to identify any problems with the user manuals and terminal equipment and to determine how well the programs operated under a more heavily loaded condition (Atherton 1971). The first year of service it was known as SUPARS I and ran in October–December 1970. A total of 349 registrants, mainly graduate students from psychology, education, and library science, conducted over 5,000 searches (Frierson and Atherton 1971). The following year, an upgraded version called SUPARS II ran in November–December 1971, and 549 registrants conducted searches. During both test periods, most users had had no previous experience with computer terminals or computer-based retrieval systems. The large number of registrants to be trained were instructed in groups, using a thirteen-minute presentation that incorporated colored slides and a tape-recorded narrative. Following the canned presentation, groups were shown an online demonstration search. In order to promote the unfamiliar concept of searching Psychological Abstracts by computer, the developers conducted an elaborate advertising campaign, including campus newspaper advertisements, posters, and letters to students and faculty. They offered, in addition to the training and demonstrations, a user's guide in the form of a "pocket reminder" (reproduced in Lancaster and Fayen 1973, Appendix E) and search consultants to handle problems and answer questions by telephone (Cook 1970).

1970 Milestone

SUPARS was the first online search system to allow users to search for and examine search strategies created by other searchers.

A special SUPARS feature permitted a searcher to retrieve online, for any term entered, all search strategies created by previous users that used the same term. This file of users' search formulations could be used to suggest alternative terms or approaches (Katzer 1971). To address concerns about intrusion of privacy that this sharing of strategies might entail, or the intrusiveness of staff monitoring online strategies, the *SUPARS User's Manual* (Lancaster and Fayen 1973, Appendix E, 468) announced:

In order to continually improve the service provided, it is necessary for the SUPARS Research Group to have access to, and be able to study, the search queries of the users of the system. In addition, one of the useful searching aids SUPARS provides for users is on-line access to selected, anonymous portions of search queries made by other users. To achieve these goals, the SUPARS system monitors and records all interactions made by all users of the service. We would appreciate a call from those users who have any questions about this procedure.

Users could retrieve these strategies; they could not be kept online and executed in their current form as was done earlier with TIP, or with features such as SEARCH SAVE or similar functions that appeared later in other online systems. The novelty here was searching on terms that were used in prior search formulations.

SUPARS should be remembered best for the various experiments and user evaluation studies associated with it (Frierson and Atherton 1971; Katzer 1972; Atherton, Cook, and Katzer 1972; Katzer and Moell 1973). It was among the earliest studies to use transaction log analyses. An unobtrusive data collection program known as STATPAC recorded each search interaction and other summary statistics of frequency of use, cost of searches, CPU time expended, and number of documents found. These data, especially from the cost/efficiency studies, were helpful in planning service modifications. Katzer (1973, 325–326) noted that examination of searches revealed also how useful a controlled vocabulary would have been for certain difficult searches:

One of our users exemplified this problem with the following incident. He wanted to retrieve documents in his subject field provided they reported results based on human experimentation. Few documents were retrieved employing this criterion, which is somewhat surprising to anyone familiar with the contents of *Psychological Abstracts*. The problem, he discovered later, was that few abstracts used the word human. Instead they employed words slightly more specific (but for his purposes, synonymous) such as male, female, boy, youth, adolescent, subject, students, etc.—and all of their plurals.

User characteristics were collected from registration forms. The investigators could thus correlate personal characteristics of users with their database usage patterns. The telephone aid service staff collected problems and questions, and assessed users' attitudes through personal interviews with a stratified random sample of twenty registrants. Although the study did not include nonusers, SUPARS was an outstanding example of integrating user feedback into the implementation of an innovative service. RADC learned what they wanted to find out about free text indexing and searching, and RADC funding for the project stopped after the two-year effort. A final report in seven volumes was published in 1971 (Cook et al. 1971).

In 1970, Atherton (later, Cochrane) served as Sarada Ranganathan Lecturer in Bangalore, India, and in 1972 as SLA's John Cotton Dana Lecturer. At Syracuse University, she played a key role in bringing computers into the library world. It was as the result of her efforts that Syracuse became the first school to introduce computer searching into classroom use. In 1971 she served as president of ASIS. In 1980, she wrote *Basics of Online Searching*, with Charles Meadow. Atherton's many pioneering contributions to information science education and research resulted in her receiving in 1981 the ASIS Outstanding Information Science Teacher Award and later, in 1990, the ASIS Award of Merit.

All of this developmental activity and evaluation at Syracuse University—AUDACIOUS, LEEP, MOLDS, and SUPARS—took place within a period of just a few years. However, these systems were not the only online retrieval projects in Syracuse, New York, during this period; we have not yet met the biggest one of all. SUNY BCN, the precursor to BRS, loaded a huge file and served medical libraries all over New York State and a few other states as well. SUNY BCN will be properly introduced in chapter 8.

University of Pennsylvania

SOLER

Picking up where we left off in chapter 2 with the Moore School of Electrical Engineering, we observe that Morris Rubinoff began in 1964 to explore using computers in IR (Rubinoff 1973). Rubinoff was an electrical engineer born in Toronto, and had a doctorate in external ballistics from the University of Toronto. He was also intensely interested in IR, indexing, and thesauri, and published many papers in these areas. One early activity, with AFOSR (Air Force Office of Scientific Research) support, involved the development and use of a repository of technical documents from ACM (Association for Computing Machinery) as the basis for developing an online system. The ACM repository library was first proposed in 1961, and the Moore School designated as the repository site (Rubinoff and White 1965b). This file was used in several Moore School research projects. In 1964, Rubinoff also planned to build a database of all computer and electrical engineering documents in the Moore School Library to use for retrieval experiments.

In May 1967, a doctoral student, Harvey Cautin, and his colleagues announced another experimental online operation. Called SOLER (System for On-Line Entry and Retrieval), the system was written in COBOL, and used a database of 2,000 documents from the ACM Repository (Cautin et al. 1967). SOLER should not be confused with SOLAR, a system of Washington State University, described later in this chapter. The AFOSR Information Sciences Directorate and the U.S. Army Research

Office provided the funding and Rubinoff headed the research team.

Even though SOLER could be accessed through dial-up to the IBM 7040, users had to wait after connecting until the 7040 became available. The message, "STANDBY" kept repeating once a minute until the operators loaded the IR and background programs and the database. The symbolic language initially developed for SOLER was system-oriented, with arbitrary symbols to represent various operations. For example, the allowable Boolean operators &, +, and ↑ represented AND, OR and NOT. The system processed AND and NOT first, in order left to right, and then OR. Parentheses could be used to override this order of processing. A phrase such as "binary computer" retrieved "binary digital computer" as well; the space character was also an operator in certain contexts. Users could limit searches to specified fields by adding non-mnemonic codes such as $A3 (which specified title field) (Cautin et al. 1967, 6). Only a few trained users tolerated this symbolic language; not surprisingly, experiments conducted in 1967 on ease of learning and use revealed that most searchers found it unsatisfactory (Rubinoff et al. 1968b).

By 1971, SOLER ran on an RCA Spectra 70/46 computer, which could support a multiplicity of files that were searchable either one at a time or collectively. The command RETRIEVE ANYWHERE allowed the same search strategy to be applied simultaneously to multiple files (Lancaster and Fayen 1973). NLM used SOLER experimentally for its Toxicology Information File. Other researchers in the early 1970s used SOLER for constructing, maintaining, and searching their own personal files.

The system offered two search language approaches, one of which was a symbolic language that permitted three search commands (RETRIEVE, COMBINE, DISPLAY). Rubinoff and his colleagues also developed a simpler command language, called "Easy English," an approach that required only that search requests be formulated in a specified syntactic form (Rubinoff et al. 1968a). It was made up of readily recognized English sentences and developed as a command language for reference retrieval from a machine database using remote teletypewriters in a conversational mode. The search software was an outgrowth of the Moore School Multilist system (Rubinoff and White 1965a). With support from AFOSR and the Army Research Office, several dissertation projects and publications resulted from this project (Rubinoff 1966; Lowe 1966; Stone et al. 1966; Rubinoff and Stone 1967; Rubinoff, Franks, and Stone 1967).

Easy English permitted requests to be formulated in the following general syntactical form:

INTRODUCTORY CLAUSE DOCUMENT CLAUSE DATA CLAUSE

Cautin et al. (1967, 14, 18) offered a few sentences to illustrate various ways the same retrieval request could be entered:

(1) PLEASE LOCATE EVERYTHING WRITTEN BY ROBERT PERKINS ABOUT EASIAC OR PSEUDO-COMPUTERS BETWEEN 1955 AND 1959 < >

(2) I NEED ALL THE AVAILABLE DOCUMENTS PUBLISHED DURING THE PERIOD 1955 TO 1959 BY ROBERT PERKINS ON THE SUBJECTS OF EASIAC OR PSEUDO-COMPUTERS < >

(3) WE'RE INTERESTED IN HAVING REFERENCES AND MATERIALS ON EITHER PSEUDO-COMPUTERS OR EASIAC AUTHORED BY ROBERT PERKINS AFTER 1954 AND BEFORE 1960 < >

The system matched words in a query with words and phrases in its dictionary. If no words matched, the system asked the user to reenter the query (Rubinoff et al. 1968).

For his 1969 doctoral dissertation, Cautin designed a new interface, called "Real English," to be even closer to natural language and to supersede "Easy English." Real English allowed users to phrase requests in any convenient form, such as declarative, imperative, or interrogative sentences, or sentence fragments.

University of Toronto

Reactive Catalogue Pilot I

In May 1967, Ritvars Bregzis, a technical services librarian from Canada who had been born in Latvia, attended an IR colloquium in Philadelphia. There he announced that the University of Toronto Library was developing an online catalog, with access to the descriptive bibliographic data (e.g., author, title, publication date). The system was an extension of a project that had been initiated in summer 1963, when the Ontario provincial government had decided to establish five new Ontario universities and had asked the Toronto library to build the five new collections, each with thirty-five thousand books, as well as to develop five identical library catalogs (Bregzis 1966). Some of the universities were to begin enrolling students in September 1964. Faced with this deadline, ONULP (Ontario New Universities Library Project) staff immediately began working with the University Institute of Computer Science and the IBM Toronto Data Centre to develop a machine system to support the catalog functions (Bregzis 1965).

By the standards of that period, this was a huge automation project. The first machine-produced catalogs were in book form. The ONULP work was completed in 1967 at which time the university authorized the chief librarian to establish a separate systems department, procure a dedicated computer facility, and work out long term plans and systems to provide services to the general library community, and not solely to the university's library. The university then began the offline retrospective conversion of its entire catalog, a project that was completed in 1974. The first computer, an SDS Sigma 7 was installed in 1968, and work began on techniques for catalog record processing from MARC tapes, and online file management (Velazquez 1979). The Reactive Catalogue database was created painstakingly on a key punch machine, in a machine-readable format closely related to the LC MARC format. The system operated on an IBM 360/50, and the first online interaction between users and machine took place sometime in 1967, via an IBM 2260 terminal that had a keyboard for input and a video screen for output. Approximately 40 K of core storage were dedicated to the pilot online system for several hours each day.

Bregzis credited BOLD and TIP for helping to shape his ideas for the Toronto system. However, his main motives in developing the online catalog were to focus on controlling the bibliographic descriptive data, increase the number of access points, and allow flexibility in combining access points. Bregzis concluded from the results up to that point that theoretical work still needed to be done on structural definition of the bibliographic record and organization of the bibliographic file in relation to machine-based storage and retrieval, as well as on query languages. He worried that "the state of the art in machine systems is pulling heavily towards compromises that accommodate machine system shortcomings at the expense of the users' inconvenience" (Bregzis 1967, 89–90). This early operating system at Toronto should be remembered most for the librarians' concern for the quality of the bibliographic description and the convenience of users. In 1971, the library's Systems Department was reorganized as a separate administrative unit called University of Toronto Library Automation Systems (UTLAS). The Reactive Catalog was part of the context that led to UTLAS. The UTLAS story continues in chapter 9.

University of Illinois

REQUEST

Starting in 1967 with support from several federal agencies, researchers at the University of Illinois at Urbana, Coordinated Science Laboratory developed an experimental interactive search system called REQUEST (Carroll et al. 1968). The system was implemented on a CDC 1604 computer, working with a bibliographic file of technical journal data, including cited references. Because of a lack of a mass storage capability at this facility, the actual computer processing was done in serial mode. Users could conduct searches in an interactive mode through a terminal display unit, and could take several online branch points—after displaying the first record retrieved, the system displayed the record on the screen and gave a searcher several online options for selection by a light pen: start another query, continue the query, exit, hold, print, or write tape output. Even though this was online searching, it was not interactive as we know it, because it did not permit search modification (other than starting a new search from the beginning), and it did not permit using intermediate output in later search formulations. It could be considered a precursor to online interactive searching that apparently did not proceed beyond this experimental stage.

A considerable amount of theoretical work in computer sciences was being done at the University of Illinois, in association with their ILLIAC IV parallel processor computer. The analytic investigation of the relative impact of file organization schemes on the response time of online search systems is one example of such work (Cordaro and Chien 1970).

Lehigh University

LEADER

LEADER (Lehigh Automatic Device for Efficient Retrieval, or alternatively, Lehigh Answer to Demand for Efficient Retrieval) was an end user-oriented prototype online system based on retrieval from the full text of documents (Hillman 1970). Donald Hillman (see figure 3.1), director of the Lehigh University Center for Information Sciences in Bethlehem, Pennsylvania, from 1967–1983, and a philosophy and information science professor since 1964, was born in England and educated at Cambridge University. He began working on the theoretical basis for LEADER in 1962, by postulating that an information storage and retrieval system should combine the functions of document retrieval, data retrieval, and reference retrieval, in order to be able to provide a wide variety of useful responses to different types of information inquiries. With NSF support, Hillman worked in the early 1960s on theoretical studies of retrieval system design and relevance issues, paying particular attention to the appropriateness of Boolean algebra for retrieval system design (Hillman 1964a, b, c). At a conference in 1964, Hillman reported that he already had done empirical testing with computer processing of a collection of 45,000 technical document abstracts (Hillman 1965, 210–219). The first implementation of Hillman's theories took place in 1965–1966, with the writing and testing of programs for full-text analysis. After more software was developed in 1966–1967, a small-scale online prototype, with a database of approximately one thousand documents in the field of information science, began operating in summer 1967 (Hillman 1968).

Probably the most important feature of LEADER was a sophisticated program for reducing the full text of documents to surrogate form. An elaborate form of automatic indexing reduced all input sentences to noun-phrases that described a document's "aboutness," weighted to their relative importance in the original document, with trivial words eliminated. Inquiries could be in natural English, that is, in the form of declarative sentences without restriction as to vocabulary or form. Terms could be truncated. Requests were processed in the same way that documents were processed, and the program looked for requests and documents that matched above a preestablished threshold, in a manner similar to the SMART system. This approach of computer analysis of source documents was in several ways also similar to the text analysis and question answering approach used with SDC's Synthex. Interestingly, it was at this time (September 1966) that Simmons at SDC concluded that no completely automatic parser could be constructed.

The system could converse with users to clarify and refine requests. After a search statement was submitted, a user was presented with phrases derived from the documents that most closely matched. The user could accept or reject these

Figure 3.1
Donald Hillman at Lehigh University with staff member Nancy Steenblock, is perusing a printout from a search of LEADER. They are communicating with the computer from an IBM terminal via a regular voice-grade telephone line. 1967. Photo from private archive of Donald J. Hillman.

phrases; if he rejected them, an alternative set was displayed. Extensive browsing and tutorial features also facilitated user-system interaction, and the system could monitor and record each user's interactive dialogue. Anderson, Kasarda, and Reed (1967) reported on the automatic search procedures and methods for modifying the number of documents retrieved. Hillman (1973, 588) felt strongly that ordinary prose could far more efficiently describe users' interests than "the artificial constraints of Boolean forms (themselves of highly dubious if not nugatory value)." The system automatically retrieved the conjunction of terms; it did not offer either an implicit or explicit OR or NOT logic. Output could be viewed in the form of document references or complete textual passages, in ranked order of pertinence, as judged by the system.

Parts of the prototype LEADER were implemented on a GE 225 computer in 1965 and on an IBM 1800 computer in 1966. As a temporary measure, other parts operated on two external time-shared services, IBM QUIKTRAN and IBM DATA-TEXT, located in Philadelphia. QUIKTRAN's main processor was an IBM 7040/7044 with IBM 7320 drum storage and IBM 1301 disk storage devices. Users communicated with the central system through either an IBM 2741 terminal or IBM 1050 data communications system over regular voice-grade telephone lines. The DATATEXT system, using an IBM 1460 computer, permitted direct online keyboarding of the database text from a terminal instead of the costly and more cumbersome card punching ("Lehigh's LEADER-MART" 1972).

Working with Andrew Kasarda, Hillman completed a full scale version of LEADER by 1969, using a database of the full text of technical articles and reports in information science and engineering. The file size was limited to 10,000 items, but regular weeding eliminated items of low quality or little interest (Hillman and Kasarda 1969). LEADER initially covered engineering and materials; it was later expanded to include business economics and urban studies, marine and environmental studies, computer sciences, and mathematics. In 1970, it was close to meeting its objective of providing fully automatic online interactive IR for the eight Lehigh interdisciplinary research centers. The full system was running on a CDC 6400, the fourth successive hardware configuration used to date. Input and output were accomplished with an IBM 1442 card reader/punch, an 1816 typewriter console that transmitted at 11 cps, and a 2260 CRT terminal that transmitted at 240 cps and could display both bibliographic data and text. The time-sharing system used was at first IBM's TSX, and later, the INTERCOM 3.0 time-sharing system written at Lehigh University (Hillman and Kasarda 1969; Kasarda and Hillman 1972). LEADER was written primarily in FORTRAN.

NSF grants funded all theoretical and developmental work on LEADER from 1962 to the early 1970s. As we will see in chapter 9, LEADER was renamed LEADERMART in 1971 and incorporated into a public online service that survived only a short time. From a conceptual view, however, Hillman's design was unique and perhaps ahead of its time.

Stanford University

SPIRES

SPIRES (originally Stanford Physics Information Retrieval System, later changed to Stanford Public Information Retrieval System) was the brain child of Canadian-born Edwin Parker, a quantitative social scientist at Stanford University's Institute for

---

1968 Milestone

LEADER was the first online search system to store, provide access to, and display a significant amount (10,000 source documents) of full-text information online.

Communication and Research. Parker had been studying the effects of communication media on human behavior and also had been trained as a computer programmer. Rather suddenly ("in the middle of the night, standing in front of the computer doing data processing"), he wondered about the social and economic effects of computer technology. Parker (1988) recalled, "Then, as I speculated about what new services, what kinds of things could happen as a result of this new technology, I decided I'd jump right in and start building some of it." He imagined that the technology would be extremely expensive, and he did not want to wait until it became commercially available. Parker therefore planned a research and development project, in order to get support from NSF, USOE, and other agencies. Even though he was interested primarily in social change, he wanted to experiment with an actual system and real environment to be able to understand what was happening. For inspiration, Parker studied the Intrex report (Overhage and Harman 1965) and traveled to MIT to talk to staff involved in TIP and Intrex; many of his ideas for SPIRES came from TIP. He also met Salton and studied his SMART system. The Stanford and Lockheed groups continuously exchanged information.

SPIRES was planned originally as a five-year effort to develop and study a system for filling information needs of Stanford scientists (Parker 1967, 1969). It was used first for experimental purposes and later as an operational retrieval system. NSF provided most of the financing, Parker served as principal investigator, and Richard Bielsker was technical programming manager.

In late 1967, a small, one-terminal pilot was demonstrated on an IBM 360/75 computer with an IBM 2250 terminal. From that point, SPIRES I was built "rapidly and unsystematically," incorporating as much as possible the valuable suggestions made by users during the first months (Martin and Parker 1971). In February 1968, SPIRES I was ready for public use and was offered for an hour and a half each day, five days a week (Marron et al. 1973). The designers decided to create an online rather than a batch system because of the obvious time-saving benefits of the former and because Stanford could provide the necessary computer system. From the beginning, the designers' goal was a system that could support multiple files and users. Most of 1968 was spent developing the software necessary for a multiple-user online system and finding a time-sharing system that could tolerate the massive storage requirements. The IBM time-sharing system did not allow enough users to make it practical for this application, so the Stanford Computer Center supplied a locally grown time-sharing system called ORVYL. Parker (1969, 9) reflected on the decision in his SPIRES annual report for 1968:

None of the proposed large scale general-purpose time-sharing systems have yet been successful. For us to tread where IBM and others have so far failed would be foolhardy. We may be foolhardy anyway, but we chose not to wait for someone else to develop a general-purpose time-sharing system. Instead, we forged ahead . . . If we succeed, we are heroes, and if we fail we are merely visionaries who were ahead of our time. . . . our chances of producing such a system are good. But we don't recommend it for others unless they are confident they can work at the present frontier of computer systems development.

SPIRES was written in PL/1, operated on an IBM 360/67, and used IBM 2741 terminals. Transmission rates were 10 and 15 cps (Fife et al. 1974). In Parker's opinion, the lack of an economical CRT display constrained the design significantly. Most terminals "were teletype-class or big mechanical typewriter-like printers . . . clunky, mechanical, slow" (Parker 1988). Weighing about seventy-five pounds, they required two persons to carry them. Another constraint on the first version was file size. Parker envisioned a file the size of the LC and a large population of users. In reality, the technology available could support only small files and a few users.

The first target population was high-energy physicists, whose specialty was the only one for which a high percentage of the world's population was in residence at Stanford because of the Stanford Linear Accelerator Center (SLAC). The physicists were computer literate and intensely concerned with information; they were all interested in searching several document collections, including the SLAC preprint collection, *NSA*, the DESY index of high-energy physics documents, and a collection of physics journal articles (Parker 1971a). Parker (1988) recalled:

In 1967 I taught for three months at our Stanford-in-France campus in Tours. I went in order to get a better understanding of what energy physicists needed in the way of information. There was another high-energy physics facility in Hamburg, Germany, so I traveled across to Hamburg to interview energy physicists there and find out how they were handling information. It was a fairly conventional research-oriented approach of scouring the world to find everything that's going on that's relevant. I also co-opted Louise Addis, the librarian at SLAC, in order to get her input and her understanding of the information needs.

From interviewing the physicists, Parker discovered that they also wanted something that he could not provide: an online file of the parts catalogs from Hewlett Packard, Tektronix and other companies that provided the specifications and availability of all the different pieces of hardware and gadgets ("trinkets from Tektronix") that physicists might use in putting together experiments. Parker (1988) recalled, "It was too diverse. It was going to be too big a file, and there was no practical way to pull it together and make it happen then."

Bielsker wrote *SPIRES Reference Manual* in January 1969. In it he acknowledged "personnel who are primarily responsible for the design and development of the SPIRES prototype system . . . James Marsheck, Hilma Mortell, Edwin Parker, and William Riddle . . . other persons who have directly aided this development effort . . . Louise Addis (SLAC Library), Diana DeLanoy (Project BALLOTS), and Eleanor Montague (Project BALLOTS)" (V). The manual included the external design specifications, a training guide, the system stop list of about four hundred words (including such terms as *accompany*, *accord*, *address*, *forthcoming*, *notwithstanding*, *oh*, *whence*, *wherein*, and *whither* that are not likely to appear on any current stop list), the list of journal names frequently referenced by the SLAC physics community, and the list of databases currently available to SPIRES users. The files were ERIC, a small Geology article collection, Library In-Process File, NSA, and High Energy Physics Preprints.

The query language was intended to be usable directly by students, faculty, secretaries, and library clerical staff without intervention by trained librarians or programmers. In reality, however, users were a combination of end users (physicists) and intermediaries (chiefly Louise Addis, SLAC librarian). Parker (1969, 10) reported that another design decision, to make the system available only locally, was based on predictions about coming technological developments:

We presumed that although batch processing systems (like MEDLARS) may be more efficient as a centralized system, interactive systems will have to be de-centralized to avoid the expensive communication costs. This judgment may change . . . if there is a drastic revision of domestic telephone tariffs after the introduction of domestic communication satellites. Nevertheless, our best guess now is there will always be need for local or at least regional services, even though there may be network switching to a national information center or centers for infrequently used material. Local systems should be more responsive to local needs than any centralized national system can hope to be.

The programmers built the first version of SPIRES not to maximize internal machine efficiency but rather to develop rapidly a system that users could interact with and provide evaluation feedback, to let them know if they were on the right track. They expected that they would build later versions with a more efficient and elegant internal structure. They were frustrated, however, because their work was interrupted frequently for demonstrations of partially developed systems and for tests that always resulted in suggestions for changes. The gradual development was based on an open-ended plan of successive iterations in six phases, to increasing complexity in the design. Parker (1969, 11–12) offered two reasons for this plan:

One is that there is much that is ad hoc in the development of computer systems. We have no theory to permit us to predict with certainty the range of modifications necessary when a new complexity or generalization is introduced in one part of the system. . . . we can't predict which straw will break the proverbial camel's back. In fact, we don't even know the weight of some of the straws we are adding. A more important reason for planning successive iterations is that the major unknown is how users will interact with the system. We need to study how users interact, what frustrations they have, what mistakes they make, what features they find useful or not useful.

A related project began in the Stanford University Libraries in mid-1967 with a large eighteen-month USOE grant to plan and design Project BALLOTS (Bibliographic Automation of Large Libraries Using a Time-Sharing System). The grant was renewed with additional funding in 1969 for another eighteen months. In 1968 the University decided to join the talents of the two separate projects, SPIRES and BALLOTS. Parker's work, with NSF funding, had been a separate behavioral science research project, activated almost a year before Project BALLOTS. The BALLOTS I prototype became operational in the Stanford University Libraries in February 1969 and used several terminals in the Main Library for online searching (Veaner 1969). The SPIRES and BALLOTS integration permitted sharing of facilities, hardware, and software, thus reducing overall costs. A major goal of the joint project was to develop a cost-efficient system for processing bibliographic records that would benefit library staff in performing technical processing functions. Parker was not as interested in this goal as he was in improving the quality of user services. He assumed, however, that the first goal was necessary in order to justify the costs involved in realizing the second. He did not want SPIRES to be just an experimental toy that faded into the dust when the NSF grant funding ran out. By merging with BALLOTS, support was continued from USOE, CLR, and several private foundations.

In mid-1969, SPIRES was available from 8:15 a.m. to 10:00 a.m., Monday–Friday, via any of the 120 terminals serviced by the Stanford Computation Center. At this time, sixty terminals could be operating simultaneously. Successful remote demonstrations of SPIRES had been made at SDC, LC, OCLC, and Columbia University Libraries. The BALLOTS/SPIRES Project demonstrated the feasibility of conducting online interactive bibliographic file searches with multiple users working simultaneously in the same or different files.

The last quarter of 1969 was spent evaluating the SPIRES I prototype. As the original NSF proposal had promised, SPIRES was used to study user interactions with retrieval systems. While online, users could key in suggestions, problems, or complaints. Staff responded to comments that included a telephone number or address. They used the suggestions to improve the system or reduce confusion by clarifying the instructions. The physicists who used SPIRES revealed that they admired the fast response time, but found the slow printing of the terminal output to be vexatious. Rather than waiting at terminals, they preferred to collect their printouts later or have them mailed to them (Addis 1970). The evaluation indicated that a milestone had been reached with the successful operation of SPIRES I and that technical feasibility had been demonstrated. The anticipated benefits of a production version, however, could not be realized by implementing it on Stanford's 360/67 because of two major problems: file integrity of the software of the 360/67 as implemented at Stanford, and the expected costs of operation ($15–$20 per hour). The developers therefore turned their efforts in 1970 to SPIRES II (Parker 1971b).

SPIRES as an acronym for Stanford Physics Information Retrieval System soon became inappropriate as the project began in its second year to work with the library's Automation Division, which broadened the project's perspective and goals. The name SPIRES then came to stand for the Stanford Public Information Retrieval System. The support and continued development of SPIRES required a complex collaboration involving Stanford's Library, Computation Center, and Institute for Communication Research.

Meanwhile, the scope definition document for BALLOTS II was published in February 1970. In November 1970, A. H. ("Hank") Epstein was appointed project director. BALLOTS continued to evolve, and be modified during the 1970s, and completed its initial development phase in 1975 (Epstein 1973). Other Stanford staff members associated with BALLOTS were Allen Veaner, Lenny Stovel, Timothy Logan, Wayne Davison, and Douglas Ferguson. Veaner directed BALLOTS and USOE funded it. (The *BALLOTS project* 1975; *Guide to BALLOTS* 1976).

SPIRES II went into service October 19, 1972, as a self-supporting, general-purpose system offering several databases in a variety of subject areas, some of which were bibliographic, but others contained student registration data or medical, biological, or environmental numeric data. Most were tiny, except for the LC MARC file which by June 1973 contained over 68,000 records. SPIRES II was written in PL360. The query language consisted of two main commands: SELECT, followed by the name of the file desired, and FIND followed by a search term, which was remarkably like TIP commands. Search terms could be linked with Boolean operators, as well as qualifier operators such as BEFORE, AFTER, WITH, STRING, BETWEEN, and MASK. David Phillips, director of the Stanford Computation Center, directed the SPIRES II project.

Stanford Research System

Meanwhile, across the Stanford campus, David Thompson, a faculty member in industrial engineering, was working with colleagues Lawrence Bennigson, David Whitman, and Dale Seastrom to investigate ways to structure a database to minimize retrieval time for any single item. In 1967 they reported results of their investigations (Thompson, Bennigson, and Whitman 1967, 1968). The analyses were followed by designs for a different type of online retrieval system, which was described publicly at conferences (Thompson 1969; Seastrom and Thompson 1972), and in the journal literature (Thompson 1971). Supported by a grant from NLM, the Stanford Research System goal was to improve medical IR. Although Thompson compared his system to BOLD, AESOP, Intrex, AIM-TWX, SMART, AUDACIOUS, and other experimental and operational retrieval systems, he did not mention the SPIRES work going on at the same time across campus.

The Stanford Research System used the computer in the Stanford Biotechnology Laboratory, an Adage AGT-30 Graphics Computer (a minicomputer with a small, 8,000-word core memory supplemented by a 2.5 megabyte disk memory unit). The sole means of user input was with a light pen to make selections from the alternatives displayed on a $14'' \times 14''$ CRT screen.

On the assumption that a computer, in addition to responding to requests for information, could be of significant assistance to naive users in formulating searches, the Stanford Research System project explored techniques for providing machine guidance in formulating queries from unstructured information needs. The system included two subject indexes: a portion of the ACM Computer Index, and a portion of *MeSH* as adapted by the Brain Information Service at UCLA into hierarchical decision tree branches displayed on the CRT. Thompson (1971, 94) described the displays:

During the man-computer dialogue, the first display presented to the user shows the most general division of subject matter, which the user selects among by choosing the keyword seeming to be closest to, or inclusive of, his question. Doing so causes the selected alternative to branch into its successive sub-alternatives and progressively in this manner on down through the remaining branches in the decision tree while at the same time stacking all decisions selected in progressive order on the left hand side of the CRT. . . . When, upon reaching any appropriate level of specificity in the classification index and specific document references are desired, light-penning the bottom line of the screen labeled 'THERE ARE XXX DOCUMENTS UNDER THIS DESCRIPTION,' (where XXX is the number of document titles indexed by the last selected index keyword) will bring up the surrogate of the first document.

The hierarchical structure was chosen because it seemed to replicate closely the structure of cognitive thought processes, thus allowing the simplest, most direct transfer of an information need into the system structure and vocabulary. Moreover, by allowing searchers to use their passive rather than active vocabularies, the interaction vocabularies were expanded "by at least an order of magnitude" (Thompson 1971, 91). A subset of the MEDLARS file was used in later experiments (Seastrom and Thompson 1973).

Thompson did not consider the Research System to be a complete system but rather only a research tool to demonstrate and test theories about human-machine interface. The orientation was toward naive users who wanted to start with general terms and work their way down to a desired level of specificity. It was not designed to support the search habits of sophisticated users who wanted to enter their own keywords or coordinate terms with Boolean operators.

DIRAC

Another system used in an experimental mode on the Stanford University IBM 360/67 time-sharing system was actually developed at Northwestern University by Jacques Vallee prior to his coming to Stanford (Vallee et al. 1971). Vallee had worked in 1965–1966 at Northwestern with J. Allen Hynek to develop and demonstrate a linguistic processing system called ALTAIR (Automatic Logical Translation and Information Retrieval). ALTAIR accepted questions in English text form and converted them into a form for database searching. Examples of questions that could be processed were: "How many bright stars are double-line spectroscopic binaries?" and "How many multiple stars are double?" Although the database was a star catalog with numerical values rather than a bibliographic or full-text file, Vallee's experience with this system was relevant for his later work with interactive search systems (Vallee and Hynek 1966). In 1970, Vallee designed a retrieval language called DIRAC (Direct Access) for online interactive searching in a system used at Stanford. DIRAC could be used for searching numeric and bibliographic databases, but was designed primarily for use with scientific data banks. The first experiments included files of astronomical data (three catalogs: supernova, bright stars, bright galaxies), medical clinical data (307 cases of prostate carcinoma that were treated with the Stanford Linear Accelerator), and clinical laboratory management data. In 1970, DIRAC was used for a collection of bone marrow examination reports at Stanford University Hospital (Wolf, Ludwig, and Vallee 1971). The main novelty in DIRAC's design was the concept of a generalized file management system that interfaced with, and would be driven from, an interactive text editor (Vallee, Krulee, and Grau 1968; Vallee 1970).

University of Alberta

SARA

In September 1967, Roger Halpin completed his master's thesis at the University of Alberta, Department of Computing Science (Halpin 1967), focusing on the development of a demonstration online retrieval system called SARA (Storage and Retrieval Alberta). SARA was programmed in APL language for use with an IBM 360/67 with IBM 2741 terminals. APL at that time did not provide a means to communicate with input-output devices other than IBM 2741 terminals. Consequently it could not call up or use any disk or tape storage devices; their use had to be simulated in main memory. SARA used a file of manually indexed bibliographic records and some abstracts of publications about Western Canadian history.

SARA was designed for online, real-time operation, with weighted search terms and Boolean search logic. It included arithmetic equality and inequality searching for searching by historical dates, and a hierarchical subject search capability to expand the search formulation automatically to include broader, narrower, or related search terms. Index terms were stored in an inverted file structure. Only two commands were used in searching: FIND and PRINT. Response time was almost instantaneous. A search result was a posting count, along with a prompt to see if the searcher wanted to see the document numbers of the retrieved records. If a user wanted to see document numbers, SARA provided five numbers with each prompt. The PRINT command operated by a searcher's entry of the document number of interest, followed by instructions regarding which part of the records were to be printed (e.g., 2613, TITLE, ABSTRACT).

SARA presumably served its objective of partial fulfillment of the requirements for Halpin's degree. Although Halpin hoped that it would be continued, we have no information regarding any more development of SARA. Halpin acknowledged his professor, Doreen Heaps, a participant in another Alberta online system described next, for her interest and assistance.

Personal Documentation System

Another Canadian development was a small pilot online system that was planned, implemented, and tested in 1967 and early 1968 at the University of Alberta in Edmonton. Called Personal Documentation System, it was designed for individual faculty members to create their own personal bibliographic databases. Doreen Heaps of the Department of Computing Science directed the project and Paul Sorenson, a graduate student, did the initial programming. The system was implemented on an IBM 360/67 at the campus computer center, with IBM 2741 typewriter terminals on campus. The computer could be used in a time-shared manner by over 200 users, but the search system was not really designed to be used in an interactive, recursive mode (Heaps and Sorenson 1968). The system was also used for experimental studies in online query languages (*Report on information* 1972). According to Janice Freeman (1997), little use was made of Personal Documentation System.

Other University of Alberta Studies

Department of Computing Science staff participated in several supporting studies in the late 1960s, including such topics as coding and storage techniques for computer file searching (as used for SDI service on *Chemical Titles* tapes from 1968–1971), automatic subject classification, development of an online thesaurus for use with a water resource file (Alber and Heaps 1971) and automatic query modification. A pilot study was made of the feasibility of a computer system to search a library catalog (the Boreal Institute Library at the University of Alberta) in both batch and online mode with the UDC scheme used for subject access. Implemented in 1972, it may have been the first online search system in regular operation for a UDC-indexed library (Benbow 1972). As a doctoral dissertation project, J. J. Dimsdale (1973) conducted studies on the optimal design for an online library catalog system suitable for a collection of one million titles.

University of California-Berkeley

In September 1963, the University of California (UC) founded the Institute of Library Research (ILR), a university-wide institute to conduct research to address problems faced by libraries, particularly the pragmatic, operational problems of the UC libraries (nine campuses, many branch libraries), and to support and extend programs of the UC library schools. Robert Hayes of the School of Library Service at UCLA was appointed director of ILR, and Raynard Swank, dean of the UC-Berkeley School of Librarianship, was associate director until that position was assumed by M. E. Maron in 1966. One branch of ILR was located at the UCLA campus where Hayes was already established, and another branch was located at Berkeley where Swank and Maron were located. Ralph Shoffner was appointed project manager of an Operations Task Force that was to work on specific library projects such as the preparation of a book-form union catalog and union list of serials for the total UC system. ILR staff performed much of the research on online library systems at UCB (see figure 3.2). Some work was done on both campuses, but it is described in this section because Berkeley is where most of the projects were conducted. Charles Bourne served as the director of ILR from 1971 to 1977.

File Organization Project

From 1967 to 1971, USOE supported a study at the ILR Berkeley branch of online systems with very large files of bibliographic records. The project was to develop and implement a research facility that could be used for investigating problems of file organization and interactive search for online retrieval systems. Maron was principal investigator, Shoffner was the project director for Phases I and II, and Allan Humphrey was the project manager for Phase II. Various bibliographic databases were prepared, ranging in size from 500 to 94,000 records. Experiments were conducted to test various methods of code compression, input conversion, and file organization for online systems. Programming was completed for some aspects of the system, and a crude author-only online search capability was demonstrated with a file of 75,000 catalog records, but a more complete online retrieval capability was not implemented during the first year (Cunningham, Schieber, and Shoffner 1969). The Phase II programming and development associated with this project are described in the next section. The final results of this project are included in several separate reports (Aiyer 1971; Shoffner and Cunningham 1971; Silver and Meredith 1971).

Figure 3.2
Allen Humphrey, Vivian Frojmovic, and Naresh Kripalani, all of the Institute of Library Research at UC-Berkeley, scan results displayed on an IBM teletypewriter terminal. 1968. Photographer: Dennis Galloway. Photo from private archive of Allan Humphrey.

Information Processing Laboratory

From 1967 to 1972, USOE supported the development, operation, and evaluation of the utility of a computer-based lab for library science education and research, and as a means of teaching librarianship principles to library school students. Based at the ILR Berkeley branch, Maron was principal investigator, Humphrey and Joseph Meredith were project directors, and Donald Sherman was another participant. Online interaction was provided for the lab by a network of remote terminals linked to a central campus computer. Software was developed to facilitate demonstration and teaching of principles of library science (Maron and Sherman 1971; Maron, Humphrey, and Meredith 1969). Several specific systems were developed in support of this laboratory: LABSEARCH, REFSEARCH, and CIMARON.

LABSEARCH

Three LABSEARCH programs were developed to provide tools to students and faculty to study retrieval using statistical term association techniques (Mignon and Travis 1971). The file consisted of 284 indexed bibliographic records and files of term association data. The search programs operated initially from a Teletype, which was replaced by an IBM 2740 terminal connected by a dedicated phone line to an IBM 360/40 in the Berkeley Computer Center. The system operated initially with four IBM 2311 disk drives, and was augmented later with a larger capacity IBM 2314 disk drive. C. Ravi designed and coded the LABSEARCH programs, which were also installed at UCLA in 1970 for library school use there.

REFSEARCH

As part of a study to develop computer-assisted instructional materials for a course in general reference work, ILR staff developed an experimental system called REFSEARCH. It was designed to search a small collection of reference books and test notions about how librarians select relevant published sources to answer reference questions. Humphrey was project director and coded the REFSEARCH software. Starting the work in June 1967, the team completed the initial development, including preparation of a sample database, in 1968. They used an IBM 360/40 as the central processor, with an IBM-2314 storage device, and an IBM-2740 remote terminal station (Maron, Humphrey, and Meredith 1969). The first version of REFSEARCH was implemented in November 1969. By May 1970, students had logged about 1,000 online connect hours. Users queried a database of descriptions of 144 general reference works from the practice collection of the UCB School of Librarianship, using initially an IBM Selectric typewriter and then three Sanders 720 CRT terminals connected to an IBM 360/40 at the campus computer center (Meredith 1971a, b). REFSEARCH is noteworthy because it was the primitive beginning to ILR's development of online retrieval programs.

The final REFSEARCH was online, but not interactive; it was essentially fast batch. The search logic permitted only AND relationships among search terms, and the terms themselves had to be expressed as numeric codes (e.g., 528 = mathematic(ian)s). Within four seconds, the system responded with posting counts and titles of the retrieved reference works (i.e., *American Men of Science*). Students did not use REFSEARCH extensively, even after the Sanders terminals were installed in 1969. After CIMARON became available, REFSEARCH was abandoned (Humphrey 1995).

CIMARON

The development of an Information Processing Lab for research and education in library science was continued as Phase II to mid-1971, and resulted in the full implementation and integration of the CIMARON system. Aiyer (1971) and Silver (1971) reported on the project's final products. The File Organization Project and the Information Processing Laboratory project jointly supported CIMARON development. Arjun Aiyer developed CIMARON for the study of searching large files of LC MARC formatted records. CIMARON permitted use of a variety of search keys (author, title, subject, publisher, publication date) and two modes of operation (SEARCH, BROWSE). SEARCH accepted queries in the form of Boolean expressions and offered many display options. In BROWSE mode, a searcher could scan the index files, viewing terms and their posting counts. CIMARON worked efficiently with large files; for example, it could search a file of 100,000 UC-Santa Cruz catalog records in a few seconds.

> **1970 Milestone**
>
> CIMARON was the first online search system to demonstrate phonetic searching.

A novel CIMARON feature was a phonetic search capability (functionally similar to, but significantly more sophisticated than, the Soundex system used then with some manual filing systems) for author searching, in which authors were searched whose names were phonetically similar to the author name in the query. James Dolby (1970), then a faculty member at San Jose State University, developed this search algorithm. The Dolby algorithm examined the phonetic composition of names more deeply than Soundex did (Humphrey 1997).

By the end of Phase II in 1971, over 150 UCB students had used the ILR search packages on an experimental basis over a period of several academic quarters (Maron and Sherman 1971). Nonetheless, ILR systems development ended with the end of the grant.

Queen's University of Belfast

QUOBIRD

Separated by an ocean and unaware of developments in the United States and elsewhere, faculty and students of the School of Physics and Applied Mathematics (later, Department of Computer Science) at Queen's University in Belfast, Northern Ireland, began in 1967 their own studies of the feasibility of online reference retrieval. They were hoping to replace their slow tape-driven systems (Carville, Higgins, and Smith 1971). They could find no existing software to serve their purposes, however, nor could they find information about online retrieval systems design in the literature. With partial support from OSTI, they wrote many trial programs, with many false starts, and operated a pilot system for two years before they had an online system that nearly met their design criteria for speed, effectiveness, and cost. They expended much of their effort in developing algorithms for access that used the disk space efficiently and that minimized disk accesses, thus ensuring reliably fast response time and reducing costs (Higgins and Smith 1971).

Only after L. D. Higgins, Francis Smith, and M. Carville were well along in their development in the early 1970s did they discover that their pilot resembled Intrex, ORBIT, and work at the Moore School at the University of Pennsylvania. They found that their technical approach was especially close to that used in SPIRES and their method of subject indexing similar to that used in Intrex (Higgins and Smith 1969). These independent but parallel efforts reveal something about the nature of invention—in spite of the lack of direct communication or opportunities for cross-fertilization, developers working autonomously sometimes produce similar approaches when they share similar goals.

Named QUOBIRD (Queen's University On-line Bibliographic Information Retrieval and Dissemination System), the experimental system could handle only a small file of 1,000 references and abstracts on atomic and molecular physics drawn from the INSPEC tapes. The pilot ran on an ICL 1907 computer, with a typical response time of one second or less, which was considered an essential performance criteria. The INSPEC indexing extracted all the significant words from titles, figures, tables, sections or chapter headings in the documents. Carville, Higgins, and Smith (1971) intended the retrieval program to be extremely easy to use. They did not expect users to construct complex Boolean statements: "the user will probably not even understand the word 'Boolean'" (206). However, they did require users to respond to system inquiries, which included the request to specify whether "union" or "intersection" was desired between two terms.

Hampered by the existing software and hardware limitations, the QUOBIRD developers envisioned in the future the feasibility of an economical and powerful storage and retrieval system. Their ultimate aim was to develop a system for retrieval from large files of a million or more documents. However, QUOBIRD did not develop into an operating service. Although ICL did try to market QUOBIRD as BIRD, they were not successful (Negus 1980). BIRD was considered for use in a 1973 British Library project but was passed over for other systems.

University of Michigan

AUTONOTE

A University of Michigan research team developed AUTONOTE (Automatic Notebook), a personal online retrieval system designed for use by individual researchers (Reitman et al. 1969). AUTONOTE ran on the Michigan Terminal System, a time-sharing system implemented on the university's IBM 360/67. In 1969 it was operating in an online time-shared manner to support users working with textual, bibliographic, or other types of private file data. Boolean retrieval could be done on the basis of descriptors assigned to the file material by users. Remote terminal access was provided by Teletype equipment and IBM teletypewriter terminals, but the fastest access (120 cps) was achieved with a CRT display and keyboard from Computer Communications, Inc. Searches were completed generally in less than ten seconds. AUTONOTE was not developed with the objective of providing a major online system or service; it originated as part of a study of scientific thinking, and then gained acceptance as a general means of facilitating personal information processing, similar to Engelbart's effort at SRI.

University of Oklahoma

GIPSY

GIPSY (Generalized Information Processing System) originated at the Tulane Medical School as TIPS (Tulane Information Processing System), a program developed by James Sweeney for medical records. When Sweeney moved from Tulane to the University of Oklahoma, he brought his program with him, and enhanced it for general database use. As director of the University's Computing Center, he was able to apply it to other applications. In 1968, GIPSY could operate in either batch or online mode, with serial searches of full text or other data (Kays 1995). In 1968, the U.S. Geological Survey used GIPSY with a database of 50,000 citations and abstracts for the *Bibliography of North American Geology* (Moody and Kays 1972).

Using IBM 1050 terminal equipment, GIPSY became operational in July 1969 at the University of Oklahoma, as a search system in the fields of psychiatry, regional planning, and technology. In the early 1970s, GIPSY software was used extensively for batch searching of ERIC file tapes. The National Oceanographic Data Center used it for its internal Biology Information Retrieval Program. GIPSY was used for a major study in 1969–1971 with full-text legal material corresponding to Oklahoma statutes (Thomas 1972). GIPSY was installed at the Smithsonian Natural History Museum and the U.S. Geological Survey in Washington, D.C., for use with paleontologic and other data applications. It was so widely used in the Washington area that it had its own informal users group. Olaf Kays (1995) recalled his fascination in watching the faces of Smithsonian terminal operators as they keyed in database entries, working with trays of dead rodents on their desks: "They gingerly picked them up, one at a time, read the information on the tag, and typed the data into GIPSY." Another U.S. Geological Survey (USGS) application was for the Geographic Names Information System (GNIS), which contained almost two million geographic names and associated data for the United States and its territories. This GIPSY should not be confused with the GIPSY (Generalized Information Processing System) developed by the International Atomic Energy Agency and described in chapter 9.

In the COSATI 1970 annual report, the Department of the Interior's Office of Water Resources Research section noted that pilot development had begun for a new remote-access retrieval system utilizing their database of over 26,000 abstracts produced for publication, *Selected Water Resources Abstracts*. The GIPSY system had been tested and demonstrated for a limited group of users, and a number of remote terminals would be established in the coming year for user training and evaluation tests (*Progress in scientific* 1970).

In October 1971, Sweeney was awarded U.S. Patent No. 3,614,744 for aspects of this program. While still at the University of Oklahoma, he began the design of GIPSY II. However, he transferred to Georgia Tech before it was completed and it remained in an uncompleted state (Kays 1995). The University of Oklahoma continued the support and distribution of GIPSY through contractor services.

University of California-Los Angeles

Brain Information Service

The Brain Information Service at UCLA was a component of the neurological information network established by National Institute of Neurological Diseases and Blindness (NINDB) of the U.S. National Institutes of Health (NIH). In 1966, the Parkinson Information Center at Columbia University was the other component, and in 1967, the Specialized Information Center for Hearing, Speech, Disorders of Human Communication at Johns Hopkins Medical School became the third operating member. NINDB was reconfigured into the National Institute of Neurological Diseases and Stroke (NINDS), and in 1969 it supported *Epilepsy Abstracts* for online retrieval (EARS, described in chapter 7).

The Demonstrations and Exhibits abstracts for the 7th International Congress of Electroencephalography and Clinical Neurophysiology contained an announcement (UCLA Brain Information Service 1969, 730) of a live demonstration to be held in September 1969: "The Brain Information Service will demonstrate its retrieval system. Retrieval will be via typewriter terminal, which can be operated by a librarian or by a scientist. The terminal will connect to the Health Sciences Computing Facility 360/91 at UCLA. The programs and terminal are the same as a system now operating in the BIS office at UCLA and connected to the HSCF computer." The database to be demonstrated contained 100,000 citations to articles in basic neurology published since 1960 that had been extracted from the NLM MEDLARS file. Searches would be conducted using an indexing vocabulary of 17,000 terms in alphabetical and hierarchical listings. We have no further information about this system other than it was apparently still active in 1971 (Brain Information Service 1971).

Northwestern University

BIDAP

The original BIDAP (Bibliographic Data Processing) program software was a set of batch-mode computer programs developed at Northwestern University as an outgrowth of the IBM-produced KWIC program for the IBM 709/90/94 computers. James Aagaard of the Vogelback Computer Center and Kenneth Janda of the Political Science Department did the initial BIDAP development, using it in the production of KWIC indexes to titles in the *American Political Science Review* (Aagard 1967). It had a capability to produce KWIC or KWOC indexes, and the means to maintain a cumulative master file. After its initial development, the program was modified and used by the Aerial Measurements Laboratory at Northwestern in connection with a continuing literature survey project for Wright-Patterson Air Force Base (WPAFB), reviewing, abstracting, and indexing publications in the telemetry field. A batch search capability was added to BIDAP's KWIC/KWOC capability in order to implement a quick-reaction capability for WPAFB. This enhanced version of BIDAP was submitted to the IBM SHARE organization for others to use and the Defense Intelligence Agency (DIA) became a user (Aagaard 1997). BIDAP was never converted for online use, but we believe it was instrumental in the Data Corporation online search software development and thus it is a part of the prehistory of LEXIS.[4]

RIMS, RIQS, RIQSONLINE

Another online system that operated successfully for several years in a university environment was RIQS (Remote Information Query System), a general data management system at Northwestern University in Illinois that allowed university users to build their own files, query them online, print from them, and alter them (Borman, Hay, and Mittman 1973). The first version of RIQS was called RIMS (Remote Information Management System). The name had to be changed, however, because of a conflict with an existing commercial trademark. With AFOSR support, development began in 1965 on a system to operate via remote access to the CDC 6400 at the campus computer center, and to combine the capabilities of the currently available batch processing programs (TRIAL, INFOL) being used there, with added capabilities provided by the remote terminals. RIMS was a disk-oriented system; the records did not need to be processed sequentially. As a prelude to the development of RIMS, the TRIAL software was modified to be operated from a Teletype or a CDC 200 User Terminal, which was demonstrated in 1969 on several databases, including a bibliographic file (Krulee and Mittman 1969). Under Benjamin Mittman's supervision, and with partial support from the USAF Office of Scientific Research, two Northwestern doctoral candidates in computer science, Donald Dillaman and Robert Chalice, with assistance from Lorraine Borman, created RIQS over a two-year period, beginning in 1969 (Mittman, Chalice, and Dillaman 1973; Dominick and Mittman 1973).

Dillaman and Chalice wrote RIQS primarily in FORTRAN IV. RIQS operated in both batch and online modes on the CDC 6400 and could be accessed from a variety of Teletype or CDC 200 terminals at 10, 15, or 30 cps. RIQS was intended for maintenance and searching of small- to medium-size files of bibliographic, textual, or numerical data (Martin 1974). For the online version, called RIQSONLINE only small files could be loaded because the available online disk storage was limited (Mittman and Krulee 1966).

Wayne Dominick (1975, 216) of Northwestern University used both RIQS and RIQSONLINE to report the following:

> The purpose of this study was to develop monitoring techniques for the RIQSONLINE information retrieval system and to provide the framework for conducting performance evaluations. . . . The methodology employed was to instrument the RIQSONLINE processor with monitoring routines designed to collect data on user on-line instructions with the system and to produce a RIQS-compatible data base of all monitored information. With this approach, the RIQS system is used both to monitor itself and to process the monitored data.

Because RIQSONLINE was designed to handle numeric databases, it also incorporated extensive capabilities to collect, store, and process data on use.

Queries were in English-like phrasing, with no controlled vocabulary and no searching on word stems. Queries could be refined using Boolean operators AND, OR, NOT, but full text phrases could not be searched with proximity operators. Designed to handle both textual and numerical data, RIQS was used for bibliographic and data management applications. Only parts of the file were inverted; much of the searching was directly on the full text of the records. Response times were thus sometimes excessive, especially during peak periods such as midafternoon near the end of the academic quarter (Borman and Mittman 1972).

RIQS began operating in September 1969 as a prototype with two bibliographic databases: the U.S. Government Research & Development Reports describing research in progress and SPIN (Searchable Physics Information Notices), the database of physics journal literature from AIP that contained only 1,127 records.

An evaluation of RIQS with the tiny SPIN file revealed that older researchers and library patrons preferred their own traditional searching methods over the online system. Astronomy, chemistry, and physics faculty refused to operate RIQS without the continuing intervention of a librarian. Astronomy and civil engineering students, however, enthusiastically adopted the technology and responded with "amazement and pleasure at the ease of use, the effectiveness of the system, the projection to other types of applications" (Borman and Mittman 1972, 170) The lack of acceptance by older users may have been partly a result of the small size of the files.

In 1972, Mittman and Dominick described a performance monitoring system they had implemented for RIQS and RIQSONLINE that could generate reports, create plots, or produce input for a statistical program. Examples of collected data included real time and CPU time per query, number of records searched and retrieved, number of terms searched, number and type of searcher language or syntax errors (Mittman and Dominick 1973). They also successfully coupled the RIQS search software with the SPSS statistical package to allow search output from numeric files to be imported into SPSS for analysis and report generation. RIQSONLINE continued in regular production use in the Chicago area during the early 1970s. By 1974, "educational and non-profit institutions in the Chicago area were making frequent use of its 50 small databases" (Fife et al. 1974, 56). Users were medical researchers, political scientists, chemists, astronomers, anthropologists, physicists, urban systems engineers, and computer scientists, primarily using files of their own data or bibliographic references.

University of Washington

Urban Data Center

With support from NSF and the U.S. Department of Transportation, the University of Washington Urban Data Center began developing in 1969 an interactive online retrieval system to support resident NSF and Urban Mass Transportation Administration research staffs, and to aid in the general management of literature, data, map, and software libraries. The system was apparently unnamed and was unusual in that it was implemented on a general-purpose computer (IBM 1130), a popular small computer normally used for scientific and research applications. The equipment included the computer system, a single disk drive (total of 630K characters of storage), 8,192 words of core storage, and a single typewriter terminal. The search system was online and interactive. However, once a search was initiated it was essentially a batch process that used all of the machine resources in a serial search until it was completed. Users had no mechanism to view intermediate search results or alter the course of the search. Retrieval speed depended upon the number of file characters searched. A typical title word search took 2.5 seconds per record; a search of the full file of 1,400 indexed bibliographic records required an hour. J. Michael Storie (1971) reported that the system was well-tested and working, capable of supporting file management problems (e.g., course descriptions, personnel capabilities) other than bibliographic.

University of Pittsburgh, Department of Chemistry

In 1968–1969, the Chemistry Department of the University of Pittsburgh ran an SDI service for their department, using a subscription to the Chemical Titles database, and an IBM 360/50 at the campus computer center. A group was established within the department, named the Pittsburgh Chemical Information Center (PCIC). The group experimented with IBM's TEXT-PAC software and CAS's CASCON software to search CA Condensates tape files (Grunstra and Johnson 1970). The Pittsburgh Time-Sharing System was used for this batch process and was found to be unsuitable and inefficient. The relevance of this SDI activity to our narrative is that after that experience, they decided in 1969 to try a compromise approach, and offer "semi-interactive" searching: "The user formulates his search request at a time-sharing terminal and stores the finished request for subsequent transmittal (along with other search requests) to the batch-processing computer, at which time efficient, noninteractive searching is carried out" (Bloemeke and Treu 1969, 157). These early experiences in searching Chemical Titles did not prove to be favorable. However, CIC staff members were convinced in 1969 that an interactive online system might meet some of their objectives, and they continued to explore that possibility (Caruso 1970). Efforts to develop improved search systems continued into the 1970s (Arnett and Kent 1973) and are described in chapter 9.

Harvard University/Cornell University

SMART

Starting in 1961, with continuous NSF support, Gerard Salton began a long-running theoretical and experimental program to explore and evaluate various indexing and retrieval techniques. To facilitate this work, he developed a set of computer programs that could be used as a lab tool for modeling and evaluation. The collective programs were called SMART, an acronym that over the years took on several meanings (System for the Mechanical Analysis and Retrieval of Text, System for the Manipulation and Retrieval of Texts, and Salton's Magical Automatic Retriever of Text). SMART incorporated a large number of automatic search and analysis procedures, and made it possible to evaluate the effectiveness of each procedure by processing the same search request against the same document collection in many different ways, comparing results for each case. SMART was not designed or implemented as an online system, although it was designed for use by researchers in an interactive manner. In practice, a searcher received and evaluated preliminary results from one search, indicated which items were relevant, and reentered this information into the batch search system that then modified the term weights or made other adjustments in the search statement and reexecuted the search.

The SMART programs were never meant to be used for anything other than a research tool; they were not meant to be an operational service. Nonetheless, SMART had some of the most sophisticated language processing features then or later available. SMART processed both requests and texts in unrestricted natural English and used statistical, syntactic, and semantic procedures, including comparison with a fully hierarchical thesaurus of concepts that were meaningful in a particular subject matter, for the analysis of information and the identification of relevant items. It was highly interactive, in order to allow a user to successively broaden or refine the search so as to retrieve the right kind and right amount of information for the particular need. According to Borko (1985), "The SMART system combined both online and batch processing in one of the most automatic retrieval systems being used experimentally."

Salton was an applied mathematician born in Nuremberg, Germany, and educated at Brooklyn College (B.A. and M.A.) and Harvard University (Ph.D.). Working at the Harvard University Computation Laboratory, Salton built his document retrieval system to operate on the IBM 7094 (Salton 1964). In a review of several retrieval techniques, Rocchio and Salton (1965, 294) noted that, "the automatic SMART document retrieval process, presently operating on the IBM 7094 computer in a batch-processing mode, is used to simulate interactive search procedures." Salton moved to the Computer Science Department at Cornell University in 1965, taking the SMART system with him. He continued to receive NSF support as well as support from NLM. Other persons named by Salton as important contributors to the SMART effort were E. H. Sussenguth Jr., J. J. Rocchio, Michael Lesk, E. M. Keen, and Robert Williamson. Salton and his colleagues used SMART to test a large variety of automatic retrieval and analysis procedures and methods, iterative search feedback procedures, and automatic procedures for dictionary construction (Salton 1968, 1969, 1971a,b; Lesk and Salton 1969). As a result of the tests and performance evaluations, Salton was able to formulate general rules for automatic language processing. He seemed confident in the late 1960s that automatic text analysis rather than manual subject indexing would be the norm in the future.

As of the early 1970s, SMART contained several databases: ADI (82 full-text papers in the field of documentation), CRAN-1 (the aerodynamics document collection of 1,600 indexed abstracts used in the Aslib-Cranfield experiments of the early 1960s), IRE-3 (780 abstracts of articles in computer science), ISPRA (1,200 abstracts in documentation), and MEDLARS (the medical documents of 270 indexed abstracts from NLM MEDLARS) for these investigations (Salton 1964; Brandhorst and Eckert 1972). Though Salton did not intend for SMART to be more than an experimental system for lab use, Cochrane (1990) recalled that he was sometimes criticized for using files that were far too small to produce evaluation results significant for real world applications. Salton (1965) acknowledged that his small-scale experiments ignored cost of retrieval, response time, influence of physical layout, or personnel problems. He defended his methods by saying that he had repeated the tests in enough different ways to neutralize the flaws and his results could be replicated in a real user environment with a large-scale operational retrieval system. Nevertheless, skeptics questioned the existence of simple "rules" and whether his results could be generalized (Rees 1967).

Salton was discouraged during his years of work that no major online research services chose to use any of his suggested retrieval techniques for their operation. Lesk (1996) recalled that in 1967 Cyril Cleverdon had urged Salton to set up a public search service, using Salton's retrieval algorithms and the ACM full-text file. Bourne remembered Salton's briefing to DIALOG senior management in the late 1980s; Salton argued that online services should move beyond the traditional Boolean search approaches. The industry reaction was generally that the SMART algorithms had not been demonstrated with large files (a million or more abstracts in a single file) and there would be additional demands for computer resources (more processing power and storage) for loading and maintenance of files under the new schemes. Such additional costs could not be justified, given the small profit margins that the services were experiencing. Additional and extensive training of existing users would also be required. Finally, there was a possibility that searchers would not realize any real improvement in performance or cost-benefit when these newer approaches were used with very large files. Somebody else would have to conduct a large-file demonstration before an existing service could risk a major disruption in service to their customers.

SMART never grew beyond a tiny laboratory tool. Salton and his colleagues at Cornell continued to use it for retrieval experiments throughout the 1980s. Over a period of many years, these experiments contributed greatly to the knowledge base of computerized information indexing, storage, and retrieval. Although an alternative name for SMART was Salton's Magical Automatic Retrieval Technique, no magic was involved, just a long, painstaking, and systematic trail of theory development and testing. ASIS awarded Salton the Best Information Science Book Award in 1975 and the Award of Merit in 1989 for his significant research contributions.

Washington State University/U.S. Forest Service

SOLAR

With support from the Forest Service of the U.S. Department of Agriculture, Washington State University (WSU) researchers developed an online bibliographic retrieval system. The developers were P. C. Mitchell, as part of his 1971 dissertation work, Jon Rickman, and W. E. Walden (Mitchell, Rickman, and Walden 1973). Actually, system development was a cooperative effort by WSU and the U.S. Forest Service. WSU became involved because its plant pathology faculty shared with the Forest Service an interest in the problem of white pine blister rust, and its computer science department was staffed and equipped to solve IR problems (Rickman, Harvey, and Shaw 1972). The system was named SOLAR, which initially stood for "Store a large collection of abstracts and to provide the On Line Automatic Retrieval," and later for "Storage and On-Line Automatic Retrieval." It appears that the system was operational in 1970, and by mid-1971 was operating with Teletype access to the IBM 360/67 in the campus computer center (Washington State University 1971). CBAC tapes were scanned locally for all relevant documents from over thirty periodicals, and two small files were constructed for local users and stored on an IBM Data Cell. One file was a collection of citations and abstracts in plant pathology, and the other was a file on drug reactions and interactions. The system was intended for local users as a research support tool with special databases, rather than serving as a search service for an extensive audience.

SOLAR was advanced for its day. It offered an online subject thesaurus, automatic indexing and searching of plurals and other suffix variants, weighted term searching for output relevance ranking, display of posting counts of the number of records retrieved by a search, and the full text of article abstracts—all on the same system. All SOLAR index entries and query terms had their suffixes removed. A table of sixty-five possible suffixes was checked by the programs for word endings that could be removed (for example, SPRAY-ER-S). Search term weighting had been used previously in batch search and SDI systems, but had been used infrequently (e.g., TEXTIR in 1965) before 1970 in an online system. SOLAR in 1971 was designed to handle large collections of abstracts, and was expected to work well even with 100,000 abstracts online. The stored abstracts could be retrieved and displayed at searchers' terminals.

In 1973 SOLAR also had the capability to accept English statements as queries, converting them into Boolean query form (as had been done earlier in the LEADER system) and saving query formulations for future use. The system allowed multiterminal (Teletype, Datapoint 3300, IBM 1050) access to as many as thirty-seven files. The system was still in regular operation in 1973, with plans to continue beyond that time.

University of Newcastle upon Tyne

MEDUSA

The remote city of Newcastle upon Tyne and its university perch on the cold shores of the North Sea on the eastern coast of England, about fifty miles from the Scottish border. In early 1971, Anthony Harley of the University Computing Laboratory (later head of the U.K. MEDLARS Service) reported on a novel approach to improving the quality and speed of searching the MEDLARS file in batch mode. MEDLARS service had been available in Britain since May 1966. The batch service was being operated by the National Lending Library for Science and Technology (NLL), located also in northern England at a former Royal Ordnance Factory in Thorpe Arch, a tiny town near Boston Spa. NLL processed search requests once a week. Harley felt that the chief disadvantage of the slow batch operation was that "the searcher cannot discover if he has asked the right question until the results come back, by which time it is too late to alter it" (Harley 1971a, 59). Harley (1977, 320–321) noted, "In 1966, we had a quarter-million citations, on about twenty reels of tape. It was necessary to assemble a batch of search questions and then scan the tapes from end to end, copying all those citations which met the specifications of any of the searchers in the batch. Afterwards, they were routed and printed. The whole process took several hours." For the first four years, the batch service was available for free. However, when a small cost-recovery charge was instituted in 1970, the number of users dropped significantly (Barber, Barraclough, and Gray 1973).

In 1968, OSTI awarded a three-year grant to the University of Newcastle upon Tyne Computing Lab to develop an experimental online system for scientists' own use, test its effectiveness in comparison with normal methods, and alleviate the most aggravating aspect of waiting for a batch processed search—that of finally getting a bibliography that is useless because the strategy was not formulated correctly. In 1971, Harley announced that the online system was ready for testing, and he reported samples of the interactive system dialogue. Users could formulate and test a search by running it against a small file of recent references on disk storage. The file of about 50,000 records represented only English-language records from the most recent five months of *Index Medicus* and *Index to Dental Literature* rather than the full MEDLARS file. It was loaded in the IBM 360/67 computer at Newcastle and accessed via ordinary telephone lines from IBM 2741 typewriter terminals (Barber, Barraclough, and Gray 1972). The system was designed to allow medical workers to formulate their own searches without using the printed list of *Medical Subject Headings* (*MeSH*). A user could get help in developing a strategy by exploring online a dictionary of 8,000 MEDLARS terms and synonyms and the hierarchical relationships among them. After selecting terms and combining them with Boolean operators, a user could test a strategy using the SAMPLE command, which caused the system to display the indexing terms associated with the items retrieved. From this immediate feedback, a searcher could modify the strategy or send the completed search formulation to be run with batch processing in the full MEDLARS file. The experiment was performed by offering a free search of the last two or three years of MEDLARS to medical workers who wanted one, in exchange for their trying the online system themselves and performing relevancy judgments. Each search question was processed in the traditional MEDLARS search intermediary manner as well as by a medical worker at the terminal. The results were then combined to formulate a third search (a batch search in MEDLARS) to provide the final product for the requestor. A typical online session lasted one to two hours, but used only a little over a minute of CPU time (Harley 1971a,b; Negus 1980).

In later reports the system was called MEDUSA, but it never developed into a major operational service. Nonetheless, the project concluded that "search formulation by the users is a practical possibility. The intricacies of a fixed vocabulary and Boolean logic can clearly be overcome" (Barber, Barraclough, and Gray 1973, 439). The stumbling block was time: "The scientist spent very much longer sitting at the terminal than the professional searcher and so long as it is necessary to pay trunk telephone charges to connect the terminal to the computer, this arrangement is too expensive to contemplate" (Harley 1975, 23).

MEDUSA was designed to support an experiment, and not to be the basis for a production operation. The emphasis was on single-file searching (MEDLARS) and providing a good user interface rather than generality or efficiency. In historical sequence, MEDUSA came along after the SUNY system was operational and after the AIM/TWX experiment, but before the MEDLINE system became operational. The MEDUSA system, as described in chapter 9, was among the U.K. systems used in 1974–1975 by the British Library for operational experiments with online search systems. The designers did implement one command that may remain as a footnote to later discussions of standard commands for online searching, a command not seen on any other online system—DESIST!

Naval Postgraduate School

In July 1961, a batch search system for the Naval Postgraduate School in Monterey, California, started to provide operational service, using a CDC 1604 computer and programs written by students and library staff members (*Mechanization study 1966*). The system, called SABIRS (Selected Automatic Bibliographic Information Retrieval System), terminated operation in June 1967 when the CDC 1604 was withdrawn from service. A newer version resumed in January 1969. In 1970, library staff were experimenting with online input of bibliographic records and planning for possible online retrieval from their current file (Markuson et al. 1971). Charles Schmidt's master's thesis (1970) reported on an online system he had developed at the Naval Postgraduate School that translated English-language search statements with stored numeric codes associated with each subject word, then retrieved bibliographic data for printout at the terminal.

University of Tokyo

TSIR-1

At a 1972 ACM conference, Takeo Yamamoto, T. L. Kunii, Shigou Fujiwara, and Hidetosi Takahashi described an online search system called TSIR-1 (TODAI Scientific Information Retrieval System, 1st version); TODAI is the Japanese abbreviation for the University of Tokyo. At the time of the conference, initial system development was almost completed and several test searches had been done. TSIR-1 was built for the Hitachi HITAC 5020 computer and time-sharing system and structured to permit access to multiple public and private files on tapes or disks (Motobayashi, Masuda, and Takahashi 1969). The equipment had a small storage capacity (48K of 32-bit word core memory and four 65K word drums), which limited the system's capability. TSIR-1 was designed for English-language databases, with indexed bibliographic records and abstracts, Boolean logic, and term weighting (Yamamoto, Kunii et al. 1972). TSIR-1 was based on prior work to process CAS tapes for use in a local file processing and SDI system (Yamamoto, Kumai et al. 1971; Yamamoto, Ushimara et al. 1971).

Summary

Thus we come to the end of our travels to visit the experimental systems in research labs and universities. We crisscrossed the United States, sojourned twice to Canada, sailed over the ocean to Northern Ireland and back, and then headed back again to England and around the world to Japan. Each system we visited made a worthy contribution to the mushrooming knowledge base. Along the way, we observed some significant milestones:

• First-time online access was provided to chemical structures, MARC records, Psychological Abstracts (with abstracts), and a significant amount of full-text information

• New aids to online searching appeared, such as access to search strategies created by other users and access to an online decimal classification authority file

• Searching was made easier by allowing users to express search queries in natural language search statements

• Online searching was incorporated into regular classroom instruction

• Document delivery was facilitated by using a terminal that could display online dialogue as well as microform images of the documents retrieved on the same screen

• Online service became available to large populations, both within and beyond the institutions that ran an online service

In the next chapter we will take another tour, this time to visit the contemporaneous developments going on in nonacademic laboratories.

4 Experimental Systems Developed in Nonacademic Laboratories, Mid-1960s to Early 1970s

Introduction

In the last chapter we examined a large number of experimental prototypes that were built and evaluated in universities in the United States, Canada, England, Ireland, and Japan. Most had a strong evaluation component, in investigations designed to test the workability of the prototypes and add to the understanding and theory base of human-computer interaction. The host universities, various government agencies, and private foundations provided the necessary support. Now we will visit more systems constructed during the same period of the late 1960s and early 1970s, but in nonacademic laboratories in the United States and Europe. Support for some of these nonacademic experiments came wholly or partly from the parent organizations. Many, however, similar to the university-based projects, obtained support from a variety of government agencies. Some also received outside funding from international or private agencies.

During this period, conferences were held that were significant in furthering the advance of online technology. An example was a workshop titled "The User Interface for Interactive Search of Bibliographic Databases," held in Palo Alto, California, in January 1971 (Walker 1971). Another significant event was a forum on interactive bibliographic systems, cosponsored by the Federal Library Committee, Committee on Scientific and Technical Information (COSATI), U.S. Atomic Energy Commission (AEC), and NBS, October 4–5, 1971 (Henderson 1973). Our knowledge of many of the systems described here comes from papers delivered at special conferences such as these, or at the regular meetings of AFIPS, ASIS, and ACM.

System Development Corporation (SDC)

Continuing along the lines of the work started in the first half of the 1960s, SDC staff developed other online file management systems that are described in what follows. Other SDC work relevant to the development of its online search service is in chapter 6.

CONVERSE

At a joint conference of FID and IFIP in Rome in June 1967, SDC researcher Charles Kellogg announced CONVERSE, a prototype language processor. SDC's CONVERSE was an experimental online question-answering or fact retrieval system, rather than a bibliographic retrieval system. The question processing system was written in META/LISPX, developed at SDC, and it ran on the Q-32 computer under the Time Sharing System. The answer-providing subsystem was based upon the LUCID data management system described earlier, using its query language called QUUP. The file for several years contained 600,000 data values from the 1960 U.S. census, computer programs, and data about the syntactic properties of English sentences.

CONVERSE attempted to attack two difficult problems simultaneously. The first was to get a computer to answer questions by forming logical conclusions from the data values in a database. The other was to translate English questions (a limited subset of English) into data management query statements. This approach had been used at SDC in the Protosynthex system. If a question could not be translated, CONVERSE had a stopgap measure built in to provide output that aided the searcher in rephrasing the question until it was translatable (Kellogg 1968a). An example of a question that could be asked and processed was: "What general kinds of statistical data are available concerning the age and income of people, the production and distribution of goods, and the extent of local taxation. Obtain this information for all cities in the West that equal or exceed San Diego in population" (Kellogg 1968c, 291). Another example of a question that CONVERSE could parse and process in 1968 was: "Which Pan Am flights that are economy class depart for O'Hare from the City of Los Angeles?" (Kellogg 1968b). It took about 10–15 seconds to translate this into a query formulation for its embedded LUCID search system. Spierer and Wills (1969) cited CONVERSE as an example of a current SDC project, but made no mention of its use with any bibliographic or full-text applications.

By the late 1970s Kellogg had abandoned CONVERSE and gone on to develop a new system that represented a simpler approach to natural language communication with computers. Although SDC research in computer linguistics and in programming computers to model human thought and language was independent of bibliographic retrieval research, it did have an impact on the design of later bibliographic and full-text retrieval systems that operated by means of natural language inquiries.

LISTS

When Donald Black joined the SDC Santa Monica group in June 1967, it was to work on a project for NCLIS. He brought with him a pioneering background in library automation, particularly with machine-readable library records and computer-produced book catalogs. Starting with his library science degree from UCLA in 1953, and followed by several years of reference library experience and teaching at UCLA, his background included several years working for Planning Research Corporation from 1958 in designing and operating intelligence data handling system, and several years of library automation experience at UCLA and UC-Santa Cruz. He participated in developing the MARC tape format, and developed an early computer-produced book catalog. Among the first things he did at SDC was to explore ways in which the new time-shared computer technology could be used to advantage in libraries.

SDC had done a study in 1964–1965 for the National Advisory Commission on Libraries on the present and prospective uses of technology in libraries, and had concluded that a computer utility could be applied to library operations. SDC later demonstrated a prototype of a library utility: a service bureau that provided specialized time-shared computer support to individual small and medium-sized libraries at reasonable cost, without requiring them to conform to the procedures or formats of other libraries (Cuadra 1971c). In spring 1967, fully funded in-house, SDC staff began to plan for building LISTS (Library Information System Time-Sharing) on the time-sharing system being developed for the IBM 360/67 and to experiment with the system (Black 1969). The experiment's goal was to determine whether online access to a large file of bibliographic data, combined with other computer-based bibliographic processing capabilities, offered a means for providing cost-effective automated services to small and medium-sized libraries. Online software and systems were becoming more widely available, as were machine-readable files (e.g., MARC), and software could be developed for batch processing of other library tasks. An SDC objective was to determine the long-term market potential for software sales or computer services.

In late 1967, just before SDC changed from a not-for-profit to a commercial institution, and just after LC had started testing their MARC tape distribution service, CLR funded SDC for an experiment to put the MARC file online. The database was to be accessible at no cost to eight libraries in the Southern California area, to see if they could make any use of it. By 1968, seven libraries of varying types had agreed to participate in a pilot operation. The libraries were in or close to Los Angeles: Beverly Hills Public Library, San Marino Public Library, Fullerton Junior College Library, Pierce College Library, SDC Technical Library, UC-Riverside, and USC. During 1968, SDC staff designed various programs for LISTS, taking advantage of the Commercial Data Management System (CDMS) then being built by SDC as part of the time-sharing system on their IBM 360/67. By year's end, however, it was apparent that CDMS was not functional to meet all the LISTS objectives. LISTS was redesigned in early 1969 to take advantage of another part of an SDC software package called Time-Shared/Data Management System (TS/DMS) or Timesharing Data Management System (TDMS), the online search system that had been rewritten to operate on the IBM 360/67 after several years of operation on SDC's AN/FSQ-32 computer (Black 1970). The TDMS story is continued in chapter 6.

Under continuing CLR sponsorship, the operational phase of LISTS began in March 1969, coincident with LC initiating its public tape distribution service (MARC II) for LC cataloging information on magnetic tape. In April, LISTS' online file searching program was operational with the MARC file. In June, after all the libraries had installed their Teletype terminals, the use of LISTS got underway. The system was available for four hours per day, Mondays through Fridays. A major revision of the file search program (called the Birch program) was released in September 1969. Other program modules to support library acquisition, online serials control (Black and Bethe 1969; Cuadra 1971a), online circulation control (Cuadra 1971b), and other processes were implemented, using the Q-32 LUCID and IBM 360 system.

At the end of the online operating period for LISTS (January 31, 1970), 30,000 records were in its MARC file. Searching was possible by LC card number, LC Classification number, Dewey Decimal Classification number, conference indicator, author-conference, publication date, and level, but not by title or subject heading. In general, the participating libraries made little use of this online search capability, probably because of the file's small size, restricted search access points, and narrow scope (and thus limited practical value). As Black recalled (1995), LISTS was not intended to be a reference tool for the public, although he recognized the potential; it was to be a technical processing system, and most of the retrieval during the test period was searching on LC card numbers to find records for copy cataloging. The developers believed that at some point the database would have enough records to be useful to the public.

An important conclusion of this experiment was that it would be more efficient, in the long run, for libraries to join together to develop a system that all could use on a common computer, than to develop a separate system at every library. Nevertheless, LISTS was a disappointment for SDC. As Cuadra (1971c, 112) explained:

I wish that we had known a year and a half ago all of the things that we know about some of the problems and pitfalls of on-line systems, particularly about the need to underestimate and undersell system capabilities, in introducing on-line service to individuals and organizations that have not had previous experience with it. It should have saved a certain amount of disappointment in an extensive experiment that we finished a few months ago.

SDC pulled the plug on TDMS (the retrieval software used for LISTS), which hurt the effort. LISTS continued beyond the CLR-sponsored experiment as an SDC library support system called ALPS (Automated Library Processing Service), described in chapter 6. Black used the LISTS experience on an SDC project to plan a system to manage the complete range of instructional materials used in the Los Angeles Unified School District (Black and Luke 1971). Black's next assignment was to work for SDC Search Service as a trainer and customer services representative (described in chapter 10).

North American Rockwell Corporation

ICS

North American Rockwell provided an example of how far online technology had moved into regular production processes in the mid-1960s. Its Space Division in Downey, California, in conjunction with IBM, decided in 1964 to implement two online files using IBM 1460 and IBM 1301 equipment: (1) information concerning 90,000 parts; and (2) information on 120,000 engineering drawings and drawing changes that had been released on the Apollo spacecraft and Saturn S-II programs. In 1967, the Information Control System (ICS) was in operation and supporting twenty-three IBM 1050 terminals on seven dedicated phone lines and was handling an average of 1,800 inquiries and 5,000 updates per week. Planning for an IBM 360 upgrade began in 1966 and was scheduled to be completed in 1968 (Brown and Nordyke 1968). ICS was not a conventional bibliographic system, but it was an example of how online retrieval technology could be used to advantage with engineering information problems.

Informatics

Informatics, Inc., began its involvement in computer-based information processing in the early 1960s, starting as a commercial systems studies and programming organization in Southern California, demonstrating strengths in the design and development of advanced data processing systems. Informatics cosponsored a major series of computer industry seminars, starting at UCLA in 1964 with a symposium on disk files; in 1965 it cosponsored with UCLA a symposium on online computing systems that drew over 700 attendees.

Informatics ran several technical information centers on a contract basis for U.S. agencies. In 1968, the company won the contract to operate NASA's Scientific and Technical Information Facility (STIF). After Lockheed completed the NASA/RECON installation at STIF, Informatics won contracts to maintain and support the NASA RECON software used at STIF and later used at the U.S. Department of Justice (DOJ) and other U.S. government agencies. We describe other Informatics online activities elsewhere where they are relevant, including activities associated with the NASA/RECON and TOXICON search systems and with Informatics' own search service.

DOCUS

Starting in 1964, with RADC support, Informatics worked on developing DOCUS (Display Oriented Computer Usage System). DOCUS provided online text manipulation, file maintenance, and file queries. Its developers, Harold Corbin and Werner Frank of the Bethesda, Maryland, office, noted that DOCUS had been implemented on a CDC 1604B computer with a Bunker Ramo 85 display console, and was being used to develop software techniques for online information processing and man-machine communication (Corbin and Frank 1966). They described an online query feature with Boolean logic and a capability to deliver retrieved records to the CRT, or to a printer, or to storage as a new database for later processing. Corbin was a member of an Informatics project team in 1966 that did a comprehensive survey for NBS of remote use of computers, including a survey of over 200 such installations (Collins 1967).

RADC System

Informatics designed an online system in 1969 for RADC at Griffiss Air Force Base, New York, incorporating techniques of automatic document classification for a large document collection. Thomas Lowe and David Roberts were the Informatics staff most closely associated with the project, which was an extension of Lowe's doctoral dissertation (1966) at the University of Pennsylvania. In a 1969 report they acknowledged the features of six other online systems then in existence (DIALOG, Data Central, ORBIT, TDMS, CCA-103, and MSIS). The developers showed a sense of humor in their functional naming of the program modules (PILE, SHOVEL, FETCH, CHOOSE, BUILD, BELCH, GULP, OUT(MESS)). This appears to have been an early version of RADCOL (chapter 9).

MITRE Corporation

ADAM

At a June 1963 conference, J. H. Burrows of MITRE Corporation of Bedford, Massachusetts, described ADAM (Automated Data Management), a software system developed with AF Systems Command support, and used to evaluate the feasibility of advanced designs of databases in certain command and control problems. At that time, it was being used to help design computer systems that could respond to queries such as: "Select out of the airfield file all those whose runway length is greater than 10,000 feet and whose distance from Boston is less than three hundred miles. List the distance from Boston, the runway length, latitude, longitude, and runway capacity, and sort the output in ascending distance from Boston" (Burrows 1964). At a spring

1965 conference, another MITRE staffer, Thomas Connors (1966), described ADAM (now named Advanced Data Management) as an online file processing system, with a multilevel, tree-structured hierarchy, providing for multiple consoles used simultaneously, remote operation, CRT graphic and character output, and light pen, push-button, Teletype, and typewriter input. Like AESOP, ADAM operated on an IBM 7030 (STRETCH) computer, and was intended to serve as a design verification tool for other programmers and analysts. In September 1965, Frank Cataldo described ADAM as a tool being built for use in designing and evaluating Military Information Systems. It was to be used in the early stages of system design to simulate the external appearance of systems that include man-machine communication and relatively large files. It was a development tool for laboratory use, not a production or operational system (Cataldo 1965). We found no evidence that ADAM was ever used for bibliographic or full-text applications, but we include it here because it was one of several major R&D projects the U.S. government funded to explore online computer-based information management technology. Also, the SDC TDMS system design (chapter 6) reportedly drew upon the ADAM experience.

AESOP

At a conference in fall 1965, MITRE staff members Edward Bennett, Edward Haines, and John Summers unveiled their experimental, prototype online control system called AESOP (An Evolutionary System for On-line Processing, or Advanced Evolutionary System for On-line Processing). With Air Force support, AESOP had been in operation since August 1965. More than just an interactive retrieval system, AESOP had a large number of general database management functions and was intended to be extremely flexible in operation and application. The AESOP designers expected that users would include both programmers as well as the highest level of executive personnel who needed direct system access. Users of the latter type needed a system that was simple to use and required an absolute minimum of training.

The first version of AESOP operated on an IBM 7030 (STRETCH) computer (65K of memory with 64-bit words) with an IBM 353 disk storage unit that held two million words. It worked with four CRT display terminals, keyboards, and printers. The retrieval program was constructed to interpret messages that users composed by means of a "communications tree" on the CRT display (Summers and Bennett 1967). Users controlled the program primarily with a light pencil; at any given moment, the variety of options available could be displayed and a user could indicate the desired move simply by pointing (Bennett, Haines, and Summers 1965; Spiegel, Summers, and Bennett 1966). It is interesting to see the competing nomenclature at that time, for example, "light pen" vs. "light pencil" vs. "light wand." In AESOP, this piece of equipment was called a "light gun," a full-size plastic pistol with the light beam emanating from the pistol's muzzle.

AESOP was designed to handle those kinds of problems that require large amounts of data to be stored, retrieved, processed, manipulated, and changed. It was used with various R&D, including an evaluation of online CAI activity within a management information system (Morrill, Goodwin, and Smith 1968). AESOP was called "possibly the closest thing to a comprehensive, integrated system for the management of memory, storage, files, and data–together with processing and display" (Licklider 1968, 218). AESOP was apparently never used to retrieve information from a large bibliographic database, but it can be remembered for its contributions to interactive displays, user control at the terminal as regards editing, printing, and programming, and user aids in query formulation.

COLINGO/C-10

In 1964, MITRE staff started COLINGO (Compile On-Line and Go), a small, general purpose file management system that became operational in 1965. COLINGO incorporated a computer control and query language that provided an operator with a grammar and vocabulary approximating English, to control program data and equipment in a data processing system. The first version of COLINGO was used on an IBM 1401 computer, and performed simple operations on single files efficiently, but had difficulty with more complex operations. Work to upgrade COLINGO to make a version for the IBM 1410 computer started in December 1964 and continued through 1966; it was named C-10 (for Colingo for the IBM 1410). The C-10 design was prompted by a desire to handle more complex file-processing operations more naturally and efficiently. C-10 was normally used in batch mode, but could be driven online through a CRT terminal when one was available. Project publications mention use of online, but we could find no evidence that it was ever used for online bibliographic or full-text searching (Steil 1967).

SAFARI

Walker (1967) described SAFARI, an experimental online system under development at MITRE meant to be used by a group of information analysts for building their own personal files of full-text information. SAFARI permitted users to scan through documents (messages, news articles, reports) displayed on a CRT, choose specific documents to be retained for further use, and permit searches to be made through the stored information to identify those records with relevant content. This was done initially on an IBM 7030 STRETCH computer in a time-shared environment, with a large CRT display console, a light gun, typewriter, and a printer. In 1967, work was underway to implement an augmented system on a time-shared IBM 360.

Cox Coronary Heart Institute

In 1966, G. Douglas Talbott reported in *JAMA* on the test results of a prototype online system that had been developed at the Cox Coronary Heart Institute in Kettering, Ohio, with support from NIH. The file consisted of six years of abstracts from over one hundred periodicals dealing with coronary heart disease, and published quarterly in the *Cox Coronary Heart Institute Abstract Journal*. The system design included storage of the original source publications on microform, with the film addresses included in the citation identification numbers. Talbott (1966, 146) believed this was "the first system to retrieve pertinent abstracts online and in real-time" and "to be the first to present the original document, almost simultaneously with the abstract, in a form readily transmissible to a remote inquiry station." He apparently was unaware of MICRO in 1965 and COLEX in 1966 that provided microform storage at a searcher's workstation with expanded versions (abstracts, extracts, tables of contents) of the information available online. It appears that, except for some brief records, these SDC systems provided additional information not available online. They did not present the microform copy, however, of all original documents at the searcher's workstation; in that regard, Cox's approach appears to have been unique. In a 1970 presentation, Porter, Penry, and Caponio, researchers associated with a different online system, mentioned the Cox system and noted that it had "not progressed beyond the pilot phase" (1971, 172). Talbott left the institute at the end of 1966, and apparently discontinued work on this system. It was never used at the institute after that.

U.S. Naval Material Command

OSIRIS

The ancient Egyptian god whose annual death and resurrection personified the self-renewing vitality of nature gave his name to an online system developed in the Information Sciences and Plans Branch of the U.S. Naval Material Command in Washington, D.C. OSIRIS (On-line Search Information Retrieval Information Storage) consisted of an automated microfiche storage and retrieval system and an online system for searching indexes and abstracts associated with the microfiche (Showalter 1968; OSIRIS 1968). OSIRIS was a prototype intended to demonstrate improved practical techniques for storing, retrieving, and displaying information. In addition to locating relevant records, the system went a step further than most automated retrieval systems of that time by allowing a user to review the retrieved record (the actual referenced document) online. An RCA 3301 computer with a magnetic card memory was used for the index storage and retrieval system; a Teletype was used as the searching input-output device. The image storage and retrieval system included a mechanical file that stored 5,000 microfiche or aperture cards in a rotary drum (50 bins with 100 cards each). Various microform image reductions were used, varying from the normal range of reduction ratios (10–45 to 1) to successful tests with image reductions as extreme as 260:1. The image storage equipment was originally designed for photographic storage. OSIRIS was demonstrated in 1966 and 1967, but unlike the Egyptian god, did not self-renew; it never went beyond the demonstration phase.

Computer Corporation of America

CCA-103

In 1967, the Computer Corporation of America (CCA) demonstrated an online search system, named the CCA-103, that used an IBM 360 computer with IBM 2260 CRT displays and could support eight terminals simultaneously. In early 1968, it was operational and available for purchase or lease. Lowe and Roberts (1969) noted that this system had no provision for a local printer. However, special features included "hurry mode" (documents streamed through the CRT at about human reading speed) and retention of temporary files so that a user could reuse or modify a previous query (similar to SEARCH SAVE as demonstrated in TIP in 1965). Boolean operators AND, OR, NOT were used, nesting was permitted, and online file modification was possible. It was among the systems COSATI reviewed and included in their benchmark demonstration described later in this chapter (Welch 1968). CCA later marketed an online multiterminal file management system (Model 204 Database Management Software System) for use on IBM 360/370 systems.

Patent Office In-House System

In 1967, the U.S. Patent Office was doing the preliminary work in-house to implement a system on a Honeywell 1200 computer that would permit a patent examiner to search selected patent files by means of remote terminals and data links (*Progress* 1968, 31). In 1969, work was under way to prepare a database of the full text of patents and related documents; searching was being done in selected subject areas in a remote batch mode, with patent examiners entering queries at remote terminals and receiving printouts at their workstations (*Progress* 1970, 26–27). Project POTOMAC (Patent Office Techniques of Mechanized Access and Classification) was established in January 1971 as a long-range developmental program to automate patent searching and classification. The first demonstrations of online interactive searching took place in December 1971. A major conclusion of this work was that the Patent Office could implement a production system in automated patent search and classification in any year in which funding was available (*Progress* 1972, 19).

Auerbach Corporation

DM-1

The Auerbach Corp. in Philadelphia developed DM-1 (Data Manager-1), described in 1967 as a comprehensive data handling system designed to provide the fastest response time available in time-shared multi-user systems by means of console access. DM-1 was developed for and funded by RADC (Resnick and Sable 1968). Data could be stored in either tape or random access devices (Dixon and Sable 1967; Ziehe 1967). DM-1 could be used for online bibliographic searching, and the software was commercially available from Auerbach in 1969. It was somewhat machine-independent, and by the end of 1969 had run on three different computer systems (Seiden 1970).

Planning Research Corporation

PACER

Perhaps the last of the large mechanized image retrieval systems of this era was PACER (Program Assisted Console Evaluation and Review), a system developed for RADC by Planning Research Corporation (PRC) in Los Angeles, with its subcontractor Informatics, Inc. PACER was intended to support the Joint Strategic Target Planning Staff and Strategic Air Command intelligence activities. PACER development began in 1967, the pilot was demonstrated in September 1968, an initial operational capability began in January 1970, and PACER was declared operational in late 1970 (*Program Assisted Console* 1972). PACER represented the first real production implementation of an individual online workstation that operated with a coordinated multimedia, multifile capability (alphanumeric text documents, tabular material, aerial photos, electronic intercept graphics), support of multiple intelligent terminals (a combined total of 48 BR-90 and RCA units), and variable function keys.

Scientific Resources Corporation

COSTAR

At a 1969 conference, Albert Sinopoli of Scientific Resources Corporation described COSTAR, an online retrieval system that had been operating since mid-1968. COSTAR was designed and developed to allow users of his company's subsidiary time-sharing service, Computer Sharing Inc., to establish an online database and interact with it for purposes of retrieval or file maintenance. Access was by Teletype terminals, working with an SDS 940 computer and time-sharing system. We have no information to indicate that COSTAR was used in any production situation for online bibliographic or full-text searching.

UKAEA Culham Laboratory

RIOT

About sixty miles from London, England, sits the tiny village of Culham, outside of Abingdon and south of Oxford. Located there is the Culham Laboratory of the United Kingdom Atomic Energy Authority (UKAEA), where Jim Hall, Alan Negus and David Dancy of the Library and Scientific Information Unit began working in 1968 on an experimental online system they called RIOT (Retrieval of Information by On-line Terminal). Hall came to the group with a background in chemistry and metallurgy and Negus had a degree in librarianship. Members of the Computing and Applied Mathematics Group at Culham helped with writing the program. OSTI, the House of Commons Library, and Aslib contributed support. The goal of RIOT was to develop a cost-effective and robust system and to use it to assess the potential benefits of online retrieval for the scientists at Culham Lab. Culham staff members were already experienced in using computers for bibliographic record handling; they had been operating an SDI system on an English Electric KDF9 computer since 1966, with Chemical Titles, Science Citation Index, and Nuclear Science Abstracts tapes (Anthony, Carpenter, and Cheney 1968; Anthony, Cheney, and Whelan 1968; Corbett 1968).

The team developed RIOT during 1968–1969 using a database of 750 computational physics literature references from 1946 to 1968. Initially RIOT was not online, but was instead a remote entry high-priority batch system. Queries were tricky to formulate and the computer responses were cryptic

(Negus and Hall 1971). After changes to incorporate longer explicit instructions for novice users, the first interactive retrieval program that ran in real time and allowed users to alter a search as it proceeded was introduced in September 1969. In April 1970, RIOT was demonstrated online at the Institute of Information Scientists conference in Reading, England.

The first version of RIOT ran on a slow and small KDF9 computer with a core storage of 32K (actually, only 14K were available to the program) and a backup disk of 4 million words capacity (computer words, not text words) (Negus 1971). Searchers used a video terminal for rapid scanning of search output and a linked teletypewriter for printing user-system dialogue or citations selected as relevant. The RIOT programmers wrote in FORTRAN because that and ALGOL were all that were available on Culham's KDF9. One small file of important reports was available for retrieval during 1970–1971, but the KDF9 was never used for large files. In principle, twenty simultaneous users could access the KDF9, but in practice there would be none or occasionally one, except when two or three terminals were used simultaneously for tests or demonstrations (Negus 1980).

Hall, Negus, and Dancy used RIOT for experimentation with small files in computational physics and plasma physics, and a database constructed for the POLLS (Parliamentary On-Line Library Study) experiment that contained social science literature references of interest to the House of Commons Library in London. In 1969, G. B. F. Niblet of the UKAEA reported on a study of the application of computers for searching of the full text of the Acts of Parliament and associated legislation dealing with atomic energy ("Second Cranfield" 1970). The POLLS prototype demonstrated in July 1970 the potential value of fast online retrieval to serve the information needs of Members of Parliament (Hall, Negus, and Dancy 1971). Negus and Hall reprinted the *POLLS User's Manual* in a 1971 article.

The plasma physics file had been run in batch mode since 1966. It provided access only to words in titles or titles augmented by additional keywords assigned by an indexer, which Negus and Hall did not see as much of a limitation since "in the field of plasma physics titles are generally very explicit and contain a high proportion of 'key' words" and the titles could be enriched by an indexer if desired (1971, 250). Because of system constraints, the restriction to searching just title words was further limited by allowing the search to be made only on the first seven characters. Words containing such stems as "electron" were split instead of shortened (i.e., search for ELECTRO and N).

RIOT offered the usual Boolean operators, but with limitations: a maximum of four AND groups, one NOT group and no more than nine terms linked by OR. If the original query needed to be altered, new words could be added but nonuseful ones (including misspelled terms) could not be deleted. A search had to be started all over again once the limit on terms was reached. Negus and Hall (1971, 257–258) described another RIOT feature designed to prevent system abuse or misuse:

An automatic cut-off operates if the user seems to be selecting few of the displayed items for printing; the assumption here is that if he does not want a hard-copy of a reference then that reference is not relevant to the enquiry. After this automatic pause (arbitrarily pre-set by the information unit) the user is of course given the choice of refining his query formulation, starting the search again with a differently phrased query, or, if he is indeed satisfied with a small percentage of relevant items amongst those displayed, continuing the search. Once this cut-off has been reached, the percentage of references shown that must be printed to prevent further cut-off is lowered.

The point of this feature was to economize on computer search time. Negus and Hall did not want searchers to use expensive computer resources to browse for serendipitous discovery of references. They did not report whether users found the automatic cutoff to be an irritation or helpful feedback alerting them to possible errors or shortcomings in the query formulation.

By early 1972, RIOT II ran on an ICL System 4-70 computer, with online access to a database of 25,000 references. The system was transferred to an

ICL System 4/70 and was live with the whole 1966-to-date file of about 25,000 records. In principle, over forty simultaneous users could access the System 4/70, but in practice, there was usually only one user. Initially, teletype units were used as terminal equipment, followed later by TI Silent 700 thermal printers. RIOT could, and did, use multiple files, but they were presented to the user as one file (Negus 1980).

RIOT was designed to be used primarily by library staff but also to be capable of being used by library users on a self-service basis (Hall, Negus, and Dancy 1972). To help occasional users, who often experienced difficulty using Boolean operators, RIOT II offered a matrix display that obviated the need for them. A searcher could build up a query statement by tabbing from box to box or rubbing out unwanted terms. As a searcher filled in a box, the number of items in the file containing the term was "posted" within the matrix. At the same time, RIOT displayed at the bottom of the screen the brief titles of the most recent five titles containing the search term, for the purpose of helping a searcher to identify additional terms. The matrix display represented a modest attempt to help searchers in lieu of a more elaborate thesaurus display possible in larger systems. "The RIOT system, with limited staff effort, relies on (a) the native wit of the searcher, (b) the fact that the data base is comparatively modest in size, and (c) the hope that the display of recent titles . . . will help to trigger off a certain number of related words in the user's mind" (Hall, Negus, and Dancy 1972, 184). Only after a user was satisfied with the formulation, would the computer be asked to execute the full search.

Costs seemed to be a major concern to the small RIOT operation at Culham Lab, especially computer storage costs, more than computer use costs. The developers could not justify keeping the databases online all day for only about three searches a day. They sought another economy by partitioning the databases so that users retrieved only a few references per search. They reduced costs also by extracting keywords from the records and storing them in a linear file complementary to the main database. This smaller file could be searched serially.

The developers of RIOT felt themselves to be ahead of their time in experimenting with this expensive alternative to manual literature searching. They were optimistic that within a decade or so, many other libraries would enjoy this technology. The British Library considered RIOT in 1973 for operational experiments with online search systems, but selected other local online systems instead.

Negus continued to work on developing online systems. A 1972 source noted his special interests as using computers in library and information work, motor racing, and draught Guinness. His work at INSPEC and Scicon Consultancy International in the 1970s on developing and implementing user interfaces to online systems led to his participating in the development and implementation of the Euronet Common Command Language in the late 1970s that is now being used in several online systems (Negus 1979).

Lawrence Livermore Laboratory (LLL)

MASTER CONTROL

At the 1969 ASIS annual meeting, Viktor Hampel and John Wade announced MASTER CONTROL (see Hampel and Wade 1969), a generalized file management system they had designed, developed, and implemented at Lawrence Livermore Laboratory (LLL) in December 1968. LLL was operated by the University of California for the AEC, which supported the work on MASTER CONTROL. The goal was to provide a single program that could handle both large and small databases, and could be used for dissimilar bibliographic or numeric databases for administrative or scientific purposes, and for SDI or online searching (Crow and Elchesen 1971).

MASTER CONTROL initially ran on a CDC 6600 computer and could be accessed through teletypewriter or CRT terminals, either at 110 baud

(10 cps) with acoustic couplers or at 4,800 baud (480 cps) hard-wired (Fife et al. 1974). Trained librarians, for whom the query language was designed, could search online or in batch mode. LLL reference librarians could search any word, word root, phrase or number in any part of the entry, using all the usual Boolean operators and field limitations. In 1971 it was available on three CDC 6600 computers with more than ten different databases available online from over 360 remote Teletype stations at LLL.

The LLL library served more than 1,500 scientists and engineers. Prior to the computer-based retrieval system, the staff could conduct only a limited number of time-consuming literature searches and could monitor only a small number of incoming technical periodicals for specific topics. After adopting MASTER CONTROL, they were able to handle many more requests for retrospective searches, provide current awareness service, and answer more reference questions. By 1974, they were handling 1,400 searches per month. They had access to many diverse files, including LLL databases, and forty-four major databases such as Nuclear Science Abstracts, Chemical Titles, COMPENDEX, and SPIN (Buginas and Crow 1973; Byrne 1975).

International Labour Office

ISIS

George Thompson and Marc Marthaler began planning for ISIS (Integrated Set of Information Systems, or Integrated Scientific Information System) in 1963. Thompson was the chief of the Central Library and Documentation Branch in Geneva of the International Labour Office (ILO), an agency of the United Nations. The first element (IBM punched card processing) of ISIS became operational in late 1965 with 5,000 records and batch searching was done using an IBM 360/30, two tape drives, three disk drives, and a database of 28,000 of their own bibliographic records and descriptions of research projects (Thompson 1968).

Following several years of batch searching, the first online searching started in August 1969, running on an IBM 360/30 with an IBM 2314 disk storage unit. Developing the online system was the responsibility of an ILO team headed by William Schieber, then in charge of systems development and data processing work in that Branch. Schieber had participated in developing online systems at UC's Institute of Library Research (chapter 3) (Thompson and Schieber 1970). Initial online use was with an IBM 1050 terminal and about 31,000 bibliographic records; access through several IBM 2260 CRT terminals became available in 1970. ISIS, which could operate in either a batch or online mode, allowed online data entry for the database. In 1969, online search results consisted of the posting counts and the abstract numbers. A searcher requiring the complete bibliographic records entered a note at the completion of the search; the records were printed offline in batch mode later in the day (Thompson 1970).

In 1970, ISIS was handling an extensive amount of regular searching. Continuing constraints on the computer storage capacity, however, limited the number of records that could be searched online. Consequently, a means was provided to permit online queries to be followed up with a batch search of the entire file (as if the online search were a test and verification of the search formulation). In 1971, ISIS was operating with 40,000 bibliographic records and providing a Boolean search capability. ISIS provided a capability to permit string searching on specific character strings in the text, and term-sequence searching. Both of these capabilities, however, were used as postprocessing features following a regular search, because they were time-consuming procedures. ISIS also had a capability called ANY, similar to the SAVE SEARCH feature on other systems at that time. ANY allowed groups of synonymous terms to be assembled and ORed ahead of time, and used later in a search. For example, ANY EUROPE generated a set in which terms in the ANY EUROPE table were ORed together (Austria OR Belgium OR Denmark OR France . . .). The ANY feature was more limited than SAVE

SEARCH because it did not allow the inclusion of AND and NOT logic operations. ISIS was among the first systems to include a major/minor search term discrimination feature. It was rather rudimentary, however, and not as well-developed as the feature demonstrated earlier on the DDC system. The ILO/ISIS story is continued in chapter 9.

InfoData Systems, Inc.

INQUIRE

Developed by Harry Kapowitz, Ron Furman, Bob Schreier, and Bob Loan, the same programmers who had developed DATRIX for Xerox, INQUIRE was a proprietary software package. As we saw in chapter 3, the programmers believed that a DATRIX-like program offered more business opportunities than they could pursue at Xerox, and they left in 1968 to form their own company, Info-Data Systems, Inc. They wrote INQUIRE in PL/1 and modeled it, like DATRIX, after Noah Prywes's threaded lists software for Multilist, rather than an inverted file structure. The program became available in 1968 and operated on an IBM 360/40 with 128K bytes of core memory, or larger.

INQUIRE was designed not so much as a text retrieval program, but more as a database management program for drug information. Nonetheless, drug companies adopted the software for text retrieval applications (Bayer 1987). As they became aware of these applications, the developers made modifications in the program's basic structure to improve the text retrieval performance. Because it was based on a threaded list structure, however, it could not operate as efficiently on a large database as an inverted file could. INQUIRE was not considered as well suited as DIALOG or ORBIT for large files and multiple terminals. Nevertheless, it was installed beginning in July 1969 in a variety of applications, both batch and online, primarily for pharmaceutical drug information, including the Warner-Lambert Research Institute and the Squibb Institute of Medical Research (Brandhorst and Eckert 1972). At Warner-Lambert, INQUIRE was still being used in a batch mode in early 1971, with search results provided on an overnight schedule from their in-house computer (Starker, Owen, and Martin 1971; Stein et al. 1973). At Squibb, it was used to create the Squibb Science Information System, containing articles on Squibb drugs, and to give online access to over 100 users (Frycki 1970). In addition to the internal database, access was provided to external files such as RINGDOC and VETDOC, produced by Derwent Publications (Bennett and Frycki 1971). In 1970, the INQUIRE software was available for purchase for $26,000 (Cuadra 1971). In 1974, the price had risen to $38,500, or the software could be leased at $1,325 per month, and it could be operated in either online or batch mode (Fife et al. 1974).

About 1975, the INQUIRE programmers decided to expand the software capabilities, to further improve the text retrieval performance. Bayer (1987) recalled: "They wrote macros to ape RECON, to build sets, hold sets, and allow you to do Boolean operations against that. They made some things look somewhat like RECON. They felt that might help them compete in the marketplace." INQUIRE did achieve some success; by the mid-1970s, at least a dozen major American and European drug firms used it for retrieval of drug data and drug literature.

ASTIA/DDC/DTIC

Organizations and Databases

Antecedents of ASTIA, DDC, and DTIC date back to 1926 with a modest USAF publication called *Technical News Service*. USAF documentation activities intensified greatly, however, starting in 1945 at the end of the European phase of World War II, when about 1,500 personnel formed technical intelligence teams and combed Germany for science and technical documents. By the end of 1945, they had collected over 800,000 documents from their screening centers. A similar document collection activity took place in Japan a little later. In 1945, the Office of Technical Services (OTS) was established with a mission to organize and catalog captured World War II sci-tech documents and to communicate the technology to American industry (Schon 1965). The processing of captured documents, along with increasing numbers of technical documents produced by U.S. agencies and contractors, introduced and identified many jurisdictional and operational problems. Seeing that coordination was essential among the information services of several military agencies, Secretary of Defense George C. Marshall signed an order in May 1951 establishing ASTIA, which could be considered the *other* Marshall Plan. ASTIA was to provide an integrated program of scientific and technical report services for DOD and its contractors. Adkinson (1978), Barden, Hammond, and Heald (1959), and Wallace (1995) provide more complete histories of ASTIA, DDC, and NTIS.

ASTIA was among the few federal agencies pursuing technological approaches in the early 1960s to improve speed and performance of operations. Claire Schultz recounted her participation in the earliest of the ASTIA efforts to introduce computers into their bibliographic processing. In 1960, after several years of pioneering experience in developing punched card retrieval systems at Merck, she was working as a UNIVAC senior systems analyst. ASTIA had recently contracted to obtain a UNIVAC computer and asked Schultz to be a consultant. ASTIA had 750,000 technical reports under bibliographic control, but only the 200,000 most recently catalogued reports were included in their automated operation, and new reports were coming in at the rate of more than 100 per day. According to Schultz, ASTIA did not have a clear idea about what to do with a new computer, and she was expected to support both the UNIVAC salesman and ASTIA while they figured it out. A pacifist, she was reluctant to become involved with DOD activities; she decided to restrict her initial participation to offering a few suggestions based on her experience at Merck.

On the day she arrived at ASTIA for her scheduled visit with Heston Heald to review their needs and objectives, Schultz was ushered into a large conference room filled with DOD personnel anxious to hear her suggestions. After her remarks, DOD staff wanted ASTIA staff to design a system and develop it in-house, and they wanted further guidance from Schultz. ASTIA management pressured UNIVAC salespeople for additional technical support, so the salespeople got the idea that UNIVAC should construct its own retrieval program to be sold with the computer. Clayton Shepherd was the UNIVAC programmer volunteered to do the programming. Shepherd, however, never got started. William Hammond, an AF officer stationed at ASTIA with responsibility for the computer system (he had been the project officer since 1958 when ASTIA made the decision to automate and had written the original proposal to automate), decided to do the development in-house (Hammond 1960). The UNIVAC equipment was installed and the first stage of the system became operational in late 1960.

Schultz continued to work with ASTIA automation, including volunteering to help develop the biology section of a proposed thesaurus, review the forms and procedures for standardizing data about DOD contractors, and review ways for the computer to verify user access to specific database information, until she left UNIVAC in 1961 to join the Institute for the Advancement of Medical Communication (Schultz 1997). Schultz served in 1962 as the president of ADI.

In 1963, ASTIA was renamed DDC, was given greatly expanded responsibilities, and acquired its own UNIVAC 1107 computer, which had a capacity to provide more information processing (Vann 1963). DDC was renamed Defense Technical Information Center (DTIC) in October 1979, and its mission was further expanded. In this convoluted restructuring, we are mostly interested in DDC, because that is the stage in the organizational metamorphosis when most of the online development took place. DDC was DOD's centralized scientific and technical report documentation service and supported DOD's research, development, test, and evaluation (RDT&E) activities. DDC's responsibilities included, among other things, the centralized acquisition and announcement of technical reports, and, when requested by authorized users, furnishing copies of reports of DOD-sponsored RDT&E. DDC's document delivery facility provided print or microfiche copies of reports in its collection and supported this service with bibliographic searches of its collection and an indexing and abstracting service, *Technical Abstracts Bulletin* (*TAB*). The DDC collection included materials with security classifications and/or release restrictions, which added processing complications. Bibliographic records for classified reports were classified as well, and therefore, the system had to provide for security-protected access to the database and secure data transmission (Bennertz 1971). The latter was accomplished by using Telecommunications Security equipment.

In addition to covering report literature, DDC served as a clearinghouse for information concerning DOD-sponsored R&D. They maintained a file of 17,000 project descriptions ("work units") known as the Work Unit Information System (WUIS), representing the current status of all ongoing DOD classified and unclassified projects. WUIS data were gathered on a standardized input worksheet (DD Form 1498: Research & Technology Résumé) known in Federal R&D circles as "1498s." The records had twenty-two searchable fields and subfields (e.g., COSATI subject code, descriptors, security classification). Most of the data related to *ongoing* R&D as reflected by WUIS, or records of *completed* R&D as reflected by the Technical Report Data Bank. WUIS searching was initiated with a batch system in 1965. In 1968, when the file had grown to over 30,000 project résumés, DDC implemented an online searching capability.

The U.S. government had a broad and continuing interest in its own organizational structure to handle unclassified sci-tech information, and it took actions in that area that related to DDC. In January 1964, COSATI and the Federal Council for Science and Technology approved the concept of a coordinated Federal sci-tech information system with three centers: (1) agriculture (centered in the National Agricultural Library, or NAL); (2) life sciences and medicine (in NLM); and (3) physical sciences and engineering (establishing the Clearinghouse for Scientific and Technical Information (CFSTI) within NBS, and building on the old OTS. CFSTI took responsibility for providing unclassified and unlimited distribution of DOD information to the general public. CFSTI began its own bibliographic file building and index publishing with *U.S. Government Research & Development Reports* (*USGRDR*) (Schon 1965). DDC continued to provide DOD and its contractors with unclassified/unlimited reports as well as to handle the more difficult task of processing classified and restricted access documents. In 1964, CFSTI and DDC agreed to eliminate duplicate input processing of their reports.

1965 was the first full year of operation of CFSTI, handling about 5,000 requests per day from its collection of over 400,000 report titles. The first CFSTI director was Bernard Fry, who later served as dean of the library school at Indiana University. In September 1967, CFSTI and DDC agreed to avoid any duplicate announcements of source publications—thus making a clear separation into two separate files: (1) unclassified DOD reports without distribution limitations, which were announced exclusively in *USGRDR*, published by CFSTI; and (2) classified reports or reports with distribution limitations, which were announced in *TAB,* the DDC confidential publication. The processing of unclassified and unlimited documents was transferred back to DDC in 1971, and users with NTIS deposit accounts were able to order reports directly from DDC (McGinnis 1997). In 1967, DDC added 50,000 reports and distributed over 1.9 million copies of reports in response to individual requests; it was a major document processing facility. In May 1968, the Technical Reports database was up to 868,000 records; WUIS contained 26,000 active summaries, with 25,000 file modifications per year.

> **1965 Milestone**
>
> The DDC database was the first machine-readable file of bibliographic records to be used in an online search system created by another organization (SDC's BOLD).

DDC was helpful to several early research projects interested in using bibliographic records in machine readable form. DDC began distributing magnetic tapes with bibliographic data in July 1963 with a tape of *TAB* unclassified/unlimited distribution citations for use with a pilot SDI system at the U.S. Army Electronics Command (Wixon and Housman 1968). In 1964, DDC provided a sample tape of 38,402 document representations to a research project at Sperry Rand regarding multilist and inverted file structures (Fossum and Kaskey 1966). In 1965, DDC sent nearly 5,000 DD-1498 records on tape to the Science Information Exchange for use in its operations (*Progress* 1966). A selection of DD-1498 records was used in the COSATI online benchmark demonstrations described later. In late 1965, DDC sent a tape of about 6,000 DDC citations and abstracts to SDC for use with BOLD, the first online system to run with a database of bibliographic records created by an outside organization. NASA was another early DDC tape recipient under an exchange agreement started in 1967. Also in 1967, DDC began providing tapes to the U.S. Army Edgewood Arsenal for its SDI activities. Regular tape distribution service for current citation information from DDC began in 1970, as did regular tape distribution service for current *USGRDR* information from CFSTI.

In 1970, NTIS was established as a primary operating unit within the Department of Commerce. CFSTI was transferred to NTIS, its functions merged with the latter's broader mission, and CFSTI as an entity was abolished.

Remote Terminal Input System (RTIS)

The sequence of bibliographic input systems used at DDC illustrates the diversity of equipment and techniques used to build machine readable files during this period. The following description of various DDC input systems comes primarily from Larry Jenkins, a computer specialist on the DDC staff since 1962, who designed, developed, and implemented some of the systems and was still working at DTIC when this text was written (Jenkins 1997, 1998).

In 1962, Remington Rand Synchro-Tape terminals were used to input and store document citations on punched paper tape. The tape was used to print out the citations onto paper galleys that were mounted on large copy preparation sheets for eventual inclusion into *TAB*. Catalog cards were produced, and the citations were retained on the paper tape. When DDC got a UNIVAC 1107 in 1963, a tape reader was acquired for it that allowed all of the paper tapes to be read into the computer and then written onto magnetic tape for what later became known as the Master Accession Direct (MAD) file.

In 1966, IBM's Administrative Terminal System (ATS) and equipment (IBM 1440 computer and 20 remote terminal keyboards) for online data input were installed at DDC for keyboarding report citation data. The new data entry system allowed DDC to move away from its Synchro-Tape operation, and allowed data to be moved more directly into the 1107. ATS was the software, and the functional process was called the Terminal Data Input System (TDIS). Referred to as the DDC RDT&E On-Line Network, or sometimes as the DDC On-Line System, or the DDC Information System, or else the DDC Remote On-Line Retrieval System, the prototype functioned between 1967 and 1971 in a combination batch and online mode.

In February 1967, CFSTI was linked to the TDIS for data input. Fourteen terminals within DDC and six at CFSTI were used to keyboard initial data and corrections for unclassified/unlimited documents into the DDC system. Interactive input processing resulted in the edited input data being written onto tape to be used as update information for the MAD file. This input system was used until 1969 when DDC got a UNIVAC 1108 system. As the 1108 had a telecommunications capability, it was then possible to give up the ATS software and IBM 1440 computer, and replace them with UNIVAC's Text Processing System (TPS), which ran on the UNIVAC 1108. The functional process was still TDIS, and the same IBM teletypewriter terminals were used, but they were used with TPS. This system was used until 1972 when the Remote Terminal Input System (RTIS) was introduced.

When RTIS was implemented, it was a standalone system, not a part of any retrieval system. One could have either RTIS or the DDC retrieval system on a terminal. It was later decided to implement an online input capability that could be used on the same terminal used for online retrieval. Jenkins designed, developed, and implemented the general-purpose input system used to input Technical Report, Work Unit, and other classified and unclassified data from both remote and local terminal sites. When the Defense RDT&E Online System (DROLS) was implemented in September 1974 (see chapter 9), RTIS was retrofitted as a major subsystem of DROLS. When that happened, both the input and retrieval systems became available in the same environment with commands that immediately took users to input, retrieval, qualification, sorting, display, or other functions.

Remote On-Line Retrieval System

In 1964, DDC was still running a batch search system, but now it offered a twenty-four-hour turn-around service for rush requests called "Rapid Response Bibliography," but often referred to as "Telex Bibs" or "Telex Searches," from their WUIS or Technical Report database (Crowe 1967; Barden 1965). Output from the Technical Report file was limited to AD report accession numbers; a recipient had to find manually the corresponding citations in the printed editions of *TAB* held in the requestor's library. DDC processed about 10,000 bibliographies per year with this early batch system (Rea 1967). DDC's tasks were performed adequately using manual and automated batch procedures until a growing volume of accessions of new reports (averaging over 200 per day) and requests for services (over 1.8 million requests for reports in 1967) turned DDC's interest to the possibility of adding online processing.

In FY 1967, DDC had completed over 20,000 batch-mode searches, with an average processing time of 3.6 workdays (their performance goal was 3.0 workdays). Their off-target turnaround time was blamed on computer downtime, reassignment of trained personnel to higher priority programs, and difficulty in recruiting quality replacement personnel. An online approach presumably was seen as one way to improve this turnaround time. In February 1967, DDC began experimental development of a remote inquiry capability on their UNIVAC 1107. The new system was called "DDC Remote On-Line Retrieval System" and "WUIS Retrieval System." It included Technical Report and WUIS batch processing. Major participants in the development were Michael Booth, Richard Bennertz, and Clinton Lemasters. Phase I was to develop an operating prototype, which was done with a UNIVAC 1107, five to seven UNIVAC Fastrand drum storage units, a prototype UNIVAC 1551 CRT terminal, a modified EXEC I supervisory system, and a limited version of the WUIS database. This prototype was successfully demonstrated during May to July 1968. It was restricted, however, to a single terminal capability in a noninteractive use of existing batch processing search programs (Bennertz 1971).

Phase II (August 1968–April 1969) was to convert the Phase I system to new hardware and software—namely, the UNIVAC 1108 under control of the EXEC 8 software system—utilizing the Uniscope 300 CRT. The Phase II system had the capability for serial (i.e., not simultaneous) access by two terminals at DDC, and operating with the complete WUIS placed on drum storage equipment. The 1108 came with 32 UNIVAC 8433 disk drives to provide mass storage capability. As disk storage became cheaper, more data were placed online.

User registration, validation, and need-to-know controls were also part of the online operations. Other enhancements added during Phase II included hard copy output at the CRT terminals, the activation of a secure remote circuit within DDC configured to operate like a remote terminal outside of DDC, and an ability to search against all WUIS data fields except text data fields.

Beginning in May 1969, Phase III focused on developing a capability for concurrent access by multiple terminals. Communication links between the UNIVAC 1108 and external terminals were established, and operational testing began (*Progress in scientific and technical communications*, 1970, 41–44). Six terminals were installed: two terminals within DDC, and one secure terminal each at AF Systems Command, National Security Agency (NSA), Naval Ship Research and Development Center (NSR&DC), and the Office of the Director of Defense Research and Engineering (ODDR&E). The terminal equipment consisted of UNIVAC Uniscope 300 Visual Communications Terminals (with a $5'' \times 10''$ viewing surface, 16 lines of display, and display speeds of 320 cps) and a 25 cps printing terminal (UNIVAC Pagewriter). Thus, DDC now had a computer configuration that provided both a multiprocessing and a telecommunications capability. At this point DDC began developing the DDC Remote Online Retrieval System that used its old batch search system as its base. This experimental system was implemented at the Secret level, and all users had to be cleared to the highest level and demonstrate the necessary "need-to-know" to have access. The first users were major military commands and labs. As access controls were established, access was expanded to other users such as federal R&D contractors, and dial-up access was provided. Because the DDC system was to work with sensitive security-classified information, special equipment and procedures had to be used with it and the information in it. For example, the telecommunications lines and equipment had to be secure; to that end, NSRDC built a special crypto-secure vault to house the terminal and telecommunications equipment, and the Air Force Systems Command used an existing vault for their communications equipment.

The initial DDC online system provided Boolean searching (AND, OR, NOT), and arithmetic searching ($=, \neq, \geq, \leq, >$) to further restrict output records by some numeric value. This was helpful in records such as the DD-1498s with field-coded numeric data (e.g., limiting search output to records of research projects with funding levels greater than \$n). At that time, this feature was seen in most online database management systems, but not in online bibliographic systems, except for the Data Central system in 1967. Searching was not recursive; users had to enter all desired terms, Boolean operators, and non-subject qualifiers before the system retrieved and displayed matching records (Bennertz 1971). The command language included nineteen "action codes," for searching, displaying, and sorting output, three "auxiliary codes" for responding to system questions, and ten "service codes" used for tutorial information. The searching codes were just that—code numbers and symbols. An early user at NSRDC who had personal experience with its development and use, Theodore Wolfe, after a two-year study of online systems, compared the complicated DDC access language with that of TIP, which used simple English words such as "search" and "find" (Wolfe 1970). This decidedly unfriendly search language nonetheless was intended to be used directly by scientists and engineers.

The 1969 system offered an option to store results of multiple searches in a Special File for merging, elimination of duplicates, and later batch postprocessing (Wolfe 1970). TIP had demonstrated this in 1964, but this feature was not available in most of the early search systems. The DDC system also included a means for truncation searching, achieving it by "masking" or "string searching," a sequential record-by-record comparison of characters in specified fields—a cumbersome and time consuming process that gave way to inverted file structures when files grew so large that the time to complete a search became unacceptably long.

This version also permitted a user to ask the system to expand a search formulation automatically to include all of the hierarchically narrower subject terms. This was done by entering a symbol ($) with the search term. This simple approach for the searcher was in contrast to DIALOG's multistep related term file lookup technique which at that time required a searcher to call up a related term display for the chosen term, and then incorporate the related term numbers into the formulation. Multilist had been the first online system with this feature, providing it in 1966. The flexibility to work with a hierarchical structure was also provided for corporate source searching. DDC maintained a Corporate Source Hierarchy for all sources submitting documents to DDC, which gave users the option to insert source code hierarchies directly into the search strategy. As organizations were closed and/or moved under another company or military/governmental entity, they were placed into the hierarchy for that organization. Some hierarchies included up to ten levels. A user who wanted to search for an organization whose source code was 108,765 entered it with the hierarchy indicator symbol ($), that is, $108,765, along with the other search terms. All the source codes for lower level parts of the organization were included in the search. The output showed accessions for all sources cataloged with any of the hierarchy codes. System users were provided with search aids such as hierarchical listings of codes with related alphanumeric names (Jenkins 1997).

DDC was sensitive to issues of subject authority control. In the DDC system, particular attention was given to controlled vocabulary searching rather than free-text searching (Woods 1971). Users searched on the descriptor field and included term weights in the search formulation (Powers 1973). DDC's predecessor organization, ASTIA, had been engaged in extensive subject authority control work since the late 1950s with their Project MARS, the *ASTIA Subject Heading List*, and the *Thesaurus of ASTIA Descriptors* (1960) and its updates. DDC was given the responsibility in 1966 for maintaining the *Thesaurus of Engineering and Scientific Terms* (*TEST*), and a professional lexicographer, Paul Klingbiel, was added to the staff to support this subject authority work. In 1966, he was among the first to use a computer to produce a search aid other than a thesaurus; he produced a term frequency listing for all the descriptors used in indexing 427,000 reports in DDC (Klingbiel and Jacobs 1966).

The 1969 online system included a weighting feature for major/minor descriptors. An input record could be assigned one or more major descriptors to indicate what it was "mostly about," along with one or more minor descriptors that indicated what it "also mentions" (Wolfe 1970, 16). The search system permitted searchers to take advantage of this indexing distinction to retrieve sets of highly relevant records. This distinction of major/minor subject terms was functionally available in TIRP in 1966, but was not as developed and articulated as the formal system of major and minor descriptors implemented with the DDC system.

The initial system provided a searcher with choices for the output records. For online output, a searcher could choose a brief set with just record numbers, or receive full records (tailored to some extent by the searcher, and sorted into order by three different attributes). Output from batch searching allowed eighteen versions of the DD-1498 format and up to six copies.

Wolfe criticized the DDC system for lacking an online thesaurus, which meant that users had to choose search terms for their topics "on a hit-or-miss basis" (1970, 30). He cited users' exasperation with the poor system reliability, as well as their optimism (26): "System reliability . . . is a constant [problem] with any new computer system, especially one which has been subject to as much revision as has the DDC Remote On-Line Retrieval System. Even so, down-time should not be as much of a daily hazard in the life of the user as it has been and continues to be with respect to both hardware and system operations." Another DDC staff member, Richard Bennertz, evaluated system use at DDC and remote sites. In his study, which took place from February through May 1970, Bennertz described the use at DDC, ODDR&E at the Pentagon in Washington, NSRDC in Maryland (the facility described by Wolfe in his earlier comparative study), the NSA in Maryland, and Redstone Arsenal in Alabama. Bennertz (1971) cited response time as an aggravating problem; he felt that the performance problems were a result of development having been "done on a crash basis [since] the resources available were minimal" (10).

Progress was made in 1970 in developing programs and technical terminology for the interface between the users' natural language and the computer's constraints (*Progress* 1971, 8–9). In May, ODC awarded a contract to Bolt, Beranek and Newman to develop an English-language retrieval inquiry system (McCauley 1972). At a 1973 conference, in the discussion period after someone else's paper, Charles Goldstein of NLM described it as a capability for both the DDC and NASA systems to convert a natural language statements into "a Boolean-structured search for a Boolean-structured database" (131). Beginning in early 1971, the system was redesigned to function efficiently as a true online system. By October, the same month that NLM began MEDLINE, the online system was operational, with 70,000 abstracts of the most current technical reports online. The complete DDC file of 700,000 bibliographic records, including the classified records, was available for searching in batch. Later, when more mass storage devices were acquired, the entire file, which continued to grow at the rate of 40,000 records a year, was searchable online. Access was restricted to searchers at DDC, the NTIS, and certain military labs and contractor facilities located around the country.

Joseph Powers (1973) of DDC noted that the prototype was operational on their UNIVAC 1108 in late 1971, with about thirty terminals. Fifteen IBM teletypewriter terminals (10 within DDC and 5 at NTIS) were used for data input of 40,000 report citations per year to the TDIS system, using the TPS software. Fourteen CRT terminals were located within DDC and around the United States at various military labs. Nine of these terminals accounted for over 42,000 online searches. Furthermore, DDC had proposed in July 1971 that the system be expanded into an operational system with 128 terminals, and that their system be a major part of the planned DDC RDT&E On-Line System, designed to provide remote online access to multiple files for input, manipulation, and retrieval of data. Fong (1971) summarized the system features as they existed in late 1971.

The volume of searching performed in the first year or so seems phenomenal compared to, for example, the number of MEDLINE searches during the same period, especially considering the restricted DDC user group. Powers reported that 42,000 online searches were done in 1970 on nine terminals; excluding weekends and holidays, each terminal at DDC averaged about thirty searches per day. Powers's definition of "search," however, was distinguished from "request." Every time a user keyed a set of terms and transmitted them, which resulted in an inverted-file search and an extraction of records from the master file for display, was counted as a search. Since searchers used the interactive system to modify their searches to satisfy specific "requests" for information, users averaged about three searches per request. Substituting the concept of "request" for "search" in the use figures yields only ten searches per terminal each day. Powers's data point up a common concern of the period in how to measure volume of online activity in a standard, realistic way.

The system was declared operational on March 31, 1972, still operating on a UNIVAC 1108. An observer noted later that in 1973, the first unclassified remote terminals were activated for training and for the first tests at the Materials and Ceramics Information Center (MCIC) at Battelle Memorial Institute. MCIC was one of the first Information Analysis Centers allowed access to the DDC system, and that was for unclassified operations only. A brief test of the DDC system and service by the NOAA/ERL library in Boulder, Colorado, in 1973 found that the average time (including mail time) for DDC report bibliographies and work unit summaries requested from DDC was seventeen working days. Phase IV, which started in the first quarter of FY 71, focused on moving the demonstration system into a more efficient production system, and expanding the network to include several other institutions. The long-range plan (Phase V) was to start in January 1974 to implement a totally new integrated online system to handle both input and retrieval processing on a secure or nonsecure basis, through a network of up to 150 terminals of various types utilizing online tutorials and displays (Bivans 1974).

In January 1973, a twenty-five-minute orientation film was released called "DDC-Your Partner in R&D." The film was made for the purpose of showing various operations inside DDC and included "shots of DDC's CRT remote installations—seldom seen by most DDC users since the units are installed in security controlled areas" (New film on DDC bibliographic services 1973). During 1972–1974, DDC assembled a team of in-house systems personnel to redesign the system; the resulting DROLS system is introduced in chapter 9.

Excerpta Medica Foundation

Warren, Vinken, and van der Walle (1969) described a database production system in operation at the Excerpta Medica Foundation (EMF) in Amsterdam to produce several printed abstract journals (e.g., *Excerpta Medica*), run an SDI service, and support a computer tape distribution service for the drug literature. The system included an extensive capability for handling biomedical terminology, including developing and maintaining an extensive subject authority file called MALIMET (Master List of Medical Indexing Terms), consisting of about 60,000 preferred terms and almost 500,000 synonyms. The system ran on in-house National Cash Register computer equipment (NCR 315-501 RMC central processor with NCR CRAM-5 random access storage units) using the Foundation's own internal software. The total system could be installed by INFONET (the Foundations's Data Processing Division) both for NCR 315 RMC and IBM 360 series equipment. The programs were "under development for an online, real-time information network and retrieval operations, employing these systems" (Warren, Vinken, and vander Valle 1969, 429).

R. R. Blanken and B. T. Stern (1975) of EMF reported on their experience with using their Mark I database and abstract bulletin production system, and their planning for a Mark II system that was expected to become operational in 1977. They noted that no true search software was written at EM until 1971, when a few searches were performed on the basis of punched paper tape input of queries. No true test of the system was possible, even though the tapes sent from Amsterdam to information centers in the United States and United Kingdom had permitted comparative studies of the EM database.

In early 1972, a terminal was installed in the EMF editorial offices to permit remote job entry of retrospective searches on the EMF internal computer system. During the first eight months of 1972, about seventy searches were run against the file of 300,000 references from their 1970–1971 editorial production. During the last four months, terminal access was also provided to the universities of Utrecht and Groningen for a user and retrieval performance study that involved about 150 retrospective searches of that database. The university activity continued into 1974.

EMF chose not to establish its own retail search service with their own computer. Instead, they made an arrangement for an American commercial firm, Informatics, in Rockville, Maryland, to provide commercial online service with the EMF database. The Informatics story, and their use of the RECON software, is told in more detail in chapter 9. EM also licensed and provided their database for internal use within interested organizations. In 1975, the file was used in an interactive online mode at Hoechst Pharmaceutical Co. in Frankfurt, Germany using STAIRS software (Blanken and Stern 1975).

Library of Congress

Bill Display System

In 1967, the LC Congressional Research Service (CRS) began using terminal keyboards to enter data for the *Digest of Public General Bills* into a remote computer (*Progress* 1968, 69). In 1969, it was using twenty-five typewriter terminals to enter this bibliographic data into its system and retrieve information online from this data entry/text editing system on the basis of subject or author (*Progress in scientific and technical communications* 1970, 103). It considered ways in which other online systems might be used to help with its task of tracking the thousands of bills presently under consideration by the U.S. Congress. CRS examined several available systems, including NASA/RECON. For various reasons, it decided in late 1970 to use an IBM product called CICS (Customer Information Control System) that was already being obtained to support IBM 1030 terminals in LC's Order Division. CRS decided to use CICS in a pilot project to develop online access for its *Bill Digest* file of about 17,000 bills, using IBM 2260 terminals. In 1971 it did implement a capability for online retrieval by Bill Number (Hamilton 1973). This system was consolidated into the SCORPIO system (chapter 9).

Allen-Babcock

VEREAD

The Allen-Babcock Computing Time Sharing Systems in 1969 included the VEREAD (Value Engineering Retrieval of Esoteric Administrative Data) system that was implemented for a group of engineers. The online record included indexed bibliographic data and searchable abstract, as well as a pointer to an accompanying copy of the source document on microfilm cartridges. With Teletype units used for terminal equipment, VEREAD allowed several users to search simultaneously (Minor 1969). We could find no further information about VEREAD.

IBM Corporation

Some of IBM's early contributions were covered in chapter 2. We continue now with some of their better-known software efforts. Most of these were intended to result in development, and sale or lease of new IBM equipment. Some were done as contract R&D by units of IBM such as the Federal Systems Division that acted as if they were independent software firms that did not have the selling or leasing of IBM equipment as a primary objective. Some of their efforts were motivated by a general research interest, or an interest in solving IBM's own internal information problems.

ATS

IBM's Administrative Terminal System (ATS) was not a complete online information storage and retrieval system. Nonetheless, as an online text input/editing system, it was an early significant component. ATS software allowed up to forty typists working at IBM 2741 terminals to time-share an in-house IBM 1440–1460 computer. Using ATS, information could be converted into machine-readable form in a more flexible manner than had been possible previously with punched card, punched paper tape, and OCR typing font systems. This approach was taken to address the problems of building large machine-readable files in a flexible, cost-effective manner. Other work was going on in the early 1960s to develop software and input systems for computer-controlled photocomposition equipment, including work at ACS on a computer typesetting system for producing some ACS journals from keyed textual input. IBM produced and contributed text processing and typesetting programs at that time to run on its own equipment. A review of new hardware developments described ATS (Annual Review Staff 1966, 195): "This ATS concept presents a serious alternative for the two basic methods of source data automation: keystroking from already typed text and automatic character reading of typed or printed text. If the material must be typed once, why not capture it in machine readable form at the outset? This concept is obviously not novel; however, the ATS configuration offers promise of a means for implementing it quite effectively with equipment that is operational and available."

Although not yet fully developed, ATS had a functional beginning in 1964, and operated at IBM's Systems Development Division Library at Poughkeepsie, New York for acquisitions and cataloging functions, including index creation and 3×5-inch card printing. It was designed for other applications as well, such as library circulation and announcement bulletin preparation, abstract and text writing and editing, communications, and statistical record keeping (Holzbauer and Farris 1966; Bateman and Farris 1968). ATS was used in the Los Gatos Laboratory of IBM's Advanced Systems Development Division in 1965 for input conversion of bibliographic records for the library (Phillips 1966). As mentioned earlier, an ATS system was installed for bibliographic database building at the DDC in late 1966.

ATS was used for a number of other applications outside the IBM Library. For example, in 1971 the Western Kentucky University Library used it in the conversion of a collection of 250,000 volumes from Dewey Decimal to LC Classification. The project took seven months instead of the estimated five years that manual conversion would have taken. The data keyed in using ATS were used to produce new catalog cards, Hollerith book cards, pockets, labels, bibliographies, and catalogs. The machine-readable cataloging data thus produced were incorporated into a real-time circulation system (Chen 1973). ATS was still being used in library work in the 1970s (Briner 1973). The LC Congressional Research Service used it in 1971–1972 for their bill digest publication and information activities; LC was reportedly the first government agency to install an in-house ATS system (Clark 1973a, b). It was also used in 1971–1972 for full-text file building on the QUIC/LAW project (chapter 9) at Queen's University in Ontario, Canada (Lawford 1973).

IBM established and operated a service bureau, DATATEXT, that used ATS-like software for online file building and maintenance from remote terminals. SUNY-Buffalo used DATATEXT in 1967 to keyboard its catalog card data. SUNY-Buffalo keyed the data on an IBM 2741 terminal in Syracuse and transmitted it via a leased line to an IBM 1460 computer at the DATATEXT facilities in Cleveland and New York City. It received tapes of the keyboarded data in return. Early in 1968 this successful test project was succeeded by an on-campus ATS/360 system that ran on an IBM 360/40 in the computer center, with seven library typists converting shelf list cards online (Pizer 1967; Lazorick 1969). It was also used for bibliographic file work at the City University of New York during their Urbandoc Project (Sessions and Sloan 1971), and by the State of New York for publishing opinions of all New York State courts and rules and regulations of all state departments (Flavin 1973). As noted in chapter 3, DATATEXT was used with LEADER at Lehigh University. ATS continued to be used into the 1990s.

Combined File Search System

The Combined File Search System (CFS or CFSS) was a package of batch programs developed in 1963–1964 and distributed in 1965 by IBM for their 1401 computers, and later used on their 360 computers in a 1401 emulation mode (Warheit 1965). Al Warheit, at IBM's San Jose facility, was most responsible for design and development of this software. For his CFSS work, he received IBM's Outstanding Achievement Award. Warheit had joined IBM as a senior systems analyst in 1959 after serving eighteen years as a special librarian at General Motors, Argonne National Laboratory, and the AEC. Warheit exemplified the IBM practice of drawing individuals with extensive practical experience into system development.

CFSS was developed originally for use at the U.S. Food and Drug Administration as a retrieval system for published technical information associated with adverse drug reactions and new drug applications (*Progress* 1970, 46–48). CFSS had capabilities for thesaurus development, file maintenance, and file searching. Service Bureau Corporation contributed the basic system to the IBM Program Library; it was not an IBM-supported set of programs (i.e., IBM had no maintenance commitment for this system). The programs were later modified and made available in 1968 to run on an IBM 360 computer (*The combined file search* 1968a, b, c).

The American Society for Metals (ASM) in a joint effort with *Engineering Index*, and in conjunction with IBM and Battelle Memorial Institute, used CFSS for their batch IR service and index publishing system in 1965 (Hyslop 1966; Vitagliano 1965; Carter, Shaffer, and DeWitt 1965). The ASM effort encouraged IBM to make several significant changes to CFSS, to work with ASM staff to design a retrieval package for the IBM 360, and to earmark substantial funding in its forthcoming annual budgets for related research (Shepherd 1965). IBM staff members who participated in the joint project included Warheit, Steven Furth, and Eugene Jackson. Freeman and Atherton used CFSS in 1967–1968 at the AIP for experiments in UDC searching (chapter 3) (Freeman 1995). Several information centers in the United States used CFSS also, including the Diamond Alkali Company for SDI service on Engineering Index tapes (Whaley and Wainio 1967), General Aniline and Film Corp. for batch searching of a collection of internal company reports (Starke et al. 1968), and City University of New York for Project Urbandoc—as an integrated group of programs that could all be run on an IBM 1401 (Sessions and Sloan 1971). We found no evidence that CFSS was ever used in an online mode—we include it here to show IBM's early experience and development in retrieval software.

Generalized Information System

Based on experience gained with military file applications and IBM's Formatted File System (FFS), members of IBM's Data Processing Division and Federal Systems Division developed Generalized Information System (GIS) (Damerau 1997). FFS had been a batch general-purpose data management system for the IBM 1410 coupled to the 1410/7010 Operating System (Minker and Sable 1967). IBM developed FFS for the U.S. Defense Intelligence Agency (DIA), based on an online system developed by the U.S. Navy. IBM developed GIS for use as a database management system and intended to provide it as part of its applications library for the 360 series of computers. GIS was given widespread visibility in 1965 and 1966 prior to its planned April 1967 availability date (Bryant and Semple 1966). It was still under development in late 1967, however, and slippages retarded its implementation for over three years (Ziehe 1967).

GIS consisted of a set of general purpose file processing programs to run in either batch or online mode on the IBM 360. GIS had basic modules for establishing, maintaining, and searching files of formatted data, and organizing, summarizing, and presenting output information. It had a capability to do text processing, synonym inclusion, and weighted term retrieval (Giering 1967b). The Document Processing System part of this set (described shortly) was made available as a field release in December 1967, as a software product separate from GIS (Sundeen 1968). IBM staff at Gaithersburg, Maryland, in conjunction with development of the initial SUNY BCN system described in chapter 8, simulated various types of searches using GIS for the software package that was being developed there (Pizer 1967).

Time Inc. Experiment

In 1966–1967 IBM and Time Inc. jointly conducted a study of full-text searching of news stories for a reference library of a news magazine. The study was done with batch searching of a file of the most recent twenty months of stories (5,000 stories, 4 million English words, 24 million characters), and 3,700 test queries that were copies of real questions received at Time Inc.'s library. IBM had had experience with full-text searching since the early 1960s, including working with the University of Pittsburgh Health Law Center's legal text search system, the Air Force's LITE legal text search system (both in chapter 7), and a system for IBM's in-house ITIRC service. The batch search system used was one of a kind, put together at IBM's Research Center at Yorktown Heights for the experiment. It incorporated word root indexes and word proximity searching. Recall and relevance judgements were made, and full-text search performance in this setting was measured (Haibt et al. 1967).

Study participants acknowledged (Haibt et al. 1967, 129) that any operational system of this type needed to operate in an online manner, and have an inquiry console providing rapid response to queries: "No such system was available at the time of the study, so an off-line system was used to give retrieval results identical to those of the proposed system. The off-line system processed queries in large batches, rather than serially, and did not attempt to give immediate response to a single query. However, the phrasing of queries and interpretation of output was done with a console system in mind." This large-scale study was thus a simulation of certain aspects of an online search system. In a May 1967 presentation of the results, Haibt and his colleagues noted, "We have since implemented a console-oriented full-text search system and it does give response times to typical queries in one-half to three minutes" (129). That online system had a complete inverted file for the text material.

Luther Haibt is the IBM staff member usually mentioned in association with this project. Margaret ("Peggy") Fischer, who earlier worked as a journalist at Time-Life (among the first female sports journalists, writing for *Sports Illustrated*), was serving as manager of the Information Processing Department at Time Inc. at the time of the study, in charge of creating a computer typesetting programs, and one of the earliest information brokerages. She continued to stay involved in information technology work for R. R. Bowker, and consulting and technical reporting for several organizations, and in professional society activities such as president of ASIS in 1977.

Document Processing System

Document Processing System (usually shortened to either DOC PROC or DPS) was a proprietary IBM software package originally meant to be a module of IBM's GIS software. It was designed for use with IBM 360 computers (Model 40 or larger) with disk files as the normal storage mode (Sundeen 1968). DPS was several years in development at IBM's Poughkeepsie facility, for internal use—primarily for the library. Al Merritt and Wally Brooks were most responsible for developing DPS. They were later active in getting STAIRS software installed in all IBM libraries (Magnino 1997). DPS was first made available as an IBM product in November 1967 (Giering 1967a; *IBM system 360*, 1967; Furth 1968). The DPS program started as a batch package for loading and updating files, generating index or concordance products, file searching, and various file maintenance tasks. Nevertheless, SDI processing was its prime function. The full-text capability was not fully developed in DPS; subject searching was done on assigned index terms and codes, and the abstract was carried along only for use as output (Magnino 1997).

DPS was used in the SUNY BCN system from 1967–1973 for their online MEDLARS service (see chapter 8). DPS was "supported for operation in the batch mode, although one installation, the Bio-Medical Center of the State University of New York (SUNY), has developed a special monitor that uses nine remote on-line consoles" (Berul 1969, 220). McCarn (1987) recalled that the early SUNY operation was essentially a remote job entry system; job cards were put into a card reader terminal, and the batch search run while a user waited at the terminal. It was not interactive: "It was a clumsy, awkward, difficult system—but it worked."

Starting in 1969, Pauline Atherton and her colleagues used DPS in a batch mode for instructional and research purposes at Syracuse University. They had been using other software (MOLDS, chapter 3), but switched when "the first efficient retrieval system, DPS, became available... during the Spring 1969 term" (Atherton and Tessier 1970). Atherton, Cook, and Katzer obtained their copy of DPS from Irwin Pizer at SUNY BCN, using it in 1970–1971 for full-text searching of Psychological Abstracts as part of their SUPARS project (Trump 1971). They modified it so that the original batch-mode processor of DPS could be made interactive. Their most complex software problem was developing a separate monitor program, and a special teleprocessing program that enabled the operating system to interface with IBM-2741 consoles while various online systems were operating concurrently.

IBM staff modified DPS in 1970 at their Cambridge, Massachusetts, facility as part of their INTIME time-shared text processing system on an IBM 360/67 for use in an online search mode (Goldfarb, Mosher, and Peterson 1970). In a report for NLM, Seiden (1970, 40) described DPS as "primarily a remote batch system with limited on-line capability to be expanded in March or April, 1970." The original DPS program allowed a user to build a file (the synonym/equivalent set) of words selected by the user or operator, to be used in addition to, or instead of dictionary words, in order to expand text searches. When these original batch programs were converted to online operation in 1970, this became an online feature.

In 1970, DPS was used in an online mode at the National Institute of Mental Health, in an implementation that permitted using communication terminals or CRT display devices. It was also used at the National Clearinghouse for Drug Abuse Information (*Progress* 1971, 15). Rae (1970) described his case study of operational problems in using the online DPS system at the Parkinson Information Center in 1970. DPS was used at WPAFB in 1973 for file building and text searching in the CIRCOL system introduced in chapter 6. Because DPS was designed mainly for batch operation, online multi-user access to CIRCOL/DPS was made possible only through a hybrid system that combined the teleprocessor executive program with the DPS retrieval system. In order to save index storage space, the index building programs deleted words shorter than a user-specified length, truncated words exceeding a user-specified length, and deleted words in the text that were on a user-specified "common word" list. The terms that passed this initial screening process were then passed against an authority file (dictionary) of terms previously determined to be acceptable to the system. Again, at a user's option, new words could be printed out for review by the system lexicographer. The DPS system, operating in an online mode with CIRCOL, included word proximity searching (i.e., word order, same sentence context, same paragraph context), stem (right-truncation) searching, and an automatic depluralization feature that treated plurals and singular forms as exact equivalents. With DPS, the entire search formulation had to be entered before searching could begin. Thus the line-by-line posting counts could not provide useful feedback during the course of the search. Nevertheless, one light-hearted touch was the system response, "GOIN' SEARCHIN" upon receipt of a search statement. Online operation of DPS was made obsolete in 1973 by the STAIRS software described later.

QUIC/LAW and INFORM/360

IBM obtained an understanding of user problems, and had an opportunity to test their equipment and software, by means of cooperative projects in which they worked with their customers in jointly exploring solutions to a problem of mutual interest. IBM typically contributed equipment and software and assigned IBM staff to the project, all at no cost to the customer. An example of such an experiment was the QUIC/LAW project from 1968–1969 at Queen's University (chapter 9). The law school provided legal expertise, all overhead costs, and use of the university's computer. IBM Canada, Ltd. provided computer equipment, analysts, programmers, and access to certain unreleased computer programs which had been developed for IBM's internal use. IBM support provided about twenty percent of total project expenses. This was all to provide support for early research on legal computing (Lawford 1973).

For the QUIC/LAW project, IBM made available a series of unreleased programs comprising a search system known as INFORM/360. In the opinion of Fay (1971, 169): "As initially constituted, the INFORM/360 system was not completely developed and had many disadvantages. Lawford's work was largely that of modifying and improving the system to overcome these shortcomings. One of the major advantages to the user of the system is the ability to communicate in conversational English instead of a complicated language of codes." The search strategy was based on statistical probability rather than Boolean logic, using term weights assigned at the time of file loading. This allowed the system to use the weights for relevance ranking of the search output records.

TEXT-PAC and Terminal TEXT-PAC

As described in chapter 2, IBM's corporate staff office, working through the IBM Technical Information Retrieval Center (ITIRC), was the major force within IBM for driving the development of a full-text search capability. This was true for the TEXT-PAC, Terminal TEXT-PAC, and AQUARIUS/STAIRS software, regardless of where within IBM the work was actually done. TEXT-PAC was one of those full-text systems. It was developed at IBM corporate headquarters in Yorktown Heights, New York, and then in Armonk, New York, under the management of Joseph Magnino and technical leadership of Sam Kaufman (1969). Two of the principal programmers (Steve Skye and Stan Friedman), who developed the expanded search logic for TEXT-PAC, were also key in developing the STAIRS search and logic capabilities.

Kaufman had earned a Ph.D. at the University of Michigan, but he said (1997) that an important factor in his being hired by Magnino was the fact that while he was working on a BS in commercial chemistry at Penn State, he had taken a course in chemical bibliography. With several years of experience in full-text processing and searching, the development and operational use of the PRIME software, and availability of the IBM 360 computer, Kaufman sensed an opportunity to design a completely new information system. It was to be called TEXT-PAC, a name Magnino chose to represent TEXT PACKAGE. Kaufman's design philosophy was that all data about each word would be captured during the first input processing program in order to avoid scanning text again in later programs. As he (1997) described it: "This information included: document ID; paragraph ID; sentence number; word length; U/L case indicator; line number; relative position of word from start of text; end of sentence; and word number in line. This information made it possible to greatly expand the PRIME search logic. Searches could be limited to a particular paragraph (ex: author), a single sentence (WITH Logic), case, root logic, masking, AND, OR, Adjacent (string), Absolute, and Negative." The data stored with each word included an indication of leading and trailing punctuation, and no "common words" were eliminated. Kaufman (1998) revealed that one reason for TEXT-PAC's rapid search capability was the fact that each record was in essence an inverted file per document: "A search record contained, in addition to the document ID: the document text minus punctuation; an inverted file with alphabetic and word position indicators arranged by word length, referencing the document text; and finally, the document in normal text printable format. This made processing multiple queries against a data base very efficient."

For retrospective searching, the batch TEXT-PAC programs could search over 125 questions during the same run. In regular operational use, searches were run daily at ITIRC, averaging 40–50 questions per day against a file of about 150,000 documents, with a turnaround time of twenty-four hours. TEXT-PAC included an input edit program to find and report up to fifteen different types of formatting or data entry errors; it could also store a dictionary or authority list (i.e., a spell checker) to flag and report any new words encountered in the input text.

One TEXT-PAC print output program used a format called Condensed Text which had a simpler record format than the full TEXT-PAC format. Engineering Index, Inc., used this simplified format for preparing distribution tapes for COMPENDEX. AIP used it for third-party use of SPIN tapes with TEXT-PAC software. ITIRC and University of Pittsburgh ran their own conversion programs to reformat CAS tapes into TEXT-PAC tapes (Grunstra and Johnson 1970).

Work started on the actual development of TEXT-PAC in 1965 after the Current Information Selection capability was incorporated into the PRIME retrospective search program and made publicly available (see chapter 2). TEXT-PAC programming was completed, and the system declared operational in 1967, with a second copy of the software installed and operational at IBM's facility in La Goude, France (Kaufman 1998). TEXT-PAC was developed initially to be used for batch rather than online searching, and it was used extensively at ITIRC. TEXT-PAC went into experimental operation at ITIRC in mid-1968, went into IBM's Program Information Department in December 1968 for public distribution, and was first described in the technical literature by Kaufman in October 1969.

Kaufman made a point to ensure data compatibility between the various ITIRC search systems (PRIME, TEXT-PAC, and STAIRS). Historical data from PRIME-1 and -2, such as a backfile of more than 100,000 documents, could be processed by a TEXT-PAC data entry program and then by STAIRS search software (described later in this section); all data captured by TEXT-PAC were compatible with STAIRS and were used as input to STAIRS without alteration; TEXT-PAC was in fact the primary data capture program for STAIRS. Even in 1972, IBM representatives were suggesting TEXT-PAC programs to prepare input to STAIRS file creation and maintenance modules that were still operating in batch mode (Furth 1973).

In late 1967, DOJ, as part of its in-house review of possible antitrust activity by IBM, requested a significant number of internal documents from forty selected IBM executives. IBM chose to coordinate the release of these documents through an external law firm, Craveth, Swain and Moore (CS&M). Magnino became involved because of his responsibility for a Litigation Processing Services Department and a Special Application Programming Department, in addition to his ITIRC responsibility. The upgraded PRIME and the early TEXT-PAC software were used to support this DOJ data collection activity.

The filing of an antitrust complaint and private lawsuit by Control Data Corp. against IBM in December 1968 triggered significant further development of IBM database management and retrieval software. The CDC suit charged IBM with monopoly of the general purpose digital computer market, and further alleged that IBM had monopolized by means of a long list of exclusionary marketing practices, any of which would constitute a huge lawsuit in itself. At that point, IBM authorized the establishment of a major litigation support activity under Nicholas Katzenbach, former U.S. attorney general (1965–1966) under President Lyndon Johnson. In order to handle the anticipated large document discovery effort, an operations support group was established. ITIRC was split into two groups, ITIRC and Litigation Support. Starting with the small group that had worked on the DOJ effort, and with organizational changes, a Litigation Analysis unit was well established by mid-1969, and additional resources were provided to speed up development of improved retrieval and file management software. Magnino's Litigation Processing group worked in support of the Litigation Analysis unit. Several weeks later, in January 1969, Data Processing Financial and General (DPF&G), a computer leasing company, also filed an antitrust complaint against IBM. Another two weeks later, on the last workday of the Johnson administration, DOJ filed its antitrust complaint against IBM, alleging monopoly of the industry and wrongful policies restraining competition. These suits were followed in short order by three more suits against IBM in 1969, and several new suits for each of several years after that.

TEXT-PAC was used for IBM's in-house litigation support activity to construct and search an index to 25 million pages of text to counter the CDC suit that was active in 1968–1973, with 3,400 outside organizations required by court order to furnish confidential market data to define the size of the computer market. TEXT-PAC was used because it was the only system, initially, that permitted upper/lowercase text processing. The CDC suit was settled out of court in 1973 with a $101 million cash and contract payment to CDC, along with sale of the IBM Service Bureau Corp. to CDC for about $16 million and an agreement that IBM withdraw from the "data services" business in the United States, for a period of six years. The DOJ suit continued through 1981 and was associated with IBM's next generation online search system, STAIRS, described later.

TEXT-PAC was available for free and widely used. It was first made publicly available in early 1969, and by April 1970, there had already been more than 240 requests for the program documentation, and sixty requests for the program tape (Kaufman 1970). ASIDIC formed a TEXT-PAC users group in 1972. The program was known to be operating in a variety of types of institutions in the United States, Europe, Australia, and Canada (Kaufman 1997). IBM widely promoted TEXT-PAC use outside of IBM for IR applications (*Searching normal text* 1970). As a consequence, many special libraries outside of IBM used it for SDI and batch searching (Grunstra and Johnson 1970; Standera 1970, 1971; Katajapuro 1971). Susan Artandi and Leny Struminger (1971) reported using TEXT-PAC at the Rutgers University Graduate School of Library Science as a teaching tool.

Within IBM, the databases being used by ITIRC were growing rapidly; they were amounting to so many reels of tape that they started to be a burden and a source of delay in the computer rooms. It was recognized that an interactive system would not only be faster and ease ITIRC's burden, it would also allow access by all IBM libraries to all databases. This led to the work on what became Terminal TEXT-PAC (Kaufman 1997). Kaufman (1969) recognized the push toward development of terminal-oriented information systems and noted that they depended on having most of the data about each word available for structuring an inverted file. TEXT-PAC captured all of the data about each word as it was entered into the system. Therefore, those databases that were already using TEXT-PAC did not have to recapture the input data in order to convert to a terminal system.

An online version of TEXT-PAC, developed by an ITIRC programming group, including some who had worked on TEXT-PAC, was tested and successfully demonstrated in Germany in 1969 as Terminal TEXT-PAC. The prototype Terminal TEXT-PAC ran under the IBM Interactive Applications Supervisor (IAS) and also had access to the INFORM programs as a subsystem for the SAVE and PURGE commands. It could use either IBM 2260 or IBM 2741 terminals. It used databases prepared by TEXT-PAC software (Kaufman 1998). Nonetheless, Terminal TEXT-PAC did not replace TEXT-PAC; for IBM its deficiency was the limit on the number of terminals (17) it could support simultaneously (Kaufman 1997).

1969 Milestone

Terminal TEXT-PAC was among the first online search systems to demonstrate word proximity searching (i.e., allowing word sequence and proximity to be part of the search formulation).

Terminal TEXT-PAC and the later STAIRS system demonstrated a pioneering online text search capability. Using word proximity searching, users could find a word within the text, find words within the same sentence (using WITH logic), regardless of their order or position, and find contiguous words within the same sentence (using ADJ logic). They also could limit the text search to specific fields (e.g., author or title). This capability did not include a means for a more global proximity searching (TERM A within N words of TERM B), or a means to consider the proximity beyond the sentence boundary to a larger boundary (TERM A within the same paragraph as TERM B). As related in chapter 7, the Data Corporation also demonstrated word proximity searching, but with the additional more powerful capability of finding TERM A within N words of TERM B. IBM and Data Corporation developers were unaware of each others' work at that time. The SRI online search system (see chapter 2) had demonstrated simple word pair or adjacent word searching in 1963 by simple character string searching, and its designers then had proposed a form of proximity searching (2 search terms within the same sentence) but had never implemented it.

1969 Milestone

Terminal TEXT-PAC was the first online search system to allow the inclusion, and meaningful use, of upper- and lowercase information in the search formulation.

Users of TEXT-PAC batch-mode software could enter search terms in either upper- or lowercase. A searcher could specify a that a retrieval be made only when the first letter was capitalized (for example, to differentiate the personal name "Carpenter" from the noun "carpenter"), or require that all letters be capitalized ("STAIRS" versus "stairs," "NOW" versus "now" versus "Now"), or specify mixed case matches—for example, "pH" (Hines 1975). Such a capability was not seen in any online system before the Terminal TEXT-PAC system in 1969, and STAIRS in 1970. Because it was the only available system that permitted upper and lower case text processing, Terminal TEXT-PAC was used within IBM in 1969 for the litigation support described in the next section, and for later internal testing of STAIRS.

Kaufman and Magnino authored a patent filed in December 1964 and issued in October 1967 to protect some of the concepts in PRIME, TEXT-PAC, and Terminal TEXT-PAC. The patent was never contested or licensed. As mentioned earlier, IBM's Litigation Processing Services Department in 1969 took a larger role in supporting development of ITIRC online programs after DOJ filed an antitrust suit against IBM. With IBM's recently announced CICS (Customer Information Control System), the ITIRC programming group was then able to get support to design what became AQUARIUS, an online search system described in the next section. After AQUARIUS testing moved along successfully, Terminal TEXT-PAC was phased out in November 1970. Terminal TEXT-PAC was intended to be a temporary system until AQUARIUS was operational (Kaufman 1997, 1998).

In 1971, the Washington State legislative offices were still using Terminal TEXT-PAC to support Washington's Legislative Information System for such tasks as bill drafting and codification and filing of administrative rules and regulations. The Statute Law Committee that performed this function operated a dedicated IBM 370/145 computer with IBM 3330 disk drives, and a total of thirty-two typewriter and CRT terminals. The terminals were used for online searching of statute texts, including Washington State Supreme Court reports (White 1973).

Kaufman did not participate directly in any other IBM search systems. He remained absorbed in his responsibility for the TEXT-PAC programs as used by external users and within IBM, including designing modifications for special IBM internal uses (for example, patent documents). He also wrote conversion programs to meet the PRIME and TEXT-PAC interface formats when ITIRC began obtaining external databases (e.g., COMPENDEX, SPIN) for its own internal use. He coauthored the publication that covered everything required to operate the thirty programs in the TEXT-PAC software system (Esposito et al. 1968).

AQUARIUS and STAIRS

As we noted earlier, internal financial support for the DOJ work expedited the solution of IBM's own real-time text retrieval problems, and further development of online search capability. When DOJ formally filed an antitrust suit against IBM in January 1969, IBM corporate staff recognized that massive amounts of material (later reported to be equivalent to a stack of documents the height of the Empire State Building) would be required for litigation defense. Magnino and Kaufman quickly drafted a proposal to build an online retrieval system employing a network of display terminals to support IBM's defense. In summer 1969, they were given approval to build a prototype. The proposed system was named AQUARIUS (A Query and Retrieval Interactive User System). By that time, they had had online experience with Terminal TEXT-PAC, the powerful IBM 360 computer, and networks of IBM 2260 display terminals. The Silent 600 portable printing terminals of Texas Instruments (TI) were becoming commonplace, and IBM had recently announced the first release of the Customer Information Control System (CICS) that supported high-volume transaction processing (Skye 1990).

From the beginning, AQUARIUS was planned as a new and evolutionary system to be eventually an IBM program product for release to the public. A prime emphasis was to provide a multi-user online terminal capability—an absolute requirement for (1) support of the forty IBM libraries (Terminal TEXT-PAC supported about 17 simultaneous terminals); (2) support for IBM managers and the IBM Suggestion Plan Department to permit plants and divisions to have online access; and (3) the in-house cooperative work and DOJ antitrust work of the IBM Legal Department. AQUARIUS was intended to provide file development/maintenance support as well as an IR capability for IBM Model 360 or 370 computers. It was developed as a total system for file creation and maintenance, as well as

IR and document delivery of unformatted text or formatted data.

As mentioned earlier, the filing of the Federal antitrust suit was followed by several private anti-trust suits against IBM, including ones by Greyhound Computer Leasing Corp. in 1969, Telex in 1972, five more suits in 1973, two more in 1974, and one in 1975. IBM used AQUARIUS for the Greyhound suit that went to trial in 1972 and finally was resolved out of court in 1981. When AQUARIUS was used for litigation support, it required a large amount of computer storage capacity, a requirement that was met with disk storage units and Kalvar film storage technology with IBM's WALNUT system. After a few years, WALNUT storage was no longer used because disk storage gained in ease of use, improved speed, and lower cost.

The telecommunications part of AQUARIUS that controlled the files and terminals was another IBM program called CICS mentioned several times earlier (Furth 1972). CICS not only supported the terminal and online functions of AQUARIUS, but also acted as an interface for other terminal applications.

Development was done at IBM corporate headquarters in Yorktown Heights and then in Armonk. The persons most responsible were Steve Skye, Stan Friedman, and Cathy Harlin. Magnino was the person credited with getting approval of the project. The team was divided into a number of smaller implementation teams, and they designed and built a library of about forty modular programs. The design of a new online system required consideration of new issues for the experienced IBM team (query and command syntax, screen design, help functions, file and index browsing, online sorting, user registration and authorization). Remarkably, they were able to deliver a system and be operating in full production mode in 1970, ready for the DOJ suit. All necessary AQUARIUS programming was completed in August 1970 (Kaufman 1998). ITIRC started using AQUARIUS in 1970 for its regular retrospective search service, but continued to use TEXT-PAC for its internal SDI service.

AQUARIUS was soon installed in all IBM libraries as part of a corporate policy to decentralize some of their library services.

In 1969, after reviewing many IBM systems and its own planned development, IBM Germany selected AQUARIUS to make a program product. The company terminated its own development and assigned a team to study and document AQUARIUS, with assistance from the ITIRC team, with the objective of having it announced as a program product in 1971. This German connection was helpful in speeding up the public release date of this new product (Kaufman 1997).

Public use of the name AQUARIUS created a copyright problem, and so it was changed to STAIRS (Storage and Information Retrieval System) when the program was offered to IBM customers as a formal product in 1970. This was only a name change, not a different system.

1969 Milestone

STAIRS may have been the first online search system to provide a significant online tutorial/help capability.

Given the time constraints of getting the litigation defense underway, the design team realized that extensive user education was not possible. Therefore they built in a tutorial and help feature. A user could call it up by simply entering a question mark or typing HELP. Depending on the context in which the command was entered, an appropriate screen was displayed.

STAIRS was designed specifically for a multi-user time-sharing environment. It was written for IBM 360 computers, using disk storage to obtain rapid access times. STAIRS provided line-by-line retrievals with posting counts, as the search statements were entered; unlike DPS it did not require that an entire search formulation be entered in full before the search started. STAIRS also labeled each search line with a number (as DIALOG had done several years earlier) so that selected parts of a search formulation could be incorporated into later steps.

The STAIRS software included features seen on only a few previous systems, including SAVE, a way to store a query for searching of other databases or for an SDI profile (Furth 1972). The software also had a multifile search capability, so that up to sixteen different files could be linked and searched by a single query, without having to reenter the query. Another useful feature was the inclusion of a "user-built" synonym list, and a synonym operator so that if a term was requested and had synonyms listed, they were searched automatically. The synonym feature had been used earlier in the 1965 TEXTIR and 1968 SUNY BCN systems, but the user-built aspect was a new variation. Another major advance for IBM software was a capability of searching phrases instead of single words. Using the adjacency operator (ADJ), a searcher could define a string of words as constituting a phrase to be searched.

Finally, STAIRS provided a capability of ranking search results according to a calculated relevancy score. The score was based on the number of occurrences of search terms in the source record and their proximity to each other. After a search was completed, retrieved records could be, at the searcher's option, sorted into order by their relevancy score before presentation to the searcher. This feature was particularly useful when the number of retrieved records was large. Output ranking by a relevance score had been done previously in online search systems, starting with TEXTIR in 1964.

The STAIRS software was used extensively worldwide, including in-house searching of large bibliographic databases such as COMPENDEX. ITIRC itself was the first regular American STAIRS user, starting in 1970 for in-house files. As it was not yet cost-effective to store large files online, STAIRS was sometimes used online just to test search formulations on small sample files before they were applied to larger files on batch search systems. BioSciences Information Service (BIOSIS) did this in 1975, testing search formulations on its own database for both its retrospective search and SDI service. In 1975, BIOSIS asked the North Carolina Science and Technology Research Center (NC/STRC) to evaluate STAIRS for it. NC/STRC did this in the course of doing one hundred online literature searches for its clients from April 1975 through March 1976, using an IBM-3275 terminal in North Carolina that was connected by a leased line to the BIOSIS computer in Philadelphia. STAIRS proved to be a flexible and easy-to-use search system (Nees and Green 1977). The International Atomic Energy Authority (IAEA) used STAIRS from 1975 for their own INIS database (Romanenko and Todeschini 1980) and IAEA used it to process data for the AGRIS file. Hoechst Pharmaceutical Co. in Frankfurt, Germany, used STAIRS for an in-house online system (Blanken and Stern 1975).

In 1972–1973, STAIRS was considered for use for CIRCOL (chapter 6). In the review, STAIRS received high marks in comparison to the DPS system then being used. A pilot trial run with a file of 24,000 records, however, showed STAIRS to have slow response times (on the order of five minutes for searches with heavily posted terms) by then current standards (Scheffler 1974). In 1973, Suzanne Humphrey, an NLM staff member, compared STAIRS software with NLM's ELHILL-2 software with respect to searching the MEDLARS citation file, and updated the comparison in 1975 with the ELHILL-3 software (Humphrey 1974, 1976). Martin (1974) reported on a more comprehensive comparative analysis of STAIRS and ten other online search system at an NSF-funded workshop at Stanford University in April 1973.

STAIRS was also used as the basis for several online services. SUNY BCN, for example, switched from DPS to STAIRS software for its operation from March 1973 until BCN ceased operation in May 1977; SUNY BCN modified the software, and changed the name from IBM STAIRS to SUNY/STAIRS (Durkin and Egeland 1974). From 1977, BRS used IBM STAIRS software, changing the name to BRS STAIRS. Lloyd Palmer wrote BRS STAIRS as new software, including features from IBM STAIRS and adding enhancements plus improved operating performances and efficiencies. BRS installed many copies of BRS STAIRS software throughout the world, which became an important revenue stream for the new company. The BCN and BRS stories are continued in chapters 8 and 9.

As we have seen, the DOJ antitrust suit filed against IBM in January 1969 triggered the STAIRS development. The trial finally began in May 1975 and lasted for six years before the U.S. government dropped the case in 1982, asserting that it had been without merit! For the trial, Magnino and Kaufman convinced IBM lawyers and CS&M (IBM's outside counsel) to put the full text of thousands of IBM and government documents into a database using TEXT-PAC input programs and to use STAIRS as the online search system during the discovery and trial phases. After the trial, CS&M stated that the firm would never go to trial again without this capability (Magnino 1997). One of the market niches that IBM had targeted for STAIRS was large-scale litigation support, and STAIRS was still being developed and used several years later for such situations. Blair (1996) reported one such application to a large full-text file (40,000 documents, 350,000 pages of text) in an unidentified case. He noted that some IBM lawyers stated that a reason for IBM's victory in a large and lengthy lawsuit was their use of STAIRS to manage the data. However, Blair and Maron's evaluation (1985) of STAIRS recall/relevance performance demonstrated that performance in online searching of unindexed full text was far below anyone's expectations.

In 1977, IBM promoted an advanced feature for STAIRS called STAIRS/TLS. TLS stood for Thesaurus and Linguistic Integrated System, and it extended the retrieval capability by providing an online thesaurus capability. STAIRS/TLS had been implemented by that time in several installations (Semturs 1978). In 1994, IBM announced that it was discontinuing its support of STAIRS.

BROWSER

In September 1971, John Williams began his announcement of a new online retrieval system with this declaration: "Many machine retrieval systems have reached a plateau of effectiveness" (1971a, 7). A year later, Phyllis Richmond (1972, 91) reacted drily, "a most interesting observation considering that few of them has even begun to touch the volume of subject matter encountered daily in manual systems." However, Williams had continued to say, "a fervent hope exists that interactive systems providing the searcher with feedback will increase effectiveness in those systems having reached a plateau" (1971a, 7). He went on to describe an online system that offered relevance feedback that had been in development since 1968. The system, called BROWSER (Browsing On-Line with Selective Retrieval), was implemented on an IBM 360 with IBM 2260 display terminals. ONR and IBM jointly supported the development.

Williams's background for the BROWSER assignment included developing and testing statistical techniques for automatic classification of documents at the IBM Federal Systems Division in Bethesda, Maryland, and working at IBM with ONR contract research support on discovering and developing techniques for automatically indexing and classifying documents. IBM staff already had experience with computer searching of patent literature. A. J. Riddles (1969), manager of IBM's Patent Operations, described the use of PRIME in 1964 for full-text searching of a file of 60,000 claims associated with over 4,800 transistor circuit patents. The file of twelve reels of magnetic tape required about an hour to search on an IBM 7090/1401 computer.

Williams and Matthew Perriens of the IBM Federal Systems Division at Gaithersburg, Maryland designed BROWSER in response to a request from the IBM International Patent Operations Department to develop and test a system that met, among others, these requirements: (1) a patent attorney should be able to formulate queries in the language normally used in writing to other patent attorneys, without the assistance of an intermediary; (2) the system ranks abstracts so that those directly matching a portion of the query may be reviewed first; (3) the system provides for searching on date, inventor, and company; and (4) the system is capable of handling abstracts written in English, French or German (Williams 1969; Williams and Perriens 1968).

To accomplish the first requirement, the database was formed with abstracts rather than formal index terms, because the natural language of abstracts provided many synonyms for the concepts of the original document. BROWSER searched on selected terms from abstracts. The last requirement, to create a system that was independent of the language of the file materials, influenced the decision not to structure BROWSER on syntax or parsing routines, or even positional indicators showing word co-occurrence in paragraphs or sentences. Since early tests indicated that the quality of retrieval was good even without phrase searching, the increased storage requirements and search time could not be economically justified.

The prototype BROWSER was used experimentally with databases of 25,000 German and 9,000 English patent abstracts, 8,000 U.S. DDC abstracts, and 1,600 abstracts from the Navy Automated Research and Development Information System (NARDIS). In 1971, BROWSER worked with 50,000 electrical engineering abstracts in German (Fay 1971). BROWSER was used also in the Patent Department of IBM Germany at Sindelfingen with a database of 100,000 patent abstracts in English and German.

The overall goal of BROWSER was to improve performance in the difficult area of patent searching, where a single missed hit could be disastrous; total recall was a primary concern. These requirements biased the BROWSER design toward high recall—that is, minimizing the number of misses rather than minimizing false hits. Williams felt that Boolean two-valued logic had limited usefulness, mainly for minimizing false hits. To minimize the number of misses, he wanted a more subtle match of degrees of relevance instead of a simple yes-no decision. Each abstract in a BROWSER file was scored with an information value that allowed a ranked search output in descending order of relevance. Williams assumed that users would want to retrieve more documents than required and to be able themselves to screen out those not precisely relevant. An added benefit would be that users might make a serendipitous discovery of additional interesting documents. Finding documents close to, as well as directly on, the topic is imperative in patent searching: users need assurance that they have not missed a relevant patent, and they must scan patents that are closely related to a new invention.

In loading the database, the term dictionary was created from titles and text of abstracts. A word scanning program eliminated stop words and truncated remaining words to word stems, or "rootwords." In building the alphabetical inverted file index of rootwords, the program assigned each term a weight, which was calculated as the ratio of the number of times used to the total documents in the base, expressed as a logarithm. This "information value" (I-value) measured the amount of information an index term conveyed in a particular data base. Since information theory states that terms having a low probability of occurrence carry the greatest amount of information, the I-value of a rootword was inversely proportional to the number of occurrences of it in the corpus; low postings equaled high I-value (Williams 1969, 7).

To search, users wrote a paragraph in their own words, in unrestricted English; they did not need to formulate a Boolean statement. Alternatively, users could use an existing abstract as a query with the objective of finding similar abstracts in the file (Williams 1971b). BROWSER reduced the search terms to rootwords and then matched them with the rootword dictionary. Terms found in the dictionary were arranged in descending order of I-value. Then, the abstracts were given a value in relation to the request that was a sum of I-values of terms matching terms in the request. The abstracts were ranked in descending information value order for display on the CRT terminal. The display showed which abstracts contained which particular combinations of search terms (anything from a combination of only two terms to the complete set occurring in a query). At this point a user could add words encountered in the abstracts examined that had not been already used or could delete terms occurring in the false drops but not in relevant hits. This relevance feedback thus allowed searchers to discard irrelevant documents and to retrieve documents containing terms that they had not anticipated.

ELMS

The goal of another development at IBM during the same period was to streamline library operations through a single integrated online system, and to give library patrons easy, direct access to all of a library's records. Designed by Robert Alexander, ELMS (Experimental Library Management System) was programmed in assembly language, operated on an IBM 360, and could accommodate up to 50 IBM 2260 CRT or 2741 teletypewriter terminals.

1970 Milestone

ELMS may have been the first OPAC.

Alexander (1967) first reported this effort and Alexander (1968) provided the first specifications for the system, which he referred to as LMS rather than ELMS. The working system, ELMS, was substantially the same as that described in the 1968 specifications. The Phase I portion, the data input and record maintenance system, using the IBM ATS system, was in operation in 1967 (Hayes 1967). Phase II provided online searching of the catalog file by means of an IBM 360 and IBM 2260 Display Stations, It was put into operation in IBM's Los Gatos Lab library in 1970, with four terminals—two in the processing area, one at the reference desk, and one in a study carrel, with a collection of 18,000 volumes (McAllister 1971; Winik 1972; *Experimental* 1972). This was among the first of the library systems that would later be referred to as OPACs (online public access catalogs). It was followed soon after by an IBM-developed library circulation system at Ohio State University that provided online access to its catalog records.

As the "E" in ELMS implied, the project was an experiment, the object of which was to explore problems of storing, maintaining and retrieving "the millions of intricately interrelated records needed to manage a large library" (Alexander and Harvey 1970, 1; Bell and McAllister 1970). The records included bibliographic descriptions, order information, and circulation status. Librarians could use it for acquisitions, cataloging and circulation. Patrons could use it to find what the library had on a given subject or whether the library had a particular item. By the time Alexander developed ELMS in 1970, a large number of experimental and operational online systems were running already in libraries and laboratories. He felt, however, that ELMS was the first to achieve the goal of integrating all library operations into a single technical processing system, thus eliminating the redundant records in on-order files, acquisitions files, in-process files, circulation files, and catalogs found in most libraries. Alexander and Harvey (1970, 3) reported:

For each document, ELMS records the source, current location, and status, as well as the bibliographic data.... it keeps track of funds, patrons, due dates and printing requirements. It keeps records on the total budget available, the amount encumbered by outstanding orders, and the amount already spent. It records the addresses of patrons, their classification (e.g., professor, student, librarian), the documents they borrow or place on reserve and can keep track of due dates and loans overdue.

The ELMS design was intended to be general and flexible enough to adapt to the needs of any size or type of library. The particular equipment used, for example, could vary for libraries with different size and speed requirements. The modular ELMS programming, with standardized interfaces between the programs, could be adapted to other libraries by substituting some of their own application programs, while retaining the I/O (input/output) and file programs.

In searching the ELMS database, library patrons could use access points such as author, title, call number, or descriptor. They could not combine terms with Boolean operators. If a search term exactly matched an entry in the database, processing was immediate. If a term were truncated or misspelled, the system displayed a segment (8 entries) of the inverted file, with the closest match to the query term in the middle of the display. If a query term were a title word, descriptor, or corporate author, the inverted file display was in permuted KWIC format. For example, if a user entered a word from a title, ELMS displayed eight titles with the closest match to the entered word in the middle.

ELMS features especially significant to online retrieval systems development included (1) conversational mode of the program, whereby each display asked one question and waited for one answer; (2) KWIC index displays to help users find appropriate search terms, in the proper form; (3) adaptability for frequent users (e.g., experienced searchers could answer routine questions before they were asked by entering all the answers at once); (4) line numbers that could be used to refer to earlier statements, and commands that could be expressed with one-character mnemonic codes; and (5) use of default conditions that anticipated the most common user responses and processed them automatically unless a user made a change. These features and others reduced the amount of keying, thus saving time and avoiding errors (McAllister and Bell 1971).

Both librarians and library patrons deemed ELMS a success. IBM librarian Ruth Winik was pleased that an ELMS terminal on the reference desk allowed her to provide fast answers to most patron and interlibrary loan questions. Winik (1972, 219) noted that many patrons seemed happy to be able to take control of retrieving library materials:

The majority of the library users enter the library, sign in at a terminal, search the files, retrieve books from the shelves, check them out and leave, without any intervention by the librarian. This is made possible because the needs of the users were considered carefully when the system was designed.... because the ELMS catalog is part of a total integrated system, on-order and circulation records appear in the display of bibliographic detail. The user thus knows at once whether a book is on the shelf, checked out, on order or in process ... if the book is checked out, the display indicates to whom and when.

ELMS demonstrated that such an approach was feasible and quite effective in handling the large volume of rapidly changing information typical of library records.

ELMS was still an active system in 1973, when Barnholdt and Hein (1973) conducted a study to determine whether or not to install and develop ELMS in a Danish research library environment. The study report noted that the system was still in use at the Los Gatos library and that Caryl McAllister of IBM was a key performer in developing ELMS. Nevertheless, in 1973, IBM withdrew ELMS and proposed to several major academic libraries that they share in development and installation costs of LIBRARY/370, a new system designed to operate on an IBM 370 computer and network to perform the acquisition and cataloging tasks for up to six subscribing libraries. ELMS was the prototype for LIBRARY/370, which was tested in at least one library, but we have no information that any of the libraries that IBM had approached had it permanently installed. In chapter 9, we will meet a later IBM system based on ELMS and LIBRARY/370, called DOBIS.

Negotiated Search Facility

The Negotiated Search Facility, established in 1969 at IBM's Research Laboratory in San Jose, California, was an online retrieval system designed to be used in the context of indexing work. The aim of the research and development team that included John Bennett, D. C. Clark, and W. Musson was to create a tool to assist indexers in the process of assigning terms to documents. The assistance would be in the form of a stored authority list to check the validity of an indexing term, view related terms, and see a tally of how many times an indexing term had been used before. Other indexing support included the facility to retrieve other documents that had been assigned the same indexing term, or to retrieve documents that had been indexed with a certain combination of terms. The NSF was useful both as a working medium for indexers, and also as a research tool for indexing studies (Bennett 1969; Clarke 1970).

Benchmark for the 1960s: The COSATI Demonstrations

Established by the Federal Council on Science and Technology in 1961, the Committee on Science Information–renamed the Committee on Scientific and Technical Information in 1964—had the responsibility for coordinating U.S. agency programs for disseminating scientific and technical information, and for developing Federal standards and compatibility among systems. COSATI served as the central point in government where the problems and potential of the expansion of sci-tech information could be considered and acted upon. It took its responsibility seriously, working on standard subject heading systems and microfiche formats, and considering various plans for a coordinated national system for sci/tech information. It arranged demonstrations of current online systems in 1967, 1968, and 1969. One COSATI panel, Panel 2 on Information Sciences Technology (IST), chaired by Ruth Davis of NLM, initiated and carried out this project—called the Federal Information Research Science and Technology (FIRST) Network—to investigate advantages and disadvantages of currently available remote terminal time-shared online retrieval systems (Landau 1969).

The database for the demonstrations had its roots in earlier COSATI activity. In 1965, the IST panel initiated three-year experimental production of the *Inventory of Information Sciences Technology Work in Progress*, as a reference tool for federal agencies. Participants collected data from major U.S. agencies about current information science/technology research, or about 1,300 project descriptions. While on loan from AFOSR, Harold Wooster conducted the first survey, which resulted in a printed directory in April 1966 that was edited and published as IST Inventory I for limited ("official use only") distribution to IST members and a number of U.S. agencies funding this type of work.

During 1967, the Panel also began investigating online query capabilities to evaluate the utility of the *Inventory*; several Panel members made presentations at a Pittsburgh conference in April 1967 that had evaluation techniques as its theme (*Progress* 1968, 5–6). File building was expanded, starting in early 1967 for IST Inventory II, and this time, DDC entered the latest information into machine-readable form for entry into the DDC-1473 Work Unit Data Bank (where information on other DOD and NASA projects was already being recorded), and prepared camera-ready copy for the printing and distribution of a limited number of copies in 1968. The DDC systems and Work Unit Data Bank were described earlier. Support in gathering, selecting, and processing of project descriptions for the second inventory was provided by Information General Corporation (IGC) under its previous name (Programming Services Inc.), under Charles Bourne's direction. DDC did the associated machine file building. This second inventory (reporting 2,468 projects) was printed in June 1967, using DDC computer support for composition and printing, and again for "official use only" distribution. This IST Inventory II file was then made available for demonstration use by the online systems identified by COSATI as commercially available and having the desired characteristics.

In 1968, COSATI, chaired by Andrew Aines of the Office of Science and Technology of the Executive Office of the President, sponsored a comparative demonstration of bibliographic online systems available then—something like an invitational state-of-the-art conference. In the spring of 1968, IST invited six companies to participate in a demonstration, using the same database (the COSATI Inventory II). The companies and their respective systems were: Computer Corporation of America (103), Data Corporation (Data Central), General Electric (Rapid Search Machine), Lockheed (DIALOG), Programmatics (TORQUE), and SDC (LUCID and TDMS). These were considered to be the major online retrieval system available at that time. GE and Programmatics withdrew because their systems could not be demonstrated within COSATI's time frame. Earlier in 1968, MITRE Corporation had delivered to the panel and participants a report containing criteria for evaluation of the systems. The report was published in August (Welch 1968).

During April and May 1968, rehearsals showed that live demonstrations could be shown only to small audiences, not the expected fifty IST members and observers. Consequently, filmed demonstration sequences were prepared in cooperation with those companies and shown along with demonstrations. Another objective of the film was to achieve a wider dissemination of the results of this benchmark comparative demonstration. Battelle Memorial Institute in Columbus, Ohio, was contracted to produce a film of the demonstrations. George Tressel produced the twenty-five-minute film during the first half of 1968, including the filming of online demonstrations of four systems. In June in Washington, DC, BMI presented the film *The COSATI Data Base* (1969) to IST in conjunction with live demonstrations of the Lockheed and Data Central systems (Summit 1969a; Welch 1968). It is an interesting historical document with some important pioneers (Giering, Summit), examples of then-current attitudes ("generally you'll find that your secretary can run the system better than you can; she types faster"), and illustrations of the systems and equipment as they operated then. The film was a significant medium for making system developers aware of other developers' work. It won the ASIS Outstanding Information Science Movie Award in 1969.

The SDC system demonstrated (LUCID) and the CCA system were more oriented to general file management applications than online searching; the Data Corporation and Lockheed DIALOG systems were the ones most oriented to online retrieval. (Prior to 1969, the names DIALOG, ORBIT, and Data Central were not in general use; only the corporate names were used—Lockheed, SDC, Data Corporation.) The project manager on behalf of COSATI was Robert Landau, a staff member in the Office of Science and Technology.

For the third inventory, the panel planned to have both a printed directory and a pilot online database with remote inquiry and report generation capability. IGC was selected again as the contractor, responsible for data gathering and editing, preparing the manuscript for the printed directory and providing the corresponding machine-readable file, and pilot operation of an online search system with multiple remote terminals (using a subcontract to Data Corporation) (Bourne, North, and Kasson 1969). COSATI awarded a contract in August 1968 to IGC to review over 20,000 current R&D project descriptions (DD-1498 forms or equivalents), gathered from fifteen federal agencies, in order to identify all (over 2,500) records for projects receiving 1968 funding and relevant to information science. The project descriptions were edited, indexed, and entered into a computer file by early 1969, using IBM 360 DATATEXT system, to prepare both masters for a printed product (Bourne 1969) and a database to be used for later comparative online demonstrations. The final edited database was printed by a line printer in upper and lower case on preprinted form stock to provide master pages for the printed product. NTIS made it available in microfiche form. The product was intended also for researchers' reference and current awareness, and as a common database for retrieval studies such as the Cranfield and SMART efforts.

One of IST's major goals was to encourage sharing and cross-utilization of the products of federally supported R&D in information science technology. Towards that objective, IST began an online experiment in April 1969, providing two databases online for remote access searching: the 1967 and 1968 COSATI Inventory of Information Science Technology Work in Progress databases, containing a total of 3,500 R&D project descriptions (*Progress* 1970).

As mentioned earlier, the IGC contract also included funds for subcontract support to Data Corp. to mount the Inventory III file online and offer demonstrations to various Federal agencies. The resulting tape for IST Inventory III was delivered to Data Corporation in April 1969. In April 1969, William Gorog, chair of Data Corporation, noted that with a contract and technical direction from COSATI's IST Panel, Data Corporation was currently loading five databases: (1) Inventory of Current R&D in the Information Sciences; (2) citations to a special library collection at Battelle; (3) citations to computer sciences at NBS; (4) citations from volumes 1–3 of *Annual Review of Information Science and Technology*; and (5) a glossary of 3,000 information science terms ("New storage retrieval system" 1969). IST made available these five databases during the first half of 1968 to the four companies that had volunteered to demonstrate their online systems. Two of the companies (Lockheed, Data Corporation) demonstrated their systems with one or more of those files at the 1968 ASIS annual meeting. This COSATI Inventory III database and the Data Corporation online system were demonstrated to many groups throughout the Washington, D.C., area in 1969. Landau arranged to have it demonstrated at a public meeting in Philadelphia in May 1969. The system received trial use on a scheduled four-hour-per-day basis for several weeks for the federal agencies that chose to participate. According to Meadow (1973), "COSATI tried to put the so-called COSATI Inventory on the system at Mead Data Central. It barely got started before it was stopped for lack of funds, as well as a lack of interest, I think" (130). Data Corporation staff prepared a user manual that was in press in November 1969 when the IGC report was written.

The COSATI activity was important because it provided a mechanism for system designers to share their work with many others and gain a better understanding of the features of competitive systems. It permitted many potential sponsors or users of online systems to obtain a better appreciation for how the systems really worked and what they could do. Summit (1980c) of Lockheed claimed that, as a result of the 1968 COSATI demonstration, Harvey Marron of USOE became convinced that OE's ERIC file would be well served by this technology, and initiated contracts at Lockheed for online services on the DIALOG system. Those contracts marked Lockheed's shift from system developer to service vendor as recounted in chapter 5.

software programming between 1969 and 1971. Because it did not emerge as a major publicly available retrieval system until the 1970s, however, we will wait until chapter 9 to meet it.

Summary

In the second half of the 1960s and into the early seventies, we saw a few nonacademic laboratories (SDC, IBM, MITRE) continue R&D they had begun in the early 1960s. During this period, however, many more commercial and governmental labs got into the act with their own projects. Many online prototypes emerged that were intended to become full-fledged production systems. The working lives of most of these systems, however, tended to be short; they were continually being superseded by newer generations of faster, more efficient, or more effective systems. Even though the designers and developers attended conferences and workshops to learn from each other, they conducted many individual experiments, all of which in one way or another added to the general knowledge pool of online IR.

A wide spectrum of R&D efforts emerged during this period. Nonetheless, we did not cover them all in this chapter. In the next several chapters, we explore developments that were happening concurrently that eventually grew into large, widely used retrieval systems. In chapter 9, we pick up the birth and maturation of the online industry in the 1970s. For example, the roots of what came to be known as the Information Bank started with a contract between the New York Times Company and IBM Federal Systems Division for systems analysis and

5 Lockheed DIALOG and Related Systems, 1961–1972

Introduction

The earliest versions of four major commercial online services, which later came to serve a large and diverse clientele, appeared in the mid-1960s, about the same time as many of the experimental systems of the previous three chapters. In that early online era, these prototype versions of DIALOG, ORBIT, LEXIS, and SUNY/BCN (later BRS) were not necessarily more innovative or sophisticated than those we have seen already. However, they were reasonably easy to use, provided satisfactory customer service, were economical enough to run on a large scale, and flexible enough to run multiple files and to serve a variety of users. Their success, in fact, seems attributable in part to these factors: the developers' practical orientation to potential users' needs, aggressive solicitation of users, and promotion of the merits of online searching.

The next four chapters track the tangled stories of these four systems. Throughout the mid-sixties to early seventies, each of them generated significant milestones. All evolved over a several-year period, with various prototypes and experimental versions that were applied to small files, limited user populations, and extremely restricted hours of service. Drawing a simple line of development for them is difficult, since they tended to be restructured, sometimes quite drastically, as developers adopted new equipment and programming languages, and adjusted interfaces and service policies to respond to feedback from early users. DIALOG and ORBIT spawned derivative systems that became other online services.

DIALOG's ancestry traces back the farthest, and with the most detail. Documentation and interviews indicate that DIALOG was conceptualized at Lockheed Missiles and Space Company in Palo Alto, California. The DIALOG story actually begins in 1961, with a batch-processed system called MATICO, the database of which was used in October 1964 for testing ADA, Lockheed's first primitive retrieval system based on third-generation computer technology. The prototype for what looked liked the basis for the current DIALOG, and was actually named DIALOG, was not demonstrated until 1966. The notion that DIALOG was RECON (an online system created for NASA) before it was DIALOG has been circulated throughout the online retrieval literature. In truth, however, the Palo Alto Research Laboratory developed an initial version of the DIALOG software as a proprietary product before making it available to a NASA facility in 1966. NASA staff gave the name RECON to this first full-scale application of DIALOG, and began offering online service on RECON in early 1969. (They had conceived of the idea of an online system to be called RECON as far back as 1964 and had also given the RECON name earlier to a Bunker-Ramo online retrieval system developed for NASA.)

Along the way of telling the DIALOG story, we encounter other organizations and other software developments that contributed to developing DIALOG or one of its spinoffs. NASA contributed its large database to the RECON project. Bunker-Ramo Corporation actually developed a RECON before Lockheed did, and Bunker-Ramo's evaluation contributed valuable specifications and design ideas to Lockheed's RECON. Informatics continued the maintenance of RECON after the NASA contract to Lockheed ended. USOE offered its ERIC file for a Lockheed evaluation study. DOJ adopted the DIALOG-developed RECON for its JURIS project. Other early adopters of DIALOG or DIALOG spin-offs included the European Space Research Organization (ESRO) and the AEC. In the pages following, we introduce the players, examine the projects, and review the evaluation studies one by one.

The most influential individual in the DIALOG story was Roger Summit, who had begun his career at Lockheed in the early 1960s. Summit had traveled to California from Dearborn, Michigan, to earn an A.B. in psychology at Stanford University. After serving in the Navy, he worked for Arthur Anderson & Company as an accountant and systems analyst, and then at Southern California

Gas before returning to Stanford where he earned an M.B.A. In June 1960, between his oral exams and his dissertation for a Ph.D. in management science at Stanford, he obtained a summer internship to be a member of the staff of Information Processing at Lockheed. He took the job to pay for the next year's tuition and did not expect to stay past summer. His supervisor gave him two assignments: one was in computer simulation and yielded the Aerospace Business Environment Simulator that was later used in Lockheed management-training sessions; the other was in IR. Summit was assigned to an inter-industry study group, including representatives from other aerospace and high-technology firms such as Douglas Aircraft, Boeing, and IBM, to explore and develop batch-oriented retrieval systems. That exercise introduced Summit to IR, and he found it so interesting that he stayed on as a full-time employee in the fall of 1960 as a programming analyst. He continued school on a part-time basis until completing his Ph.D. in 1965. From this beginning, Summit was destined to become a major figure in the online industry, and in 1991 he received the ASIS Award of Merit for his contributions as a "guiding force behind the creation of the online information industry" ("Summit and Gore" 1991).

Summit (1981) reflected that three events in 1964 were critical to DIALOG's development: (1) a Lockheed vice president read, with great interest, a report on LC automation (King 1963); (2) IBM announced its third-generation computer series (IBM 360); and (3) Lockheed management received a proposed IR study plan. Taken together, the LC report provided the stimulus, the new computer technology provided the means, and the proposal resulted in the recognition and funding necessary to establish the Lockheed Information Sciences Laboratory in January 1965 (Summit 1981).

We are getting ahead of our story, however; let us begin with internally supported R&D and an automated library-processing system called MATICO.

Lockheed Support for Information Science R&D

In the early 1960s, Lockheed supported a wide range of internal R&D at their Palo Alto Research Lab. Some studies in computer and information sciences were quite advanced for their day. In 1962, for example, the Electronic Sciences Laboratory (ESL), directed by W. F. Main, had projects in pattern recognition, algorithmic studies of written English, mechanical linguistics, and mechanical translation. At this early date, the mechanical-translation effort was aimed at formulating useful means for automatic translation between Russian and English as well as translation between Chinese and English. Richard Tanaka headed the Computer Research Group of the Research Lab.

In 1964, the R&D support programs included for the first time projects clearly identified as library or IR activities: library systems research (as an indication of its corporate support for this line of inquiry, Lockheed committed $145,000 of internal research funding for this research program); reference retrieval in a library; IR and machine organization; fact retrieval; automatic indexing of text material; mechanical linguistics; algorithmic studies of written English; sequential machine synthesis; pattern recognition; multivalued logic; and hospital information systems. The principal investigators and senior scientists involved in these studies (introduced later in the DIALOG story) included Robert Whitely, Daniel Drew, Oscar Firschein, M. Fischler, A. J. Nichols III, Jim Dolby, Howard Resnikoff, Ken Gielow, Gordon Uber, Lois Earl, H. R. Robison, and Summit.

In April 1964, Tanaka submitted a proposal for an "LMSC Information Storage and Retrieval Study Plan" to Lockheed management (LMSC was an abbreviation for Lockheed Missiles and Space Company). In response, management committed the company to a serious program of information storage and retrieval research, directed by Tanaka. The Information Sciences Lab was established within ESL in 1964, with Eugene Duncan as the director. By October 1964, the storage and retrieval effort had fifteen professional staff members. The team included at least two specialty groups—a language studies group and an electronics research group.

Library research for 1964 had three major components: (1) state-of-the-art review of relevant background information; (2) definition and implementation of a first-generation online reference retrieval system—to permit experimentation to begin; and (3) initial investigations to define a generalized information center that would incorporate research results and advanced techniques in its operations. Lockheed had not yet decided what its role should be—system manager, R&D contract facility, or equipment manufacturer; the company had not even considered the idea of being an international information utility. However, the company was aware of the significance of establishing its competence by successfully completing several study projects (Stromer 1964). Firschein (1993) recalled, "In 1964 the group was trying to determine promising areas of information science research, and so it tended to wander off in all directions in their topic areas. Only Summit, because of his business school background, had an end user in mind—the others were more research minded." By late 1964, Lockheed had defined a focus for its information activities. However, it was clear that further R&D would require new I/O equipment for their R&D facility. Merrill (1964, 1) opined:

It appears highly likely that LMSC will pursue the development of information retrieval systems for hospitals, travel bureaus, libraries, real estate offices—to name a few. As part of this diversification activity, a program is planned for the development of I/O equipment suitable for use in these various retrieval applications. To illustrate the significance of this work, the Hospital Group feels that their competitive position depends, to a large extent, on having a satisfactory I/O system.

Lockheed gained more exposure to large-scale information handling problems in 1965; after conducting a study of present and proposed information activities and the requirements of California state agencies, the company prepared a plan for developing and implementing a system. With the encouragement of Governor Edmund G. ("Pat") Brown (as part of a state government attempt to assist defense industry contractors to diversify and shift to other lines of work), Lockheed expanded upon the work started in 1963 with internal support to analyze hospital practices and investigate hospital information systems (Fuller 1965). In 1964, Lockheed spent over $120,000 to support in-house R&D to transfer their missile- and space-related skills and capabilities to the solution of similar problems in communications and operations of different types of hospitals. Over the next few years they conducted studies in medical and hospital information systems.

Also during 1965, Lockheed committed $49,000 of internal research funding to a research program for online library reference retrieval. Summit was principal investigator, with Drew as an associate. This program was a follow-up effort for the ADA experiment described later in this section, with the objectives of improving the man-machine interface to the search system and expanding file size capability to about 200,000 references. Another internally supported project was for Drew to start the design of the LACONIQ time-sharing monitor to be used with online search systems developed at the Lockheed laboratory.

Monetary support of the Information Retrieval group, especially for machine language translation, gradually disappeared. The group splintered to support other products. Firschein, Drew, Earl, and Summit continued to work at the Lockheed Palo Alto Research Lab. Firschein worked on image processing, pattern recognition, and artificial intelligence and occasionally participated in the DIALOG group for special assignments. In particular, he was project leader for the DIALIB project in 1967–1977, and was instrumental in starting DIALOG's Classroom Instruction Program and ONTAP training and practice files (all described in chapter 9). Resnikoff and Dolby were interested in language issues (e.g., word hyphenation, line justification, reverse dictionaries). Their algorithms for automatic hyphenation of words were used in the design of an automatic justifier-hyphenator device that a Linotype manufacturer had licensed. While Summit was a junior member of this group, he continued with Lockheed and DIALOG until his retirement in 1991.

First Building Block: MATICO

In 1962, Kenneth Carroll and Summit stated, "no truly effective, economical, efficient program for an automated search of literature now exists" (18). They described work they had begun the year before at the Lockheed library (the TIC, or Technical Information Center) to build MATICO (Machine-Aided Technical Information Center Operations), a system designed to improve the efficiency of card production and filing for the catalog of a collection of 200,000 technical reports. Although MATICO was not an online search system, it was an indication that Lockheed staff were thinking about the computer processing of bibliographic records as early as 1961, and Summit described MATICO at a 1962 IBM information retrieval workshop.

Carroll had come to TIC in 1959 as supervisor of the Literature Search section, working for William Kozumplik, TIC manager. Kozumplik had come to Lockheed with extensive experience with special Air Force libraries such as the RADC, the Air University, and the Air Force Special Weapons Center. He was receptive to new ideas and new technology. Carroll had prior experience in library mechanization, and in his new position he was responsible for initiating and expanding computer applications to library operations, with the goal of improving TIC's effectiveness. In his pursuit of new technology for the library, it was natural that he seek out other staff interested in mechanized information handling. He discovered kindred spirits, including Summit and Dan Gold. The outcome of their collaboration was threefold: (1) development and implementation of MATICO; (2) Information Sciences Lab staff awareness of some specific idiosyncracies of library information handling; and (3) continued availability of a test facility that received attention outside of Lockheed. The publications and presentations that resulted gave Lockheed visibility in the professional and federal arenas—few librarians, information workers, or federal agencies had heard about Lockheed's information activities before then.

Assigned to work with Carroll, Summit's role was defining the system specifications, and Gold's role was programming. With IBM punched cards for source-data input, they used an IBM 7090/1401 computer complex to generate printed catalog cards in proper filing order and to write the cataloging data onto magnetic tapes for an SDI service on new acquisitions, for producing book catalogs in specialized areas of the collection, and for creating KWIC indexes. They based their KWIC indexes and SDI service on the pioneering work of Hans Peter Luhn and Terry Savage at IBM. Later, TIC staff also searched the magnetic tapes in batch mode; requesters stated their topics in natural language terms and staff entered the terms into MATICO, which translated them into descriptors that had been used to index the technical reports. The batch program searched in two ways—through an inverted file of descriptors and through the unit records. The output was full bibliographic data, and abstracts when available, on $3'' \times 5''$ cards (Drew 1964c).

MATICO continued in operation for several years, processing as many as 1,200 documents per month. In 1964 ADA used the MATICO database (see next section). Although MATICO was not an online search system, it was a visible computer-based library technical processing system, and thus was evidence that Lockheed staff were working on computer processing of bibliographic records in the early 1960s. MATICO also served as a marketing tool, promoted to information professionals and potential sponsors as an example of Lockheed's "leading edge."

In early 1965 completion of the next phase of MATICO development became an obvious prerequisite for the successful pursuit of other business opportunities in computer-based information processing. That is, marketing purposes made the presentation of continuing and expanding Lockheed developments in the area of computer-based information processing important.

DIALOG Prototypes and Precursors

ADA/CONVERSE

ADA came into being at the urging of the president of Lockheed, Eugene Root. His executive vice president, Herschel Brown, had read a report on LC automation (King 1963) and found the possibilities impressive. Brown was due to retire, however, and was unable to follow up. Root wanted to give Brown a special retirement tribute and decided to present him with an operational online system at his retirement party.

Main, the ESL manager, and the ESL group received the assignment in September 1964 to build an online system. Main called in two of his staff, Drew and Tanaka, and passed the assignment to them. Drew, a senior scientist, was to be the technical person, and Tanaka's job was to fight any political or logistical battles. Main suggested that Drew talk to Summit because Summit had experience with library automation. Summit was in the last throes of his doctoral work; he was unhappy that he could not assume a leading part in the project (Drew 1996).

Because of the impending retirement ceremony, only a few weeks were available to complete the project. The team had to work with what they already knew and what was immediately available to them. Under Drew's management, eleven experienced professionals labored to meet the tight schedule for system demonstration. Their first proposed design appeared in a September 1964 internal report by Drew, Graziano, Satterfield, and Summit. Drew (1964d) also described the design in an October internal report. The proposal was an opportunistic attempt to take advantage of a special-purpose online computer, the ADA (Automated Data Acquisition) system available elsewhere within Lockheed, at a time when few online systems of any kind were in operation anywhere.

Only one computer was available that could be used in an online mode, installed as part of the ADA production control and inventory system at the loading dock of the Lockheed Sunnyvale, California, facility. Whitely set up a communications link from the Lockheed Palo Alto Lab to the Sunnyvale loading dock. ADA had been operating since 1962 on two RCA 301 computers with three Bryant disk files (using 1-meter disks with a 44-megabyte capacity per unit), along with data input stations (IBM single-card readers) and output (print-only) Teletype stations. ADA was installed for regular production use, collecting and reporting procurement, manufacturing, inventory, and personnel information from remote manufacturing and receiving areas. Staff, however, envisioned its potential for online reference retrieval experimentation.

Drew coordinated the project with Summit, whom the ADA management team considered the IR expert. Summit was involved with the interface design and the decision to implement a Boolean search capability. Drew credits Summit with introducing inverted file structures to him. The six-week period after the team learned of the equipment availability gave little time for designing programs and writing specifications. While ADA had programs for basic tasks such as file building and maintenance, the team had to write other programs for retrieval functions. They did not have sufficient time to implement more than Boolean AND and NOT operators, nor to implement output set numbers or recursive searching. Thus the search interaction allowed only the refining or whittling down of a prior answer set. MATICO machine-readable records were the test file. Storage space restrictions, however, limited the size of file that could be accommodated on the disk (100 records were used in the first operating model, but extended to 1,600 records by the end of 1964, and to 8,000 records in mid-1965).

Even with its limitations, ADA was ready for testing during the first week of October 1964. In the TIC *New Reports* for October 15, 1964, Graziano announced that an ADA Inquiry Station was now located in both of the TIC libraries (Sunnyvale and Palo Alto), along with their associated remote data input unit, remote output page printer, cabinets of pre-punched tab cards, and posted instructions for scientists' direct use. They noted that this was an experimental prototype, representing an extension of MATICO, and that they hoped to have 1,700 reports in the system by October 15, the same week that Kessler and his collaborators at MIT announced TIP at the ADI annual meeting (Kessler, Ivie, and Matthews 1964).

On October 21, Tanaka (1964) sent an internal memo to the ADA team commending them for their fine work: "The time allocated was very short, and the target date could not have been met without superb cooperation from many organizations and individuals." In a May 1965 paper, Drew, Summit, Tanaka, and Whitely described how the standard ADA query device, an IBM 1-card punched card reader, was also restricted for this application (an awkward device, the team admitted). Next to the card reader was a file cabinet containing prepunched cards prepared for insertion into the reader. Searchers were instructed to find all the cards appropriate for their search from labeled card file drawers. Each card in the cabinet contained an allowable search "term" (author's name, title word, corporate author, secondary report number, date of publication, or subject heading—about three assigned to each document) describing one or more of the collection documents. Each catalog record had up to forty-four of these prepared keypunch cards. Searchers also could insert two standard control cards, the NOT card and the END card. If a user inserted two term cards with no intermediate control cards, the system assumed Boolean AND logic. If the user inserted the NOT card between two term cards, the system negated the second term. Users had to enter each card, one at a time, into the card reader, then insert the END card last, to signal that search entry was complete.

Creating an alphabetical inverted file of the master records achieved speed in ADA's search. This system used master records only for display-ing search output, which it accomplished with a slow and noisy Teletype printer. ADA could print up to three records; if more than that matched the inquiry, it printed out only accession numbers. Searchers were encouraged to refine their requests until they retrieved no more than three references. Even then, each catalog record required a full minute to display on the teletypewriter. Although users might appreciate that the system could save them hours or days of manual searching, they still were impatient with the slow rate of output.

The development staff were aware that the first stages of the ADA design would implement few innovations in retrieval techniques. Nonetheless, "It will also be the first real-time library retrieval system of which we are aware" (Drew et al. 1964, 8). "The idea of an automated library information retrieval system designed for immediate response is not novel, but to the best of our knowledge, has never been implemented in a working system" (1). Drew and his colleagues seemed unaware of prior work and of demonstrations in California at SRI and SDC, and at MIT. On October 15, Graziano (1964) observed "it is interesting to record that, according to Charles P. Bourne of SRI, this is believed to be the first on-line system of its kind." This observation was probably based on Bourne's comments at a meeting at Lockheed on September 30, 1964, where Graziano, Kozumplik, and Whitely were discussing the progress and performance of the Lockheed system with interested parties from SRI. The Lockheed group may have felt that they were the first ones to demonstrate such a system because no previous internal reports mentioned the work that researchers had done earlier at SRI (just five miles down the road), SDC, or MIT. They were familiar with Kilgour's plan for an online technical processing system for the Columbia/Harvard/Yale medical library because they had prepared an internal report of Kilgour's presentation at the Medical Library Association (MLA) meeting in June 1964. They were not familiar with TIP and Kessler's work at MIT during the ADA project, but they learned about it later (Drew 1996) and referred to it in a May 1965 report (Drew et al. 1965) and a paper submitted to

American Documentation in July 1965 (Drew et al. 1966).

The team recognized that ADA was far from suitable as an online system, but it did provide a quick opportunity to try something that might be useful, and a platform for further experimentation (Drew 1964a,b). In December 1964, Gielow commented, "The present ADA system library retrieval is limited... entering new data into the files is quite painful. What is more, the ADA application programs require expert assistance to change" (2). ADA was online but not interactive. Users could enter search terms online, get immediate access to the computer resources for searching the database, and receive output of record accession numbers; but they could not intervene and modify the search process on the basis of intermediate results. ADA did not give users control over the output format or reformulation of requests. The system determined the type of output based on the number of records retrieved. Users had to expand searches manually. It was an online remote-batch system; however, this was true of most online systems in the early and mid-sixties.

In January 1965, Graziano reminded his colleagues that Lockheed had an opportunity to obtain federal funding from the Library Services Act of 1965. To do that, however, they would have to complete the next phase of MATICO/ADA.

Shortly after the ADA demonstration, and mindful of its shortcomings, Firschein and Drew (1965) described a way for ADA to provide the option of operating in an interactive tutorial mode to explain itself to an untrained user. As described earlier, such a feature had been implemented already in MICRO in 1965, but Firschein and Drew were unaware of it. They proposed that in response to a system query, a user would key in either N (Not familiar with this system) or E (Expert). Coincidentally, these were the same responses used in later SDC systems, but with different definitions (New, Experienced). A short time later, Drew (1965d) complained about the severe hardship of working with slow Teletype terminals, which had "obliged the reluctant abandonment of 'tutorial mode'"— tutorial mode was practical only with a CRT (3). Two weeks later, Drew and Merrill (1965) commented that experience with ADA/CONVERSE had shown a need for a more flexible I/O terminal and that the existing ADA input and Teletype output configuration would soon be replaced by a teletypewriter station. However, a CRT with alphanumeric keyboard (and additional function buttons) would be a logical replacement for the teletypewriter I/O terminal.

In a February 4, 1965, report, Firschein and Drew proposed how the *Engineers Joint Council Thesaurus* (which Drew had obtained on magnetic tape) could be used online in formulating a search. They proposed that output displays of a search formulation include posting counts for the number of times that an authorized descriptor term was used. This feature actually was demonstrated first in BOLD in 1965. They suggested how a system could offer output choices when the number of records exceeded fifteen; the solution was to provide full catalog records for the first three records, titles only for the next fifteen, record numbers for the next fifteen, and offline catalog records for the remainder. Firschein and Drew's ideas were remarkably foresighted. BOLD was the first to demonstrate an online thesaurus in 1966, and other systems later implemented default output options when a search retrieved a large set.

Also in February—but after the Firschein and Drew report—Summit (1965) described the conversational nature of the search process and proposed a command language to support it (for example, operators such as FIND TITLES WITH, FIND WORDS NEXT TO, COMBINE). In March, Drew (1965d) described a search process of "coarse sieving" that created subfiles of the total file and eliminated clearly irrelevant references so that a detailed search of the remainder was feasible. He described the use of such a subfile in the next logical search step: "This use of subfiles is clearly recursive... these subfiles are not destroyed until the total search is at an end, so that partial backtracking is facilitated" (2). He proposed the numbering of each subfile or output set; this represented the first description of using search subsets in later logical operations and recursive searching. Set and subset numbering were implemented in 1966 in the first DIALOG, the first online system to demonstrate this important feature. He had earlier proposed that posting counts be part of the system response.

Drew's March (1965d) report also proposed testing of a searcher's input statements for logical or other errors before starting the search, with an attempt to understand and propose alternative statements, using prompts such as DO YOU MEAN . . . ? He included a hypothetical users' manual to describe the features and user interface he had in mind. The manual illustrated the use of subset numbers; thesaurus lookups with related terms, broader terms, narrower terms, and synonyms; the use of a FIND command; searching by bibliographic coupling (e.g., FIND LIKE 51332 to find references that used the same subject descriptors used with document number 51332); the option of online or offline printout; and the options for output content (full catalog record, titles and accession numbers, report numbers, or accession numbers). Drew's proposal for system features was not only farsighted, it was an interesting way to write the functional specifications for a proposed system. Summit apparently appreciated this approach of specification writing (reverse engineering from the proposed users' manual) because he insisted that it be used with later DIALOG systems.

In another March report, Drew (1965b) proposed a way to accommodate alternative word forms automatically, using tables of allowable suffixes. Remember that Dolby and Resnikoff had already done linguistic R&D, particularly on word types, word stemming, and hyphenation rules.

A May 1965 report and corresponding conference presentation (Drew et al. 1965) noted that the system depended upon two other operating Lockheed systems: MATICO and ADA. MATICO supplied the database, and ADA furnished the online computer and its time-sharing monitor. These reports and later publications named the ADA system CONVERSE I. The name was intended as a verb, as in "to converse," which suggests that the later system name, DIALOG, was similarly inspired. The report also mentioned that another system was now in development, called CONVERSE II, which was designed around a teletypewriter inquiry station and the principle of allowing a "free" vocabulary at the start of the search. The Teletype (with possible later change to a CRT) would provide access to the thesaurus then in use for indexing MATICO documents and to the corporate source authority list, so that the indexing and retrieval vocabularies would become as similar as possible. Other features to be added included OR logic, searching by ranges of publication dates, accession numbers, or on word stems, larger file sizes, and more output options. Drew acknowledged D. B. J. Bridges, C. D. Satterfield, and M. R. Stark for the rapid and successful implementation of this system.

In June, Drew (1965a) provided additional details concerning the requirements and hardware organization for future online search systems. He suggested a small set of general commands (FIND, COMPARE, MULTIPLY) for elementary text processing, file manipulation, and arithmetic operations. He argued that the system should be convenient to use and noted that the principal factor in convenience was response time, which should ideally allow a user to work at a self-determined pace, not one limited by the system. He elaborated on the use of an online thesaurus that incorporated hierarchical relationships between terms.

Meanwhile, planning for an upgraded CONVERSE began after library staff who used ADA realized that major improvements were needed. CONVERSE II was to be designed around a teletypewriter station (in response to searchers' complaints about the awkward card input device), a natural language retrieval vocabulary, and recursive searching that allowed the results of one step in the search to be incorporated into the next. A Teletype would provide access to the thesaurus used for indexing MATICO documents and the corporate source authority list, so that the indexing and retrieval vocabularies would be as similar as possible. Other features to be added included OR logic, searching by ranges of publication dates or accession numbers, searching of word stems, larger file sizes, and more output options (Summit 1966b). Long-range plans for a CONVERSE III included a CRT that would provide tutorial help and increase output rate.

CONVERSE II and III never materialized. Instead, the developers reconfigured the software along a different and more flexible path. The revised design completed by 1966 was different enough to be considered not a second version of CONVERSE, but rather a new online system that incorporated lessons learned from the brief CONVERSE experience. In this way, then, CONVERSE was a precursor of DIALOG.

While developing and testing ADA, the Lockheed group realized that a more flexible and powerful online system was necessary for them to be able to meet their research objectives, which were to "establish a program to investigate the information retrieval problem. Initial emphasis will be placed on a particular problem area, namely, the library problem that includes storage, retrieval, dissemination and display elements which are applicable to other information retrieval areas" (Summit 1981, 9). They considered ways they might be able to obtain or use other equipment within the Lockheed complex, and in early 1965 they proposed to management to purchase a small computer for the Palo Alto Research Lab. Management accepted the argument that information science was basically an experimental field and that most advances would come through experimentation and testing of hypotheses. In December 1965 a new IBM 360/30 computer (serial number 3: the third 360/30 built by IBM) was delivered. This computer system, with its 120K bytes of core memory, included an IBM 2321 Data Cell storage unit with 415 megabytes of storage, two IBM 2311 disk drives (with replaceable disk packs of 7.2 megabytes each), a tape drive, an IBM 1443 offline printer, and an operating console with an IBM 2260 CRT and IBM 1053 input-output typewriter terminal. Several projects shared the computer, and because retrieval development required full use of the computer, it could be used only about two hours per day for that purpose. Nonetheless, this facility now provided the platform on which staff could develop and test a new online system, based on their previous experience.

In spring 1967, the lab computer complex consisted of an IBM 360/30 with 32K bytes of core memory, two IBM 2311 disk drives each capable of storing 7 million bytes, an IBM 2321 Data Cell that could store over 400 million bytes, and two magnetic tape units for input-output (not storage) devices (the total system storage capacity was far less than most PC workstations of today). Communications with users was done via IBM 2260 CRT-keyboard consoles (Nichols and Reiter 1967). By mid-1969 the computer system had been upgraded to an IBM 360/40 with three IBM disk packs and one IBM Data Cell storage device, and assorted I/O devices. By early 1972, the lab had an IBM 360/40 and a 360/44 computer.

Drew was the person most responsible for developing and demonstrating ADA/CONVERSE, and he made other contributions described elsewhere that were significant to Lockheed retrieval system development. Drew graduated from Reed College with a B.A. in mathematics. Before joining Lockheed in 1959 as an analyst and programmer, he worked in Angola to manage an international lumber enterprise. He attended Stanford part-time and got his M.S. in statistics. Years later he recalled the ADA project warmly for the visibility and rewards it brought to him. After delivering a paper at a conference in New York in 1965, he received an invitation from Parker at Stanford University to give lectures in a computer science seminar. The Stanford and Lockheed teams were familiar with each other's activities; Parker was on the distribution list for Lockheed's *Information Retrieval Notes*, and it is possible that the Stanford staff used that material in developing SPIRES. Drew gave the lectures and then received a job offer with a 50 percent pay raise to come to Stanford to work on SPIRES. Lockheed matched the offer, and he stayed on at the Lockheed Palo Alto Research Lab.

QUIKTRAN

While the ADA/CONVERSE development was going on, the Lockheed group demonstrated another prototype online system (Gielow 1964). In December 1964 Gielow, mindful of ADA's shortcomings, demonstrated an online retrieval capability that used an experimental version of IBM's QUIKTRAN system. QUIKTRAN had been in experimental operation at IBM since mid-1963 and was available as a standard IBM product for customer use starting in April 1965 (Morrissey 1965; *QUIKTRAN User's Guide* 1966). QUIKTRAN provided a remote-access batch computing capability, but developers had not intended it for database maintenance or retrieval. Nonetheless, Gielow used it in that way. He wrote his program as a general-descriptor search program and demonstrated it with a small real estate file. The program could search descriptors for location city, price range, and number of bedrooms and bathrooms. Like ADA, this was only technically an online and time-shared system—it was more of a remote-batch system that did not allow interactive modification of a search as it progressed, or use any of intermediate search products as partial products in search reformulations. It used an IBM 1050 terminal for access to an IBM 7040 computer, with IBM 1301 disk and IBM 7320 drum-storage units located at an IBM facility in New York City. The database contained only a few records, but enough to demonstrate the system. After the demonstration, Gielow made no further use of this system; he created it primarily to show how this programming language, an interactive form of FORTRAN, was usable for interactive searching. Also in the fall of 1964, as described later, researchers at the University of Iowa considered the use of QUIKTRAN as an approach for remote searching of legal databases.

EXPLICIT/IMPLICIT

In August 1965 Drew proposed a design for a reference retrieval language for online searching. His proposal addressed two different and incompatible search environments, which could be described in today's language as end-user searching versus power searching by a trained intermediary. These environments were to be served with separate online search dialogues: IMPLICIT was a question-asking system, rather than a query language; EXPLICIT was a search language that aimed to provide power and flexibility with specific operators. Neither dialogue depended on syntactic analysis (Drew 1965f).

Previous Lockheed designs had assumed the use of a low-speed output device, severely limiting tutorial possibilities and reducing the possibility of displaying alternatives to allow a searcher to select rather than specify. In a break from the past, EXPLICIT assumed that users had an IBM 2260 CRT with keyboard and cursor as well as an IBM 360/30 computer with disk and IBM Data Cell storage. The keyboard would have defined function buttons (YES, NO, EXPLAIN, SAVE, PRINT). As far as possible, questions were to be answerable by the use of buttons that conveyed a conventional meaning.

Drew's design included important online features that were present in earlier systems: a thesaurus with hierarchical relationships displayed for broader or narrower terms; titles-only search output (and similar display options for authors, subject headings, accession number, publication dates, or corporate source field data) for the first (or next) ten documents in the output file; weighted term searching to facilitate ranking output by perceived relevance or importance; construction of a list of search terms for future use (a SAVED SEARCH) for online searching or SDI; and an offline printing option.

Drew also proposed entirely new features that were used widely later in online systems: term posting counts with index displays; search set numbers for use in later operations; construction of a searcher-defined file of document accession numbers that a searcher could retrieve again without repeating the search (a KEEP function with a separate file name); tutorial information on demand; and user comments to the system operators. Other systems (e.g., MIT, SDC) may have implemented some of these features at about this time, but because the distribution list for *Information Retrieval Notes* included interested outside parties, this amounted to "publication" of these ideas at a date earlier than the reports that other developers distributed. Drew's August 1965(f) document identified and proposed key features that Summit used later as the basis for the initial DIALOG system. Drew (1996) modestly maintained that his August 1965 specifications paper represented not just his own ideas, but ideas from everyone working on the ADA project at that time. He did not create them after looking at outside systems; the list was developed independently from the ADA group's own experience. Drew (1996) did not remember exactly where the idea for set and subset posting counts came from: "It might have been me. It might have been Summit. We talked a lot during those times." Nonetheless, our review of all the internal reports showed that Drew was the principal spokesperson for most of the major concepts of the early Lockheed systems.

Drew noted that Summit believed that end-user searching was of secondary importance. Summit's attitude reflected Lockheed library practice, where end users accessed library systems only sporadically and preferred to have librarians do the searches. A typical use pattern was to request an extensive bibliography at the start of a new project, obtain all the pertinent documents, and update it seldom, if ever. Researchers preferred the convenience of explaining the requirements to a trained searcher and getting the results printed and delivered by mail. In contrast, Drew thought that the online user interface was a fundamental issue for consideration for industry-wide practices or standards, and he wanted to publish his internal EXPLICIT/IMPLICIT report to stimulate wider distribution and discussion. Gerald Salton, a consultant to the project, saw the paper and wanted to publish it in the *Communications of the ACM*, of which he was an editor. Drew thought that was a good idea, but Summit argued to the Research Lab management that the paper was proprietary information that should not be published. His argument prevailed, and Drew was not permitted to publish this pioneering work (Drew 1996, 1997).

Based on the experience he had gained with online search systems, Drew saw a need for an effective time-sharing system that would let a single computer support multiple online terminals simultaneously. This led him to develop LACONIQ, the executive program described next. He observed that the time-sharing software developed for MIT's Project MAC and other time-shared systems was multipurpose in design, and thus inefficient for specific applications, so he designed his software specifically for IR applications.

LACONIQ Time-Sharing Monitor

With internal support, Drew and other Palo Alto Research Lab staff started work in 1965 on programs that permitted the programming and simultaneous operation of various time-shared online application programs (Drew 1965c, 1965e). The resulting software was the LACONIQ (Laboratory Computer Online Inquiry) time-sharing monitor, with a prototype application for bibliographic searching. LACONIQ's design supported several terminals serving the same application, and also different simultaneous applications. ("Monitor" in this case was the program that monitored the assignment of computer resources to various application programs running simultaneously, not a CRT monitor.) This monitor was different from others then in use; it polled the remote consoles at the system's convenience, rather than responding to interrupts generated by users' consoles ("contention" mode). The monitor scheduled all system resources (communication lines, core storage, CPU use, I/O channels) and was the system software that allowed Lockheed computers to work in a time-shared mode.

LACONIQ was designed for the computer available to the group, which was an IBM 360/30 with multiple remote CRTs (IBM 2260 and Sanders 720 types). The researchers believed that the 32K bytes of core storage available on this system could provide satisfactory online service for four simultaneous terminal users, and an upgrade to an IBM 360/40 could accommodate twelve users.

The first version of LACONIQ was operational in December 1966, supporting three IBM 2260 consoles (two operating at remote locations). Each display station had its own small printer. By mid-1967, ten online applications were in development or in operation with this system—including text writing, updating, and retrieval from a file of engineering documents; processing of failure data on missile component parts; support of retrieval experiments as part of an ONR research program on automatic indexing and abstracting (with files of abstracts of physics articles, and a book on medical terminology); and retrieval from a file of military capabilities and resources. LACONIQ allowed quick and easy setup of an online application to permit others to create, retrieve, and manipulate files online. ADA and DIALOG were two application programs that used this early systems work (Drew 1967; Reiter 1967; Bridges 1967). In addition to Drew, Reiter, and Bridges—who published accounts of LACONIQ's development—the LACONIQ group included Stephan Burr, Ed Estes, Len Fick, Ken Gielow, A. J. Nichols, Sidney Shayer, and Gordon Uber.

LACONIQ permitted DIALOG to operate in a multi-terminal mode in January 1968 for the first time. However, its use was short-lived. In the summer of 1968, Lockheed hired Stuart Madnick, friend of employee Mark Radwin and MIT graduate student, to write a self-contained time-shared version of DIALOG. Madnick had worked previously as an implementer of IBM's Cambridge Monitor System. In just two months at Lockheed, he extended IBM's system to run a five-terminal DIALOG system on an IBM 360/30 with 32K bytes of main memory (the smallest configuration made for a 360 system), some IBM 2311 removable DASDs, and a 600 megabyte IBM Data Cell. Madnick's work remained the basis for DIALOG's operating system for several years, divorcing it from LACONIQ or any other system (Radwin, 1997). Drew's involvement with IR and further development of DIALOG concluded in 1968.

Even though the Lockheed Palo Alto Research Lab staff had been working on advanced computer approaches to library data processing for years, including cooperative work with Kozumplik and the TIC in their own Palo Alto facility, a Lockheed publication said that, "On-line real time dialog library catalog systems, admittedly more powerful, are still excessively costly" (Kozumplik and Lange 1966). The staff pursued a number of leads for R&D support. One lead in 1965 was possible NASA support for development of a prototype online reference-retrieval system. The next section discusses this funding pursuit.

DIALOG

Summit described the birth of DIALOG with the following statement, which appeared in two different publications (1968b, 49; 1969a, 67): "Beginning in 1966, personnel of the Information Sciences Group of the Lockheed Palo Alto Research Laboratory began the experimental development of an on-line retrieval language called DIALOG." With this assertion, he seemed to separate DIALOG from the previous projects—ADA, QUIKTRAN, EXPLICIT/IMPLICIT, LACONIQ, and other Lockheed work. Summit (1981) recalled that the conceptual design of DIALOG "all came together one morning in January of 1966; the preliminary design specification had been completed." This moment came six months after Drew's proposal for EXPLICIT/IMPLICIT, which had detailed specifications for the major features to be incorporated into DIALOG, as well as requirements, organization, and hardware issues for an upgrade of CONVERSE. Drew's design included basic commands, an alphabetic index display of search terms and related terms with posting counts, the creation of a numbered set for the results of each search statement, and the option of using the set numbers in later search statements. In February, Lockheed sent an unsolicited proposal to NASA, while the system was not yet operational.

In June, the name "DIALOG" appeared in print for the first time (Summit 1966c). Even after personal communications with Drew and Summit, we were unable to trace the source of the name. The origin may have been Drew's use of the word "dialogues" in the title of his August 1965 design proposal, *Two reference-retrieval dialogues* (Drew 1965f). "DIALOG" appeared in the title of the first users' manual, published in November 1966 (*DIALOG users manual*), as well as in another report that month (Summit 1966a). Summit used DIALOG in the titles of two other editions of the manual that appeared in March (1967a) and in a September 1967 report (1967b). The mid-1968 COSATI demonstration and report (which we discuss later) labels the Lockheed system as DIALOG II. The ERIC study described later noted that DIALOG II software was installed in July 1969. The identification "II" was dropped soon after that, however, and the system was then called simply "DIALOG". Realizing the commercial importance of protecting the name, Radwin had Lockheed's legal office register a trademark for it. That action had the unintentional but interesting consequences of forcing IBM to stop using the name in magazine advertising inserts sections and forcing Exxon to rename its speech synthesis and speech recognition subsidiary name from "DIALOG Systems" to "Verbex" (Radwin 1997).

In 1966(c) Summit provided the first written description of DIALOG commands and features (EXPAND, SELECT, COMPARE, and DISPLAY) for a system to be used by non-experts with the NASA bibliographic database. The system also provided EXPLAIN, TYPE, and PRINT commands, posting counts for each term searched, and an online thesaurus display with related terms. It used a logic command (COMPARE) that performed *all* simple logic operations for two given terms or set numbers (A and B, A or B, A not B, B not A) and displayed the results in a matrix rather than requiring a searcher to specify which logic relationship was needed. This required too much processing power for public use, and the requirement of an explicit logical operation soon replaced the COMPARE command.

The same report set up a schedule calling for DIALOG simulation with an IBM 360 console typewriter (to test sequence steps and command displays) on June 24, 1966; demonstration with an IBM 2260 display unit of prototype retrieval from a sample file of 100 NASA citations on July 15; and testing with a full file in August. Pending receipt of the IBM Data Cell storage unit, display terminals, and full NASA file demonstration searches of the full database operating under the LACONIQ monitor system were scheduled for August 19. A remote station for searching was to be installed at the NASA Ames Research Center on September 16. All development to this point had been done with only Lockheed funding, but in July NASA finally responded to the February proposal by awarding a contract to fund the proposed schedule.

This replacement for ADA was a flexible, user-directed language for retrieving document references. The design did not limit it to any particular database, but rather left it open for application to a wide variety of IR problems. Although its main purpose was to obviate the need for intermediaries, it included features that only frequent searchers such as library staff would use. The online programs were in basic assembly language. The query language, at least as of March 1967 (we were unable to verify the existence of all these functions in the 1966 reports), consisted of commands in the form of verbs such as EXPAND, SELECT, COMBINE, DISPLAY (for output on a CRT), TYPE (for output on the low-speed teletypewriter printer), PRINT (for output on the high-speed printer at the mainframe computer), KEEP, END SEARCH, and LIMIT, followed by specific parameters (Summit 1967a). These commands are almost identical to the DIALOG commands still in use in the 1990s. However, they appeared on searchers' keyboards as the upper case or shift values of the top row of keys. For example:

BEGIN $
SELECT   <

```
COMBINE     >
EXPAND      @
DISPLAY     *
TYPE        (
```

Searchers had to use symbols to combine terms in Boolean statements: the plus (+) for OR, the asterisk (*) for AND, and the minus (−) for NOT. The symbols were a convenience for searchers, since entering a logical operator with a single keystroke helped to compensate for the relatively slow transmission of characters to and from the program. The designers' decision to use symbols for the commands was also a deliberate attempt to help users distinguish the logical operators from the search terms (Summit 1987). DIALOG offered a template for searchers to place on their terminal keyboards to remind them of the functions associated with specific keys. (DIALOG trainers and users complained later that the templates were a nuisance and kept falling off the keyboards.) Later the program allowed the text versions of OR, AND, and NOT in search statements. By 1984, when the DIALOG Version 2 software was implemented, user documentation and training sessions had stopped making any mention of the symbols.

The predefined commands not only functioned independently of search terms, but could be entered in any order. The program's modular structure allowed searchers to build and revise their strategies, slowly and systematically, based on their needs and on feedback at every step. This split the search process into a sequence of small steps, each of which was quite simple (Summit 1971).

> **1966 Milestone**
>
> DIALOG was the first online search system to provide set numbers to intermediate search products, along with a means to make use of those sets in later operations.

The March 1967 manual provided the first full description of the DIALOG language and retrieval system (Summit 1967a). It described basic commands: BEGIN, EXPAND, SELECT, COMBINE, LIMIT, KEEP, DISPLAY, TYPE, PRINT, and END. The design included a thesaurus capability to identify alphabetically- and subject-related search terms, and Boolean operators (AND, OR, NOT). Each search response received a set number that users could incorporate in later operations during that search session. This use of set numbers was an approach not seen in any other online systems. Other design staff members of the early DIALOG days strongly resisted assigning set numbers to intermediate results; they felt that using so much of the limited, and expensive, memory space for storing intermediate answer sets was extravagant. They agreed upon a compromise approach that used the intermediate sets, but limited the total amount of memory space allocated for the working storage of each active searcher. That allocation increased every year thereafter, as file sizes and intermediate sets grew larger and larger. Fortunately, memory costs dropped every year. Several years later, Wente (1971, 102–103) commented:

A "linear" mode of search criteria entry was employed in the initial [Bunker-Ramo] test and was found through user comments to be less desirable than the parallel entry mode of the second [DIALOG] test. The linear mode allowed the user to operate on his initial search results . . . it further allowed him to revert to his previous status should he proceed too far—usually to "zero" documents retrieved after a logical "and" operation. The need to restart searches for this reason proved annoying, particularly to library reference analysts, because of the time lost and resulting repetition of steps. The alternative "parallel" entry mode created "sets" of documents which could then be combined in an unlimited manner at any point in the search, with combinations of two or more sets in turn being processable just as any other sets created by direct selection from inverted files. Library personnel particularly praised the "set" approach, while non-library users were not antagonistic to its greater learning requirement. This more powerful logic capability therefore became a clear preference for RECON.

The set number approach continued with DIALOG and its derivative systems, and many systems by other organizations incorporated it.

The first version of DIALOG did not allow entering strings of terms in Boolean expressions in a single search step. Terms could be entered only one at a time, or selected from a display. Terms selected then could be combined using Boolean operators. This two-step, indirect design also was deliberatea—intended to help novices develop and execute a search strategy interactively. Experienced searchers, however, found it to be tedious and frustrating. As DIALOG evolved, the developers made changes to accommodate the preferences of both experienced librarians and end-user searchers. Summit (1971, 92) reflected:

During the initial design, there was deep concern over the typical user's ability to deal with Boolean logic. To simplify this operation, COMBINE allowed only two input steps... and automatically produced three results sets: 1 AND 2, 1 OR 2, and 1 NOT 2. Thus the user could build a very complex expression in small steps. This philosophy was modified to allow any number of input sets, and a single Boolean operator at each step (1 OR 2 OR 3). The modification was made because many users found the earlier procedure tedious and time consuming... In the final modification, full Boolean logic of any complexity was allowed. Despite this extended facility, many users continued to deal with relatively simple expressions... there seem to be substantial individual differences in the ability to use Boolean logic effectively. The compromise we have reached is to allow recursion with single Boolean expressions for the novice as well as complex specification for the more sophisticated user.

Because the retrieval logic was independent of any database, DIALOG was applicable to a variety of retrieval problems. In 1968, researchers applied DIALOG to four small areas of experimentation, including a personnel file, a file of criminal records, a COSATI database, and a database of descriptions of 1,200 diseases. We examine these applications in more detail later.

Even though JURIS was not implemented until 1971, using a copy of DIALOG's RECON that was developed for NASA, George Kondos, operations research specialist in the Government Information Systems Division of Lockheed, was exploring the *potential* application of DIALOG to legal reference material as early as 1968. Kondos (1968) described how DIALOG could be used for retrieval in the areas of law enforcement, legislation, administration, and judicial proceedings. We introduce Kondos and JURIS again in chapter 9.

These small experiments with management, legal, and medical data augured the great variety of nonbibliographic databases to which others would apply DIALOG years later. Summit (1971) summarized his philosophy in designing and adapting DIALOG: "The design criterion most often ignored, perhaps because of historical inability to include it, is that of flexibility. It is no longer necessary to find the 'one best way' to design a retrieval system; it is now possible to design a system that is responsive to individual differences in user needs as well as individual differences in the approach to problems" (94). This philosophy of flexibility and adaptability from the beginning may have been the key to DIALOG's wide acceptance, adoption, and eventual enormous commercial success.

After its initial support for the Information Sciences Lab (through 1966), Lockheed provided fewer funds for retrieval system development. The prototype might have disappeared, just as most of the systems described thus far did, if the project management had not been chasing opportunities for external support to permit it to become self-supporting. Among the efforts to move beyond the demonstration stage to regular production search services was the initiative to obtain NASA support for continued development and use, beginning with the demonstration project at the NASA Ames Research Center discussed next.

Summit later acknowledged the critical role that government support played in sustaining DIALOG at this point, allowing it to survive and grow. In 1973 (191), in an after-dinner talk at a small conference sponsored by various federal agencies, he paid tribute:

Accomplishments over the past five years have been substantial. . . . These developments would not have taken place without active support from the public sector. Although *we* all recognize both the utility and economy of computer-assisted retrieval, the obscurity of payout made the private sector reluctant to initiate investment. The present expanding use of information-retrieval technology in the private sector seems to confirm the optimistic expectations of those among you who provided initial support.

NASA/RECON

The DIALOG development story continued with activities supported by NASA. We interrupt it briefly, however, to review NASA's history and to chronicle the contributions of Bunker-Ramo Corporation to what became known as RECON (Remote Console).

NASA

The Space Act of 1958 established NASA to contribute to knowledge of phenomena in the atmosphere and outer space, develop and operate aerospace vehicles and probes, and study the potential benefits of and opportunities for using aeronautical and space activities. The Act charged NASA with providing the widest practicable and appropriate dissemination of information concerning its activities and findings. From the beginning, NASA collected and indexed reports, books, and journal articles containing aerospace scientific and technical information. NASA initiated its computerized system in 1962, and agency staff and contractor staff entered bibliographic citations into the computer and searched them in batch mode (Pryor 1975). In 1963, they established a decentralized retrieval system by providing a batch search program and monthly issues of bibliographic records on tape (Wente 1965). The growing size of the file and an awareness of the potential of third-generation computers led to initial planning in late 1964 for an online search system at NASA.

One of the NASA staff who contributed to the design specifications, and later the successful system implementation, was government science advisor and technical information specialist Van Wente. Wente had worked as a chemical engineer for Firestone Rubber and Tire Company before beginning his government career in 1950 with the Naval Research Laboratory. He worked at the U.S. Atomic Energy Agency from 1956 until 1961, when he joined NASA. Wente's supervisor was Melvin Day, who was instrumental in moving AEC and NASA into a position of leadership in technical information services and technology during the 1960s and 1970s. He was deputy director and later director of NASA's Office of Scientific and Technical Information, and from 1967 to 1970 he was deputy assistant administrator for Technology Utilization at NASA. Day continued working in the field of scientific- and technical-information handling by serving in management positions at NSF, NLM, and NTIS.

In 1964, after discussion with Day, Summit prepared an unsolicited proposal to use a Lockheed-developed online search system for automating NASA's information system. Unknown to Summit, Simon Ramo of Bunker-Ramo had talked to Day and Wente about the same issue, and had also submitted an unsolicited proposal (Wente 1995). NASA responded in April 1965 by issuing a request for proposals (RFP) for developing a prototype online system to employ the full NASA document collection (about 200,000), in a realistic library environment for direct use by scientists and engineers (Hlava 1978).

Bunker-Ramo Corporation

As described in chapter 2, Bunker-Ramo formed in 1964 by the merger of three organizations with strong experience in aerospace, computers, and data communications. Based in Canoga Park, California, the staff of this new organization had experience with high-volume searching of large data files with nationwide data communication systems.

Bunker-Ramo's work on the development of NASA/RECON was an outgrowth of an assignment that Bunker-Ramo's president, Simon Ramo, had given to Herbert Mitchell in August 1964. Ramo suggested that Mitchell explore how the new company could apply its expertise in online desktop communications to online retrieval.

Mitchell had extensive experience with computers, data communications, and IR. With a Ph.D. in applied mathematics in 1948 from Harvard, where he helped Howard Aiken build the Harvard Mark II computer, his earlier experience included work as a logical designer and programmer at Eckert-Mauchly, UNIVAC, Sperry Rand, Honeywell, Collins Radio, and Teleregister.

Mitchell was aware of several available computer-based information systems, such as MEDLARS and a legal information service, and his own organization's brokerage information services. He considered combining several of these into a single service and quickly created a proposal for a "Direct electronic library" (Mitchell 1964). He wrote another internal document in April 1965 that described in more detail how the direct electronic library would be used for bibliographic searching, making use of the NASA database and the Teleregister Model 213 Display Station for online searching with up to one hundred concurrent users. The distribution of this document, however, included only six people, including Ramo.

Ramo presented the online system idea to Mel Day at NASA in the fall of 1964. Ramo was well-known and respected within NASA. In 1964 he received the Air Force's award for making the greatest contribution over the first ten years of the guided missile program. NASA management liked Ramo's idea, but as mentioned earlier, they received a similar unsolicited proposal from Lockheed at about the same time and issued an RFP instead of immediately awarding a contract to either company.

Lockheed, Bunker-Ramo, IBM, and seven other companies submitted proposals in June 1965. NASA chose Bunker-Ramo, believing that they had an existing system to which they were willing to add new programming in order to meet NASA's minimum specifications (Wente 1987). Other considerations were that Bunker-Ramo had extensive experience in computers and online data communications, and most importantly, they were the lowest bidder. Mitchell (1990) said that the NASA RFP seemed "to be an ideal way to get started in the broad field I had been proposing, and I persuaded our management to bid on the contract. I also persuaded management to do the programming without charge so we could have proprietary rights to it when the contract was completed. Otherwise the government would own those rights."

Bunker-Ramo conducted the test primarily at four locations—Langley Research Center, Electronics Research Center (Cambridge), NASA headquarters, and Aerospace Research Applications Center—with terminals also located at the Center for Application of Science and Technology (Detroit) and the NASA information facility in College Park, Maryland, using twenty-three remote terminals, Bunker-Ramo's programs, and a UNIVAC 1050 computer (Wente 1968).

In spring 1966, Mitchell labored on converting the database, which had 275,00 bibliographic citations and was growing at the rate of 2,000 per week. Staff in Suitland, Maryland (near the Goddard Space Flight Center), produced the data on an IBM 1410 computer. Mitchell himself took the reels of backfile tape from there to their GE computer in Canoga Park, California, to generate (on the midnight shift) the inverted files to use on the UNIVAC 1050 in New York City that would provide the online service. When the application programming was complete in May, Mitchell drove from California to New York with a users' manual and about fifty reels of the database on tape that was ready for loading. New tapes were shipped from California to New York with each NASA file update.

1966 Milestone

Bunker-Ramo's version of RECON was the first online search system to use a file of more than 200,000 records (the NASA database).

Bunker-Ramo loaded the database and became one of the first online developers to use an existing machine-readable file of bibliographic records created by another organization (BOLD had used a small file of DDC citations and abstracts in 1965). For contract purposes, Bunker-Ramo adopted the name "RECON," which NASA staff had picked in advance of the selection of any specific system.[1] They chose RECON over the alternative proposed by Breen Kerr, Day's boss at NASA. Kerr's suggestion had been MARIAN, as in "Marian the librarian," the female lead character in *The Music Man*, a stage musical that opened in 1957 and whose film version appeared in 1962. According to Wente (1987), "It was hard to talk him out of that. We worked hard to invent an acronym, or words that fit into the acronym MARIAN. Ever since, I have absolutely detested contrived acronyms."

Bunker-Ramo issued a manual in May (*NASA/RECON—Computer Library* 1966) that used the name "NASA/RECON," but the company labeled it as proprietary information and would not make it public until after June 1. They issued a non-proprietary manual in October 1966 (Meister and Sullivan 1967, Appendix, 31–58). The first edition had "Direct Electronic Library" on the cover; the second used the name "RECON." The RECON equipment included remote consoles, leased telephone lines operating at 1,200 baud (120 cps), a computer facility that included a UNIVAC 1050 (time-shared with two other users), and a large random-access storage system (Fastrand II Drum Storage Subsystem—the same drum memory used for the Library/USA demonstration at the 1964–1965 World's Fair).

1966 Milestone

Bunker-Ramo's version of RECON was the first online search system with a capability for online ordering of source documents.

The system allowed users to order documents online, including microform copies of source materials. Several NASA facilities maintained a microform archive of the material included in the bibliographic database, and some librarians placed the terminal and microform collection in the same room. NASA administration recognized the importance of timely access to the full text of source material in concert with access to on-demand searches.

In Bunker-Ramo's RECON, searchers used function keys on the keyboard rather than English-language commands to enter search expressions. The Bunker-Ramo terminal had sixteen function keys; each key represented one command. (As described later, the second NASA/RECON experiment, with Lockheed's online system, used a command language but also included defined single-stroke keys for certain major functions.)

The online system was an extension of one that Bunker-Ramo had developed earlier, the one that they demonstrated at the 1964–1965 New York World's Fair Library/USA exhibit (chapter 2). The software allowed a searcher to enter a term without using any command language. The system responded with a display of the term and ±6 alphabetically adjacent terms. When a searcher entered an authorized term from the dictionary (the *NASA Thesaurus*), the system immediately displayed the retrieved citations. The system also had an EXPAND function that showed cross-referenced terms and their posting counts. At each stage, a user saw the total number of documents that matched the search at that point. The software did not permit recursive searching; searchers had to create sets and whittle them down to desired size. If a search was unsatisfactory, a user had to retreat to previous stages one step at a time, or begin all over.

The project evaluators, Dennis Sullivan and David Meister, were human-factors specialists from Bunker-Ramo. They reported their findings to NASA and also to their professional colleagues at the 1967 ADI annual meeting. Although the system was operating at six locations, only the Langley, Virginia, facility had enough usage to warrant formal evaluation. Over a seven-week period the evaluators counted total number of searches conducted and number of successful searches, which they defined as those that resulted in a searcher viewing at least one title. Even by this modest standard, only half of the 2,409 searches could be considered successful. After users acquired experience, Sullivan and Meister met with them in small groups for informal, in-depth discussions and asked them to fill out a detailed questionnaire. They gathered reactions to RECON as well as many suggestions for desirable features of an advanced retrieval system, and they compared the speed and accuracy of the online system to the existing offline search system.

The overall evaluation results indicated that librarians were more critical of the system than were scientists and engineers. Both, however, considered online superior to manual searching and offline batch searching. Their criticisms seemed to be attributable to the prototype status of the system, and most respondents were optimistic that programmers could resolve the problems. Most of the scientists and engineers were able to use the system reasonably well with instruction and help from librarians.

NASA was pleased with the pilot and wanted to continue it for some time after the two-month test. But another Bunker-Ramo department had started a service bureau business in the brokerage industry; it used the same UNIVAC 1050 that the NASA test ran on, and the company reallocated the computer resources because the business was more profitable than the NASA contract. The stock market provided many more clients than the few bibliographic-searching clients. Internal maneuvering resulted in new prices for computer time and rental costs for the consoles and communications gear, with charges for outside contract work more than twice the amount as for internal projects. Bunker-Ramo offered to continue the trial on a month-to-month basis at twice the fee that they charged during the trial period (on the pretext of recouping the losses of the initial project). NASA refused to pay that much, instead terminating the project and leaving Bunker-Ramo with a large loss. Mitchell left the project in October 1966 and, after a brief move to TRW in January 1967, went to NASA's Goddard Space Center.

In response to a February 1968 NASA RFP for follow-up development and implementation of the full NASA/RECON system, Bunker-Ramo submitted a proposal with a high cost estimate because management wanted to recover the financial loss of the first project. They lost that gamble when NASA awarded the contract to Lockheed instead.

Mitchell's son, William, summed up the situation: "As with its airline reservation systems business, Bunker-Ramo was simply too small a company to initiate this scale of information access. Less than a dozen employees participated in the development of the NASA/RECON prototype during the 18 months of the project. The technology was present but the vision and the resources with which to scale up the infrastructure were absent" (Mitchell 2001, 5).

The Ames Experiment

Phase I—Single Terminal Operation at Ames

During the Bunker-Ramo experiment and evaluation, the Lockheed Information Retrieval Group, completely under in-house funding, continued to develop an improved online system. Undaunted by NASA's awarding the NASA/RECON prototype project to Bunker-Ramo in 1965, Summit submitted an unsolicited proposal in February 1966 for a parallel online experiment. NASA awarded a $20,000 contract to Lockheed in July to install and operate a remote terminal at NASA Ames Research Center utilizing DIALOG to access the NASA file of 260,000 citations. NASA wanted to begin the test with a full-scale system, since the time for implementation was short and any special problems of large scale would not become apparent until searchers started using it. The Ames Research Center is at Moffett Field in Mountain View, California, within ten miles of the Lockheed facilities and DIALOG project staff. Summit was designated project manager, and he acknowledged Donald Chamberlin, Peggy Don, Robert Mitchell, and Dexter Shoultz as Lockheed's principal programmers of the project, along with Keith Eckhardt of IBM (Summit 1967a). At that point, DIALOG was the culmination of six years of research in information storage and retrieval conducted in the Lockheed Information Science Group.

Shoultz wrote the first file-generation program, as used on the NASA database, in assembly language. Parts of his program continued in use for several years on other files, particularly those to create the linear (master record) index and the inverted index files. Radwin wrote more generalized file-conversion and -generation programs in PL-1 to work with Shoultz's programs and designed the full-text retrieval language extensions to DIALOG, while Shelly Giles improved the file-conversion and file-generation programs associated with full-text processing. Mitchell and Lew followed as the main systems programmers for the NASA project and rewrote and improved Shoultz's programs. Summit acknowledged Shoultz as the principal programmer for the file conversion and load routines, and the two co-authored a report on the file conversion programs (Summit and Shoultz 1967). Summit (1975b) related a story about Shoultz that illustrates the primitive state of understanding of the technology of that time. Whenever Shoultz received a file tape that was unreadable and could not be loaded, he was sure that the tape had either received a dose of upper-atmosphere magnetism or a blast of cosmic rays while being shipped via airplane, so he insisted that tapes be delivered by train.

The contract specified use and testing of IBM's new 2321 Data Cell device, which had a storage capacity of 400 million bytes of information, for storing the 300,000 NASA report and journal citations in the Information Sciences Group computer, an IBM 360/30 with 32K bytes of core storage, the smallest model made. By November 1966, indexes to the files were generated and stored on the Data Cell and two IBM 2311 disk drives. In April 1967, a single remote terminal was installed in the Ames Research Center Technical Library. It consisted of an IBM 2260 keyboard and display device, an IBM 1053 printer, and an IBM 2848 terminal control unit. The terminal and its support equipment were too large to carry up the stairs to the second floor; workmen lifted them up the outside of the building by a crane, and removed a part of an exterior wall to get them in the second-story library (Summit 1973). The $20,000 installation cost for the equipment nearly equaled the cost of the project itself. Radwin, who supervised the crane, noted that once installed, the equipment heated the room to a temperature that was uncomfortable for staff. Undoubtedly the expansion of online user sites would have stalled had not the size of terminals rapidly shrunk—not many organizations would have bothered to deconstruct a wall and rebuild it just to install a computer terminal.

The online search system used with the later Ames experiment was a big improvement over the earlier ADA. Summit (1967b ii) described the relationship of the Ames system to ADA (which he called CONVERSE): "The current system developed from an early on-line experiment called CONVERSE." The newer system provided five specific commands: EXPAND term (to display alphabetically adjacent terms and their posting counts), EXPAND related term (to display subject-related terms and their posting counts), SELECT (to search on a term and assign a set number to the items retrieved), COMBINE (to cause a specified logical operation to be executed with named set numbers), KEEP (to store retrieved record numbers of interest), and DISPLAY (to recall the record associated with a specified accession number to core storage for output). This combination of commands and Boolean operators (OR, AND, NOT) were features not seen on prior Lockheed system prototypes, and they represented the first public appearance of the DIALOG search language. A description of DIALOG as it was used with the NASA database was given in a technical report and corresponding conference publication by Summit (1966a).

Starting in January 1967, the Ames test ran for two hours each day for two months, for a total of eighty hours. Searchers communicated with the computer over telephone lines at 1,200 baud (120 cps). The telephone connection suffered substantial problems, causing about eight hours of downtime, and every Monday morning the telephone company had to reestablish the lines. Trouble with the IBM equipment caused about seven hours of lost time. In all, the system was down for almost one quarter of the time during this two-month test. Because the system supported only a single terminal, engineers and scientists at the Ames facility were invited to sign up for searching at scheduled times. The reaction was enthusiastic; within a month, the reservation list was backlogged from one to two weeks. Summaries of representative sample searches performed by NASA Ames scientists and engineers showed search times of about one hour, with favorable comments from searchers (Summit 1967b).

Phase II—Single Terminal Operation at NASA

In July 1967, during the contract's second phase, Lockheed shipped the terminal to NASA headquarters in Washington, D.C., for further testing and evaluation. NASA staff, mainly Karen Milligan, a NASA librarian, used it during a three-hour period each morning for one year, to search on behalf of other NASA personnel. Even though the sponsor and Lockheed described the project as only a demonstration and experiment, staff performed over 300 useful searches that year. They searched on an IBM 2260 CRT with an IBM 1053 terminal printer, operating at about 240 cps (Summit 1969b).

The file grew during this period to 400,000 citations, including abstracts for the 1967 items. A brief test was conducted of the feasibility and utility of the storage and display (not indexing) of 150-word abstracts for technical reports. However, insufficient usage information was collected to permit any judgement of the effectiveness of online abstracts. The records always carried a one-sentence notation of content, but abstracts were added on a regular basis in 1972 for records entering the system. The impact on storage costs, as well as the prevailing attitude that summaries and abstracts were not needed online because full microfiche copies of the reports themselves were co-located at many terminal sites, may have delayed the online availability of abstracts on NASA/RECON. The emphasis was on finding and obtaining a few good documents, or a few known documents, rather than comprehensive text-searching capabilities. Daniel Wilde (1997) of NERAC, who had started working with the NASA tapes in 1966, recalled, "In those early days, the NASA database was fairly limited. We only were interested in finding subject topics. All the access points of today were wishful thinking. We did not even retain language. Of course, over the years we rebuilt the file many times."

Lockheed installed another terminal at Ames in October 1967. Thus the system was accessible from three sites—Palo Alto, Moffett Field, or Washington, D.C.—but not simultaneously. This increased the pressure for DIALOG to transition to a multiple-terminal system. In January 1968, DIALOG operated for the first time in a multi-terminal mode. For RECON, the obvious choice for data communication during the 1966–1968 period was 240 cps over voice-grade telephone lines. NASA already had such leased lines, and they made them available to RECON at little additional cost (Wente 1971). The telephone lines caused far fewer problems at this time, but the IBM Data Cell continued to cause frequent non-recoverable failures. Overall, the system was down about 12 percent of the scheduled time during this year, about half as much as it was down during the first Ames test period (Summit 1969b).

DIALOG/RECON

In February 1968, NASA issued the second RFP for development and implementation of the full NASA/RECON, which resulted in the current version. Remembering that the RECON name had been selected years earlier, before a system existed, NASA staff quipped, "This is the *real* RECON" (Wente 1987). Basing the RFP specifications upon findings of the previous Bunker-Ramo and Lockheed contracts, they named twenty features that Bunker-Ramo's final report (Meister and Sullivan 1967) had enumerated for an ideal IR system. NASA stipulated in the RFP that the resulting RECON software would be government-owned, which permitted NASA to make it available as public-domain software. Legislation required NASA to spin off to the public the results of its activities in all areas, including software development (Wente 1995). Three organizations competed for the RFP, and in June 1968 NASA awarded a contract to Lockheed to design software—that is, to modify the existing proprietary DIALOG system—and to install the system on the IBM 360/50 at the NASA Scientific and Technical Information Facility (STIF), which is now the Center for Aerospace Information (CASI), in College Park. For Lockheed, this was a development contract to deliver software to NASA. This was not a contract for online service; that was yet to come. NASA was to operate the system to provide online service to ten NASA facilities around the country. NASA's project manager was Larry Stevens, who later worked for Informatics and Tymshare. Summit was Lockheed's designated project leader, and he assembled a group of five programmers to upgrade the current search software to NASA/RECON. Mitchell was in charge of hardware, system, and programming; he wrote the file loading program, designed the interface with RECON files, and wrote the original SELECT, COMBINE, and DISPLAY commands. Lew and the other programmers wrote the command processing and output processing programs. Drew (1997) described Mitchell as the real hero in this development project.

The expanded system needed more disk capacity and memory than were available on the Palo Alto machine. Therefore, until the Palo Alto computer could be upgraded, the developers used an IBM 360/40 at Lockheed's Sunnyvale facilities while the programmers still used keypunch machines at Palo Alto. They sent the card decks to Sunnyvale, where running a program sometimes took three to four days because the RECON project had low priority at the Sunnyvale computer center. Eventually the project got its own upgraded 360/40 with 256K of memory (less than the storage and processing capacity of today's personal computers).

The project quarters at this time were both Spartan and crowded. The computer room had no raised floor; all the interface cables and power cords were exposed. With new computer equipment and disk drives, the computer facility encroached on the cafeteria space—at one point, a staff member was using the cafeteria kitchen counter as a desk.

1968 Milestone

NASA/RECON was among the first online bibliographic search systems to operate in a multifile access mode.

In October 1968, with the addition of a second NASA file, and while still in development, RECON operated for the first time in a multifile mode. Users could choose the file they wished to search, and it was available immediately without intervention from computer center staff (Summit 1980a). Four separate files were available online shortly after: STAR, IAA, W (research résumés), and X (classified and limited access documents). NASA also created a file of all 1962–1968 correspondence and internal working group memos involving top NASA officials. This correspondence file provided the NASA administration with a powerful method of maintaining high recall and visibility of historical correspondence.

Before this, online searchers did not have an option of file choices (at least, for major databases).[2] In a 1988 presentation to DIALOG staff members, Summit admitted that he had no idea that online systems would have to deal with so many different files. From the beginning, he had thought that the total number of different files to be accommodated would correspond to the number of major abstracting and indexing services, such as *Chemical Abstracts*, *Biological Abstracts*, *Engineering Index*, and *Index Medicus*. Ken Lew wanted a specification on the maximum number of files that DIALOG and its accounting software would have to handle. Lew asked, "What's the maximum number of files that a user will ever remember? 16? 32?" Summit replied, "No. Better make it 128; I can't imagine we'll ever do more than 128." Including private or limited-access files, DIALOG exceeded that number by 1979, and later added about 100 new files per year.

From its inception, NASA had relied on a contractor to run STIF and fulfill its scientific and technical information requirements. Documentation, Inc., had been the first STIF contractor, starting in 1962 when STIF was established. They came to that position with experience in modern information-handling techniques, and operated the automated portion of STIF. In 1968, the successful bidder on the STIF contract was Informatics (they continued until 1980), who supplied about 200 people to acquire and process all the technical report material and enter it into the system, handle the microfiche production and document delivery system, prepare and distribute printed indexes, and operate the STIF computer facility. They even had their own full-time lexicographers (most indexing organizations do not) to maintain the thesaurus and the indexing system.

Informatics was already well known in the computer and information industry. Some of its activity was described in chapter 4, and more is described in chapter 9. Early in its corporate history in the 1960s, Informatics sponsored a major symposium on disk files; following this pioneering effort was their sponsorship of another major symposium in 1965 on online computing, with over 700 attendees. Their MARK IV general purpose database software was delivered in 1968 for batch processing, later upgraded for online operation, and installed in hundreds of organizations. Informatics was a major force in online systems. They even had an online retrieval system in the design and development stage, which Novell (1967) described at an information colloquium. Summit considered Informatics to be a potential threat to DIALOG, because they were so familiar with online software and large database processing, and had started in the online search service business with their own service, as we discuss in chapter 9.

With the new contract for maintenance of NASA/RECON, and after the installation of the DIALOG software on the NASA computer was completed, Informatics adopted software for file maintenance called STIMS (Scientific and Technical Information Modular System). STIMS was NASA's system for high-frequency data updates and for producing various printed indexes. Informatics did not make any modifications to the DIALOG software until Lockheed's development project was complete.

By February 1969, the system was ready and available for NASA personnel to use on a reasonably permanent basis and in March began operation with six RECON stations (Langley Research Center in Hampton, Virginia; Electronics Research Center in Cambridge, Massachusetts; Lewis Research Center in Cleveland, Ohio; STIF in College Park, Maryland; and two sites in NASA headquarters (NASA-RECON 1969; *Progress in Scientific and Technical Communications* 1970, 105; Losee 1971). The addition of fifteen stations during 1969 extended the RECON network to NASA installations across the United States. At the end of 1969 the system was operating with twenty-four consoles at nine locations (see figure 5.1). These were high times for NASA; in July 1969, American astronauts landed on the moon.

In July 1970, RECON replaced batch searching at STIF for the routine processing of literature search requests from users without online terminals (Coles 1973; Wente 1997). The search software was running on the IBM 360/50 at NASA/STIF, returning information from a file of about 700,000 bibliographic records (and growing at the rate of about 70,000 records per year) stored on a combination of magnetic disks and IBM Data Cells (Wente 1971; Losee 1971). DIALOG had completed its contractual requirements to design, develop, install, and modify the NASA/RECON system, at a total cost to NASA of about $1 million (Summit 1975a).

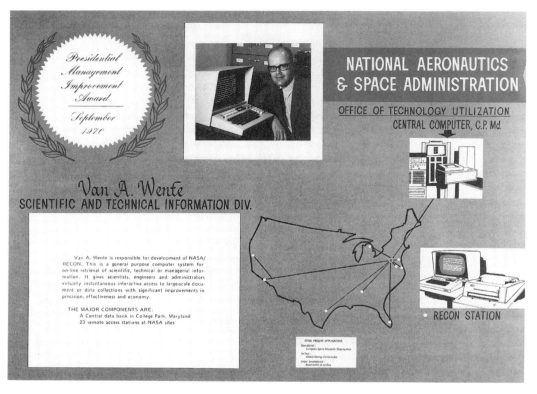

Figure 5.1
A poster was prepared of the 1969 version of NASA/RECON system, to present to the Presidential Management-Improvement Award Committee. It features Van Wente, who won the award. 1970. Photo from private archive of Van A. Wente.

Implementation problems came almost immediately. Three terminals shipped to the NASA library in College Park in spite of their massive size, managed to become misplaced in the back of the library, mixed in with book shipments. After the staff found them, AT&T had to install leased lines, and electricians had to wire each terminal with its own electric power supply because each one consumed so much power. The terminals still overheated regularly and blew the circuit breakers; each time staff had to wait until the machines cooled off before resuming searching.

Data Meister and Sullivan collected in the 1967 tests of the Bunker-Ramo RECON designs had revealed that 76 percent of search terms were subject terms, 14 percent were personal authors, 5 percent were report or contract numbers, and 5 percent were corporate sources. These and other data from users about the importance of system response time influenced NASA's decision to retain all access points but to keep only the subject terms on direct-access disks and to move the other indexes to the slower, but cheaper, data cells.

The Bunker-Ramo and Lockheed tests also had revealed users' great concern for reliability, which depended on the computer, terminal, software, and communications. Users felt most strongly about waiting at the terminal for several minutes without any clue as to when or whether the request would be processed. As a result, an acknowledgment that requests were "in process" or "in queue" was built in. For several years, users could not count on the NASA computer to keep running for more than about thirty minutes at a time. The average full search took about thirty minutes; only about 70 percent of the searches could start and finish without interruption.

While RECON operators could claim priority, if necessary, for access to the IBM 360/50 at the NASA facility in College Park (that had 512K of core storage, two Data Cells, and two 2314 disk units), RECON operated in a time-shared environment with other programming requests. The remote RECON stations communicated with the NASA computer through leased voice-grade telephone lines that were in place already for other NASA purposes. Occasionally, staff had to stop searches because RECON data transmission was interrupted to give priority to special conferences or launches. The terminal was a Bunker-Ramo 12-inch CRT—chosen for its speed and searchers' needs for browsing through online indexes and sampling records in what was considered an enormous database. Data transmitted at 2,400 bits (240 cps)—the printer, by comparison, was slow. The Teletype had a printing speed of only fifteen characters per second, so printouts of long bibliographies were not feasible on these printers; long printouts could be produced, however, at the central computer's high-speed printer and mailed to users.

In 1970, international online use of RECON was demonstrated in Buenos Aires, Argentina. Using a commercial telecommunications network, the National Argentinean Organization for Scientific and Technical Documentation successfully demonstrated online searching (Losee 1971). This was the first test of using TWX/Telex terminals with RECON and was among the first instances of international access to DIALOG. Later versions of various DIALOG and RECON systems incorporated the same communication protocols to accommodate TWX/Telex searching on a regular basis. This was of special interest to users in developing countries with poor telecommunications capability. For example, Bourne demonstrated the first online searching in Cairo, Egypt, in 1976 using this approach to access DIALOG.

In 1971, NASA/RECON supported twenty-four installed terminals. Online service was scheduled to be available for twelve hours per day. NASA was in the process of changing the terminal printers, and already had received twenty-four new printers from TI. The new TIs, relatively quiet thermal printers that operated at thirty characters per second, replaced the older and noisier Teletype units that operated at about twelve characters per second. Rental costs for CRT terminals at this time were in the range of $200–400 per month, and dropping.

In spite of the CRT's speed, response times were irritatingly slow. According to Wolfe (1970), if all twenty-one terminals were using the NASA computer simultaneously, response time was ten to twelve seconds or less. Fong (1971), however, claimed that with fifteen terminals running, the response time was approximately fifteen to twenty seconds. The discrepancy may have resulted from how Wolfe and Fong calculated the average response times, or the performance may have degraded over time. In any case, the response time for the first multiple-terminal version of DIALOG was much slower than the response times for TIP (a few seconds) or QUOBIRD (about a second)—earlier systems that had used only a single, hard-wired terminal. Adelaide Del Frate, the head librarian at the Goddard Space Flight Center who was also responsible for the center's RECON terminal, reported during a discussion at a 1971 forum (Hughes 1973, 15):

In the early days (1969–70) response time was a major deterrent. We had some bad problems, and I am sure that half the people we lost were lost because of system troubles, of which delay in response time was one ... response time is not a major problem now ... [it] is under fifteen seconds, but it depends on the type of data that you run on the terminal and the time of day. If you are on in the morning when everyone else is asleep, the response time is really great, and there is no delay at all; if you go on about noon, forget it.

Also participating in the discussion, Wente added more about response time: "Actually, we say fifteen to forty seconds—the average depends on the time of day. Fifteen seconds would be a good time in the morning, before the West Coast terminals are on the system, and we can say about forty seconds for the afternoon. Forty seconds is the average response time from the time at which you press the transmit button with the request until the response comes back on the CRT" (Hughes 1973, 17).

In 1971, NASA established a RECON users group, with representatives from thirteen agencies to facilitate sharing of system knowledge and understanding. RECON improvements during 1971 included: increased speed of response (by allowing parallel processing of user commands); an increase (from six to twenty-six) in the number of databases that could be defined for searchers; capability for word root (truncation) searches and range searches; and capability to prelimit an entire search (*Progress* 1972, 53). Del Frate and Jane Riddle (1973) commented that after three years of operational use, "System response time continues to dissuade users" (45). They also made a pointed observation about who was actually sitting at the terminals:

During these same postnatal and adolescent years, we have sadly made an almost complete about-face on the original system philosophy of direct user-computer interaction. We originally were, and in a last ditch, nucleic corner we still remain, firm believers in the tenet that the most profitable retrieval from any system is achieved by the user himself directly interfacing with the information. Now we are forced to recognize that the scientists and engineers are not using the system directly and that they prefer ... to entrust their needs to that of an emissary—an intermediary—if indeed, they use it at all.

During 1969, the file continued its steady growth to over 500,000 records. By early 1972, it had grown to 800,000. The online file was the equivalent of NASA's *Scientific and Technical Aerospace Reports*, *International Aerospace Abstracts*, and *Aerospace Medicine and Biology*. Citations had accession numbers that functioned as microfiche location codes, and the microfiche documents were available for manual retrieval from files maintained at each NASA facility, often stored close to the terminals. NASA/STIF at College Park housed the source documents (Wente 1971).

RECON operated on a main linear file of document records and a set of inverted index files. Thus, users could search separately for subjects, authors, corporate sources, and report or contract numbers. Subject indexing was by author-assigned keywords, and index terms NASA staff assigned using the controlled vocabulary of the *NASA Thesaurus*; searchers were supposed to use only terms that appeared in the thesaurus. However, scientists or engineers could enter any word or phrase, even misspelled, and the system responded with an alphabetical thesaurus display of the twenty valid terms closest to the string of characters entered. Each term was displayed with its postings count and an assigned reference number. Alternatively, searchers could display terms that were related semantically to the original search term (that is, related terms in the *NASA Thesaurus*). Instead of re-keying desired terms, searchers could choose them by entering just the reference numbers from the online thesaurus display.

Even though DIALOG/RECON did not yet in 1970 have the capability for free-text searching, professional searchers considered its controlled vocabulary and manual indexing a strong advantage over other systems. In a study that evaluated and compared five online retrieval systems, Wolfe (1970, 30–31) praised RECON for its powerful subject retrieval capabilities:

The thesaurus-controlled vocabulary ... distinguishes the RECON system and gives its user a great advantage ... the RECON user does not have to locate the appropriate subject terms for his search on a hit-or-miss basis ... To determine the narrower terms available for a previously selected term, the RECON user enters an expand command, and the narrower terms and their usage counts are displayed below the original term and its usage count ... This elegant and efficient location and display of appropriate search terms, their usage, and available hierarchical search expansion capabilities is a major Milestone in the development of on-line information retrieval systems.

Wolfe, however, criticized the query language $ < @ +); he felt that the use of symbols was a major flaw in the RECON system.

For an eleven-month period, running from August 1970 to June 1971, NASA distributed evaluation forms with 3,001 search results. The survey results showed that almost 89 percent of respondents found the searches suitable to their needs (Coles 1973). Del Frate provided another picture of the operation of a typical early RECON installation—at the Goddard Space Flight Center. Her description (1973, 2) was more revealing than the evaluation form's data:

The physical facilities for RECON are good. It is located in a glassed-in, quiet area on the second floor right outside the book collection. The emotional climate for RECON is also good. The library staff eagerly anticipated, perhaps too eagerly anticipated, the arrival of RECON; we held a well-publicized advertising campaign; the staff from NASA headquarters gave a series of technical lectures to the potential users; we held weekly instruction sessions and gave assistance before and during user searches. Until this week we had for RECON the almost full time use of a professional librarian with substantial NASA and good user experience, Miss Jane Riddle, the government information-systems librarian, whose help really made this report possible.

After a year of operation, Del Frate observed (2, 4) that some disgruntled users left and did not return:

We thought—perhaps I really should say we prayed—that the downtime, the response time, and the delays in the updating cycles would be minimal after the break-in period. As you can see from the statistics on one-time users, we lost a lot of people in the first peak months when we were having system troubles. We tried but could not bring these people back. They will never come back, although the system has been greatly improved and these things do not now constitute a major deterrent to the use of the system.

Librarians, rather than end users, conducted most searches. The scientists apparently felt that it was more cost efficient for librarians to search; many reported that they would not conduct their own searches even if RECON were in their own buildings. Del Frate and Riddle (1973) concluded that end-user use would not increase appreciably until the need for a search arose often enough to allow users to develop proficiency in searching. They were dismayed at the lack of direct user involvement. "The user is deprived of the stimulating synergistic benefit of direct exchange and the system is deprived of the most valuable feedback of all during its formative years: direct user suggestion and criticism" (45).

Users at Goddard did not use RECON much for current awareness. They employed only some features, and most searches were for subjects rather than authors, corporate report numbers, or other access points. Another discouraging discovery was that users, when discussing what they thought RECON covered, revealed a poor idea of the database scope, content, and updating schedule. This lack of knowledge seemed to contribute to over-anticipation and loss of faith in the system. Del Frate recommended that the system display at the beginning of every search a description of the scope, content, years covered, type of data included, sources, and journals covered.

At the conclusion of this second NASA contract in 1969, DIALOG was installed and operating on the NASA/STIF computer under the name of NASA/RECON. The online service continued operating from the computer in Maryland. Its activities in the 1970s are chronicled in chapter 9. As mentioned earlier, DIALOG staff involvement terminated with the software delivered to NASA at the end of the contract. RECON maintenance and modification then became the responsibility of NASA and its contractors. As a result, NASA/RECON proceeded down an independent path of features, capabilities, and performance.

When the project concluded, NASA placed a copy of the DIALOG software in the public domain by giving a copy to the University of Georgia COSMIC (Computer Software Management and Information Center) software depository. They also deposited a copy of the NASA/STIMS software used for file development and maintenance in conjunction with RECON. NASA had established COSMIC early in 1966 to collect and disseminate to the public computer software that was developed by or for government agencies. The DIALOG software put in the public domain represented not only the enhancements developed with NASA support, but also the much larger asset of the entire DIALOG system that resulted from Lockheed's significant R&D investment every year since 1965.

In 1970, after the DIALOG software was in the depository, copies were available for other organizations to use as the basis for their own systems, including DOJ for JURIS, AEC for AEC/RECON, LC (to provide online service to Congressional offices) (*Progress* 1971, 35–36) and Informatics, Inc. (described earlier in this chapter and in chapter 9). Informatics staff had operational familiarity with this software from working with it at NASA, which no doubt influenced Informatics management to obtain a copy of the DIALOG software to use for other Informatics applications, such as the TOXICON online system and Informatics' own search system (chapter 9).

Other Early Applications

In 1967–1969, Lockheed staff used DIALOG in an experiment with personnel files of the Space Systems Division, to allow additional detailed information to be added to individual employees' files regarding special skills. This skills register permitted fast online searching of a large number of personnel records (initially 6,000 records, but later expanded to about 18,000) to find employees with specified attributes (Summit 1968b, 1969a). While Division management considered it a great success, they failed in their repeated attempts to convince the personnel department to take over the system and operate it company wide.

In 1967, Lockheed staff tested DIALOG with criminal identification records. They prepared a file with data about the physical characteristics of specific individuals, descriptions by witnesses, and other characteristics. The objective was to assist in the identification of suspects. They demonstrated the system in Palo Alto at the annual meeting of the California Peace Officers Association in February 1968 (Summit 1969a). The use of computers to support law enforcement was a popular topic then; the Lockheed work paralleled SDC contract work in support of the LAPD (chapter 2).

In 1967, the Palo Alto Research Lab conducted a study for NASA's Manned Spacecraft Center on data management issues in major areas of concern to NASA (e.g., biomedical, lunar/earth, resources). Eugene Duncan was the project's technical director and Summit wrote the requirements and specifications for a lunar/earth database system (Summit 1968a).

In 1968–1969, with a grant from the U.S. National Institute of Mental Health, Lockheed collaborated with the National Council on Crime and Delinquency (NCCD) to support a pilot demonstration of online searching of the Uniform Parole Reports database. The collection held 57,000 records of data associated with persons released from U.S. prisons in 1965, 1966, and 1967. Users searched the file on the IBM 360/40 at the Research Lab. Radwin conducted online demonstrations with it to large audiences at NCCD in June 1969 in Boston (Summit and Radwin 1969), and at the American Congress of Corrections in August 1969 in Minneapolis (Wenk et al. 1970). Online access to the file permitted analysts to obtain answers quickly to such questions as the relationship of recidivism to the original offense (e.g., for persons released on parole for homicide, what was the frequency of various types of offenses committed during the first year on parole?) (Wenk, Gottfredson, and Radwin 1970). The file remained online into 1972, with 106,000 Uniform Parole Reports (UPR) and about 6,000 Parole Decision Records (PDR) describing parole information and a follow-up period of two years for each case. An interesting innovation that Radwin added, to assist users' analytical work and hypothesis testing, was a feature to create tables from specified X-axis and Y-axis values; the counts in the table cells were the results of automatically ANDing the corresponding X and Y attribute values. This 1970 contract was for the provision of online search service for NCCD and National Parole Board staffs. This was the first *service* contract for DIALOG, and as such, could be considered the starting date of the Lockheed search service.

In 1968, another Lockheed research group used DIALOG to support experiments with a database of 1,200 diseases from Current Medical Terminology, indexed by etiology, signs, symptoms, complications, pathology, and lab procedures. This was associated with a long-range ONR-sponsored study of automatic indexing and abstracting (Earl and Robison 1969).

In May 1968, Battelle staff filmed a demonstration of DIALOG with the COSATI database, along with demonstrations of other online search systems. They gave a demonstration to COSATI members in June 1968 (see chapter 4 for more details). In mid-1968, Noreen Welch described the demonstrations in detail and provided a description of DIALOG features as they existed in April 1968. Welch described the Lockheed system as DIALOG II. Lockheed dropped the "II" soon after and did not use it again until it reappeared with much fanfare in 1984 for a considerably upgraded and enhanced version of the software called DIALOG-2.

In 1971, the Information Systems Programs Office of the Palo Alto Research Lab started contract work for GTE Sylvania's Electronic Warfare Laboratory on a project for the U.S. Army. The goal was to explore the use of DIALOG to maintain a file of bibliographic records from Sylvania, DDC, and other sources, on electronic warfare information. They planned in 1971 to convert the file to standard DIALOG form and install the software on Sylvania's IBM 360/50 computer for their use at their Electronic Defense Laboratory in Mountain View, California (near the Lockheed facilities). This effort continued for several years, with an examination of alternative ways to provide information service on this database to the U.S. Army Electronics Command. The long-range objective was to provide the army with a full-capability minicomputer-based Army Electronic Warfare Information System (AEWIS) retrieval service that operated on a PDP-11/20 or PDP-11/45 computer at the army's Fort Monmouth, New Jersey, research facility. William Pitts built such a system under a Lockheed contract with the army, and later as an independent contractor (Radwin 1997).

DIALOG/ERIC

ERIC

ERIC began in 1964 as an obscure unit within USOE with the name Educational Research Information Center, reflecting its mission to serve what was then the Division of Educational Research. Being viewed as serving only the relatively small and noninfluential educational research community, however, put ERIC at a competitive disadvantage in the fierce budget battles within USOE. In July 1967, the name changed to the Educational Resources Information Center (Burchinal 1983), and ERIC's scope enlarged to cover the literature that represented the broadest definition of education, and to serve the broader practitioner community. Today, ERIC is part of the National Library of Education and is characterized by its combination of decentralized subject-specialty clearinghouses and a central processing facility.

From the beginning of ERIC's operation in the late 1960s, computer tapes were a by-product of preparing the printed abstract journal and other index publications. These tapes were available on loan beginning in 1968, which changed to purchase in 1970. During the 1970s, the tapes were extremely popular for batch-search and SDI operations at many educational institutions; at one time in the late 1970s, about 100 subscribers received ERIC tapes and updates. At the time of ERIC's establishment and initial operation, major USOE participants were Lee Burchinal, director of the Division of Information, Technology, and Dissemination; Harvey Marron, chief of ERIC; and James Prevel.

As a result of demonstrations they had witnessed, Marron and Burchinal agreed to a test of online searching for ERIC, knowing that they would find a way to provide this form of searching on a regular basis. They became convinced that this new online technology would serve ERIC well, and they initiated a series of DIALOG/ERIC contracts. Marron, as early as May 1967, had stated to the ERIC clearinghouse directors that online computer search capability was not as far off as had been originally anticipated when they made the decision to purchase the Termatrex manual file search equipment (Trester 1981). He later said that the driving force behind their interest in online services was a realization that they could not just continue to try improving the status quo with their current systems (Marron 1995).

The Stanford Experiment

In December 1968, USOE awarded a new type of contract to Lockheed—not to develop an online system but rather to use DIALOG software on Lockheed's computer to provide an online retrieval service, at least on an experimental basis. Summit (1987) considered this contract a "point of demarcation" when DIALOG "transitioned from a development organization to a services organization, and we never went back." Actually, this initial contract was for an experimental or demonstration service on a file of 15,000 report citations; the regular service contract did not come until 1971. Burchinal recalled later that USOE had little experience in giving contracts to commercial organizations, and their contracting authority came under restrictions associated with the use of research funds. They had to proceed carefully with their contracts office and hence characterized their projects as experiments or tests. Paisley (1995) confirmed this contracting uneasiness; the story he had heard was that ERIC wanted to install a DIALOG capability for all ERIC clearinghouses and USOE regional offices. The USOE way of proceeding, however, was to evaluate a system first. So they implemented the evaluation with the understanding that only unexpected problems could derail the plan to make DIALOG available at a large number of sites.

1969 Milestone

DIALOG, with the ERIC database, provided the first instance of extensive availability of abstracts online for search output.

In early 1969, Lockheed staff loaded magnetic tapes containing 12,300 bibliographic citations and abstracts from the ERIC index, *Research in Education*, and a backlog of Division of Education Research contractor reports from 1956–1965 that preceded the beginning of ERIC, on the IBM 360/40 computer in Palo Alto (Summit 1970a). The citations and abstracts were stored in full uppercase (all capital letters), as was the practice for all files and computer search systems at that time. Furthermore, abstracts were available for only displaying or printing; they were not searchable because disk capacity was limited and thus online storage space was insufficient for all the corresponding index entry titles required for searching. As described in chapter 2, the SRI system in 1963 had been the first online search system to store the text of abstracts and documents and provide them as search output. However, that was for a very small database for demonstration purposes. Syracuse's SUPARS project in 1970 (chapter 3) appears to have been the first instance of indexing and online *searching* of an extensive database of abstract text, along with the abstracts in search output.

A key competitive strategy of DIALOG was to offer searchers the maximum possible record content, along with the maximum possible added-value processing (e.g., constructing indexes to all possible record fields, full-text indexing, word and phrase indexing), at the lowest possible price. This was the long-term strategy to acquire a critical mass of users that would lead to market leadership and dominance, and also to make it extremely difficult for anybody else to prepare a meaningful business plan and enter the marketplace as a potential competitor. Summit (1987) recalled that when his group decided to store the ERIC abstracts online, they worried they might go bankrupt because the abstracts were so expensive to store. They discovered, however, that they made *more* money *with* abstracts, because many searchers displayed the abstracts online, which used more connect time than just displaying citations. The additional revenue more than compensated for extra storage costs. With the advantage of hindsight, we might say that this was easy to anticipate, but in fact it was a revelation to DIALOG management.

From March to October 1969, a remote terminal was installed at the ERIC Clearinghouse on Educational Media and Technology at Stanford, also in Palo Alto (Burchinal 1970). USOE asked ERIC clearinghouse staff to help evaluate the online service because of their interest in IR techniques and because they were only a few miles away from the Lockheed Information Sciences Lab, which facilitated personal communication and kept communication charges relatively low. The clearinghouse director, William Paisley (1995), joked that staff were eager to use the system because the terminal room had to be kept air-conditioned, a rare luxury. Paisley noted that the air conditioning was discussed at a staff meeting as the major payback for the extra effort required by the evaluation. The opportunity to work with DIALOG did not impress them since they had "better" systems on campus (SPIRES, and the SUMEX facility proposed for the Stanford University Medical School by Joshua Lederberg), and they were familiar with the work of COSATI, MIT, NLM, and others.

Lockheed staff wrote an ERIC/DIALOG users manual (Summit 1970a, Appendix A) and launched the Stanford service in the spring of 1969. In response to mail and telephone requests, clearinghouse personnel conducted more than 800 online searches and printed out more than 51,000 citations and abstracts over a one-year period. During the Stanford evaluation, DIALOG developed a small fan club of education faculty who were working on books and found that they could save many hours by searching the education research reports on ERIC. Some of them came weekly, and with a little training from Michelle Timbie became competent searchers even before certain clearinghouse staff members learned how to use the system. This was among the earliest instances of encouraging end users to do their own searching.

1969 Milestone

DIALOG was the first online search system to provide an on-demand online display of the current search formulation and associated posting counts.

In July 1969, Lockheed installed a new version of the software called DIALOG II—not to be confused with the DIALOG II Summit described in the March 1967 users' manual discussed earlier in this chapter, or with the DIALOG-2 system in December 1984. The upgrade removed a number of the limitations. This DIALOG II, through the use of parentheses, allowed the grouping of set numbers in complex logical expressions. It also permitted users to SELECT multiple or ranges of set numbers, to display the set history, and to have more flexibility in displaying records retrieved (Timbie and Coombs 1969).

In the fall of 1969, Lockheed loaded the *Thesaurus of ERIC Descriptors* so that searchers could display conceptually as well as alphabetically related terms online. Access was available for a two-hour period three days a week. In September 1969, a second terminal was installed for a nine-month test period at the USOE Regional Office in

San Francisco, and a third terminal was installed in late 1969 at ERIC headquarters in Washington, D.C. Among the reactions to demonstrations was a comment from an elderly woman who said, "My, my, . . . That's the way we used to do it before the computer came along"—meaning that online systems allowed searchers to interact directly with indexes (Summit 1973, 193). By the end of 1969, ERIC contained 24,558 records (Brandhorst 1995).

ERIC clearinghouse staff members Timbie and Coombs produced a detailed study of users' reactions in December 1969. Timbie herself ran about 75 percent of the searches on the system, which operated six hours a week, on Tuesdays, Wednesdays, and Fridays. The other 25 percent of system availability was designated for other users to become acquainted with DIALOG. Outsiders were attracted to the system; spontaneous repeat use by faculty consumed some of this time. Timbie and Coombs asked nine outside users to participate in reaction "case studies." They directed each user to study the manual in advance, and to arrive about thirty minutes before the system became operational that day, in order to ask questions and examine the terminal. When the DIALOG program was loaded on the Lockheed computer, the visitor sat down and conducted a session alone, with Timbie hovering nearby to answer questions, coach, and prompt the searcher to make use of different system features. When the online session was over, she served coffee and then conducted a structured, tape-recorded interview to explore each user's reactions to all aspects of the system.

The most common negative reaction was irritation over the delays in waiting for the execution of a command. Timbie and Coombs (1969, 34, 36) reported that other negative comments included annoyances with the hardware, the searching process, or the ERIC database:

- The innovative system can be frustrating for people who don't like changes.
- The letters on the CRT have an unpleasant shape.
- The touch of the keyboard is too different from that of most typewriters.
- There are delays that make users wait for the system.
- They worry that the search was expensive.
- They find weaknesses in the indexing.
- Building combined sets one at a time, rather than doing it with one complex statement, is inconvenient.
- The CRT causes bleary eyes after a while.

They also noted: "As an estimate, once every two weeks (6 sessions, or 12 hours) there was serious difficulty . . . with the system" (2). They believed that many hardware and software problems that interrupted scheduled service were "the natural result of Lockheed staff continuing to develop the system while it was in use." The programmers addressed many of these complaints, in modifications made to DIALOG in August 1969.

Among the strongest features of the online system cited by the outside searchers were the unexpected, serendipitously retrieved citations: "The biggest problem was staying with what I had originally pursued, instead of getting off on other interesting things" (43). Other positive comments were (Timbie and Coombs 1969, 32):

- The system opens new avenues for thought; it "widened horizons."
- The system releases inhibiting mechanisms.
- It exhilarates, creates interest.
- It provokes users to order their approach.
- Having the printed record to refer to is handy.
- They like the possibility of being able to access the system from anywhere in the country.
- It is simple to use, easy to work with.

As the most experienced and skilled searcher involved in the project, Timbie did not quite agree with the last comment. Although the system was in one sense simple to use, she felt that considerable experience and time was needed to master the operating rules (Timbie and Coombs 1969, 5):

> Two hours is enough time for the average user to become quite capable of using the DIALOG system.... Two hours is not long enough, however, for a user to gain familiarity with all the different avenues of inquiry possible with the system. (This is not a criticism of DIALOG: with two minutes of instruction the average driver could use a Formula Two racing car to go to the corner grocery, though a skilled driver could benefit from months of experience before going on the circuit with it. It is an admirable design precisely because it can be used under such different circumstances and at different levels of complexity.)

Timbie and Coombs attributed the success of the ERIC/DIALOG project in large part to good working relationships between themselves and the staffs at Stanford and Lockheed and with Prevel of USOE.

After the first year, Summit predicted that the demand for use of ERIC online would range from 10,000 to 125,000 requests per year (Summit 1970a). The high end of this projection was achieved within only seven years; by 1977, users conducted 125,000 ERIC searches each year on DIALOG (Summit 1987).

The ERIC Online Service

For the experiments, ERIC consisted of only report citations from *Research in Education*. In 1970, it was augmented by separate files for records from the *Current Index to Journals in Education*, *Current Project Information*, *Pacesetters in Innovation*, and *Field Reader Catalog*. All files were simultaneously available online and searchers could switch from file to file with a single command. *Current Project Information* was simply a file of the projects in progress. *Field Reader Catalog* was a file of potential proposal reviewers and subject experts. These two files were never integrated into ERIC, and both are now obsolete. *Pacesetters in Innovation* announced a special body of literature for a particular OE program office; those records also were not integrated into the main database (Brandhorst 1997).

While the experimental service was running, USOE issued an RFP for contractors to provide service on a more regular basis. Lockheed's November 1970 proposal was the winner in the competition, and in 1971 USOE executed a contract with Lockheed to establish and operate an online search service for USOE, using ERIC. Summit was designated as the Lockheed project manager with Radwin as assistant project manager and subcontract manager. This was a significant, but expected extension from the prior Lockheed work to provide an experimental service on terminals at Stanford, USOE-San Francisco, and ERIC headquarters. In 1971, as a measure to reduce costs, provide local service support, and avoid problems of long distance data transmissions, Lockheed contracted with TRW Service Bureau to run the DIALOG programs on their systems, and to provide search services for the eastern segment of the DIALOG/ERIC network. In January 1972 the service transferred to Boeing Computer Services in Seattle, where it remained until June when all DIALOG service ran on the IBM 360/40 computer in Palo Alto (Summit 1972). In January 1972, Project RISE in Philadelphia gained access to the DIALOG/ERIC service; this was the first online ERIC terminal in the east that was outside the immediate Washington area.

By 1972, Lockheed had permission to offer the ERIC and NTIS databases to *any* subscriber; this was a key step for the beginning of the commercial Lockheed Retrieval Service. At the end of 1972, Lockheed was still under contract to provide online service to USOE, and ERIC contained a total of 122,325 records in five related subfiles.

Paisley later noted that the impact of DIALOG on American education during the 1970s was subtle, but nonetheless great. The 1969 addition of CIJE coverage to the report database combined the refereed journal literature with the unrefereed report literature (unlike almost all other files then or since), and made the database far more useful than its only important competitor, H. W. Wilson's *Education Index*. Also, the database was available online and was searchable from anywhere in the country. A terminal, microfiche reader/printer, and a photocopier became an instant educational information center in scores of state libraries, regional school units, and even school district offices. ERIC on DIALOG was an early and striking example of information empowerment. The rise of education extension services for school improvement (analogous to agricultural extension services) can be attributed to confidence at the local level that needed information was at hand. When the first educational extension agents went out in states like Oregon, Utah, and South Carolina around 1975, one of their calling cards was an offer of free search services. They funneled search requests to DIALOG searchers in the regional office or state library, then returned the results to their clients. These extension services flourished and became interconnected via the National Diffusion Network. And so, partly because of DIALOG and ERIC, educational extension service emerged as a new professional role and became a channel for school improvement efforts (Paisley 1995). Brandhorst (1993) prepared an extensive annotated bibliography of publications about ERIC from 1960 to 1992.

ESRO/RECON

ESRO

A group of ten European countries and Australia founded ESRO in 1962 as a multinational organization devoted to space science. ESRO and the European Launcher Development Organization (ELDO) created the Space Documentation Service (SDS) in 1963 as ESRO's information center. In November 1965, SDS became operational in Paris. Earlier, prolonged negotiations had taken place between ESRO and NASA for an exchange agreement. It was clear that ESRO could not quickly build a useful indexed reference file (in print, microform, and machine language) and a new retrieval system to search that file. However, ESRO, in cooperation with its member countries, could act as a focal point for obtaining and processing European aerospace reports and submitting them completely processed for entry into NASA's system. NASA in return could provide the magnetic tapes of 400,000 references to unclassified documents in the aerospace field from *Scientific and Technical Aerospace Reports (STAR)*, *International Aerospace Abstracts (IAA)*, microfiche copies of documents, and programs for searching the files. Each party felt that this exchange worked to its advantage. A one-year experimental exchange started in mid-1965.

ESRO obtained copies of NASA's SDI and batch search programs, and for a few years used a contractor to run them in Paris. They announced a more permanent agreement in 1968 when SDS moved from an external contract operation to an in-house computer operation. However, this long-distance operating mode entailed many frustrating delays and communication problems (Martin 1969). Also, the large volume of batch searching was a problem, and ESRO staff looked seriously at a new large-scale batch system that NASA was developing for an IBM 360. However, RECON's appearance halted their consideration of any batch system. Although the cost of designing and implementing a European online system was too much for ESRO, they could afford to pay Lockheed to modify RECON "for operation in the rather different ESRO environment," and they did so with NASA's agreement (Isotta 1970b, 29).

The SDS head was Noel Isotta, whose early career included working as a television transmission engineer for the BBC in London and as an electronic information officer for the British Ministry of Supply. Other SDS staff members who were instrumental in developing this system were Peter Kallenbach, Gerd Mulhauser, and David Raitt.

ESRO/RECON

In 1969, ESRO awarded Lockheed a contract to modify, install, and maintain a version of RECON for direct use in Europe. DIALOG staff loaded the software and NASA database of 400,000 bibliographic records onto the IBM 360/65 computer of the European Space Operations Centre at Darmstadt, Germany. Lockheed management's proposal to

ESRO included the stipulation that all computer programs supplied under the contract shall remain Lockheed property, and that ESRO was to be given only a restricted license to use those programs.

> **1969 Milestone**
>
> ESRO/RECON was the first online search service to run in Europe and provide online search service in Europe.

In July 1969, the first terminal was installed in Paris (Romerio 1973). The online link was made in July between Darmstadt and Paris and the system was fully operational by September. Raitt (1970) noted that about 500,000 references were stored on Data Cell storage units at the Darmstadt facility. Terminal equipment consisted of a CCI keyboard and TV display unit along with a Teletype printer for output (Isotta 1970a). By 1971, five terminals were operational—two in Paris at ESRO headquarters, one in Darmstadt, one in Noordwijk in the Netherlands, and one in Kent in Britain for the Ministry of Technology. The file was growing at a rate of 6,000 records per month (*Information activities* 1971). Kallenbach (1972) reported that the RECON network then comprised ten terminals in seven European countries. Although other developers had demonstrated search systems before in Europe, this was the first operational *service* in Europe. Lockheed continued under contract to ESRO to maintain the RECON software through 1972.

In order to persuade potential users to adopt and pay for the new service, Isotta sent a five-person team to tour the ten sites and demonstrate it. Their "almost superhuman task" was to speak to scientists intelligently about a wide variety of research and development topics, in any of ten languages (Isotta 1970b, 30). Another challenge they encountered was that of the telecommunications networks, because of a lack of uniformity in the requirements for network interconnection of the various European Postal Telephone and Telegraph (PTT) agencies (Isotta 1972a). By the end of 1972, SDS was operating entirely with leased lines, and general dial-up capability was added later.

With NSF underwriting the cost for telecommunications, Isotta demonstrated the ESRO/SDS system at the ASIS annual meeting in October 1972 by searching the Darmstadt system from Washington, D.C. The data communication link was the INTELSAT IV communications satellite; this was an early public demonstration of the feasibility of international satellite data communications networks (Sophar and Berninger 1972). The advance publicity for the demonstration gave about equal attention to the online system demonstration as to the satellite data transmission demonstration.

The Royal Institute of Technology library in Stockholm was added as a node to the ESRO/RECON system in October 1972. The service offered several databases, including STAR/IAA, Metadex, Compendex, GRA (NTIS), NSA, and Electronic Components (Hjerrpe 1975). Lockheed continued to provide programming support, including system and feature changes, until ESRO assumed that responsibility in the early 1970s, and ESRO made all later changes to RECON. ESRO is now the European Space Agency (ESA), and the Space Documentation Service is now the Information Retrieval Service (IRS). The ESRO/RECON story (i.e., the ESA/IRS story) continues in chapter 9.

AEC/ERDA/DOE/RECON

AEC/ERDA/DOE

The Manhattan District Project to develop the atomic bomb accumulated a large amount of information in the field of atomic and nuclear energy in the early 1940s. By 1944 the project had developed a large, effective information service. In 1946 the newly-established AEC (Atomic Energy

Commission) absorbed the project. *Weekly Title List*, a current-awareness publication, started in June 1946 and grew to become *Nuclear Science Abstracts* (*NSA*), a major bibliographic aid to nuclear research and engineering.

In 1960, AEC began serious consideration of using computers in its technical information program as it looked for ways to assist in the indexing and production of *NSA*, and in the provision of information and document delivery services. AEC staff used advanced techniques for that time, such as high-speed cold-type photocomposition equipment (Linotron typesetting from magnetic tapes, Listomatic camera photocomposition from punched cards, 120-character IBM printer chain) for the production of their printed products. Planning began in 1967 for the creation of computer tapes to drive the Linotron photocomposer (then in testing at the Government Printing Office) and to provide magnetic tapes for distribution to other interested parties. They developed KWIC and SDI services and products, and even a batch-oriented search system called RESPONSA, starting in 1963, with a large file of over 400,000 records, as the primary search system until RECON replaced it (Hutton 1968). Early in 1968, AEC's Division of Technical Information Extension (DTIE) worked with the AEC facilities contractor, Union Carbide's Computer Technology Center (CTC), on a bibliographic search program called RANSAC, but they set that work aside with a change of computer equipment at the Oak Ridge National Laboratory (ORNL). Adkinson (1978) provided a more complete history of AEC's sci-tech information activities.

In the fall of 1968 the director of DTIE, Edward Brunenkant, pressed for the creation of an effective retrieval system, one that could handle sci-tech information, legislative material, and research in progress, and could display at a user's option bibliographic information, keywords, or abstracts. At about the same time (November 1968) Data Corporation gave a demonstration in Oak Ridge of their full text Data Central search system (see chapter 7) to AEC's Annual Technical Information Panel Meeting. As a result of that demonstration, DTIE requested that CTC study the feasibility of obtaining Data Central (Kidd, Price, and Yount 1969). CTC was to look at acquiring Data Central either by leasing the computer and programs and storing and accessing data from Data Central in Dayton or Washington, or by purchasing the programs and installing them at CTC for use on government-owned computers at Oak Ridge. The CTC investigation stipulated file updates every two weeks, six terminals at major user sites, and costs computed over a three-year operating period. The resulting cost estimates were high—the Data Central programs alone were priced at $160,000. As William Vaden, deputy manager of DTIE, described it, "We didn't even have enough money to purchase the program, let alone modify it and run it. As a consequence, our interest dimmed and we began to look elsewhere for possibilities" (1969).

Acquisition of DIALOG

The CTC study identified other systems for consideration, including AUDACIOUS and SPIRES. DTIE staff also went to NASA to review their experience with RECON. In discussions with Wente of NASA, they learned that since the operating program was government-owned, AEC had no need to pay for any system development. NASA encouraged DTIE to build on what had already been developed and paid for at government expense. It was noted, however, that modifications would have to be made to the AEC database because of differences in data elements and record structure. Hughes and Brooks (1975, 190) explained that another reason for chosing RECON was its features, and also:

Because so many other agencies were planning to adopt the system as well: compatibility, and a start at standardization in the most visible part of such a system—the user commands—were becoming evident. In the same spirit AEC retained the name RECON for a system even though major changes and special adaptations were made. A new user sitting down before one of our consoles for the first time will know a great deal about the system just from the name if he has seen RECON systems elsewhere.

After demonstrations of RECON and discussions with NASA, AEC began negotiating with Lockheed for a contract to modify the AEC database and create an online system that had NASA/RECON characteristics. In May 1969, Lockheed proposed to AEC an experiment in which Lockheed would: (1) convert one volume (75,000 records) of *Nuclear Science Abstracts* to a RECON-compatible format and update it twice; (2) provide online service for two hours per work day via a terminal in Oak Ridge; (3) prepare a user's manual; and (4) conduct a study of the applicability of online retrieval techniques to AEC files. Summit was the proposed project manager. A contract was executed for the period June 1969 through March 1970, with a total funding of almost $60,000. The system would be known initially as AEC/RECON and later as DOE/RECON (Vaden 1992; Frazier 1978).

The contract stipulated that DTIE would supply indexed citations for twenty-four issues of *NSA* (about 50,000 records, without abstracts) and one update of twelve issues. Lockheed loaded a total of 150,000 records during the course of the experiment. Lockheed was to develop programs to load these files in their Palo Alto computer in a format compatible with the RECON software, with the intent of eventually moving the file and programs to CTC at Oak Ridge. One remote terminal was to be located at Oak Ridge, with provision for two more later. System operation would be limited to two hours per day on three days per work week. A 240-cps line was to be used from Palo Alto to Oak Ridge, ready for use by the end of 1969, and with query testing scheduled for early January 1970. The purpose was to determine RECON's applicability to the AEC databases. The first successful test was in January 1970, working with one volume of *NSA*, 240 cps CCI terminal equipment at Oak Ridge, and the IBM 360/40 computer in Palo Alto. AEC staff called this system RECON III and identified it as a modified version of the system that Lockheed designed for NASA ("Information retrieval at DTIE" 1970).

After testing, DTIE staff were convinced that RECON held the greatest promise of an online retrieval system for AEC, and they should secure it permanently. They felt that the nine search elements gave a powerful search capability (descriptors, personal authors, corporate source code, *NSA* category code, journal source CODEN, author affiliation country code, report number prefix, contract number prefix, and patent country code). The first terminal was installed at DTIE in Oak Ridge (see figure 5.2). In 1970, terminals were added at Lawrence Radiation Laboratory (Berkeley), Bettis Atomic Power Laboratory (Pittsburgh), and AEC headquarters library (Germantown) to further test the capabilities and response of RECON at times when multiple remote terminals were online. Summit (1970b) created a manual for users.

In July 1970, using a remote CRT terminal in Paris and with AEC funding, ESRO staff searched the AEC/RECON database and search system, still loaded on the Palo Alto computer. The link from Paris to the computer was via a leased line on a Saturday morning. This single demonstration to an ESRO audience was short, but it was the first instance of international access and use of the AEC/RECON (DIALOG) system. Isotta had requested the demonstration; he wanted to demonstrate the feasibility of a worldwide IR system (Vaden 1992). This was a very early international online search (preceded only by the BOLD and TIRP demonstrations in 1967), which used the new TAC #5 trans-Atlantic cable, in service for only four months prior to this demonstration; cables, not satellite communications were the principal trans-oceanic means of data communication then (*Progress* 1971, 3).

Installation and Operation of DIALOG at AEC

In October 1970, Lockheed proposed to install the RECON software and NSA file on the IBM 360/75 at ORNL, for AEC personnel to operate and use. The installation and maintenance was to be done over a fourteen-month period through calendar year 1971, with the understanding that AEC would initially operate the system with one local and four remote terminals. Lockheed staff transferred the AEC/RECON system and database to an IBM

Figure 5.2
Typical equipment layout for user to access AEC/RECON. 1970. Photo provided courtesy of the DOE Office of Scientific and Technical Information.

360/75 computer at ORNL starting in December 1970, in an exhausting process that took about twenty-eight fourteen-hour days. The installation was a joint effort, carried out by David Meinhardt of Lockheed and Woody Gove of Oak Ridge, with assistance from other Oak Ridge and IBM staff. After the installation was complete, the DIALOG software was operational at Oak Ridge for thirty hours per week, with the five-terminal network (see figure 5.3).

AEC personnel provided an international demonstration of AEC/RECON for ten days in Geneva, Switzerland, in September 1971, in conjunction with the Fourth U.N. International Conference on the Peaceful Uses of Atomic Energy. The system was based on the original Lockheed software but included new features and improvements that Oak Ridge staff had developed. The AEC staff conducted the demonstration with the IBM 360/75 computer at Oak Ridge, 240 cps CCI terminal

Figure 5.3
Gloria Haire introduces a user to a new method of accessing Nuclear Science Abstracts via AEC/RECON. 1970. Photo provided courtesy of the DOE Office of Scientific and Technical Information.

equipment in Geneva, and a database of 188,000 NSA records.

By the end of 1971, the end of the Lockheed maintenance contract, twelve terminals had been installed on the AEC/RECON network. Unfortunately, however, the early operation "was plagued by recurring problems related to both programs and hardware. At one time there were five known simultaneous problems. Operation slowly improved during the first year as they learned the things to avoid, and as Lockheed provided patches" (Hughes and Brooks 1975, 191). Robert Freeman (1995) recalled that when he was at NOAA in 1972, they had AEC/RECON terminal number 10 in the network, and that they had to remember never to turn off the power to the terminal during the work day, because that would cause the entire network to go down! Lockheed continued to maintain a copy of the NSA database on their own computer into 1972, perhaps thinking that they could provide service to others from the Lockheed facility. However, NSA did not appear on the list of public files when Lockheed went to commercial service in 1972.

Vaden (1979, 3) noted that after the RECON installation, Al Brooks and other ORNL staff "completely reworked RECON, retaining most of the original design features involving the user interface, but built from scratch the improved, original file maintenance software." He also noted that DOE/RECON would not have existed in its current form without the contributions of Charles Price, William Multhouse, Woody Gove, Karl Haeuslein, Ray Plemens, Frank Hammerlin, Barbara Corey, and Charles Hammons. He singled out Jo Robinson, then at Lawrence Berkeley Lab, for working miracles in coordinating their workshops.[3] Oak Ridge staff members Haeuslein and Culkowski (1975) described the rewritten version of the original DIALOG/RECON system: "Even though the search system has been reprogrammed, we have attempted to maintain the general concepts and the sound ideas of Roger Summit and Dave Meinhardt" (iii). Meinhardt had joined Lockheed in 1970 after experience as a computer specialist at the CIA. He had worked on the ERIC online project before being assigned to the DOE project.

By the end of 1972, the file contained more than 250,000 bibliographic records (all the citations appearing in NSA since 1967). AEC/RECON was operating with one IBM 2321 Data Cell and three IBM 2314 disk packs. The records were indexed only by assigned subject headings, subject heading code, author, corporate author, journal title, country where the described research was performed, report number prefix (the system did not have enough storage capacity to store the entire report number), contract number prefix (not enough storage capacity for the entire contract number), and country that issued a described patent. Abstracts were neither indexed nor stored in the system at this time, and users had no means to search for title words.

DOE/RECON served primarily in-house searchers, using AEC's own leased line facilities; dial-up service was not added until early 1976. Online access and resources were always limited to DOE staff, their contractors, certain other government agencies, and other selected libraries and information centers. AEC staff and their contractors maintained and modified the system and added more databases. They operated their RECON software primarily in an experimental mode through 1975; this is described in more detail in chapter 9.

In January 1975, a new U.S. federal agency, the Energy Research and Development Administration (ERDA) was formed and assumed all AEC activities. After the establishment of the U.S. Department of Energy (DOE) in October 1977, it incorporated ERDA activities. With these multiple name changes, the online search system also had corresponding name changes (AEC/RECON, ERDA/RECON, and DOE/RECON). As soon as DOE made the full database available to the private sector, several commercial online services started providing unlimited worldwide access with more convenient and more powerful search systems, resulting in greatly expanded online accessibility and use.

Other Projects and Proposals

Lockheed management was insistent that the DIALOG project and staff become self-sufficient with regard to their continued funding, and encouraged Summit to continue to seek outside project support. With that incentive, he pursued projects from outside agencies in 1970 and 1971. Examples of these were: San Mateo County Dept. of Public Health and Welfare (their health and welfare statistics database); ARCO (American Petroleum Institute's Petroleum Refining Literature database); NCCD (file of parole reports); and Oregon Human Resources Agencies. These projects involved loading a sponsor's file (or one the sponsor had obtained) on DIALOG, and the sponsor's provision of a specified amount of online access to the file. These were not R&D projects, and they were not projects to provide public service. They followed the general pattern set with the NASA and ERIC projects of providing a specific constituency with access to a specified database. DOJ also used a copy of the RECON software for a project called JURIS, which was part of the DIALOG family tree (see chapter 9). In 1972, Lockheed included a statement in their proposals that the DIALOG software was available for lease or purchase, an offer that was less valuable since NASA had put the 1969 edition of DIALOG in the public domain.

DIALOG (Lockheed Retrieval Service)

The Decision to Start a Commercial Service

By the early 1970s, Summit was becoming frustrated that his bosses at Lockheed required him to devote at least half of his time to revenue-generating projects besides DIALOG; apparently, they did not believe that an IR service could pay the bills. He thought that if management would just leave him alone, he could make DIALOG into something profitable. He decided to leave Lockheed and accepted a position as a vice president of Informatics, Inc., in Washington, D.C. (a firm that was already actively involved in installing DIALOG/RECON software for other organizations and was starting to provide public online search services). Driving down the San Francisco peninsula with his family one day he realized that he did not want to leave the beautiful Palo Alto area. After talking again to his boss at Lockheed, Summit convinced the company to allow him to form DIALOG as a Program Office, as Summit's full and exclusive responsibility. Many years later, Summit learned that Lockheed administrators had been ready to dump DIALOG at that time; he believes now that he could have bought DIALOG in 1972 for less than $200,000. In August 1988, Lockheed sold DIALOG to Knight Ridder, Inc., for $353 million.

The beginning of the commercial search service was intertwined with an event that took place almost simultaneously with the DIALOG staff in Palo Alto and the SDC ORBIT staff in Santa Monica, and involved both organizations. In 1972, Carlos Cuadra, manager of the SDC Library and Documentation Systems Department, was trying to convince *his* management of the commercial potential of an online retrieval service. When they too remained unconvinced, he prepared a questionnaire to ascertain the potential interest outside SDC. He mailed it to about 7,000 subscribers of an NTIS current awareness service. The head of Lockheed's Technical Library received the questionnaire and passed it on to Summit, who recalls reacting with a jolt: "I remember how disquieting it was to see that survey, because we felt that we were in a little pocket all to ourselves in the online retrieval business. We felt we did not have much competition until we saw that survey" (1987). Summit immediately took the questionnaire to his management as proof that such a service had commercial potential—after all, another major organization was already doing market research! The realization that someone else was on the verge of beginning a commercial service, and the conviction that indeed money was to be made in IR, provided the incentive at Lockheed to give the final approval in early 1972 to begin Lockheed Retrieval Service.

The Start of the Commercial Service

Commercial service initiated in December 1972, with Summit as the Information Retrieval manager, Radwin as senior technical associate (both in Palo Alto), and Robert Donati as Eastern representative, based in Washington, D.C. Radwin had earned degrees in electrical engineering from MIT in 1964 and 1965, respectively and was working on his Ph.D. in industrial management and as a research assistant associated with the Project MAC time-sharing system. He curtailed his study to join the DIALOG staff at the Palo Alto Lab in 1967. He participated in DIALOG design, development, and application, including work with personnel, medical, and criminal justice files. Before DIALOG started its public online service, his work as a senior scientist of the Research Lab had focused on the telecommunications aspects of the service, creating the DIALINDEX product, and on developing and extending DIALOG's full-text search capability. Donati had graduated from UC-Berkeley with a B.A. in mathematics in 1953. He joined Lockheed in 1956, and at the start of DIALOG commercial services he was serving as the Eastern representative for the Information Sciences Division, providing marketing and customer services support.

Lockheed had been in the online service business since 1966, with contracts to specific populations, but had never provided service to the general public. The new public service was named "Lockheed Information Retrieval Service," also known as LRS. That name appeared on search printouts and marketing materials until mid-1976, when the service's name changed to DIALOG Information Retrieval Service, or just DIALOG for short, and the organization name continued as Lockheed Information Systems. In mid-1981, Lockheed established the DIALOG Information Retrieval Service as DIALOG Information Services, Inc., a wholly owned subsidiary of Lockheed Corporation; at this point, the name DIALOG referred to the name of the search software, the search service, and the organization.

Starting in late 1971, DIALOG provided contract online service on ERIC to institutions identified by the USOE. In August 1972, in response to an RFP from NTIS, Lockheed started providing contract online services with the NTIS database and online access to five terminals to NTIS itself—to support a public information service (NTISearch) that NTIS had initiated in August 1971 with batch searches and microform equipment (Tancredi and Ryerson 1972). The DIALOG system was still running on an IBM 360/40 system in Palo Alto, and the DIALOG group, with Summit as program manager and Radwin as assistant program manager, was reporting to Duncan, director of the Information Sciences Division. The move to provide a public commercial service was to offer the service in addition to this established base of operation. In fact, Lockheed's April 1972 *Proposal to provide an online bibliographic information search and retrieval system* to NTIS stated: "LMSC will actively solicit additional subscribers for this service on substantially the same operational basis as that offered to NTIS. Additional income produced by a multisubscriber service would lower the cost of the system to NTIS. An extensive communications network controlled by LMSC is undergoing further development to support this service" (2–1). This was an early indication that the DIALOG group would try to sell online access to users other than database providers and their immediate constituencies, as they had done so far. After the decision to start a commercial service, however, the company had to accomplish many things that had not been necessary while it was doing contract programming work or running experimental services to limited populations under contract to a single agency. For example, licensing additional databases and establishing all of the administrative machinery for customer password management, usage and royalty accounting, and customer billing operations was now necessary. Furthermore, Lockheed management required that this was all to happen without Lockheed investing any significant resources. The service was obliged to pay its own way, out of revenues earned from its operations.

Meanwhile, down in Santa Monica at SDC, Cuadra received only 1 percent of his questionnaires back. But that's the next story.

6 SDC ORBIT and Related Systems, 1963–1972

Introduction

As Roger Summit had suspected would happen, SDC also inaugurated an online commercial search service with access to the MEDLINE and ERIC databases in late 1972, the same time as Lockheed's. The roots of what came to be known as ORBIT go back to 1962. They were not in Protosynthex, TEXTIR, LUCID, CONVERSE, BOLD (although the BOLD work especially laid important foundations), or other systems developed at SDC (described in chapter 2), even though they were all written in JOVIAL. ORBIT's rootstock was a large-scale semiautomatic batch retrieval system called CIRC. In 1966, SDC staff at WPAFB in Dayton, Ohio, rewrote the CIRC programs for online retrieval and tested them in an experiment called COLEX, applying them to a database of foreign technical literature. The programs for the online version of COLEX at first were called General Purpose ORBIT, later just ORBIT. Between 1966 and 1972, the programs evolved through several incarnations. Thus COLEX is the true online forerunner of ORBIT. The success of the trial led to the permanent installation of the system—by then called CIRCOL—at Wright-Patterson.

The U.S. defense community may never have discovered ORBIT had it not been for a fortuitous coincidence. Two senior managers joined NLM, Ruth Davis and Dave McCarn, bringing with them experience with SDC online systems from the DOD even before NLM was involved with COLEX. McCarn was at the DIA when they supported SDC's development of the COLEX online system, described later. Davis was familiar with COLEX and other online systems from her research and engineering management position in DOD. Both managers were instrumental in NLM's granting a development contract to SDC in 1969 for inauguration of the AIM-TWX experiment, to provide nation-wide access to a database over low-speed public communication lines.

The AIM-TWX contract between NLM and SDC, and the one between NASA and LMSC examined in the last chapter, shared some features. Both were contracts for developing a version of existing proprietary software tailored to a specific subject matter, audience, and database structure. Both involved large, rapidly growing databases and were designed for populations scattered around the United States. Both contracts ended in the early seventies, leaving the developers to find alternative support for expanding their activities. Both DIALOG and ORBIT were lucky to have managers who believed in their value and who promoted them ardently, with energy and determination, even without a great deal of support from their own organizations. As Summit sustained DIALOG, Carlos Cuadra labored against great obstacles to develop and rescue ORBIT. The ORBIT story begins with the short history of a system aborted before it ever got off the ground, then the story moves to Dayton, Ohio, to examine the joint efforts of SDC and several government agencies.

SDC was an exceptional organization in the 1960s and 1970s. The many significant R&D projects there that were not related directly to ORBIT developments provided a stimulating environment populated with creative, curious individuals who had the freedom to pursue research goals without worrying about bottom-line profits. The following are a few examples of such activities not described previously in the book:

• Simmons continued his natural language processing research.

• Carter conducted a study in 1965 for COSATI on national document-handling systems for science and technology.

• Staff conducted a COSATI study in 1966 of a national abstracting and indexing system.

• With NSF support, Katter worked on document representations.

• Doyle and Blankenship worked on automatic classification techniques.

• Cuadra and Katter conducted research on relevance assessment.

• Staff surveyed library technology for the National Library Commission.

- Katter and Harris conducted a DOE-funded evaluation of *ARIST*.
- With DOE funding, Cuadra and Pearson reviewed automation in the Federal library community.
- Wanger conducted an NSF-funded study of the impact of online searching.

These projects and studies were chronicled in Baum 1981, along with a tremendous amount of other computer-related research and development in which SDC took the lead nationally.

TDMS

In 1966, SDC staff began to design a general purpose online storage and retrieval system to run on the AN/FSQ-32 computer in Santa Monica. The system was first called Time-Shared Data Management System (TDMS), and later called Tactical Data Management System for Air Force use. TDMS was an outgrowth of TSS-LUCID, an experimental data management system that had been operating at SDC on a time-shared computer since 1964. Over two years of experience with TSS-LUCID by more than fifteen organizations influenced the design of TDMS. An earlier online version was a full-fledged database management system called Query and Update (QUUP) that included DBase II software (Shiban 1967). QUUP was the Q-32 online query and update capability for TSS-LUCID databases. In 1966, the Foreign Technology Division (FTD) staff of the USAF Systems Command saw a demonstration of remote online access from Dayton to a database on SDC's Santa Monica computer, using SDC's online search programs (Kershaw, Crowder, Davis, Loges, and Merendini 1966). The demonstration influenced their thinking about SDC and online systems; that story is continued in the following sections.

TDMS in 1967 was a single-file system that used disk storage and CRT terminals, with both Boolean and arithmetic search capabilities for text or bibliographic records, and meant to be used in a conversational mode (Giering 1967a; Ziehe 1967). TDMS was demonstrated in spring 1968 (Bleier 1967; Bleier and Vorhaus 1969). Welch (1968) described the characteristics of TDMS while it was being considered for use in the COSATI benchmark demonstrations (chapter 4). TDMS created indexes for every record field, and to some contemporary observers this was an extravagant use of storage space (Baxamoosa 1970).

Although designed for the Q-32 computer, SDC actually implemented TDMS to operate on any IBM 360 model 50 or larger. It could operate in either batch or online mode. A commercial version of TDMS developed in 1968 was called Commercial Data Management System (CDMS or TS/CDMS), and SDC convinced a couple of oil companies to use it for interactive marketing reports the following year.[1]

TDMS development relied on support from various U.S. federal agencies, including ARPA. SDC staff included Robert Bleier, Alfred Vorhaus, R. D. Wills, V. L. Raucher, H. S. Schwimmer, and J. R. Shiban.

FTD staff used the TDMS software in 1969 for a DIA-supported project for online maintenance of a thesaurus used with the CIRCOL project (described later); they used TDMS for that application because the ORBIT system at this time did not have a complete file-updating capability (Black 1987). SDC used TDMS software also with the LC MARC file for the CLR-sponsored LISTS project the same year (chapter 4). At the time that the LISTS project ended, SDC had an operating system for ARPANET, and SDC management decided to offer online service bureau operations to anybody who wanted to buy them. As Black (1995) described it:

We took the LISTS project and tried to come up with a package that would allow people to get MARC records and an ordering component, and tie them together with the MARC records. All this was going to run on TDMS. SDC made a lot of pronouncements over a period of four or five months about how they were going to support this and give it a chance—and so our group came up with this ALPS (Automated Library Processing Service) system which would allow for library processing on a monthly fee basis.

SDC had now decided to participate in the library online service and database business, although not in the same way for which they later became known. Black (1995) continued: "We did a road show, went to six cities and gave two-day presentations, showing off the system. Jules Mersel was involved with the ALPS project and made a good sales presentation. I gave part of the presentation, and Carlos Cuadra gave part of it. A couple of library systems were thinking of subscribing. Some time in spring 1969, SDC pulled the plug on TDMS. So there went the product." And TDMS and ALPS went with it. Cuadra (1997) recalled that at one of those shows in Albany, "When we were showing how quickly the search software found the number of MARC records in the catalog, we were momentarily struck dumb when an attendee had the temerity to ask, 'How do you know it's right?'"

SDC and WPAFB

CIRC

The combined efforts of an SDC team located at WPAFB, the Foreign Technology Division at WPAFB, and other DOD agencies such as DIA produced the CIRC (Centralized Information Reference and Control) system. They developed CIRC to support the analysts in monitoring the foreign sci-tech literature, especially that of the U.S.S.R. and other Eurasian Communist countries judged to be hostile to the United States. The goal was to maintain an assessment of these countries' capabilities in selected technical areas, and to identify new developments of military, strategic, or economic significance. Input to CIRC consisted of foreign technical documents and publications, including reference books, reports, newspapers, trade literature, and journal literature—mostly open source literature. A large, long-term contract that went by the code name STEP (Science and Technology Exploitation Program) provided document selection and processing.

LC staff started and ran this AF-supported project shortly after the Sputnik technology surprise but later moved it to Dayton for the Air Force to run. The system incorporated translations of the materials when translations were available; when they were not, translations were provided on request. In 1965, the system was fulfilling requests for translations of Russian material by means of postedited machine translation products, using an AN/GSQ-16 (XW-2) Automatic Language Translator machine built by IBM, owned by FTD, and used only for Russian-to-English translations (See 1967). In 1968, this was one of two operational machine translation systems in the United States translating from Russian to English (Chai 1968). This special-purpose computer eventually was displaced by proprietary software such as SYSTRAN. Prior to 1967, the automatic extracting (abstracting) programs SDC designed and developed under contract to RADC were applied to CIRC material that the Machine Translation Facility at FTD processed (Kershaw, Crowder, Davis, Loges, and Merendini 1966).

CIRC development and operation was restricted to equipment already available at WPAFB: a Friden Flexowriter to prepare punched paper tape, IBM 7094 and 1401/1403 computers, and Kodak Lodestar/Recordak 16-mm microfilm storage, retrieval, and printing equipment. Input was punched on paper tape and then transferred to magnetic tape. Records, including abstracts, extracts, or tables of contents, were microfilmed for fast access by a reel-and-frame accession number on a motorized microfilm viewer-printer. This was a continuation of an approach that SDC had used in the SATIRE and MICRO systems (chapter 2).

The system produced retrospective, known-item, and current-awareness subject searches, accession lists, and bibliographies on selected topics of continuing interest, which by September 1965 users could print on card stock, one card per record, for easy manual sorting, weeding, and filing. In 1965, the SDI volume was 140 profiles with weekly updates, and by 1967 the number of profiles had grown to 200 (Taulbee 1967b). In February 1966, a center was opened for handling retrospective search requests.

CIRC was not the earliest batch search system. Similar systems had been in operation in the private sector for several years before CIRC began. However, CIRC did operate on a larger scale than most of its predecessors, and received considerable management attention and support. The developers of CIRC did not design it for research; they meant it to be an application program. Although the retrieval program began operating in December 1964, this was not announced to users at the time (Kershaw, Crowder, Davis, Loges, and Merendini 1966). By July 1965, the file had 40,000 records—each with full bibliographic information and subject indexing. At this point, Davis (1966) considered CIRC to be among the more advanced mechanized document-centered systems with a large database. By September 1966, the file comprised 65,000 records on five reels of tape and was growing rapidly at a rate of 60,000–70,000 records per year, which likely was faster than any other searching system then. In 1967 the system was serving nearly 4,000 users and had the potential to serve 7,000 more; the file contained close to 200,000 documents and was growing at a rate of 7,000 documents per month (Taulbee 1967a).

Cuadra (1997) recounted that in the early CIRC days, the FTD librarian was appalled when analysts came to the library looking for materials as a result of receiving reports from the new computer system because they ripped many library cards and abstracts out of the file drawers—apparently to simplify their note taking. Cuadra was excited—not by the theft and logistical problems created, but because the system was inducing more people to make increasing use of the library.

SDC accomplished the CIRC design, systems analysis, and programming under contract to FTD. The work started in July 1962, with SDC staff levels ranging from twelve to thirty professionals and with a total of ten man-years of Air Force and federal employee labor and fifteen man-years of contractor labor (Kershaw, Crowder, Davis, Loges, and Merendini 1966). Cuadra headed the effort that led to the CIRC batch system, but he left it to join the SDC Research and Development Division before the online COLEX and CIRCOL systems started. In 1965, SDC-Santa Monica staff members studied the list-processing program techniques from Noah Prywes's work at the University of Pennsylvania (chapter 2), for possible application to the CIRC system (Bichel and Smith 1965).

Much effort was devoted during the CIRC history to convert a system of free term indexing to a controlled subject term approach: "A total of 2 Air Force and 3 contractor man-years were required to develop vocabulary control, including programming time" (Kershaw, Crowder, Davis, Loges, Merendini, and Thomas 1966, 92). The CIRC indexing vocabulary was planned to be coordinated with the vocabularies of DDC and other DOD agencies. A system with over 100,000 CIRC index terms was transformed in 1966 into a thesaurus of 10,000 terms that controlled the indexing vocabulary and was carefully structured in three parts: one hierarchical, one alphabetical, and one permuted. Indexers assigned from two to fifteen descriptors to each document. A modified version of this thesaurus, consisting of 22,000 controlled subject terms, was prepared by a team from SDC-Falls Church, Virginia, in 1968–1969 as an effort to develop an integrated thesaurus to satisfy the needs of all sci-tech intelligence activities monitored by the DOD intelligence community (Dovel 1969). The controlled vocabulary/indexing was dropped in 1973 in favor of free-text searching (DiFondi, Mangio, and Roberti 1973).

Orrin Taulbee, John Welch Jr., and others at Goodyear Aerospace Corp. conducted a CIRC evaluation in 1966–1967 (Taulbee 1967b). The study included a questionnaire and follow-up interviews of a sample of users from three different intelligence services (Treu 1967; Barrett, Thornton, and Cabe 1968). Taulbee concluded, "The CIRC system has been implemented over a number of years on a piecemeal basis, making use of existing resources wherever possible ... under the circumstances and with the resources applied, a commendable job has been done" (1967b, 226). It was, however, still a batch search system with Boolean search capability and use was cumbersome; in spite of original specifications calling for dependable total-file search with a twenty-four-hour turnaround time, preparing searches for input could take as long as three days to code. (Barrett, Thornton, and Cabe 1968). Taulbee observed that sixteen of nineteen test participants in early 1967, who were all satisfied with their computer printouts, had experienced an average response time of nine days. The average response time for the three unsatisfied test participants was *thirty-five days*. These response times were for the search service to receive, code, and obtain output to be returned to requesters. Additional time was needed for the control and signing off of transmittals.

Computer time for searching on an overloaded IBM 7094/1401 was limited and restricted to second shift; 120 hours per week were requested in 1966 for CIRC operation and evaluation of new programs, but only 80 hours a week were received. The initial search program operated on a maximum of ten requests per batch, and printed a maximum of one hundred records per request; with another program this was later upgraded to batches of twenty-five requests. Furthermore, disagreement between SDC and the FTD computer center over when CIRC programs were to be run, and a lack of experienced computer operators appeared to be as consequential as limited computer resources in contributing to production delays. Serial processing was fast becoming impractical, and by mid-1966 program and file conversion to the IBM 2302 disk storage was begun. By early 1967, CIRC still did not receive enough computer time to fulfill all of its requests. By mid-1969, however, there were plans to upgrade the IBM 7094 to a 360/65.

Another challenge for the system designers was that some documents were subject to security classification, which created headaches in sorting and restricting the output according to the security clearance of the recipient. FTD personnel morale was also worrisome; many staff feared losing their jobs or wondered how they would fit into the new system. A few appreciated the opportunity to be on the cutting edge of development and receive on-the-job training, but most did not want added responsibilities without a pay raise (Kershaw, Crowder, Davis, Loges, and Merendini 1966).

CIRC continued in operation while FTD management considered ways to improve the performance of their retrieval system and ran a major experiment with an online system (COLEX, described next).

COLEX

Given the demands for CIRC's products and services, the experience of trying to assemble it piecemeal over several years, difficulties in obtaining sufficient computer time to develop and operate this important intelligence information system, the findings of the evaluation studies, and the knowledge that operating such a system in online mode is technically feasible, AF and DOD management decided to test an online approach in earnest. At a May 1965 conference, Barrett had announced that SDC was looking at time-sharing for remote inquiry, to allow multiple users to query the same computer file from Teletype consoles. As mentioned earlier, in 1966 the FTD staff had seen a demonstration of remote online access from Dayton to a database on SDC's Santa Monica computer, using an SDC search program. Presumably, the staff had also seen a breadboard model in mid-1966 of Data Corporation's online system in development for another Air Force lab at WPAFB. Therefore they decided to conduct a major feasibility demonstration of online retrieval, with DIA providing the funding and RADC as the contracting agency. Duane Stone of RADC was project monitor (and also oversaw the later SDC thesaurus development). SDC-Santa Monica received a contract, starting October 1, 1966, to conduct the experiment—called COLEX (CIRC On-Line Experiment)—and supply necessary supporting data to determine the value of an online time-sharing retrieval capability to the scientific and technical intelligence community (Baker and Smith 1968b).

The first phase of the funded experiment ran through October 31, 1967, and a continuation phase ran through June 1968. However, Cuadra (1976, 54) said, "In 1965 ... [ARPA] initiated daily on-line access from 13 organizations across the U.S. to what was then considered to be a very large data base: 200,000 items of non-U.S. technology literature." Cuadra did not name the system, but it seems clear from the reference to thirteen stations that he meant COLEX. This suggests that an experimental national online network may have been in use even a year before the official COLEX project began, but no other documentation is available to confirm the exact start date of online operation.

SDC staff from the Santa Monica, Dayton, and Falls Church offices participated in COLEX. The Santa Monica group included Katter, Blankenship, and Burket—all reporting to Cuadra. All were involved later in developing the public versions of the NLM and ORBIT search systems and SDC Search Service. Authors of SDC reports associated with COLEX included J. Smith, A. W. Baker, J. P. Hoffman, and J. C. Cornelli. L. Cegala and E. Waller of the Falls Church office authored the *COLEX User's Manual* and were the online system monitors for COLEX operations (Baker and Smith 1968b).

Black (1987) commented on the genesis of COLEX and the resulting ORBIT system, starting from the batch CIRC system:

Intelligence analysts were sprinkled around the country at various locations. They were taking the documents and microfilming them and putting them on 16 mm microfilm cartridges—the kind where you can punch in a number and it would go zip and stop at that document. They produced index cards for this stuff that they were microfilming and they would send batches of this stuff out to all of these analysts. These guys were not librarians; many of them, I suppose might have had secretarial help. But they were clearly not ready, willing, or able to file all of these cards that they were given. So it was a big mess and yet they were supposed to be keeping on top of all this technology that was passing under their eyes."

It is noteworthy that SDC-Dayton staff did not make any direct use of the available SDC-Santa Monica software (described in chapters 2 and 4) for COLEX or CIRCOL.

COLEX operated on the Time Sharing System (TSS) (chapter 2) on the computer at SDC-Santa Monica, instead of on the WPAFB computer. SDC hardware then consisted of a AN/FSQ-32 computer, a PDP-1 computer, drum storage, disk storage, sixteen tape drives, and associated punched card equipment. The COLEX system consisted of nine computer programs: seven produced the COLEX database on an IBM 7094 and two operated on the Q-32 for retrieval operations. Typical of most SDC retrieval projects of the 1960s, all the programs were in JOVIAL.

The experiment used the main database and thesaurus from the CIRC project for producing the COLEX database. For the first phase, October 1, 1966, through October 31, 1967, the project used a sample of unclassified records (54,685 at the beginning, and 67,500 by the end of October 1967) from the CIRC file. FTD's IBM 7094 computer was used to create the file (Baker and Smith 1968a). From November 1, 1967, through February 23, 1968, the file consisted of 67,500 references. During February 1968, a new version of COLEX was installed and the file expanded to include unclassified references to all 217,822 CIRC records, 80 percent of which were citations to Soviet publications. Increasing file capacity was possible by adding a second disk to the Q-32, which increased storage capacity from 33 million to 67 million characters and permitted a big expansion of the online file. By any measure, the online bibliographic database was huge then. Because the computer's online storage capacity was limited to 150,000 records, however, not all were available online at the same time.

1968 Milestone

COLEX was the first online search system to use time windows to handle large or multiple databases.

The operational solution was to divide the file by accession dates: references for the first 110,000 documents comprised one file, and references for the remaining 107,822 documents comprised the second. The first file was available to users on Tuesdays and Thursdays; the second was available on Mondays, Wednesdays, and Fridays (Smith, Hofmann, and Cornelli 1968). The COLEX service was the first to use time windows as a makeshift way to provide access to a very large database. SDC Search Service later used time windows during the early days of its operation.

> **1968 Milestones**
>
> COLEX was the first operational national online search service network.
>
> COLEX provided the first large-scale use of an online search system.

COLEX was the first operation of what could be considered a national online searching network. Even though it was an experiment, it was fully operational and remained in regularly scheduled operation from March 1968 until sometime in 1969, when it transitioned from an experiment to regular production. COLEX was operating before the launch in October 1968 of the four-node SUNY BCN network (chapter 8) and the February 1969 seven-node NASA/RECON system (chapter 5). TSS could handle up to fifty in-house and remote users simultaneously during the evaluation period. Remote users were limited only by the availability of Teletype and telephone equipment and service. The COLEX programs accommodated sixteen simultaneous users, but only thirteen stations at twelve agencies were designated for the experiment. The thirteen COLEX user stations either had dial-in service (TWX or Dataphone) to the Santa Monica computer, or leased lines that permitted users to be online simply by turning a knob on the Teletype.

The telecommunications equipment proved to be highly unreliable and searchers endured many interruptions and delays. In one instance, when a Teletype was unable to transmit properly, the evaluators stated with satisfaction that the telephone company repaired the malfunctioning equipment within six hours of notification, "even though the telephone company was involved in a labor dispute at the time" (Smith, Hofmann, and Cornelli 1968, 9).

Most users were at U.S. military or government organizations, such as the Air Force Systems Command, Harry Diamond Laboratories, RADC, Redstone Arsenal, DIA, or the Oceanographer of the Navy. Beginning in January 1968 NLM was also given access, as Station No. 12, to all COLEX services except classified microfilm. In addition to desiring access to the database, NLM wanted to acquaint librarians with the computerized accession techniques.

COLEX searchers could retrieve records by using up to ten English-language multiword descriptors, each of which could be designated an optional or a "must" term (i.e., only the document references that contained the term were retrieved), authors' names, or by a code for subject area. They could qualify output by country, type of document, and publication year or range of years. The COLEX retrieval program operated in either of two modes. The first mode, an instructional or self-teaching mode, allowed an untrained user to operate the program via detailed instructions and retrieval options explanation. In the second mode, the same retrieval options were available, but the instructional material was shorter. Either mode of operation was available at any time, This was an approach implemented years earlier on the SDC MICRO system ("A Search: 1967 style" 1967).

The system ranked output by responsiveness to a query—in descending order according to how many of the search terms appeared in the record. The system provided messages such as "16 documents exist for this retrieval request. 1 document contains 2 of the descriptors. 15 documents contain 1 of the descriptors." This feedback was helpful to searchers when it came time to specify the number of records to be printed online or offline. Searchers could view references in a standard format or they could specify particular fields of bibliographic information desired in the output (Baker and Smith 1968b). Searchers who wanted more detail than the database records provided had access to abstracts, extracts, or tables of contents stored on CIRC microfilm in a Lodestar viewer-printer at each COLEX station. Providing expanded versions of the online records in microform at the search station was a continuation of SDC's approach from SATIRE in 1962 and MICRO in 1965 (chapter 2). Black (1987) recalled using COLEX: "It was the very first ORBIT. That vintage ORBIT was kind of a laughing matter in many respects. They put it together relatively fast. It was kind of a semi-menu system but it wasn't really a menu system. It would ask you questions, and it allowed you to go through a series of logical progressions and you could keep narrowing down."

Evaluators studied the online system during March through June 1968. They collected and analyzed a large amount of data, including users' names and station numbers, any comments, start and stop times, number and length of searches, search keys and qualifiers used, and number of records printed online and offline. Additionally, they gathered user reactions by means of frequent contact between them and the COLEX System Monitor via telephone, Teletype, and face-to-face visits. Users were enthusiastic about the large CIRC file but unhappy that it was not updated on a monthly basis as promised. They liked the variety of access points, disliked the long time (several minutes) required to generate an offline printout (a new search could not start until the offline printing was complete for the previous search), and they recommended that the short form of the COLEX Retrieval Program be even shorter. Users had many complaints about the microfilm and Lodestar viewer/printer, including that reels were misaligned, film broke, hard copies from the microform printer were unreadable and hard to handle and store, and overall the excessive maintenance required to keep everything working. Users made recommendations about the thesaurus, searcher aids, hours of access, training needs, end-user searching, and various features of the retrieval program. Some of these suggestions were relatively easy to implement, but others related to limitations in the hardware or software that would not be resolved for several years.

Looking back, Borko (1985) said that the COLEX experience was the beginning of the basis for SDC's proposals to do major online systems development for NLM. As described later, this early exposure to SDC's online retrieval program influenced NLM to award a major development contract to SDC.

A side note illustrates again how the paths of the pioneers in this field crossed and interconnected. While at DIA (a sponsor of the SDC COLEX project), early online developer Richard Giering used DIA's terminal to search COLEX. As chief of the Military Capabilities Section, he had been using DIA's data processing equipment since 1965 to develop and maintain inventories of enemy ground forces in specific geographic areas. While he was working under the constraints of a formatted file system and batch processing computers, he heard about a research project at Northwestern University—sponsored by the Recon Lab at WPAFB—that had developed a set of IBM 7094 programs to do batch searching of textual data stored on computer tape. He obtained a set of the programs, called BIDAP (chapter 3), and started to experiment with them on an IBM 7094 computer at DIA. (More details of his experimentation are in chapter 7.) BIDAP was meant for batch processing, and Giering's use of it was on a dedicated console, which provided fast batch service. In that way, it technically could be considered online, but it was not interactive and did not have multiple users.

In a fortuitous coincidence, an Air Force intelligence analyst overheard Giering talking about his work and arranged for this text search approach to be used with some current Air Force work at the Recon Lab. Giering quickly arranged to help Data Corporation install the BIDAP software on the RECON CENTRAL computer in Dayton for use by

Air Force personnel. From the COLEX terminal at DIA, Giering used BIDAP programs now being operated online at RECON CENTRAL. He also used the COLEX terminal to access search programs that he had installed for DIA's use on Data Corporation's RECON CENTRAL system. Thus the early programs that were the conceptual seeds of the Data Central and LEXIS systems were being used by a system designer on terminals supplied by the developers of early SDC ORBIT software. This was the kind of cooperative coupling and technology transfer that their mutual sponsor, DIA, wanted. Unfortunately, although the Air Force and civilian project personnel at WPAFB associated with COLEX and Data Central activities knew of each other's existence, they remained unaware of the details of each other's systems (Giering 1995). McCarn was also at DIA during this time and carried his experiences with COLEX and Data Central with him to NLM in 1968 to become one of the developers of AIM-TWX and MEDLINE. Captain Giering retired from the Army in early 1967 and went to work for Data Corporation, where he was instrumental in developing their online systems and beginning LEXIS (see chapter 7).

Experience with the COLEX terminals was common among individuals who later worked on online systems. This included SDC, DIA, and NLM staff who were associated with developing COLEX and later SDC-developed systems (ORBIT, AIM-TWX, MEDLINE), DIA and Data Corporation staff who were associated with Data Corporation and its derivative systems (Data Central, Mead Data Central, the OBAR service, and the beginnings of Mead LEXIS), and the AF project monitors who later worked with other online systems.

CIRCOL

DIA deemed the COLEX experiment a success and gave approval in 1969 for the system to continue at FTD as an operational system called CIRCOL (CIRC-On-Line) (Dovel 1969; Spierer and Wills 1969). An important change was the addition of abstracts online to provide freedom from the microfilm and make it easier for users to make relevance judgments. Considering how large the file was, and how limited—by current standards—the storage capacity was, the decision to add abstracts to the online database was a bold move. Another change was running CIRCOL on an IBM 360/65, using IBM Data Cell storage devices, and in 1970 replacing SDC's CIRCOL software with IBM's DPS (chapter 4), which had text indexing capabilities.

The COLEX experience had revealed a critical need for "a current and comprehensive thesaurus reflecting all terms and their relationships required by each organization and so structured as to satisfy the needs of indexing, retrieval, and dissemination throughout the intelligence community" (Dovel 1969, 14). To meet this requirement, DIA directed the development of a computerized thesaurus that could be updated regularly online. Using the functions of AUTOLEX (automating lexicographic), the thesaurus project ran on SDC's TDMS, rather than ORBIT, because ORBIT in fall 1969 did not yet have an updating capability. This thesaurus was not a success because TDMS was not designed to be a lexicographic tool and was awkward in this application. While not fully satisfactory, however, the test results suggested that the concept of online thesaurus maintenance was worth exploring.

In 1970, CIRCOL operated for about four hours each day with approximately thirty IBM 2741 or 2740 teletypewriters accessing it from various parts of the country. The service was available free of charge for government agencies (Fong 1971). In April 1970, the file contained 365,000 records, all processed by manual indexing and including only assigned topic tags and titles for each document. Searchable abstracts were added sometime between April 1970 and July 1971 (King, Neel, and Wood 1972), and by July 1971 the file had grown to over 530,000 records. While the online system initially captured only the title for the retrieval process, later it captured the text from abstracts, extracts, and even brief full documents, with the intention of eventually discontinuing manual indexing of the titles and text material (Canfield 1973).

In 1970–1971, Donald King, Peggy Neel, and Barbara Wood of Westat Research conducted an evaluation study of CIRCOL to compare the retrieval effectiveness of human indexing from a controlled vocabulary with the natural language of abstracts and title text. The evaluation, using real-life searches from users (Canfield 1973), indicated no significant difference (King, Neel, and Wood 1972). In 1973, DiFondi and Roberti of RADC and Mangio of FTD reported on the King evaluation of free-text searching on the CIRCOL system as part of an investigation of indexing practices for that system. In critiquing the Westat study, Lancaster and Fayen (1973) judged that "the interactive capabilities of the on-line system were not exploited and, in fact, many of the results were derived by simulation. The study therefore sheds little light on the characteristics of on-line systems per se" (175). Nonetheless, DIA used the study results in deciding to discontinue indexing with a controlled vocabulary, thus reducing indexing costs to one-fifth. The favorable user reactions they collected after the discontinuation reinforced for them the wisdom of the decisions to load abstracts online and provide natural language searching of them.[2]

In a use study conducted in 1972–1973, Frederic Scheffler (1974) observed that information specialists tended to do subject searches. End users, who were FTD intelligence analysts, however, used CIRCOL mainly for searching on personal names. Scheffler concluded that certain searching habits, such as creating large sets, degraded response time whereas techniques to reduce the size of sets such as limiting by date or qualifying by country codes greatly shortened response time. A supplement to the user manual encouraged searchers to adhere to these time-saving techniques.

Scheffler also investigated the suitability of IBM STAIRS software with a CIRC database as a possible alternative for the IBM DPS software then being used for CIRCOL. Scheffler concluded that STAIRS, with certain modifications, would be suitable for the FTD/CIRC applications; it was easy to use and provided excellent response times.

During the course of Scheffler's study, the CIRCOL file grew to 850,000 records, with 15–20,000 new records added each month. The DPS file building software used a stop list to avoid building index entries (and using storage space) for common words and words shorter than a specified length, and to truncate words longer than a specified length. The system then compared the remaining candidate index terms against a list of authorized terms and printed out any new terms for review by a lexicographer. An automatic depluralization feature treated plural and singular variants as equivalents.

AF representatives identified with CIRCOL included DiFondi and Roberti at RADC, and Mangio, James Canfield, Donald Quigley, and James Shawley at WPAFB. SDC personnel associated with CIRCOL included Jane Anthra, Raymond Barrett, William Nance, and John Scroggins. Scroggins later became chief programmer for the first ORBIT system. The Dayton ORBIT software later incorporated parts of the CIRCOL program.

In January 1971, a document with no author or other identification except a title ("Central Information Reference and Control System (CIRC II)") defined system design requirements for a CIRC II retrieval system to replace the existing CIRC. CIRC II was to provide both batch and online search capabilities. A major portion of FTD's IBM 360/65 computer time would be available for development and operation of CIRC II; implementation would occur within two years after approval of the design requirements. The document cited a need to have source documents completely machinable, and promised that frequently the entire text of short articles or documents would be input. The design called for copies of all microfiche created during input processing to be available at all terminals to give searchers rapid access to source documents. Some terminals would have interfaces with automatic microfiche filing equipment to facilitate retrieval and re-filing.

CIRCOL, now identified as CIRC II, continued in operation at FTD into the 1980s, providing SDI and online search service. It still operated under a time windows system, with unclassified information available during morning hours, and classified or secure portions available in the afternoon hours. Its primary service objective was to meet the intelligence needs of DOD's sci-tech intelligence production agencies (Swanson 1981).

General-Purpose ORBIT

COLEX was the implementation of a special-purpose, JOVIAL-based program designed just for these applications. During 1967–1968, SDC-Dayton programmers developed a version of it called General-Purpose ORBIT. It was "general purpose" in its intent to be used with virtually any type of document collection and to be accessed at the IBM 360/65 computers at SDC in Santa Monica or in Falls Church, from any location in the country ("Man/machine" 1967). This was the first of the SDC programs to bear the ORBIT name, and the major developers were Nance and Scroggins of the SDC-Dayton facility. The programmers in Santa Monica were Don Blankenship, Bob Burket, Dave Kenton, and Dwight Harm (Cuadra 1997). The system began operating in 1967, running on the Q-32 at Santa Monica.

In September 1967, *SDC Magazine* described "what is probably the most comprehensive system presently operational—the SDC-developed ORBIT (On-line Retrieval of Bibliographic Text) system" ("Man/machine" 13). Although the explanation of what the letters in ORBIT stood for was a little different than Nance and Lathrop (1968)—they said it was "*O*n-line-*R*etrieval of *B*ibliographic *I*nformation *T*ime-shared"—this seems to be the first public use of the ORBIT name. (This system was later referred to as ORBIT I.) The article did not mention who was using the system, but the database description and sample printout suggest that this was the FTD application, and the timing coincided with the COLEX phase of the FTD project. The article stated that ORBIT ran on a computer in Santa Monica, with access from Teletype terminals, and that more than a dozen research facilities across the country were authorized to dial in. Searchers could use subject descriptors, author names, or any of the twenty-two COSATI subject areas, with qualifications possible (e.g., limit by date, language, document type) on the answer sets. The article's mention of online access by a dozen facilities across the country is coincidental to COLEX access by twelve stations. It also described a database of 65,384 documents, which is very close to the number of documents from the CIRC file in the COLEX system near September 1967. SDC's COLEX and initial ORBIT system (ORBIT I) were the same, and they both ran on the Q-32 in Santa Monica. ORBIT I only worked on the Q-32; it never went anywhere else.

In 1968, while the ORBIT software was running the FTD application from the Q-32, SDC was developing the General-Purpose ORBIT system to run on IBM 360/50 and 360/65 equipment. General-Purpose ORBIT was also available to run on a buyer's local computer. It was intended to enable librarians to convert existing manual catalogs and indexes for their own collections to an online storage and retrieval system. A manual was available to guide librarians in describing their own file design and storage and retrieval requirements in an interactive, online dialogue mode (Nance and Lathrop 1968).

General-Purpose ORBIT could operate in an instructional mode with either a long or short form of dialogue. The long form involved detailed messages and questions to users that were eliminated or abbreviated in the short form. Access points included any bibliographic element that contained fewer than thirty-six characters, for example, subject descriptors, author names, or subject codes. Qualifiers such as country, type of document, subject area, or date allowed a searcher to narrow a query. The output was document references and/or abstracts that General-Purpose ORBIT rank-ordered by matching a requester's search criteria. Searchers were able to select which parts of a record to print, and could print the records either online or offline. Built-in error checks prevented searchers from making expensive mistakes; for example, the system automatically rechecked requests for lengthy online printing. The searching program was flexible: "The requester may reinstate his previous subset of documents if by chance his qualifying logic reduces the output below that anticipated" (Nance and Lathrop 1968, 11). Another aspect of ORBIT's flexibility was that remotely located users could access it from a variety of typewriter terminals, teletypewriters, or keyboard plus CRTs. Interlibrary loan transactions in American libraries during this period commonly used teletypewriters.

In 1969, the Copper Development Association (CDA) sponsored an experiment to use ORBIT with their bibliographic database on copper technology. Beginning in May, remote terminals in CDA headquarters in New York and at the Copper Data Center office at Battelle Memorial Institute in Columbus, Ohio had online access. CDA member companies were expected to have terminal access by the end of 1969 (Covington 1969). (CDA also used Battelle's BASIS, discussed in chapter 9.)

ORBIT II

In 1971, ORBIT II replaced General-Purpose ORBIT, but they had little in common beyond the name. Although they shared the same capabilities, ORBIT II was a major refinement that ran on OS/MFT-OS/MVT, not TDMS. Designed to run on an IBM 360/40 or larger computer, ORBIT II was intended to provide extremely rapid retrieval (a few seconds or less), to many users (more than 150), from very large files (over 100,000 records of indexed materials) ("ORBIT for bibliographic" 1971). Upgrading to ORBIT II was part of the NLM ELHILL development, described later. The decision to upgrade SDC's existing online bibliographic search software may also have been a result of management's desire to develop revenue-generating products. As seen in chapter 2, SDC corporate support shifted from extending Protosynthex and BOLD to further developing the ORBIT software. Black (1995) recalled that SDC's upgrading of ORBIT I to ORBIT II was part of a general R&D operation to continue developing platforms for research projects, as a follow-up to BOLD. At that time, SDC management did not have any notions about a public online service.

A project team at SDC-Dayton had written General-Purpose ORBIT, but a team at SDC-Monica wrote ORBIT II. The major creators, Blankenship and Burket, had worked on the SDC-Dayton program, but they wrote the new program in PL-1, incorporating only a small portion of the old JOVIAL program. ORBIT II was a new program, not an upgrade of the existing CIRCOL system, one so radically different that Cuadra and his staff at SDC-Santa Monica seriously considered giving it a name other than ORBIT. Cuadra (1990) recalled that the team fought about the name before settling on ORBIT, "even though hardly a line of code was the same as the original." He recalled the birth of ORBIT II (1997):

I recall, from being in the computer room with Bob Katter, Bob Burket, and David Kenton, that ORBIT II, written in PL/1 and running under OS, made its first successful run that night. Someone in our gang has a photo showing the programmers with brand-new sweatshirts on which "ORBIT II" (I think) was stenciled. A printout from the above eventful night reads as follows:
ORBIT TOO IS OPERATING. WELCOME TO THE WORLD OF AUTOMATED INFORMATION RETRIEVAL, AND CONGRATULATIONS ON PASSING THE FIRST BARRIER. YOU MAY NOW INSERT SUCH COMMANDS AND REQUEST AS YOU DARE.

The first public mention of ORBIT II appears to have been in January 1970, when Seiden described it as a commercially available conversational bibliographic storage and retrieval system, running on an IBM 360/67, that was used as a test vehicle for NLM planning, with applications for Parkinson's disease, MARC, ERIC, and others. At a 1970 conference, Cuadra (1971b) remarked that the ORBIT II program package for online searching of large bibliographic files, using an IBM 360/40 or larger computer, and accommodating 150 or more concurrent users, was available for $22,000. This was "a fraction of the cost of developing them. I happen to know, because my own staff did the work, that the ORBIT on-line retrieval system cost over $200,000 to develop. And it would cost about that amount for someone to try to replicate a system of this complexity" (115). He made essentially the same statement at a seminar of the Chicago Association of Law Libraries (1971a).

Just as DIALOG was saved from extinction by the opportunity to apply it to NASA's file of aerospace literature records, the major break for further ORBIT development came in the form of a government contract from an agency that already had a large, important machine-readable file—in this case bibliographic records for medical literature.

Modern Bibliographic Control of Medical Literature

What is now known as the NLM was founded by John Shaw Billings in 1865 as the Army Medical Library, and in 1952 it became the Armed Forces Medical Library. In 1956, two U.S. senators, Lister Hill of Alabama (named for Joseph Lister, the English physician who introduced antiseptic surgery), and John F. Kennedy of Massachusetts, cosponsored the act that created the modern NLM. The Hill-Kennedy bill authorized a new building to house the library, to be located on an old golf course next to NIH in Bethesda, Maryland. Hamilton (1987) related that Senator Hill was especially concerned about the deplorable state of the old Army Medical Library: "Located in an ancient, red-brick Washington building without an elevator, toilet facilities, or adequate lighting, [it] had fallen on hard times. Years passed in which the library did not purchase a single book; the job of director usually went to a senior Army medical officer on his final tour of duty. Since the end of World War II, several commissions had debated what to do about this situation" (209).

The director of NLM through its transition period was Frank Rogers, who had earned his M.D. at Ohio State University in 1942 and an M.S. in library science from Columbia University in 1949. After finishing his library degree, he immediately joined the Army Medical Library and was assigned the directorship as a lieutenant colonel in the U.S. Army Medical Service. He served until September 1963, at which time he became librarian of the University of Colorado Medical Center, where he used his influence and intimate knowledge of NLM to establish in Colorado the first NLM regional search center. During 1962–1963, Rogers served as president of MLA, and afterward he received many awards and honors for his contributions. Rogers was succeeded at NLM in 1964 by Martin Cummings, who kept the post for twenty years.

In 1968, NLM joined with NIH, and Congress authorized the creation of a new research facility, to be built as a skyscraper wing of NLM and called the Lister Hill National Center for Biomedical Communications. The mission of the center was to develop new methods and systems for improving medical information transfer (Cummings 1985). Adams (1972) reviewed this early NLM history and its players and Rogers (1963, 1982) did likewise for the origins of MEDLARS.

Understanding how NLM came to adopt SDC ORBIT software for one of the earliest large-scale online retrieval operations requires an appreciation of the tremendous pressure on NLM in the 1960s to control the mushrooming medical literature. The story begins twenty years earlier, immediately following World War II.[3] The enormous proliferation of medical research and publication at that time was a direct result of several influences, including a shift in research to newly recognized problems, the development of science in countries that had previously not published much in these fields, and a huge growth in federal research grants in the United States making many new projects possible. Consequently, lengthy backlogs of papers waiting to be published developed quickly. Within a decade, thousands of new biomedical journals started in order to absorb the backlogs (Brodman and Ohta 1967, 901). Such a tremendous increase in medical periodical publication in such a short time overwhelmed the bibliographic services, including

Index Medicus—which NLM and its precursors had published since 1879—that existed to keep up with indexing and abstracting the literature from all over the world.

More efficient methods of bibliographic control were needed to cope with the overwhelming volume. As early as 1948, staff at the Welch Medical Library at Johns Hopkins University were developing a file of medical journal titles on punched cards for input to a first-generation computer. Other attempts to mechanize the production of medical indexes, using Listomatic cameras and Flexowriters to type duplicate cards automatically, followed in the 1950s ("The National Library of Medicine Index" 1961). Cummings asserted that the roots for MEDLARS lay in a grant that CLR made in April 1958 to NLM to plan for the automation of its main bibliographic service. Without that pivotal step, MEDLARS would not have followed: "People think of this as a great big government invention. But the fact is, the Library couldn't have started on it without that little grant from the Council" (Council on Library Resources 1993, special insert, 5).

MEDLARS: NLM's Contribution

Other NLM staff who participated in early MEDLARS included Joseph Leiter, Winifred Sewell, Charles Austin, and Melvin Day. When Day joined NLM, he brought with him the experience of managing NASA/RECON development (chapter 5). Leiter, a Ph.D. graduate in biochemistry from Georgetown University in 1949, was involved in cancer chemotherapy data screening at the National Cancer Institute before moving to NLM in 1965 as associate director of Library Operations. Austin joined NLM in 1962 as chief of the Data Processing Section. Sewell's participation is described later.

In the 1950s, projects on mechanized indexing of medical literature resulted in an effective system for production of several printed access tools (*Index Medicus, Cumulated Index Medicus, Bibliography of Medical Reviews*). In late 1960, however, NLM management realized that more powerful bibliographic control and access was needed. A retrieval system could not be successfully grafted onto a publication system that dealt mainly with problems of composition, so they decided to start by designing a new retrieval system and then a publication system. In November 1960, NLM engaged an analyst to draw up specifications for a system that Rogers and Taine named MEDLARS, for Medical Literature Analysis and Retrieval System.[4] The preliminary specifications were unsatisfactory, so Rogers and Taine rewrote them completely. In early 1961, NLM distributed the specifications to many interested organizations (Taine 1963a,b).

Rogers can be credited for leading the innovations at NLM in the late 1950s and early 1960s. Although Adams (1965b) recognized Rogers as the developer of MEDLARS, others argued that Rogers and Taine were both its creators—Taine as project officer and manager, and Rogers as major technical contributor. Adams's role was to pursue secondary objectives of MEDLARS, which included a vision of how the search facilities, interlibrary loan, and general library services improvement could penetrate the whole medical library community.

Adams earned a B.A. in English at Yale University in 1930 and a B.S.L.S. from Columbia University in 1940. He joined the Army Medical Library, and in 1946–1949 served as the acting librarian. From 1950–1959 he served as librarian at NIH, then later at NSF. In 1961, he returned to NLM as deputy director. His return to NLM during the same period as the Knox study (described later), the negotiations between NIH and NLM, and the subsequent transfer of NIH funds to NLM for new systems development (described above) was probably not coincidental. With Estelle Brodman he planned NLM's extramural program (later embodied in the Medical Library Assistance Act), and he made a major contribution to MEDLARS planning and development before retiring from government service in 1970. He was extremely active in professional activities, nationally and internationally, serving as the president of both ADI and MLA.

Support for MEDLARS development seems to have come from the law that established the National Heart Institute (NHI) within NIH and authorized the Surgeon General to establish an information center on research, prevention, and treatment of heart disease. In 1960, the NHI Council became concerned about the lack of sufficient bibliographic coverage of cardiovascular diseases. In order to secure guidance on the best way to correct this, NIH Director James Watt commissioned a study with an external contractor, J. Douglas Knox. Knox recommended that NHI establish a joint working group with NLM and a collaborative plan whereby NLM would be responsible for the mechanized storage and retrieval of the world's biomedical literature, with selective retrieval geared to the needs of the cardiovascular scientist. NHI would be responsible for planning the utilization of this information. Watt and Rogers discussed the possible use of computers in this plan. The Knox Report led to negotiations between NLM and NHI, and in 1960, $500,000 was transferred from NHI to NLM for this purpose.

Claire Schultz also participated in developing the initial MEDLARS system specifications. As a UNIVAC representative, she had been involved in developing the UNIVAC-based system at ASTIA (chapter 4). At a demonstration of the ASTIA system, Schultz conversed with Rogers and Taine about possible uses of computers at NLM. The three later discussed how the RFP process could be a means of gathering more ideas about computer applications, and they defined tasks for bidders. Although NLM asked Schultz to help formulate the invitation to bid, she declined because of her perceived conflict of interest in simultaneously preparing UNIVAC's proposal response. Schultz (1997) commented that, given her preproposal participation, "One would expect that UNIVAC had an inside track toward winning the contract! Not so. Because I was so well acquainted with what NLM wanted, I did not include a proposal for a preliminary study of the problem—as many others did—including GE. That was considered by the proposal-readers as a fatal flaw."

Soon afterward, Schultz left UNIVAC to join the Institute for the Advancement of Medical Communication. As described in the next section, NLM was now in the position of having a successful bidder (GE) who likely wanted their study to lead to an installation of one of their own computers, and an NLM staff who knew their own problems well but did not know much about computers. NLM's solution was to engage Schultz as a special consultant to serve as an interpreter at all weekly planning meetings between NLM and GE staff, and protect NLM from buying a GE computer if it were not the correct choice. Schultz became president of ADI in 1962 and recipient of the ASIS Award of Merit in 1980.

Win Sewell joined NLM in May 1961 as a subject heading specialist in the Index Section. She was appointed deputy chief of the Bibliographic Services Division under Taine in December 1962 and became a full-time participant in the MEDLARS program. She created *Medical Subject Headings* (*MeSH*) for MEDLARS, as well as the NLM infrastructure to maintain and update *MeSH* as the subject authority file. For the MEDLARS project, NLM reserved for itself the preparation and use of *MeSH*, and did not ask their contractors to provide more than a capability to search with the *MeSH* indexing structure. While director of NLM, Rogers countersigned every subject heading and hierarchy that Sewell proposed (Sewell 1997). To this day, *MeSH* is among the most vigorously maintained subject authority systems, even to the extent of requiring commercial online vendors of the NLM database, as part of their license agreements, to do annual file maintenance runs to make all the subject heading changes in the online records to correspond to annual changes in *MeSH*, a requirement that has been a hot issue for the vendors.

MEDLARS: GE's Contribution

NLM issued the RFP to develop MEDLARS in February 1961 to seventy-two companies for competitive bidding. By the April 1961 deadline, NLM had received twenty-five proposals (Adams 1972;

Rogers 1964). Rogers and Taine read and evaluated the proposals, assisted by representatives from HEW, DOD, NBS, and the CIA. Rogers (1982, 81–82) commented:

> It was discouraging. Proposal after proposal offered schemes that bore little discernable relationship to the specifications we had issued. Many of the proposals indulged in what I considered to be mere fanciful speculation. Finally, I reached the bottom of the pile, and the last proposal happened to be the one submitted by the General Electric Company. It almost immediately conveyed to me the sense of being on the mark, and when Taine and I carefully reviewed our assessments of the whole lot, we found ourselves in easy agreement on selection of the General Electric proposal.

Cloyd Dake Gull had spent several months working full time in preparing GE's proposal. His most recent experience had been working since January 1958 for GE's project team on the DEACON information retrieval project (chapter 2). As Gull (1997) described it:

> The MEDLARS award process started with 72 companies attending the bidders' briefing, 26 proposals received and reviewed in about six weeks time, from which the top three companies would be invited to make an oral presentation also, over Memorial Day weekend. GE was notified to make its presentation just before Memorial Day. Lindon Saline (our manager), Bob Vredenburg (marketing manager), and I made the presentation. Scott Adams and the U.S. Public Health Service [USPHS] contract officer attended for NLM. As the presentation progressed, the contract officer became visibly upset with our presentation. We could not think what we had done or left undone. Finally, in exasperation, he said, "Write this in your proposal there, and that over there." We did so, of course, and labored through to the end. Adams said nothing. When the presentation was finished, we adjourned to a restaurant and went over the points. We did not see where we could have gone wrong, but we were not very hopeful since there were two companies to be heard from, and we didn't know who they were. It was Monday before we learned what happened. NLM and USPHS had chosen GE for the award and had canceled the other presentations, but they neglected to tell us that we had been chosen!

GE had a corporate interest in IR issues, starting in the early 1960s. Several of the GE staff members who worked on the MEDLARS project had prior experience with a major targeting information retrieval system for AFCIN (Air Force Chief of Intelligence).

NLM executed a multi-phased contract in August 1961 with the Information Systems Operation of GE, located in Bethesda, about "a stone's throw" from the new NLM building (Taine 1963b, 160). Richard Garrard was GE's manager for the MEDLARS Project and was assisted by Carl Kalo and Panos Galidos. Taine was the project director for NLM. The three-year, $3 million GE contract called for the delivery of an operational system on January 31, 1964. Gull's participation was limited in the preliminary design phase because he had been elected president of ADI and also had a prior commitment to teach for six weeks at the University of Washington's library school. Nonetheless, the preliminary system design was complete on January 31, 1962 (*Final technical report* 1962; Garrard 1965). The Honeywell-800 computer for the system was delivered and made available to NLM in March 1963, and test searches were run that fall. MEDLARS began operation at NLM on January 1, 1964 (Adams 1965b), and the NLM staff took over the operation in February (Adams 1965a). Once installed, the original MEDLARS system remained in operation for more than ten years. On February 28, 1975, the last production job was run on MEDLARS I. ("End of an era" 1975). The project had required thirty man-years of programming.

Considering that GE was then producing its own computers, the GE staff recommendation of a Honeywell computer was a surprise to many. As reported by persons familiar with the decision, the contractor and consultant staff analyzed the computers available and determined that the Honeywell was the least expensive and had the most capability. As special consultant to NLM, Schultz made her own independent study of all candidate computers on the market. She described a meeting where she was scheduled to present the results of her research on behalf of NLM (1997):

Representatives of many government agencies attended the meeting, as well as the brass from GE. I was nervous, but had done my homework, so there was surprisingly little difficulty. One of my premises was that the mainframe computer had to do the job for at least five years because it would be too disruptive to have to change computers within that time. An OMB person put serious pressure on me at the morning coffee break to recommend IBM equipment. Toward the end of my presentation, GE suggested that two 225s could be used in tandem instead of a single computer, but my data knocked down both suggestions. I recommended the Minneapolis Honeywell 800 (not the UNIVAC III as some expected) and the recommendation was accepted.

Gull (1997) confirmed that GE staff had studied eight computer systems thoroughly and found that the Honeywell 800 was the most reliable. Unfortunately, no one had considered that the Honeywell tape format required twice as much space as other formats then in use, and that nobody else was using the Honeywell format (which caused problems for them later). Further, they had no idea that Honeywell was getting out of the computer business. While the selection turned out to be a bad decision, no one at the time could have foreseen it.

The major functions of the total MEDLARS system were to (1) produce the printed *Index Medicus*; (2) offer specialized subject bibliographies, either on pre-selected topics, or by special request from individual scientists, by means of batch searching; and (3) make the MEDLARS file widely available to other libraries and research institutions for use within their own programs (Cummings 1965a). The major objectives for MEDLARS as stated by NLM management in 1961 were somewhat different, but they did include the specific goal of making "possible the prompt (a maximum of two days) and efficient servicing of requests for special bibliographies, on both a demand and a recurring basis, regularly searching up to five years of stored computer files." Two design criteria that impacted the accomplishment of that objective were (1) a decision to train search specialists to formulate retrieval requests, rather than allowing customers to formulate their own search statements; and (2) a decision to use serial tape files for storing journal article citations rather than random access devices. This latter decision was the result of a careful analysis of comparative costs and retrieval efficiency of equipment available in 1961–1962 (Austin 1968). Literature searches or "on-demand bibliographies" were not in great demand in the early 1960s; early in 1965, NLM was receiving requests from a national constituency at the rate of only about twenty a day (Kilgour 1966), close to the 2,500 on-demand bibliographies for FY 1964 projected in the 1962 GE MEDLARS preliminary design report (*Final technical report* 1962).

From the beginning, MEDLARS worked well on another task, production of *Index Medicus*. The input and data validation process was another important part that worked well, but received little attention in the specifications; the original specifications had no requirement for either online or remote I/O.

In response to a contract requirement for a fast photocompositor, GE subcontracted with Photon Company for an innovative, unique electronic device called GRACE (Graphic Arts Composing Equipment). GRACE could handle many type fonts and foreign languages (needed for medical terminology, including genus/species names as well as non-U.S. journals). It was estimated to have the typesetting power of fifty-five Linotype operators. As Gull (1997) told it:

During proposal writing, GE learned about GRACE, which was the invention of a couple of MIT professors. Although there was no finished model of GRACE, GE proposed to acquire the first one from their company, Photon, and to use it in MEDLARS. As time went on, Photon employees proved incapable of making GRACE work, meaning GRACE would not be delivered on schedule. GE foresaw that this failure would, in turn, cause GE to fail to deliver on schedule. GE sent a couple of their engineers to Cambridge to make GRACE work. The GE engineers soon made GRACE into the first successful computer-driven photocomposition device, and MEDLARS was delivered on schedule.

The GRACE equipment was used to produce *Index Medicus* beginning in August 1964 (Cummings 1976a). This development helped to establish electronic photocomposition as a viable alternative to prior methods of typesetting, while using a machine-readable file as the source of the operation. GRACE was then the fastest phototypesetter in the United States. NLM used GRACE until 1969, when it was replaced with a faster commercial model, Photon ZIP 901, and its equipment retired to the Smithsonian Institution. As mentioned earlier, NLM had already demonstrated a pioneering spirit in generating mechanized approaches to production of their printed catalogs.

Initial MEDLARS Experience

During 1963 NLM ran several hundred test searches under what might be called laboratory conditions. In January 1964 NLM announced its intention to make search services available and solicited search requests from local research scientists. Prior to this announcement, Adams and Taine (1964, 110) expressed an opinion typical of the time regarding the use of computers for searching:

The sophistication of machine search is of such an order that economical use of computer time suggests a screening of the questions put to it. Thus MEDLARS search is not intended to substitute for verification of the spelling of a reference, or for lists of papers published by an author, or on a single subject. For such questions, a conventional search of the printed monthly issues of *Index Medicus* is fully as efficient and more economical. MEDLARS use will be reserved for more complex questions.

NLM began processing demand searches in April 1964, and in the next twelve months ran over 1,100 searches for physicians, researchers, health officials, and teachers who agreed to evaluate the bibliographies for completeness and relevance (Adams 1965b). The demand for MEDLARS increased rapidly. The results of this experience revealed two difficulties: (1) processing requests was time-consuming and only a small number of NLM staff were available for the task, which made it impossible to accommodate a large volume; and (2) weaknesses in *MeSH* resulted in retrieval of many irrelevant citations. Accordingly, the library adopted a policy of providing search services only under test conditions.

A sharp three-party exchange of letters to the editor about exaggerated claims for MEDLARS (e.g., "publication of aspirations as achievements") noted that MEDLARS batch searching done in 1964 used a database of only a little more than one year of *Index Medicus* citations, and that NLM had to hold back on demand bibliographies because they were too time-consuming even with that small file (Shaw 1965a, 1965b; Cummings 1965b; Garrard 1965).

When MEDLARS staff began processing requests, the computer took about forty minutes to read all the tapes. At an April 1965 meeting, Adams reported that they had 265,000 citations in the database, and were inputting records from 2,400 journals at the rate of about 14,000 per month (Adams 1965b). At a late 1965 presentation, Shumway (1966) observed that even though MEDLARS indexing began in 1963, fruitful machine search of the MEDLARS tapes for citations was limited to the period since January 1964, and no retrospective indexing was planned. He stated that 370,139 citations were stored then on MEDLARS tapes. Austin (1968) admitted, "Many program 'bugs' continued to appear in the search routines. These problems . . . resulted in poor demand search production in 1964" (54).

By mid-1965, NLM still did not have sufficient staff to handle the workload and still was deferring the date when it would open to all search requests (Adams 1965a). Shumway (1966) reported a twenty-day average response time for searches, with some backlog, and a restriction on type of searches accepted. NLM gradually accepted more requests and in fiscal year 1965 processed 1,800 searches (Rogers 1974). For August through December 1966, the average turnaround time ranged from twenty-four to sixty-four days. For January through June 1967, the average turnaround time had improved to thirteen to twenty-four days (Lancaster 1968a).

During 1965, Cyril Cleverdon, librarian of the College of Aeronautics in Cranfield, England, visited the director of NLM. Cleverdon described his ideas on evaluating the efficiency and effectiveness of information systems by determining their recall and precision ratios. Cummings saw this as an opportunity to evaluate MEDLARS output and identify areas for improvements. On Cleverdon's recommendation, Cummings hired Wilf Lancaster to evaluate MEDLARS, and he retained Cleverdon as a consultant (Miles 1982). The evaluation, among the earliest of a computer-based retrieval system, took place in 1966–1967 and resulted in one of the earliest publications with empirical recall/relevance data (Lancaster 1967, 1968a, 1968b, 1969a, 1969b, 1971a; Lancaster and Jenkins 1970). Lancaster had pointed remarks about MEDLARS performance, including problems with indexing of source material, query formulations, and the user-system interface. (Lancaster became important again in connection with the AIM-TWX evaluation.)

NLM's Regional Search Centers

During the MEDLARS design phase, Rogers asked Adams to consider secondary objectives for the system. After consulting with the GE team, Adams proposed the decentralization of MEDLARS. Recognizing the likelihood of the demands for machine searching outstripping the resources available from a central service facility, Adams asked GE to conduct a preliminary feasibility study of decentralization (Adams 1965a, 1965b). Other secondary objectives were storage and retrieval of text on microfilm to provide copies to searchers, the handling of library technical processing (e.g., acquisitions, circulation), and the use of online input and query stations. Adams described technical difficulties with meeting those objectives: The machine-readable file and updates were in a tape format accepted only by a Honeywell computer, and the associated search programs were in a programming language (ARGUS) that could only be used on a Honeywell.

As mentioned earlier, an immediate MEDLARS objective was to perform on-demand batch searches in response to reference questions. The initial MEDLARS had such a capability, but it was underused. NLM had the machine capacity to handle a greater volume of search requests, but the staff could not cope with the expected demand and did not have approval for the additional staff positions needed. This led to the decisions to decentralize the services in regional centers and to establish a policy of constrained use for the current service. Cummings (1965a, 119) offered his view of the start-up experience:

Another serious problem... has been the shortage of trained search specialists. This has necessarily limited the number of searches which can be formulated. Hence, full machine capability has not yet been approached. In fact, we reached only about 25 percent of the machine's operating capability.... It is hoped that this problem can, in part, be alleviated through the decentralization of MEDLARS. A contract has been negotiated with UCLA for the reprogramming and reconversion of Honeywell tapes for use on IBM 7090 and related equipment. We plan to establish six or eight university-based regional MEDLARS centers so that the means of access to, and retrieval of, the literature will be shared freely and extensively with the entire biomedical community.

NLM chose the Biomedical Library at UCLA to serve the western United States and to be the first in a proposed network of geographically dispersed MEDLARS search centers. NLM contracted with UCLA in 1964 to (1) reprogram copies of the MEDLARS file from an ARGUS to a COBOL format (a language accepted by many IBM computers), so that the tapes could be run on local IBM machines; and (2) establish a pilot demonstration search center to test the programs under actual operating conditions ("NLM contracts with UCLA" 1964; Lewis 1966). Harvard received a contract to perform a similar conversion. Concurrently, NLM acquired a small computer to convert their Honeywell tapes to IBM-compatible tapes. Austin was the NLM project monitor and the project managers at UCLA were Louise Darling (biomedical librarian) and Wilfred Dixon (director of the Health Science Computer Center) ("UCLA gets contract" 1965). Cummings commented on the significance of the contract: "The decentralization of MEDLARS is a logical and necessary development to enable the system to help meet the mounting demands of the biomedical community for current medical information" ("MEDLARS decentralization" 1965, 14). However, even though UCLA produced programs for an IBM 7094-7040 computer, reprogramming problems prevented the MEDLARS system from becoming operational there (Garvis 1966; Austin 1968).

MEDLARS decentralization from 1964 onward, by means of contracts with external organizations, was intended to provide additional capacity and a basis for a biomedical information network. From NLM's point of view, the principal activity of the centers was to produce on-demand bibliographies by conferring with requesters, formulating search statements, forwarding the search statements to the computer center (NLM or local), and reviewing results with requesters. Adams (1964) talked of plans to move toward decentralization; he mentioned the planned release of the MEDLARS tapes to any library at approximate cost—something that never happened.[5] NLM's decentralization decision was well-received by the medical community. Both Adams (1965a) and Cummings (1965c) reported that forty institutions had expressed an interest in becoming a MEDLARS search center.

In December 1964, the DeBakey Report of the U.S. President's Commission on Heart Disease, Cancer, and Stroke identified ways in which research money being spent in these areas could be made more effective by bringing research results into practice (*The President's Commission* 1964, 1965). Throughout the report were numerous references to medical libraries; it was probably no coincidence that DeBakey was director of the NLM Board of Regents about this time. This report, and others, led to the Medical Library Assistance Act (signed into law in October 1965) and the Regional Medical Library Programs (Cummings and Corning 1971).

The first regional NLM search center was at the University of Colorado, which received an NLM contract in February 1965. The manager was Frank Rogers, who had left NLM and become director of the Dennison Memorial Library and professor of Medical Bibliography. He arranged for time on a Honeywell-800 computer within the Reclamation Service of the U.S. Department of the Interior in Denver. This computer was compatible with the system then in use at NLM, so no major programming was needed in Denver, and it became operational within a month. Initially, in order to allow orderly growth, services were limited to University of Colorado Medical School faculty (Rogers 1966b; Austin 1966; Adams 1965b). With a new contract, the system began in September 1965 to serve the entire medical community in the Mountain Time Zone (Darling 1966). In addition to serving the Colorado community, it had been processing NLM's backlog of searches (*Progress of the United States Government* 1965, 20–21). The Colorado center was the first success among the regional search centers—it was the first to start doing its own searches; the other five MEDLARS stations mailed formulated searches to NLM for processing there, even after they had been in operation for two to three years. One novel program that the Colorado staff wrote allowed annotation of user printouts from the tapes received from NLM to show the Colorado library's holdings ("New MEDLARS Center" 1965).

In August 1965, when Irwin Pizer became chairman of the SUNY Task Force on Medical Libraries (chapter 8), he planned for the participating SUNY medical libraries to form a network that might become a MEDLARS center serving other medical schools in upper New York, Pennsylvania, and Ohio. Pizer approached NLM about that possibility, and in September drafted a proposal, "A Computerized Bio-Medical Information Resource." Bridegam and Meyerhoff (1970, 106) observed, "The computer-mediated retrieval of *Index Medicus* citations and the decentralization of search capabilities of MEDLARS tapes had medical institutions literally scramble to become MEDLARS centers."

The next steps in NLM decentralization included contracts established in 1966 with the University of

Alabama Medical Center (to serve the South), the University of Michigan Medical Center Library (to serve the Midwest), and Harvard University (to serve the Northeast). OSU and Texas Medical Center established MEDLARS centers using their own funds; the Medical Library Assistance Act provided further support of MEDLARS search service at the regional libraries (Austin 1966). In 1967, in order to decrease turnaround time and lower NLM costs, NLM decided to have all university-based MEDLARS stations do more of the intellectual work related to processing requests (search formulation and review of output) and have NLM perform the machine processing centrally (*Progress* 1967, 51). By the end of 1967, all five stations had sent personnel to NLM for six months of intensive training in indexing, *MeSH*, and search formulation.

These regional centers, however, made heavy demands that were troublesome for NLM: "The resulting expansion increased the problems dramatically by the spring of 1968, when there were eight MEDLARS Centers in the U.S. and two abroad" (Leiter and Gull 1968, 257). NLM was feeling the stress of a lack of resources for serving the demands of outside researchers, while institutions around the country were eager to become active participants in providing on-demand searches. By the end of 1972, eleven regional search centers were operating, four of which had computer processing capability.

Rogers (1974, 75) described the process during the late 1960s as follows:

The MEDLARS files were serially ordered. Citations for about one month of indexing would just about fill one reel of tape.... If one wished to search the most recent 750,000 citations in the file, one had to pass the forty tapes which held them. At about 3 minutes per tape, this process of reading took 2 hours, followed by another period of logical comparisons, formatting, and printing. At a computer cost of $250 per hour, it is obvious that the economics of doing searches one at a time is not favorable. The solution was, of course, to batch—to collect some optimum number of searches and to process them all at once against one reading of the entire tape file.

The long turnaround time associated with batch searches was especially problematic for clinicians, who therefore tended to use the printed *Index Medicus* instead. For those willing to wait, the system could be frustratingly slow and ineffective. After formulating a search, punching it on cards, and mailing it to NLM, a librarian at a regional medical library had to wait from six weeks to three months to receive a client's bibliography. Sometimes NLM did not return a bibliography, but rather sent a maddening message such as, "You misformulated your search; please try again" (McCarn 1987). If a client made the request at a library other than a regional medical library, the results would be further delayed because of the extra leg of round-trip communication and shipping. The cumbersome nature of the batch process led some searchers to use the SUNY BCN online system (chapter 8) to test and modify their search formulations or to obtain interim search products before submitting them for searching on the more comprehensive MEDLARS batch service. Another frustration for searchers was that the batch system was limited in search capabilities; for example, no title word search capability existed.

Concerned about quality control issues in searching, NLM instituted strict control measures, but this inhibited the growth of MEDLARS searches. Leiter and Gull (1968, 257) summed up these restrictions:

All persons who are selected to perform indexing and searching activities for MEDLARS, either at (NLM) or in the MEDLARS Centers elsewhere, are required to take a six-month course of instruction at NLM divided between indexing and searching techniques. There are three classes conducted during a year by regular NLM staff members, and in 1968 as many as 20 trainees were accepted in one course. Each trainee must have a formal education in the biomedical field, and full competence in handling the English language. After the searchers graduate and reach their stations, they are supervised by a senior searcher and their work is subject to revision. One or more searchers from each Center is required to come to (NLM) at least annually for a one-week workshop.

No other computer-based search service ever put such an extensive training requirement on its searchers. NLM's justification was their belief that indexers only have to know the current indexing rules, but searchers need to know the rules used in all previous years. With the introduction of online searching in October 1971, the training program was shortened to three weeks. Several years later, the program was reduced to successful completion of a NLM computer-assisted-instruction program followed by only one week of training. A total of 254 search analysts were trained at NLM in 1977 (*MEDLARS and Health* 1982).

The total volume of MEDLARS batch search activity grew steadily between 1965 and 1968. NLM processed a total of 3,035 specialized bibliographies in 1966 (Cummings 1967a). They also produced several popular "Recurring Bibliographies" that amounted to regular periodic alerting publications. By the end of 1968, about 70 percent of all MEDLARS searches were done in the Centers and a continually decreasing fraction were done at NLM. Thus more of the searching was being done closer to the users. In 1965 the average batch size was eight searches per run, and by 1968 the average batch was forty searches. Search time stayed roughly proportional to the size of the file searched, which forced constraints on searching the older files.

Austin (1968) reviewed the previous four years of MEDLARS experience and observed that some of the initial objectives had not been met: "It has not been possible to accomplish a two-day search turnaround time with the present batch processing system. Also, because of computer time limitations, demand searches beginning in early 1968 include only references from January 1966 on (only 2+ years of coverage), instead of references from the entire file" (60). The rationale for dropping the pre-1966 tapes from searching may have been their lack of *MeSH* subheadings—they could not be searched in the same fashion as the later tapes (Sewell 1997). Another problem was that early NLM indexing had no term for "human." Consequently, output included all the results of *all* animal research, including humans. Searchers had to NOT out a list of terms (e.g., monkey, beagle, mice) in order to increase the relevance of retrieved records (Angione 1999a).

By early 1970, the MEDLARS file was written on forty-eight reels of tape; it took two and a half hours to read the one million citations (Rogers 1982). MEDLARS search services peaked in NLM's fiscal year 1971, with 18,000 batch searches in the United States (4,000 at NLM; 14,000 at other U.S. centers), and an additional 5,600 at foreign centers (Rogers 1974). Searches routinely covered a span of the most recent thirty to forty-two months.

MEDLARS searches were free. Operating costs for both machine and labor continued to decline with experience; they dropped from an average of $168 per search in 1965, to $85 per search in 1967—figures that are greatly in excess of the typical costs experienced with later online services (Rogers 1966a, 1966b, 1968; Cummings 1967a).

As mentioned earlier, Lancaster reported on a recall and precision performance evaluation of MEDLARS in 1966 and 1967. Salton (1971b) also evaluated MEDLARS performance, and other NLM staff members followed up (Jenkins 1972). Hogan (1966), for example, was critical of turnaround time, noting that it took more than three months to obtain results from NLM in response to a request from her library in Arkansas. Stevens (1970) felt that it was appropriate to review the original objectives statement against the results actually achieved. He did so in a careful, factual review. For example, a stated objective had been to make possible prompt (a maximum of 2 days) and efficient servicing of requests for special bibliographies, on both a demand and recurring basis, regularly searching up to five years of stored computer files. Stevens pointed out that this objective had not been met—only a two-year database was being searched, and the average turnaround time was two weeks. The original projections called for 22,500 searches to be provided in 1969—in 1968, however, there were only about 9,200 searches.

In May 1971, NLM restricted each MEDLARS Center to a specified quota of searches. Michigan's was ninety searches per month, with at least 25 percent to be from outside the University of Michigan (Hirschfeld 1972). Processing times for 75 percent of demand bibliographies were fifteen calendar days or less; over 90 percent were processed within twenty calendar days (Leiter and Mehnert 1972).

For index production, however, MEDLARS was much faster than previous methods and offered more depth of indexing than had been possible before. Brodman and Ohta (1967, 904) asserted that MEDLARS revealed a number of indexing deficiencies, which spurred the staff to revise the subject heading list, find "new indexers with adequate scientific and linguistic backgrounds," and improve the indexers' training.

NLM's International Search Center Partners

In addition to their search services in the United States, NLM tried to respond to international requests. According to Cummings (1997), NLM was overloaded with requests from forty countries for tapes and services. In establishing priorities for response, Cummings and Mary Corning decided to work first with medical institutions in countries that had both technical expertise and knowledge of how to serve users. Thus they started with the U.K. and other European countries. NLM arranged to establish MEDLARS centers with OSTI in the United Kingdom and with the Karolinska Institutet (School of Medicine, Stockholm) in Sweden. Regular customer service from Karolinska started in June 1967 using an IBM 7094-1401 computer, and expanded in June 1972 to provide online MEDLINE service from a local IBM 360/75 (Falkenberg 1975). The British and Swedish arrangements were based on NLM providing magnetic tapes, technical documentation, and training programs, and the international partners providing evaluation and technical feedback. This approach was expanded later to require the participating organizations to furnish indexed bibliographic data (their local or regional source data) to NLM for inclusion in the MEDLARS file (Corning 1972). From 1965 through 1972, MEDLARS centers were established also in Australia, France, the Federal Republic of Germany (West Germany), the World Health Organization in Geneva, Canada, and Japan, and later in Iran, Mexico, South Africa, and Brazil. Like their U.S. counterparts, they made heavy use of the production of specialized bibliographies using batch search software and NLM's machine-readable files. Later they had the option of direct online access to the NLM computer (Cummings 1976b).

Some new centers were slow to build up a volume of use. The Australian National University, for example, participating in a pilot study by the Australian MEDLARS Service of the National Library of Australia, offered their service beginning in February 1970, but it was June 1970 before they received their first request—and the printout was delayed for two months because of computer problems. Their second request was not until January 1971 (McEwin 1971). After a year of a pilot operation MEDLARS became fully operational in Australia in April 1971 (Hodgson 1972).

NLM granted to their international partners the exclusive right to provide online service for the geographic area covered in their joint agreement. This resulted in a de facto worldwide search service monopoly for NLM and its partners. The receipt of MEDLARS input data from its international partners was extremely important to NLM. The lingering effect was that NLM restricted all U.S. commercial online services from offering access to NLM files outside the United States, even though some of them had MEDLINE for U.S. customers since the late 1970s. Thus, for many years, U.S. search services were contractually prohibited from making MEDLINE available to the international markets served by the NLM partners.

The British MEDLARS service, operating out of the NLL (later renamed the British Library Lending Division) at Boston Spa, processed their first batch of retrospective searches in May 1966 on the English Electric KDF9 computer at the University of Newcastle upon Tyne (Harley 1975; Bower 1971). NLL librarians formatted the searches, which were computer processed at the university. Growth in use was rapid in the United Kingdom, reaching a peak of about eighty searches a week, with a quarter of these being done under contract for the French MEDLARS center. Shortage of processing capacity at Newcastle led to the use of other KDF9s at Salford University and Nottingham University (Harley 1977).

In describing the experience at Newcastle in 1969, Barraclough (1970) said that after the librarians formulated them, search requests were grouped in batches of thirty, and run through the entire collection of thirty tapes—which took from six to eight hours of computer time. More than 48 percent of searches had a turnaround time of twenty-one days or more. This experience led them to obtain a three-year OSTI grant for designing and testing an experimental online search formulation and sample retrieval system. As part of the experiment, an IBM 2741 terminal was installed at NLL, connected by phone lines to an IBM 360/67 computer at Newcastle (Harley 1971a). NLL staff used this online system with a sample MEDLARS file of 40,000 recent records to test and modify search formulations before sending them away for batch processing against the full MEDLARS file (Harley 1971b).

In 1972, OSTI funded work by the United Kingdom Chemical Information Service (UKCIS) to write a new set of MEDLARS retrieval programs, this time for the ICL system 4/50 computer because of obsolescence of the KDF9, the degraded state of the original programs, and the impending NLM-introduced changes in the vocabulary. UKCIS expected the new set of programs to be in operation about mid-1972. In the meantime, the turnaround time for the batch searches on this system had "improved" to 73 percent completed within fifteen working days, from only 31 percent completed within fifteen working days in the prior six months ("MEDLARS: Searches processed" 1972).

In 1971, the four MEDLARS processing centers in Europe, experiencing operational inconveniences in searching the old backfile (1964–1965 MEDLARS tapes), decided to try an experiment in cooperative processing. Each center was receiving few requests for backfile searches; thus it took a long while for each center to accumulate what they judged to be a worthwhile batch for processing: "The total demand in Europe . . . justifies about one batch a month" ("European MEDLARS cooperation" 1971, 139). They agreed that each center should take a turn processing a batch for everyone. The first run took place in June 1971 in Cologne at DIMDI (Deutsche Institute für Medizinische Dokumentation und Information).

MEDLARS Upgrading: Planning for MEDLARS II

MEDLARS continued in operation until 1972, even with its many deficiencies, which everyone involved understood well. In 1967, after four years of operating experience, it had fully accomplished only three of its nine original objectives and partly accomplished six of them, and it was experiencing the shortcomings of a pioneering system. Austin (1966, 150) observed, "In some respects MEDLARS actually was obsolete before it was ever operational because the design was frozen in '61, and about two and a half years was required to implement it." Austin (1968) reflected on the prudent approach that had been taken on the initial batch MEDLARS system design: "The Library did not attempt to experiment with untested theories in designing the system, because of the large volume of literature to be processed and the number of users to be served. The conservative approach has resulted in four years of continued successful operation. What is more, there is no evidence of the system breaking down as the volume of literature increases, as some in this field predicted" (69).

The conservative approach may have helped the service to survive, but not to thrive. After four years of MEDLARS public service, even an NLM publication conceded that "MEDLARS is a developmental system with certain inherent limitations," and cautioned that, "The bulk of search requests will be processed and released by the Library within 15 working days after receipt by the Search Section. Requests which pose unusual problems will be reported on within one month" (*Guide to MEDLARS* 1968, 7–8, 10). The *Guide* asked users not to request author searches ("Author indexes are available in INDEX MEDICUS and CUMULATED INDEX MEDICUS"), or verification of specific citations ("This information is readily available in INDEX MEDICUS and elsewhere"), or citations "on a single subject, or concepts which may be easily coordinated, e.g., bladder neoplasms, cardiovascular complications in pregnancy. These citations may be found readily in INDEX MEDICUS under the appropriate headings" (7). Another NLM publication (*The principles of MEDLARS*, n.d., 45) repeated the restrictions, noting specifically, "The MEDLARS system is not designed to search on authors' names." This sounded much like the comments that Adams and Taine (1964) had expressed four years earlier. Looking back over this period, Miles (1982, 379) summed up, "The time from the submission of the request, through the formulation of the request by an analyst at NLM and the processing in the computer, to the review and mailing of the bibliography to the patron, was usually 3 to 6 weeks."

It was clear that the increasing volume of published medical literature and the growing service demands soon would overwhelm the MEDLARS capacity. Consequently, NLM initiated plans in 1967 to expand and upgrade the system, and issued an RFP in August 1967 for MEDLARS II (discussed later).

In April 1967, Ruth Davis joined NLM as associate director for research and development. The R&D program became known as the Lister Hill National Center for Biomedical Communications, and in August 1968 Davis became its first director. She was a computer expert for intelligence information systems such as CIRC/COLEX and had served as a staff assistant in the Office of Director of Defense Research and Engineering at DOD. Prior to that, she managed the computer center for the U.S. Navy's David W. Taylor Model Basin. She was a major participant in the 1970 COSATI online database benchmark and Battelle film (chapter 4). She left NLM in 1970 to become director of the Center for Computer Sciences and Technology at NBS.

As part of NLM's strategy to upgrade MEDLARS, Davis recruited a former colleague from DIA, Davis McCarn and hired him in October 1968 to lead the long-range planning as deputy director of the new Lister Hill Center. McCarn had earned a B.A. in mathematics from Haverford College, had served as a USAF mathematician, and had worked at DOD, where he had management responsibility for intelligence data handling systems. He was one of three who went to the DIA in 1962 to write the plan and take over the intelligence system computers in the Army, Navy, and Air Force. At DIA, he had become familiar with the COLEX system, the Data Central system at WPAFB, and other online systems in development or operation. In fact, McCarn was the person most responsible at NLM for technical development of its online activities, including AIM-TWX, ELHILL, and MEDLARS II. He left NLM in 1978 to form his own consulting company and later joined H. W. Wilson Co. in 1980 as director of Computerized Bibliographic Services. In 1986, he wrote Grateful Med, a widely used online interface to MEDLINE.

From DIA, Davis brought in Ralph Simmons, who had been in charge of developing an online system for the Air Force. As NLM's head of Information and Computer Sciences, Simmons' first task was establishing RISC, a room with terminals for online access to computers in other organizations. In RISC, NLM staff became familiar with various files and computer techniques of possible use to NLM. They used this facility, for example, to experiment online with SDC's ORBIT and a neurology database, described later.

Joint Ventures between NLM and SDC

NLM's Trial Use of COLEX and SUNY BCN

Davis' group established RISC to coordinate NLM's access since January 1968 to COLEX and other external online systems. COLEX contained only a tiny amount of information relevant to medicine, but the link gave NLM staff a chance to become familiar with online developments; it was a window for observing an operating online service. The NLM portion of the COSATI report for 1967 activities commented on the RISC project (*Progress* 1967, 49–50):

This center will house on-line communications terminals to provide access to remote computer centers . . . permitting access to remote data-banks; on-line programming using the advanced programming languages available at computer centers; and experimentation in several application areas by NLM personnel. Computer systems currently contemplated for access from the RISC include . . . COLEX, the SDC computer facility at Santa Monica . . . (CIDS) . . . Project MAC at M.I.T.

McCarn's primary objective with RISC was to convince NLM staff that online searching was viable. The first opportunity to accomplish this was with the COLEX system. As mentioned earlier, NLM staff had been able to use COLEX in trial mode starting in January 1968. In late 1968, NLM also was able to access the online medical literature retrieval system that had been operating since October 1968 at SUNY-Syracuse (see chapter 8 for SUNY BCN development). McCarn considered installing the SUNY system on NLM's computer but decided that it was too expensive because of special terminals that SUNY used.

McCarn (1970b) did, however, analyze detailed usage data from SUNY, including the size of SUNY online files compared to batch runs on MEDLARS, number of doctors in New York state compared to other states, and number of outside users of the SUNY system. His calculations suggested that availability of an online system in a library would result in twice the use of citation information as would access to MEDLARS. At this time, NLM was struggling with its decentralized batch system, and SUNY's successful launch of an operational online service with MEDLARS data in October 1968 could have been a spur to NLM's online development. For NLM, engaged in an intense public relations campaign to establish a reputation for itself as a major national and international library and leader in the field, being upstaged by the SUNY group with its relatively modest resources no doubt caused bruised egos and reassessment of their own efforts. However, none of the current or former NLM staff members contacted on this point could remember anybody at NLM worrying about competition from SUNY, or SUNY's impact on NLM's image. However, the contrast between the NLM batch and SUNY online search service remained conspicuous for the next eighteen months (until the start of AIM-TWX) by articles and comments on the relative performance of the two search services (Darling 1970).

Online Neurology Database Experiment

Besides COLEX, NLM also observed SDC's online progress during an experiment with ORBIT conducted between April and October 1968 at the SDC office in Falls Church. NLM contracted to use ORBIT by means of remote access to the Q-32 in Santa Monica. NLM purchased only enough disk tracks of storage to store about 10,000 document references plus the ORBIT programs. Since file size was constrained by the amount of storage allotted on the SDC time-shared system, NLM could use only a small subset of the MEDLARS file. NLM selected only references to journals and monographs in the area of neurology (primarily Parkinson's disease). The choice of database was related to NLM's cooperative work with NINDB in support of the Neurological Information Network (Bering 1967). NLM extracted the references from their Honeywell system and provided them to SDC. SDC then converted the records into the format required for their system and built the online indexes.

The main participants from the SDC-Falls Church office were Scroggins, J. K. Mizoue and R. D. Glass (Scroggins 1968). Although the SDC time-sharing system at that time could handle up to eighteen remote users simultaneously, the neurology literature experiment seems to have been used primarily for demonstrations. In the letter to Ralph Simmons at NLM that accompanied Scroggins's 1968 final report, he wrote modestly, "It was demonstrated at the recent [October 1968] ASIS Conference in Columbus, Ohio with a small degree of success." No evaluations of the experiment were published.

In 1969, SDC staff in Santa Monica switched the neurology database experiment from the Q-32 to the 360/67. They did the switch to increase the flexibility and useful life of the system (Katter 1970). After the switch, they modified the program for use in the experimental program at the Lister Hill Center. Katter identified this modified program as ELHILL, described later.

After the neurology database experiment, SDC still used the term "NLM ORBIT." In a June 1969 SDC publication that reflected work under contract to NLM regarding considerations for BCN, Katter and Blankenship discussed plans for empirical studies "beyond current NLM ORBIT," and their plans to incorporate resulting improvements in "NLM experimental ORBIT" as quickly as possible without further empirical investigation. They talked of the "NLM experimental ORBIT" program being easier to modify quickly for use as an experimental developmental tool.

BCN

During the mid-1960s, NLM started planning for a national BCN. Cummings (1966) reported that NLM was in the process of developing their own plan for a national library system for the health sciences. The signing of the Medical Library Assistance Act gave this effort major impetus. On behalf of the Office of Science and Technology of the Executive Office of the President, NSF awarded a contract to Herner and Co. in Washington, D.C., to recommend a design for the U.S. Medical Library and Information System. Saul Herner, Mary Herner, Melvin Weinstock, Roger Sisson, Linsey Dorney, Harold Bloomquist, Lois Lunin, Edward Leyman, John Martinson, and Richard Schneider conducted the study (Herner et al. 1966; Weinstock et al. 1966). The Herner team reviewed the NLM network plan and a SUNY plan, and compared them both against their proposed plan. The Herner team used outside experts who were active in systems development, and who are mentioned elsewhere in this book, including Pizer (SUNY BCN), Furth (IBM), and Kilgour (Yale University and OCLC).

In 1967, NLM staff concentrated on further planning for national networks, to be based on a projected Center for Biomedical Communications (CBC) (*Progress of the United States Government* 1968, 48–50). Cummings (1967b) articulated NLM's concept of a Biomedical Library Network, including the proposed CBC. The plan was complete in June 1968, and it outlined a logical, orderly production of a biomedical network during the next five years.

Davis remarked in October 1968 at the SUNY BCN dedication exercise, published in 1969 (113):

Actions on the part of the staff of NLM and others in the medical library profession over the past few years, supported by specific legislation, have resulted in the establishment of the nucleus of a national biomedical library network. Under the Medical Library Assistance Act of 1965, regional and medical libraries have been established through Federal funding, and NLM has contracted with a series of institutions to provide specialized MEDLARS services for users located in their respective areas. In addition, various separate institutions have made major accomplishments directed toward improved biomedical communications—with the work here at SUNY being particularly outstanding.

During the same month, Simmons (1969) used the expression "the Biomedical Communications Network" in the title of a conference paper. He noted that in August 1968, Congress had passed a joint resolution authorizing the establishment of a National Center for Biomedical Communications, had designated it the Lister Hill National Center for Biomedical Communications, and had established it as a part of NLM.

NLM now had its network, and one of its four major objectives was the Biomedical Communications Network's (BCN) design, development, implementation, and management. The name itself was confusing for observers of the information scene; SUNY had already established a BCN in

1965 and it operated as an online service in October 1968 as SUNY BCN. Pizer and others later incorporated another BCN as a nonprofit organization in 1976 to succeed the SUNY BCN system and to serve as a marketing agent for the BRS search services (chapter 9) (Simmons 1969).

NLM's BCN was to be managed by a staff of sixty-four and a budget of $16 million by FY 1974. Congress, however, never appropriated funds for it, although funds were available for contractors to support the network. NLM executed such a contract with SDC-Santa Monica in 1969 to support studies aimed at providing information and assistance to NLM in planning the BCN (*Progress* 1970, 56–57). Under the direction of Carlos Cuadra the SDC planning studies included (1) Katter and Blankenship's review (1969a, 1969b) of the online interface; (2) Katter's 1970 review of user experiences with online services and of items to be considered in the "experiment for introducing the on-line remote access retrieval of bibliographic citations of biomedical literature"; and (3) Seiden's 1970 feature analysis and comparison of available online systems. These preliminary studies led to specific activities such as the neurological online database experiment described earlier, and other actions described later, including the AIM-TWX experiment and the MEDLINE system. At this time, NLM was clearly working toward developing a major online information network. McCarn and Leiter (1973, 321) described NLM's first steps in online systems:

In the fall of 1967, the NLM began to experiment with on-line bibliographic search services. It first installed and evaluated the on-line service (ORBIT) for the foreign literature [the FTD COLEX project] ... ORBIT was then used to experiment with a data base in neurology. These experiments helped in specifying the capabilities necessary for an on-line service for the biomedical literature. To verify these specifications, the NLM also contracted, in 1969, for a review of extant on-line bibliographic retrieval systems. As a result of this evolutionary and analytic approach, the NLM began in early 1970 to develop an on-line search system.

That system was AIM-TWX, discussed next.

Putting It All Together—Database, Telecommunications, Online System: AIM-TWX

The planning exercise at this stage revealed at least three requirements for an online medical information system, "one of which was a good retrieval system, the second of which was a useful database, and the third was communications that were cheap and alive" (McCarn 1987). The challenge of filling all three essential requirements led to NLM's next stage of development: experimentation with a large-scale operational system designed specifically for retrieval of medical literature. The requirement for "communications that were cheap and alive" was easily and quickly filled by utilizing AT&T's existing TeletypeWriter Exchange Network (TWX). TWX interconnected extremely slow teletypewriters (10 cps) across the United States through its own system. The medical library community had been using the TWX network heavily for interlibrary loan (McCarn 1971). TWX terminals had been installed in more than 500 libraries and could be used for online searching without the purchase of additional terminal equipment. AT&T's TWX network paralleled the Teletype network of Western Union. They were different, however, in that the analog to digital processes were different. "It was a very big deal to get the authorization and hardware to get both types of terminals to talk to the SDC computer" (McCarn 1995).

The "useful database" was a five-year file of Abridged Index Medicus (AIM), which contained about 100,000 citations from the hundred most frequently used English-language journals in clinical medicine, lifted from the MEDLARS file of citations from 2,300 journals. NLM had considered a "junior" edition of *Index Medicus* as early as 1963, and had compiled a sample issue in 1965 for review and comment. Noting that an abridged edition, covering a limited number of most heavily used English-language journals, had been contemplated, Rogers expressed hope that MLA's committee would study the proposal and present its specification for a junior version of *Index Medicus* (Adams

1964). NLM began producing AIM in January 1970, drawing a subset of about 13 percent of *Index Medicus* records. Its immediate acceptance by the biomedical community suggested that a database covering the literature in those journals would be useful, so the AIM file was updated monthly. By spring 1972, when NLM discontinued the AIM-TWX service, it had grown to about 180,000 records and covered 122 journals. The combination of database and communications system gave the project its name: AIM-TWX.

A third element, however, was still needed. The "good retrieval service" was ORBIT, which SDC agreed to modify to meet the special requirements of MEDLARS searching. NLM's access to and familiarity with SDC's online COLEX system since January 1968, and their experience with the neurology database, were probably instrumental in their decision to use SDC software for AIM-TWX. According to Katter and Pearson (1975, 88), NLM's commitment to SDC came in 1969: "NLM investigated several on-line data processing packages and, in 1969, settled on System Development Corporation's ORBIT as the basis for the pilot AIM-TWX on-line searching service." Black (1987), an SDC participant in the project, believed the AIM-TWX project started because NLM staff asked SDC to implement such a system for them, at a time when SDC's management was pressing the staff to "look for things that generate money." In fall 1969, NLM contracted with SDC to provide the experimental service to enable NLM to test its feasibility, use, and acceptance. SDC-Santa Monica staff, under Cuadra's direction, developed this version of the ORBIT software under contract to NLM.

The changes that NLM asked SDC to make to ORBIT consisted of three system extensions related to the MEDLARS file: (1) MESHNO, to get the *MeSH* Classification Number of a specified *MeSH* subject term; (2) EXPLODE, to cause a generic hierarchical expansion of a specified *MeSH* Classification Number; and (3) TREE, to display terms related hierarchically, which allowed searches to be expanded or limited (Cuadra 1990; Cobbs 1971). For example, TREE could generate a display of all the subject terms that are under the "leukemia" subject hierarchy in the *Tree Structures* section of *MeSH*. From the online display, a searcher could incorporate the hierarchy in a search strategy, a feature used previously only on a relatively small scale in BOLD, the Stanford Research System, MEDUSA, and early DIALOG. Katter (1970, 21) summarized the new features in a planning paper for the design of the experiments to introduce online access to the biomedical literature:

Some of these desirable features were already partially available in the Q-32 ORBIT retrieval system being used as an experimental vehicle for the NLM studies. In order to increase the flexibility and useful life of the system, the Parkinson's disease data base was first switched from Q-32 ORBIT to 360/67 ORBIT, and then the 360 ORBIT program was modified into a special version for use in the experimental program being conducted by the Lister Hill Center. This specially modified ORBIT program is called ELHILL.

The name ELHILL came from the Lister Hill Center, which had been an eponymous tribute to Senator Lister Hill. ELHILL is simply a phonetic version of "L. HILL" as initially written by the SDC programmers. They wrote ELHILL in 1970 to run on smaller IBM computers so that it could be installed at NLM and foreign medical centers (*Progress* 1971, 13).

SDC loaded the AIM database and ELHILL software on their IBM 360/67 in Santa Monica. NLM decided not to use the IBM 360/50 already at NLM because of SDC's estimation that it would cost more than $100,000 to make their software operable on NLM's equipment, as well as the fact that providing online service during normal working hours would seriously disrupt MEDLARS II development and other programs running on the NLM computer (McCarn 1970b). Cuadra (1975, 48) observed, "The reason that AIM-TWX and MEDLINE are part of SDC's history is that we developed the systems for NLM and for two-and-one-half years operated them on our computers." In October 1971, while SDC was running the AIM-TWX service on its Santa Monica computer, it was also installing an expanded version of the system (a version of ORBIT II) on the IBM 360/50 at NLM that was eventually called the MEDLINE service (Katter 1973). NLM and SDC had both expected that after MEDLINE became operational both systems would continue to be available nationwide. At a 1971 conference, McCarn (1973) stated, "The (SDC) computer now housing the AIM-TWX system will also be tied into the overall network; users will then be able to select either AIM-TWX or MEDLINE after dialing into the network" (99).

Commands in ELHILL, as in ORBIT II, could be entered in any order, with a minimum of punctuation. The program offered explanatory messages, online tutorials, an index display capability, and an online thesaurus. Author searching was possible with AIM-TWX, but because of storage space limitations, only the first few authors of a publication were put in the online index. This practice continued with the initial versions of ELHILL.

Left-truncation searching (looking for terms that *end* in a specified character string, as described earlier with the TIP system) is a feature particularly helpful in searching chemical or pharmaceutical information. ELHILL had this feature, as well as the more common right-truncation feature. Left truncation was so demanding of computer resources, however, that it was unpublicized and available only to pre-approved users with certain classes of passwords (Black 1987). It was not popular, and was done only on a CA backfile that did not require any update processing (Black 1996).

An online ordering capability (the command was called ORDER) was included in the ORBIT II software from the beginning, at NLM's request. NLM had been doing a heavy business in photocopying and interlibrary loan, and wanted to facilitate this process for all participants, particularly for NLM and the Regional Medical Libraries. Because NLM operations staff was not ready to provide such a service, however, it was not used when it was implemented. It was not until NLM provided DOCLINE and Loansome Doc in 1991 that NLM provided the service foreseen by this 1970 software. Online ordering is discussed further in chapter 9.

Printing could be accomplished online, or offline on the high speed printer, with air mail delivery of the printout. A command called PRINT HITS printed the output references in rank order by the number of terms in the record that were in the search request. It ranked highest the documents that had the most number of ORed terms. SDC first used this feature in TEXTIR in 1964. This is essentially the same as the ranking features of some of today's Web search engines. While a potentially useful feature for ELHILL, according to Woodsmall (1991) searchers did not make much use of this capability. It was later removed from the system in order to free up four bits from the search code to permit their use in a date ranging feature.

An online questionnaire captured searcher reactions, and searchers also could send free-text comments to the system operators and receive online bulletins (Katter and McCarn 1971).

PROG:
WILL YOU PLEASE ANSWER A FEW
QUESTIONS? YES, NO, OR SHORT.
USER: yes
PROG:
FOR EACH QUESTION, INSERT A
NUMBER AND A CARRIAGE RETURN. WHO
IS OPERATING THE TERMINAL? :
1.PHYSICIAN, 2.NURSE, 3.MEDICAL
STUDENT, 4.OTHER STUDENT, 5.OTHER
HEALTH PROFESSIONAL, 6.INFORMATION
SPECIALIST, 7.OTHER.
USER: 5
PROG:
IF THE OPERATOR IS HELPING OR
REPRESENTING SOMEONE ELSE, WHO IS
THIS OTHER PERSON? USE CATEGORIES
ABOVE, OR 0 FOR YOURSELF.
USER: 0
PROG:
INSERT APPROXIMATE NUMBER OF
TIMES OPERATOR HAS PREVIOUSLY RUN
ELHILL.
USER: 1
PROG:

```
WHAT WAS MAIN PURPOSE IN USING
ELHILL THIS TIME? :
1.DEMONSTRATION OR TRAINING,
2.EXPERIMENTATION AND EXPLORATION
OF SYSTEM CAPABILITIES, 3.TO
OBTAIN NEEDED BIBLIOGRAPHIC
CITATIONS, 4.OTHER.
USER: 3
PROG:
WHAT MAINLY PROMPTED NEED FOR THE
BIBLIOGRAPHIC CITATIONS? :
1.PATIENT CARE PROBLEM.
2.EDUCATION, 3.RESEARCH, 4.OTHER,
5.DON'T KNOW.
USER: 1,3
PROG:
WERE THE ON-LINE SEARCH RESULTS
OF VALUE? : 1.MAJOR VALUE,
2.CONSIDERABLE VALUE, 3.MINOR
VALUE, 4.NO VALUE, 5.DON'T KNOW.
USER: 1
PROG: **GOOD-BYE FROM ELHILL!
PGM STOPPED
/logout
LOGGED OUT 10:13 12/04/70
TERMINAL TIME 01.77 HOURS
CPU TIME 001 MINUTES 07.1
SECONDS.
```

[Online questionnaire used in AIM-TWX, reproduced in Lancaster and Fayen 1973 159].

The AIM-TWX pilot online searching service officially became operational during its presentation at the MLA conference on May 31, 1970, after a month of pilot operation. There were four non-NLM users on June 1, and thirteen official non-NLM users during June (Woodsmall 1991). In McCarn's (1987) estimation, the database (a 5-year file of 200,000 AIM citations) was big enough to be "useful," and the ORBIT II program was of a sound design and functioned well. The communications system, however, "was a disaster: the TWXs were clumsy and they were fairly busy with interlibrary loan anyway, and they were administratively in the wrong part of the library." When AIM-TWX started operation it was also possible to access the system via "portable" terminals. Black (1995) recalled: "It was more like a 67-pound terminal! It even came with wheels on it. I went out to UC-Riverside to give a demonstration. They gave us a room on the second floor of a motel that had no elevators, and I had to go up the steps one step at a time. We thought Nirvana had been reached when TI came out with their first portable terminal (about 45 pounds), and the next one after that was about 35 pounds."

In spite of the limitations of the TWX terminals, the experiment started off strong. The ninety users were a self-selected group of librarians, students, and practitioners, including physicians in Indiana through the TWX terminal at the South Bend Public Library, who had indicated that they had access to TWX terminals and desired to use the system. NLM limited the size and composition of the group so that the system would not become overloaded and potential users would not be rejected because of busy signals, and a variety of user groups could participate in the trial (McCarn 1971). NLM also allowed some pharmaceutical companies to access AIM-TWX. Cuadra (1997) observed, "Since NLM couldn't take money directly from commercial organizations for such access, the PMA [Pharmaceutical Manufacturers Association] member companies paid SDC for their access to this service (there was no separate PMA tape to load), and SDC gave a credit to NLM on their service invoices from SDC."

In most online systems, a larger number of users (password holders) are authorized than the number of persons who can use the system simultaneously. The AIM-TWX system was configured to limit the number of simultaneous users to less than twenty (Coles 1973). Cuadra (1971a) reported that there were thirty-three different authorized institutional users, and that they occasionally had as many as sixteen or seventeen of them using the system simultaneously. The service was offered from 8:00 a.m. to 12:00 p.m. Pacific Time, Monday through Friday. The Lister Hill Center funded the computer costs; the users paid for the terminals and the TWX toll calls, which cost from twenty to seventy cents per minute. The average search took about fifteen to twenty minutes, using about thirty to forty seconds of computer time.

The pioneer users were not trained; they received only instructions from the terminal about how to call in to the system. They were then expected to plunge in. Even though NLM had contracted with SDC for training, McCarn (1970b, 307–308) at this point did not deem it necessary: "The SDC system is a system which can be used without training." McCarn (1987) contrasted the ease of use of ORBIT then with the obstacles to accessing DIALOG:

ORBIT was so user friendly. It was really simple to use that system; it was almost self-explanatory. You got an impression on how to use ORBIT by looking at it. DIALOG you did not. They had those paste-up boards and they assumed you always had to have leased lines and you used those funny top row keys, like asterisk and exclamation point. ORBIT was designed to run at 300 baud over public communication lines and still be intelligible and relatively efficient at low communication speeds.

McCarn recalled being surprised to learn that some of the biggest institutional users were hospitals. Hospitals had exerted great pressure on NLM to start the printed *Abridged Index Medicus* because the clinicians wanted only a few good references, not exhaustive recall. The online AIM let the clinicians, or their designates, search directly and quickly to find a few references. At an October 1971 conference, Katter (1973) observed: "The medical librarians who resisted the use of AIM-TWX at first, almost to a person, like very much to use it now .... This has also meant additional staff in several places, for example, in orthopedic hospitals, which simply started being flooded with various kinds of requests for services" (183).

One of the subscribers to the service was the Medical Library at the University of Virginia, whose director, Wilhelm Moll, conducted an evaluation of the use of AIM-TWX during a four-week period late in 1970. He characterized the experiment as "one of the most stimulating and exciting periods in the history of this library" (Moll 1971, 458). In preparation for the trial, Moll's library printed and sent announcements to all Virginia hospitals and to the medical staff of the Medical Center. A press release resulted in feature stories in several media. As a result, a rash of search requests came in, which kept the library staff working overtime. The manuals NLM sent were difficult for University of Virginia staff to understand, but they considered them so vital that "every one of the operators was under strict orders not to remove the booklets from a shelf near the Teletype machine" (459).

For the actual searching, the four staff members operated in two teams with two searchers working together. One person keyed in strategies and displayed results on the Teletype. The other team member recorded the findings in a log, kept the search requests and results in order, and, most important, used *MeSH* to reformulate search statements as needed, which seemed to be necessary even when the initial search formulation had been carefully prepared in advance. The service was not without a few glitches (Moll 1971, 461):

Although the library had been promised a four-hour period daily ... the periods of actual use were shorter due to many "cut-offs" which separated the user from the system either temporarily or permanently for that day. The causes cannot be explained entirely. They may have been due to machine, line, or computer malfunctioning ... it should be stressed that interruptions were quite frustrating, especially when a physician had taken time off from patient care or other duties to be present in the library while the search was being conducted. Hopefully, some of these problems will be ironed out in the not too distant future to guarantee an uninterrupted service.

Overall, however, the Virginia Medical Library staff were thrilled with online searching; they considered over 80 percent of the searches successful, and the tremendous response from the medical practitioners in Virginia indicated a great demand for an online service. Moll (1972) conducted another evaluation from August 1971 to January 1972, with similar results.

From November 1970 through February 1971, Lancaster conducted a formal evaluation of AIM-

TWX. Cummings recalled (1997) that this may have been the first time that a government agency paid an outsider to evaluate any government information system. He noted that Mortimer Taube, one of the foremost library and information system consultants of the day strongly advised Cummings against doing the study, saying, "It would be devastating." Lancaster was born in England, attended the Newcastle upon Tyne School of Librarianship, and moved to the United States in 1959. Lancaster's credentials to conduct the study included prior experience with the ASLIB Cranfield Project, his prior employment (1964–1965) at Herner and Company, his prior employment (1965–1968) at NLM as Information Systems Specialist, his comprehensive evaluation of the MEDLARS batch search system in 1966, his authorship of a book on IR, and his position as director of the Program in Biomedical Librarianship at the University of Illinois Graduate School of Library Science. The respect his colleagues accorded Lancaster is evident in his winning the ASIS Best Information Science Book Award in 1974 and 1978, the ASIS Outstanding Information Science Teacher Award in 1980, and the ASIS Award of Merit in 1988.

Lancaster's evaluation aimed to determine how effectively biomedical practitioners, with a minimum of introduction to the system, could conduct their own online searches. The searching was done at four MEDLARS centers that had online search capabilities. Lancaster identified aspects that needed improvement. For example, he felt that the principal limitation of ELHILL was that it required "virtual perfection" in the entry of search terms and commands; making mistakes was easy, and the system made little attempt to compensate for human error. Scanning searchers' printouts, Lancaster found examples of missing or superfluous punctuation marks, spelling errors, and transposition of words in *MeSH* thesaurus terms, all of which caused the system to reject search terms. "The inexperienced user has enough to tackle in grasping the search methods and commands as well as familiarizing himself with the vocabulary. He should not be bothered with the need for perfection in spelling and punctuation" (1972, 13). Lancaster criticized the lack of any entry vocabulary; AIM-TWX accepted only *MeSH* headings and subheadings. Even the *MeSH see* references were omitted from the online retrieval system, and Lancaster felt that *MeSH* did not have nearly enough cross-references anyway.

Lancaster had a vision for the system's future. He wanted to eliminate use of Boolean algebra in searching, which retrieves only those references that match a search strategy exactly and rejects all others. Lancaster felt that dependence on Boolean logic was a consequence of the way the early computer-based systems had developed: "They were viewed as more mechanized versions of semimanual systems such as those employing edge-notched cards or the optical coincidence principle" (1972, 17). He envisioned a system that could retrieve a partial match and use algorithms to rank document references according to the degree of match with the search statement. Completely automatic translation of searchers' natural-language terms to the controlled vocabulary terms of the retrieval system was also on Lancaster's wish list. Apparently he was unaware of General Purpose ORBIT or LEADER.

In spite of these complaints and suggestions, Lancaster was positive about the overall performance of AIM-TWX (1972, 11): "AIM-TWX appears to meet a definite need. The great majority of the searches conducted . . . could not have been conducted in *Index Medicus*. They involve conceptual relationships that would be virtually impossible to handle without some facility for term coordination. Moreover, in many cases the searches involved terms that would not necessarily be *print* terms." Lancaster was pleased with the level of satisfaction expressed by the subjects who participated in his study, the chief objective of which was to investigate how effectively biomedical practitioners could conduct searches on their own, with a minimum of training. He concluded (11):

On the whole I believe the results to be surprisingly good. Although a few users went badly astray, the majority were able to conduct productive searches. The precision achieved in most cases was high and the cost in time appears to be well within tolerable limits. It is not to be expected that the requestor himself will perform as well as would a trained analyst. He probably would not use *Index Medicus* as effectively either. He cannot master the complete vocabulary, indexing policies and the niceties of search strategy in a matter of minutes. Nevertheless, acceptable results were obtained in most cases by a simple and straightforward approach. It is noteworthy that many of these users were seeking only a few relevant references. They did not require high recall.

At the time that AIM-TWX started officially, the SUNY system (chapter 8) already was providing online service to its network of users (including NLM), using a file of about three years of MEDLARS citations and over 60,000 monograph cataloging records. AIM-TWX had a more limited database but provided capabilities—for example, direct searching by author, publication date, journal title, or language—not available in the SUNY system then, except as a further qualification on a record already retrieved from a keyword search. Both systems allowed term truncation, but AIM-TWX did not provide any subject search capability (i.e., title words) beyond controlled vocabulary searching; some users referred to it as a "thesaurus-bound" system. AIM-TWX provided more useful and immediate feedback, for example, posting counts for each line of a search formulation as it was executed. SUNY supplied such data only after the entire search formulation was executed. Furthermore, AIM-TWX output included descriptors with each record, but SUNY did not. AIM-TWX seemed especially well suited for getting five to ten references into clinicians' hands rapidly (rather than an exhaustive search). Management staff of NLM and SUNY BCN both must have perceived the other system as competition to their own.

In a reflection on early library automation, Pizer (1984, 344) commented on his SUNY experience:

As NLM began its AIM-TWX experiment with end-users, it too found similar answers to many of the questions on which SUNY had provided data. Users had a very low tolerance for a system which required them to proceed through a lengthy series of questions and answers in order to formulate their search. They were impatient with response times which, although rapid in comparison with manual searching, seemed endless when sitting waiting for a keyboard response. Users preferred to have a trained intermediary perform their searches, especially as few users searched the system with enough frequency to become highly proficient, and most were not able to keep up with system changes which altered searching formulations.

Professional searchers[6] of that period recognized the important differences between the SUNY and AIM-TWX systems. As one pioneer searcher, Ann Van Camp (1971, 2) declared: "AIM-TWX is best suited to only certain categories of our user population. First and foremost are reference questions from practicing physicians in Indiana that are concerned with patient care. Those questions that are not one-term searches are usually well suited to the AIM-TWX system . . . AIM-TWX should be the on-line system of choice for medical students."

The principal objectives of the AIM-TWX experiment were to evaluate the potential benefits of such a service to users, and to provide empirically-based answers to a range of questions concerning technical aspects. The response of the medical community to the service was encouraging; AIM-TWX demonstrated the viability of a network and revealed the demand for an expanded online system. The planners at NLM projected that it would be far less expensive, however, if NLM ran the new service rather than contracting it out to SDC. Planning and preparation for such a service at NLM began early in 1971. NLM staff seemed to be operating under the assumption that SDC would continue AIM-TWX in parallel with NLM's MEDLINE. As mentioned earlier, McCarn (1973, 99) stated in 1971, "The [SDC] computer now housing the AIM-TWX system will also be tied into the overall network; users will be able to select either AIM-TWX or MEDLINE after dialing into the network."

Black (1987) recalled that, after the initial AIM-TWX service started, "it turned out to be wildly successful, and NLM's budget was strained. And the next year there were a lot more people clamoring to have access. Everybody who used it loved it. They said, 'We want more, give us the whole MEDLARS database.'" McCarn's perspective (1987) was similar: "In three months we had 90 users and it was costing NLM an arm and a leg out there at SDC. It quickly became abundantly clear that no matter what the management at NLM thought, or what the designers of MEDLARS II thought, there was a really big need for interactive searching, at least in the medical community."

NLM discontinued AIM-TWX service in April 1972. It had served more than eighty institutional users, and its successful use and acclaim had convinced NLM management to proceed with plans for a fully operational, nonexperimental online search service (*Progress* 1972, 33). Along with the visible success of AIM-TWX was evidence of the continuing conflict of the federal versus private sector over competition for providing goods and services. Private-sector publishers and service providers had already voiced their concerns about the difficulty of competing against free or subsidized federal information services. In particular, after a Nixon political appointee toured NLM and saw a copy of a recently printed brochure describing the new AIM-TWX, the administration quickly contacted NLM and ordered it to destroy the brochures immediately to prevent NLM from competing with the private sector. NLM destroyed all but a few copies (Katter 1998).

Cuadra (1976) acknowledged the importance and contribution of AIM-TWX when he identified it as the main stimulant to online retrieval services in the United States. Nonetheless, he maintained that the impetus to the *growth* of United States online services came mainly from commercial organizations such as SDC and Lockheed.

Online retrieval services had come quite far by this point. As McCarn (1974) asserted, "In 1971 there were only two major on-line services . . . SUNY . . . and AIM-TWX . . . . Both covered the medical literature as indexed by NLM, and in total, there were 85 institutional users" (147). The next great step forward of expansion MEDLARS II could not be taken until major changes were made.

MEDLARS II Implementation

Early MEDLARS II development was concurrent with NLM's online experiments. In summer 1966, NLM contracted with Auerbach Corporation to draw up specifications for a new system. An upgrade of the existing MEDLARS, it would accommodate new features, including online searching and retrieval of bibliographic records. In June 1967, NLM published a Request for Qualifications Statement notice in *Commerce Business Daily*, asking for statements from firms interested in bidding on a project to design an updated MEDLARS. In August 1967, after reviewing the submitted qualification statements (including one from Lockheed), NLM issued an RFP for MEDLARS II development. After receiving proposals from seven prospective contractors in November 1967, NLM awarded a contract for over $2 million to Computer Sciences Corporation (CSC) in June 1968 (Leiter and Gull 1968; Miles 1982). NLM projected the first implementation phase for fall 1969. Unfortunately, however, the CSC project did not go smoothly (see next section).

Meanwhile, when McCarn arrived at NLM in October 1968, he was astounded to see that the specifications included a capability for online input but scarcely mentioned online searching. The CSC contract had been signed already, so it was too late for McCarn to stop the project. One modification to the RFP gave a sense of an online capability to test search strategies, but it specified no actual online production search capability.

The CSC Fiasco

All through the AIM-TWX project, planning proceeded for a major upgrade of MEDLARS, to be called MEDLARS II. NLM had awarded a contract to CSC, a major software development firm based in Los Angeles, for the technical development. An announcement of the project reported that CSC was developing a package of interrelated application programs called COSMIS (COmputer Systems for Medical Information Services), and that a batch-mode system was expected to be operational by mid-1969, with an online capability available to users by 1970 ("MEDLARS II" 1968). NLM installed an IBM 360/50 in 1970 to be used in the development and testing of MEDLARS II.

Details of the CSC design and progress on the contract are not documented in the literature. Without naming individuals or organizations, but with the conviction of personal experience, McCarn (1970a) described the problems that arise within an organization when computer system contractors and program managers fail to communicate well with each other. What seems evident now is that during the course of the contract, NLM and CSC both gradually realized that their expectations for the new system differed. The original requirements of the contract specified a system that could be maintained efficiently, that is, an effective *database management* system for which additions, changes, and deletions to the file could be processed quickly and economically. McCarn worked hard to convince other NLM staff, and the AIM-TWX experiment reinforced his view, of the great value of online retrieval. After the eager acceptance and quick success of AIM-TWX, NLM changed its requirements to include an effective and high performance *retrieval* system. These two goals, unfortunately, were incompatible for large files at the time. A database management system efficient for file maintenance was likely to be slow in searching and retrieving records; one that was consistently fast for retrieval normally required that maintenance be done periodically in batches to avoid interruption of online service. McCarn (1987) recalled:

What CSC was building, however, was a database management system where you do everything in linked lists and you can update the lists but you just cannot find anything fast. Everybody at NLM began to say, "We always wanted online. Didn't you understand that?" They started trying to get CSC to make changes and make it possible to do online searching and pretty soon it was just all turned into a terrible mess. CSC was caught in a changing set of requirements that made meeting the government's expectations impossible.

One possible solution to resolving this "terrible mess" was to cancel the contract.

NLM Regents Alfred Zipf of the Bank of America and Bruno Augenstein of Rand Corp. asked their own organizations' computer staffs to check on CSC's work, and the reports they received were critical. Zipf approached SDC in March 1971 for a technical review of NLM's project. Donald Cohen of Rand headed the review panel. The regents were concerned that CSC had been on the project for several years, had spent millions of dollars, and had not yet written code for retrieval; furthermore, the resulting product might not be satisfactory to NLM (Black 1995, Miles 1982). The reviewers concluded that the routine MEDLARS II production alone would take more hours per day of computer processing (and seven days per week) than would be available from the planned computer equipment, and thus the proposed system was infeasible (Black, Cady, and Katter 1971). They recommended terminating the project. NLM then asked SDC to do a computer simulation, or model, to predict how well the CSC programs (as then developed and described) would run. Cuadra (1990) recalled: "The end result was SDC's conclusion to NLM, that by the time it was done, it would not run. It would be much too big for the machine they had. It would be much too slow. They concluded that after having spent at least a million, maybe two million dollars, they needed to pull the plug." Ralph Simmons, who had been overseeing the retrieval system development, worked out a new contract that NLM signed with CSC in June 1969. CSC still fell behind schedule, and NLM became increasingly pessimistic about the company's abilities to meet the deadline. Thus, in April 1971, NLM cancelled the CSC contract for MEDLARS II and awarded a contract to SDC instead. A federal statement on this matter (*MEDLARS and health* 1982, 12) said tersely, "The original contractor could not fulfill its obligations, and a contract was negotiated with SDC." CSC apparently was not financially disadvantaged; they had reportedly been working with a cost-plus-fixed fee contract, so they walked away from the project with no significant financial loss and later became a major software company.

Cuadra (1990) remembered that the CSC muddle was never openly discussed at that time within the profession; no one involved could see any advantage in doing so: "Obviously, NLM did not want to say anything about it because they might look foolish for having selected the contractor or for not canceling it a week earlier or a month earlier or a year earlier. CSC certainly did not want to get a bad rap. And SDC had no reason to want to engage in libelous or semi-libelous publicity. So everyone was very quiet. It kind of went away."

The lesson of the bungled contract, nevertheless, was not forgotten by either party. NLM awarded a sole-source contract to SDC but insisted that it be a fixed-price deal, and for an amount that was reportedly less than the amount already paid to CSC for the unfinished work. SDC made no use of any of the CSC work product and handled the MEDLARS II contract quite differently.

SDC: The Development of MEDLARS II and ELHILL II

In a review of AIM-TWX, McCarn (1971) wrote that NLM had reviewed the extent to which the ELHILL II online search programs that SDC was developing could meet the service objectives of the planned MEDLARS II system; and he concluded that ELHILL II could do the job. Furthermore, operating on NLM's planned IBM 370/155 computer, it could accommodate forty or more simultaneous users. This observation was apparently based on the Black, Cady, and Katter study results reported to NLM in April 1971.

In June 1971, NLM awarded to SDC a major development contract to complete MEDLARS II. The plan was to design the system around the structure and logic of AIM-TWX, adding an improved file generation and maintenance system, and a new set of programs for photocomposition. The scope of some of the earlier objectives was reduced. Bob Katter directed the small SDC team of analysts and programmers working primarily in Santa Monica. The retrieval subsystem was the responsibility of Bob Burket, Ray Baker, and consultant Don Blankenship. (Burket and Blankenship were involved in the first and second incarnations of ORBIT.) Karl Pearson and Don Black performed the library systems analysis for the SDC team. The original software design was the joint product of Burket, Blankenship, and Kenton, who later became an NLM staff member. Burket installed MEDLARS II software at most of the NLM overseas partner facilities.

SDC's being on the other side of the country from the NLM staff in Maryland added extra costs for travel and communications. Nonetheless, Katter and Pearson (1975, 95) viewed the separation as having tangible benefits: "These arrangements provided for full SDC control over its own staff, kept NLM and SDC from interfering with each other, reduced to a minimum the meetings and conferences that might otherwise have wasted manpower, and gave the programmers a considerable degree of control over the computer resources required to meet their needs." On the other hand, Katter was determined not to commit the same error as CSC, in failing to meet NLM's expectations. Accordingly, he took a tape recorder to the requirements meeting at NLM. Cuadra (1990) recalled:

Not a little one like that [the one being used in this interview] but a monster. Katter trotted out the recorder and said, "The past problem was not any one person's fault, or any one organization's fault. The Library did not know enough about computers and programming to make requirements that were ironclad, clear, and perfect. The programmers and designers on the other side did not know enough to know they were being given requirements that were impossible or wrong." Katter decided that it was important for our sanity, and for everyone's protection that the requirements be clear, agreed upon, and that both parties come somewhere toward the middle, and it be captured and documented. So everyone would sign off and say, "Yes, this is truly what I asked for and I really mean it and that is what I want."

Like Hal Borko, Carlos Cuadra, and Roger Summit, Katter was trained as a psychologist (Ph.D. in psychology from the University of Oregon in 1958). He joined SDC in 1958 and worked there until he left in 1976 to join private companies in the Los Angeles area. While at SDC he developed ORBIT II, managed MEDLARS II design and implementation, managed program development for SDC Search Service, and participated in many R&D efforts on the analysis of the information requirements of various professional user groups and on the analysis and design of online terminal interfaces for online activity. He is generally recognized as the technical leader in the development of MEDLINE and ORBIT. In his post-SDC positions, he worked with national intelligence agencies in the design, development, and evaluation of user languages and interfaces for various IR systems.

At NLM the project was under the overall direction of McCarn, who, with his technical staff, devoted much time to preparing functional requirements and planning system implementation and installation. Katter accorded them much of the credit for the success of the enterprise. SDC delegated the responsibility of facilitating close coordination between NLM and SDC in the project's early stages to a consultant from Rand, Don Cohen, who assured the NLM staff that the design approach SDC was taking was viable and effective. He assisted the NLM staff in defining their system requirements and developing firm control over the project. A symbol of the cooperative endeavor took place in fall 1972 when the NLM and SDC project leaders happened to be in Europe at the same time; they jointly lit a candle to the success of the system in the Cathedral at Reims. A more substantial mark of their successful teamwork was that "the functional requirements, once published, stood throughout the implementation phase virtually without change" (Katter and Pearson 1975, 95).

MEDLARS II was complete in 1974, and NLM accepted it in January 1975. Miles (1982, 389) reported NLM's point of view:

The new system possessed all the capabilities of the original MEDLARS, it was faster, it was cheaper per unit cost of processing, it permitted higher standards for data, and it was more responsive to interactive searching and retrieval. New files with different record formats could be designed and implemented without interfering with other activities. The scope and variety of data bases and publications could be amplified more readily, and components of the system could be installed easily in other libraries.

MEDLARS II differed also from the original MEDLARS in other important ways, such as fewer errors in the bibliographic records, a greater potential for creating new information products, and provision of a baseline test bed for investigation and experimentation. The major enhancement of MEDLARS II over MEDLARS I was the shift to online interactive searching and retrieval, a vast improvement over the batch-mode capability of the original MEDLARS.

MEDLINE

Although the medical community responded enthusiastically to AIM-TWX and it continued in operation until spring 1972, planning for its successor had begun by 1971. McCarn and Leiter (1973, 321) affirmed, "Experience with AIM-TWX demonstrated the viability of a network and identified the need for an expanded on-line system from the NLM." NLM management elected to have SDC build MEDLARS II because they felt that they had already bought the ELHILL software and wanted to build on the retrieval system (McCarn 1995). The proprietary rights to ELHILL, however, still represent a contentious issue. Former SDC management staff still argue that NLM never bought ELHILL. Cuadra (1997) commented:

To the best of my knowledge, NLM never "bought" ELHILL. What they did was pay, as part of the $1.2M MEDLARS II contract, for the addition of exactly three commands to SDC's commercial ORBIT system. NLM claimed that it either owned all of ELHILL or had a right to have/hold and use a copy of it in any way it saw fit. Since SDC had developed ORBIT and did not think it had given NLM any rights to it, it filed suit. A lower court decided for SDC, a Court of Appeals reversed that decision, and the U.S. Supreme Court, through a 4 to 4 tie, with one Justice recusing himself, failed to reverse the Court of Appeals. I remember being told by folks in the legal department of SDC that the words in our "agreement" with NLM that allowed NLM to claim rights to ORBIT/ELHILL were written by my former boss on an envelope. He had a law degree and probably assumed that he had protected SDC's rights in ORBIT. SDC's attorneys must have agreed or they would not have allowed SDC to go to court.

The MEDLARS II project was not fully complete until fall 1974, but SDC developed the online retrieval subsystem relatively quickly by using the proven ORBIT system (in its ELHILL incarnation, which by this time was called ELHILL II to support retrieval on a much larger file). NLM named the expanded system MEDLINE (MEDLARS Online) and brought it up on NLM's computer in Bethesda with a user group of twenty-five institutions and a database of 1,100 journal citations from 1969 to date, at the end of October 1971 (McCarn 1973). By the end of 1971, NLM replaced its IBM 360/50 with a 370/155 to obtain greater processing power. Over 450,000 references were in the database, and the users had grown to ninety-two institutions (*Progress in Scientific and Technical Communications* 1972, 33–34). TYMNET provided data communications for MEDLINE (chapter 9); replacing the slow TWX terminals with higher speed equipment and lines was a big step forward. When MEDLINE became available, patrons chose it over the MEDLARS batch service. As the MEDLINE service grew, the regional centers sent in fewer requests to NLM, and NLM discontinued the MEDLARS demand search service in January 1973. As described in chapter 8, SUNY BCN was a national online network before MEDLINE, but MEDLINE was the first such network accessible via a *local* phone call (because of TYMNET). Addi-

tional NLM files eventually came online, starting with CATLINE in 1973. TOXLINE actually has a separate history of startup and development, which chapter 9 covers.

Among the original users were the NLM regional medical libraries, large medical school libraries; then other schools, nonprofit research institutions, hospitals, clinics, and independent medical libraries, but no private sector institutions such as the medical research laboratories of pharmaceutical companies. The participating institutions did not pay for use of MEDLINE. NLM's story after transitioning to MEDLINE continues in chapter 9.

U.S. Department of State Installation

At a conference in October 1971, Sheldon Rosen of the U.S. Department of State commented during the open discussion after Katter's paper (1973) that the U.S. Department of State in Washington, DC, was using the same online search package (then unnamed, but presumed to be ORBIT II) that SDC had supplied to NLM. The Department was making its own changes to the system to accomodate different users and requirements. The modified system, DOSIR (Department of State Information Retrieval), contained sensitive Department information (Katter 1998).

The COSATI annual report for 1971 activities (*Progress* 1972) noted that planning was underway in 1971 for an integrated document and data system to operate at the U.S. Department of State beginning in the first half of 1972. Remote sites around the headquarters building with typewriter and CRT terminals would provide online access. Index records and their proxies would reside in the computer, with the source documents stored on microform.

DOSIR was meant to have low visibility. Black (1996) said that information about it was available only on a need-to-know basis so no public documents described DOSIR. Nonetheless, the existence of ORBIT at the State Department was confirmed by its appearance in a table in Martin's feature analysis (1974). Former SDC staff members who were involved with the project also confirmed it and recalled that the initial installation was in March 1971 with an online upgrade in September 1971. Burket of the SDC-Santa Monica office was most responsible for the installation. ORBIT continued to run at the State Department through 1995 (Cuadra 1997).

ERIC Projects

SDC completed a series of projects for the USOE (before it became the Department of Education) involving the ERIC database. One of these required Judith Wanger and Neil Sherman, then based in SDC's Falls Church office, to travel around the United States giving ERIC demos.

Lee Burchinal (whose association with ERIC is described in chapter 5, and who also had arranged an ERIC online service contract with Lockheed in 1968) remembered that when Wanger traveled to give demonstrations, she was "lugging a terminal about the size of a five-drawer file cabinet (1995)." This extremely slow Teletype was so large and heavy that it required two large packing cases for shipping. When she moved later from Falls Church to Santa Monica, Wanger became SDC Search Service's first official salesperson. Diana Delanoy in the Santa Monica office helped manage ERIC and tried to drum up usage for it in pre-SDC Search Service days.

The SDC Search Service later picked ERIC because it was cheap, easy to obtain, well known by the SDC staff, had been available online with DIALOG since 1969 and had received considerable attention. For SDC, this was an experiment to find out what was "out there" and what else they could do with this service.

Disk space was a problem then, so the "time windows" scheme described earlier with COLEX was used, making ERIC available for two hours per day. Cuadra (1997) remarked that the phrase "disk space was a problem" proved to be a portent for the fates of SDC's and Lockheed's systems: "While Roger Summit was busy buying up slow, cheap IBM Data Cells, SDC was buying high-quality IBM hardware and charging SDC Search Service full 'retail' prices for disk storage and compute-power. Armed with the cost numbers involved, any junior accountant could probably have foretold the results of the DIALOG-SDC competition."

At a 1974 ASIS meeting, Cuadra noted that SDC had demonstrated ERIC online in 1969, and this experience had convinced them of the value of ERIC and online searching. In early 1972, SDC started formal marketing of ERIC by announcing that it would provide an online service named SDC/ERIC and mailing information about it to prospective users. This was all before the start of the SDC Search Service.

SDC Search Service

In 1969–1970, while SDC software was being used in several pilot projects (e.g., Los Angeles police files) and in experimental services such as COLEX, CIRCOL, Copper Data Center, and AIM-TWX, Cuadra was still focused on R&D projects and contract studies. The idea of starting a public search service had not yet occurred to him. In a presentation, Cuadra (1980, 36) remarked:

Ten years ago I was honored by the American Society for Information Science by being named Distinguished Lecturer for 1970. In this role, I traveled around the country, discussing the promises and pitfalls of online information services. At the time, there were no commercial online retrieval services in operation and, although the company I worked for was operating an online service in support of [NLM], I had not conceived of anything like SDC Search Service.

In an 1990 interview, Cuadra (1990) confirmed that "the decision to go commercial crept up on SDC." Some of the creeping interest at SDC may have resulted from outside coaxing. McCarn (1987) remembered from his NLM experience:

I wrote a letter to George Mueller [Mueller became president of SDC in 1971] trying to convince him to go into the online service business. They let AIM-TWX die at SDC and they did not move into online service for months after that. If they had been planning, they would have used the government's money to get their service up and off the ground and get more databases that weren't NLM's so that when NLM dropped out they would have had a whole clientele and everything.

According to Black (1987), SDC decided to venture into a public online service after gradually realizing that a market niche not being served by NLM was available to them:

Carlos [Cuadra] and myself and Judy [Wanger]—the three of us that were involved in the decision to start a commercial search service. We had to persuade SDC management that it was a good idea. The thing that persuaded them was the fact that now NLM had started running MEDLINE, but they (NLM) were getting so many requests from medical schools and others for access, that they cut off all commercial organizations from direct access to the NLM computer. So PMA came to us and said, "We'll give you the tape" because they got the tape as a quid pro quo for doing indexing for NLM on the drug literature, and in return for that NLM gave them the tape. PMA then sent us the tape which we could put up instantly since we were still running MEDLINE for NLM. That persuaded management that there was a potential business there. Since PMA wanted CHEMCON we immediately put up CHEMCON.

Cuadra (1997) remembered:

When we were considering in 1972 the idea of creating the commercial online service business called SDC Search Service, we had some assurance of getting income from the PMA companies that had been using AIM–TWX and MEDLINE and from other PMA companies that wanted to use MEDLINE. We asked PMA folk, "What else do you need?"—knowing that it wasn't ERIC—and learned that it was chemical bibliographic data, which translated to Chemical Abstracts Condensates.

Cuadra was familiar with *Chemical Abstracts* from serving on their Board of Directors from 1969–1972. Cuadra invented the CHEMCON name for the CA Condensates database; he alleged (1997) that it was such a good name that even the DIALOG sales staff occasionally referred to it that way. Chapters 9 and 10 look more closely at the behind-the-scenes role that PMA played in helping to establish the SDC Search Service.

While SDC was modifying their ORBIT software to produce the ELHILL version for NLM in 1972, Cuadra was attempting to convince SDC management that ORBIT had great commercial potential. As discussed in the last chapter, he mailed a questionnaire to about 7,000 NTIS subscribers—a copy of which reached Summit, who took it to Lockheed management to alert them of the competition in the online retrieval business. Cuadra knew of Summit's online activities, but he knew nothing of Summit's alarm. When Cuadra received only seventy of the questionnaires back (1 percent), with almost no encouraging responses, he was disheartened and dismayed. He maintained (1990) nonetheless that he had not been defeated; he locked the questionnaires away in his desk and told no one the results:

I did not let that particular cat out of the bag for maybe four or five years. Instead I went to management and said, "We must start an online retrieval service." That was the first time I learned that there are some kinds of needs that people do not know they have until you can satisfy them. You have to show them what you've got before they know that they really want it and they always wanted it and they always needed it but they did not know it. I was a psychologist before, so I should have known better about surveys and instruments, but I had never dealt with something that did not exist before. So I asked my management for permission to go ahead. I got a 90-day: "Let's try it." No one was convinced at the time it was going to fly. We had no marketing plan and no sales folks. So they said, "Let's look at it in 90 days."

So in late 1972, at about the same time that Lockheed was launching its Information Retrieval Service, the fledgling SDC Search Service received a chance to load and test files, find a market of users, and prove its viability to SDC management, all within *three months*.

Carlos Albert Cuadra, who was eager to push ahead in spite of little encouragement from potential users and only half-hearted support from his management, characterized himself modestly as a "rat psychologist and piano player." In fact, however, Cuadra had already demonstrated leadership in information science research and development and library automation. He was well known for having established in 1966 the *Annual Review of Information Science and Technology* and editing it for ten years. He had won the ASIS Award of Merit in 1968, the ASIS Best Information Science Book award in 1969, and the ASIS Distinguished Lecturer award in 1970. Three U.S. presidents appointed him to serve as a member of NCLIS.

After earning his Ph.D. in psychology at UC-Berkeley in 1953, Cuadra worked as a staff psychologist at a Veterans Administration Hospital before joining Rand Corp. in Los Angeles. At Rand he saw SAGE, the computerized air defense system that was the first large-scale online system. Cuadra (1971c, 107–108) described it:

> It was the pioneer in direct and immediate man-computer communication. The SAGE computer, a special-purpose device built by IBM and called the Q7, was, in 1957, the world's largest computer. At the time I was working with the SAGE system, the Q7 was the first and only computer I had ever seen, and because everything about computers was too new to me I was not at all shocked that the computer provided for rapid access from about 150 very elegant consoles. . . . the SAGE system firmly established the concepts of on-line interaction and time-sharing.

As a field training specialist, Cuadra's assignment was to go to radar sites in Montana, North Dakota, and elsewhere to monitor simulation-based training exercises for the radar personnel.

> If you can imagine people in Northern Montana who see one flight a day, that crosses Montana on its way to Seattle. They were supposed to take care of 800 Russian missiles and 5,000 Bears and Bisons [Soviet military aircraft] coming over the pole. They had no skill, and no way to get the skill tracking one airplane a day. So the Division invented this notion of cutting off all the external communications to a radar site and pumping in synthetic data so it looked on the scope like a major invasion. You had to shut down air defense for two hours, that was one of the tricky things. By simulating the attacks and building up the load from one airplane to ten airplanes to 100, you could train people to higher levels of competence. The key concept was not only simulation but feedback. After the exercise they said, "Here is what came in. Here is what you called it. You called this Russian Bear American Airlines 209, you misidentified." The combination of exercise and noncritical feedback was supposed to help people get better. I was supposed to be there as a consultant, but it was against my natural nature, so I got put in charge of hiring people to do that. I never had to go out in the field; I got to hire the people who went to Grand Forks, North Dakota.[7]

Cuadra's "natural nature" was not to write programs or design systems, but to manage and be involved with customer service and training, presaging his managing the SDC Search Service. When the Research and Training division split off from Rand in 1957 and became its own corporation (SDC), he stayed with it and in 1968 was promoted to manage the Library and Documentation Systems Department (by 1971 renamed the Education and Library Systems Department). From 1974 until he left SDC in 1978 to create his own company, he was the general manager of SDC Search Service.

The two major organizations in the early online search service industry—SDC and Lockheed—had different philosophies and approaches to their products. SDC staff closely associated with the online search system were R&D-driven. With a history of published accomplishments, SDC hired staff with training, experience, and inclination toward solid R&D work. The online services were focal points around which staff could pursue their R&D interests. Building a business empire based on online searching did not seem to be a major goal for the SDC staff. Lockheed staff closely associated with the DIALOG system displayed little skill at R&D ventures (with the exception of the DIALIB project run by a professional researcher loaned to DIALOG by another Lockheed department). The Lockheed Retrieval Service, whose leader had a Ph.D. in management science, focused on business and growth interests. DIALOG senior management were not particularly interested in R&D for its own sake, or even as project revenue, except as a means to bootstrap the growth and development of the online search system. Among the management, the prevailing attitude was that using staff for R&D projects did not yield as much as using that staff to build the business. They relied on empirical data from operating experience and discouraged market analyses or theoretical studies.

Chapter 9 continues the public story of the early years of ORBIT as a major player in the online industry. Chapter 10 looks behind the scenes to see the continuing struggle at SDC to keep the search service alive.

7   Computer Searching for the Legal Profession: Data Corporation, OBAR, Mead Data Central, 1964–1972

Early Experimentation with Searching Legal Information

The LEXIS system in wide use today (as part of Lexis-Nexis) was not conceived by computer programmers, systems engineers, IR specialists, or librarians. Lawyers made the first initiatives; they felt that a critical need existed in the legal profession for new methods of locating cases, statutes, regulations, articles, and other material relevant to legal research.

The earliest demonstration of text searching capability was probably the experiments within IBM in 1958, with an IBM 650 computer. The system was limited to five-character word matches, however, which resulted in answers that were difficult to use. Using other systems and non-English text material, researchers within IBM further demonstrated the technical feasibility of full-text searching at that early date (Magnino 1966).

Even before the advent of online facilities, Canadian and U.S. universities were testing computer searching and manipulation of legal and other text material, including linguistic analysis, concordance and index building, and file searching, all in the late 1950s and 1960s. The project descriptions in this background section are all for batch-mode activities, included here to show the important precursors to later online legal information systems.

Oklahoma State University ("Points of Law")

Robert Morgan, a business law professor at Oklahoma State University, began in 1957 to develop a system by which computers could be used for legal research—probably the first system for computer storage and retrieval of legal material. He conducted his pioneering work without outside financial support, and without access to extensive law library facilities (Wilson 1962b). His method became known as the "points of law" approach, in which manually indexed and coded representations for single legal concepts ("points of law") were stored in machine-language form. Coded representations of the concepts of interest to a searcher were submitted for computer searching of a magnetic tape database, yielding a printout of the relevant case citations (Morgan 1962).

Morgan gave his first public demonstration of the system in December 1960, at the annual convention of the Oklahoma Bar Association, with batch searching on an IBM 650 RAMAC computer to retrieve selected tax materials. This was soon after Horty's 1960 demonstration of searching full-text legal statutes (see next section). In August 1961, at the ABA annual meeting in St. Louis, Morgan demonstrated batch searching of the Internal Revenue Code, Regulations, and selected cases in the Federal Gift Tax field, using an IBM 1401 computer.

Drawing on his background as a pilot in the USAF for eleven years, Morgan made a proposal in October 1958 to the Air Force judge advocate in an attempt to interest the Air Force in utilizing computers for storing and retrieving court martial records and other military law materials. We believe this formal written proposal was the first detailed statement of a system for computer storage and retrieval of a complete body of law. No one, however, took immediate action on his proposal, and Morgan died in 1962. The Air Force did eventually embrace the idea, initiating the development of the LITE system under the direction of another pioneer of that time, John Horty. A description of Horty's work follows.

University of Pittsburgh Health Law Center

The Health Law Center at the University of Pittsburgh began a two-year study in 1956 of the legal aspects of hospital operations—the objective was to study and compile in one location the laws of various jurisdictions pertaining to hospitals. Later, the project expanded into a general study of health law (Robins 1968). The study, which involved five or six attorneys full-time plus other nonlegal personnel, was under the direction of attorney John Horty. It led to the development of a manual on hospital law that included each state's laws regarding hospitals. Horty (1960b) related that the project personnel initially felt that the law did not vary much between states. They were mistaken, however, and found that the statutes differed greatly from state to state. They also found that indexing systems that worked well in other areas of the law gave them trouble in the area of hospitals. At the completion of their initial project and reference manual, they found that they were still having difficulty finding things in the printed manual. At that point, they started talking to the staff at the university's Computation and Data Processing Center. The staff were interested in helping to explore other solutions, and they initiated further discussions with IBM representatives, including Hans Peter Luhn (Horty 1960b). They proceeded with a plan to keypunch a sample of the Pennsylvania health statutes (about 6 percent) and develop programs for the university's IBM 650 computer to search that material.

Horty demonstrated this batch-search system for legal statute text at the 1960 annual meeting of the American Bar Association (ABA). The presentation relied on technical assistance from IBM's Yorktown Heights Research Center, and a full-text database of 2,650 sections of Pennsylvania statutes concerning health and hospital law (Horty 1960a, 1965, 1966; Horty and Walsh 1963; Harrington 1984–1985). Horty's pioneering demonstration appears to have been the first example of a text-searching system that provided word-proximity searching (word A within the same sentence as, and no more than n words after, word B). The retrieval research program at the university was conducted jointly by the Computation and Data Processing Center and by the Health Law Center (Horty 1962). CLR provided initial support with the first grant for legal retrieval research that Horty's group received. Support for their later experiments in the 1960s came from IBM and the American Bar Foundation, as well as NIH, USOE, Ford Foundation, and Pittsburgh industrial firms (Link 1973; Kehl et al. 1961).

Horty (1962) conducted one of the first studies to evaluate computer searching and used his own experiments for data. He attempted to determine the efficiency of the retrieval system by manually searching six queries that had been searched previously on the computer, then compared the relative performance of both types of searches. In 1963, Horty also became involved in a contract between the Air Force Accounting and Finance Center (AFAFC) and the University of Pittsburgh for developing LITE, a full-text batch-mode legal search system for the USAF, which is described in a later section. Horty left the university in 1967 to form his own organization, Aspen Systems Corporation, also described later.

Western Reserve University (WRU) Indexing System

At the 1959 ABA meeting, Jessica Melton and Robert Bensing of WRU suggested a way for using computers for legal research. They showed how the unique WRU indexing system—already used with test projects in the machine handling of metallurgical and medical literature—could be used with legal literature. For their demonstration, they indexed the Sales portion of the Uniform Commercial Code and several cases that had been cited in connection with it, posed questions to the file, and reviewed the answers for relevance (Melton and Bensing 1960; Melton 1962).

Southwestern Legal Foundation

In the early 1960s, Robert Wilson, research director at the Southwestern Legal Foundation in Dallas, oversaw experiments of the use of computers for processing full-text legal statute information on magnetic tape to produce printed-word indexes. For a pilot project, Wilson experimented with a full-text file of all federal and state appellate court decisions in the field of arbitration and award in five southwestern states. The file comprised about 200 decisions—about 525,000 words of official text. Researchers prepared the file by keypunching, in uppercase only, from the source text (Wilson 1962a; Robins 1968).

Wilson also experimented with batch searching on an IBM 1401 of a database of 260 federal court decisions (over 400,000 words) dealing with taxation of oil and gas transactions in the petroleum industry. Project OGRE (Oil and Gas Reports, Electronic) began in April 1960 and was complete by the end of 1963 (Wilson 1966). The documentation is unclear regarding whether Wilson developed and used his own search software. Eldridge and Dennis (1963a) mentioned that Wilson "has undertaken experiments with the Horty-Pittsburgh system as applied to case law" (89–90).

An interesting feature of Wilson's experiments was the use of microfilm rather than magnetic tape for storage of the full text of the case law, with frame numbers recorded in the computer index as part of the document number. This approach of storing only a microfilm address in the computer record, and storing the full record on an accompanying microform file, appeared a few years later with several online search systems as a measure to cope with limited and expensive computer storage space.

An IBM systems engineer, Harm Schreur (1963), described an inverted file approach for batch searching of legal text at the Southwestern Legal *Center* (but he was probably referring to the Southwestern Legal *Foundation*). Schreur noted that in index building, they grouped each word and its variants (e.g., account, accounts, accounting) into the same index entry. Synonyms could be included in these word groupings. They made no attempt to note the exact position of a word within a text, but instead used an approximation approach in which a document was broken arbitrarily into a maximum of thirty sections, and the index word was tagged by section number. This allowed a searcher to specify that two or more words must appear in the same section, and thus obtain some semblance of word proximity searching. This was among the earliest attempts at word-proximity searching, but it was not as complete as Horty's prior work.

George Washington University—Datatrol Corporation

In August 1962, John Lyons of the Graduate School of Public Law at George Washington University addressed the ABA annual meeting to describe his collaboration with Datatrol Corp. in a demonstration of computer searching of indexed documents dealing with antitrust problems (Eldridge and Dennis 1963a). For a pilot experiment, 350 documents were indexed, and their full citations, including indexing and a short abstract, were keypunched to build the file. Search request cards were also keypunched and fed into the IBM 1401 computer. The resulting printout included the entire file record (Lyons 1962). This approach used Edmund Stiles's association factor for the actual search technique.

A large part of the search strategy of this system was developed by William Hammond and programmed by Walter Filleman, both of Datatrol. Datatrol staff were knowledgeable about the indexing issues. They had done prior work in that field, including their NSF-supported study of the convertibility of the indexing vocabularies of ASTIA, AEC, and NASA. In 1963, Datatrol developed a generalized IBM 1401 search system to support in-house experimentation on various retrieval concepts. That program permitted multiple simultaneous searches, varying degrees of indexing sophistication (including the optional use of links, roles, and term weighting), and output-relevance ranking. In 1964, they made the programs available for commercial use in a legal setting, giving them the name Evidence Retrieval and Correlation, but with an intended use that today would be described as "litigation support software" (Long 1964).

American Bar Foundation (ABF) Project

In December 1961, ABF joined with IBM to conduct a long-term study (the American Bar Foundation Project, or ABF-IBM Project) of the application of computers to legal-information problems. Within IBM, Steven Furth found the funds to support the extensive computer processing required. CLR gave a grant to ABF to support the transcription of the file by Horty's group at the University of Pittsburgh. William Eldridge of ABF, as the project director, supplied advice about the nature of the legal file and its use and managed an extensive evaluation of the results (Dennis 1967). Sally Dennis, an advisory systems engineer from IBM's Chicago South Sales Office, was the principal IBM participant who designed the special automatic indexing and searching programs.

The project team immediately attended to the practical problems associated with indexing legal material. They used IBM KWIC programs to complete two index publication projects of interest to the ABF constituency. They then focused on identifying activities that would not duplicate the work of other groups, and would be of broad utility to the legal profession. They planned to build experimental systems only, and not to develop a commercial service. The research that seemed most appropriate for their investigation was indexing and file organization techniques associated with computer-based handling of large volumes of legal material, and in May 1962, they proposed an eighteen-month study to do that. Their proposal, which ABF approved, included the general requirements for such a system, and some experiments using cases from the *Northeastern Reporter* and four different indexing methods (Eldridge and Dennis 1963b).

By August 1962, manual indexing of the database was well under way and specifications were being prepared for full-text keyboarding of it (Eldridge and Dennis 1963a). The full text of 5,200 recent court opinions (about 10 million words) from the 1959–1962 editions of *Northeastern Reporter* were keypunched for the experimental computer searching of legal opinions. The source text then was subjected to a computer processing routine to calculate an "associative factor" for each meaningful term (i.e., not a stop word), based on the statistical probability of the occurrence of the term with the occurrence of other terms (Dennis 1965a). IBM 7090 computers performed all processing. A user searched by submitting a question in the form of a sentence to the same computation procedure, and matching the query computation result with the corresponding data for the source text words. The degree of match for the various term pairs was represented by a score. Thus it was possible to deliver the output records in order of probable relevance to the query (Robins 1968).

File building and software development were complete in 1965, at which time Sally Dennis conducted an evaluation study, searching forty-three queries. A four-lawyer panel judged the search results for recall and relevance (Eldridge 1965; Dennis 1965b, 1967; Mermin 1967). This was among the first formal evaluations of computer searching of full-text material. Kayton (1966) used this database in another research project. Other IBM research and development projects related to text searching are chronicled in chapter 4.

LITE

As mentioned earlier, Morgan of Oklahoma State University wrote a proposal in October 1958 to try to interest the USAF in the use of computers for storing and retrieving military law materials. In 1961 the Office of the Staff Judge Advocate (USAFC) in Denver, Colorado, began to study the potential use of computers for retrieval applications. Among systems that received their attention was Horty's at the University of Pittsburgh. While they probably also reviewed Morgan's work, Morgan had died in 1962 and the State of Oklahoma was not in a position to follow up. As a result of their study, AFAFC submitted a proposal in August 1962 for developing and testing a full-text magnetic tape search system. The USAF headquarters approved the proposal in July 1963 (Davis 1966a, 1966b). In October 1963, AFAFC gave a sole-source contract to the University of Pittsburgh, with a subcontract to IBM. The contract, which was to run through November 1964, called for a test facility in the Denver area, training Air Force personnel in use of the system and in developing selected full-text files (e.g., the entire *U.S. Code*, a portion of the published Decisions of the Comptroller General). Batch searching of full-text legal statutes was thus established, in a production operation called Project LITE (Legal Information through Electronics) (Volino 1972).

During a six-month period in 1964, with the 17-million-word database on an IBM 1410 operating in batch mode, AFAFC staff conducted a companion study of searching 215 queries manually and via LITE. The results showed that searching via LITE was efficient and usually produced the same or more relevant citations than searching manually (Davis 1965, 1966b). At the end of the test period, AFAFC awarded successive contracts to the University of Pittsburgh for 1965–1967. This follow-up work for computer search service and file building and maintenance was performed on IBM 1410 computers, with drum storage, all operating in batch mode. With this contract support, the University of Pittsburgh Health Law Center and the IBM Federal Systems Division developed LITE for legal information retrieval, along with several major LITE files and the LITE organization in Denver (Furth 1968).

LITE was a joint effort involving Horty and others at the University of Pittsburgh, and Jack Garland and others at IBM. Garland, who had both a law degree and an M.S.L.S. in library science, was a lead person on the IBM team. The original intent was to move the operating LITE system to Washington, D.C., at an early stage. Air Force General Paul Scheidecker was reportedly the major force behind Project LITE. Unfortunately, he died shortly after the project started, leaving behind no forceful advocate to bring that about (Chartrand 1994).

LITE provided computerized legal research service to DOD starting in 1965. From 1967 until 1970, various commercial contractors supported LITE operations. In early 1970, LITE operations transferred to a contractor who quickly defaulted, which caused a suspension of operation until March, when LITE was authorized to run its own operation (without contractors) at the AFAFC computer center in Denver, using IBM 360/65 equipment (Wilkins 1972). Up to this time, all of the contractors had run LITE with the batch file building and search software developed by the University of Pittsburgh and IBM.

In 1968, the Air Force authorized leasing of the LITE files and computer programs to U.S. parties outside the federal government ("LITE source" 1968; "Leasing of LITE materials" 1968). The files included such works as the full text of the *U.S. Code*, published Decisions of the Comptroller General, Armed Services Procurement Regulations, Fiscal Year 1966 and 1967 Appropriation Acts, unclassified International Law Agreements, and Court of Military Appeals Decisions ("LITE research capabilities" 1968). In 1971, the Air Force considered transferring LITE to the DOJ; DOJ staff had already converted the U.S. Code database to the DOJ JURIS online system from the LITE database (Stevens 1973). The text parsing programs of LITE, however, were used in the JURIS online system (chapter 5), and the JURIS staff also converted the U.S. Code database from the LITE system to JURIS (Basheer 1973).

In 1972, LITE was still operating as a batch-mode, full-text (over 90 million words) retrieval system at AFAFC, running over 1,000 searches per month (McCarthy 1971; Mallow 1973). Users were still entering search statements with punched IBM cards. The master text files were stored on IBM 2314 disk units, and the file in 1972 required ninety-five disk packs, with a maximum of twenty packs accessible to the search software at any one time (Sieburg 1972). Even though the name "LITE" changed to "FLITE" (the "F" was for "federal"), it never became an online system ("Computerized legal research" 1981).

University of Iowa College of Law

As part of a 1965 study of opinion-writing practices of federal district court judges and of various publishers' practices in publishing those opinions, Allan Vestal of the University of Iowa College of Law used an IBM 7044-1401 at the university's computer center. Over 2,500 opinions were analyzed and coded, with the resulting indexing information coded in numeric form and punched on IBM cards. Each card represented a single federal district court opinion, and contained twenty-five coded characteristics. For search and analysis purposes, the punched card file, program, and associated control cards were read into the computer, and the resulting output was printed on a high-speed printer ("Jurimetrics: The Electronic Digital Computer" 1965).

University of Pennsylvania—LAWSEARCH

In 1965, University of Pennsylvania Law School researchers began work using computers for legal IR. They developed a system called LAWSEARCH that operated in either a batch or on online mode, using Multilist (described more fully in chapter 2). LAWSEARCH should not be confused with the Project Lawsearch sponsored by CLR in 1961–1964, which studied the use of Termatrix optical coincidence cards in legal literature indexing and searching.

University of Florida College of Law

In October 1966, Betty Taylor, librarian of the University of Florida College of Law, demonstrated an online search system that used on-campus IBM equipment and a hard-wired computer terminal to search an index to articles published in Florida legal periodicals. The records included the periodical citation along with up to three subject heading codes (Levinson 1967).

University of Manitoba Faculty of Law

In 1968, Stephen Skelly of the Faculty of Law and staff members of the Institute for Computer Studies at the University of Manitoba developed and demonstrated a batch-mode bill-drafting system for the Manitoba Attorney General's Department. It included a capability for remote-terminal searching of the full text of all Canadian Regulatory and Statutory Laws, federal and provincial, that had been processed into the system. Skelly (1968a, 1968b) mentioned the possibility of online interrogation of case law.

University of Montreal—DATUM

The DATUM Project (documentation automatique des textes juridiques de l'Université de Montreal) at the University of Montreal in Quebec was a joint research venture of the law faculty and the computer center to provide, for the legal profession as a whole, bilingual searching of both English and French legal case law text. The DATUM staff wrote programs that were used on a test basis at Dalhousie University, Halifax, Nova Scotia. Initial plans were to provide a file of twenty-five years of case law in the original French or English version. The first demonstrations were in May 1970. In July 1971 they were operating with a database of about 140 million characters of case law on a CDC-6600 computer in Montreal with disk storage.

The project team started their own consultation search service, performing computer searches for interested users at a cost of $15–25 per search. As part of their research, in 1971 they installed a Teletype terminal for remote batch retrieval at a large law firm in Montreal. Mackay (1973) noted that a query submitted from the terminal was normally answered in a few minutes. He mentioned the availability of a special feature to print portions of the text with the search words underlined. Although highlighting was a relatively new feature, it had been used already in Data Central, as we shall see. One planned feature was an automatic bilingual thesaurus generated for this system ("DATUM Project" 1970). Such a capability would allow a search term to be automatically augmented by synonyms, translations, and other equivalent terms, so that a searcher could retrieve French as well as English texts, even if the query was in one language only. If this feature was implemented, it may have been the first instance of a bilingual user-interface option. Such a feature was demonstrated with the University of Montreal RETRO system in 1973 (chapter 9).

State Bar Association Activities

Many American lawyers in the 1960s were concerned about the excessive amount of time and effort required to access legal materials, and several state bar associations conducted investigations on their behalf. For example, in 1966 the executive committee of the New York State Bar Association (NYSBA) sponsored the Lawyers' Center for Electronic Legal Research. At about the same time, the Philadelphia Bar and the Missouri Bar each surveyed the research habits of their members in order to determine how a computer could best assist them. Other bar associations took similar actions (Rubin 1974) because lawyers believed that their credibility, confidence, and quality control were threatened. Harrington (1970, 1145) explained:

Early in the [Ohio Bar] association's investigation of existing programs and of prospective ones promised by various software companies, it became apparent that a computerized research system would be more likely to be of service to the profession if at least a substantial degree of control were exercised by the organized Bar. In the first place, many lawyers were properly skeptical of computers because they knew that for years the sponsors of some systems had been promising much more than they could perform. It was judged that only the organized Bar could readily regain their confidence.

A bar association represented the interests of the legal profession and ensured that any computerized research system would meet their professional standards of thoroughness, accuracy, and confidentiality.

New York State Bar Association

The New York State Board of Regents chartered the Lawyers' Center for Electronic Legal Research (LCELR), which became a nonprofit, educational organization. Its initial studies were directed at analyzing present methods of legal research, examining the feasibility of creating a national network, extending databases and access to them, and testing all systems of electronic retrieval of legal information (Plowden-Wardlaw 1968).

The NYSBA executed a contract with Mead Data Central (MDC) in January 1971 for a cooperative study of the feasibility of providing a computerized legal-IR service in New York. The study covered the research patterns, size, and composition of the New York Bar, and the attitude of the Bar toward computer searching of legal research materials. MDC was obliged to load a file as defined in the contract (Flavin 1973). Additional New York Bar and MDC activities are described later.

The New York Bar Association started their formal research organization earlier than did the Ohio Bar Association with Ohio Bar Automated Research (OBAR). It was OBAR, however, that took the most direct steps in initiating computer search service to the legal profession.

Ohio State Bar Association

During the period 1964–1967, a group of Ohio State Bar members began exploring the concept of computer-assisted legal research and its technology. In 1965, they heard John Horty speak on this topic at the annual dinner of the Ohio State Bar Foundation. The president of the Ohio Bar at that time, James Preston, resolved that his presidency would be remembered for the initiation of a computer-assisted legal research service for Ohio lawyers.

Also present for Horty's after-dinner speech was William Harrington, an attorney who had earned his J.D. from The Ohio State University College of Law, and had become Research and Legislative Counsel to the Ohio Bar in 1958. After Harrington attended the dinner and learned of Preston's vision and commitment, he volunteered to take charge of the Ohio Bar computer project and immediately began a review of available technology. He went to Pittsburgh to work with Horty's system, and arranged for demonstrations by various technology suppliers. Harrington and other Ohio Bar attorneys set out to write specifications for a system—they hoped to be able to improve and expand upon

Horty's system. Harrington (1984–1985) judged those specifications to be among the most important achievements of the Ohio Bar group. The service definition they crafted in 1966 called for a nonindexed, online, interactive, computer-assisted legal research service to search the full text of legal materials, not headnotes or digests. This is still the core service definition for today's LEXIS online service. While online retrieval of full-text information had been demonstrated and reported as early as 1963 with the SRI system (chapter 2), it seems unlikely that any of the Ohio group were aware of SRI, and no evidence points to the source of their inspiration. Harrington's specification for online searching discouraged many technology vendors, and few companies offered to build the service.

By December 1966, Central Media Bureau, a New York company engaged in a contract with the New York Times to develop the programs for computer-based production of the *Times* printed indexes, appeared to be the only choice of vendor. The lawyers opened negotiations for a contract for the Ohio Bar to fund software development for the defined service. News of the negotiations was important enough to be picked up by the *Wall Street Journal*, where it caught the eye of William Gorog, a businessman and president of Data Corporation of Dayton, Ohio. Gorog immediately called Preston, just before the contract with Central Media Bureau was signed. Gorog proposed that his company be of assistance, and invited Harrington to visit Data Corporation in January 1967 to see their online software, which had been demonstrated for the first time only six months earlier (reportedly intended to be used with medical literature). Harrington came away from the Data Corporation presentation convinced that this interactive online system (nonindexed and full-text) represented the most advanced and sophisticated retrieval software he had seen. The lawyers immediately suspended negotiations with the New York firm, and in that same month created the OBAR organization to manage the computerized research program. The history of other attempts to develop commercial computer-based legal search services, as well as the history of Data Corporation, must be considered before discussing OBAR.

Early Commercial Legal Search Services

Law Research Service/Inc.

A product of the New York–based firm Law Research Service/Inc., the commercial Law Research Service began in 1964. The firm's president, Elias Hoppenfeld, was a practicing attorney in New York and had been working since 1960 with the idea of using computers to help with research tasks of practicing attorneys. In 1965, Hoppenfeld (1966) described Law Research Service operation to the ABA Electronic Data Retrieval Committee. According to Mermin (1967), the description was not informative about what was stored in the computer or specifics of the indexing. Nonetheless, Hoppenfeld stated that, given the current options of full-text or descriptor searching, the latter approach was preferable because the cost of computerizing the full text would not afford a profit. For the company's first database, the best choice was the New York State law, because the average practitioner was mostly concerned with state decisions. Hoppenfeld (1966, 49) told the ABA committee that the file conversion task had been tedious and that he had been nervous and skeptical about the outcome:

This long period of creation was one of spending, spending, and spending money without any income at all to the investor . . . When you add that this was a pioneering venture, with no real record of success, it made the course and time even more difficult . . . many of the people connected with the venture had their doubts even though market research people believed that the attorneys did desire the service, we could not be certain that they would accept and use it and lastly who knew that the computer people who said they could make the "brain" work, could do it.

The tape file eventually consisted of over 1 million case abstracts, including all the New York cases officially reported since 1846, and all officially reported federal cases.

> **1964 Milestone**
>
> Law Research Service was the first computer-based bibliographic search service provided on a regular basis by a commercial organization.

The search system was implemented on a UNIVAC III computer. For the initial demonstration, they invited 250 judges and all came. When the service became available in 1964, it was in batch mode and the cost was $250 for ten queries ("Jurimetrics" 1965). A client filled out a standard query form, and mailed or delivered it to the service. At the service, a lawyer-editor in the legal specialty designated by the client reviewed the query, assigned appropriate search terms, keyed the query formulation onto punched cards and fed the cards into the computer. The UNIVAC III searched the relevant magnetic tapes, and a high-speed printer printed out the selected case names and citations. The editor reviewed the printout for relevance, chose the four most relevant cases, and had the full text of those cases and their dissenting opinions printed from the microfilm reader-printer. The resulting package was then mailed or delivered to the client.

Within one year of start-up, they had conducted over 20,000 searches and enrolled over 5,000 attorneys, comprising the majority of the largest law firms in New York State. With experience, some clients asked to do their own search formulation and code selection from a printed thesaurus, so the service added that option.

Hoppenfeld proclaimed that they intended to change their operation to an online system, in which attorneys could key in a query using a remote computer console in their offices, with the query going directly to the computer, and the search results going directly back to the client. The proposed system change required a change from the UNIVAC III to a computer with a disk file and random access memory (unstated, but presumably an IBM machine). To support the growth of this enterprise, they made a stock offering that was sold out in two days.

> **1966 Milestone**
>
> Law Research Service may have been the first online search service provided on a regular basis by a commercial organization.

Hoppenfeld announced their intention to create the various state databases immediately, and to place remote computer consoles in their representatives' offices for online searching. They hoped to be in operation in the majority of the states by end of 1965. This service's operation in a true online mode, and if and when it was first used commercially online, is unconfirmed. However, it is probable that it happened in 1966. When it began operating in batch mode, Law Research Service was the first commercial (i.e., operated by a commercial organization as a business venture) computerized bibliographic search service. With its shift to online mode, it became the first commercial online bibliographic search service. No other commercial online service became available until several years later, with the 1969 Data Corporation/OBAR service and the 1971 DIALOG/ERIC federally funded service.

When the online system was implemented, a searcher used a Teletype terminal to directly interrogate the computer using ten-digit descriptor code numbers, and within minutes received court citations on the terminal. Mail services supplied full-text printouts that searchers ordered by Telex from a manual copy service. The online service limited the output to the ten most recent court decisions for each descriptor, in chronological order, with the most recent and highest court decisions first. Logical operators (AND, OR) were available to work on the separate lists of cases for each descriptor. Apparently little information was published to describe the technical details of the operation, or to describe how the file was analyzed and stored (Robins 1968; "Computer retrieval" 1968).

In 1968, the company had 150 branch representatives in thirty-nine states. In 1970–1971, it was involved in litigation with its California franchises over an alleged lack of correlation between legal queries submitted and case citations produced (Beard 1969, 1971). This may be a milestone for the first time that a computer search service was sued for poor performance. Regrettably, no further information about the outcome of this organization and service is available.

COMSEARCH

In 1966, the Miche Company in Charlottesville, Virginia, announced a new search service called COMSEARCH. It had a manually indexed file of all reported opinions involving habeas corpus of the U.S. Court of Appeals for the Fourth Circuit, from the creation of that court in 1891 to 1966. Queries were to be mailed to the University of Virginia, where they were batched and searched on a Burroughs B500 computer. Search results, consisting of résumés of the retrieved opinions, were then mailed back to the requestor. The search cost was $25 for the first subject category and increased as more categories were searched ("COMSEARCH—Computer search of habeas corpus" 1966).

Data Retrieval Corporation of America

This commercial organization in Milwaukee had a contract in 1967 with the State of Wisconsin to furnish a system of full-text storage and retrieval of Wisconsin statutes, with a retrieval service to be available on a fee basis to private attorneys. Data Retrieval Corporation was apparently also working with a co-citation searching system (Mermin 1967).

Aspen Systems Corporation

In 1967, about the same time that the Ohio State Bar Association confirmed its decision to provide a full-text legal database service and chose Data Corporation's system instead of Horty's, Horty left the University of Pittsburgh and established Aspen Systems as a commercial enterprise engaged in computer storage and retrieval of legal data. Horty created Automated Law Searching, Inc., as a subsidiary of Aspen to assume the responsibility for maintaining and expanding the file ("Computer retrieval" 1968). Horty's full-text search system became the basis for ASPENSEARCH (chapter 9). By 1968, Aspen had built the full-text file of statutes of almost all fifty states, at a time when MDC had the statutes of four or five states and was making much hoopla about it. By 1969, Aspen had created the largest full-text database ever seen: Aspen System 50, the complete *U.S. Code* and the statutes of all fifty states. As Aspen's president, Horty stated that the primary users of Aspen System 50 were legislative bodies and government agencies ("Full texts" 1970). Pemberton (1997), who served for several years as Aspen's director of communications, disclosed: "Aspen actually had 46 states on disk . . . for some reason there were problems with the remaining four. So when we got an order for a 50-state search, we'd run 46 on the computer, then search the rest manually, then keystroke the results from the manual search so we could print it out and make them look like they were done on the computer." Aspen provided full-text data input service in the early 1970s, such as the opinions of the New York State courts (Flavin 1973). By 1972, Aspen was providing litigation file support services to many institutions (Feinman 1973).

One of the Mead participants, Carl Fisher (1997), recalled a 1973 meeting with Lawrence Berul (who replaced Horty at Aspen in the early 1970s) to negotiate Mead's acquisition of the full text of Pennsylvania case law materials from Aspen. Mead canceled the deal because the Aspen file was all in upper-case characters.

Data Corporation and Data Central

Beginning in 1964, a private computer programming and support company in Dayton launched an independent line of development that culminated several years later in a contractual relationship with Ohio lawyers to produce a new online system. The seeds of what evolved into today's LEXIS system were planted at that firm, Data Corporation.

Recon Central Project

Bill Gorog had been educated at the U.S. Military Academy and Ohio State University. After receiving his M.S. in industrial engineering in 1951, he began his career as a marketing manager at the Bulova Watch Company where he helped develop one of the first electronic watches. In 1956, he joined Data Corporation in Dayton, becoming the chair and chief executive officer in 1963. Under his direction, the company developed an online full-text retrieval system. They did this with internal funding as well as external support through a contract with the USAF at WPAFB, also located in Dayton (Rubin 1974). Richard Giering (1995), the principal developer of the system, provided most of the information in the following story.

In 1964, Data Corporation was active in highly sensitive super-high resolution photography associated with aerial and satellite photo reconnaissance systems, as well as sensitive visual and electronic targeting activities. All of this involved R&D in camera equipment and film processing technology. Under NASA contract, Data Corporation used this technology in the Lunar Ranger and other moon-related programs. The company was also doing research in high resolution photo display techniques, and multicolor ink jet technology that later became a Mead spin-off, Mead Digit, which was sold to Kodak.

Among Data Corporation projects was operation of a special library that supported the Reconnaissance Laboratory (Recon Lab) at WPAFB. The library was called Recon Central,[1] and its primary mission was to serve the Reconnaissance Division of the Avionics Laboratory by providing a data storage, retrieval, and reproduction facility in the field of reconnaissance and surveillance technology. The library responded to individual requests for information and served as the reference source for scientists and engineers in the Reconnaissance Division who produced state-of-the-art summaries, technical reports, and other publications for the reconnaissance community. Starting in 1964 and continuing for several years, Data Corporation produced a series of handbooks on airborne reconnaissance equipment, film processing, and support activities for infrared, ultraviolet, and radar systems. This support was at a time when the United States was engaged in developing and using highly classified spy satellites (with the first successful photo-reconnaissance satellite flight in 1960) and U-2 overflights (Klass 1995; Brugioni 1996).

In 1966 the library collection contained 16,000 items—8,000 were aperture card microfilm images of document abstracts. The remainder were technical reports, program and requirements data, and DD-1498 data about relevant current R&D projects originating from FTD, DDC, AEC, and NASA. About one hundred new items (mostly abstracts) arrived each day. The reports were indexed with a controlled vocabulary of 3,400 keywords drawn from 28,000 total keywords that DDC, NASA, and FTD used to index the documents represented by the 8,000 abstracts stored in the aperture card collection (*RECON CENTRAL* 1964). Retrieval was via a "peek-a-boo" optical coincidence card system, but staff had a study contract to consider the use of an IBM 360 for online searching from remote terminals (Kershaw, Crowder, Davis, Loges, Nerendini, and Thomas 1966).

Data Corporation received support in mid-1964 to study the feasibility of using full-text computer processing to aid in the operation of Recon Central. Robert Roalof and Len Crouch, Air Force representatives of Recon Lab, and Gorog of Data Corporation were among the participants. (Giering 1980, 1983). Gorog had been using IBM equipment at the Recon Central facility and was talking with

Air Force officials about a possible upgrade to the newer IBM 360 machine that was becoming available. He knew of work that had been done at DIA to demonstrate the benefit of a full-text searching approach. He used Northwestern University's BIDAP programs (chapter 3) and DIA staff experiments with BIDAP to argue their utility to Recon Central. The officials agreed and let Data Corporation acquire an Air Force IBM 360 as part of the existing facilities contract. The computer was located in a vault at the Recon Lab because computers, data entry equipment, and other special equipment used with highly sensitive data were often shielded in vaults or screen rooms to prevent electronic eavesdropping of the electromagnetic signals radiating from the equipment.

The initial computer search system for Recon Central was a single-terminal fast batch, noninteractive system, but technically it could be called online in the same way that the SATIRE system (chapter 2) could be called an online system. Requesters gave their search requirements to the computer operator, who entered the search statement at the computer console. The computer executed the search and printed out the results. The data (new and replacement records) were entered into the system in a true batch mode.

1967 Milestone

Data Central was the first online bibliographic search system to incorporate an arithmetic search capability.

Data Corporation's 1964 study confirmed the theoretical feasibility of a full-text approach. In 1965 the contract was expanded to include construction of a "breadboard model" of a single-terminal fast-batch online system. A breadboard model is a working prototype intended only to demonstrate performance, not meant for delivery. It takes its name from the practice in electronic labs of putting experimental electronic circuits together on laboratory bench tops, table tops, or actual breadboards; this was then the standard way in which the Recon Lab worked while developing reconnaissance hardware. In mid-1966, software was demonstrated for the first time at Data Corporation. The software included arithmetic search features (e.g., greater than, less than) required for the searching of numeric data fields such as dates, or film or equipment specifications (e.g., lens descriptions, film speeds). Arithmetic searching had been proposed for the 1963 SRI online system (chapter 2) but never implemented. The contract scope was further expanded to prepare for on-site feasibility testing.

Data Corporation's mid-1966 online demonstration took place about a year after Bunker-Ramo started the NASA/RECON project and made their first demonstration (chapter 5), before DIALOG had received a contract to install their demonstration terminal at the NASA-Ames facility (chapter 5), and several months before a contract was awarded to SDC for the COLEX online project to begin (chapter 6). The Data Corporation equipment was an IBM 360/40 with an IBM 2321 Data Cell with access restricted to 40 million bytes (that crashed regularly), two IBM 2311 disks (7 million bytes each), and an online console typewriter. The feasibility model required this dedicated system to support one terminal and one file; the emphasis was on the demonstration of the retrieval program, not time-sharing. In late 1966 the model was complete and feasibility was proven. In early 1967 Data Corporation's own computer was installed in the Recon Lab. Limited services began at Recon Central, and planning started for the development of a production system. At this point Giering joined Data Corporation and assumed leadership of developing their online search system. Giering had earned a B.S. in engineering and mathematics from the University of Arizona and had training in data processing. As chief of a Military Capabilities Section, he had served as a U.S. Army captain at DIA before retiring from the Army to join Data Corporation.

Giering's work with Data Corporation actually began as an unpaid consultant in 1966 while he was still on active duty at DIA and developing and implementing a computer-based information system for military capabilities intelligence data. In military terms, the system was called Defense Order of Battle System, which is another name for an inventory of enemy ground forces—numbers, strength, location—for a designated geographic area. The system used the Formatted File System (FFS) software. FFS was a proprietary name for an IBM software product derived from work for the DOD; IBM later commercialized it as the Generalized Information System (GIS), described in chapter 4. The FFS software required many coded representations for the data (e.g., V-127 for a Russian Tiger tank) and would have required many code books and authority files in any operational application. Giering saw that this would not be practical in the field; he thought that a means for searching the text of situation reports and action reports from the front lines was necessary. At this point he saw the value of a full-text approach. As seen in chapter 6, he discovered a research project at Northwestern University that had developed a set of programs for the IBM 7094 to do batch searching of text stored on computer tape. He obtained a copy of the programs, called BIDAP (chapter 3) and began to experiment with them on an IBM 7094 at DIA in late 1966.[2]

Giering's first experiment with the BIDAP programs was to use them with airborne photo reconnaissance analysis reports. The reports were narrative comments by a photo interpreter about a single photo image (e.g., "There is work underway to lengthen the runway"), and each photo image had its own separate printed report. Intelligence analysts regularly received large stacks of those printed reports for review. Giering proposed replacing that practice with on-demand searches of the narrative text itself. The BIDAP software was meant for batch processing, and Giering used it with a dedicated machine (i.e., fast batch, with no other jobs or users on the system) and an operator either at the computer console or at a remote terminal. Thus it was technically online, but not interactive, and not with multiple simultaneous users.

Using sample queries for topics of current interest, he demonstrated this approach to other U.S. Army intelligence analysts at DIA and found immediate acceptance of the idea. As described in chapter 6, an Air Force intelligence analyst at an adjacent desk overheard the conversation, jumped in, and arranged for this approach to be used with the Recon Lab at WPAFB. Giering worked to help Data Corporation install the BIDAP programs on the Recon Central computer for Data Corporation and Air Force personnel use. Coincidentally, DIA was funding the CIRC/COLEX/CIRCOL work at WPAFB and had installed a computer terminal at DIA for COLEX. Giering used that terminal to work with the BIDAP programs that were now being operated at Recon Central. This may be considered the moment that Giering began developing an online search system for Data Corporation. Thus, the SDC COLEX system and the beginning of the Data Corporation system crossed paths at this time, primarily because two persons in different branches of the armed services happened to have desks located together in a government office building in the Washington area.

1967 Milestone

Data Corporation's online system was among the first online bibliographic search systems to operate in a multifile access mode.[3]

Although Data Corporation had demonstrated its online system in mid-1966, the first demonstration of the software *on-site* at Recon Central took place in March 1967, using three separate files: (1) R&D project description records (DD Form 1498s, described in chapter 4 as part of the COSATI demonstration project; (2) textual research reports; and (3) hardware specifications of varying complexity from textual documents to numeric descriptions, and combinations of text and numeric information. The system used an inverted file from both the text and the structured fields, and Boolean logic. The first demonstration was limited to a single console typewriter, but soon thereafter the system had the capability to support either the console typewriter or an IBM 1050 hardcopy terminal—but not both simultaneously.

Also in spring 1967, Recon Central staff members used the Recon Central system and the SDC-developed CIRC system (chapter 6) to evaluate and compare full-text searching with searching of assigned keywords. This happened after the DIA sponsors of the CIRC system at WPAFB heard about Data Corporation's system and decided to examine it more closely. DIA obtained a copy of the unclassified portion of the CIRC database and arranged to have it loaded on the Data Corporation system. In Giering's view (1995), from a technical perspective, the comparison favored Data Corporation's approach. The evaluation report, however, was buried, and apparently nothing further came from the comparative evaluation. Research uncovered no documents reporting the results of the evaluation.

It is clear that Data Corporation staff, their Air Force sponsors, and DIA staff were aware of SDC's work in time-shared IR systems. Likewise, the CIRC, COLEX, and CIRCOL developers and their sponsors (FTD and DIA) knew about Data Corporation and its work. Unfortunately, strict secrecy requirements, "need-to-know," and the associated compartmentalization of their respective activities, as well as the proprietary interests of the two commercial contractors involved, prohibited any transfer of the details of system functions and performance between the Recon Lab and FTD activities. The two groups knew of each other's existence, but not the details of their work.[4]

When Giering joined Data Corporation in 1967, his first assignment was designing and implementing the time-sharing capability as a first step in expanding to a "production system." However, in October 1967, Air Force funding for a full production system terminated. Although no proof of such a speculation exists, this decision may have been related to the AF decision at the same time to fund COLEX (chapter 6). The demonstrated Recon Central system capabilities remained in operation at the Recon Central library with the limited breadboard version. The full production system proposed to the Air Force was to include such features as time-sharing for multiple simultaneous terminals, other terminal types, more generalized file definition, more recursiveness, optional and personalized synonymy, KWIC displays, and more generalized input-output options. As described next, Gorog obtained entrepreneurial funding and began in-house development of the full system as a proprietary product. Not until two years later did Recon Central (by that time called Avionics Central) install Data Corporation software (described later).

Development of Data Central Online System

With the termination in October 1967 of Air Force support for developing a production online system, and with the beginning in September of a project with a new sponsor (OBAR, described later), Data Corporation began in-house to develop a generalized full-text database management system to be called Data Central. Data Corporation funded the work, with the objective of developing their own proprietary product. Giering (1967b) was convinced that such a system could be generalized to work with all kinds of files; it was unnecessary to distinguish between numeric, bibliographic, or full-text database management and search systems. At the start-up, Giering (1967a) reviewed existing and proposed intelligence data handling systems, including his own proposed Data Central, DIA's IBM 1410 Formatted File System (Mark II, III) and 7094 Formatted File System, the National Military Command System Support Center's NIPS system, IBM's 360/50 Formatted File System and GIS, Informatics Mark IV, and SDC's TDMS.

In late 1967, Giering assumed responsibility for designing, implementing, and testing a time-share capability as a first step in the expansion to Data Corporation's own production system. The result was the full implementation of the time-share capability in early 1968 on the original breadboard version at Recon Central. The breadboard version was used, instead of the newer production system, as an attempt to interest Recon Lab management in buying into the time-shared capability and supporting an upgrade to their current system. Up until then Gorog and other Data Corporation management were unsure that a production capability could be achieved within the planned time and budget constraints. The implementation of the time-sharing capability, however, convinced them; in spring 1968 they assigned Giering to manage the complete conversion of the breadboard into a commercially viable production system that could process all types of files, and the associated business, including planned data centers at Washington, D.C., Dayton, and WPAFB. This was to be an in-house project, funded by Data Corporation. Beta testing of the production version of Data Central began in mid-1968 at Union Carbide, using chemical compound files. The feasibility test resulted in Union Carbide purchasing this early model in summer 1969 for installation in their Charleston, West Virginia, facility.

Comparing the 1968 system with other systems available then shows the different philosophical approaches to system design. Giering (1983) described it as the first "recursive full-text search system." Observers at other organizations later described it as the first *semi*-recursive full-text search system because it only narrowed the previous search result, and only a single answer set was retained. They also stated that it had no index display function. It is true that only a single answer set was provided, and that prior, intermediate search results could not be used later in the same search operation. The concept of recursiveness was being implemented with both the Data Corporation and Lockheed systems, but by different modes. The two teams of designers had different ideas about which features had priority. For example, Lockheed gave high priority to index displays and the use of set numbers; Data Corporation gave priority to full-text searching, KWIC, and color displays.

In mid-1968, Data Corporation opened a service bureau that hosted several online files and experiments, described later. This was shortly after Horty left the University of Pittsburgh and founded Aspen Systems Corporation and its computer service bureau of full-text legal information. The Data Corporation facility was located in an industrial area of Arlington, Virginia—just outside Washington, D.C. The office was on the second floor above a large metalworking shop. Working the phones and the terminals was difficult when the metal stamping machines were in operation, jiggling the floors. Giering (1995) recalled that he arranged to receive advance notice of scheduled heavy stamping, or cutting of I-beams, so he could shut down all the computers to avoid the problems that the shaking and vibration of the building and everything in it caused. Robert Bennett (1997) described the building as having "rat holes and falling metal slabs."

In October 1968, the Recon Lab permitted the first public demonstration of the combination of Data Corporation's time-sharing software with Recon Central's search software. The new commercial system, when complete, was Data Central, a generalized IR system with text-searching capabilities and online remote access. This first demonstration of Version One was at the ASIS annual meeting in Columbus, Ohio, using multiple IBM 1050 terminals and Teletypes, and databases of OBAR legal texts, a personnel file, and COSATI-sponsored R&D project descriptions (DD Form 1498s). Giering had been in a great rush to get the system operable in order to demonstrate at the ASIS meeting, where he showed that his system could easily accommodate four terminals and multiple files. This was probably the first public demonstration of an online search system specifically designed for full-text searching—no other full-text online search system was on the market at that time. To process full-text material, the system automatically derived an inverted file, or keyword dictionary, from all words in the file except for a stop list of common words deemed to possess no retrieval value.[5] Every word in the inverted file and combinations of them were searchable.

OBAR

Even before Air Force support was phasing out, Gorog made the overture to the Ohio Bar to demonstrate Data Corporation's software to them and to convince them of the feasibility of using the Recon Central techniques in the full-text search of legal documents. Along with Gorog, Giering and Eugene Bold represented Data Corporation in the discussions, and Harrington and Preston represented Ohio Bar interests. By fall 1967, the participants decided that the Ohio State Bar Association, via its new subsidiary corporation called OBAR, was to provide an online service and contract with Data Corporation to supply the necessary software and database support. This was an ambitious project, considering that OBAR was less than a year old.

The Ohio Bar Association formed OBAR as a subsidiary nonprofit corporation in January 1967, with Preston as president. Even with its own staff to manage its computerized research program, OBAR remained closely associated with and under the control of the Ohio Bar; OBAR's executive vice president, Harrington, was also research and legislative counsel for the Ohio Bar, and the OBAR trustees were the members of the Ohio Bar executive committee. Attorneys in Ohio had already gained some familiarity with computer searching of legal materials. The Ohio Legislative Service Commission had contracted Horty at the University of Pittsburgh to produce a full-text file of the Ohio Revised Code and the Ohio Constitution, which they received in 1966 (Eriksson and Johnston 1967). Searches of the file convinced many attorneys of the utility of such a service. In September 1967, after seeing presentations by a number of computer firms, OBAR signed a contract with Data Corporation, represented by Gorog and Giering (Troy 1969). Under the contract, Data Corporation was to adapt their full-text retrieval system to law documents.

The 1967 contract was for a feasibility test that required the loading of a 50-million-character file. After the successful feasibility test, the contract was amended to call for online service and other features. The contract and amendments thus provided the following: (1) Data Corporation would modify its retrieval software to make it more suitable for legal research (OBAR would pay a fee for the modifications and would own the exclusive right to use the resulting software for legal research); (2) Data Corporation would convert Ohio case law and statutes into machine-readable form for use with the system (OBAR would pay the cost of conversion and own the database); (3) Data Corporation would run the operating system, providing all necessary hardware, software, communications, and personnel to support the service for Ohio lawyers; (4) OBAR would market the service; and (5) sales revenues would be divided between OBAR and Data Corporation (Harrington 1984–1985).

The modifications deemed necessary to make the software acceptable to OBAR included all the features mentioned earlier to move the breadboard version to a production version—namely, introducing proximity logic based on number of words separating search terms rather than their coincident appearance in the same sentences or paragraphs; changing the stop word list, including a means to have different word lists for different applications; and extending the communications capability so that the OBAR service would be Teletype-compatible in addition to being compatible with IBM terminals. Later contract amendments essentially nullified the elements of exclusivity, OBAR's paying for and owning the database, and the division of revenues.

The first step in the project was Data Corporation's attempt to prove that Data Central (this is close to the time that the name came into use) could support legal research. The system supported four online devices. The first database for OBAR consisted of fifty recent volumes of Ohio Supreme Court Reports (50 million characters). The file was keypunched and loaded for testing. The planned addition of the full text of all reported Ohio case law, plus the Ohio Revised Code, would total at least 450 million characters (Troy 1969). One result of the keypunching, however, was a realization of the huge magnitude of the data conversion. Neither Data Corporation nor OBAR had sufficient funds for building such a large file (Giering 1995).

The OBAR corporation sold debentures to members of the Ohio Bar to raise the funds for the contract (Harrington 1970). With these bonds and additional loans, OBAR raised and committed $250,000 to start the OBAR system and service. In the opinion of Preston (1971), Data Corporation "would probably never have entered the legal field, except for the Ohio State Bar Association" (190).

An important event took place at this time: Mead Corporation's acquisition of Data Corporation. The OBAR story continues later in this chapter.

Acquisition of Data Corporation by Mead

Fortunately for the development of Data Central, the funding problem was resolved, at least for start-up costs, in 1968 when Mead acquired Data Corporation and made available a substantial amount of investment capital (Harrington 1984–1985). Pemberton (1994) reported that Mead purchased Data Corporation for $6 million.

Bayer (1987) related a legend of how Mead, a Dayton paper manufacturing company, happened to purchase a computer software firm:

Bill Gorog [president of Data Corporation] made a lot of money and became a wealthy man. His backyard literally backed up over the fence to Jim McSweeney's [president, soon to be chairman, of Mead]. They were backyard buddies in a fine neighborhood in Dayton. They got to talking about how Gorog thought that the software could be used beyond this reconnaissance application, and how they had already approached the Ohio Bar and had already formed OBAR. Gorog and McSweeney were just talking about this as business people do, and somewhere along the line McSweeney said, "This is a good idea. We want to do something with this." Mead was at the beginning of its diversification phase, and the decision as I understand it (the story could be 95 percent legend and only 5 percent fact), was made over their common backyard to develop the OBAR concept with money that McSweeney and Mead Corporation could bring to the party.

Giering (1995)—who was in a better position than was Bayer to know the true story—said that the legend was common knowledge among Data Corporation employees at that time, and that Bayer's story is only slightly incorrect:

Data Corporation was jointly and equally owned by Bill Gorog and Lysle Cahill. Bill was the driving force behind cameras and computer technology, while Lysle was more interested in photography (film, etc.) and other reconnaissance applications. As I remember the story, it was Lysle who was Jim McSweeny's neighbor. While it is my understanding that OBAR was mentioned in the backyard discussion, it counted for no more or less than a number of other activities . . .

Gorog (1997) confirmed that Cahill, not Gorog, was McSweeney's neighbor, adding:

There were two main reasons why Mead bought Data Corporation: (1) unknown impact of computers on the paper industry; (2) ink jet technology. At that time, people were saying, 'Computers are going to eliminate paper overnight.' Mead wanted to hedge their future position. Furthermore, Mead was exploring new printing technology, and had some good techniques, but Data Corporation had the technology and experience in the electronics side of the ink jet printers. So OBAR and ink jet technology were the main reasons behind the acquisition. Jim McSweeney, who started as a non-college trained time clerk, was very perceptive, and had a nose for the right things at the right time.

Harrington (1984–1985, 550) supplied another perspective on the acquisition:

[Mead] did not acquire Data Corporation to become a partner in the OBAR experiment, but to acquire other Data Corporation technology more closely related to Mead's traditional lines of business in forest products, paper, and printing. Indeed, it has been said that Mead was not even aware that Data Corporation was committed by contract to an effort to build a computer-assisted legal research service. Nevertheless, Mead rescued the OBAR experiment from imminent financial failure and in time invested the tens of millions of dollars the development of a nationwide system for computer-assisted legal research would require.

Giering (1995) agreed with Harrington's comment about Mead's lack of awareness of Data Corporation's extensive work in OBAR and legal research at the time of the acquisition. Giering recalled that in early 1969, when he was the director of Data Corporation's Information Systems Division (ISD) and responsible for all of the computer business, members of the Mead staff came to Data Corporation to "find out what they had gotten, and how it could fit into their corporate family," and it was quite a shock for them to find that ISD had such a significant ongoing business, while simultaneously pursuing developmental activities toward even bigger future opportunities (e.g., OBAR). Bennett (1997) also confirmed that Mead did not know what they were buying when they acquired Data Corporation. They bought it for other reasons, and then they took inventory and found the OBAR activity. That is when they brought in A. D. Little and Jerome Rubin to look at it: "What is this thing? Is there anything to it?"

In the months following the acquisition, Data Corporation continued with its ventures as before, but the entire enterprise would soon change.

Data Central System Enhancements: Version One

The developing Data Central system offered a powerful combination of retrieval capabilities. In summer 1969, Version One of the commercial system was demonstrated for the legal service from Dayton and for several government service contracts. Giering (1995) considered Version One to be the "first real production model." At that time, Mead had IBM 360 computers in Dayton and Arlington Verginia.

> **1969 Milestone**
>
> Data Central was among the first online search systems to demonstrate word proximity searching (i.e., allowing word sequence and proximity to be part of the search formulation).

Searchers could specify distance between search terms. The SRI online search system (chapter 2) had demonstrated simple word pair or adjacent word searching in 1963, and its designers had proposed a form of proximity searching (two search terms within the same sentence) but had never implemented it. Data Central was among the first online search systems to demonstrate this capability (IBM Terminal TEXT-PAC—chapter 4—was the other one). This system also included capabilities for truncating search terms and searching with a "universal" or "wild" character (for example, SM*TH for "Smith" or "Smyth"). First demonstrated with the MIT-TIP system in 1965 (chapter 2), this wild character was a significant feature of Version One. Plural or possessive forms of words containing five or more letters in the singular, regularly formed search word, were automatically retrieved when the singular form was entered. Thus, PICTURE retrieved items containing PICTURES, PICTURE'S and PICTURES'. Irregular plurals such as GOOSE and GEESE were handled as synonyms where they each had to be included in a list. The search logic included standard Boolean and arithmetic operators. Version One was modifiable to fit many computer and terminal hardware configurations, including high speed (120 cps) black and white CCI (Computer Communications, Inc.) CRT terminals as well as other terminal types. Several organizations adapted it to various kinds of applications.

> **1970 Milestones**
>
> Data Central was the first online search system to highlight the terms in the retrieved records that caused a record to be retrieved.
>
> Data Central was the first online search system to allow users to generate a KWIC display of a specified number of text words on either side of a search term in the retrieved text.

The KWIC release of Data Central was introduced in fall 1970. This version allowed an online user to obtain a personalized abstract or extract of a record retrieved. Whereas the usual use for KWIC processing was to provide an index display of selected words in the context of other words in the title of a publication, KWIC in the Data Corporation system displayed the keywords used as search terms, as they were found in the file record, along with the surrounding context words; the display took the form of sentences containing the search terms, and when strung together for the same record, gave the sense of a meaningful extract. At the same time, the full-text display included color highlighting ("KWIC" for Data Corporation also meant keyword-in-color). Giering's incorporation of the KWIC feature probably stemmed from his familiarity, as described earlier, with the BIDAP batch programs that he had used at DIA.

The introduction of terminals with screens not only made the system faster and easier to use, it made the KWIC feature feasible. KWIC highlighted the words in the source text that caused the item to be retrieved. A variety of ways to achieve the highlighted effect were tested. For black-and-white terminals, the words could be accented by blinking them, dropping them a little below the level of the others on the line, varying the light intensity, or simply flagging them with an arrow or asterisk (Lancaster and Fayen 1973). The search terms could also be highlighted showing them as black-on-white, with the surrounding text displayed as white-on-black (Rubin 1974). For printing terminals such as the Teletype or IBM 2740, highlighting could be underlining or surrounding the term with asterisks or other special characters.

> **1970 Milestones**
>
> Data Central was the first online search system to use a color CRT output device.
>
> Data Central was the first online search system to use color contrast in search output displays to highlight the search term in the retrieved record.

The first color terminals were put into use in June 1970, with various colors for various parts of the records. Using Sony television sets for screens, the first color terminals displayed the output "in gaudy colors—case names in green, citations in yellow, KWIC words in red, ordinary text in white—all on a bright blue background" (Harrington 1984–1985, 551). A later terminal that provided four colors for output display showed field designators in green, terms matching the query in red, fifteen significant words on each side of the term in yellow, and all other information in blue (Fong 1971). This highlighting feature allowed lawyers or their assistants to skim through large amounts of material and print out each place a decision was cited, with the accompanying comments on each side, to study for relevance later. The feature had been available on the original Data Central program, but in this context it was dubbed "OBARizing" (Preston 1971, 191).

> **1970 Milestone**
>
> Data Central was the first online search system to allow searchers to page backward to reexamine previously displayed records.

The use of CRTs was not the only improvement at this time. Rubin (1974, 49) commented that "MDC removed most of the mystifying computerese and refined the man-machine interface by adding ... the ability to flip back and forth from page to page and from case to case." The enhancements endowed "computer-assisted research with the iterative quality of book research, . . . [and] greatly enhanced the MDC system to the point that it was regarded less as an interesting experiment and more as a tool with practical value."

Giering (1972) described the characteristics of the system as they existed then. Giering (1983) recalled attending the AFIPS meeting in 1971 in Palo Alto, California, where many of the early designers described their systems. He remembered coming away feeling terribly happy because his system seemed to be "the best of the bunch" at that time.

OBAR System Expansion

From 1967 through 1969, a great deal was accomplished in developing the OBAR retrieval system. Preston and Harrington traveled throughout Ohio selling OBAR bonds and encouraging law firms to become subscribers to the service. In mid-1969, testing of the OBAR database started with a limited number of Teletype terminals in law offices, while Data Corporation continued developing their commercial system. Data Corporation sales staff and OBAR representatives arranged full beta testing in law firms around Ohio, starting in 1970.

In the middle of 1969, an evaluation confirmed that OBAR had demonstrated feasibility of computer-assisted legal research. Nevertheless, Harrington (1984–1985) observed: "The computer system and its communications were unreliable, the search protocol was less than transparent, there was an unacceptable degradation in response time when more than a few lawyers were doing research at the same time, and the data base was too small for much practical research" (549).

OBAR was using Data Corporation's system as a service bureau; the contract was not just for software development. OBAR was actually one of several clients for Data Corporation's new service bureau. In offering this legal research service, OBAR took flak from outside critics who were strong advocates of the then-popular West Publishing's printed products with the West Key Number system—a manually assigned key number that represented key phrases in a controlled indexing vocabulary. OBAR nonetheless stood its ground and continued supporting the innovative service.

1969 Milestones

Using Data Central, OBAR was the first large-scale use of online full-text searching.

Using Data Central, OBAR was the first large-scale online system to operate with full-text statutory and case law.

In spring 1969, OBAR began adding more retrospective legal material to the database. By February 1970, it contained 550 million characters. Beginning in 1969 Data Corporation, through OBAR, offered a limited number of Ohio lawyers a prototype online full-text statutory and case law retrieval system. Harrington mentioned in 1970 that the attorney general of Ohio was the first OBAR subscriber, but he later contradicted that statement, saying that Squire, Sanders, and Dempsey had been the first and that the law firm also loaned money to OBAR to support the venture (1984–1985). Giering (1995) affirmed that the Ohio attorney general *was* an early user, but he believed that Data Corporation furnished it free of charge; thus he may have been the first *user*, but definitely not the first *subscriber*. Data Corporation installed teletypewriter terminals in fifteen locations, including private law firms and public law offices. The Teletypes communicated directly with the computer over long-distance telephone lines. Preston (1971) said that price schedules were still in the experimental stages, but he suggested $75 per hour. Giering (1995) admitted that pricing was experimental because no other service was in the marketplace, and they had no guidance on the product's price sensitivity. They had concerns about price in relation to such factors as volume of data available online, terminal type, and line speeds used. The $75 figure was an average; in discussions in-house and with lawyers around the state, the fee ranged from much less to costs of double that figure.

In spite of the simplicity of the interface design and the tailoring of the system to lawyers' needs and preferences, the lawyers' need for a day or two of training became apparent, as did the need for a manual (*Search instructions for OBAR*, reproduced in Lancaster and Fayen 1973, 460–466).

Harrington (1970) reported that the number of installations had grown to twenty, but that not all users were enjoying great success: "Effective use of the computer requires precision of legal terminology and logical organization of thought. There is definitely a skill to be developed in the use of the computer, and not every lawyer develops it as readily as any other" (1148). He maintained nonetheless that the OBAR system had proven to be practicable and workable, and was in increasing use in law offices in all major cities of Ohio. In response to the wishes of Ohio lawyers, a complete library of all Ohio primary legal research materials was online, including the full text of the Ohio constitution and code plus the full text of all reported decisions of the supreme court, courts of appeals and lower courts of Ohio. Harrington (1974) confirmed that this was what Ohio lawyers wanted at that time.

Such comments reflect the experience during the beta test period for Version One (the commercial system). MDC staff concluded that the beta tests were less than a complete success because of (1) lack of reliable service; (2) terminal equipment that was slow (10cps) and noisy (clattering Teletypes were out of place in law offices); and (3) a database that was too small. While the Ohio case law went back to about 1903, the lawyers wanted it all, regardless of the cost-effectiveness of loading the old data. Rubin (1998) remembered the OBAR system's inadequacies: "With more than one user online or a search of any complexity, a search could run five or six hours or even more." These problems appeared to be solvable and the system could be fully developed, but more money would be required than OBAR had available or could raise, and probably more than Data Corporation could commit by itself at that time.

A company reorganization in February 1970 resulted in the removal of all OBAR activities from Data Corporation and their placement under the control of a new organization, Mead Data Central.

Harrington (1970) characterized the computerized legal research system that had been developed cooperatively between OBAR and MDC by four important features that in combination distinguished it from any other system offered to the legal profession at that time. These features were as follows: (1) the system searched the full text of the material; there was no indexing, digesting, or other editing or tampering with the original materials; (2) it was a full time-sharing system, which meant that each lawyer could communicate directly with the computer without the intervention of a third party; (3) the program permitted lawyers to conduct a continuing dialogue with the computer, which allowed them to review legal materials quickly and thoroughly; and (4) the search product was the full text of the material. Furthermore, a lawyer could search "entirely on the basis of his own judgment as to what materials he wants to see and how he wants them searched, with a high degree of accommodation to his own personal research preferences and habits. The lawyer is not compelled to adapt himself to the computer's method of search; the computer adapts itself to him" (1146).

Based on the experience of the first group of users, MDC made a number of modifications during 1970 and 1971, including replacing the slow teletypewriter terminals with CRTs that were twelve times faster. Rubin (1974, 49) remarked:

The original (1969) MDC-OBAR system was crippled by the teletypewriter terminal, which could type only ten characters a second. Thus the extent to which a lawyer could refine a search request to produce the most relevant cases was limited by the terminal's inability to print out retrieved cases quickly enough for the user to determine relevance. In 1970, MDC remedied the problem by replacing teletypewriter terminals with CRT terminals (accompanied by hard-copy printers), which could display lawyer-system dialogue at a rate of 120 characters a second.

Results from a 1970 study by James Carlisle (Yale University) of lawyers and law students using the MDC system for full-text retrieval influenced the decision to move from Teletypes to display terminals. At that time, about forty law firms in Ohio had Teletypes; by January 1971 all had CRTs ("Session IV" 1971).

Although the OBAR/MDC system was serving only a few Ohio lawyers in 1970, the OBAR and MDC executives—including Harrington of OBAR, H. Donald Wilson, president of MDC, Rubin, vice president (later president) of MDC, and Bennett, MDC's director of training—all were attorneys and all had expansive visions for the future. They anticipated that ultimately as many as 300 communications terminals might be located in Ohio. According to Harrington (1970, 1147, 1148), they even looked beyond the boundaries of Ohio:

Negotiations are already well under way with several other state bar associations who wish to establish computerized research systems. As those states build data bases of their state law, the data will be made reciprocally available. It used to seem that this goal was as much as ten years away, but the technology has progressed more rapidly over the past year than anyone anticipated. The day may be near when a lawyer can reach the law of any state or any part of the federal law by using a communications terminal in his office to command a computer.

It was never intended that the O.B.A.R. system should be for Ohio lawyers only. The Ohio State Bar Association committed itself to the initial work of building a system that would be of value to all lawyers. Mead Data Central, Inc. is committed to the building of a national system.

To assist MDC in expanding the system, OBAR staff fielded hundreds of inquiries, visited many states as well as ABA meetings, and received delegations from the bar associations of many states.

Mark Bayer (1987), an early employee who conducted demonstrations of the system to lawyers, described his experiences as "missionary work."

We used to carry these big old machines around . . . We had a Model 25 Teletype machine, along with a 110 baud external modem with an acoustic coupling unit for the telephone handset, all mounted on a big piece of plywood that we put in the back of a station wagon. We employed a driver just to help carry this equipment up and down the stairs from their second floor Iron Works office, load it into the company station wagon, and help get it out of the car and into the demonstration location. We had to carry it up and put it on a desk in a law firm *and* we had to do something behind the scenes—we had to kick users off the computer, stop programming, and take everything possible out of the foreground, if not the background, and run almost a single-user system to get meaningful, reasonable, response times. We used to plot and scheme like you wouldn't believe, to give a demonstration at a major law firm, to convince them that this was "representative service."

Chapter 10 introduces others who were willing to "plot and scheme like you wouldn't believe," in order to convince potential users of the value of these fledgling services. These "missionaries" were indispensable agents for achieving the ambitions of the online entrepreneurs.

In an early 1972 presentation, Robert Asman (1973), president of OBAR, described for an audience of lawyers—mainly those who had invested in OBAR bonds—the OBAR projects and experiences in glowing terms. He discussed OBAR retail search services for institutions that could not justify the establishment of their own terminal facility, and pilot projects with law schools (including assistance in the development of a law school's "OBAR Room." He mentioned the agreement between MDC and OBAR, but it was clear that it was the OBAR service that was being promoted and used, and *not* the MDC service. The OBAR system interface and search products in 1971 said, "You are now in communication with (Data) Central," and there was no mention of Mead. Giering (1995) observed that interface wording caused contention, and this particular message was at the heart of the disagreement. Many institutional customers of Data Central were using the same computer with different files; OBAR was only one, albeit a large one. The computer interacted simultaneously with several different user populations while giving each user the impression that they were connected to a computer dedicated to their particular database and application. OBAR wanted the log-in message to be legal-oriented such as: "You have reached the OBAR legal research service." The log-in message dilemma contributed to a September 1971 split within MDC, discussed later (Giering 1995).

When the Ohio State Bar Association began investigating existing programs, it became convinced that the legal profession would be served best if the Bar retained substantial control (McCabe 1973). The Ohio legal fraternity accepted that argument and worked to make the search service subordinate to the legal profession. Mead inherited that situation when they acquired Data Corporation, and continued to embrace a philosophy of partnerships with bar associations. MDC continued that partnership pattern when they signed a contract in January 1971 with the NYSBA to provide for the gradual introduction of MDC service in New York. Under the terms of that contract, NYSBA would attempt to obtain from the State of New York the right to use the copyrighted legal material and would sponsor the MDC system as the official system of the New York State Bar. Flavin (1973, 52), reporter for the State of New York, commented: "We had confidence in the system and the company from the beginning. Nothing has happened since to shake that confidence. Quite the contrary, Mead Data has shown clear indication of its good faith by carrying out the agreement as written, particularly by investing a rather large sum of money."

Mead continued discussions with other state bar associations in 1972 to arrange for the system's availability under those associations. A major reason for working with the bar associations was an expectation of enhanced prestige and contacts when Mead was working with high-powered lawyers and judges. A secondary reason was to acquire the source materials of those states; in Ohio, and in many other states at that time, the copyright to the printed court decision publications was in the hands of the respective state bar associations.

During 1970–1972, MDC accomplished much: marketing the idea of full-text retrieval to lawyers and bar associations outside Ohio, expanding the file to over 500 million characters, and ironing out some of the technical problems in natural language retrieval. In spite of the debate raging in the information science field at the time concerning indexing by means of the automatic processing of full text versus indexing by means of human assignment of terms from a controlled vocabulary, MDC continued undeterred in its mission to launch a nationwide legal information research system. During this same time, OBAR as an organization faded from the picture. It sold its proprietary interests and the Ohio database to MDC in return for ten years of royalty payments, and for all practical purposes it ceased operations in February 1971. After five years of intense involvement with this online search system, Harrington returned to private law practice in Columbus, but he continued as a consultant to MDC. Diana Fitch McCabe published an article in 1971 that identified obstacles to using OBAR (McCabe 1971). From her vantage point as an employee, she saw that OBAR, instead of meeting the promise that the founders had for it—to give solo or small-firm attorneys as much research power as large firms had (and thus benefit lower-income and middle-class clients)—was instead developing into a service that only large firms could afford. That pattern of Mead actually discouraging smaller firms from using its system continued into the late 1970s. Some observers felt that this was a strategic error that later allowed an opening for WESTLAW. Bennett (1997) took issue with that suggestion—he felt that the new service, LEXIS, would have died if they had catered to less wealthy clients at that time: "We were charging the equivalent of $165 per hour, and if we couldn't make a go of it with the big law firms that could afford to pay, then it wouldn't have worked with the small law firms. So we went where the money was, to confirm that there was a sufficient market there to permit the business to get started." OBAR annual revenues reached $2 million in 1972. By the end of 1972, the Ohio market test of the second-generation system was complete, and the system was ready for nationwide marketing. The tale of the transformation of Data Corporation/MDC activities into the Mead LEXIS service, and the launch of LEXIS in April 1973 as a publicly available commercial service, continues in chapter 9.

In addition to the individuals who participated in the planning, research, and development, OBAR owes much of its success to early users, who made an invaluable contribution. Asman (1973, 47) said:

> The success of this... depends upon the patience and endurance of the users. If our subscribers in Ohio survive the barrage of questionnaires, interviews, consultants or experts, if they can sit through our search framing classes, training sessions, meetings, speeches, and slide presentations, if they can live with our equipment experimentation and our pricing strategies, and if they can tolerate our incessant curiosity, you have them to thank for being willing to be the most thoroughly dissected live animal in this hemisphere.

Some of these "dissected live animals" are introduced in chapter 10.

Other Applications of Data Central

Union Carbide's Study

In fall 1968, Edward Brunenkant, director of the AEC's Division of Technical Information (DTI), indicated his desire to create an effective retrieval system for long-term AEC program interests. He invited Data Corporation to come to AEC's DTIE at Oak Ridge, Tennessee, to demonstrate Data Central in November 1968. The demonstration was effective, and DTIE requested that AEC Oak Ridge contractor Union Carbide and its CTC conduct a review of the possibility and relative costs of using Data Central over a three-year period to provide online access to six organizations (major user sites), with an initial file of one volume of *Nuclear Science Abstracts* (75 million characters). Union Carbide's study examined alternative means, with cost estimates, of using Data Central to provide remote online access to *NSA* (Kidd, Price, and Yount 1969; Buchanan and Kidd 1969). They concluded that Data Central might be employed in either of two ways: (1) use it to store and access a file at a Data Corp. facility in Dayton or in Washington, D.C.; or (2) purchase and adapt the software and install the system on the government-owned computers at CTC in Oak Ridge. The files were to be updated every two weeks, and the system was to support six terminals.

Upon completion of the study, DTIE was surprised to find out that the costs would be much higher than they had expected. The three-year costs would be about three-quarters of a million dollars for an Oak Ridge installation, and about 2 million for service bureau operation by Data Corporation.[6] The software by itself was priced then at $160,000. As Vaden (1969) of DTIE declared, "To say that we were astonished at these cost estimates would be putting it mildly. We didn't even have enough money to purchase the program, let alone modify it and run it" (2). So they looked again at alternative possibilities, including an earlier system at Oak Ridge (RANSAC) that used a weighted-term approach with Eurotom indexing, Stanford's SPIRES, and NASA/RECON. In discussing RECON with Wente of NASA, DTIE staff learned that because the RECON programs were already government-owned, AEC could obtain and install them at little additional cost. Following RECON demonstrations and discussions with NASA staff members, Lockheed received a nine-month (June 15, 1969, to March 31, 1970), $60,000 contract to install the RECON software at AEC, instead of using Data Central (Vaden 1992). DTIE did not solicit a proposal from Data Corporation for AEC/DOE's internal online system. (The AEC/RECON story is in chapters 5 and 9.)

The Oak Ridge effort was not a complete loss for Data Corporation. By mid-1969, the company had sold and installed a beta version (pre–Version One) of the system at Union Carbide's Charleston, West Virginia, facility for use in tracking research in the chemical field. (This facility had served as a beta test site for the system.) At this time, Data Corporation had two commercial service bureaus (at Dayton and Arlington) and one government contract facility (Recon Central).

BEER Database Application

Following up on a feasibility study begun in 1968, the BEER (Biological Effects from Non-Electromagnetic Radiation) database, a bibliographic database of all relevant documents in the field was loaded onto the Recon Central system in summer 1969. BEER was produced by the U.S. Army's Walter Reed Army Medical Center. It later moved to the Arlington service bureau, where it continued at least into 1972.

TIMPS/ENVIRON Database Application

The TIMPS (Technical Information Management and Planning System) file was loaded on the Data Corporation system in 1967 and ran there until 1973, when it went to Informatics and was renamed ENVIRON (Bayer 1980). In 1969, the U.S. Federal Water Pollution Control Agency used Data Central as a service bureau to load the ENVIRON (Environmental Information Retrieval Online) project descriptions on Data Corporation's Arlington computer. The U.S. Environmental Protection Agency (EPA) used Data Central in 1971 for a large file containing legal, technical, and management data; data on pesticides, toxic spills, research, and chemical companies; and files on all water-quality monitoring stations throughout the country. In Henderson 1973, Powell stated, "We have an on-line system that is presently on-line about 8 hours a day, with the software package as well as the time-shared capability provided by Mead Data Corporation" (42). The file was used with terminals in most EPA regional offices, and continued at Data Corporation at least into 1972.

PADAT

From 1968 to 1970, the APA worked on a plan for developing a national information system for psychology. A national retrospective search service was among the possibilities considered. King and Caldwell (1970) studied and reported on such a plan. Data Corporation established a contract with APA in summer 1969 to provide an experimental online search service called PADAT (Psychological Abstracts–Direct Access Terminal). Data Central's Arlington service bureau made *Psychological Abstracts* available online to subscribers of the print product in 1971 and 1972. This was before APA put their file on DIALOG and other online services. Data Corporation's service bureau converted significant amounts of APA data, both by in-house keyboarding and by offshore contractors, and some was converted by Inforonics.[7] The database comprised bibliographic records with abstracts (Lancaster and Fayen 1973; Gechman 1972). In 1971, APA offered three ways to access Psychological Abstracts in machine-readable form: (1) a quarterly tape subscription service called PATELL (PA Tape Edition–Leased or Licensing); (2) a retrospective search service called PASAR (PA Search and Retrieval); and (3) the PADAT online service.

EARS

In 1969, NIH awarded to Data Corporation a contract to load *Epilepsy Abstracts* online. The EMF made the file available in machine-readable form as a by-product of their publishing operation, and Data Corporation loaded it on Data Central's computer in Arlington.

The system acquired the name EARS (Epilepsy Abstracts Retrieval System) for the experiment after online access to some of the data was first demonstrated in May 1969 (Porter, Penry, and Caponio 1971); J. Kiffin Penry and Joseph Caponio (1969) gave a public demonstration in September 1969 in San Diego, California, at the Congress of Electroencephalography and Clinical Neurophysiology, using only Volume 1 (1,301 abstracts) as the EPIL database. Congress attendees were able to interact with the system, using a Teletype or CRT terminal to the Arlington computer. They could search on the full text of the complete informative abstract, as well as on the article title (English or other language) and primary or secondary indexing terms.

Between April and July 1971, the NINDS supported an experiment and evaluation in which biomedical practitioners at six U.S. medical centers used this system. The records consisted of the 8,000 citations and their abstracts and assigned index terms in *Epilepsy Abstracts*. The database was available for four hours per week (later extended to 8) via Teletype terminals. A total of forty-seven searches were completed during the experiment—sixteen different users at six centers (Porter, Penry, and Caponio 1971). (Other reports based on this study were Lancaster 1971b; Rapport, Lancaster, and Penry 1972; and Lancaster, Rapport, and Penry 1972.)

The EARS tests and the AIM/TWX tests (chapter 6) both were concerned with online access to medical literature, were comparable in scope, and took place at almost the same time. Although Lancaster participated in both evaluations, NLM's AIM-TWX experiments received much wider attention. MDC lost an opportunity here for publicity; the EARS evaluation received little publicity because MDC senior management did not care much then about NLM or any market not directly related to the legal one. During spring and summer 1971, MDC management agonized over which direction the business should pursue. One faction wanted to *concentrate* on legal research, while another wanted to exploit the technology across the marketplace, *including* legal research. During this period, MDC lost many opportunities in the nonlegal marketplace.

NINDS used the EARS contract to experiment with abstracts of articles in neurology, and to estimate costs for a projected NINDS online retrieval system for neurology.[8] No follow-up contract with MDC existed, however, to provide such a service.

Avionics Central

In mid-1970, the Air Force library known as Recon Central was renamed Avionics Central, to match a change in the Air Force lab name. Up until that time, Recon Central had continued to use the breadboard version of the Data Central search system, which it had received as a deliverable from the development contract with Data Corporation. With an improved production version now available, Avionics Central contracted with MDC in October 1970 to obtain a copy of Data Central to replace the limited breadboard system. Avionics Central then began dial-up service with CRT terminals. Avionics Central used MDC software at its own facility to provide "private-file" service to other organizations. Avionics Central's use of MDC's Data Central software at its own facility to provide private file service to other organizations, as if it were a commercial service bureau instead of a federal agency, was in competition with MDC and led to major disagreements between those parties in later years.

HEW Database Application

In January 1971, a database in support of audiovisual materials (e.g., equipment, slides, films, AV project information) was loaded for HEW. This application continued into 1973 when a concerted federal effort was made to integrate all AV files into one application. In 1971–1972, HEW also had a bibliographic file online with Data Corporation that was a catalog of all publications produced by any of HEW's components (e.g., FDA, NIH).

Mead Personnel Files Application

In mid-1971, a database was loaded to support the complete personnel files for all Mead employees. This application included structured data as well as full-text information such as résumés, job descriptions, annual evaluations, and reports on labor grievances and negotiations. The system also generated various required reports for governmental and in-house use. This was a dynamic file that required an extensive file-maintenance capability.

COSATI Demonstrations

The story of the 1969 COSATI demonstrations, film, and comparative study of contemporaneous online bibliographic search systems is in chapter 4. Data Corporation participated and Welch (1968) described the Data Central features for the study. The demonstrations were done with the limited breadboard system.

With contract support from COSATI, Data Corporation started in mid-1969 loading files that included (1) summary data of federally-sponsored information sciences R&D projects; (2) bibliographic records from Battelle's Information Research Center; (3) bibliographic records from NBS on the subject of computer science; (4) bibliographic records for all references in volumes 1–3 of *Annual Review of Information Science and Technology*; and (5) a 3000-term glossary of information science terms. The contract support for Data Corporation was provided by means of a subcontract to IGC (with Bourne serving as project leader at IGC), the contractor responsible for preparing the database for the COSATI inventory of federally sponsored information sciences R&D projects. The IGC contract started in August 1968 (Bourne, North, and Kasson 1969).

In May 1969, with encouragement from Landau of the U.S. President's Office of Science and Technology, Data Corporation demonstrated its system in Philadelphia at the Sixth Annual National Colloquium on Information Retrieval. Landau (1969) announced to the attendees, "The system that you will see downstairs this evening, which is run by a company called Data Corporation, is a network which is already operating in the government now, and a group of agencies is experimentally testing the effectiveness of this system" (362).

SSIE Test

In early 1970, staff of the Smithsonian Science Information Exchange (SSIE) at the Smithsonian Institution loaded a file of research project descriptions (Notices of Research Projects) on the Data Central system for use in an experiment of free-text versus controlled-indexing retrieval. The experimental objective was to compare natural language searching with the conventional subject indexing then being done by SSIE staff. The test used a terminal at SSIE to access the computer at Data Corporation's Arlington office and was complete in early 1970 (Hersey et al. 1970, 1971). The surprising results were that both recall and precision for subject indexing were higher (recall was 30 percent higher and precision was 15–20 percent higher) than for free-text retrieval. However, the researchers concluded that both approaches had some merits.

Arthur D. Little Market Research Study

In early 1969, at Mead's request, Data Corporation began discussions with major international consulting firm Arthur D. Little (ADL) for a market research study of how Data Central technology could be exploited, from a business standpoint, without regard to a specific market. The consulting work culminated in a report in fall 1969. The study concluded that the nonlegal market was too small—that is, no market identified outside the legal research business was big enough to consider.[9]

As a result of the evaluation, the contract was revised to explore the feasibility of a full-text online interactive legal search service. Mead funded and directed the second study to find out if the market were sufficient to justify a major investment, how much further development of OBAR would be required to make it marketable, and how much money the development would cost. ADL sent one of its partners, Donald Wilson, to Ohio as head of a consulting team. Wilson, a lawyer, brought in Edward Gottsman as a consultant in system design.

Seeing the need for a practicing lawyer on the team, the strategic planning group at Mead asked Jerome Rubin also to participate as a consultant. Rubin, a physicist and Harvard-trained lawyer, had practiced law for twenty years, had represented ADL in legal matters, and had an interest in technology. Gorog and Giering represented Data Corp. in the study.

Spin-Off of MDC from Data Corporation

The ADL team for the second study reported in early 1970 that its market survey indicated that computer-assisted legal research was potentially a profitable business. Making a marketable business on the basis of the OBAR experiment, however, would require extensive redevelopment of the software and a major investment. Rubin (1998) recalled that, in the presentation to Mead, "ADL told Mead that it had nothing but an idea, that the OBAR/Data Central software was essentially worthless, but that appropriate software could be developed, and that there was a potential for a significant business." The formation of a new organization, Mead Data Central, was completed by February 1970 to handle that new business, but Data Corporation continued as a separate organization. Rubin (1973) reported: "To manage the project, Mead incorporated the Information Systems division of Data Corporation as a wholly-owned subsidiary. The new company, Mead Data Central, Inc. took over the contract with OBAR and the long-term dedication to providing an efficient and effective computerized research service to lawyers" (36). Years later, Provenzano (1987, 41) reported on an interview with Rubin:

When the A. D. Little team returned with a favorable prognosis, the Mead Corporation decided to 'roll the dice' and fund the project. Jerry [Rubin] formed a venture management firm with H. Donald Wilson, RW Development Corporation, to run the project on a contract basis. Rubin served as president with Wilson as vice president. Mead also formed a subsidiary, Mead Data Central, in which Wilson and Rubin held the same titles but in reverse. After one year, Wilson left Mead Data Central to pursue other interests in venture management.

In an orderly transition, Jerry became president of MDC that same year. Faced with a database in the infant stages of development and a wholly inadequate retrieval system, he brought in a new management team including new technical management and began to build a system.

From that point, publications and pronouncements by the Mead staff associated with legal information services talked about the "OBAR system" and "Mead Data Central" but made no mention of Data Corporation.

The parent Mead Corporation spun all the information science business from Data Corporation to MDC. This included the Arlington service bureau, the information science activities of Recon Central, support for the Union Carbide contract, and OBAR legal research activity (Harrington, Wilson, and Bennett 1971). The restructuring separated the legal research applications from all other existing and potential applications and organized them under a new subsidiary. MDC was to be a wholly owned subsidiary to concentrate on computer-assisted legal IR systems and to develop and market a national legal research service (Harrington 1984–1985).

The staff and activities of the Information Systems Division of Data Corporation (Giering and Peter Vann were codirectors of the Division before the spinoff) became the nucleus of MDC. Many Data Corporation officers and employees transferred to MDC. Technology issues remained Giering's responsibility, and Vann had marketing duties. Giering's group continued to operate as it had before, developing its own software and information services. The new MDC corporate mission was to exploit the business that would result from the Data Central online system. Wilson was the first president of MDC. Giering and Vann from Data Corporation and Rubin were named vice presidents.

In September 1971, MDC decided to concentrate on the selling of legal information, and split the business activity into two groups. The legal search service remained with MDC, and the nonlegal contracts were returned to Data Corporation. In-house, the split was described as the "legal" market and the "illegal" market. While Data Central initially was used by both, during the next eighteen months MDC developed a completely new system that was based on the same technology, but with improved reliability and stronger multi-user capacity, and directed to the legal profession. At that point, the Data Central system and capabilities became the purview of Data Corporation. In March 1972, Data Corporation was renamed Mead Technology Laboratories (MTL) and started marketing its full-text search system under the name Data Central System. It was packaged for IBM 360/370 computers and priced at a lease rate of $1800 per month. MTL continued to work with a variety of databases and users.

As a result of the September 1971 decision, Rubin became president of MDC and Wilson became vice chairman of the board. Rubin released Giering and several other employees he had inherited from Data Corporation; he built a new team comprised primarily of persons from outside Data Corporation. Giering and Vann returned to Data Corporation with the nonlegal business in the newly reconstituted Information Systems Division, and continued developing a general purpose system called Data Central. At MDC, Rubin established some independence from Mead and led the development of a new system dedicated to legal research, later to be known as LEXIS. Rubin (1998) recalled:

I hired Ed Gottsman (a member of the ADL team) to direct the development of an entirely new system (which I later christened LEXIS). Bob Bennett and I designed the new system during the winter, and Bennett, with my kibitzing and amending, wrote the functional specs. Gottsman imposed some feasibility criteria on the specs and took charge of building the system. The functional and performance specs went through several iterations as Bennett and I worked closely with Gottsman, Dana, Brynuck, and Thomson on the technical side, and by late summer of 1972, I approved the definitive specs and turned Gottsman et al. loose to do the coding. During this same period, I also defined our business plan and our pricing and marketing strategy and started sponsorship negotiations with state bar associations and NCAIR. At the same time, Bennett and I defined the contents and structure of the databases (or, as we called them, the libraries), began the massive job of accurate data conversion of the New York and Federal libraries (unlike the OBAR data, which were unacceptably dirty), and designed the training program (including writing the material and making a video).

Bennett joined MDC in September 1970 and soon became a vice president. He assumed operational control after the September 1971 reorganization and remained as executive vice president until he left in September 1981. Before joining Mead, Bennett had worked at the CIA in the Office of the General Counsel; while away from the CIA for a year's training at MIT, he became familiar with the LITE system and became interested in legal text searching. At that time Ed Gottsman, who was working at the CIA as part of an ADL contractor team, introduced Bennett to Jerry Rubin. Bennett joined the Mead team with responsibilities for market testing, service definition and design, terminal specifications, and database contracts; he spent much time with the prototype tests in the Ohio law firms (Bennett 1997). The system that Rubin and his new crew developed was not fully designed until fall 1972 and not actually launched as LEXIS until May 1973. Rubin and Bennett both left the company in September 1981. Chapter 9 discusses LEXIS further.

8 State University of New York Biomedical Communication Network, 1965–1976

Introduction

The tour of universities in chapter 3 described Syracuse's rapid developments between 1966 and 1970, including AUDACIOUS, MOLDS, and SUPARS. However, the most important and enduring project in Syracuse during that period was the Biomedical Communications Network of the State University of New York (SUNY BCN), which evolved years later into the commercial BRS Search Service.

Chapters 5 and 6 described the tangled, convoluted evolution of DIALOG and ORBIT. The developments of OBAR and Data Central in chapter 7 were also complex. By comparison, the formation of SUNY BCN appears unswervingly deliberate and purposeful. Transforming the initial concept, however, to a working online system within three years and without an existing model of a public search service to follow, required imagination, coordination, foresight and, probably, some beginner's luck.

Planning for the service began in 1965 with the establishment of a special task force to study the automation needs of the medical library community. At this point the task force had a vision of improved user services, but had no hardware, software, communications, database, or funds to support any of it. They set for themselves a target date of September 1968 to achieve their task, and they missed the target by only one month. Actually, the system was operational in September, but the dedication ceremony took place October 18, 1968 ("Biomedical Communication Network" 1968). They managed during the planning period to obtain funding support from the state of New York, acquire the magnetic tape records for five years of medical journal literature records from NLM, index a portion of the monographic literature in their own libraries and input it in LC MARC format, construct a new thesaurus, acquire hardware and software from IBM, and pull all of it together into a fully developed, operating online service providing access from remote locations. SUNY BCN was not the first online search system, and it was not the first to operate with multiple online users, but it was the first to provide online service on a regular scheduled basis to a geographically dispersed network of users, with the intent of continuing as a regular service rather than operating as an experiment only. The COLEX system (chapter 6) was in operation at an earlier date as a major network, but by definition COLEX was still an experiment until sometime in 1969, when it was authorized to continue as a regular service under the name of CIRCOL.

A Network of Medical Libraries in New York

The New York Medical Community Vision

The commercial retrieval system known later as BRS Search Service (but no longer operating with that name) was conceptualized in 1965 as part of a network of New York medical libraries. Lacking hardware, software, communications, or even a database, a small group of visionary medical librarians and medical practitioners sparked the idea, based only on a need for improved, faster information services that health professionals could use themselves. An enthusiastic 31-year old librarian named Irwin Pizer led the group. Born in Wellington, New Zealand, Pizer came to the United States and in 1960 earned a degree from the Columbia University School of Library Service. He served a one-year internship at NLM, which proved to be propitious, considering his later cooperative ventures with NLM. He then worked in the School of Medicine Library at Washington University in St. Louis, Missouri, where he participated in Estelle Brodman's experiments in applying computers to library technical processes (Pizer, Franz, and Brodman 1963; Pizer, Anderson, and Brodman 1964). In 1964 he left Washington University and, bringing with him this automation experience, moved to New York State to take the position of librarian of the Upstate Medical Center Library and assistant professor of medical history at SUNY-Syracuse. He was lucky to join an energetic and well-funded medical community, one on the brink of a major new automation project.

New York State Funding

SUNY officials established Intracom in 1965 as New York State's equivalent to the national confederation of universities called the Interuniversity Communications Council, Inc.—better known by its trade name Educom. In July of that year an Intracom subcommittee, the Task Force on Medical Libraries, began to function. The three SUNY medical libraries heads—Pizer, Miriam Libbey, and Helen Kovacs—and three medical faculty members served on the task force. On August 17, 1965, the group elected Pizer as chairman (Bridegam and Meyerhoff 1970; Pizer 1967). The charge to the group was to plan a program that "would enable the three medical libraries in Buffalo, Syracuse, and Brooklyn to make more effective use of the resources contained within them" (Pizer 1966, 151). Pizer drafted a statement of their plan, calling for an online, user-oriented, networked system that integrated searching for book and journal materials. By "user-oriented," he meant that users—students, faculty, or practicing physicians—could search a system themselves, "without the necessary intervention of a professional librarian or indexer, or anyone previously trained in the formulating of search strategies" (Cain 1969, 250). This latter goal never was realized and was virtually abandoned by 1971.

The task force adopted the plan, and the state of New York funded the project beginning in January 1966. Bridegam and Meyerhoff (1970, 105) reported: "The Vice-President for Health Affairs at SUNY at Buffalo, Peter H. Regan III, was not only interested in computer applications to medical libraries but had sufficient drive to persuade the Bureau of the Budget of the State of New York to support the project and obtained funding from the Legislature. . . . Both Pizer and Regan were able to persuade the President of [SUNY] to try a pilot project which estimated to reach a steady cost level of $600,000 in 1969–70." Thus SUNY launched the BCN, beginning with a three-year developmental phase. Pizer was appointed director, and active implementation began in September 1966 (Cain and Pizer 1967). Pizer already had been working with an external group on related library-planning studies. Coincident with the January 1966 funding of the project, he was one of several authors of a report on an NSF-funded study by Herner & Corporation to develop an optimal design for a national network of medical libraries (Weinstock et al. 1966).

Pizer set a target date of September 1968 for initiation of the operation to provide public online service. The task force drew up hardware and software specifications and investigated the products available from various manufacturers to determine which had the capabilities they envisaged. They were aware of the technological possibilities that were available; in fact, several task force members had personal experience with library automation activities. The task force staff collectively knew of many proposed and demonstrated library automation systems (e.g., Kilgour's plans for a centralized online bibliographic search system for the Columbia-Harvard-Yale Medical Libraries, the King, and other studies of library automation for LC), as well as current thinking about library networks (e.g., NLM studies and plans for regional or national medical library networks, and public response to the 1965 task force proposal itself).

Parallel to the task force efforts was an Arthur D. Little study of a plan for a library processing center for SUNY (*A plan for a library* 1967). Pizer had already indicated an interest in shared cataloging, and he was instrumental in the first cooperative cataloging system that used online technology (several other library systems such as the Columbia-Harvard-Yale Medical Libraries had been working already with a batch cooperative system but had also been planning for an online search system). In cooperation with NLM, the Francis A. Countway Library of Medicine in Boston, and the Upstate Medical Center Library, SUNY BCN developed the framework for such an online system, and in April 1970 SUNY's SCATT (Shared Cataloging Access

Through Terminals) became operational, providing online access to a file of in-process books being cataloged at each of the participating libraries. After a year's experience with that system, NLM announced that development of a similar file (to be called CATLINE) was concurrently under way at NLM; that caused the project participants to agree that cooperative cataloging was viable and to shut down the joint project (Egeland 1975b; Onsi and Pelosi 1970).

Contributions from NLM

Even before the SUNY task force was established, Pizer had envisioned a system with remote terminals that could be used for bibliographic searching and interlibrary communication. He had hoped that the participating SUNY medical libraries might become a MEDLARS center serving other medical schools in upper New York, Pennsylvania, and Ohio. As a regional center, the libraries would gain access to communications with the other centers as part of a national biomedical information network. Seven days after he was appointed task force chair, Pizer approached NLM about this possibility. His earlier internship at NLM and participation with NLM staff in the Herner study of a national medical library system undoubtedly made this an obvious initial step for him (Bridegam and Meyerhoff 1970).

Joseph Leiter, then deputy director for NLM Library Operations, supported the plan by designating the SUNY medical library network as a Regional MEDLARS Center. Later Leiter served on the SUNY BCN User's Task Force Committee from its beginning in April 1972, and participated in board meetings until he resigned from it in March 1976 because of a perceived conflict of interest (Van Camp 1995). NLM also made available five years (1964–1968) of MEDLARS records on tapes (750,000 records) for SUNY's use during this start-up period. NLM's generosity resulted partly from a desire to collect developmental and operational data from the SUNY experience that could guide NLM in its own online service planning. At this time (1966) NLM staff may have seen demonstrations of online systems such as DIALOG, COLEX, and Recon Central, and they may have been considering options for the provision of online service with the NLM data. However, they probably did not have any direct personal experience. As seen in chapter 6, Davis and McCarn, who did have firsthand experience with such systems, had not yet joined NLM. NLM did not get COLEX access until January 1968; they did not run their ORBIT neurology database experiment until April 1968; they did not start AIM-TWX until June 1970. Ultimately, their observations of the SUNY effort did have an important impact on the planning of their own MEDLINE service.

Meanwhile, the Upstate Medical Center Library also hired Alexander Cain of the British Museum as library systems analyst to oversee monograph selection, organization, and subject indexing for the database (Cain 1967). In 1967 BCN was also working on an NLM contract to convert a machine-readable file of NLM's Current Catalog monograph records (produced under MEDLARS) to the LC MARC format, and to convert a machine-readable file of all relevant monographic materials held in the Syracuse Library. This major component of the SUNY network was to structure the bibliographic records in the database in MARC, the machine-readable cataloging format developed at LC. Pizer (1969, 106) noted: "Since it is likely that this is to be the national format which all other libraries will either use or arrange to be compatible with, the Network adopted the MARC format as its standard, and was designated as a LC MARC center in the pilot project in October 1967." Cain and Pizer (1967, 259–260) felt that "it would be foolish to go our own way"; they rightly presumed that the MARC format for computerized bibliographic records would become a national standard for American libraries.

Thus many linkages connected BCN and NLM in these early years, and there can be no doubt that NLM's support of and cooperation in BCN was significant in its success. Years later, Pizer (1984, 344) acknowledged NLM's support: "Part of the success . . . was due to the far-sighted leadership of Dr.

Joseph Leiter ... His faith in the development of systems outside of NLM, and the uses that such systems could be to NLM in the provision of data for planning and modification of the developing MEDLARS II and III systems, opened the way for a period of fruitful and jointly useful collaboration." At the SUNY BCN dedication exercises in October 1968 (shortly after NLM had published its own plan for a Biomedical Communications Network in June 1968), Ruth M. Davis (1969, 55), then director of Lister Hill National Center for Biomedical Communications, expressed her views of the NLM-SUNY relationship:

The new SUNY network will hopefully take its place as a part of this future expansion and will be one of the free vigorous constituents of the national network providing services to the students, faculty, researchers, and medical practitioners reached through the facilities of the SUNY system. It is expected that, as plans develop, the SUNY network will be given an opportunity to participate in the extension of these services beyond its university bounds to provide for needed biomedical information support to the entire State through cooperative actions with other institutions and organizations.

Contributions from IBM

Pizer wrote the final version of the BCN planning document in January 1966, including budget figures for an IBM 360/40 computer. Later in 1966, he developed specifications and asked eight companies to submit proposals. IBM was the only bidder to submit a comprehensive proposal. IBM simulated various types of searches, using samples of both the book indexing data and the MEDLINE data, at its Gaithersburg, Maryland, facility, using its Generalized Information System (GIS) for the software package being developed there for the IBM 360. Steve Furth of IBM was among the experts consulted during the 1965–1966 Herner study of the NLM system. Not surprisingly, IBM won the contract. This role for IBM seems consistent with their participation in other projects that had high national visibility and opportunity for showcasing of IBM equipment. Such projects provided IBM an opportunity to obtain firsthand understanding of user requirements and suitability of IBM's current and proposed equipment. IBM, of course, had a strong self-interest in marketing a computer system for libraries that had potential for replication and broad transferability.

In September 1966, with the launch of the operation, IBM assigned a full-time systems engineer, James Dorr, to the project (Bridegam and Meyerhoff 1970). The software adopted and adapted to the SUNY online operation was the IBM DPS (chapter 4), first demonstrated at SUNY in October 1968, and continued as the basis for the BCN service until mid-1973. An early name for the SUNY BCN online version of the retrieval software was SYMBIOSIS (System for Medical and Biological Sciences Information Searching)—a name, according to Pizer (1969, 102), that was "intended to convey the idea of a mutually beneficial interaction between man and machine." In spite of its originality and cleverness, this name did not appear anywhere after 1969.

Databases, Indexing, and Thesaurus Projects

In addition to MEDLARS, SUNY BCN assembled two much smaller files. One was the SUNY Union List of Serials (30,000 titles). The other, called Netbook, contained 20,000 catalog records for monographs published since January 1962 that were held in the three SUNY medical libraries. The records from this union catalog were included in order to improve the quality of subject access to that literature and to test the theory that if researchers could find out what was in specific parts of books, the use of such material would increase significantly. Pizer (1967a, 58) noted: "We are also interested in trying the [in-depth book indexing] experiment with medical literature and to obtain proof either for or against the oft repeated statement that the book literature is not important in the medical practice, or in education."

The Netbook project advanced in 1966 when the Upstate Medical Center Library hired Janet Egeland, who had just completed her master's degree in social psychology. Employed as a reference librarian, her job was to participate in the Netbook experiment, along with two other subject analysts, by creating index headings on a chapter-by-chapter basis, assigning seven or eight headings per chapter or other small indexable unit. Under Egeland's supervision, she and the other indexers thus indexed the monographs with about the same thoroughness as journal articles in *Index Medicus* (Egeland 1972). The conversion of book records to machine-readable form was accomplished using the IBM DATATEXT service. Keyboarding was done on IBM 2741 communication terminals at SUNY that were connected to a computer in New York City. Three subject analysts worked on the task at a rate of about eight books per day per analyst (Pizer 1967). This multiyear experiment continued through December 1969, by which time about 8,000 titles had been processed into the Netbook database. The experiment and federal support was terminated at that time, reportedly because this type of indexing was too expensive. However, the Netbook file remained online from 1968 to July 1971, when it was removed to make room for more online journal citations. The NLM book database remained online until December 1972.

The SUNY-Buffalo library also had a catalog keyboarding project, but not with in-depth indexing. A test project was successful, and in June 1967 the conversion project at SUNY-Buffalo started with four terminals. Early in 1968, DATATEXT was succeeded by an on-campus ATS system that ran on an IBM 360/40 at the university computer center and worked with data from seven typists keyboarding shelf-list catalog cards in the library (Lazorick 1969).

This in-depth monograph indexing was interesting for the library field. Because it was so resource-intensive, it was a radical departure from traditional subject descriptions of books by libraries—other than by some special libraries. Although in-depth indexing of medical texts, and an online catalog of books and monographs, with deep indexing, catalog card production, and remote terminals were elements of the earlier Columbia-Harvard-Yale Medical Catalog (online) project, SUNY BCN seemed to be an expansion of that approach.[1] The in-depth indexing was an experiment, using the entire collection of 1962 books at the Upstate Medical Center Library to see to what extent the resulting greater ease of accessibility and refinement of subject analysis would increase the usefulness of this literature. Cain and Pizer (1967, 259) had noted:

A study of circulation at the Upstate Medical Center... revealed, contrary to experiences in other medical libraries, a greater number of charges for monographs than for serials and we hoped that, by making content information of monographs available in depth to the user, we could demonstrate a truer pattern of use... Because of the experimental nature of the... project, it was decided that only those monographs held in Syracuse would be so treated (11,000 titles).

The next major thrust with deep indexing of monographs, again with the preparation of machine-readable records for online searching, was Pauline Atherton's CLR-sponsored Subject Access Project at Syracuse University's School of Information Studies from 1976–1977. The indexers augmented over 2,000 online catalog records chosen at random from the University of Toronto Library (in 10 different fields in social sciences and humanities). The records were loaded as a private file (called BOOKS) on the SDC ORBIT system for experiments and evaluation tests in the relative cost and retrieval performance of monograph catalog records with and without subject description augmentation (Atherton 1977, 1978a,b). The indexers augmented the records using rules to add words and phrases from the tables of contents and back-of-the-book indexes to the records. Atherton obtained a copy of the DPS software from Pizer's project across the Syracuse campus and used it for the early stage of her BOOKS project.

One of Cain's projects was to construct a thesaurus for indexers, beginning with 17,000 words that frequently appeared in the article titles in *Index Medicus*. He then mapped these entry terms to equivalent or more generic terms extracted from

MeSH and, for nonmedical topics, *Library of Congress Subject Headings* (*LCSH*) (Cain 1969). NLM bolstered this indexing and thesaurus work in 1967 by delivering a deck of 18,000 cards comprising the 1967 *MeSH* terms. The SUNY project planned to duplicate the decks for the other network libraries (Pizer 1967).

SUNY BCN

Membership

Many of the basic elements of a network had been in development in other medical libraries in 1965. However, according to two directors of participating libraries, Bridegam and Meyerhoff (1970, 106): "Great drive, ingenuity, firm development support from IBM, and a commitment of funds by the State of New York produced results which had eluded others." SUNY BCN formally began operation in October 1968.

1968 Milestone

SUNY BCN was the first online search system to provide service on a regularly scheduled basis to a geographically dispersed network of users, with the intention of continuing to operate as a regular service rather than just running as an experiment.

The network began operation as a regular production service, with the intention of continuing in that capacity—it was not an experiment or trial operation. Thus it became the first online search service network as we might define it today. Formal dedication ceremonies were held on October 18, coinciding with a joint meeting of the upstate New York chapters of ASIS, MLA, and SLA ("Biomedical communication" 1969).

The SUNY project objective was "to establish a network which would link the State University's three medical and health libraries located in Syracuse, Buffalo, and Brooklyn" (Herner et al. 1966, 45). The initial objective of linking online only the three SUNY libraries was modified by broader consideration of New York state needs. Lucretia McClure was among the non-SUNY searchers at the University of Rochester Medical School Library, and a former member of the SUNY BCN Ad Hoc Committee on Network Operations. McClure (1995) noted that the Rochester library started the SUNY online service in October 1968 along with the three SUNY institutions. They installed an IBM 2740 next to the library reference desk. "The library staff searched in the mornings, and they let users come in and search in the afternoons." Soon SUNY-Stony Brook joined, and by 1969 the network included the four SUNY medical libraries and several non-SUNY institutions: the medical libraries at the University of Rochester, Albany Medical College at Union University, Harvard University, and Columbia University as well as the New York State Medical Library and NLM. The addition of NLM was related to the mutual interests of both NLM and SUNY in establishing and supporting regional networks. Harvard, which was neither part of SUNY nor a New York library, joined because Harvard was a MEDLARS Regional Search Center; as SUNY and Harvard already shared some cooperative ventures, it was a logical extension.

A news story ("Biomedical Communication Network" 1968, 2) about the dedication and start-up of BCN stated:

Designed originally to tie the four medical centers of the university together in order to amplify their resources and thus provide vastly improved services to the medical community of the participating schools, it became obvious quite early that the usefulness of the system to be developed would be greatly enhanced through cooperation with the private schools within the state. The Network has now evolved into a facility which will be connected between federal, state, and private institutions.

The article identified the BCN charter members (2):

As the Network begins operation there will be nine participating libraries: the Health Sciences Library of the

State University at Buffalo, the Edward G. Miner Library of the University of Rochester Medical Center, the SUNY Upstate Medical Center Library at Syracuse, the Albany Medical College of Union University (at Albany), the SUNY Downstate Medical Center at Brooklyn, the Biomedical Library of the State University at Stony Brook, the Francis A. Countway Library of Medicine of Harvard University in Boston, the Parkinson Disease Information Center at Columbia University Medical Center in Manhattan, and the National Library of Medicine in Bethesda, Maryland.

In 1970 several other non-SUNY, non-New York institutions were added to the network. In August, a terminal was installed at the Medical Center library at Ohio State University, the twenty-first to be installed on the SUNY BCN system ("Computer is researcher's" 1970). The Indiana University School of Medicine joined the network; at that time they had the distinction of being the participant with the most distant terminal from the SUNY computer. The University of Illinois followed.

Thus the first fully operational online bibliographic retrieval service for biomedical literature was not centered at NLM, but in upstate New York. While the NLM experiment with an early version of ORBIT on a file of neurology citations had also taken place in 1968, the SUNY BCN system was operating with a full-sized database—a year and a half before NLM's experimental AIM-TWX service began operating in June 1970. SDC's COLEX (chapter 6) began its test and evaluation period in March 1968, but this was self-defined as an experiment; it was 1969 before approval was given to move COLEX to regular production mode under the name of CIRCOL.

The development costs of SUNY BCN were in excess of $1 million, mainly borne by the state of New York. Outside sources, primarily NLM, provided additional support. The anticipated costs of the first full year of operation were $600,000 ("Biomedical Communication Network" 1968). This was probably a record amount at that time, and for some time to come, for a computer search service in the public sector.

The network, under Pizer's leadership, was designed to be a loose organization and to function "rather like a federal association," with the director preparing budgets, implementing goals, communicating with the library profession, and being the final arbiter in decisions relating to the network's systems (Cain and Pizer 1967, 258). Policies were to be set in conjunction with a Network Advisory Committee that the director appointed. While acknowledging that such an organizational structure helped the network to "pursue its goals directly and made the attainment of operational deadlines easier," some members grumbled about the director having too much authority and wished for a "better means of group decision" and fairer representation (Bridegam and Meyerhoff 1970, 110).

Evidence of differences in goals and objectives between Pizer and some Network Advisory Committee members was the aborted effort in 1969 to implement an interlibrary loan service that would have been triggered automatically by a user's search results. Pizer envisioned that whenever a user retrieved citations to relevant documents that were not in the user's library, the system would order the documents from the nearest network member library, unless the user indicated otherwise. Pizer (1972b, 58) reported that the automatic interlibrary loan was designed and ready to function by 1969:

At that point, the problems which face a library network, but which are unrelated to its technology, became evident. As the librarians of the member institutions were faced with the reality of accepting a larger number of interlibrary loan requests than they had been accustomed to receiving, they balked. The Network Advisory Council felt that the anticipated avalanche of requests would render normal service in this area unworkable, thus the automatic interlibrary loan procedure was never tried, even on a limited basis.

By 1971, the database contained over 1.3 million citations to both journal and monograph information, and the network had sixteen institutional members. All of the terminals were located in the libraries of participating medical centers, so most users were individuals within the medical centers who made regular use of the library. Policies for who was allowed access to the network were set by each member medical center, not by network administration.

Databases

> **1968 Milestones**
>
> SUNY BCN was the first online search system to use an online bibliographic database of more than 500,000 records.
>
> SUNY BCN was the first online search system to offer a database with in-depth indexing to books and other monographs.

The MEDLARS file (750,000), the SUNY Union List of Serials (30,000), and the netbook database (20,000) provided a total of 800,000 bibliographic records online in 1968 from SUNY BCN. Start-up services in 1968 included online access to (1) the most recent five years of MEDLARS data (over one million records); (2) the combined book catalog records from 1962–1968 of the three SUNY medical libraries, along with the NLM book catalog records from 1966 to date (30,000 unique titles); and (3) the Union List of Serials for all SUNY libraries, along with the serials titles from member libraries of the Central New York References and Resources Council (25,000 titles). (The union list had initial problems because NLM changed journal codes without informing the programmers until after the old codes had been stored in the system). About 6,700 of the book titles were accompanied by their in-depth indexing with an average of about seven assigned subject headings per chapter.

The scope of the database collection changed in 1972 with the addition of SUNY-Albany, the first nonmedical library to join. Because it was nonmedical, SUNY-Albany pushed for access to files with nonmedical content and put up the initial money to get the ERIC database online (Van Camp 1988). The original system objectives formulated in 1966 for the SUNY system included a means for searching multiple secondary sources. Pizer (1966, 162) had signaled his intent to add other external databases such as Chemical Abstracts and BIOSIS (Biological Abstracts).

Operations and Equipment

Network headquarters—with more than twenty-five full-time staff consisting of librarians, programmers, systems analysts, subject specialists, computer operators, and related technical staff—and the central computing facilities were at the Upstate Medical Center. A computer center in the library was built, consisting of a two-floor area of 16,000 square feet, 2,500 square feet of which were devoted just to the computer. Pizer (1984, 344) observed:

One of the great advantages of the SUNY Network was that it was entirely under the control of the library. This greatly simplified the interactions between librarians, programmers, and computer technical staff. The computer facilities were located in the library, and the proximity of library and computer helped the staffs of both units better understand the complexities of each operation. One benefit was that there was no competition for priorities regarding computer time and projects.

Van Camp (1995) recalled that all of the BCN terminals were on AT&T dedicated lines; they were not dial-up terminals. Because the terminals were dedicated, the system was accessible only to subscribing institutions. The system was up initially for four hours a day, five days a week, but by October 1969 it was available to the network for 37.5 hours a week (from 10 a.m. to 4:30 p.m. Monday through Friday).

In 1969 the annual membership fee was $5,000, which included rental of the terminal, telephone line charges, and computer time. Given the number of searches performed that year, the average cost per search was about $3.30 (Bridegam and Meyerhoff 1970). By 1971 the annual subscription fee was $7,500, which allowed unlimited usage, and in 1972 the fee increased again (Van Camp 1988). Most

SUNY BCN users were high-volume users; that is, they ran many searches. They used both SUNY and NLM's MEDLINE because they needed both systems to handle the volume. Their SUNY BCN contract gave them unlimited use for a fixed fee. This large and growing volume of use, and the fixed fee schedule, spelled trouble for BCN (as it did years later for other networks such as America Online). Pizer (1972b, 61) revealed his concern about the escalating charges when he asked, "Why should a library pay SUNY $8,000 to $10,000 a year when it could participate in the MEDLINE network for the cost of a TWX terminal, which it may be already using?"

When it began service, BCN used an IBM 360/40 computer. Data were stored on an IBM 2321 Data Cell (the same model that Lockheed and Data Corp. used) and an IBM 2314 Direct Access Storage Facility, which together provided more than 600 million characters of storage. The terminals were IBM 2740s that the medical library used also for interlibrary loan. An IBM 1403 printer provided offline printing with mixed upper and lower case characters—it was unusual at that time to see large volume computer printout in anything but uppercase characters. The equipment, however, had problems. Pizer lamented that the system did not realize the operational capacity claimed by the vendor; it could not handle a large number of terminals simultaneously and did not have a capacity for large growth. Pizer (1972a, 63–64) commented:

Unfortunately, we were doing our hardware selection some years before Mr. Kilgour, and we did not undertake mathematical simulations of network load or of core capacity, or response time. We were, consequently, at somewhat of a disadvantage when evaluating the proposals received. The vendor whom we selected assured us that the proposed system could handle hundreds of terminals with the computer model which was suggested. It turned out, however, that as we began to load the data bases, we found that so much core storage was used up with instructions and in controlling the initial group of 25 terminals, that the addition of more terminals was out of the question. This was a major problem that was unforeseen by the computer manufacturer, partly because there was no operating network of comparable size and scope at that time.

In addition to the limitations of the interface and resistance of network members to some of the planned innovations, the terminal hardware and mass storage device handicapped SUNY BCN. Formulating a search strategy with the *MeSH* terms would have been much easier with the use of a CRT terminal to display the hierarchical structures of the vocabulary. Furthermore, the slow (15 cps) IBM 2740 typewriter terminals were noisy, which was particularly problematic in the library settings (Rae 1970). Also, just as Lockheed's use of IBM Data Cells for the Ames experiments and for RECON had caused much down time, SUNY BCN likewise experienced frequent service interruptions with Data Cells. Pizer (1984, 356) described the problem of trying to store large quantities of data online:

In the 1960s IBM was still trying to develop large-scale storage devices which could solve this problem, and the SUNY system was designed using an IBM Data Cell. This was a machine somewhat larger than a 20 cubic foot refrigerator which contained cylinders of magnetic film in strips, with the cylinders being mounted on a drum. The location of data on a strip was recorded in a machine index, and when accessed the appropriate strip would lift from its storage cylinder, wrap around a read head, and then return to the cylinder after use. The machine was filled with an inert gas to maintain its pressure and internal atmosphere, and was a mechanical marvel. Unfortunately, IBM was never able to solve the many mechanical problems which such a machine was subject to, and the device passed into history as a curious, but unsuccessful mass storage device.

In defense of the Data Cell, it was used successfully (but not trouble-free) for many years with the Data Corporation and DIALOG systems, and Lockheed was among the last IBM customers to retire its Data Cell equipment, reportedly to be sent for display at the Smithsonian.

The development for BCN during 1967–1968 was directed by Lloyd Palmer, who adapted the DPS software. He also led the continuous effort to develop system upgrades and enhancements to the

BCN system after its start-up. The modified DPS program ran on the BCN system from 1968–1973, and was later replaced with IBM STAIRS.

User Interaction and Training

As a trial strategy designed to require that searchers interact directly with the system without help, no staff assistance was available for the first three months of operation. The staff quickly acknowledged that the trial was unsuccessful; searchers decidedly needed trained staff at hand to redo unsatisfactory searches, to give instruction in using commands, finding search terms, and formulating search strategies, and to conduct searches for those who were disinclined to search for themselves or who were unable to wait for an available terminal (Egeland 1971). Bridegam and Meyerhoff 1970, 107) described the situation: "Despite the fact that a person has read and reread instructions of machine searching and received a half-hour orientation, it is the exceptional user who will not require the assistance of a librarian for at least his next five or six searches. Providing this assistance and other related services greatly increases the staff requirements of the library." These findings seem comparable to the current experience of librarians working with end users of online and CD-ROM databases. McClure (1995) recalled, "There were no search aids, and few manuals at that time." They did let users come in and do the searching starting in 1968, although they were usually accompanied by a reference librarian who was familiar with *MeSH* and medical terminology. McClure (1972, 1) reported, "Afternoon hours were made available for searching by the Library's public. The response was immediate and enthusiastic. Frequently the afternoon schedule was filled days in advance by students, faculty members, and research personnel."

Because BCN staff assumed that medical practitioners were not likely to master Boolean operators, they presented the underlying relationships in such a way as to elicit what a user wanted without having to express it in Boolean terms. Egeland (1971, 109) explained:

The query language helps the user set up his search within this logical framework by having him enter his subjects in *groups*, depending on the relationship he desires between them. This approach alleviates the need for the user to even be aware of the actual Boolean concepts he is using . . . Rather than confusing the user by explaining that he may employ any one of several forms of logical relationships . . . he is simply told that subjects entered in the *same group* will be searched unrelated to or independent of each other and that subjects entered in *separate groups* will be searched in a coordinate relationship to or dependence on each other. It was found after experience with a great many users that the easiest way to explain the logic of searching is to explain that the subject or subjects in one group will be cross-matched with the subject or subjects in all other groups in the search and the merged output from this cross-matching process returned.

Pizer (1972a, 62) noted, "We have also found that the problems of constructing a system which the researcher can use unaided by a professional input analyst are considerable, and it may be that they are not worth the effort to solve."

Until 1971 searchers were not informed of the total number of hits, and output was limited to no more than ten citations to books and ten citations to journal articles. Egeland (1971, 109–110) gave two reasons for this latter constraint:

(1) The user cannot stop the search once he received the message YOUR INQUIRY IS BEING PROCESSED. If he realizes at this point that he has made an error in the subjects he has typed in or that he has entered a subject in the wrong group, for example, he cannot terminate the inquiry. If he decides that he is not going to be interested in seeing all of the output after looking at a few citations, there is no way he can stop the printout after looking at a few citations, there is no way that he can stop the printout unless he simply turns off the terminal altogether; (2) The actual print time of the 2740 communications terminals used for retrieval is too slow to make it practical to allow a user to utilize long periods of on-line machine time to print out large numbers of citations. The number 10 was arbitrarily decided upon in the early stages of Network operation.

If a user wanted a complete bibliography, the same search statement had to be reentered up to nine times until all citations had been typed. Later, as they better understood users' needs, they removed the restriction on number of citations that could be printed at a time.

Fortunately, this cumbersome approach with output was temporary. When SUNY BCN was using the DPS software, the entire search statement was reprocessed to get the next ten citations, but this was not true after BCN changed to the STAIRS software (Van Camp 1995). Joy Stiller (1970, 107), a searcher at NLM, compared this with the AIM-TWX system (using ORBIT software) that was "friendlier in this regard." After printing five citations, the ORBIT program at that time (1970) prompted a user repeatedly to see if more output was wanted; in response to a simple affirmative reply, ORBIT printed five more and it did it without reprocessing the entire search statement. In contrast, the batch NLM MEDLARS search system at that time routinely printed up to 500 citations in a search printout (Darling 1970).

The SUNY software was limited also in that one could not search for author, publication date, journal title, or language, except as a qualification of the sets retrieved on a keyword search. Nor did it provide intermediate search results; it revealed the number of citations found only after the entire formulation was entered. Again, this deficiency contrasted with AIM-TWX, which gave search term hit statistics from each line as it was entered. According to Bridegam and Meyerhoff (1970), SUNY BCN users, however, were delighted to learn that the printouts were their own property! Stiller (1970) emphasized that search analysts preparing complex strategies for MEDLARS could use the SUNY BCN system to explore the database and refine the request before submitting the strategy to the NLM batch system.

Access to the online service could be achieved via either of two modes of search interface, one of which was called "Query Search," designed for practicing physicians, clinicians, and students. Query Search did not allow direct entering of commands or recursive use of sets previously created. Instead, the program presented to searchers a series of questions to be answered by YES or NO or multiple choice selection, "very much like an automated reference interview" (Pizer 1969, 102). Then searchers typed in *MeSH* terms, which could be truncated. The program translated the terms and the answers to the questions to construct search equations with Boolean operators. This interface was designed to minimize users' typing because "most people are such poor typists" (Pizer 1972a, 67).

The problems of spelling and typing errors were addressed also by adding to the online thesaurus the most common misspellings of words (e.g, opthamology for ophthalmology) and variant forms of words such as the English spellings "gynaecology" and "anaesthesia." Thus searchers could make mistakes or enter variant spellings and still retrieve automatically the desired records. The query language was designed on three levels of detail, so that users could select the one that matched their level of experience and system familiarity (Bridegam and Meyerhoff 1970).

In addition to the Query Search mode, experienced, trained search personnel had access through two versions of a Search Direct mode that was faster and more flexible, and by 1970 it permitted searching for words in titles in addition to *MeSH* headings (Egeland 1971). The ability to search directly for keywords in titles was an important SUNY BCN capability that NLM did not implement on MEDLINE until 1975—through a cumbersome, indirect "textword" (TW), or "text fragment" (TF) and "stringsearch" feature, and not until December *1990* with a comparable direct search capability. Online title word searching had been demonstrated elsewhere as early as 1963 with the SRI system. MIT's TIP and DIALOG included title word search capability in their systems in 1964.

The SUNY system did not have the *MeSH* explosion feature (at least not by April 1971, when it was requested at a users' meeting, as reported by Spiegel and Crager in 1971). This feature, which used the hierarchical "trees" in *MeSH*, was available for NLM MEDLARS searches. Furthermore, the MEDLARS output included all assigned subject headings with an article citation (thus providing a mini-abstract or telegraphic abstract)—something the SUNY system did not do—a continuing manifestation of the relatively high costs of online storage capacity (Darling 1970). For several reasons, including a proprietary rights dispute between NLM and several publishers of abstracts, abstracts were not added to MEDLARS and MEDLINE until 1975, and then only for a limited number of records from those journals that gave permission for use of their abstracts. The provision of abstracts for *all* incoming records did not start until 1989.

In spite of the increased demands on the staff and costs of membership and access, the member libraries discovered a number of benefits to offering online services, some of which were practical, and some of which enhanced the librarians' status. Bridegam and Meyerhoff (1970, 108) described these benefits: "As a new service, the terminal draws curious faculty, staff, and students into the library. While they are there, the staff can explain other library services and bibliographic tools which would be of use to them. Enthusiastic faculty members bring visiting colleagues to see demonstration searches. The medical center personnel view the library as a progressive department, making use of the available technological advances."

The designers of online systems, including the earliest, considered the problem of how to provide users with the source publications that corresponded to the retrieved references. Even the first of the proposed online reference retrieval systems (1962 SATIRE) addressed this issue by providing microform copies of the cited publications at the searcher's workstation; this pattern was implemented in several SDC systems (1965 MICRO; 1966 COLEX). Other early systems (1963 SRI; 1967 OBAR) addressed this issue by storing the full text of the records themselves.

A third approach, providing a holdings record—that is, an address to a library location instead of a microfilm reel-frame location—was done before the online days in some batch and SDI systems, and has continued to the present. This approach appeared, for example, on a regular production basis in 1968 at the University of Colorado NLM Regional Search Center, as described in chapter 6. The idea was expanded in 1975 with an SDI system run by UC that annotated the output records for over 6,000 profiles for users on nine campuses to show (tailored for each recipient) the closest library in the California system that had a copy of the journal in each citation, and the call number for each cited journal in that library (Bourne 1976b).

1968 Milestone

SUNY BCN was the first online search system to incorporate library holdings and availability information in specific output records.

Pizer's plan (1967) was to deliver not only the library call numbers for SUNY-held books included in the output, but to go a step further and check the SUNY circulation system database to determine availability of the books, as well as take the appropriate follow-up action (report the status; generate interlibrary loan request, overdue notice, or return request). He planned a similar system for journals for the fifty-eight libraries represented on the SUNY Union List of Serials. Library holdings information was incorporated in the BOOKS database, but not their MEDLINE file.

By 1971, the query language had been through three major revisions, but still was not satisfactory to a majority of users. Patrick Rae (1970, 174), a librarian at a member institution, observed, "Users have found that the existing dialogue is not clear and raises many questions . . . Often a user leaves a terminal session puzzled, frustrated and unaware of the great assistance that the system could have given him." Also, it was apparent that the medical practitioners obtained results that were far less relevant than those obtained by trained searchers who understood the *MeSH* indexing. Users who were dissatisfied with their own searches tended to blame the system rather than their own inability to formulate a search request. Once the novelty of conducting a search wore off, "even the users who had at first expressed willingness to sit down at the terminal and do their own searches became less and less interested in spending the time that was involved" (Egeland 1971, 111). As more terminals were added and more searches were conducted, response time degraded and users often had to wait for terminals that were in use. In a survey of 241 users, only 18 percent said that they preferred to operate the terminal; 78 percent wanted to delegate their searches to a trained searcher (111–112):

Some users were delighted to have the opportunity to experiment with the machine, while others were not willing to try performing their own searches. There was a hesitancy on the part of some users to operate the terminal for fear that they would make errors and cause the whole system to break down ... Other users simply would not take the time to perform the mechanical operations necessary to enter a request and seemed to assume from the beginning that they were not expected to perform their own searches.

By 1972, trained analysts conducted the great majority of searches. The end-user query language was phased out, and only the direct search language remained.

Response time for several of the early online systems was measured in minutes rather than seconds. In October 1971, the average response time for the SUNY BCN system with the new IBM 370/155 system was 135 seconds, but by January 1972 it had improved to 35 seconds (Pizer 1972b; "Network statistics," 1972). While this would be considered poor performance by today's standards, it was quite acceptable in those days.[2] Some searchers found ways to make more productive use of their time during these slow searches, by such tricks as running several searches simultaneously on multiple terminals and multiple systems.

> **1968 Milestone**
>
> SUNY BCN was the first online search service to hold an annual users conference.

In order to provide a forum to discuss and compare experiences in using the retrieval system, including machine and query formulation problems, options on charging for services, how much information to retrieve, and suggestions for improvements, SUNY BCN held regular user meetings, work sessions, and workshops, before and after the online service became available (Spiegel and Crager 1971). The May 1971 workshop held at SUNY Upstate Medical Center Library provided an example of regional technology transfer; it included a special presentation on SUPARS at Syracuse University (chapter 3).

In 1971, BCN searchers debated the issue of when it was appropriate to run a BCN online search and when it was better to use the MEDLARS batch service. Because of the considerable differences in search capability, with each system having its own strengths and different response times and products, the question was hard to answer. Spiegel and Crager (1971, 52) supplied samples from user meeting transcripts that reveal elements of the debate:

I think that basically SUNY is supposed to be answering simple questions and when anybody wants a comprehensive search, they want it done by a MEDLARS analyst, to go through MEDLARS, and that SUNY is supposed to be used, for example for somebody who wants a study of genetics in the Amish people, which is very difficult to pick it out from the printed index because you can only get it by title ... I also think that SUNY should pick up a big overload for the one population that MEDLARS at this point can't serve at all and that's the clinician population. Because he does need 10 or 15 citations. It may require a fairly complex formulation to get at what he wants, but he doesn't want to be overloaded with it and he needs it within this week or as soon as possible.

Move to Albany

McCarn (1970b) observed that the SUNY system could not be expanded to a national audience without major modifications. His analysis of the performance characteristics (307) showed that "the existing computer hardware and software were not fast enough to support any appreciable increase in use ... use of this system might prejudice users and the service against it because of unavoidable service delays." Users requested improved service and complained about worsening system response times. In replying to such requests and complaints, the network administrators explained that they were circumscribed by shortages in staff and funds (Snyder 1981). At a 1969 presentation Bridegam and Meyerhoff (1970) reported that twenty-one terminals could be attached to the computer without causing delays—more would cause problems. Of course, this limited the number of institutions that could participate directly in network service. In a news report ("Operating history" 1972), the situation was analyzed:

To outward appearances, the Network was thriving. However, behind the scenes there were severe budget problems. To make the Network self-supporting as sole users of the IBM 360 would have necessitated an impractical increase in fee to each of the users. In addition, there were no funds available for developmental work or for other improvements in the system. Thus ... the Network moved its operation from Syracuse to Albany. Here, some of its financial problems could be alleviated by the fact that it joined with a number of other computer services supplied by the [SUNY] Central Administration.

Thus, in July 1971, as part of a consolidation of SUNY data processing activities designed to expand services and run operations more efficiently and cheaply, the administration of SUNY BCN transferred from the Upstate Medical Center to the SUNY Central Administration in Albany. The system was loaded on a larger computer—an upgrade to an IBM 370/155. During the move, service for network users was discontinued for only four days—the network continued to run on the IBM 360/40 from July until it was installed on the 370/155 on September 1. The small, dedicated IBM 360/40 was abandoned and the programs were loaded on the larger computer of the Central Administration. Response time improved markedly after the changeover.

The move to the 370/155 made it possible to accommodate more than twenty-one simultaneous users. Unfortunately, however, because of the limitations in the design of the original system, it still could not handle more than about twenty-seven terminals. New subscribers could be added only by reallocating existing terminals from institutions that had more than one (Pizer 1972a).

SUNY BCN was planned and operated as a facility/service for the constituency of the entire SUNY system. Although it was not intended to be a publicly available search service, there were exceptions. As noted earlier, the participation expanded in 1969 to include the first organization from outside the SUNY system (other than the University of Rochester, which was a charter member with the original three SUNY participants). Four new institutions joined the network after its move to Albany: Jacobi Library at Mount Sinai Medical College in New York City (August 1971 as Terminal 25); the Food and Drug Administration at the Public Health Service in Rockville, Maryland (October 1971 as Terminal 2, originally a Syracuse number); the Albert R. Mann Library of the New York State College of Agriculture and Life Sciences—a SUNY College at Cornell University in Ithaca, New York (February 1972 as Terminal 26); and the Library of Health Sciences at the University of Illinois at the Medical Center in Chicago (February 1972 as Terminal 27). In February 1972, the New York Academy of Medicine dropped out when the grant funds for their participation expired ("Network adds" 1972). By the end of February 1972, seventeen institutions were actively using the system, and the volume of search activity had been growing rapidly over the prior seven months.

Koenig (1995) recalled that when he was at Pfizer in the early 1970s, he arranged for Pfizer access to MEDLINE data for a limited amount of searching on SUNY BCN on an informal basis because Pfizer and the rest of the U.S. pharmaceutical industry had been denied access to NLM's online services by NLM policy. Pfizer did chemical substructure searches for SUNY, and SUNY did MEDLINE searching for Pfizer on a quid pro quo basis. Because of New York state regulations, SUNY BCN could not charge for services for which Pfizer would have gladly paid. These circumstances led to further joint attempts by Pfizer and SUNY to develop projects of mutual interest, one of which was a proposal to compare MEDLINE and Excerpta Medica searching—described later.

In moving to Albany, the online system was transferred from a single dedicated computer serving only SUNY BCN, to a central university facility that was larger, but which ran the BCN system in addition to all of the regular university administrative work, such as student registration records for the entire SUNY system. Furthermore, BCN was the first teleprocessing application installed at this facility. SUNY BCN faced even more difficult resource and priority constraints in its new home. In a reflective mood, Pizer (1971) remarked: "The political problems ARE enormous and real.... More than one project has come to grief because such problems played an important role. The early Columbia-Harvard-Yale medical cataloging project was one example, and we are now witnessing the rapid decline of the SUNY Biomedical Communication Network for this reason."[3]

Nonetheless, the immediate purpose of the consolidation was accomplished. The Network remained operational with reasonable fees, and development work began to improve the online search capability. However, when the Network moved from Syracuse, it came under the management of the director of the Central Office Computer Center, Ronald Quake. Therefore, after leading the BCN from its beginning to the point of being a major national online system with international recognition, Pizer left SUNY to join the University of Illinois at Chicago as librarian of its Medical Center, but he maintained contact by joining a Users' Task Force Committee. He emerged later in a dominant way in finding a replacement for the BCN (see chapter 9). Pizer died in 1991, after a notable career ("Irwin Howard Pizer, 1934–1991" 1992). Cain later went to the National Library of Scotland, and Leiter continued to serve the network as a member of the Users' Task Force Committee. Meanwhile, Egeland had moved up from indexer to online searcher, then search trainer, finally becoming the director of User Education and Training Services. She desired to remain in Syracuse, so she left the network when the headquarters moved from Syracuse to Albany. She became associate librarian at Upstate Medical Center Libraray, and continued as chair of the Network's Ad Hoc Committee on Network Operations, to advise Quake, until her resignation from that position in September 1972, when she moved to Minneapolis. From her Minneapolis home, she resumed a connection with the network in January 1973, with responsibility for user education and training, and public relations. She continued with BCN until April 1976, when she left to help start BRS (chapter 9).

As the new director of the Central Computer Center, Quake thus assumed overall responsibility for the computer operations of BCN. A graduate of Union College, Quake had worked as an insurance salesman, a systems engineer for IBM, and a systems analyst for UNIVAC. He left SUNY in 1973 to join the New York State Division of Criminal Justice in Albany, as director of the Bureau of Identification and Information Services, where he was responsible for the largest statewide computerized criminal history record system in the United States before returning in 1976 to join BRS.

SUNY BCN and STAIRS

Switch from DPS to STAIRS

For almost two years after the move, the Network continued to use DPS to search the MEDLINE file of approximately 1.5 million medical journal and monograph citations provided by NLM. However, as early as 1971, a BCN Ad Hoc Committee on Network Operations started work to select software to replace DPS (McClure 1973).

In 1970, IBM made the STAIRS software commercially available. The modified DPS programs that ran the online MEDLARS database service from 1968 to 1973 were not flexible enough to permit both controlled-vocabulary searching and full-text searching of multiple files. Consequently, a decision in 1973 to broaden the scope of database coverage beyond the medical field required the acquisition of new search software. Performance testing of STAIRS began in October 1972, with over 200,000 citations loaded online for user familiarization and testing. A workshop was held in December 1972 for search analysts to learn the new software ("New network software" 1972; "Online performance test" 1972). After extensive comparative evaluation of three software packages, STAIRS was chosen. It was used to load the MEDLARS file and begin production operation in March 1973 (McClure 1973; Egeland 1974, 1975b).

By the end of 1972, all network members were using terminals with speeds of 30 cps. The institutions renting terminals from the Computer Center were using either the UNIVAC DCT-500 or NCR 260 terminals. Other terminals in operation throughout the network were either the TI Silent 700 or the Execuport 300 ("New user terminals" 1973).

EMF Database Plan

BCN staff had always wanted to add more external databases online besides MEDLARS; this objective was included in their original planning in 1966 and was reaffirmed by the Ad Hoc Committee on Network Operations when it formed in 1971. The first choice of network users was to add records from the EMF. Pizer (1972b) announced that SUNY was about to start a four-month experiment to load 50,000 citations from the 1971 files of Drug Literature Index published by the EMF. If that test were successful, they would add the most recent two-year file of 500,000 citations from Excerpta Medica for access from all SUNY terminals. However, by mid-summer of 1972, the SUNY network had decided not to use the Drug Literature Index for a test file, but instead to use two or three months of recent records from EM files. A comparative test was planned of both full-text and controlled-vocabulary searching of Excerpta Medica records, and controlled-vocabulary searching on the MEDLARS file. This would be followed by the loading of the most recent two-year collection of Excerpta Medica records for regular production searching as a BCN database. In fall 1972, the *SUNY BCN Network Newsletter* reported that BCN had reached agreement with Information Intersciences, Inc. (3i Co.)—U.S. representatives for the Excerpta Medica publisher—to put EM online for experimental searching. Egeland was named project coordinator. Four network centers had agreed to participate in the test, which would run representative searches against both the Excerpta Medica and Index Medicus files. The newsletter stated that the Excerpta Medica database was then being loaded and that a pilot study would begin in early 1973. However, neither the experiment nor production searching of the Excerpta material came to pass on the SUNY system.

Earlier, at the EMF itself, Peter Warren, Pierre Vinken, and Frans van der Walle (1969) described a database production system then in operation in Amsterdam to produce several printed abstract journals (for example, *Excerpta Medica*), run an SDI service, and support a computer tape distribution service for drug literature. This system also included an extensive capability for handling biomedical terminology, including development and maintenance of an extensive subject authority file called *MALIMET* (*Master List of Medical Indexing Terms*), consisting of about 60,000 preferred terms and almost 500,000 synonyms.

Blanken and Stern (1975) noted that no true search software was written at Excerpta Medica until 1971, when a few searches were performed on the basis of punched paper tape input of search questions. A true test of the system was not possible, even though the database tapes sent from Amsterdam to information centers in the United

States and the United Kingdom had permitted comparative studies of the Excerpta Medica database. Excerpta Medica also licensed and provided their file for internal use within interested organizations. In 1975, staff at Hoechst Pharmaceutical Co. in Frankfurt, Germany, used the database in an interactive online mode, using STAIRS.

Koenig (1995) told the Excerpta Medica story from a different angle. When he was at Pfizer, the staff desired the Excerpta Medica file as well as MEDLINE. *MALIMET*, the Excerpta Medica vocabulary, was much richer in its pharmaceutical agent terms. For example, it could support a search on PCPA or parachlorophenylalinine, a hot topic in the 1970s, whereas MEDLINE could only get as close as "serotonin antagonists." Koenig worked with Quake and Egeland to put together a plan for an online study to compare search effectiveness of MEDLINE versus Excerpta Medica databases. SUNY BCN would load a portion of Excerpta Medica (supplied by Pfizer). Pfizer would make a "contribution" to SUNY BCN for file loading, staff time, and related expenses. Pfizer would get MEDLINE searching, and they would jointly conduct and publish some research. Egeland, Quake, and Koenig thought this was a clever way to allow SUNY BCN to "charge" Pfizer for services. The real agenda was for Pfizer to contribute the Excerpta tape and money to SUNY BCN to permit them to load the data, and for Pfizer in return to get MEDLINE access through SUNY BCN while jointly doing the study.[4] Pfizer corporate headquarters were in New York, and Quake's charter was to support the state of New York—but not commercial institutions. The deal was about to be settled and the trial service started, when it was canceled abruptly because SDC announced that it would offer MEDLINE with the PMA tapes to any interested user. Also, Egeland reported that the contract negotiated with the 3i Co. had been invalidated because the company was no longer the U.S. distributor for the Excerpta Medica tapes ("User committee meets" 1973). SUNY BCN and Pfizer now had no need to go through the extra effort of a special comparative test.

Other Database Studies

In March 1973, SDC's new software (ELHILL IIC) became operational at NLM. Van Camp (1973) did a comparative analysis of the new SUNY and MEDLINE systems in 1973 based on over 1,000 searches done between July 1, 1972, and April 1, 1973, on each of the systems.

Plans were confirmed in September 1973 for a cooperative research project with BIOSIS and SUNY BCN to determine the applicability of *Biological Abstracts* for online searching ("SUNY and BIOSIS" 1973). As mentioned in chapter 4, BIOSIS was using STAIRS in-house at that time for their own production processes. SUNY's switch to the STAIRS software was an important first step in being able to add other files. Lloyd Palmer, then manager of System Programming for SUNY Central Office Computer Center, wrote the program modifications to convert IBM STAIRS to what became known as BRS STAIRS. The new software permitted natural language as well as controlled vocabulary access, which DPS could not (Egeland 1975b). Under the direction of Egeland, then acting director of SUNY BCN, and Kay Durkin, planning officer in the Research and Development Department at BIOSIS, BCN staff conducted a pilot test of the BIOSIS database extensively with SUNY users before adding it in 1974 (Durkin and Egeland 1974). This was a major experiment to evaluate the use of BIOSIS with the STAIRS software on the SUNY online service, on over 700 test searches.

Gradually, BCN added additional databases in subject areas other than medicine: ERIC in October 1973, and Psychological Abstracts in March 1974. ERIC was loaded online under STAIRS at the urging of the staff at SUNY-Albany, with that library providing additional financial support to the Central Office Computer Center to make it happen.

Backup for NLM's MEDLINE

After March 1973, the Central Office computer served not only its primary SUNY BCN subscribers, but also functioned as a backup for NLM's MEDLINE. Supported by a $250,000 federal contract with NLM, the SUNY central computer added thirty additional ports to handle online searches during peak periods when the NLM computer was overloaded, and to extend the NLM hours of service ("SUNY operates computer ports" 1973; "SUNY-Albany joins NLM" 1973). Thus users dialing through the telecommunication network could be switched automatically from the NLM computer to the backup computer at SUNY without redialing. BCN users were assured that "the contract for MEDLINE processing will in no way affect the operation of SUNY's own (BCN), nor will the addition of 30 MEDLINE ports impact the performance of the existing Network service" ("NLM contract awarded" 1973).

In spite of this support to NLM from SUNY, the two systems, because they were operating with different search software and different computers, were considered by some users to be competitors. Other users felt that they complemented each other. In either case, users began examining the differences between the SUNY system and the emerging MEDLINE system. Opinion was divided over which one was superior in retrieval capabilities. Spiegel and Crager, users at the College of Medicine and Dentistry of New Jersey, were among the first to make such comparisons. They compared performance in fulfilling search requests, without remarkable results (Spiegel 1972; Spiegel and Crager 1973). Even in 1972, significant limitations still existed; for example, it was still not possible to do online search of the MEDLARS file by author name on either the SUNY BCN or NLM systems (Pizer 1972b). Humphrey (1974, 1976) analyzed and attempted to clarify the distinctions in the structure of the two search systems.

In 1973, some medical libraries had their choice of online access to MEDLINE from two different sources: from NLM or from SUNY. The NLM file provided access from 1970 to date in two separate files, SUNY provided the same period of online coverage plus a retrospective batch search from 1964–1970 with the same search formulation.

SUNY also provided a title scan feature that permitted title word searching, something that the NLM system could not do—however, after SUNY installed the title scan feature, NLM management encouraged their programmers to put in the stringsearch feature. The decision rule at one institution was to use NLM MEDLINE unless the subject matter of the search was peripheral to clinical medicine, a comprehensive search prior to 1970 was needed, or a specific term was required. In those cases or when the MEDLINE system was not available, the SUNY system was to be used (Egeland and Foreman 1973).

Expansion and Demise

A new subject index to the SUNY BCN System User Manual was prepared as a class project in Atherton's course on abstracting and indexing at Syracuse University in 1975 ("User manual; New index" 1975). (Unfortunately for the students, their project received only limited usage because the SUNY BCN did not survive past 1976: in March 1976, when it had about thirty-two institutional members, it lost all state funding.)

In 1975, BCN reached out beyond its original East Coast operations and proposed an extension of online service to the nine UC campuses. The reasons for the offer are unclear, given Egeland's summer 1975 statement that BCN was at capacity in the current computer center hardware environment and that the waiting list of institutions who had requested membership in the network whenever the service could be expanded to additional users was growing (Egeland 1975a). UC librarians felt that support of this BCN might introduce competition in the online industry, and prompt a reappraisal of the prices charged by the commercial services. Because the UC campuses already had low cost access to NLM's MEDLINE service, their interest was primarily in access to BCN's BIOSIS, ERIC, and Psychological Abstracts databases.

SUNY BCN eventually expanded to thirty-two medical and university libraries located between Massachusetts and Minnesota. By the end of 1975, there were more non-SUNY participants (including federal and out-of-state institutions) than SUNY participants. Allison and Allan (1979) wrote in a postmortem: "It was given permission to continue, provided it could demonstrate that it had fulfilled its objective (it had) and that it could be self-supporting. It was forced to increase its charges slightly, and earlier than expected, but it was able to survive that crisis. In fact, it was able to hold its feet steady for the second year of operation (with some small reductions in some cases) through the growth of the network."

The transfer in 1971 to the university computer center in Albany, intended to improve access for network users, actually degraded service. At Albany, the network had to compete in a shared online environment in which its priority was lower than that of other university users, and later lower even than for the NLM contract access (Van Camp 1995). Apparently the university administrators did not appreciate the importance of the network. The NLM contract money went to the SUNY Central Office Computer Center, not to BCN. The NLM service contract also may have contributed to the degradation of the service. As mentioned earlier, under the terms of a $250,000 contract, SUNY assumed the obligation from March 1973 to provide online computer search service support to NLM password holders. SUNY continued the NLM contract to provide the ports to handle the overflow from NLM until the early 1980s (Pizer 1984). In any case, response time degenerated each year, and users grew increasingly dissatisfied. On March 1, 1976, near the end of SUNY BCN, when the service and response time were getting worse, Pizer and representatives of the user groups went to the SUNY Chancellor's Office to plead with the executive vice chancellor for more support. McClure (1995) recalled that it was a contentious meeting in which a SUNY administrator said, in the context of the California users wanting to come in, that "New York state taxpayers couldn't possibly fund things that would help people in other states." The possibility of trimming SUNY BCN then to include only New York institutions did not seem to be a viable alternative; *greater* participation was needed in order to reach a critical mass.

In spite of the problems and issues SUNY BCN faced throughout its ten-year lifespan, the developers and users viewed it essentially as a success. The subscribers and searchers generally were pleased with the service, the operation ran economically, and the administration remained open to suggestions for changes to accommodate user needs and preferences. SUNY BCN fell victim to changing institutional priorities, as well as, apparently, financial hardships in New York and university administrators who failed to realize its importance. Pizer (1984, 346) offered yet another explanation: "One of the reasons that systems fail is that the vision of the designers exceeds the capabilities of the technology that is available."

The demise of SUNY BCN was not really final; within a year it had been reincarnated as a full-blown commercial search service called BRS. Egeland, Palmer, and Quake played leading roles, along with Pizer's attempt to build a *second* BCN, in the rise of BRS (see next chapter).

9 The Online Industry: The Public View

Introduction

In the early 1970s, the online world witnessed quiet, but pivotal transformations. The major developments were announced publicly at the time, but much of the activity and decisions were proprietary and not documented in the open literature. For example, the date, or even month, that SDC Search Service or Lockheed DIALOG, went "commercial" is difficult to ascertain.[1] In 1991 and 1992, groups—even within at least one major online service—that were planning special events to note the twentieth anniversary of the online industry had a difficult time determining a specific date in 1972 when the online business or industry "started." At the end of 1976, BRS (Bibliographic Retrieval Services) burst on the scene with balloons and fanfares as the newest entry into an established online "industry." In 1971, however, the industry hardly existed, and its birth was a quiet event. The rapid maturation and expansion of the industry from about 1970 through 1976 was astonishing, and is the subject of this and the next chapter.

A survey (Fong 1971) conducted at the start of the decade of the services, interface languages, processing software, hours of operation, staffing, and other features of the various online services as they existed then did not reveal which ones would succeed within a few years as commercial enterprises or major government-sponsored systems and which would not. Nevertheless, this period was a demarcation point for the systems whose early development we traced in the past four chapters. SDC Search Service and Lockheed DIALOG were transformed into commercial retrieval systems. Developments and research with OBAR and the Data Corporation system led to LEXIS. SUNY BCN adopted the IBM STAIRS software and acquired databases in new subject areas. NLM's MEDLINE, and ESA/IRS continued to penetrate their specialized markets. At the time that these established systems were changing, new systems not seen before were introduced for public service.

To give the full flavor of what was happening in the industry during the rapid expansion in the seventies, we tell the story twice, from different angles. In this chapter, the milestone activities and innovations are chronicled as they were presented to the public, through the published literature, search services newsletters, press releases, and public appearances of online industry representatives. In the next chapter, the same events will be probed from a different angle, through the eyes of industry insiders and the first users. When we speak of the "seventies" in this context, we mean the period through 1976 (and sometimes a little beyond), at which point the online industry began to take off. That is another story.

As in the 1960s, many exchanges of information among developers and users occurred in the 1970s. Some took place at periodic gatherings called by project sponsors and funding agencies to facilitate the transfer of technology they were helping to develop, and others took place at meetings sponsored by professional societies. In chapter 4 we mentioned a few of these significant meetings. Another important gathering of designers was a Stanford University workshop on feature analysis of interactive retrieval systems. This NSF-sponsored event was held in April 1973 (Martin 1974).

Much of the development work in the 1970s was disseminated in the form of conference, symposia and workshop proceedings, technical reports, and various journals of library and information science and technology. Not until 1977 and 1978 did a few core journals that focused on online and database activity begin: *On-Line Review* (March 1977, Learned Information), *Online* (January 1977, Online, Inc.), and *Database* (September 1978, Online, Inc.).

From the Sixties to the Seventies: Experiments to Full-Fledged Public Services

Within a short period between late 1971 and spring 1973, the first commercial services were launched from the prototypes of the sixties, earlier operational systems such as SUNY BCN were greatly enhanced, and AIM-TWX and MEDLARS were transformed into MEDLINE. All of these represented system upgrading, more new users, new databases, and expanded telecommunications access. We begin this section by picking up the continuing stories of the each of the systems previously examined, and follow them with introductions to the new systems of the seventies. Then we explore the general kinds of new hardware and telecommunications that made rapid expansion possible.

Lockheed Retrieval Service and DIALOG

In chapter 5 we brought the DIALOG story to the point in 1972 when DIALOG first became available as a public online service. We examined the 1971 renewal and expansion of the ERIC service contract that gave a big boost and foothold for the public commercial service, along with the 1972 NTIS service contract. The story continues here with the start of the public service.

Once Roger Summit had the approval from his superiors at Lockheed in early 1972, he announced the commercial online service. About that time, DIALOG was established as a separate profit center within the Lockheed Palo Alto Research Lab. Like a Lockheed jumbo jet, however, the service got off the ground slowly. The first customer was Lockheed itself, followed by GE's Atomic Power Division in San Jose, California, in 1972, who wanted to be able to search *Nuclear Science Abstracts*. They did not know about DIALOG, but they knew that AEC was conducting computer searches. When they approached AEC to obtain that service, they were referred to Lockheed. Thus the first commercial customer came to Lockheed without any marketing, demonstrations, or other incentives (Summit 1987). Such was not to be the case, of course, with most of their later customers. Another early business/industry customer for the use of databases other than NASA, DOE, and ERIC was the Calspan Corporation in Buffalo, New York. Calspan signed up in December 1972, primarily for the NTIS database, and first used its online terminal in January 1973. Barbara Kunkel and Betty Miller were the pioneering searchers at Calspan.

In January 1972, Project RISE (Research & Information Service for Education), in Pennsylvania, was among the first customers for the Lockheed online service who were not part of the constituencies already supported by the NASA, DOE, and ERIC service contracts. RISE used the ERIC file and had the first ERIC/DIALOG terminal in the eastern United States outside Washington, DC. Other organizations who contracted for use of ERIC were the Iowa State Board of Education and the Center for Exceptional Children. In March 1972, the USOE service contract was expanded and extended, and the first ERIC/DIALOG User Group Meeting was held in Arlington, Virginia. San Mateo County Educational Reference Center (SMERC) in California started service in May 1972. Contra Costa County Public Library (California) and Stanford University started dial-up service in December 1972.

The formal kickoff for Lockheed's commercial service seems to have been at the SLA meeting in June 1972. The search service was christened Lockheed Retrieval Service (LRS)—or alternatively, Lockheed Information Retrieval Service—and it used the DIALOG search software. Its renaming as DIALOG Information Retrieval Service did not happen until mid-1976. Gordon Schick joined DIALOG in 1972 and worked with Lew and Giles to continue file design and development, including supporting administrative programs. Other early staff members included Mitchell, Radwin, Schoultz, and Fred Zappert.

DIALOG's computer facility grew rapidly during the seventies. An IBM 360 Model 50 was installed in September 1973. In July 1974, the seventh IBM Data Cell was installed, increasing total storage capacity to 3 gigabytes. A Model 65 in December 1974 increased storage capacity to 4.2 gigabytes. In October 1975 a second Model 65 computer, along with an additional six billion characters of online storage, raised the total to about fifteen billion characters (more than double the early 1975 capacity). As a result of this expansion, additional ports were added, working storage space was increased for individual users, and several more files added.

During the first year only a few files, all bibliographic, were available to a small number of customers. File number 1 was ERIC, which had over 122,000 citations by the end of 1972. The other 1972 file was NTIS. Since August 1971, NTIS had been providing a public retrieval service (NTISearch) from its database, using a computer output microfilm (COM) subject index of descriptors and identifiers for the database, and a mechanized microfiche retrieval system—Image System's Compact Automatic Retrieval Display (CARD)—to provide copies of filmed images of the retrieved citations and abstracts. Because of the satisfactory user response, NTIS solicited proposals in February 1972 for an online search capability to provide this function. NTIS awarded a contract to Lockheed for use of DIALOG as the basis for NTIS to provide this service. A strength noted in Lockheed's proposal was the recent implementation of a full-text search capability, including word proximity searching, to permit searching on title, descriptor, identifier, and abstract words. Internal Lockheed R&D funding in 1971–1972 made this extension possible. However, the bid to NTIS did not actually propose that abstracts or titles be parsed for online searching. At the same time, a capability was added for truncation term searching (i.e., stem searching) and for user-defined output format designators. The proposed output speeds were either 30 or 240 cps, and the terminal options were limited to the KSR33 Teletype (10 cps), GE Terminet (30 cps), or the CCI CC30 CRT Terminal (240 cps) with GE Terminet (or equivalent) printer. While the proposal to NTIS included a statement that DIALOG was available for lease or purchase by NTIS and other users, NTIS chose not to exercise that option. This was the genesis of the loading of the NTIS database on Lockheed's system. As part of the agreement, Lockheed was permitted to make the NTIS file publicly available online (Tancredi and Ryerson 1972).

The NTIS proposal included language to the effect that Lockheed would solicit additional subscribers for this NTIS service on the same operational basis as that offered to NTIS, and that additional income produced by a multisubscriber service would lower the cost to NTIS. That must have sounded good to NTIS, because it appears that they let Lockheed offer their file for public use without requiring any royalty payment. Lockheed's renewal proposal in April 1975 noted that because of substantial commercial NTIS usage, they could now offer a royalty payment.

At the beginning of 1973 the number of DIALOG customers was thirteen, and the number jumped to thirty-seven by summer. The number of public databases grew correspondingly during this same period—increasing from two at the beginning of 1972 to eight at mid-1973. The number of online records grew from 100,000 to 1,330,000 by mid-1973. Other early files were Exceptional Child Education Resources (ECER), Abstracts of Instructional and Research Materials in Vocational and Technical Education (AIM/ARM), Nuclear Science Abstracts (NSA), PANDEX Current Index to Scientific and Technical Literature, and TRANSDEX (citations of translations) (Donati 1973). The producer of the PANDEX and TRANSDEX databases, Crowell Collier Macmillan, discontinued them, so Lockheed had to withdraw them in January 1975. NTIS and ERIC were well known from years of availability in batch search systems. ECER and AIM/ARM had also been available earlier, but were more specialized in content and known primarily by education professionals. The Council for Exceptional Children in Arlington, Virginia, produced ECER. In 1972, a terminal was installed there, and Lockheed boasted in a proposal that "it operates two hours per day, every working day."

The service added a few more files during 1973, including Psychological Abstracts, AGRICOLA (known then as CAIN—for Cataloging/Indexing), INSPEC, and ABI/INFORM. By the end of 1974, the DIALOG service offered eleven files; by the end of 1976 it offered more than fifty—although this number is a little inflated because some databases were split into separate files by date ranges and each file had its own number. INSPEC, first available online in October 1973, may be the bibliographic database that has been publicly (and continuously) available online longer than any other database produced by a nongovernment organization. AGRICOLA was loaded as part of a contract to provide online service to the National Agricultural Library (NAL). A condition of that initial contract was that it was to be available on a royalty-free basis for use by other interested users. In November 1974, a searcher at NAL entered a Search/Save (stored search formulation) on DIALOG, where it stayed for the next thirteen years—probably the oldest and longest-running stored search formulation in online history.

Summit later judged access to telecommunications networks to be their most significant development for 1973. Customers could access DIALOG through a local phone call in major U.S. cities at a flat charge of $10 per hour. This allowed the concentration of their worldwide demand at a single computer center. TWX access at 10 cps was added in August 1974 to serve users in countries that did not have good data communications networks. By the end of 1976, DIALOG had TYMNET access to sixty-nine U.S., five Canadian, and four European cities, and TELENET access to forty U.S. cities and three Canadian cities—a total of seventy-seven different U.S. cities. The online content and value of DIALOG and the other search services had sufficient value to drive the extension of the TYMNET and TELENET networks to over fifty countries in the second half of the 1970s. These online services and the associated packet networks were the true precursor of today's Internet and World Wide Web.

In fall 1973, online service was scheduled from Monday to Friday for 8.25 hours per day. Given the equipment and system configuration, a fifteen minute break in the middle was necessary to accommodate the offline printing activity and perform file and system maintenance activity. In January 1974 the shift break was eliminated and service expanded to 11.5 hours per day, except for Tuesdays, when the system shut down an hour earlier to permit preventative maintenance to be done on the equipment. At the end of 1974, online service was scheduled for 12 hours per day, Monday through Friday, except for 11 hours per day on Tuesdays and Fridays. Saturday service and evening service began in March 1975.

1973 Milestones

DIALOG was the first online search service to advertise in journal publications.

DIALOG was the first online search service to produce a regular newsletter for its customers.

Users of Lockheed's online search service (the organization will be referred to as Lockheed rather than as LRS, since that abbreviation never caught on) were mainly librarians, functioning as intermediaries for the end consumers. These users were first made aware of the service in January 1973 in *Special Libraries*; a news item ("NTIS search," 58) announced that the NTIS database was available "to the public on a fee basis," and more information was available by writing to Dr. Roger Summit at the Lockheed Palo Alto Research Laboratory. The Lockheed staff was so small in 1973 that all inquiries were directed to Summit or to Bob Donati (on the East Coast). By May, advertisements began appearing regularly in *Special Libraries*, presumably aimed at special librarians. Batch search services such as DATRIX had been using journal ads for years before the online services, so the use of ads was not unique, but they mark a stage in the growth of online services. The banner of the first advertisement was "Lockheed announces a simple, low-cost way to search major bibliographic databases. Online." A straightforward description of the service and databases available followed the headline. After the first advertisement, Lockheed changed "announces" to "offers" but otherwise kept the text the same. None of the advertisements during the first year used the name DIALOG; only "Lockheed Information Services." In 1974, Lockheed publications made reference to "Lockheed

Retrieval Service," "Lockheed Retrieval Services," "LRS," and "DIALOG." In mid-1975, Lockheed was still labeling its log-in statements and search printouts with the name "Lockheed Information Retrieval Service" without mentioning the name of the software (DIALOG). In January 1976, the TYMNET log-in procedure required users to enter the name of the node desired (changed from LMS to LRS) and the name of the system password (DIALOG); the Lockheed system responded with "Enter your DIALOG password." In a June 1976 presentation, Donati referred to "the Lockheed DIALOG system." The first issue of *DIALOG*™ *Chronolog*, the newsletter of "Lockheed Information Systems" appeared in May 1973. The name "DIALOG Information Retrieval Service" did not appear on the *Chronolog* masthead until the July 1976 issue.

From the beginning, DIALOG management adopted a goal of expanding online service to the broadest extent possible, to serve all possible users with all types of information. This goal inspired almost a missionary zeal and dedication, and it underlay much of the decision making at DIALOG during the 1970s.

An early published evaluation of an online search system, from the standpoint of productivity and efficiency of searching, rather than comparative feature analyses or issues of recall and relevancy, was a study involving DIALOG. Bourne, Robinson, and Todd (1974) conducted it at the UC Institute of Library Research for the National Institute of Education, under subcontract to Lockheed Palo Alto Research Lab. A practical interest in getting more productivity out of DIALOG prompted the study. It examined operations and performance of nine terminal installations using DIALOG for searching ERIC, in an attempt to identify factors that influenced productivity of terminal use. It looked at response time by time of day and day of the week, search commands and logic used by searchers at each terminal installation, the mix of complex, medium, and simple queries, and the extent and impact of the variant forms of descriptors in the file. Guidelines were prepared for searchers to consider for pre-search and terminal activities. Timing studies were done to suggest procedures that could increase search speeds. The empirical data were based on all search activity during fifteen selected days in October–November 1973.

By the early seventies, DIALOG management had obtained direct experience with the information needs of special libraries and users in the federal government and industrial sector. They were anxious, however, to expand into the public library and academic sectors. Accordingly they submitted a proposal in December 1973 to NSF for an experiment to supply online service to selected institutions in those market sectors. Summit asked Oscar Firschein to prepare the proposal and then go to Washington to review it with NSF personnel. In March 1974, NSF awarded a two-year contract to Lockheed for the DIALIB (DIALOG in Libraries) project to study the feasibility of online service for the general public, using four California public libraries. Summit chose the DIALIB name, even though the Lockheed patent lawyer bitterly opposed it because he felt that it weakened the DIALOG trademark (Firschein 1987).

Summit was the DIALIB project director and Firschein was the full-time principal investigator for the next three years. Firschein had been involved earlier with DIALOG through the Lockheed Computer Research Group activities, but most of his energies were spent in information science research related to image processing and artificial intelligence. An external contractor, Applied Communication Research, Inc., was used to evaluate the experiments. As stated in the NSF proposal, the major objective of DIALIB was

... to determine the impact on libraries and users of providing on-line access to a universe of technical, social, and educational information heretofore unavailable to the general public. Thus we are interested in the retrieval system and its associated data bases as a 'change agent,' and are concerned with the effects both inside the library as well as outside, on the society at large. In addition ... we will determine realistic pricing policies for public library on-line retrieval service.

When he announced the award, Lee Burchinal, head of NSF's Office of Science Information Service, reiterated that the major objective was to investigate ways in which public libraries could be used as linking agents between the general public and the vast amounts of information that had been cataloged, abstracted, and stored in large computer-readable databases. Burchinal (1975, 7) stated that another goal was "to determine if sufficient demand can be aggregated from infrequent or low-volume users to support advanced retrieval services at public libraries or other organizations. If successful, various combinations of information companies and local service groups might develop."

The initial participants for this project were four public libraries geographically close to the DIALOG facilities (Santa Clara County Library, San Jose Public Library, Redwood City Public Library, San Mateo County Library). Several other libraries (Minneapolis Public Library, New York METRO system, Long Island Library Resources Council, Houston Public Library, and Cleveland Public Library) were added later. All participating libraries were provided with terminals and access to the DIALOG service. DIALIB was eventually extended to three years, June 1974 through July 1977. During the first year searches were conducted for free, during the second year they were priced at half, and the third year was full-cost recovery searching. The Redwood City Public Library withdrew at the end of the second year, and the Santa Clara County Library shortly thereafter. The variation in user fees over the three-year period provided a unique opportunity to investigate the impact on demand, search behavior, and user attitude at various fee levels (Cooper and DeWath 1976; Summit and Firschein 1977b; Firschein, Summit, and Mick 1978). Bourne was a member of an advisory board to this project, and recalled how interesting it was to hear the participants' attitudes and experiences. For example, one participant was reluctant to install Teletype terminals in the library because they were "an electrical appliance" and posed a hazard to users. DIALIB was covered extensively in the professional literature (Ahlgren 1975; Summit and Drew 1976; Mick 1977; Cooper 1977; Firschein and Summit 1977; Summit and Firschein 1977a).

In August 1974, DIALOG held its first users' meeting, in Washington, DC, with over one hundred users. At the May 1975 users meeting, DIALOG announced that Search/Save was to be advertised soon for general use for all files; the March–June 1975 *Chronolog* proclaimed its availability. While this feature had been first demonstrated with MIT's TIP, and had been implemented in DIALOG in December 1972, at about the same time as IBM first announced the SAVE feature for its STAIRS software, DIALOG did not make it available for public use at that time. Search/Save allowed a searcher to recall a stored search formulation and incorporate it in another search. This feature made it possible for searchers to construct, use, save, edit and reuse search formulations that represented repeated-use building blocks of larger formulations (e.g., formulations to represent elementary and secondary education levels in the education files, or heavy metals in the sciences files); in some instances, users and database suppliers published such formulations as a service to facilitate effective searching by others.

Bourne, Robinson, and Anderson, all at the UC-Berkeley School of Library and Information Science, in separate collaborative tests during 1975–1976 with Lockheed and SDC, produced the first lab workbooks for library school students to use in learning online searching (Bourne 1976a, 1977). The draft workbooks were tested with online lab classes run by Bourne, Robinson, and Anderson at Berkeley, and by Atherton at Syracuse. Lockheed chose to offer the workbook in conjunction with its Classroom Instruction Program, and reissued it several times into the 1980s to keep up with changes in DIALOG. SDC placed less emphasis on support to library schools, and chose not to use the workbook. Bourne, Anderson, and Robinson later joined Lockheed to work for the DIALOG service.

In addition to DIALIB, another of Firschein's 1976 projects was to propose and help implement, with Bourne and others then at ILR, the first of

DIALOG's publicly available Online Training and Practice (ONTAP) files. The first ONTAP file of 35,000 ERIC records was unique in a training sense because the file also contained the predetermined record numbers that comprised the answer sets for a set of search questions that accompanied the file. This permitted the students to test their search strategy and answer set for a given question against a predetermined absolute answer set, and obtain an immediate recall and precision score. This ONTAP file was later used for research and instructional purposes at other institutions (e.g., Markey and Atherton 1978; Markey and Cochrane 1981; Bellardo 1984, 1985).

In 1975, the Information Industry Association (IIA) gave Lockheed (jointly with SDC) the Information Product of the Year Award. The award noted their unique contribution in "head to head" competition and "cited their efforts in providing a 'major breakthrough in the control and retrieval of a wide range of bibliographic data' and in 'shaping the procedure by which a range of the information needs of the American society will be met'" ("Members" 1975, 57).

The award was given in spite of teething problems with the new and growing DIALOG service. At the May 1975 users meeting, DIALOG staff noted that during the previous December and January, a 10–20 percent outage of scheduled time had occurred, but they had now brought this down to 2–5 percent. Management considered this to be good performance (years later, their availability performance objectives were 99.9 percent). The system was further limited to fifty communication ports (i.e., fifty concurrent terminals logged on), which caused frequent out-of-port conditions and angry users who could not log in when they wanted to.

By the end of 1976, DIALOG had managed to implement or improve some features and provide 120 cps dial-up access; add a second IBM 360/65 computer, provide eighty-four hour per week access to more than fifty databases and a total of more than 12 million records (on a system with 14 billion characters of storage), with service to thousands of customers in several countries in North America and Europe. In 1988, Lockheed sold its wholly owned subsidiary, DIALOG Information Services, Inc., to Knight-Ridder, Inc., for $353 million. In 1992, Summit retired from DIALOG and received a Distinguished Service Award from the IIA.

The Lockheed Scandal

Unfortunately, the public DIALOG story is not complete without reference to the scandal that kept the name of Lockheed Aircraft Corp. on the newspaper front pages and magazine covers for nearly two years between 1975 and 1976. The earliest references to the unsavory story described Lockheed as an "ailing aerospace giant," in an unhealthy U.S. airline industry that was suffering from excess capacity and huge increases in the cost of jet fuel (Fuller 1974, 83). The problems for Lockheed were cited at least as far back as 1971; a magazine writer said that Lockheed had been "sliding toward bankruptcy" ("Bribe overruns" 1976, 194). To keep the company afloat at that time, in spite of a heavy debt load, the U.S. Congress, with much debate and controversy, had granted a guarantee for bank loans of $195 million. Desperate to keep selling their enormously expensive airplanes, Lockheed representatives looked for markets abroad, especially in Japan and Western Europe. According to testimony from Lockheed's chairman of the board in front of a Senate subcommittee investigating multinational corporations, the cost of doing business in these countries was "kickbacks" (a deliberate substitution for the word "bribes") to influential politicians and businessmen (Pauly 1975, 54). The committee and the Treasury secretary were horrified that the government had given loan guarantees to a company that candidly admitted to at least $22 million in overseas payoffs ("Rules for Lockheed" 1975). No matter that such activities may not have been actually illegal by American law, or that other American companies were likely doing much the same thing, the fact of the loan guarantees and that Lockheed was the largest American defense contractor made the company the focus of the scandal. Adding to the shock value of the story were the revelations in each of the countries involved of the alleged corrupt politicians or national leaders (including Prince Bernhard of the Netherlands), and a powerful underworld figure in Japan who was accused of receiving $7 million as a paid Lockheed operative ("Scandals" 1976). Another magazine writer blamed the Lockheed scandal for the "biggest political storm" in Japan's postwar era, calling it "Japan's Watergate" (Stentzel 1976, 262). In late 1976, a journalist snidely referred to Lockheed as "that international symbol of trouble" ("Meanwhile" 1976, 33). Student protesters picketing outside Lockheed facilities in Palo Alto, California, shouted that Lockheed was a "merchant of death" (Caputo 1987), perhaps interweaving their indignation about the scandal with their protests against the Vietnam War.

As a Lockheed product, the online service enjoyed the reputation of its parent company as a leading technology innovator, but also suffered the snide criticisms arising from the scandal, and from Lockheed's involvement in developing "things that go bump in the night"—all kinds of black and mysterious defense projects such as the U-2, SR-71, spy satellites, and the deep-sea secret retrieval of a sunken Soviet submarine—even though the online service had nothing whatever to do with building or selling military aircraft, missiles, or space hardware, except in the sense that DIALOG had been conceived as a retrieval system to cope with the rapidly increasing amounts of technical data that aerospace engineers needed. Ten years after the scandal, Pemberton (1988, 7) referred to DIALOG as "an oasis of integrity" during that "difficult period of Lockheed corporate history... those dark days of 1975–76." Nonetheless, in the mid-1970s, DIALOG trainers and service representatives could not escape the fallout of the scandal. Their private feelings about having had to absorb the criticisms are described in the next chapter.

SDC Search Service (ORBIT III)

Like Lockheed, SDC announced in early 1972 an online service, also aimed at end-user searchers. A news item in January (LEASCO 1972) described the service as a collaboration between SDC and ERIC: "A new service for searching the ERIC data base from a user's own office or library terminal.... The ERIC data base, and other current educational materials, are stored in SDC's large-scale, time-shared computer in California which is connected to a multiplexer unit in Washington, DC. Users dial a special number, then connect the phone receiver to their terminal and start typing information requests." SDC called the service SDC/ERIC. When SDC brought the ERIC database online in 1972, it contained about 73,000 citations; at the end of 1972, it contained over 122,000 citations (ERIC on-line 1972; Brandhorst 1995). More of the ERIC story is in chapters 5 and 6. The data communication capability provided with the new SDC Search Service was the new TYMNET network, first made available in February 1972 for both the NLM and SDC systems. Because NLM made the arrangement, that story is told later in this chapter.

In August 1972, SDC offered online services to member companies of the PMA. The only database was MEDLINE—PMA's copy that SDC had loaded on its own computer. PMA had obtained the file on magnetic tapes from NLM in exchange for indexing and supplying documents that NLM could not otherwise obtain; in this way PMA was functioning as the foreign countries who had similar arrangements with NLM. SDC insisted on a commitment of $1,000 of searching per month, to which each of the large pharmaceutical companies could readily agree because they had no other effective way to obtain online search service with MEDLINE. In the next chapter the contentious behind-the-scenes negotiations among NLM, SDC, and PMA will be explored further.

The first to sign on was the Pfizer library, which thus became the first paying customer of SDC Search Service. Koenig (1987) related how he got started with SDC when he was at Pfizer: "I don't remember anyone coming to us or any hands-on training. I just remember that we signed up and started using it. We already knew something about online searching. We were SDC User Number 2. For years I wondered who Number 1 was. And then when Pauline Angione worked at SDC I asked her to look into it." Angione referred him to Cynthia Hull of SDC who told him that User Number 1 was a chemistry professor at a small California college, and the husband of someone on the SDC staff. He was a beta test site and was not charged. But Pfizer was the first *paying* customer of SDC (Koenig 1995). Hull also told Koenig that of the first paying SDC customers, most were pharmaceutical companies (roughly 65 percent). SDC was marketing to an audience that already knew how to use computer-based information services. Black (1987) identified Exxon Research and Engineering Company in New Jersey as among the first customers, with Ben Weil and Barbara Lawrence as the searchers there. Lawrence, Weil, and Graham (1974) mentioned their 1973 efforts to gain competence with ORBIT and DIALOG on the CA Condensates and NTIS databases. Black remembered conducting SDC's first training session at SDC. Three people attended.

SDC's third database was Chemical Abstracts Condensates (CA Condensates, CAC, or CHEMCON). The decision to load CAC was based on discussions with the pharmaceutical companies involved in the experimental online NLM service; when asked which other online file they wanted, they all answered "CAC." SDC had it online in February 1973. Mary Jane Ruhl, a chemist by training and ORBIT staff member who had helped with the SDC CHEMCON design, gave its first demonstration at an ACS meeting in Columbus, Ohio (Black 1987). This third database caused major headaches for the staff and threatened the survival of SDC Search Service (see chapter 10).

The actual full-fledged commercial service started in December 1972, with Carlos Cuadra as manager. Another SDC staff member who was a major participant in the start-up was Judith Wanger (Cuadra's chief assistant), who designed many of the online files, and directed training and marketing activities. In March 1973, *Special Libraries* ran a brief news item announcing the service and databases available: ERIC, CHEMCON, CAIN (Cataloging/Indexing, later known as AGRICOLA), and MEDLINE (which was available only to a restricted customer set). This announcement did not use the name ORBIT, and neither did the first SDC ad in *Special Libraries* that appeared in November 1973. Even though the ad appeared ten months after Lockheed's, SDC designed it to be eye-catching and to denigrate its competitors' advertisements:

Promises! Promises!
  'Dozens of databases! Millions of bibliographic records! Billions of characters of storage! On-line! Immediate! Cheap! Effortless!'
  How many times have you heard this? And, how many times have you been suspicious of the claims? They sound too good to be true. And, unfortunately they usually are.
  We at System Development Corporation don't put much stock in promises. We just tell the facts as they are.

The ad continued by listing the major strengths of SDC's online service and suggested that readers could get more information by writing to Search Specialists Judith Wanger in Santa Monica or Linda Rubens in Falls Church, Virginia.

By late 1973, the search service in Santa Monica was solidly established, with over fifty organizational users. Five files were offered: MEDLINE (biomedicine), CHEMCON (chemistry), ABI/INFORM (business), ERIC (education), and CAIN (agriculture). In 1974, COMPENDEX (engineering), GEO-REF (geosciences), NTIS (U.S. government technical reports), SciSearch (science citation index), APILIT (petroleum literature), and APIPAT (petroleum patents) were added. The last two were available only to American Petroleum Institute members at that time.

For a new service, this was a large number of files that made severe demands for storage capacity. Online storage was expensive, as charged by the SDC computer center to SDC Search Service, and posed a formidable financial strain. The search service solution was the approach that SDC had taken earlier with COLEX and CIRCOL for FTD—namely, the use of time windows. Until the end of 1976, SDC Search Service allocated the computer storage space to different files during different parts of the daily operating schedule. This permitted the SDC Search Service to choose an amount of online storage that it was able to afford, while balancing that against the impact on users. Consequently, even though a database was advertised as available online, its accessibility might be restricted to a specific time slot (e.g., 8:00–11:00 a.m. for COMPENDEX). By late 1973, over two million records were available online with SDC Search Service.

> **1974 Milestone**
>
> SDC Search Service was the first online search service to provide publicly available online document ordering service.

In March 1974, SDC began the first public operation of online document ordering from a search service. Called Electronic Maildrop®, the service supported document requests made to NTIS (for the NTIS database) and CIS (for the CIS and ASI databases). Bunker-Ramo had demonstrated an online document ordering feature in 1966 in the experimental NASA system (chapter 5). NLM had a document ordering feature in MEDLINE right from the beginning, with the ORDER command. NLM included this feature in the original specifications, in order to permit other medical libraries to get documents from NLM. At that time, most MEDLINE users were hospital libraries. Unlike later systems (e.g., DIALOG's DIALORDER) that were much easier to use, a user of the ORDER feature had to key in the bibliographic details and user name and address as part of the request—resembling an electronic mail feature, with all messages going to NLM. This ORDER capability was always present in the software but never announced until SDC had a document supplier who could provide the delivery service and unload the order file daily in order to pick up the requests. SDC's "Dear ORBIT User" letter in December 1976 announced:

In January, we will expand our ELECTRONIC MAILDROP® service to provide on-line ordering of over 5,000 journals covered by (ISI) OATS® (Original Article Tear Sheet) service, which can be used regardless of the SDC Search Service data base in which the reference is found; [and] dissertations available from University Microfilms International (UMI). Procedures for using ORDER OATS and ORDER UMI to obtain full-text copies will be announced in our January newsletter ... Many of the users of the NTIS, CIS, and ASI data bases have found the ELECTRONIC MAILDROP a particularly useful part of our service, because it saves them considerable time and paperwork to order on-line.

By April 1974, ORBIT was in its third incarnation, written in PL/1, and known as ORBIT III. ORBIT III was available for purchase or lease, ran on IBM 360 or 370 computers with disk storage, and could handle simultaneously up to forty files, each of which could contain at least 1 million records (ORBIT III 1974). The program allowed limiting by fields, range searching for dates, and standard Boolean operations and nested Boolean expressions but did not permit users to search easily on natural language terms as phrases nor specify distance between terms. However, according to Black (1996), ORBIT III did offer a STRINGSEARCH command that allowed retrieval of phrases in titles and abstracts. String searching was limited to a specified field in the record and searched all words in the field (stop words did not apply to string searching). Other than in string searching, ORBIT operated with a long list of stop words, some of which were meaningful terms for certain users.

In addition to loading the software on SDC's mainframe, SDC loaded it on the computers of NLM and NLM's foreign partners, SUNY at Syracuse, and the U.S. Department of State; the State Department may have been a pilot or demonstration project by SDC (Fife et al. 1974). SDC's first users' meeting was held in June 1975 in Chicago, in conjunction with the SLA annual meeting. As noted earlier, the IIA gave SDC and Lockheed a joint Information Product of the Year Award in April 1975.

During 1975, the number of users doubled and its files grew to a total of 7.7 million records. In 1976, the rate of new customer signups was even higher. During 1976, the processing capacity of SDC's computer, an IBM 370/158, was greatly expanded with an upgraded CPU. Even more important was a 50 percent increase in main memory—billions of bytes of additional disk storage that permitted the time windows of file access to be dropped in September 1976. New features were added, including the left-hand truncation feature that gave users of one CA file (CHEM7071) an expanded capability to search chemical name fragments.

By the end of 1976, SDC Search Service was considered a major public online service, with over twenty significant databases, TYMNET and TELENET access, and considerable visibility in training and marketing. There was, however, still room for improvement. After several years of commercial experience, SDC realized that it needed to upgrade its search software to include more powerful text search capabilities such as word proximity and word adjacency. It implemented this on a file-by-file basis—by reprocessing the source records and building new index files. In late 1976, for example, ERIC still had subject access only by assigned descriptors and identifiers, and the NTIS database could not be searched on subject indexing phrases (i.e., multiple-word terms were entered in the online index as separate terms).

Cuadra and several SDC Search Service staff, including Blankenship, Burket, Wanger, and Cuadra's son Neil, left in 1978 to form a new organization, Cuadra Associates, Inc., still in operation as of this writing. Black left SDC to start his own consulting and database service, Information Services Associates.

National Library of Medicine and MEDLINE

When we last looked at MEDLINE in chapter 6, it was the end of October 1971, and NLM had just brought up a part of the MEDLARS database online on NLM's computer in Bethesda. The retrieval software, based on SDC's ORBIT, was ELHILL II (enhanced in 1974 to ELHILL III) (Katter and Pearson 1975). After a few months of additional work, NLM fully implemented the file (at this point naming it MEDLINE), adding bibliographic records and subject indexing for 1,200 journals (increased to 2,200 by 1974), worldwide in scope, selected from the larger MEDLARS database, and covering the current year plus the three most recent years (Rogers 1974). Clearly the scope of MEDLINE was far beyond the AIM-TWX database.

> **1972 Milestone**
>
> NLM and SDC MEDLINE, with TYMNET, provided the first instance of use of a public data communication network with an online search service.

In February 1972, NLM announced the new MEDLINE service, which would provide free online bibliographic searching for medical schools, medical libraries, hospitals, and research institutions throughout the United States, Canada, England, and France ("NLM introduces" 1972). The experience with TWX and the TI terminals showed that cost and performance of data communications were critical to user institutions. Therefore, in February 1972, with the beginning of online searching by external users, MEDLINE access was obtained through direct dial-up phone lines or TYMNET. This was the first use of a public data communication network with an online search service.

By June 1972, MEDLINE searches were being performed at a rate of 70,000 per year. The growth during the first year was staggering. The number of searches performed per month increased from 5,000 in July 1972 to almost 18,000 in June 1973 (National Library 1974). By July 1974, NLM had over 200 using institutions in the United States, and a growing number of users in other countries, and was operating at a level of over 220,000 online searches per year (Kissman 1974). The explosive growth might be attributed to the fact that the service was free at that time. However, over 400,000 searches were performed in 1975 and 600,000 in 1976, in spite of the implementation of modest user charges ("MEDLINE: Where" 1976).

In March 1973, NLM's new software, ELHILL-IIC became operational—coincidental with the new SUNY BCN software, IBM-STAIRS, becoming operational (see figure 9.1). The NLM MEDLINE search service was still free, while SUNY BCN was charging subscription fees to each participating institution. However, many institutions paid for and used SUNY as their primary service because it had search functions (especially after the change to the STAIRS software) not available with NLM's MEDLINE.

Initially, the new service could support up to twenty-five simultaneous users, which was immediately inadequate. NLM quickly expanded the service to accommodate fifty users at a time. Even

Figure 9.1
A search analyst at the National Library of Medicine examines a printout of bibliographic citations obtained through MEDLINE, while her colleague checks the system's controlled vocabulary (*Medical Subject Headings*) for additional terms. c. 1973. Courtesy of the National Library of Medicine.

this capacity proved insufficient by early 1973. During busy periods, response time degenerated to three minutes ("NLM's MEDLINE" 1973). In early 1973, "MEDLINE was averaging about 30–35 simultaneous users" ("MEDLINE service" 1973, 77) and "had reached its saturation point (so that) during periods of peak use, requests (other users) could not be logged into the system" ("SUNY operates" 1973, 1074). In March, after a competitive procurement process in which SUNY BCN outbid SDC, NLM then contracted with SUNY (at $240,000 a year) to provide an additional thirty ports of MEDLINE search capacity on the SUNY-Albany computer, for use by NLM-authorized searchers. A duplicate of the file was loaded on the SUNY computer. As described earlier, this meant that SUNY was then simultaneously running both IBM-STAIRS and ELHILL search software on the same computer. The SUNY computer provided online service for nine hours a day, and NLM's operated for eight hours a day, with four hours of overlap in the afternoon when usage peaked. Authorized users did not use the same password for both systems. Thus MEDLINE was available to authorized users for a total of thirteen hours a day, five days a week (Rogers 1974). These extra MEDLINE ports on the SUNY system also provided redundancy for searchers in the event that one system crashed or otherwise was unavailable. The MEDLINE overload ports continued on the SUNY system until the early 1980s, years after BCN had lost its state funding and users and had been forced to shut down. NLM also upgraded its own computer in 1973, replacing an IBM 370/155 with a 370/158, to increase capacity and improve performance.

By the end of 1973, NLM was providing online service to more than 250 U.S. institutions. Because problems of growth and potential system saturation still existed (*MEDLARS and health* 1982), NLM established a charge of $6 per connect hour and $0.10 per page of printout ("Report of the National Library" 1974). The surprised user community reacted with a prediction that MEDLINE usage would decline. Actually, that was the response that NLM had expected and wanted. About a third of the libraries doing the MEDLINE searches had already established a patron use charge; the new NLM charges accelerated this practice (usually $5–$10 per search). Chapter 10 includes a further discussion of NLM's pricing strategy.

During 1973 and 1974, NLM staff created several new databases and services. SERLINE (Serials On-Line), a union list of 6,000 biomedical serials in common use, with holdings data for 100 medical libraries, supported interlibrary loan (McCarn 1974). SDILINE (Selective Dissemination of Information On-Line) was a database of one month of MEDLARS (the month preceding appearance of *Index Medicus*) that allowed online searching of users' continuing research topics (called "profiles") (McCarn and Leiter 1973b). CATLINE (Catalog On-Line) included all NLM cataloging data from 1965 forward—about 100,000 monographs (Rogers 1974). CANCERPROJ covered ongoing cancer research projects and clinical trials, and EPILEPSYLINE contained citations and abstracts related to epilepsy (Cummings 1976b).

During the early MEDLINE days, potential users were required to take a three-week training course in Bethesda before they could get a password. The first course was in late 1971, and it consisted of training on each *MeSH* category and hands-on ELHILL training. Part of the rationale for this comprehensive instruction was that NLM data had always (since 1879) been indexed and searched by a controlled vocabulary. The staff felt that a searcher had to think like an indexer in order to find indexed material. Furthermore, staff members argued, NLM indexers had to know only the current indexing rules, whereas searchers had to know the rules used for all the years represented in the database. This view was later tempered by a realization that not enough searchers could ever be trained to meet the growing demand for searching (see figure 9.2.).

NLM and the National Science Library (NSL), located in Ottawa, Canada, formalized an arrangement for Canadian access to MEDLINE in January 1972. The contract specified that NSL could offer access to MEDLINE to a limited number of

Figure 9.2
A search analyst conducts a MEDLINE search on a terminal at the National Library of Medicine. 1975. Courtesy of the National Library of Medicine.

Canadian centers. J. E. Brown of the NSL decided which libraries were allowed to participate, from among the formal applications submitted by librarians. Each participating library was responsible for purchasing or renting a terminal and for telephone line charges to its nearest TYMNET node. NSL absorbed the charges for accessing MEDLINE for an initial six-month period, then charged $5 per connect hour to help defray the operating costs ("Allocation" 1972).

As mentioned in chapter 6, as part of exchange agreements, NLM provided copies of the ELHILL software to its foreign partners so it could operate ELHILL locally. Thus NLM sponsored a series of national search services, most of which eventually provided service beyond NLM's files. The British Library was the first foreign MEDLARS center; MEDLARS customer services started there with batch searches in 1966. The British Library used the same ELHILL III software used by NLM as the basis for BLAISE (British Library Automated Information Service). BLAISE provided online service on the MEDLARS and LC MARC files when it began public operation in early 1977 (Holmes 1977a). As of late 1972 eight non-U.S. MEDLARS centers existed, some of which were experimenting with online systems.

The Karolinska Institutet (School of Medicine, Stockholm) was the second MEDLARS foreign center—and the first MEDLARS user on the

European continent. MEDLARS customer services started there in 1967 in batch mode. In June 1972, it started running MEDLINE and a test file on an IBM 360/75. It expanded the database to about 320,000 citations in January 1973. The scheduled online time from 1972–1974 was ten hours per week; in 1975 it increased to twenty-five hours per week. All service was free of charge during this period. By the end of 1975, with continuing support from the Swedish Medical Research Council, it was supporting a total of fifteen terminals in Scandinavia, Poland, and Finland, providing access to Biological Abstracts, CAC, CBAC (Chemical-Biological Activities), and Psychological Abstracts. In 1975, the initial MEDLINE at Karolinska was replaced by MEDLARS II and ELHILL-III, also on the IBM 360/75 (Falkenberg 1975).

A MEDLARS center to serve Australia was established at the National Library of Australia in 1969. Initially, the Karolinska Institutet programs were used to provide batch mode service (Middleton 1977). In August 1974, SDC staff successfully loaded and tested ELHILL III at the Department of Health's IBM 360/65 installation in Canberra. In October 1975 it was available for operational use (free) for two hours per day. Because of online storage space limitations, however, online access was restricted to only about three to seven months of data, including abstracts (about 40 percent of the records).

In 1974, it was possible on an experimental basis to search the text of English-language abstracts that had been added to MEDLINE for about a thousand journals. This was in addition to title word searching already available. It was done by a serial scanning of the string of abstract words, instead of searching a fully inverted file, and was thus a slow procedure. String searching was so slow that any practical use of it was restricted to a modest set of records (<1,000) that had been selected from the total file (e.g., a user could select all records in a MeSH disease category, and then string search for any of those records that had a specific pharmaceutical compound in their abstracts). This implementation, made as a regular feature in 1972, was a trade-off of index storage space for preprocessed records against on-demand computer processing. Unfortunately, the string search capability was only available on the most current MEDLINE file (1972 to date), not the backfile (1969–1971) because it was offline. Thus a complete search of the file required two different search strategies. In late 1975 the NLM MEDLINE backfiles (1969–1971) were still being searched in batch mode, but with search formulations entered through online terminals.

Also in 1974 NLM decided to transfer the TOXLINE database to NLM, and TOXLINE search service was transferred from Informatics' system to NLM's MEDLINE system in April. Hummel (1975) reported on a comparison study of the search software used before (NASA/RECON as run by Informatics) and after (ELHILL) the transfer.

The SDC work to design and implement the total MEDLARS II began in fall 1971 and was completed by fall 1974 (Katter and Pearson 1975). In January 1975, the completely new MEDLARS II (multifeature system for database production, index publication, online searching) became operational (Beckelheimer et al. 1978). Planning and procurement for MEDLARS III began in 1974 and continued into the 1980s, with the expenditure of several millions of dollars (Smith and Mehnert 1986).

In 1975, NLM made demonstration passwords available at no charge for library schools to use MEDLINE on the SUNY or NLM systems, to train students in online searching. An indication of NLM's concern about the load on its system was the condition in these password agreements that the NLM system was not to be used from 1:30–4:30 p.m. EST but the SUNY system could be used whenever it was available. If they had been aware of it, SUNY BCN users would likely have groaned at this policy; they were complaining then about the heavy load and poor response time on SUNY's system.

Chester Pletzke, director of the Midwest Regional Medical Library, initiated and sponsored the first regional or national meeting of MEDLINE searchers. Pletzke wanted meetings for MEDLINE searchers similar to the ones SUNY held for SUNY

BCN searchers. He arranged a series of meetings ("MEDLINE Clinics of the Midwest") at the John Crerar Library in Chicago. The first clinic, held in September 1975, included a speaker from NLM to provide a MEDLINE update, Egeland from SUNY BCN, and several speakers from that region.

NLM then decided to hold its own annual MEDLINE users meeting. It held the first one in conjunction with the MLA annual meeting, a practice that has continued to this date. The early meetings were helpful because users had no NLM user manuals or search aids at that time, only *MeSH*. Searchers first learned of new features from the meetings rather than from NLM publications.

By the end of December 1976, the number of subscribing libraries was over 600. The rapid growth was alarming to NLM staff, who tried to monitor it in order to prevent system overloading and consequent performance degrading. NLM implemented several strategies, including the earlier price increase in July 1975, to regulate the growth and spread the use evenly throughout the day. A 1976 NLM statement ("MEDLINE: Where" 1976) noted:

The imposition of hourly terminal connect charges in 1973 and, in 1975, a raise in the rates coupled with a new policy of variable charges based on 'prime time' and 'non-prime' time use, were actions taken to spread costs equitably and to provide a mechanism for managing growth. The network continues to expand in an orderly fashion, and repeated improvements to the system have managed to stave off the reaching of a saturation point.

By the end of 1976, NLM had established itself as the dominant supplier of online access to its own MEDLINE database. However, it was operating with a relatively small online file (two years, incrementing with updates to a maximum of three years of the most current data) compared with some other online services in operation then.

Readers may wonder why NLM paid another U.S. computer center (SUNY) to handle NLM's overload search activity for several years, and gave their database to institutions in foreign countries for their local online services, while at the same time vigorously prohibiting any U.S. commercial online search service from providing service on the database—even to U.S. institutions. Overseas competitors of U.S. institutions could access the file online on their own national systems. Prior to 1970, NLM tapes were not available outside the Library for sale or lease. As we shall discover in the next chapter, SDC tried to obtain a copy of the file under the Freedom of Information Act (FOIA), but was denied in a legal action that lasted until 1976 (Curran 1977). In 1970, the NLM Board of Regents recommended that the policy be changed to permit leasing the tapes (this was at about the time that NLM's AIM-TWX service on SDC was made available for free). SDC and Lockheed tried mightily during the 1970s to obtain permission to make MEDLINE available online. NLM would not permit it to be used by a commercial firm, however, until it finally licensed the database to BRS in 1976 for service to start in 1977, and with severe operational restrictions (e.g., service only in the United States) and a requirement for a minimum $50,000 a year royalty payment. When the database was finally made available to the commercial online services, it received extensive use, resulting in a large increase in the total U.S. and worldwide use. It was for years the most heavily used file on BRS. The commercial services provided improved search features not available on the NLM service. For example, beginning in September 1981, DIALOG offered the *entire* MEDLINE file online (1966 to date, with over 3 million records); other online services, including NLM, were still doing offline backfile searches to cover the same time period. It was not until 1982 that NLM permitted the commercial online services to make their online MEDLINE files available worldwide—after being prohibited from competing with the NLM's bilateral international partner monopolies from the beginning of the MEDLINE service.

A number of comparisons were made of the SUNY and NLM search systems when used with essentially the same database (Spiegel and Crager 1973; Egeland and Foreman 1973; Humphrey 1974,

1976). Moll (1974), who had evaluated NLM's AIM-TWX (chapter 6), reviewed the 1972–1973 MEDLINE use at his institution.

Another BCN (BCN-2) and BRS

In 1976, the SUNY Biomedical Communication Network, established in 1966 at Irwin Pizer's initiative (chapter 8), was faced with a namesake imitator–also established at Pizer's initiative. The *second* Biomedical Communications Network—which for clarity's sake will be referred to as "BCN-2"—was established in the State of Illinois in early 1976 as a not-for-profit national educational organization of libraries and information centers interested in development and refinement of online services. The non-SUNY members of SUNY BCN started it, with Pizer as a member of the Board of Directors. Another board member, Leiter (NLM's deputy director of library operations), arranged for NLM linkage to BCN-2. The choice of name to match that of SUNY BCN was no accident. It likely led many people to assume that this new online service was a nonprofit affiliation of the very visible SUNY activity that had gone on for years. Some speculated that BCN-2 was intended to be a front organization to see whether other libraries had any interest in a commercial online service to replace SUNY BCN. Pizer sent a BCN-2 letter to the non-SUNY members to solicit their participation (Van Camp 1995). Initial mailings from BCN-2 made no mention of BRS and read as if BCN-2 were going to offer its *own* search service.

Pizer sent a form letter on BCN-2 letterhead, undated (but asking for a response by February 15, 1976), to all U.S. medical school libraries, pharmaceutical company libraries, and university libraries with holdings of 200,000 or more volumes, inviting them to become members of BCN-2. The letter stated:

We believe that by reorganizing as a nonprofit professional association we will be in a better position to assure the continuation of the Network in the following ways:

1 Speaking with a more powerful voice as a group of users who are independent of the computer provider of services.

2 Being able to contract with a vendor of services in such a way as to insure that performance standards are met. (Pizer 1976).

So it was clear that Pizer and BCN-2 had an objective of working on behalf of user institutions to arrange for the desired computer services. Pizer (1976) continued:

We have been presented with a proposal from an independent group of highly reliable experts to provide computer services for the Network. Contracting with this group will achieve the following benefits:

1 Retention of the present price structure.

2 Availability of an increased number of databases.

3 Availability of the complete databases which are now being used, and the guarantee of timely update of the files.

4 Ability to provide additional terminals and allow new members to enter the Network, thus helping to keep costs down.

These benefits can only be gained if a majority of the present subscribers to the SUNY Network agree to act in concert. We hope that you will join us in taking this necessary step to assure the evolution of this important national resource . . . Considering these facts brings many of us to the conclusion that the continued operation of the Network under the present and foreseeable conditions is not viable, and far from satisfactory . . . It is not inconceivable, however, that SUNY will agree to correct existing conditions and plan to continue to operate the Network, and may wish to make a proposal which will meet the objectives we have raised. We have asked the Chancellor of the University for a definite statement of the SUNY position by mid-February [1976].

In a February 18 letter, Pizer (1976) wrote, "Many of you were interested in knowing the identity of our alternative vendor, but unfortunately, we cannot yet reveal this information. I can assure you that the persons involved are reliable, experienced, and can truly produce." It seems clear that the planning and organizing by Quake and Egeland were well under way at this time. Another BCN-2 letter, dated March

2, noted, "Our alternate vendor has been proceeding with plans for service and will have a final proposal ready for BCN [Pizer did not specify which BCN] consideration by April 1" (Pizer 1976).

Later statements on behalf of BCN-2 to current BCN participants and prospective BCN-2 subscribers made the proposed service sound much better than the current service. Pizer's March 11 letter listed the databases that were expected to be available: MEDLARS, TOXLINE, BIOSIS Previews, CA Condensates, CANCERLINE, Psychological Abstracts, COMPENDEX, ERIC, NTIS, CAIN, and INSPEC, and "other data bases will be added as justified by user demand" (Pizer 1976). However, the new organization did not meet this expectation when it began service. The starting date was projected to be September 1, 1976; the start date slipped to January 1977. The letter stated specific computer performance specifications from a user point of view—online response time, offline print distribution time, search capability (full inversion of all author, title, and abstract terms), file update frequency and currency, and data communications capability (access by TELENET or TYMNET). This may have been the first time that an online service publicly committed to a set of performance specifications.

By May 1976, Egeland and Quake published a *Final prospectus* for Bibliographic Retrieval Services, Inc., for distribution to interested participants (*BRS* 1976). With no money, but determined to keep the service afloat, they devised a pricing plan that included an annual subscription fee based on levels of monthly usage (e.g., 5–80 hours/month corresponded to $125–$800 per month), exclusive of royalties and data communications charges, and with discounts for not-for-profit educational and government agencies. Egeland asked the present SUNY BCN participants for a $7,500 annual payment on speculation, to help get BRS up and running. The $7,500 subscription provided access to all available files for up to a total of seventy connect hours per month. These charter members continued to get preferential rates in subsequent years. Statements made to prospective participants in 1976 indicated that Egeland was trying to get together a guaranteed 4,000 hours per month access from educational institutions; with that commitment, they could promise to a start-up within five months. They planned to mount the IBM-STAIRS software on a service bureau computer at Finserv Computer Corporation in Schenectady, New York.

The first public announcement of the organizational plans for the new service was made in Minneapolis on June 15, 1976 at the first annual meeting of BCN-2. Pizer presided with 112 people in attendance, representing more than sixty institutions. The meeting minutes noted that the head of Finserv Computer Corporation described the firm and its plans for providing a dedicated online service to BRS via an IBM 3781-45 computer. Egeland would be responsible for training and education. She described BRS as a dedicated operation offering online service to the academic community at an acceptable price. To the meeting attendees, it was clear that this new BRS organization was the group that Pizer had mentioned in his February 18 letter, when he wrote, "the persons involved are reliable, experienced, and can truly produce" (Pizer 1976). The minutes identified the founding members of BRS as Jan Egeland, Ron Quake, and Lloyd Palmer.

The October 12, 1976, update from BCN-2 reported that BRS had worked hard during the summer, had formally organized, sent out contracts, obtained its computer, begun loading and testing the files (BIOSIS, ERIC, and Psychological Abstracts were then operational), and had made presentations at professional meetings. All non-SUNY members of the old network and NASIC had signed their BRS contracts, and group contracts were being negotiated with the Federal Library Committee, the Denver Bibliographic Services Research Center, and the University of California. In the meantime, SUNY had sent out a letter to its users offering a six-month contract, but with no commitment to maintain or improve the level of online service or to continue it beyond March 1977. Things did not look good for the continuation of the original SUNY BCN. The last (undated) BCN-2 letter gave itself a pat on the back: "In its first year of existence, the BCN has been instrumental in finding an alternative vendor for search services for its members. In encouraging the founding of BRS, Inc. to meet the needs of our libraries, we have made a major contribution to the development of competitive information retrieval services in the United States."

Thus the three persons most responsible for BCN, Egeland, Quake, and Palmer, built a new search system that replicated the SUNY system and improved it. With the encouragement of medical librarian users, they also created a new organization—a commercial company to be operated outside of SUNY. Quake became president, Egeland was vice president for marketing and training, and Palmer was vice president for systems development. They made the decision to form a new company in spring 1976; by December, they were ready to provide commercial online services. Palmer was responsible for all BRS computer operations, systems design and development, and getting "the system up and functioning properly in the very short time frame of five months" (Provenzano 1987, 37). He had worked as a systems engineer for IBM in Albany, New York, and had joined the SUNY Central Office Computer Center staff in 1970 as manager of systems programming. Immediately before joining BRS, Palmer worked at the New York State Division of Criminal Justice Services (coincident with Quake working there), supervising a large computer system for criminal justice agencies. Palmer left BRS in fall 1977 to rejoin IBM.

The first general meeting of BRS subscribers was held in Syracuse in December 1976, a month before BRS actually started providing public service. Quake introduced the meeting, and then turned it over to Pizer as temporary chairman. The new organization began service in January 1977 and the first eleven databases containing nine million records became commercially available online from BRS. Telenet provided dial-up access, but with speeds limited to thirty cps.

Within four months of its establishment, BRS had inherited the hard core of biomedical users from the defunct SUNY network and had signed contracts with several major library consortia including BCN, CLASS, BCR, MIDLNET, NASIC, the Federal Library Committee (FEDLINK) and the UC system (Zimmerman and MacKinnon 1979; Van Camp 1994). SUNY ceased operating BCN in May 1977, because all of its non-SUNY subscribers had transferred their search business to BRS. SUNY arranged for BRS to provide service to the remaining SUNY participants. Nevertheless, SUNY did continue the NLM contract to provide ports to handle NLM's overflow until the early 1980s (Pizer 1984). In October 1980, Egeland and Quake sold BRS to the Thyssen-Bornemisza organization for an unspecified amount. Provenzano (1987, 36) quoted Egeland, who said, "It was an offer we simply could not refuse."

TOXICON/TOXLINE

The 1960s witnessed a growing alarm that humans and their environment were being assaulted increasingly by the adverse affects of "burgeoning chemical technology which yearly introduces thousands of new and potentially hazardous chemicals into the environment" (Kissman 1975b, 67). The science of toxicology literature is dispersed over the disciplines of biology, analytical chemistry, biochemistry, pharmacology, and medicine. In June 1966, a panel of the President's Science Advisory Committee called for a coordinated, computer-based system for toxicological information that would be accessible and affordable to anyone in government, industry, or academia who legitimately needed such information, including "health professionals working in the areas of environmental pollution, industrial or occupational health and safety, pharmacology, toxicology, medicine, agriculture, and other bioscientific disciplines" ("NLM Toxicology" 1972, 315).

The response to the panel's recommendations was the establishment in January 1967 of the Toxicology Information Program (TIP) at NLM (not to be confused with Project TIP at MIT, described in chapter 2). TIP concentrated on pesticide toxicology as a first step. In June 1970, Henry Marcel Kissman, a pharmaceutical chemist and information specialist, moved from being the director of the Science Information Facility of the U.S. Food and Drug Administration to direct TIP. Kissman was born in Graz, Austria. His doctorate was in organic chemistry and he specialized in computer sciences and chemical documentation. Under Kissman's leadership, TIP expanded its activities to environmental pollutants, drug interactions, and other topics. It also encouraged (in conjunction with BIOSIS), the development of a new computer tape subscription service called Toxitapes for Industrial and Pharmaceutical Toxicology, caused NLM's AIM/TWX file to be expanded by the addition of fifteen journals from the area of clinical toxicology, and developed *Abstracts on Health Effects of Environmental Pollutants* (a new abstract journal and computer tape service) that was later used as the basis for the online HEAP (Health Aspects of Pesticides Abstracts Bulletin) database (*Progress* 1971, 76–77). In 1971, TIP formed the Toxicology Information Response Center at Oak Ridge National Lab to perform literature searches and build toxicology databases. In 1972, TIP initiated TOXICON (Toxicology Informational Conversational On-line Network, or Toxicology Information On-line Conversational Network), a national online toxicology IR system (*Progress* 1972, 34; Kissman and Hummel 1972a; Miller, Gerstner, and Beauchamp 1974). As noted in chapter 7, NLM had experimented in 1969 with full-text searching of a limited collection of toxicology-related reference material (Epilepsy Abstracts) using the Data Corporation. online system. That demonstration convinced TIP management of the utility of full-text online searching.

This TOXICON system started providing online service in October 1972. TIP designed TOXICON to make toxicological data available online from remote terminals, using full-text searching with word proximity retrieval capability and five relevant databases. The TIP project staff chose to use search software other than that already available to NLM because their needs were different. NLM software used literature indexed by NLM with a controlled vocabulary (*MeSH*) for subject searching; toxicology had nonindexed citations and abstracts, which needed a text searching capability of titles, abstracts, and keywords to meet its subject searching objectives (Kissman 1975b, 1995).

In early 1971, Mead Data Central, Informatics, and Battelle Memorial Institute responded to a request for proposals from NLM for a full-text retrieval system; SDC and Lockheed declined to bid. The RFP was based on TIP's full-text experience gained in the use of the MDC system with the HEAP database. The HEAP experience with the Data Corporation full-text system served as the prototype for TOXICON. Evaluation of the proposals led to a contract for Informatics in March 1971. Informatics proposed to use DIALOG's NASA/RECON system (which was by this time in the public domain, from COSMIC at the University of Georgia) with Informatics making enhancements to support full-text searching. During 1972–1973, Informatics modified the RECON and STIMS software; they added such additional features as highlighting (by asterisks or color) of search terms in the output records—seen earlier on the Mead system but not on DIALOG. The TOXLINE service was publicly announced and demonstrated in April 1972, and service instituted in October 1972 (Hummel 1975). Informatics used a commercial computer service bureau, COMNET (Computer Network Corporation) in Washington, D.C., to provide the actual online service, running the STIMS/RECON system on an IBM 360/50 with IBM 2314 disk drives, and accessed via the Tymshare network (Schultheisz, Walker, and Kannan 1978).

The TOXICON service used NASA/STIMS software for file maintenance (which was done at NLM on its IBM), the Lockheed-developed NASA/RECON software for online retrieval, and the ALPHA time-sharing system (proprietary software developed by COMNET) (Kissman 1975b). The online service ran on an IBM 360/65 with an Ampex disk storage device and nationwide access was via TYMNET. The files consisted of (1) a bibliographic master file of 180,000 records, many with abstracts; (2) full-text files of articles and reviews ranging in size from a few pages to a complete book; and (3) plans for files of specific numeric and textual data as animal toxicity studies, adverse drug reports, poisoning cases, effects of environmental chemicals or pollutants, and chemical identification data. The sources for all these data included *Toxicity Bibliography, Health Aspects of Pesticides Abstract Bulletin, Abstracts on Health Effects of Environmental Pollutants, Chemical-Biological Activities, International Pharmaceutical Abstracts,* and *Hayes File on Pesticide Toxicology,* which covered the period 1950–1966 (Kissman and Hummel 1972b). Other sources, including subsets of existing medical and chemical databases, were added later. Because of the great variety of sources and data types, no controlled vocabulary indexing was done. Instead, users could search records via all words from titles and abstracts, keywords from full-text documents, as well as chemical substance names. The challenge, successfully met, was to merge the contents of all the source files into a database that appeared to users as a single file.

TOXICON was a public service. With a subscription through Informatics, any scientist worldwide could gain access from 8 a.m. to 10 p.m. EST, Monday to Friday, and from 8 a.m. to 6 p.m. on Saturday. A $350 start-up fee covered training and manuals. Usage fees were $45 per connect hour (which only partially covered the operating costs), and $5 per 1,000 lines of offline printout. There was no monthly minimum charge (Kissman and Hummel 1972a). As the prime contractor for TOXICON, Informatics trained users, supported customer services, and billed users (Kissman 1973). J. Robert Harcharik was director of TOXICON services for Informatics.

TOXICON was renamed TOXLINE in April 1973 because NLM staff had learned of prior claims to the name ("TOXICON renamed" 1973). NLM decided in December 1973 to transfer TOXLINE from Informatics' contractor service bureau operation to the in-house NLM system—along with a shift from RECON/STIMS software to ELHILL software in 1974. Kissman continued as director of the service. Unfortunately, when NLM switched the TOXICON service to the NLM computer, it immediately denied access to the U.S. pharmaceutical companies and other private-sector users of that file. Access via Informatics had been unrestricted and available to the entire public worldwide. Now, access via NLM was restricted to authorized NLM password holders. Service was offered from NLM's IBM 360/50 on April 1, 1974, and discontinued through Informatics in April 1974. At the time of the transfer, Informatics was still using the RECON-based system on the COMNET service bureau with access via TYMNET, and NLM was using a modification of the ORBIT programs that NLM identified as SDC's ELHILL-2 software—which was also being used then for the MEDLINE service. Connect costs went down with the move, from $45 to $15 per hour, offline prints were reduced to 10 cents per page, and initiation fees and training charges were eliminated ("TOXLINE transferred" 1974).[2] Users were required to learn the MEDLINE query language, but more than half of current users already used MEDLINE anyway. Further, the word proximity search capability that had been available on the Informatics version of the RECON software was not available on the ELHILL software; a slower and more cumbersome string search capability was the ELHILL alternative to proximity searching. Immediately before the transfer, about seventy-five institutional TOXLINE subscribers were using a total of about 350 connect hours per month on a database of over 300,000 records. By July 1974, the TOXLINE user community had grown to 105 organizations (Kissman 1974, 1975b; "NLM offers" 1974).

The TIP service offered several bibliographic databases in the areas of toxicity, chemistry, environmental pollutants, pesticides, and pharmacy, as well as a new file called Toxicology Data Bank (TDB). TDB contained "evaluated data as found in a selected set of sources, such as textbooks, criteria documents, reviews, or the files of specialized information centers, on compounds known to be hazardous and to which populations are exposed"

(*National Library* 1975, 23). CHEMLINE, a chemical dictionary for about 60,000 compounds, was an aid to TOXLINE searchers because of the diversity of nomenclature used in the literature. It was made available for online searching in January 1974 on the Informatics RECON IV system. A second version was made available from NLM on ELHILL-2 software in June 1974. A third version was made available on the NLM system in January 1975 using ELHILL-3 software and NLM's IBM 370/158 (Schultheisz, Walker, and Kannan 1978). This was the first online chemical dictionary file. Also at this time, TIP decided to have the textual descriptions of the data indexed with *MeSH*. Users could therefore retrieve either on the controlled terms or on the natural language words from titles and abstracts (Kissman 1975a). For his work on toxicology information systems, Kissman received in 1973 the HEW Superior Service Award. He retired from NLM in 1992.

Schultheisz (1981) provided more detail about early efforts to accommodate input formats of the various data sources, as well as the special data parsing rules used for index entry processing. Kissman and Wexler (1985) reviewed the TOXLINE history and federal efforts to support a toxicology information system over the previous twenty-year period.

Mead Corporation

LEXIS

The OBAR system (chapter 7) continued throughout 1971 and 1972. Harrington (1984–1985, 552) noted:

By the end of 1972, the Ohio marketing test of the second-generation OBAR (OBAR II) had been completed, and the system was almost ready for nationwide marketing. Before it could be offered as a service to the lawyers of states other than Ohio, however, it would need a new name. The new name was LEXIS.

Although some people assume that the word 'LEXIS' means 'law information service' ('LEX' for law and 'IS' for information service), the name is not an abbreviation or acronym. It originated with a firm of consultants in New York whose business was to suggest corporate and business names. Their theory was that names with an X or two in the middle (such as Exxon) were intriguing. Hence LEXIS.

Rubin (1998), however, rebutted Harrington. He claimed that he himself "personally coined the name LEXIS (and later NEXIS). It was in fact derived from LEX (for law) and IS (for information service). When I coined the name LEXIS, I was aware of the memorability and design advantages of names containing an X or two; the firm that coined the names Xerox and Exxon had been a client of mine when I was practicing law." By September 1972, having been convinced that the design would meet the needs of legal researchers and was economically feasible, Mead Data Central was ready to produce the new system. LEXIS was a brand new product with a new software package and its own terminal, designed for ease of use. Giering (1995) alleged that the internal LEXIS capabilities (e.g., full-text word searching, KWIC display) and functions were unchanged from the original Data Central system. However, others who had been affiliated with LEXIS claimed that LEXIS had no relationship to the original Data Corporation or OBAR system. Rubin (1998) recalled:

Bennett and I (and some consultants, including Gottsman of ADL and Professor Tony Oettinger of Harvard) were unable to persuade Don Wilson to scrap the OBAR system and start over from scratch. In the late summer of 1971, Mead insisted that I take over as president and undertake the effort Bennett and I had been urging. Because of my partnership with Wilson, I was reluctant to do so, but Mead said that the alternative was to shut MDC down and Wilson encouraged me to accept. Once I became president, we were not upgrading OBAR; we were building an entirely new system and service.

As we will learn, the new system and service was in fact quite different from OBAR, but retained important elements such as full-text storage and retrieval.

LEXIS was launched on April 2, 1973, but with a partial waiver of charges for the first month. MDC's goal was to establish a national legal electronic library encompassing all U.S. federal law, and the law of the fifty states. At its commercial launch in May, MDC offered LEXIS on a charter subscription basis to lawyers in New York, Washington, DC, and Ohio (Rubin 1973). The new service included Ohio and New York case law, and a federal tax library. By the end of 1973, the online file included two billion characters of text, covering Ohio law, New York law, federal tax law, the *U.S. Code*, and the *United States Reports* (Supreme Court cases from 1938 to date) (Rubin 1974). The records associated with each state or federal agency were kept in separate files that had to be searched separately. A challenge for LEXIS throughout the 1970s was to expand the scope of the database as rapidly as possible, and to strive for truly national-level coverage. LEXIS managers viewed the costs of adding all the primary legal materials of each of the states as well as federal materials as extremely high, but not prohibitive. By 1974, LEXIS was well on its way to becoming a nationwide system for legal research.

Starting with Missouri, more state databases were added, until eventually all U.S. states were covered. From the beginning, Mead's strategy for file acquisitions was different from other online services. Mead chose to invest and develop their own proprietary databases by keyboarding or otherwise obtaining royalty-free machine-readable text; most other online services, with the exception of NLM's, obtained their machine-readable databases from other organizations. Mead arranged for large volumes of text to be keyed into machine-readable form, mostly by using offshore contractor facilities. Their development of their own proprietary database became extremely important in the long run. For other search services such as DIALOG and SDC, the absence of their own proprietary databases became particularly troublesome in the 1980s and later when growing royalty rates resulted in decreasing profit margins.

The first president of MDC was Donald Wilson, who left after the first year. He was succeeded in 1971 by the vice president, Rubin, introduced in chapter 7. While the computer center, software programming, and back-office operations continued to be located in Dayton, Ohio, corporate headquarters, including marketing, sales, communications, training, and planning, were in New York City. MDC operated with the cooperation and support of the bar associations of Ohio, New York, Texas, Missouri, and Illinois. The National Center for Automated Information Retrieval (NCAIR), an organization of judges, lawyers, and certified public accountants, set up committees to advise on content and assist in source collection (more in name than in fact) (Fisher 1997; Harrington 1974). Other professional organizations contributed professional expertise and, in some cases, original library materials, in paper or machine-readable form, and they exerted influence over content, structure, database coverage, and services. Nevertheless, as a private company, MDC bore the financial risk and gained the profit. MDC and Lockheed were the first, and most successful commercial participants in a field that was otherwise full of systems developed and operated with government funding.

Subject access in LEXIS, as in OBAR, was based on word and phrase searching of the full text of documents, generally with little or no formal a priori digesting, abstracting, or indexing. The indexing and abstracting that was done did not come from any central source–case law material from a handful of states contained an abstract (called a "syllabus," and generated by the issuing court). While some published case decisions contained "headnotes" written by West Publishing indexing staff, using an uncontrolled or lightly controlled vocabulary, these headnotes were not included in LEXIS because they were copyrighted. Rubin (1974, 40) asserted: "Full-text research permits the researching lawyer to release his imagination from the confines of conceptual rubrics and to bring his own judgment freely into play. Even if in information theory every word in a book can be called an index term the difference between finding cases in a traditional index, with its limited number of statically-defined pigeonholes, and finding them using the living language of the courts is significant on a practical level."

At its beginning in 1973, the system was intended to serve two hundred simultaneous users without service degradation. LEXIS grew quickly that year to serve over 3,000 lawyers, judges, and tax accountants in New York, Illinois, District of Columbia, Massachusetts, Missouri, Texas, and Ohio (Rubin 1974). Tax professionals were targeted as a distinct user group because of the information-intensive nature of their work and the fact that federal tax research involves "a discrete body of primary sources–the Internal Revenue Code, Regulations, tax cases decided by the courts, Revenue Rulings, Revenue Procedures" and others that could be organized into a single file (Rubin and Woodard 1974a). Both lawyers and accountants viewed LEXIS as a useful tool for fast, objective, and flexible access to the rapidly increasing volume of U.S. legal materials.

According to Rubin (qtd. in Provenzano 1987, 41–42), a key objective of their business plan was "to crack the librarian barrier. Our goal was to get a LEXIS terminal on every lawyer's desk. To ensure this, MDC offered perpetual training to every lawyer in a firm at no additional charge." Limiting the marketing and use of LEXIS to law libraries would have resulted in a smaller number of actual direct users. Unlike the approach taken by other online services with their target constituencies, LEXIS marketing and direct sales were directed from the beginning at the end-user attorneys, not the law librarians.

In consultation with lawyers, the designers also decided that the intended users wanted a retrieval program based on conversational English, with search options displayed in menus. They expected that users would know, or would learn quickly how to formulate strategies by choosing appropriate natural language terms, using Boolean OR, AND, and BUT NOT to specify logical relationships, and distance operators to specify how close together two terms had to be (e.g., W/6 meant within six words). After a user keyed in a word, phrase, or combination of terms, LEXIS responded with a count of how many cases satisfied that request. The program then asked the user to choose a format and display the cases found or to modify the search by adding further terms. Through this interaction with the program, users could refine their searches until they were satisfied with the results. They could receive prompting and still retain control over a search.

MDC trainers developed a seminar and taught it at MDC learning centers. It was a combination of instructor's introduction or a video and hands-on instruction. This training was reinforced with diagnostic and tutorial messages built into the program. In teaching word proximity, trainers provided suggestions on how to obtain the equivalent of sentence and paragraph searching. Two terms within twenty-five words of each other approximated two words within the same sentence, and within one hundred words approximated a paragraph (Giering 1995). They wanted users not only to learn the mechanics of searching, but also to understand the role of the computer in legal research. Rubin (1974, 45) explained:

Far from complicating (or usurping) his task, the MDC system encourages a user to engage in the familiar facets of the research process . . . but with true *assistance* from the computer. The distinction between assistance and intervention is important to dispel two related misconceptions which frequently crop up, especially among the uninitiated. One is that the computer replaces the researcher; the other is that the computer, with some human direction, locates answers to legal problems. The first idea, in simple terms, anthropomorphizes a mechanical device. The second idea, in slightly more subtle terms, reduces research to question-answering and raises the process of electronic retrieval to reasoning. Both ideas give the computer more credit than its due. While the computer can be applied to the analysis of legal issues . . . the computer applied to legal research is no more nor less than a tool for locating the law.

The original LEXIS philosophy, reflected in system design, marketing, and training, was that only an end user (the person with the actual problem) knows which material accurately answers the problem at hand, and thus an end user should be the searcher. LEXIS never assumed that a professional intermediary or surrogate searcher would be used. Other major search systems started out with a stated philosophy of end-user searching (e.g., MEDLINE for clinicians, RECON for engineers and scientists) but quickly changed—at least until the early 1990s—to designing for professional intermediaries ("power searchers").

Rubin and Woodard (1974b) noted that over 100 LEXIS terminals had been installed in users' own offices, nearly 4,000 lawyers and accountants had been trained to use those terminals, and the database contained about 4 billion source characters. In terms of total characters stored, LEXIS and DIALOG during the early 1970s probably had the two largest online database collections of all the systems described in this text.

In 1974, LEXIS shared an IBM 370/155 computer in Dayton with other Mead projects and applications, which were run at a lower priority. A second CPU was available to LEXIS for backup support, and the mass storage consisted of IBM 3330 disk storage units. The communications processor could handle up to sixty-two terminals simultaneously, using a leased-line 720 cps network that allowed individual users to operate at 120 cps. This configuration of computer and communications equipment permitted more than 90 percent of all user search requests to be executed in less than fifteen seconds (5 seconds average), and—with additional communications processors—was reportedly able to support four hundred simultaneous users. The central site availability was 99.5 percent, a good performance figure in those days (Rubin and Woodard 1974b). In 1975, an IBM 370/155 with 2 megabytes of working storage and 5 billion bytes of replacement disk storage was providing the service from Dayton, accommodating about 200 terminals at a data communication rate of 120 cps (Abramowitz 1975).

LEXIS' first competition for online legal search services did not come until 1975, with the announcement of West Publishing's WESTLAW service. By the end of 1976, LEXIS was the dominant online service in the legal marketplace, with the largest collection of full-text statutory and case law material available online (Sprowl 1976a).

However, LEXIS at this time still did not contain a complete national library; it contained the full text of decisions from six different states, and uneven coverage of Federal material (Sprowl 1976b). Rubin continued with MDC until September 1981 when he and top aides, Bennett (chief operating officer), Fisher (vice president, product development), and Gottsman (vice president, strategic planning), left to pursue other activities. In 1985, Rubin received the IIA's Hall of Fame Award for creating LEXIS.

Reflecting on the significance of LEXIS for the information industry, Rubin (qtd. in Provenzano 1987) observed, "It was the first commercially successful online system with significant profits. It proved the benefits of a full-text system. And it changed the modus operandi of the legal profession." (42). An objective of the original LEXIS business plan was making a profit in three or four years. It proved to be on target—in 1977 LEXIS had their first operating profit on an annual basis four years after its commercial launch. This "long term" (for Mead) strategy created tension between MDC and the parent Mead Corporation. Rubin recalled (qtd. in Provenzano 1987, 41), "It was one battle after another to get money from them. The money was spooned out and the sword of Damocles hung over our heads. Mead threatened to fold MDC at practically every MDC board meeting." Mead eventually gained a huge profit by hanging on to LEXIS; in 1968 Mead purchased Data Corporation, the corporate platform on which LEXIS was born, for $6 million. They reached $65 million in revenues by 1981. By the end of 1993, the company had sales of $551 million and earnings of $50 million (Pemberton 1994). In late 1994, Mead announced that it had agreed to sell its business unit that included the LEXIS/NEXIS online operations for $1.5 billion in cash to Anglo-Dutch publisher Reed Elsevier PLC.

Mead Technology Laboratories

As we saw in chapter 7, Data Corporation was renamed Mead Technology Laboratories (MTL) in

October 1972. For the next several years it continued to develop and provide contract support services for its Washington, D.C., client base, as well as for the Avionics Central client base. MTL activities were parallel to, but separate from, OBAR/LEXIS development. In late 1973, the Data Central online service was still being offered from MTL's Arlington facility (Marron et al. 1973). In mid-1974, the Arlington service bureau office was closed, and the support service transferred to Dayton.

By mid-1975, additional features had been implemented on the MTL system. These included flexible display features that allowed users to jump back and forth between pages of full-text material, and an online output editing capability. Relevance ranking of output, based on the number of search terms in the records retrieved, was offered as part of a sort feature. Recursive searching (using data retrieved as a result of one search as the parameters for another search) was implemented, along with a capability to handle other types of terminals.

In June 1976, the Boston Globe contracted with MTL for a feasibility test of a program to automate its news clipping library, using data from the *Globe's* automated typesetting process, all to be done without interference with the production of the daily newspaper. Significant disagreement was expressed within the library profession as to whether this was feasible or practical. Clipping and filing were labor-intensive activities within news organizations, with significant budget and service implications. Another contentious issue was the impact of trying to sell access to users outside of the newspaper. The *New York Times* experience (detailed later) was closely monitored in this regard. The major participants for this project included George Collins (the *Boston Globe's* librarian), Jennifer Chao (assistant librarian), and Dick Giering of MTL. In September 1976, the *Boston Globe* contracted with MTL for the first newspaper production database system. In October 1976, the *Globe's* automated library began operation, and in July 1977 the *Boston Globe* stopped the manual clipping of the newspaper.

Once the *Globe* had become a production operation on the Data Central Service Bureau, some of the MTL management—seeing the LEXIS profits, and feeling that MTL could generate more of the same—wanted to set up an additional sales force, obtain rights to the news library data, and begin to sell it. Mead management, on the other hand, saw the investment that had been poured into LEXIS and had serious misgivings. Rather than stay with the proven and profitable (although with smaller margins than LEXIS) service business, MTL continued to pressure the parent Mead organization to permit MTL to enter the information selling business. MTL gambled and lost; the complete information service business was taken from MTL in 1978 and transferred to MDC. Giering left Mead in December 1977 to help form a new organization, Infotex Associates in Dayton, concentrating on developing and installing turnkey systems of text entry–photocomposition–file maintenance for newspapers and other publications. In late 1980, MDC halted support of the Data Central business and the Data Central system was scrapped.

ESRO/RECON and ESA/IRS

In chapter 5 we saw the ESRO/RECON online system begin operating in September 1969. In 1972, ESRO/RECON was providing access to nearly 1 million references (with an average of 600 characters each), with no practical physical limitation in storage expansion other than number of available Data Cell storage units (each with a 400-million-character capacity). The RECON software was designed originally for searching only the NASA database, but later, the feature developed by Lockheed to accommodate additional files was incorporated in the ESRO system. Lockheed was still under contract to ESRO in 1972 to maintain an operating version of RECON, and in 1972, ESRO added the METADEX (*Metals Abstracts*), GRA (*U.S. Government Reports Announcements*), COMPENDEX, and NSA databases.

When ESRO started developing its network, no dedicated high-speed lines were available for data transmission. In 1972 there were national data lines, but no international lines specifically for data. Its network was constructed of leased lines with a speed of 120 cps, to support a pilot four-terminal operation between Darmstadt, Paris, and Noordwijk (Holland). According to Kallenbach (1972, 198), "For present system loading with 10 terminals, an average response time for any elementary command is between 8 and 12 seconds which is fast enough considering the loss of concentration by the interrogator."

In spite of the language differences and telecommunications problems in Europe, as well as other geographical and political barriers, the ESRO/RECON facility and its DIALOG software continued to develop. In 1973 it was moved from Darmstadt, Germany, to the European Space Research Institute (ESRIN) in Frascati, Italy. Back in the country of his father's origin, Noel Isotta (introduced in chapter 5) continued as head of the service. By this time the developers recognized a need for a dedicated computer to run the large system and consequently installed an IBM 360/50 at Frascati. By mid-1973, the ESRO/RECON service supported five files with a total of 1.25 million references and provided service in seven countries. Martin (1973) reported on a major study of users, noting four different European institutions' searching experience.

In August 1974, Lockheed staff installed an upgraded version of the DIALOG software at the Frascati facility. From this point forward, all software changes to the ESRO system were made by ESRO staff. In November 1974, the service was supporting twenty-four terminals in eight European countries, and providing access to almost 3.5 million references in eleven files. Unfortunately, even with the rapid search speeds of this online system, some end-users were still seeing turnaround times measured in weeks because of the inefficiencies of other parts of the infrastructure. Swedish information requesters in 1974 were experiencing an average turnaround time of eighteen days from the time they mailed a search request to the Swedish node of ESRO/RECON (the Royal Institute of Technology) in Stockholm, until the time that they received their resulting search printout by mail. The delay was partly due to a policy that required all searches that yielded ten references or more to be printed offline in Frascati—much of the holdup was attributable to the poor performance of the Italian postal system. In order to ensure that the printouts were not lost in the Italian mail, SDS sent them twice weekly by courier to Paris, for mailing from Paris (Hjerppe 1975).

By the end of 1974, twenty-seven terminals were operating and at least sixteen databases were online, including many produced in the United States such as the NASA and American Institute of Aeronautics (AIAA) files, COMPENDEX, METADEX, CA Condensates, and GRA. The system was now operating with approximately 2,000 megabytes of disk and Data Cell storage for the databases. Network communications over the PTTs between the participating countries and Frascati were still troublesome and expensive, and a number of alternative communications networks were considered to provide greater reliability, increased traffic capacity, and wider variety of interfacing capabilities (Isotta 1975). All the terminals were of one specific type, running at 240 cps, and connected to a dedicated leased-line network. A local dial-up facility was also added at this time, but only in the Rome area, to permit access by any Teletype-compatible terminal. The Commission of the European Communities was planning to develop EURONET, a European data communications network. SDS started to set up its own European data communications network (ESANET), however, because of the slow development of public data networks in Europe. Furthermore, European telecommunications costs were then five to six times the costs of U.S. telecommunications and were hampering the growth and utilization of online services in Europe.

Kallenbach (1972, 198) noted that thought had been given at ESRO "to the computer storage of search experience by storing selected search profile strings, which can be regenerated when a search on a similar problem is performed." Isotta (1975) reported that a feature had recently been added recently to the ESA system, to permit a search formulation to be stored for subsequent recall and use in other search formulations. This feature had been implemented on MIT's TIP in the 1960s, and several other later experimental systems, but this may have been the first instance in which this feature was made available on a major service (ESA and Lockheed). During a discussion at the December 1975 EUSIDIC meeting, Isotta (1976) noted, "the search-save procedure whereby you can carry a search over from one file to another ... is available on the Lockheed and SDS systems."

In 1972, Isotta recognized that his organization needed to have a semicommercial outlook and to charge users for services. SDS was operating then with a significant subsidy from ESRO. It had been suggested that the full costs of the operation should be recovered from earned income by 1975. Isotta (1972b, 191), however, acknowledged:

Income derived from computer searches alone would never be sufficient to meet the heavy operating costs and it would be necessary to rely on terminal installations outside ESRO, for which customers would pay a substantial annual rental ... If terminals are to be installed outside ESRO, it will be necessary to add to the data base by incorporating other commercially available files ... substantial income can not be earned without confirming the 'semicommercial' type activities of SDS within a civil service organization, requiring not only the charging of customers ... but also the expansion of marketing effort in order to find new clients.

At that time, Isotta (1972b, 191) had a low number of terminals in mind: "The number of terminals needed to arrive somewhere near a breakeven position is a network of at least twenty-five terminals, an apparently ambitious number for Europe."

ESRO was interested in reaching an audience beyond Europe. In 1975, with support from UNESCO, the network added a node at the National Documentation Centre in Rabat, Morocco to facilitate online searching by users in North Africa (Raizada 1977). The extension included providing an operational Arabic-language terminal interface, filling the screen from left to right in English, and the other half from right to left in Arabic characters; this had not been done to date with any of the other public online services. Eight terminals were installed with this Arabic-language capability; they were used for data entry and searching of a private file, and searching the other ESA databases. By the end of 1975, the SDS dial-up facilities covered Germany, the United Kingdom, France, and Italy. The supplementary TYMNET options with extensions to Sweden, Denmark, and Belgium resulted in a total of thirty-seven dial-up ports into Frascati (Isotta 1975).

In May 1976, the ESA was established to consolidate under a single body the complete range of ESRO and ELDO activities (Mader 1981). The name Space Documentation Service (SDS) was changed to Information Retrieval System (IRS); ESA/IRS became a major European online search service for science and technology, providing access from France, Germany, the Netherlands, Spain, Scandinavia, and the United Kingdom. Prominent in ESA/IRS activities in the 1970s were Isotta, Kallenbach, Mulhauser, and Raitt, all introduced in chapter 5.

By the end of 1976, ESA/IRS had taken on a semicommercial appearance and attitude, with an expansion of marketing and sales, offering twelve databases and online service to users beyond the boundaries of Europe. They started a pattern of developing and implementing innovative features and services not previously seen elsewhere. ESA/IRS staff continued to modify and enhance the original DIALOG software after its installation. In 1976, IRS started developing an entirely new software, named ESA-QUEST, to replace RECON. To users, however, ESA-QUEST still closely resembled DIALOG search software.

NASA/RECON

As we saw in chapter 5, Lockheed installed its DIALOG software as NASA/RECON on the NASA computer in Maryland in 1969, with twenty-four consoles operating at nine different sites. In 1974, NASA/RECON was providing 11.5 hours/day service with twenty-three different databases with a total of over one million bibliographic citations. All twenty-four terminals that were active in the United States then were wired into a 300 cps voice-grade leased line network.

Slow response time continued to be the most serious problem in the 1970s. Harold Pryor, the director of NASA's STIF, noted that its online system was, "reasonably reliable, being up about 92 percent of the time" (1975b, 89).[3] Response time varied between five and eighty seconds—the average was fifteen seconds and the median less than twelve seconds. Pryor attributed the slowness to the large demands (twenty-four terminals on leased lines that could be used simultaneously) being made on the relatively small IBM 360/50. He suggested that the problem could be solved only with a new computer.

In late 1973 and early 1974, STIF conducted 114 one-hour interviews with scientists and engineers at thirteen facilities, to assess the usefulness of the NASA information system, including NASA/RECON. The interviewers received positive comments about RECON but were "also advised with equal vigor that RECON's response time on many occasions was too slow" (Pryor 1975a, 518). Bivans (1974) reported that a study at the NOAA/ERL Library in Boulder, Colorado, revealed that for searches requested from NASA, most came back in eleven or twelve working days; one required sixteen working days. To speed up response time, new software was developed and new hardware added. Before the end of 1974, users noted a 40 percent decrease in response time.

Up until 1974, all NASA/RECON citations were contained in a single large database (about 1 million records) containing 11 separate "file collections." This segmentation reduced response time because searchers worked with smaller sets of records for data transfer, logical processing, and output processing. In 1974, bibliographic records for the NASA Library Network (NALNET) book holdings and selected LC MARC records were added as separate files (Jack 1982).

By the end of 1976, NASA and Informatics had considerably improved response time—it was about two to three seconds, even at peak times when twenty to thirty users were online. The principal designer for this improvement was Ray Blasik, an Informatics employee. Other key personnel were Robert Johnson of Informatics and William Brown (NASA project manager). Changes made by NASA and its contractors to the software included full-text searching in 1977, multitasking to reduce response time, and new search commands (Wente 1997). Reliability of both hardware and software, however, continued to be a problem (Wente 1995). As of this writing, NASA/RECON still operates in the Center for Aerospace Information (CASI) as STIF is now called, as a contractor-operated system for NASA organizations.

AEC/ERDA/DOE/RECON

As mentioned in chapter 5, DIALOG completed the installation of the RECON software at DOE's Oak Ridge facility in January 1971, operating primarily with the NSA database.[4] In 1972–1973, the original DIALOG RECON program operating at Oak Ridge National Lab was rewritten by Union Carbide staff on behalf of AEC, acting as contractors and operators of the Oak Ridge facility. The rewritten AEC/RECON was put in daily operation in September 1973 on an IBM 360/75 computer, where it continued to operate throughout the period covered by this text (Haeuslein and Culkowski 1975). CRTs manufactured by Computer Communications, Inc. (CCI), were used as the primary terminal devices. The AEC/RECON software permitted users to search any of sixteen individual files, but only one at a time. Even after reprogramming in the early 1970s, the planners apparently did not feel that the system would ever need to handle the larger number of files that is common practice today. The new AEC/RECON software also limited itself to having eleven separate index files (keyword, author, country of origin, report number series, corporate source (old code), corporate source (new code), CODEN, NSA category code, contract number, patent nation, and subject descriptor (not for NSA). Contrast this to online file design practices today that may provide scores, or even hundreds of separate index files for specific databases. This file design closely reflected the focus on the NSA database as it existed then. The linear (i.e., display) file (the source data itself, not the generated index entries) was written in the STIMS (Scientific and Technical Information Modular System) record format. NASA developed the STIMS format. AEC's use of the format was partly motivated to support database standards in this field.

A new AEC/RECON user manual was published in May 1974 to reflect the changes (Gillcrist 1974). The original *Nuclear Science Abstracts* ceased as of June 1976 with the publication of *Atomindex*, an international abstracting service in the field of nuclear science, and the beginning of the searching system produced by the INIS from records prepared in cooperating national or regional centers and sent to the IAEA in Vienna (Walker and Luedtke 1979).

DOE staff operated the RECON software primarily in an experimental mode through 1975, using DOE's own leased lines, and serving a restricted constituency of DOE staff, their contractors, certain other government agencies and other selected libraries and information centers. In 1976, public access to the DOE/RECON online service was made available through WRISC (Western Regional Information Service Center) at the Lawrence Berkeley Lab in California, and the DOE Regional Energy Information Centers in San Francisco and Denver. Dial-up service was added in early 1976.

Key staff in the 1970s included Charles Gottschalk at the DOE Office of Technical Information, Leon Yount (RECON manager), and Vaden, Gove, and Haeuslein at Oak Ridge National Lab. By the end of 1976, there were forty dedicated lines and over 130 dial-up users. The most active files were the Energy Database (the continuation and renaming of the NSA database), NSA, and Water Resources Abstracts. The RECON software was running on a shared computer concurrently with a large number of non-RECON users and actually using less than 20 percent of the CPU time. It was experiencing poor reliability; most problems were caused by failures in old equipment and installation of new disk memory units. The system still did not have a full-text search capability to permit searching words and phrases in the titles or abstracts (*ERDA/RECON Newsletter* 1977).

Lehigh University LEADERMART

As described in chapter 3, Donald Hillman at Lehigh University worked on LEADER throughout the 1960s. In September 1969, with NSF support, planning began for an end-user-oriented system as part of an interactive online search service. These plans evolved into a commercial service named LEADERMART (LEADER plus "MART," for the Mart Science and Engineering Library at Lehigh, which jointly operated the system with the Center for Information Science). Martin (1973) reported that LEADERMART was first put into service during March 1971 and became fully operational in September 1971 for on-campus scientific and engineering research centers (Hillman 1977; "Lehigh's LEADERMART" 1972).

1971 Milestone

LEADERMART was the first fully operational public online search service, providing service to any interested user.

LEADERMART was developed with a general objective of promoting interdisciplinary research and encouraging interaction among the science and engineering disciplines, with services to professionals associated with interdisciplinary academic research centers, as well as employees of agencies of the federal government and users in industry and business. The approach was oriented toward science in general rather than toward any particular discipline, so that information of widely different origin might be communicated across disciplinary boundaries (*Summary of proceedings* 1971). Thus, LEADERMART was made available to *any* interested subscriber, without restriction, which made it the first truly publicly available online search service. As a result of contractual or self-imposed constraints, the other operational online systems at that time were all working in support of designated and restricted constituencies and were not encouraging, soliciting, permitting, or signing up any "walk up" customers.

When asked why Lehigh decided to launch a commercial system, Hillman (1996) supplied several reasons: "The NSF grant supporting LEADER was as much a development grant as a research grant. Lehigh undertook to maintain the system AFTER the NSF funding had come to an end ... [and] the Mart Science and Engineering Library, led by an energetic new Director, was expanding its services beyond the campus confines. There was a well-established policy of service to industry which furnished a natural fit for LEADERMART." Also, perhaps more important, "the cost of providing information services to the university's interdisciplinary research centers exceeded on-campus resources. Off-campus revenues thus became a necessity." Consequently, external, fee-paying customers were sought. Although designed to serve the needs of Lehigh, Hillman envisioned LEADERMART as part of a national information network. One report ("Lehigh's LEADERMART" 1972, 183) noted:

It became clear early during the LEADERMART project that the full potential of the LEADERMART System and Service would not be realized if it were restricted to on-campus users. As a result, the original objectives were modified and extended to include off-campus users via system expansion. In addition, it appeared both possible and practical to integrate other existing retrieval systems into a network ... of major and minor access modes thus eliminating the need to duplicate retrieval service functions.

Hillman's definition of off-campus users included users in private industry such as pharmaceutical firms. Thus he was moving to direct competition with other online services such as Battelle's BASIS, Lockheed's DIALOG, and SDC Search Service that were courting those users. As early as 1970, Hillman talked of outside support needed; in response to a question at a 1970 conference about the projected fixed cost of operating LEADERMART when the Mart Library took it over, Hillman said, "The annual cost is estimated to be $250,000, some of which we hope to meet with funds from local industry and research groups" (Hillman 1970, M-15). Koenig (1987) recalled that Hillman "identified the pharmaceutical industry as a likely candidate. He went to all of us information managers in the major companies" asking for "something like $50,000 each." As an inducement to the pharmaceutical and chemical companies, Hillman proposed to put online the CA Condensates and MEDLARS databases.

Hillman began demonstrating LEADERMART to the librarians of major chemical and pharmaceutical companies in 1971. Early users included Barbara Prewitt at Rohm and Haas, Barbara Lawrence at Exxon, and Koenig at Pfizer. Lawrence (1997) recalled a briefing at Lehigh where she and Prewitt were curious, but a bit suspicious, about non-Boolean searching because of their prior Boolean-based searching on batch and SDI systems.

The task of developing the retrieval system was assigned to Lehigh's Center for Information Science (Hillman 1970). LEADERMART was implemented on a CDC 6400 computer. Its output consisted of citations or complete textual passages from one or more source documents, in any way a user specified. The search process began when a query was entered in the form of sentences describing a user's problem. Each input sentence had to be grammatically well formed, but with no restriction on vocabulary. Hillman (1970, M-9) provided a sample: "I would like to know whether modular bounded functionals have ever been used in theoretical studies of retrievable sets, and if so by whom and with what results. If there has been no application of this type, I would be interested to learn of any work in retrieval theory that makes use of Borel functions. If there is no such work, please direct me to retrieval studies involving topological measures or metric spaces in general." Each inquiry was analyzed by the same procedures used on the text of the input documents. The program fashioned an appropriate response by comparing the conceptual structure of an inquiry with the general structure of the file. The comparison was conducted by a user-computer dialogue in which LEADER instructed and interrogated the user via the CRT; thus each inquiry was negotiated through successive modifications of a user's stated interests.

With the University of Georgia, Lehigh established an information service for the EPA's National Environmental Research Center in Cincinnati. As a first step, Hillman set up a cooperative arrangement with Georgia to share access to bibliographic databases (Kasarda and Hillman 1972). An NSF-funded telecommunications link was installed in 1972 between the Georgia system and LEADERMART ("Lehigh's LEADERMART" 1972).

When it first became publicly available, LEADERMART had about two years of COMPENDEX online, which was the first online access to this database (*Summary of proceedings* 1971). Later, LEADERMART added more files, including CA Condensates, Mathematical Reviews, and the LC MARC II file (which formed the basis for Lehigh's online library cataloging system). In addition to these databases produced elsewhere, LEADERMART offered three special purpose files, constructed and maintained at Lehigh. One was Tall Structures Abstracts, which contained literature on tall buildings such as environmental systems, gravity loads, temperature effects, earthquake loading and response, fatigue and fracture, nonlinear analysis, and masonry structures. A second contained abstracts acquired from the American Society of Civil Engineers. The third contained about three-hundred full-text records of information science documents for experimental purposes, especially in testing the text analyzer. By 1972, all of these files contained a total of nearly a half million records; approximately 300,000 titles and abstracts were online at any given time (Kasarda and Hillman 1972).

As of April 1973, the large bibliographic databases had been removed from the system. We could not determine exactly why; perhaps the retrieval approach did not work well with citation-only records, or the royalty costs were too high, or the processing and storage costs were too high. A further mystery is whether the operators really believed that they could have a commercially viable service without those databases.

1971 Milestone

LEADERMART was the first online search service to institute connect-hour charging.

The charge in 1971 for access to any of the databases was a standard $55 per connect hour, except for government and academic users, who were charged $45 per connect hour, and members of the Lehigh University community, who received the service free of charge. By 1973, LEADERMART was accessible from approximately thirty terminals, on and off campus, but only about twelve could be connected concurrently to the CDC 6400 with its 65K of core memory. Since the computer served all other university computing requirements, LEADERMART access could be limited during peak usage periods, and response time was related to the number of users connected (Marron et al. 1973). The system suffered occasional software and hardware problems such as "balky" disk units and tape drives that interrupted normal service and file updates, and "noisy" telephone lines that disconnected users at remote locations (Hillman 1973).

From the mid-1960s on, Hillman had been convinced that end users were able to conduct their own literature searches, without intermediation or assistance. He invested a large amount of time in designing a system that he thought would be easy to use. Thus he was astounded to learn that users were having considerable difficulties in using LEADERMART. Hillman (1973, 593) analyzed the situation:

By far the most intriguing outcome of our interactions with different user groups was the paradoxical emergence of evidence that 'easy' systems are hard to use. This puzzling phenomenon remained unexplained until it became clear that those who reported most difficulties in using LEADERMART were not the end users of the information provided. With hardly an exception, they were information specialists or middlemen interposed between the system and the user. As a result, LEADERMART was not being employed by the kind of research worker for which it was directly designed. . . . [Although] some open-minded and flexible information specialists were, of course, able to use LEADERMART with great proficiency. However, intermediaries of rigid habits are invariably mismatched with a user-oriented system.

Besides attributing the intermediaries' problems to their inflexible, ingrained searching habits (e.g., they insisted on having explicit Boolean operators), Hillman (1973, 593) felt that they were not capable of fully understanding their clients' needs—"it is impossible to do someone else's browsing"—and they could not effectively use conceptually related terms displayed in rank order of calculated pertinence. Hillman suggested that users of an automated information system should be the "gatekeepers," or highly motivated, inquisitive information seekers. He did not propose how the needs of everyone else, especially in places where no gatekeepers existed, should be met.

Another LEADERMART initiative was an NSF-supported "operational experiment" started in 1974 by the Pennsylvania Science and Engineering Foundation (PSEF), to determine how to market scientific and technical information innovations (Hillman 1974b). The objective of the PSEF project was to bring information services to the public, especially small to medium-sized industrial firms. PSEF was to be the organizing agent, and was to use LEADERMART to explore cost-effective marketing strategies to firms throughout Pennsylvania (Burchinal 1975). A team from state government (PSEF), academia (Lehigh and Temple University), and business (Metascience, Inc.) was assembled to formulate and test different techniques for marketing new products to information specialists. The emphasis was on developing marketing models (Hillman 1974a). Hillman (1996) observed, "No suitable marketing organization was available that would have permitted LEADERMART services to be commercialized."

In spite of Hillman's marketing and extensive NSF support, however, LEADERMART did not become a commercial success; instead it suspended its operations. Just as staff were beginning to build a customer base, Lehigh University decided that it could no longer afford to keep LEADERMART going. According to Hillman, the decision to terminate the LEADERMART service was completely economic. The cost of running the system on the CDC 6400, a scientific computer that was ill suited for data processing applications, was astronomical—$10,000 per month just for file update operations. The computer had an awkward habit of overwriting the record block table as stored data on the disk drives approached maximum capacity, resulting in the loss of all files. Because they updated everything from slow magnetic tape drives, they lost nine hours every time they had such a glitch while updating the CA Condensates file.

In order to provide printouts in mixed uppercase and lowercase characters, LEADERMART installed the ALA standard printer train containing the large character set that permitted printing of LC catalog card data as well as information from full-text databases they were likely to use. This character set contained about twice the number of characters as were used in the standard sixty-three-character set for the CDC 6400. The installation slowed down all computer printing on campus by about 40 percent, and definitely detracted from LEADERMART's popularity with other Lehigh computer users.

The CDC 6400 time-sharing system had not been developed when the LEADER application began (they used a Lehigh-developed system instead); it was completed under contract to Lehigh about a year after LEADER started. As a result, the time-shared operations that were crucial to any interactive applications were unreliable at best. Furthermore, the university community was growing restless with the frequent processing interruptions caused by LEADER's demands on resources.

Among the reasons for termination of the service, Hillman noted that most significant was the university's total lack of experience in knowing how a service to external users should be established and sustained. With the exception of the library community, Lehigh's thinking at the time was inward-directed and insular. Research grants were to be pursued, and the research, once done, was to be followed by more research, all funded by outside agencies. The idea of developing a service was quite foreign to the prevailing culture. LEADERMART was therefore allowed to die. To be sure, its natural language processing technology survived as a tool for further research, but essentially the system was withdrawn from the marketplace. The LEADERMART story is a sad tale of a system that was unusual and advanced for its time but which could not survive in a university culture that isolated itself from mainstream developments. The system came too soon and cost too much. A supreme irony is that Lehigh University has now reversed its stance on commercial activities and has even established a company to commercialize faculty inventions and developments (Hillman 1996). Perhaps the marketing was not aggressive enough. Perhaps the users, many of them librarians and information specialists, did not feel comfortable with a system that asked them to write the request in a narrative paragraph, rather than to build the query through a succession of iterative steps. Among the hypotheses for its demise was the view that LEADER was perhaps too user-friendly. In 1974, Summit and Firschein (1974, 298) surmised that, in attempting to formulate queries for users, the program actually took control of the search away from them. If users did not understand what was going on inside the program, they could not participate in modifying the results: "Perhaps some users did not want to leave the 'thinking' to the computer but rather preferred to express their query in explicit form; or perhaps Boolean capability was required because of unsuccessful experiences or boredom with the many iterations of the natural language capability." As we noted, Hillman's design was unique and perhaps far ahead of its time. Koenig (1987) pointed out that if one had written a paper years later on LEADERMART as it was in 1970 or 1971 and taken it to a conference

on expert systems with AI [artificial intelligence], changed the wording very slightly, almost nobody except us old-timers would know that this was a 17-year-old paper being recycled. In fact, it would be an interesting experiment to do that, for someone to take one of those old Don Hillman papers and update it, present it and see whether anyone noticed that it wasn't current. That was a remarkable system that he put together at that time. If only Hillman had been successful in getting support from the pharmaceutical companies. How very close we came to having a quite different paradigm of what online searching was like, and a version of online searching that would be much more user friendly and much more oriented toward the end-user.

Koenig himself wrote a paper (1992) about the failure of LEADERMART to compete in the commercial marketplace. LEADERMART did not fail because of the lack of interest and support of potential users. Several institutions used and liked it. Prewitt (1974) did extensive experimentation with it at Rohm and Haas Company and found it to be useful. Prewitt had just begun to teach bench chemists how to do their own online searches when Lehigh removed LEADERMART from the commercial market.

Hillman became the director of the Center for Information and Computer Science at Lehigh and continued working on LEADERMART after the service was discontinued. With NSF support in 1974–1975, LEADERMART was used as a basis for further research, and its existing capabilities were enhanced in developing a new front-end question analyzer called QUANSY, and a new file organization approach for data retrieval.

New Public Search Services of the Seventies

Also during the first half of the seventies, several new online retrieval systems appeared that served distinct user populations. They contributed to expanding the audience for online retrieval by serving previously unfilled information needs.

QUIC/LAW, QL/SEARCH, and QL Systems

QUIC/LAW was a Canadian system for legal materials that lasted only from 1968 to 1973. However, the software later became the basis for QL Systems and WESTLAW. The Law Faculty at Queen's University, Kingston, Ontario, developed QUIC/LAW and the project was directed by Hugh Lawford, a law professor at Queen's, and Richard von Briesen, a computer expert who also taught as a law professor. Queen's University, IBM Canada Ltd., the TransCanada Telephone System, the Canadian government, and the governments of British Columbia and New Brunswick supported the project. The QUIC/LAW Project was established to investigate possible uses of computers by lawyers, with particular emphasis on the use of computers to assist legal research (Lawford 1973; Herron 1979).

QUIC/LAW was developed in the context of other legal IR research going on in Canada then, including plans at the University of Manitoba for computer searching of all Canadian Regulatory and Statutory Laws (federal and provincial). A full-text database of over 2 million words for the Revised Statutes of Manitoba was completed in 1970. Another example of Canadian legal research was the Treaty Project that worked with the QUIC/LAW Project to develop a capability for storing and retrieving thousands of records of treaties, and the full text of Canadian treaties. The Treaty Project experimented with a sample group of about 600 bibliographic treaty records as a database for QUIC/LAW. The DATUM project (chapter 7) was also part of the Canadian legal research work going on at this time.

A joint study with IBM started in 1968 and continued through 1969. Lawford (1973, 67–68) reported, "IBM provided computer equipment, systems analysts and programmers and access to certain unreleased IBM computer programs which had been developed for IBM's internal use." These unreleased programs comprised a search system known as INFORM/360. When Lawford received it, INFORM/360 was not fully developed, and had many disadvantages. According to Fay (1971), Lawford's work was modifying and improving the system to overcome the shortcomings. The search strategy of the software was based on statistical probability rather than on Boolean logic, and used term weighting as a basis for selection and output relevance ranking. All "insignificant" words (e.g., a, an, the, which) were ignored in searching. The project used ATS for file building, after making considerable modifications.

QUIC/LAW was designed to be used by end-users, not intermediaries. In 1969, users could search the full text of documents by keywords linked with Boolean operators, or they could enter a query in natural language (e.g., give me all the documents on the eutrophication of Lake Eire). The system displayed the retrieved references in rank order by relevance to the query, using statistical techniques: "If one retrieves 150 cases, he will see the most significant one first" (Lawford 1973, 70). In 1972, the system was still in a test phase, sharing an IBM 360/65 at the University of Ottawa, with eight terminals scattered over considerable distances and the jurisdiction of five telephone companies to test communications techniques, and with plans for an expanded test with terminals in law offices and government agencies.

Queen's University offered online searching of two legal databases: full texts of Supreme Court of Canada decisions from 1923 to date and the 1970 Revised Statutes of Canada in French and English ("Electronic legal" 1974; Gechman 1972). In addition to the two legal databases, two scientific databases were offered: POLLUTION—67,000 selected bibliographic records and abstracts extracted from

ISI, Chemical Abstracts, and Biological Abstracts tapes, and ENVIRONMENT—a small test file of bibliographic records, also known as the Canada Water, WATDOC, or Canadian Environment database. POLLUTION was later replaced by Pollution Abstracts, and ENVIRONMENT replaced by Oceanic Abstracts. These two scientific databases were the first bibliographic files on QUIC/LAW; before it had only carried full-text legal files.

The published literature does not disclose the reasons for the demise of QUIC/LAW, other than to suggest that it was too costly. One study of its performance ("Electronic legal" 1974, 53) did expose serious flaws and expressed the core of many users' frustrations with computer-based retrieval systems:

An experiment to see if QUIC/LAW could find an actual case on a specific point revealed a serious computer error. The question posed was: 'Is there any case in which a tugboat was kept available for the original owner following expiration of the formal contract of hire?' (an exact description of the 'St. John Tugboat v. Irving Oil Refinery' case). QUIC/LAW produced four cases, with the 'St. John' case ranked fourth. The computer was then fed the keywords, 'tugboat,' 'contract' and 'expiration,' to which it responded that no case containing those words existed. In desperation the QUIC/LAW personnel tried to retrieve the case by feeding in 'Tugboat' and 'St. John.' On a further negative reply the QUIC/LAW staff retreated in confusion.

Because of the rapid growth of the QUIC/LAW Project and the prospect of commercial use of the systems that had been developed, Queen's University asked in 1973 that the project be incorporated as a separate entity outside the university. Lawford (in a paper by Rushbrook and Lawford 1976, 228) commented:

QL Systems Limited originated as a research project at Queen's University, the QUIC/LAW Project, to investigate potential uses of computers by lawyers. When the project became too costly for the University to continue, the staff of the Project first offered to donate the project's programs and other work to the Canadian government and, when that offer was refused, set up a private company to carry the research into commercial operation.

Lawford and von Briesen incorporated QL Systems in 1973 to carry forward the work started by the QUIC/LAW Project. Lawford became the president and von Briesen became vice president. The QL computer was in Ottawa. Using its proprietary software, QL Systems later developed the first Canadian commercial retrieval service, QL/SEARCH, concentrating on bibliographic (e.g., METADEX, Pollution Abstracts, Oceanic Abstracts, Selected Water Resources Abstracts, ABI/INFORM) and full-text databases (Canadian legal material such as the statutes of Canada and the provinces). As a Canadian company, its objective was to make the system bilingual. The company had English-language files of interest to Canada, particularly databases from the United States, but it also worked on developing French-language databases in which all the records were only in French. By the end of 1976, five of its files were entirely in French. Users also had the option to receive messages in either French or English.

In 1974, QL Systems loaded World Aluminum Abstracts and made it available online with full-text searching of the title, abstract, and subject indexing fields, at a cost of one dollar to sign on, and a dollar per search (Rushbrook and Lawford 1976). From a pricing point of view, this may have been the first instance of a log-in charge and a per search charge for an online system. From the beginning of the commercial enterprise, the system was given the name Shared Information Service to stress the importance that the management attached to the sharing of services and costs of providing the information (Herron 1979).

The QL/SEARCH software was installed in several other locations in Canada and the United States. Starting in December 1974, it was tested with full-text material at *The Globe and Mail* (Toronto) (Rhydwen 1977). An agreement was made for the QL software to be used, starting in January 1976, by *The Globe and Mail* for their online retrieval service that consisted of the full-text news and other editorial content of that newspaper, starting with 1976 material. Search service for users outside of *The Globe and Mail* started in January 1978, through QL Systems (Nash 1979).

By the end of 1976, QL Systems had expanded to include twenty-one files (16 Canadian and 5 French-language) concerned with Parliament and government, law, environment, energy, pollution, business, mining, communications, and the Canadian North. It was serving over 120 customers (including a few customers outside of Canada) and operating at its Kingston computer center. A modified version of the QL/SEARCH software was also used by West Publishing Company in 1976 as the basis for its WESTLAW online service.

QL Systems was the first Canadian commercial online retrieval service, and the management put an emphasis on making this system bilingual (French and English), with French-language databases and with system messages and responses available in French or English. At the time of this writing, QL Systems was still a major Canadian online search service.

BASIS-70

The first of the seventies generation of online retrieval systems to be implemented was BASIS-70, developed at the world's largest private research organization, the Battelle Memorial Institute (BMI) in Columbus, Ohio. BASIS-70 had extensive in-house funding support and was based on extensive Battelle experience in operating several information analysis centers (IACs). The principals associated with BASIS included John Murdock, John Fried, David Columbo, and David Penniman. Murdock, a physicist, joined BMI in 1951. In 1953 he participated in developing and managing one of the first IACs in the United States and continued to participate in information research and system design, including overall responsibility for information research at BMI's Columbus Labs. He served on national committees relating to information systems. Fried, who joined Battelle in 1964 with degrees in civil engineering and mathematics, was the chief of the BASIS-70 Project and was responsible for its design, development, and implementation. Columbo, with degrees in mathematics and computer and information science, joined Battelle in 1969. His 1969 master's thesis at Ohio State University ("Automatic Retrieval Systems and Associated Retrieval Languages") provided much of the initial review and evaluation of available technology for use with BASIS. Bernard Dennis, with degrees in mathematics and physical sciences and in public school administration, joined the BASIS team after the system was developed, and managed the Washington, D.C., operations to help market BASIS. Prior to joining BMI in 1964, Dennis developed and managed the first computer-based technical information center in an industrial organization—in 1958 at GE in Cincinnati.

Murdock selected the name BASIS from among the entries in a naming contest. Although he wanted a name that was not an acronym and had no inherent meaning, the name BASIS came to stand for Battelle Automated Search Information System. The "70" was added in the beginning to suggest that the system was forward-looking to the 1970s, but was dropped within a couple of years (Murdock 1990). The intended use for BASIS was to meet "a wide variety of information and data projects at Battelle," that would include bibliographic storage and retrieval as well as management information, engineering data, and physical properties of various metals and plastics (Fried 1971, 143).

The software was installed and the system became operational in Columbus in July 1970 (Penniman 1971). The files available at start-up included several sponsored files, each to be used in providing online service to a contracting institution's own user group. This included bibliographic databases for the Copper Data Center (5,000 records from CDA), the Defense Metals Information Center (DMIC) (2,000 records from the USAF Materials Lab), and 3,000 records relating to the ecology of the American Isthmus region (particularly eastern Panama and northwestern Columbia); databases of facts about properties of plastic materials (sample of 55 plastic materials manufactured by Durez Plastics Co.), and properties of selected metals (200 records on selected alloys from MIL-Handbook-5. "Metallic Materials and Elements for Aerospace Vehicle Structures"). Penniman (1994) noted, "The first external application, with a real contract from a real sponsor came from the Chemical Rubber Company (CRC) who put up a database of properties to test market an online handbook. They decided not to proceed with the product after the test, but it was our first outside contract with a sponsor not already doing work at Battelle in the information center area. CRC was our first marketing success." CRC was a major handbook publisher, and the planned system would permit users to specify desired characteristics of chemical compounds, and retrieve the names of compounds meeting their criteria.

By January 1971, BASIS-70 was providing access to ten small files. By December 1971, approximately thirty small files were loaded. Later, the software was installed at the U.S. National Security Agency (Fife 1974) and in an institution in Japan (Martin 1974).

In late 1970, at least two of BMI's regular IAC sponsors, DMIC and CDA, whose manual files were being built and maintained at Battelle's Columbus laboratories, were pressing to obtain remote online access to their files before the end of 1971. Battelle had operated the DMIC since 1950 and the Copper Data Center since 1965. From May 1969, CDA had also been searching their database online with the competitive ORBIT system, using one terminal at the CDA headquarters in New York and another terminal at the Copper Data Center office at BMI (giving Battelle staff a good chance to study and use ORBIT). CDA expected that their member companies would be able to have their own online access to this ORBIT-based file by the end of 1969 (Covington 1969). BASIS-70 was developed partly in response to that pressure.

The BASIS-70 design specifications called for an RCA-7 computer, so staff implemented BASIS on an in-house CDC 6000 series computer, and referred to it as "interim BASIS" or "Phase I BASIS" until arrangements could be made to acquire an RCA-7. Unfortunately, RCA left the computer business after the Battelle staff chose that equipment for BASIS-70. So the Phase I version continued, with several upgrades, to be the regular BASIS system. The system was intended to (1) provide a smooth transition between Battelle's manually operated IACs and a computer-based system; (2) meet the demands of their current IAC sponsors for remote access to their files before the end of 1971; and (3) provide a system that could be used as a benchmark for testing users' reactions to features that would be offered in the RCA-7 version of BASIS-70. The original intent was to implement Phase I BASIS-70 in a transitional basis only, however, the system was so well received they decided to continue it as a separate functional service on the CDC 6400 even after the delivery of the RCA-7.

Battelle objectives during 1970–1971 included development and delivery of search software, and the pursuit of research and development objectives. They were less interested in running a commercial search service. One activity discussed within BMI was the possibility of offering a group-sponsored project to ten or twelve organizations who supported their own CDC 6400 series computers. In return for a modest contribution by each sponsor ($4,000–$6,000), a research program in online technology would be supported that was expected to be of benefit to all of the sponsors, and a copy of the BASIS software would be installed on each sponsor's system. This group-sponsored project did not go forward, but it showed the willingness of Battelle at that time to make the BASIS software widely available to other users at a modest cost.

Like other designers, the BASIS developers aimed to fashion a system for direct use by scientists, administrators and managers, and especially engineers. They visualized a system with modules of all the types of information and support that an engineer might need: models, mathematics, bibliographic data, and the full text of documents (Murdock 1990). Eventually, most BASIS files were bibliographic, but some did contain management information, engineering data, or other numeric data. Although the BASIS design was done after they studied the online systems of DIALOG, SDC, MDC, and others that were operating then, the BASIS designers wanted to move beyond that first generation of online systems. As observed in chapter 4, BMI staff had been involved with the major online systems in 1968 when they produced a movie of the COSATI benchmark demonstrations of online systems. As a designer, Fried (1971, 145) felt that the two keys to direct end-user searching were reliability of performance and ease of use. BASIS, he felt, was easy to use: "With BASIS-70, users need not be experienced in library search techniques nor in computer programming. The system provides all the necessary guidelines to conduct a search. Although the efficiency of a search is enhanced if the user has a sound understanding of the contents of the data base being interrogated, an effective search can be conducted without previous familiarity with the file." An example of design that was intended to facilitate ease of use was the automatic response of the program to a search term that produced zero hits: NO SUCH TERM. WANT ADJACENT TERMS? YES/NO. A YES produced five lines of the alphabetic index with the middle line being the searcher's original term. This display was equivalent to the EXPAND feature implemented on DIALOG several years earlier, but automatically suggesting it to the searcher in the event of a zero answer set was novel. Automatic suggesting of alternative terms did not exist in other systems until years later—with the sole exception of MIT's TIRP in 1966 (chapter 3). Also, unlike many other systems, BASIS executed Boolean OR operators before AND because "users frequently want to enter several terms to mean the same idea" (Fried 1971, 147). BASIS operated with a large list of stop words (the stop list consisted of all words or character strings with three characters or less), some of which were meaningful search terms for certain users.

The programmers showed their sense of humor with the terminal interface responses programmed into BASIS of 1970–1971. For example, the response to entry of an invalid ID was "Will the mystery guest please login," and the response to a new search was "Your slate is clean." Despite these user-friendly enhancements, however, BASIS in the 1970s was used, as were virtually all the online systems of the period, primarily by librarians. Unlike today, it would have been startling to see a scientist, engineer, or executive working at a keyboard (Murdock 1990).

Written mostly in FORTRAN, the BASIS software was moderately flexible compared to others available then. BASIS allowed searching of natural language terms with word proximity operators or of controlled vocabulary in databases with assigned indexing. However, as in the original version of RECON, a searcher could enter only one term at a time and had to wait for a response on the number of hits before entering another term. After entering all desired terms, a searcher could use Boolean operators to connect the line numbers representing the terms. Fried (1971, 146) viewed this constraint as an advantage—it was a way to give a searcher a 'sense of feel' for the magnitude of retrievable items at each point duing the search: "This frequently results in a totally different search pattern than if all search criteria were entered before any items are retrieved. Knowing the number of items that satisfy each search term and logical combination at any point during the search gives the user a better awareness of his progress and allows him to continue his search more effectively."

By January 1971, BASIS-70 was available weekdays via standard telephone lines from 9:00 a.m. to 12:00 a.m. It could be queried remotely via telephone lines using Teletype (at 10 cps) or CRT terminals at speeds up to 480 cps. TYMNET communication service was connected to BASIS and made operational in March 1972.

Battelle was a not-for-profit organization, established originally to conduct research and development in metallurgy and related engineering areas, that was by charter not permitted to advertise—and thus could not promote the BASIS service. To get around this constraint, BMI established an arrangement in early 1972 with an external organization, Science Information Association (SIA) of Washington, D.C. For a couple of years therefore, individuals outside of Battelle were made aware of BASIS and contracted for online access indirectly through membership in another organization, SIA.

Bob Landau and Norman Cottrell of SIA, along with Murdock of Battelle, marketed BASIS and its two large databases, NTIS and CHEMCON, which were added in 1973. Landau also provided training for new users.

Landau had earned degrees in electrical engineering, public administration, and the law. In the mid-1960s, he directed the COSATI Information Science and Technology Inventory that resulted in the development of a common database that was used in a demonstration and movie of online systems (chapter 4). His last federal assignment was as an information science advisor in the Office of Science and Technology in the Executive Office of the President. In early 1970, he left the U.S. government after eighteen years in the intelligence community, to form several of his own organizations.

Prior to his SIA work for the BASIS service, Cottrell had been active in developing computer-based information services. With a degree in economics from the University of Washington, he served in the U.S. Naval Intelligence during World War II, gaining four years of intensive experience in highly analytical and advanced intelligence systems. He joined Sperry Rand in 1945, and when he left there in 1963, he was director of marketing for its Federal Systems Division. He served as director of documentation for the American Society for Metals and chair of the Information Systems Committee of the Engineers Joint Council in New York. Cottrell also served on technical information committees for COSATI and the U.S. National Academies of Science and Engineering.

In early 1971, Landau performed financial analyses at SIA for the proposed online service, with extensive tables of cost figures associated with various combinations of file storage, search activity volume, search duration, and hours of daily service. Lancaster and Fayen (1973, 384–392) reprinted these cost tables and analyses. In a September 1971 internal memo, Landau made the observation that none of the then available online systems had yet been able to successfully offer online accessibility to "large" databases (over 10 million characters)

for more than a two-hour window per day. The SIA/BMI group had an initial goal objective of a fifteen-hour per day service, but because of the prohibitive costs for direct access storage (much higher than it is today), they were forced to trim their service for large databases to four hours per day on weekdays and nine hours on Saturdays. They planned to split their database offerings into time windows, as had been done earlier on COLEX and CIRCOL (see chapter 6). They also looked for service opportunities with more moderate-sized databases. Databases being considered for inclusion were primarily compilations of sci-tech project descriptions (SSIE), citations to the sci-tech report literature (NASA, NTIS, AEC), and citations to other professional literature (ISI, COMPENDEX, ERIC, PANDEX).

1973 Milestone

BASIS was the first online search service to provide access at any time to an online collection of more than 1 million records.

A sample six-month portion (last half of 1972) of the CA Condensates file was available online in early March 1973 for demonstration purposes, and the full CAC file (July 1970 to present with about 1 million records) was available as a single file in May 1973.[5] The complete NTIS database (January 1970 to date, with 140,000 records) became available on BASIS in February 1973 and was accessed regularly by SIA members. No abstracts were indexed or stored with the NTIS file, but subject access was available by searching title words, keywords, and other subject codes.

SIA staff had marketing underway in 1972 to sign up interested organizations for BASIS subscriptions and to provide training sessions for searchers. The *SIA Newsletter* was started for distribution to actual and potential subscribers to the service, with particular attention paid to the market for the NTIS and

CAC databases. In the early seventies, the BASIS computer could support sixty users simultaneously and TYMNET access was available from major U.S. cities at significantly lower costs than normal long-distance telephone rates. By March 1974 there were nine-hundred users, most of them at BMI's Information Centers; only about fifty were outside subscribers through SIA (Landau 1990). U.S. government subscribers included EPA, NBS, the Department of Transportation (for the TRIS-ON-LINE service), and DOD. Other subscribers included Calspan Corp. and Exxon.

Penniman conducted a pioneering research project to analyze online users' search behavior. His 1974 study at Battelle reviewed over 230 hours of BASIS searching during April–May 1974 in 934 interactive search sessions (Penniman 1975a,b).

With this strong start, Battelle was on its way to becoming a major online service. However, certain non-technical issues blocked the way. A review of Battelle's history will explain why its online service did not flourish. BMI started in 1929 with an endowment from Gordon Battelle "for the encouragement of creative research and the making of discoveries and inventions." For years it grew only modestly; its big turning point came in 1944 when its subsidiary (Battelle Development Corp.) signed a royalty-sharing agreement with Chester Carlson to help him develop and market his image reproduction system based on static electricity. This was seven years after Carlson invented xerography and had been denied backing by many major business organizations (Bixby 1962). In 1947, Battelle signed a contract with the Haloid Company (later Xerox Corp.) to put the invention on the market. The eventual extraordinary success of the Xerox product line is well-known history. In the 1960s, Battelle traded its xerography patents to Xerox in exchange for stock. Battelle's Xerox stock holdings grew in value to more than $225 million, at which time it attracted the attention of the Attorney General of Ohio who questioned in a lawsuit whether the intent of Gordon Battelle's will was being faithfully carried out and whether the Institute should be allowed to accumulate and retain such wealth. Presumably Ohio state officials had visions of considerable tax revenues resulting from any resulting change of status. The U.S. Internal Revenue Service also wanted tax revenues from BMI activities that the IRS claimed were taxable. The 1975 court decision in this law suit resulted in some divesting of activities, an IRS tax bill of $47 million, and a court-ordered donation of $80 million to various charitable causes (Armstrong 1982). This was the milieu for Battelle management as they reviewed the internal proposals for establishing an online service.

In April 1974, Cottrell said in a letter to SIA participating subscribers: "The original goals of SIA and Battelle's Columbus Laboratories (BCL) were to pilot program demonstrate the technical and economic feasibility of on-line accessibility to large data bases. It has now been clearly demonstrated that on-line systems like the . . . BASIS system can deliver highly selective information quickly and inexpensively in a form attractive and easy to use." Cottrell went on to comment on the economic feasibility issue, noting: "Cost/revenue breakeven has not been achieved in the present program and the assuredness of its being reached in the short term is not sufficiently high to attract continuing financial support. The [CAS] and [NTIS] databases are now available through commercial on-line suppliers at costs comparable to those of SIA rates to its members. It had never been planned that SIA/BCL would compete with 'production' commercial systems." He concluded by saying that SIA planned to transfer access for SIA online users from BASIS to SDC's system and to concentrate on making new and specialized databases for its members.

Landau had met with Summit at Lockheed and Cuadra at SDC earlier that year to discuss a smooth transfer of service for the SIA subscribers. Landau decided that users should be transferred to SDC, primarily because SDC was the only commercial provider at that time offering access to CHEMCON. Another influence on his decision may have been that Landau and the Battelle staff were more familiar with ORBIT from their prior exposure to the COLEX, CIRCOL, and Copper Data Center work. The transfer took place on May 1, 1974, and the SIA/BCL public online service on the major databases effectively terminated. Battelle's BASIS public online service was an equal competitor to SDC Search Service and Lockheed's DIALOG when it was discontinued. From that point on, the BASIS service restricted itself to specialty files and private files for limited groups of users. SIA turned to offering brokered SDI and retrospective search services for its members, as well as R&D and consulting assignments.

An interesting experiment in 1975–1976 was the exploration of possible use of BASIS for online subject searching in support of the OCLC bibliographic utility. OCLC's search capability at that time was limited to searching on codes built from selected characters from selected title words or author names in order to find catalog records for known works; it did not have a general title word or subject heading search capability. With support from CLR, an experiment was performed to determine the feasibility of using the BASIS software at OCLC for this purpose—the details are described later in the OCLC section.

By the end of 1976, BASIS was still operating, available for nineteen hours per day, but used only under service contracts to support private files of special constituencies. The BMI Columbus facility was using the BASIS software to provide online search service for the Copper Data Center (Settles and Black 1978), the Metals and Ceramics Information Center, the Battelle Energy Information Center, and the Transportation Research Information Service (TRIS). The BASIS software was distributed widely throughout the world and used with in-house systems running on CDC-6600, DEC-10, UNIVAC 1100, Xerox Sigma 9, or IBM 370 computers, and it was used later in other public online services such as the British Infoline-I service.

WESRAC DATACOM

In 1967, NASA and the USC Graduate School of Business Administration jointly established a nonprofit organization in Los Angeles, called the Western Research Application Center (WESRAC). WESRAC was one of NASA's Regional Dissemination Centers for collecting and disseminating new knowledge resulting from aerospace research to business, local government, and research organizations in the western states. WESRAC initially provided a batch tape search service (Komoto 1970). Retrospective batch services cost around $300–$400 per search. Using USC's IBM 370/158, WESRAC developed an online system, DATACOM, and provided commercial dial-up online access at 10 or 30 cps to the NASA, NTIS, ERIC, and several other databases. The online service was priced at about $25 per connect hour. It appears that the online service began in 1971, but we can not determine the exact date.

While DATACOM had limitations, it was available to be used by any interested party. Only accession numbers, report titles, and descriptors were in the online file, and only descriptors were searchable. Furthermore, the files were available only for brief periods during the week; the NASA database was available only on Monday and Wednesday mornings, the NTIS database was available on Tuesday and Thursday mornings, and ERIC was available weekday afternoons (Zais 1974). DATACOM was still in operation in early 1975; we know nothing about it after that.

Informatics Search Service

We met Informatics, Inc. of Rockville, Maryland, in their relationships with NASA/RECON and TOXLINE, and in the story of how Roger Summit was offered a vice presidency there, accepted it, then backed out after the Lockheed management gave him permission to start a commercial online searching service at Lockheed. The fate of the Informatics and DIALOG service might have been quite different if Summit had taken the position. Instead of DIALOG, Informatics might have been the industry leader in public online services by the end of the seventies. Instead, the directors of Informatics, Robert Harcharik, Howard Coleman, and Larry Stevens, set a much more limited goal—providing contracted information services for a few government agencies and private companies.

As mentioned in chapter 5, the complete set of RECON retrieval programs that Lockheed developed for NASA were considered to be in the public domain; NASA had deposited them in the COSMIC software depository at the University of Georgia, with a copy to be made available to any requestor. In 1971, under Harcharik's direction, Informatics (the NASA/STIF facilities contractor at that time) acquired a copy of NASA/RECON from COSMIC and started modifying it for their own use. Informatics' staff had developed a database management system called MARK IV (chapter 5), so they named the modified NASA program RECON IV.

In addition to its work for NASA, Informatics also solicited work from NLM. It was pleased when, after successful experiments with full-text searching with the MDC system in 1970, NLM initiated a competitive procurement in early 1971 for a full-text retrieval system. According to Hummel (1975, 24):

Mead Corporation, Informatics, Inc., and Battelle ... responded to the request for proposal, but surprisingly both SDC and Lockheed submitted a no-bid. Evaluation of the proposals led to a contract being let to Informatics, Inc. in late March of 1971. The system proposed by Informatics was the ... (NASA) version of the STIMS/RECON package with system enhancements to facilitate free text search. During the succeeding year, RECON was modified and the TOXLINE files were built. The TOXLINE service was publicly announced and demonstrated in April of 1972, and service instituted in October of that same year.

The TOXLINE search service was run on the Informatics computers through April 1974.

In October 1972, because NLM's computer was not large enough to run TOXLINE, as described earlier, different search software was needed for the nonindexed TOXLINE materials. NLM awarded a contract to Informatics to make the TOXLINE service available on an IBM 360 that was operated by a service bureau called COMNET. Long-distance access was available via TYMNET.

Thus began the Informatics search service. Major participants were Coleman, Richard Lemon, Mike Kelly, and Mark Bayer.

SIA, who acted as the marketing representative for the BASIS service, also served as a representative for the Informatics TOXLINE service. TOXLINE as provided by Informatics was not a publicly available service; it was initially available only to academic institutions and medical schools (Bayer 1995). The CA Condensates, CBAC, ENVIRON, and POPINFORM databases were added in 1973. This was the first online search service use of the latter three databases; CAC had gone online with SIA and SDC in 1973. Actually, the full CBAC and CAC files did not go online here; only selected portions were online, as subsets of the TOXLINE file. Bayer, who joined Informatics in 1973 as a search service manager, developed a litigation support file, called Genesis, that was tailored for needs of lawyers representing the large American oil companies (Bayer 1987). Informatics used Genesis as the basis for much of its private file litigation support work in the following years.

In January 1974, Informatics offered CHEMLINE, the first online chemical dictionary file offered publicly, as an adjunct to TOXLINE, to compensate for the diversity of nomenclature in the literature (Schultheisz, Walker, and Kannan 1978). As described elsewhere in this chapter, a policy decision by NLM led to the transfer of TOXLINE operation and service support to NLM, beginning on April 1, 1974, and discontinued through Informatics on April 25, 1974. The change was not unexpected; from the beginning the contractual arrangement was presumed to be temporary.

Also in 1974, Equitable Life Insurance Company acquired Informatics, and allowed the search service to use the in-house computer at Equitable to continue its contract work. The online service operated with any of the then-available 10–30 cps "low-level" teleprinter terminals and was available from 8:00 a.m. to 10:00 p.m. throughout the work week.

A late 1974 Informatics news release announced that Informatics and the EMF had reached agreement in principle for Informatics to obtain an exclusive license to market the Excerpta Medica database in North America, and that Informatics planned to provide access to it on its own interactive Literature Search and Retrieval Service in Rockville. In early 1972, a terminal was installed in the Excerpta Medica editorial offices and retrospective searches were done as remote job entry on their own database of 300,000 records (Blanken and Stern 1975). Experiments with online use of their file continued during 1972–1974, including trial searches from other institutions that compared the Excerpta Medica and MEDLARS databases (Verheijen-Voogd and Malhijsen 1974). Informatics began providing online access to the EM database for several large companies such as Procter and Gamble, Squibb, Abbott Laboratories, and others (Bayer 1987). The file initially contained only records for a six-month period (May–October 1974), or about 182,000 records. James Powell and his colleagues at the Upjohn Company in Kalamazoo, Michigan, evaluated online use of Excerpta Medica on the Informatics system in late 1974 and early 1975. They awarded high marks to the database for appropriate indexing vocabulary and wide coverage of the drug literature, which resulted in the retrieval of items that could not be found in MEDLINE or TOXLINE. Powell (1976) reported that users were not pleased, however, when unfamiliar journal titles appeared in the printouts. He praised Informatics for allowing online access to the thesaurus but criticized them for the slowness in computer response time—although the users discovered eventually that response time was much better early in the morning. Another source of user frustration was the communication link between Kalamazoo and the Informatics computer. Users often had to dial two or three times to establish a connection, and searches were cut off while in progress. Powell criticized the RECON IV software for allowing only subject access; users wanted to be able to search by authors' names as well, not only to find known citations, but also for subject searching, since "many scientists and physicians associate the names of prominent investigators with certain research areas" (1976, 156).

The MEDLARS and Excerpta Medica files have always overlapped in coverage of the literature; in that sense they could be considered competitors. Excerpta Medica has generally been more current, and with more data (e.g., abstracts) than was provided with MEDLARS records, and it was stronger in its coverage of the drug literature; the Excerpta Medica database could be considered a premium product (Bourne 1980b; Houghton, Webster, and Smith 1982). However, in 1975 the Informatics service with the Excerpta Medica database priced at $120 per hour had little chance in competing with the NLM MEDLINE service at its subsidized $15 per hour ($8 per hour non–prime time) rate. Further, the EM online access was limited in scope and capability (e.g., no *MeSH* terms, and no full-text searching) and required a large up-front monthly fee. Not surprisingly, Informatics was forced to discontinue its online Excerpta Medica database service.

By the end of 1976, the Informatics search service was still in operation but serving primarily private file customers for online service in support of their proprietary goals such as litigation support. Informatics was still offering their Mark IV search system and enhanced application programs, and was also active in contract R&D work. An example was RADCOL, an online search system developed for RADC.

New York Times Information Bank

The concept of a fully automated system for online retrieval of news and current events was conceived at the New York Times in the early sixties. The architect of the idea was John Rothman, who was born in Berlin, Germany, graduated from Queens College, and received a M.A. at NYU, and a Ph.D. from Columbia in 1956; both degrees were in English and Comparative Literature. He joined the Times in 1946 as an indexer and in 1949, he became the assistant editor of the printed *New York Times Index*. In 1964 he was promoted to editor. In this position he was able to present to senior management his ideas for computerizing the *Index*—born on the same day in 1851 as the *Times* itself—and the clipping files, or morgue, that had been collected since the turn of the century. By the mid-sixties, the morgue contained about twenty million clippings that were deteriorating in their folders, and were often out of order, lost, or stolen. Over 10,000 clippings of newspaper articles were being filed each week under individual subject headings. At the least, the morgue was difficult to access, because the indexing system was haphazard, inconsistent, inaccurate, and permitted only one subject access point (Rothman 1972). The Times had four separate information facilities: (1) the clipping library or morgue; (2) the *NYT Index*; (3) the Reference Library; and (4) a photo library—all administratively separate facilities, each with its own indexing vocabulary and procedures. This meant that a journalist had to go to four separate floors and search four different systems to conduct a comprehensive search. Rothman (1968) proposed the consolidation of this activity, starting with the clipping file and the *Index*. The Times managers were receptive to Rothman's ideas because the experience of the 1962–1963 newspaper strike was still fresh in their minds; they wanted to use computers to cut costs and increase the efficiency of the staff (Provenzano 1987).

The possibility of applying computer technology to the *Index* was investigated, beginning in 1965, according to Rothman (1968, 86), "in part to end the waste of time and manpower inherent in the manual process, and in part as a first step toward a comprehensive, centralized, automated information retrieval system." According to Pemberton (1994, 13), a former Information Bank employee: "The original NYT Information Bank was conceived first as an in-house replacement for the paper's clipping morgue that would save $4 million a year. When former Executive Editor Abe Rosenthal flatly refused to give up the morgue, the enterprise tried to stay afloat with commercial sales, but was far ahead of its time and wound up losing millions." Longgood (1973, 21) quoted Rothman: "I realized that the cost of automating the morgue for the staff's use alone would be prohibitive. So I proposed that if the cost could be spread by making the library available to outside subscribers, it could be made financially feasible."

The first development phase was computer-assisted production of the printed *Index*, which began in 1966 and represented the beginning of the database ("NY Times Info Bank" 1972; "New York Times Index" 1968). Central Media Bureau, Inc., of New York was engaged in 1966 to design the index-building system, write the programs, and conduct the computer operations until the Times obtained a sufficiently large computer facility. Central Media Bureau's system started successful operation in January 1968. Central Media also produced a thesaurus of 20,000 entries in loose-leaf and machine-readable format (Rothman 1968). However, although the computerized file building started in January 1968, only data for October 1969 to date (about 500,000 records, but only a relatively short time span of coverage) was used with the initial online system; additional backfiles were not added until after 1973.

Rothman (1968, 87) had a vision and a grand plan for the system:

The ultimate system envisaged will comprise detailed abstracts of all textual material stored in a computer, full text of all such material in microform and all graphic materials stored in automated retrieval devices interfaced with the computer, and a world-wide communications network enabling staff members and outside clients to retrieve information from the system on a real-time basis. A direct hook-up to other public affairs information centers for background and reference materials is a further possibility.

But like most people at the time, Rothman did not exhibit a strong conviction that there was a potential here for an entirely new information service industry.

Within a year following the project to convert the *Index* to a computer-based system, the Times decided to finance a major project that ultimately absorbed and superseded the entire clipping library and its records from 1851. By selling access to outside subscribers, the company expected that costs could be partially offset and the *Times* eminence as an information source enhanced. This was unprecedented for the Times; this was the first time in its history that it permitted outsiders to have the same access to its research files that staffers had. The company also recognized that the cost of the proposed computer installation was much greater than the cost or revenue associated with another volume of the *Times Index*. Therefore, to maximize the computer's use to the Times staff and outsiders, it decided that the computer would also index other publications. Its original guess was that perhaps thirty additional journals would suffice; eventually it was over sixty, including ten other newspapers (Weil 1975). Rothman (1973, 18) offered the official rationale: "The *Times* undertook this project for two reasons: to absorb already existing information services and offer improved facilities to its staff, and to offer a new service to the outside world and thus create a new source of revenue."

Before the days of online searching, the company prevented others from indexing the *Times* and threatened anyone who attempted that with lawsuits. Nonetheless, in 1972 they were quick themselves to start indexing other publications—although they did obtain prior permission from all the publishers. According to Pemberton (1982, 1997), the Times senior legal staff sensed a potential problem in the abstracting of sixty-five journals that were to be included in the file. So they asked each publisher for permission to do so—and all but two publishers agreed. *Esquire* did not and was excluded from coverage; the *Wall Street Journal* initially declined but later agreed after obtaining the rights to use some *Times* material for their services. Rothman (1973, 16) noted that Times staff microfilmed all of the other publications without the permission of those publishers, but said that this material "will not be made available to anyone outside the *Times* staff until arrangements with the copyright owners have been made. Such arrangements will be sought eventually, when there is sufficient demand, but have not been initiated as yet."

The senior management and legal staff had another opportunity to revisit the indexing rights question in 1977 when a new commercial database supplier, with financial assistance from the DIALOG service, announced plans to produce National Newspaper Index, which would include up-to-date indexed coverage of the *Times*, including the article headlines; this would be an extremely competitive product (Pemberton 1982). That interesting story is beyond the calendar scope of this text.

In a March 26, 1969, news release, the Times announced the development of the Information Bank, a real-time, interactive retrieval system, "which will make available vast resources of material to major research and reference libraries, government agencies, journalists, scholars, and other media, including radio and television networks, with speed, thoroughness and comprehensiveness." It was clear that this was going to be more than an in-house system. At the news conference it was announced that the system was being developed under the direction of Rothman, then director of information services at the Times, IBM would assist in design and implementation, and Arthur D. Little would assist with market development; their responsibility was to determine the size and scope of the potential market, evaluate the kind of response the system and its service might expect from potential customers, and forecast what changes were likely to occur in the kind of service the system would be capable of producing.

At a hearing before a congressional committee on April 30, 1969, Rothman revealed the company's intention to make its online service available to the public in early 1971 as a subscription service (as it turned out, they were almost two years late). The projected fees were on the order of $100 to $2,000 a month, depending on the kinds of service a user wanted. The Times was serious about marketing; it started right away by hiring Jeff Pemberton in September 1970 as marketing manager. A journalist by training, he had worked at the *Wall Street Journal* and in Washington for Aspen Systems where he participated in the marketing, public relations, and database preparation for ASPENSEARCH, described later. Pemberton (1997) noted: "I joined the IB in September of '70 as marketing manager. John Rothman was already the director of the project. Ivan Veit, Executive Vice President of the Times, was the godfather of the project, the guy who John convinced of its merit, and who persuaded Punch Sulzberber to approve. Bob November (a Harvard M.B.A.) was brought in early to represent the business side of the project since John had no business background." According to Peggy Fischer who worked at Time-Life during the 1960s, Chet Lewis, chief librarian, was Rothman's boss at the Times and should also receive credit for supporting and developing the Information Bank. Fischer (1995) recalled that during the 1960s, there were three large and notable library reference services: New York Times, Time-Life, Inc., and LC's Congressional Reference Service. Lewis was involved in the activities and staff of these services at that time and later brought his experience to the Information Bank.

The IBM Federal Systems Division in Gaithersburg, Maryland performed formal systems analysis and programming of the software for online retrieval between 1969 and 1971 ("Information Bank picture" 1980). F. Terry Baker headed the IBM team that did the major programming (132 man-months) for the online system. Formal testing was to start in April 1971. The program was late, but operational by fall 1972. Times reporters were the first users.

From the IBM project team's perspective, the system was designed to support 64 local terminals (IBM 4279/4506 digital TV display subsystems) and up to 120 remote lines with display or typewriter terminals, and operate on an IBM 360. Indexing data were to be stored on IBM 2314 disk storage, abstracts of all articles stored on an IBM 2321 Data Cell, and photographs of the full text of articles placed on microfiche and accessible through four TV cameras contained in the RISAR microfiche retrieval device. Searching was to be done with Boolean logic statements. Searchers were to view character-display abstracts of the source articles on the terminals, and when a camera was available, view the image display (Baker 1972). The system was to have a built-in thesaurus, and an expectation of being current to within forty-eight hours of publication, for both abstracts and microfiche (Pemberton 1971). In early 1973, the data retrieved were scheduled to be current within seventy-two hours of publication (Univ of Pitt 1973). Later that year, the update currency was described as no more than ninety-six hours (four working days) after publication, working with a volume of about 9,000 records per month ("The New York Times Information" 1973). Compared to most online systems of that time, this one was exceptionally current. Bachelder (1976, 18) affirmed the daily update process and added, "Most material is current to within six weeks of publication, while *New York Times* material is available four working days after publication."

The delay of the start-up date for the online service until late 1972 was due, as with many other new system start-ups, to several factors. One was the plan to include microfiche images of the full text of the source material in a new computer-controlled microfiche storage and retrieval system intended to deliver copies of source material on demand. While this was advanced technology at the time, IBM management already was familiar with advanced microform technology from their WALNUT system development and operation in the early 1960s. The Times management was familiar with microform technology, having bought American Microfilm in the mid-1960s in order to make their own *NYT* film product. Designed to Times specifications, this system was called Foto-Mem RISAR (Record Information Storage and Retrieval). It had a storage capacity of 2.5 million pages on 25,000 microfiche. RISAR was designed to retrieve individual fiche on command, position them before a video camera, and send an analog TV signal of an individual frame to a video terminal (the same terminals used for digital signals from the online search system). The Foto-Mem unit did become operational, but its reliability ranged from 50 to 70 percent; this was judged to be inadequate for regular use by the News Department.

To replace the automated fiche image retrieval system, Times management eventually removed the fiche from the machine and put them in manual card files; a person wearing white gloves pulled fiche on demand to load them under one of four TV scanning cameras for the images to be sent to remote viewing terminals in the Times building. The special terminals displayed both digital signals for Information Bank searching and analog signals for video display of the fiche. The terminals cost $10,000 each; IBM had designed them for Japanese newspapers and the display of Japanese–language characters (Pemberton 1995, 1997). At an April 1973 Stanford conference on interactive retrieval systems, the Information Bank could not be demonstrated because "it required a terminal that was not available on the West Coast" (Martin 1974, 12). Meanwhile, the company that was developing the image storage device (Remote Console Information Corp.) went bankrupt, and the Times had to pursue other alternatives (Pemberton 1981).

In November 1972, after the investment of $3 million in development, the online retrieval system was operational at Times headquarters, accessible from more than sixty IBM 4506 CRT terminals in the building—one on every reporter's desk. The building was wired with coaxial cable. An IBM 370/140 with eight IBM 3330 disk drives was the core of the online system. In 1973, the computer facility consisted of an IBM 370/145 with five IBM 3330 disk storage units; at users' workstations were CRT terminals usually accompanied by hard-copy printers (Rothman 1973; "The New York Times Information" 1973). This expensive network of high-priced hard-wired terminals in the newsroom was later torn out by a managing editor who preferred the traditional paper-based morgue.

Also in November 1972, the program was used outside Times headquarters; it was installed in the Hillman Library at the University of Pittsburgh. The service was underwritten by the Times and NSF for two years, and students, faculty, and researchers, as well as Pittsburgh's business and industrial community, civic leaders, and representatives of the various news media were allowed access to it ("Univ of Pitt" 1973; Weil 1975). For the next fourteen months this was the only Information Bank installation in an academic institution, and it led to a dissertation about the system (Moghdam 1974). Allen Kent was in charge of the program, which was developed as part of a campus-based information system, funded by a five-year NSF grant, for the purpose of developing a synthesis of traditional and technological innovations in information transfer to serve both academic and nonacademic constituencies on campus and in the community. This was not the first instance of regular academic use of online searching—as we saw in chapter 3, in 1970 the Syracuse University community made extensive online use of Psychological Abstracts from their campus system.

The Information Bank began providing service to its first paying customer in February 1973 and commenced full commercial operation in May 1973 at just about the time that SDC Search Service and DIALOG were beginning serious marketing. The file contained nearly 400,000 records covering the period between late 1969 and March 1973 (New York Times 1973). By 1975, the database had grown to about 1 million records (Bachelder 1976). Records in the Information Bank encompassed all news and editorial matter from the *Times*, plus selected material from over sixty other newspapers and periodicals, and consisted of complete bibliographic data, detailed abstracts, appropriate descriptors, and other search elements. This totaled 14,000 articles per week (Longgood 1973).

The first commercial customer was the CIA, and most of the first customers were spy agencies or military intelligence in Washington, DC. LC was next and then NSA. The Army Library in the Pentagon, DIA, and the State Department were in the first ten. Soon it had fourteen outside customers, including NBC, Associated Press, IBM, and the UN (Provenzano 1987; Longgood 1973). The Times believed that its best marketing strategy would be to start in Washington, so it set up its first marketing office there. By summer 1973, full-scale marketing was under way—directed at business, government, academic, public libraries, and other information centers in industrial corporation and news-gathering agencies. Chapter 10 describes an insider's view of their marketing ordeals. By the end of 1973, the service had twenty subscribers (Greengrass 1974).

The system had no TYMNET or TELENET access when it first became publicly available. Subscribers could lease direct lines in order to obtain a dedicated 240 cps service. In 1975, the Information Bank was accessible only at 120 cps, and in 1976 it was accessible to users with 30 cps communications and terminal capability (Rogers 1978).[6]

In 1974, access hours were 8:00 a.m. to 12:00 a.m. on weekdays, and 9:00 a.m. to 5:00 p.m. on Saturday. By 1975, the service had about seventy subscribers in the United States, Canada, and Mexico, including a few public and university libraries. Most of the subscribers, however, were still corporations or U.S. government agencies, who typically located the online service in the information center or library (Bachelder 1976). The system had the capacity to handle between 250 and 300 subscribers (Weil 1975).

The search language was extremely simple to learn. All of the instructions for browsing the thesaurus, keying in terms, using Boolean operators and limiting by dates, sources, descriptor, and abstract weights were presented in stepwise fashion on the screen. In fact, a search could *only* be constructed in this lockstep way; the searcher could not control the sequence of commands or skip steps. It had a limited search capability; searches could be made on four basic term types: personal name, organization name, geographic location, and subject (by controlled subject headings). Free-text searching of the title, abstract, or other parts of the bibliographic record was not possible. After the strategy for a particular inquiry was fully framed, the system searched the files, and abstracts of the documents that met the specifications were displayed. The online system was limited by its IBM designers to a maximum output of 112 abstracts in any one search. If a user wanted all the abstracts up to that number, they would be displayed consecutively, at a rate chosen by the searcher. If more than 112 abstracts were retrieved, the searcher had to add additional descriptors to reduce the number of records to no more than 112 (Weil 1975).[7] Along with the online system to retrieve and view abstracts, users could access a microfiche collection and use a reader-printer to view the microfiche and obtain a hard copy if desired.

Rothman, who had been director of the Times Library and Information Services, became the director of the online service. In 1969, he had appeared before a hearing of the U.S. Congress House Committee on Education and Labor and had given testimony about the background, justification, and future development plans for the online system.

In spite of the literature and presentations targeted to librarians and other information professionals, the Information Bank was, as many systems of that period, designed for end users—students, business executives, government officials, news media staff, and others. Sally Bachelder (1976, 21), a marketing representative, explained how easy it was to use: "The Information Bank is designed with the end-user in mind. All instructions for operating the system appear on the CRT screen; it is not necessary to digest a thick instruction manual. In addition, the structure of an Information Bank inquiry never varies, so the infrequent user can easily navigate the search process. By using conversational English and avoiding all function keys, the Information System is a simple system to master." Rothman (1973, 16) himself commented on the user interface messages: "These messages and the diverse options and instructions that they present were designed with the newspaper reporter and editor in mind. . . . The system is largely self-teaching and self-service; the interposition of librarians or information specialists is not required." In reality, however, the system was used, like others of that time, almost exclusively by librarians and designated researchers. Bachelder assumed that two reasons accounted for this phenomenon. First, experience and sustained usage were necessary to become familiar with the controlled indexing vocabulary, which was essential to successful subject searches since no natural language search capability was available. Second, infrequent users were much slower than were frequent users, and business executives and government officials did not want to take time to conduct searches.

The simplicity of the access structure that was designed for infrequent users frustrated the experienced searchers. Pemberton (1983, 10) described how negatively information professionals reacted to searching it: "The head of the Systems Department of a large West Coast library told me that, 'I don't even want to be in the same room when somebody's running an Information Bank search.'" Pemberton continued:

Curiously, and ironically, this retrieval system, which evoked such a negative response from an adult information professional, could be learned by a child with no instruction whatsoever. I once watched a *Times* reporter bring his 10 year old son into the newsroom and use an Information Bank terminal as a baby sitter. The father did not know how to use the IB and there was no instruction book around. But in a few minutes the lad had learned the system and was having a grand time. But, as Paul Berthiaume confided to me... "the trouble with this software is that once people get proficient with it they get to hate it."

According to Pemberton, part of the frustration in using the system could be attributed to the indexing that did not allow searching on newly coined jargon, slang, acronyms, or technical terms that had not been incorporated into the thesaurus. The reporters especially were frustrated when they could see these words in abstracts but could not use them as search terms. Although the system provided in-depth indexing with a controlled indexing system and a published Information Bank thesaurus, it did not allow free text searching of words in titles or abstracts.

Another experienced searcher, Marydee Ojala, was an early user of the Information Bank service. Ojala (1987) noted:

It rapidly became apparent that the software was inadequate. Designed for people unfamiliar with computer based reference services, [it] was tutorial in nature, guiding the searcher through each step. During the 1970s, information retrieval systems flourished and database searchers became increasingly sophisticated. Complaints about the rudimentary software mounted as searchers began comparing it to other systems. The menu-driven approach, though useful for beginners, slowed down the searching process and aggravated searchers.

Independent of the views of the outside customers, the internal users (Times reporters) and their management were very critical of the system. Fischer (1995) recalled talking to Rothman at that time and hearing him tell of the great resistance he got from the journalists to using the terminals. In 1978, Pemberton wrote, "The *Times* news department (as opposed to the non-newspaper subsidiaries which include the Infobank) has always considered the Information Bank a massive failure because of poor indexing and lack of natural language searching" ("Potentially huge database" 1978, 68). This dissatisfaction was in spite of the fact that in-house users' terminals were hard-wired to the computer center with $350,000 worth of cable to provide extremely high transmission rates; apparently being fast was not enough. In the same article, Pemberton divulged that the online system had failed to replace the paper clipping file: "Instead of allowing the Infobank to replace the old clipping morgue (as originally planned), Managing Editor A. M. Rosenthal took the morgue under news department control, boosted its budget and tore out the expensive network of more than 60 hard-wired Infobank terminals in the newsroom" (68).

From its home in the New York Times headquarters building in mid-Manhattan, the entire online operation was moved in 1975 to an office park in Parsippany, New Jersey. The relocation was needed for additional, lower-cost space, and, according to Pemberton (1983, 11), to eliminate the threat of a strike from the indexing staff:

The [indexers] take considerable pride in their ability to reduce a complex, far ranging page one story into a cogent, tersely written abstract. They also believe that this cannot be done on a production line basis and that they must be protected against management efforts to rush the job. Their protection is the Newspaper Guild, a feisty union that has not been reluctant to strike the Times... There were frequent brush fires and skirmishes between management and the unionized indexers. Parsippany was to end that ... Eventually all indexing—for both print and electronic products—would be done in non-union Parsippany.

Along with the move, the Information Bank was separately incorporated in 1975 as the New York Times Information Service. Rothman left to become director of research and information technology for the Times, where he stayed until 1981 when he was appointed head of the New York Times Corporate Archives.

By the end of 1976, the Information Bank had added 62 other periodical publications (including 10 other newspapers) to its database, extended the *New York Times* file coverage back to January 1, 1969, compiled a database of 1.3 million abstracts, and published the fourth edition of the thesaurus that included close to 700,000 terms. The Information Bank had no significant competition in the online newspaper database business up until 1976. Competition came that year when Giering at MTL started to develop and install a newspaper text editing and retrieval system for the *Boston Globe*. Another competitor, the National Newspaper Index database, was started by Information Access Corporation in 1977.

The Information Bank apparently lost the battle of the bottom line, experiencing losses in every year except one after it became a commercial venture, and consuming a reported $20 million investment. In 1983 the New York Times company granted an exclusive license to MDC to distribute the Information Bank data, and the service discontinued its online operations ("New York Times Co." 1983). The Times then appeared to forget that this pioneering service, one of their most ambitious, most expensive, and most visionary outreach projects, ever existed. A recent book published by the Times about its history over its entire life span included not a single word about the Information Bank or its fourteen years of very visible public activity (Shepard 1996).

CAN/OLE

In spring 1973, after several months of preliminary planning, the staff of the Canada Institute for Scientific and Technical Information (CISTI) and the Computation Centre of the National Research Council joined forces to create an online IR system (Heilik 1976b). A participant, James Heilik (1976a, 47) characterized this activity as "little more than an exercise for the CISTI programmers to learn something about on-line operations." CISTI actually began operating the online service, called CAN/OLE (Canadian On-Line Enquiry) in spring 1974 (Peel 1977). R. A. Green of the NRC Computation Centre in Ottawa designed CAN/OLE, and he and three programmers from CISTI did the programming. Peter Wolters was also associated with both CAN/OLE and CAN/SDI.

Since 1969, CISTI had been operating a highly successful SDI service (CAN/SDI) with thousands of subscribers. The CAN/OLE project was initiated in response to the growing demand of the subscribers for a retrospective searching capability. Leblanc (1978, 170) reported, "One aim of CAN/OLE was to provide a needed extension to CAN/SDI, that of allowing rapid on-line access to retrospective files. Very few changes in CAN/SDI were made to implement CAN/OLE." With government subsidies, CAN/OLE permitted Canadians to gain online access to commercial American and British databases and several government-supported Canadian databases. The system charged all Canadians equally, regardless of their location, and had a search capability in both official languages, English and French (Alley, Lawford, and Wolters, 1978).

The online service began with 2.1 million references in five databases: Biological Abstracts, CA Condensates, COMPENDEX, INSPEC, and the Union List of Scientific Serials in Canadian Libraries (UNION). Storage capacity initially was so limited that the files had to operate in time windows—the COMPENDEX/INSPEC combination was available Monday, Wednesday, and Friday from 9:30 a.m. to 1:30 p.m., and from 2:00 p.m. to 7:00 p.m. on Tuesday and Thursday afternoons. The Biological Abstracts/Chemical Abstracts pair flip-flopped schedule times with the first pair. The system had to be shut down every day at midday for a half-hour period to switch the databases.

From the beginning, the UNION database was available online to show the locations of over 37,000 serials held in 236 libraries across Canada. This was helpful for online document ordering and delivery requests and was a feature that none of the other public online services had at this time (except for bibliographic utilities such as OCLC or RLIN). The major U.S. online services had tried to get the equivalent U.S. serial holdings file but could not get it; LC refused to make the CONSER tape (with library holdings data) available to the public online services.

> **1973 Milestone**
>
> CAN/OLE may have been the first online search system to offer a bilingual interface option.

A bilingual search interface was a feature of CAN/OLE that was also introduced in the RETRO system in 1973. A searcher could choose the preferred language of the interface (French or English), and when chosen, the system messages as well as the commands were in the language chosen. From the documentation available to us, it is does not appear that this bilingual capability extended to allowing search terms to be used in either language. The ILO/ISIS system appears to have been the first one to provide that capability.

By autumn 1975 at least fifteen Canadian university libraries were subscribers. By the end of 1976, CAN/OLE had grown to provide access to over three million records for more than sixty government, industry, and academic institutions across Canada (Heilik 1976b).

WESTLAW

It was not until 1973 that the management of West Publishing Company of St. Paul, Minnesota, after watching several years of OBAR and the early market testing of LEXIS, decided to enter the market with an online system of its own (Sprowl 1976b; Harrington 1984–1985). As a commercial publisher, West had been in the legal information business since the nineteenth century, publishing indexes to state and federal court cases in heavy bound volumes. West Publishing was curious, but conservatively cautious about this new technology. In 1975, two years after the public birth of LEXIS and its online full-text searching, West announced the availability of their new online case law retrieval system called the West Computer Law Retrieval System (in 1976 the name was changed to WESTLAW[8]), and the first subscriber went online in April 1975 (Larson 1977). This commercial service used a modified version of QUIC/LAW (Sprowl 1976b). In the beginning, the service had a database that contained headnotes taken from West's National Reporter System, with more than eight years of state court decisions and more than fifteen years of U.S. federal court decisions (Ginnow 1975).

The initial system searched the "headnotes" (the basic retrieval tools that West had used for years) but did not search the full-text of the court decisions. Arnold Ginnow, editor-in-chief at West, reported in 1975 that a study had been done to determine whether a system using West headnotes would retrieve relevant cases without the necessity of a search of the full text of each opinion. West's management was concerned because a full-text file would be much larger than a corresponding headnote database, and the extra cost of storing and searching the full text would be significant. Ginnow concluded that the headnotes produced retrieval at least as good, if not superior, to retrieval from a full-text search.

In April 1976, West started test-marketing WESTLAW at a price much lower than the price for LEXIS. The WESTLAW database was prepared in-house by West staff, and the service provided from the company's IBM 370/145 in their St. Paul headquarters. Subscribers received IBM 3275 CRT terminals that were equipped with an IBM 3284 printer (West Publishing 1976).

By the end of 1976, WESTLAW was emerging, along with LEXIS, as a major legal online search service. They were both positioned and designed to be marketed to the legal community and, as such, competed with each other more than they competed against the other online services. Most WESTLAW development took place, however, after the period covered by this text.

RETROSPEC

Cybernet Timesharing Ltd. in London developed an online service for its Sigma 7 computer using the newly developed FREESEARCH search system. The Institution of Electrical Engineers cooperated in allowing a subset of about 18,000 records (*Computers & Control Abstracts* section) from its INSPEC database to be run on the Cybernet system as an experimental online service for U.K. users from April 1973 to March 1975. The service was called RETROSPEC-1. The system was accessible through regular telephone dial-up service and provided Boolean and weighted term-search capabilities (Holmes 1977b, c).

The RETROSPEC-1 database, marketed jointly in England by INSPEC and Cybernet Timesharing in 1974, was accessed online with terminals at research centers in Teesside and Motherwell. Mann (1974, 1) analyzed the prospects for the database: "The free language indexing of the records can be criticized as being inefficient and would make regular usage of the database unlikely. It was felt, however, that the interrogation programs were useful and that the experience derived from them could benefit the proposed in-house system for library and information services."

Dow Jones News/Retrieval

Dow Jones Information Services began the Dow Jones News/Retrieval service in 1974 to serve brokers and professional investors. William Clabby was the managing editor of this service at its beginning. The service started as a menu-based system, but later permitted command-based searching, primarily for full-text files. The full-text material consisted primarily of lengthy abstracts from the *Wall Street Journal*, *Barron's*, and the Dow Jones news wires—however, the file was limited to the most recent ninety days of acquired material. Simplified searching was a major design objective. Jeff Pemberton wrote the first instruction manual for this service in 1976. In 1996, he commented drily, "Forrest Gump would have had no problem with it" (Pemberton 1996, 5).

Dow Jones later expanded its market scope by offering additional unique databases of interest to the business sector. At its beginning, Dow Jones was sold only on a contract basis to high-volume users (brokers only) and all customers were hard-wired to the Dow Jones computers; this was changed in 1977 to allow TYMNET dial-up access by low-volume users.

1975 Milestone

Dow Jones News/Retrieval may have been the first online bibliographic or full-text retrieval system to provide file updates on a real-time basis.

By 1976, Dow Jones was boasting of only a two-minute lag between the time a story moved over the Dow Jones news wire and when it was loaded on the system and available for searching. We are not aware of any earlier example of real-time updating of full-text or bibliographic information for online searching.

Info Globe

The *Globe and Mail*, based in Toronto, Ontario, is considered one of Canada's leading newspapers, in fact, the "newspaper of record" for Canada, corresponding to the role in the United States of the *New York Times* or the *Washington Post*. The online information division, called Info Globe, started in

1975. At that time the Globe and Mail made an agreement with QL Systems to use QL's online retrieval software for the paper's clipping file. The system was developed in cooperation with QL's in-house library to replace or augment its large clipping service; hence the company decided to start with full-text newspaper coverage (news and other editorial content) beginning with January 1, 1976 material (Rushbrook and Lawford 1976).

Info Globe was a full-text search system, working with the *Globe and Mail* file and several other full-text databases, but with no online thesaurus. The full-text capability, however, was constrained in that every word with more than 60,000 postings was put on a stop list and hence could not be searched. For the period covered by this text, the chief users were the Globe editorial staff who used the system heavily on 960 cps terminals. Some European users also accessed the system during this period. Info Globe did not become publicly available until 1979, at which time the file covered the period from November 14, 1977, to date.

JOIS

The Japan Information Center of Science and Technology (JICST) was established as an information service organization of the Japanese government in 1957. JICST was a producer of a bibliographic database in science and technology, but also started providing an online bibliographic search service in April 1976, using its JOIS-I (JICST Online System-I) software and files such as CA Search, MEDLARS, and its own JICST database. The online service was provided in both an English-language (JOIS-1) and Kanji (Chinese character) mode (JOIS-K). By 1980, the total number of citations online was more than 6 million. JOIS used a Hitachi HITAC M-170 computer and an extensive data communication network throughout Japan (Suwa 1980).

New In-House Search Services of the Seventies

ILO ISIS

The ILO ISIS system (chapter 4) of the International Labour Office started its online operation in 1969. The ISIS software was intended for internal ILO use, but ILO later distributed it to other institutions throughout the world. For example, in 1972, ILO made ISIS available to the Swedish government for use with its national computerized library network (Schieber 1971, 1972; Tocatlian 1975). In return, the Swedish library information system (LIBRIS) was made available to ILO and the UN family of agencies.

1976 Milestone

ILO/ISIS may have been the first online search system to allow search terms entered in one language to retrieve records indexed by corresponding terms in another language.

In 1973 the International Development Research Centre (IDRC) in Canada acquired and installed ISIS to run on local IBM 360 equipment. Under the terms of their agreement with ILO, IDRC was required to develop ISIS further in some way. IDRC chose to add a multilingual search capability. Because of the international context in which the IDRC information system was developed, and planned to be used, IDRC already had a multilingual thesaurus (English, French, Spanish, German, and Arabic, with Portuguese and Indonesian planned). IDRC's objective was that, by keying in an English term, a searcher could also retrieve documents indexed by the equivalent terms in French or the other languages (and vice versa). By May 1976, only the French and English search capabilities were implemented because all the databases available to the searchers were indexed only in French or English (Schafer and Brandreth 1976).

RADCOL

As we saw in chapter 4 and earlier in this chapter, Informatics staff developed RADCOL (RADC Automatic Document Classification On-Line) for RADC at Griffiss AFB in Rome, New York. The project had started in the late 1960s and continued through the mid-1970s. RADCOL was unusual in that it automatically classified documents based on an analysis of the text (Lowe and Roberts 1969). Informatics staff members associated with this project included Peter Kurtz, Thomas Lowe, and David Roberts.

NASA-LISR

An online search system was developed at NASA's Lewis Research Center in Ohio and put in service during 1970. At first it was called the Lewis-NASA Line Information Storage and Retrieval (LISR) system, but it also used the name NASA-LISR. It was intended for use as a database management system, and to be as compatible as possible, from the user's point of view, to RECON, but its major use was with descriptions of photographs of the United States taken by the ERTS satellite. A revised version of LISR was in operation for a few months in 1972 until NASA discontinued its support. NASA-LISR was among the online systems reviewed in the 1973 conference on feature analysis of interactive systems (Martin 1974). Charles Goldstein was a NASA Lewis staff member associated with NASA-LISR.

Northern Colorado Educational Board of Cooperative System

This unnamed system had its roots in federal legislation and the early ERIC system. Around 1967, as a result of the National Defense Education Act and the Elementary and Secondary Education Act, individual project staffs dutifully completed and submitted detailed proposals, plans, and reports as required by these grant programs. The growing piles of these reports triggered the start of ERIC and other means to get control of this material. In 1967 the Boulder Valley Public School District in Boulder, Colorado, submitted a proposal to keypunch ERIC abstracts and local materials and load them onto the CDC computer at the NBS facility in Boulder. Staff would search the abstracts at the request of school teachers and administrators. The proposal was funded, and it evolved into one of three nationally recognized prototypes for computerized educational resource centers in the late 1960s and early 1970s. Funding grew, and this center, the Northern Colorado Educational Board of Cooperative Services, became a high-volume search service for school districts in that region.

Roy Tally (1995) supplied most of the description of this system. Tally applied for a job with the project in spring 1968. With a degree in foreign languages, he was hired as an abstractor-indexer, even though he admitted later that he had no formal training or experience for that position. From 1968 to 1972, the ERIC files were searched with a succession of batch mode systems. The project installed its own minicomputer in 1969, and before 1971 a disk-based file and an interactive front end. Tally moved to Madison, Wisconsin, in June 1972 to work with the ERIC file at the Wisconsin Department of Public Instruction. He continued to search the Boulder system from his UNIVAC Uniscope 100 terminal in Madison, using a dial-up phone connection at 480 cps speeds. Because he was the only user, "Response time was great!" At this time, the system allowed a searcher to query the ERIC thesaurus, select authors, descriptors and identifiers, create sets, and view document titles online.

In 1972 Tally went on to work cooperatively with University of Wisconsin staff to help develop the WISE-ONE system. We have no other knowledge about the Boulder system, other than that it was online and in full operation for a year before WISE-ONE appeared on the scene.

WIRE/WISE-ONE

In 1970 Becker and Hayes proposed the WIRE (Wisconsin Information Retrieval for Education) project. WIRE became the name for an online search service that was started with federal funding as a demonstration project by the Wisconsin Department of Public Instruction to provide Wisconsin educators with individualized access to current educational research and resource information. It followed a batch-mode system for the ERIC database called WISE (Wisconsin Information System for Education) that had been written for the University of Wisconsin's CDC 3600 computer by Thomas Olson, a computer science student (Spuck et al. 1974).

WISE-ONE was the name given to the online search software that ran on the UNIVAC 1110 at the UW-Madison computer center. WIRE, the online service, started operation in November 1972, with access to the ERIC file of over 100,000 bibliographic records and abstracts. The project operated on a cost-recovery basis, with a charge of $10–$25 per search. Search requests were submitted to a central facility for searching. With funding from the UW School of Education and Wisconsin state agencies, Olson, Donald McIsaac, and Dennis Spuck of the School of Education and Tally of the Wisconsin Department of Public Instruction developed the WISE-ONE software (McIsaac and Olson 1973; "Information retrieval" 1974). The WISE-ONE program was also a class project in computer science at the university (Olson et al. 1975). The objective of the four partners was to create a statewide system for education using the resources of the university, WISE-ONE, and the Wisconsin Department of Public Instruction and make it available to educators at all levels. They also wanted to save the cost of their expensive connection to the Boulder computer center. WIRE was available directly to school district administrators, teachers, and specialists.

With federal support, the campus Center for Studies in Vocational and Technical Education ran a WISE-ONE demonstration project on the UNIVAC 1108 at UW-Madison from December 1973 through June 1974. Nine terminals were located in volunteer districts in the state, and access provided to ERIC via dial-up phone lines at rates of 10 to 30 cps. The four separate files could not be searched simultaneously.

The search system used Boolean operators, but provided access only by author's last name or assigned subject headings. For ERIC reports, the online output was limited to ERIC accession number, author, and title. For journal articles, output was limited to these data plus journal name, volume number, and pagination. Abstracts could be printed offline for next-day mailing by a command that formulated the search statement for a batch run on the ERIC tapes.

A SAVE command was available to preserve search strategies or portions of search strategies temporarily. The volume of searching during the demonstration project grew to a peak of 222 searches per month at the end. In late 1974, in order to make better use of project resources, terminals that had been in eight districts were consolidated in the four districts where the user population had expressed the most interest, or where the district operating personnel seemed most anxious to disseminate ERIC information (Lambert and Grady 1975).

Through 1974–1975, the group gradually converted the WIRE service over to use the WISE-ONE system. Because the computer center supported interactive dial-up computing, searching was interactive from the start. In 1974, online access to ERIC was available to any interested party, at a rate of $1–$3 per connect hour. Over a thousand searches were performed during the years 1972–1976. WISE was still in operation online at the end of 1976 (WISE search 1977).

JURIS

In early 1970, lawyers and librarians at the Justice Department in Washington, DC, began planning an information system that would improve the quality and uniformity of the department's legal briefs and opinions and speed up judicial proceedings (Morrissey 1970). Their goal was to give lawyers in every legal office throughout the country rapid access to a central source of all significant prior research material generated within DOJ. This included legal handbooks, form books, appellate briefs and legal memoranda, along with legal policy and procedures documents, summaries of significant reported decisions, case file intelligence, and evidentiary material for protracted cases (Kondos 1971). At that time, over 2,500 DOJ attorneys were handling over 60,000 civil and criminal cases annually, involving varying degrees of legal research.

These goals spawned JURIS (Justice Retrieval and Inquiry System), conceived as an online, interactive system with access from remote terminals. A pilot was started in late 1970 or early 1971, in which a single terminal in the main DOJ building in Washington was connected to NASA/RECON about ten miles away in College Park, Maryland. The database used in the pilot contained the full text of 600 appellate briefs and 130 selected legal memoranda in the area of search and seizure, the DOJ *Manual on the Law of Search and Seizure*; the 26,000 sections of the *U.S. Code* (extracted from the Air Force LITE file) and proposed revisions of the criminal code, and extracts from 500 general evidentiary documents for a protracted case (Losee 1971; Kondos 1971). The goal was a preliminary testing of the concept. Soon after, the NASA/RECON program (a DIALOG copy), obtained through COSMIC, was installed in the Justice Department where it was modified and transformed into what came to be known as JURIS. George Kondos, a DOJ staff member, assumed the major responsibility for JURIS from then until well into the 1980s. Kondos was introduced in chapter 5 when he wrote an article on the potential of DIALOG for legal information.

In 1971, there was consideration of transferring LITE to the DOJ. DOJ staff had already converted the U.S. Code file to JURIS from LITE (Stevens 1973). In 1972, JURIS consisted of a mix of programs from several sources: (1) NASA/RECON software developed by Lockheed (the main bulk of JURIS); (2) NASA/STIMS file maintenance programs; (3) USAF LITE (chapter 7) text parsing programs for processing full-text information; and (4) program modifications made by the JURIS project staff (e.g., special utility routines for tape format conversions such as LITE to RECON). Plans announced in 1972 called for installation of four remote terminals in the main DOJ building and one station outside at a U.S. Attorney office in one of the ninety-three judicial districts, with the remaining ninety-two districts to receive their terminals within a year (Basheer 1973). JURIS was designed to operate on an IBM 360/40. Response time on the pilot system was in the range of 1–10 seconds.

Starting in 1972, DOJ used JURIS also for in-house private file work for litigation support, including several major racketeering and organized crime cases. During 1972 and 1973, however, JURIS remained in the experimental stage. By mid-1974, even though seven terminals were operating (in 5 U.S. Attorney offices, 1 at LC, and 1 at the Department of Agriculture), the database was still too limited to be of much research value. Therefore JURIS was used mainly for training, occasional search requests, and demonstrations to attorneys, key department officials, legal and technical representatives from other government agencies and various states and foreign countries. Even so, a small test of the system suggested a five-to-one savings in attorney time over traditional research methods. Attorneys who did not have access to a JURIS terminal were encouraged to request searches by phone or mail (Kondos 1974).

To supplement the small JURIS file, DOJ contracted in 1974 with Mead for access to LEXIS. LEXIS provided the federal case law material, so that part of the original JURIS goal was accomplished. From then on, DOJ concentrated its JURIS use on special in-house files and applications, particularly to support investigations and litigation. Over the next several years, JURIS was used extensively in-house to support the building and searching of hundreds of private files associated with DOJ investigations and court activity; for example, it was used in the antitrust litigation against West Publishing (Rubin 1998).

In early 1974, based on functional specifications written at Justice in 1972 for the design of a system that built on the experience gained to date, DOJ staff completely redesigned and rewrote the NASA/RECON software being used for JURIS to add a full-text search capability, and to make it compatible with LEXIS so that attorneys could access LEXIS case law or JURIS memos and briefs from the same CRT terminals. Mead Data Central supplied the terminals to Justice. The new system, operational in mid-1974, also permitted expansion to over one hundred terminals without degrading response time (Kondos 1974).

With more terminals, the department expanded its training program in 1974–1975 by bringing hundreds of U.S. attorneys and assistants from their field offices to Washington and New York for intensive two-day training sessions. In July 1975, a "circuit riding" program sent trainers to the field offices for on-site instruction. By August, almost a third of the 3,000 DOJ attorneys had been trained in LEXIS and JURIS. Many made helpful suggestions for materials to add to the JURIS databases.

Using Boolean logic, a JURIS user could search combinations of key words, either in the document as a whole, or specified within a single sentence or within a range of a certain number of sentences. The search terms could be nouns, verbs, judges' names, or numerical citations. A searcher could display the documents retrieved or just a KWIC display in which the terms and a specific number of words on either side of them were shown, in order to judge relevance. The entire document could be displayed or just those pages containing the search terms—a helpful feature in long documents. Creating another set of displayed documents with different terms was accomplished by merely typing in the new terms. Another set of documents was compiled, separate from the first. Searching JURIS thus involved building sets of data into a search "tree," so users could branch off in different directions.

A special feature of JURIS in 1974 was a display of the entire search history on the terminal, with the sets of documents listed by set numbers to which the searcher could refer. Hambleton (1976, 202) described this feature: "At any time the user can go back to an earlier set without erasing those sets compiled later. Other systems allow a searcher to modify his tactics from level to level, but at any point, if he retraces his steps, all information collected beyond the point to which he returns is lost. The JURIS searcher may at any time return to an earlier set and then return to that last of items compiled without losing any data."

From July 1974 through May 1975, DOJ assessed the operational and economic advantages of automated retrieval systems for legal information. Searchers could access either JURIS or LEXIS from the same terminal. In mid-1975, at the end of the evaluation, the results indicated overwhelming user acceptance, with great time savings and more satisfactory research when using a computer. DOJ management then approved further JURIS development and authorized a new terminal designed specifically for JURIS and its users. The newest version of JURIS was expected to be operational by spring 1976 (Hambleton 1976).

In August 1975, MDC and Justice were unable to agree on terms for a new contract, so the LEXIS subscription was canceled. Federal case law had not been added to JURIS since 1974, so the file had little case law. A remedy for the problem was to borrow the case law database on magnetic tape from FLITE (Federal Legal Information Through Electronics), an old Air Force project. Version 2 of JURIS was implemented in early 1976 and continued operating without further significant modification into the 1980s.

DDC DROLS

As mentioned in chapter 4, the DDC online system became operational on March 31, 1972. During the period 1972–1974, when about thirty users were accessing the system, DDC assembled a team of in-house systems personnel to redesign the existing system as a real-time multi-activity online system that used one program to accommodate up to 128 concurrent users. The primary designers were

Victor Furtado, Kathy Vlahopoulis, Norma Ayala, and Larry Jenkins (McCauley 1972).

In September 1974, the redesigned system, renamed DROLS (Defense RDTE On-Line System), was put in operation and immediately provided improved response time, an input system, and more capabilities including online document ordering. A UNIVAC 418 (later replaced by a Xerox 1200 printer) was obtained to provide a printing capability for the offline bibliographies (Moholm 1995).

By the end of 1976, with the DDC bibliographic database containing over 750,000 records, DROLS was firmly established as an online search service. However, it still had limited capabilities in comparison with other systems at that time. For example, DDC initially chose not to make the title and abstract fields of their records searchable.

TOOL-IR

With support from the Japanese Ministry of Education, researchers at the University of Tokyo developed an online bibliographic retrieval system, TOOL-IR (University of Tokyo On-Line Information Retrieval system), to work in an integrated seven-campus system to serve academic personnel in all of Japan's universities, colleges, and polytechnic institutions. Starting in the early 1970s, the development produced both a batch system and an experimental online system called TSIR-I (TODAI Scientific Information Retrieval System, first version). TSIR-I used a HITAC 5020 computer with a time-sharing system. Test searches were first demonstrated in 1972 (Yamamoto et al. 1972).

Using several HITAC 8700 and 8800 computers and associated disk storage units, TOOL-IR began partial operation at the University Computer Center in September 1974. In April 1975, the most recent fifteen months of CA Condensates and all of the bibliographic and numeric data from the Crystallographic Data Centre were made available online, with INSPEC expected to follow soon after. Command verbs were in English, and the basic syntax was English-like in the sense that the command verb (e.g., SEARCH) came first, followed by objects and complements. Starting in June 1975, this facility was scheduled to operate as an online regional center for Chemical Abstracts Service and the Crystallographic Data Centre (Yamamoto et al. 1975).

PIRETS

As noted in chapters 3 and 7, the University of Pittsburgh had been active in computer-based information systems since the late 1950s. Accomplishments included Horty's pioneering work on full-text legal searching in the late 1950s, the NSF-funded Pittsburgh Chemical Information Center (1967–1970), and the NASA/industry-funded Knowledge Availability Systems Center (KASC) that served as a NASA Regional Dissemination Center from 1964, providing batch searches from the NASA database.

In August 1972, a new system, PIRETS (Pittsburgh Information Retrieval System), became operational on DEC PDP-10 computers at the University Computer Center. PIRETS was used for batch-mode searching through KASC, or for online searching of a very small file (e.g., one month's issue of the METADEX database) with remote Teletype-compatible terminals. The emphasis was on batch searching and SDI service. The online mode from remote terminals using small database samples was intended primarily to assist in query formulation and testing for the batch searches (Hartner 1973). PIRETS was a full-text search system, using Boolean operators and left- and right-truncation features in a serial search of the entire file. This work was done as part of the NSF-supported Campus-Based Information System (CBIS), under the direction of Allen Kent. Dale Isner was the principal designer (Marron et al. 1973) and Libby Duncan and Libby El-Hadidy were also associated with PIRETS (El-Hadidy 1995).

PIRETS was developed to provide free bibliographic search service to students, faculty and staff at Pittsburgh, using the CAC and NASA databases. After several years of development, the service was made available to the university community in

September 1974. The ERIC and Social SciSearch databases were added at that time. PIRETS was designed to allow novice users to do their own searches without an intermediary (Borgman and Trapani 1975).

PASS

In 1972, staff at the University of Tulsa, on behalf of the petroleum industry, started developing an interactive search system called PASS (Petroleum Abstracts Search System), to be used with Petroleum Abstracts. PASS was programmed in FORTRAN IV and ran on a Xerox Sigma 6 computer (Martinez 1973). In the late 1970s, the University of Tulsa's Petroleum Abstracts database was made available online through SDC as a controlled access database to the organizations subscribing to the Tulsa information service. It appears that the University took this approach rather than run their own online service.

RETRO

The Defence Scientific Information Service (DSIS) of the Canadian Defence Research Board (DRB) was responsible for developing and operating an online bibliographic search system called RETRO (not to be confused with RETROSPEC of Cybernet Timesharing, Ltd.). RETRO was used with a collection of scientific and technical publications of interest to Canada—much of it with a security classification. DSIS started working with computer-based bibliographic systems in 1967. In 1968–1969, DSIS staff converted bibliographic data to a machine-readable file and started an SDI service. In 1971, they developed a prototype search system (the DSIS Retrospective Search Simulator) to explore operation of an online system for this community of users. When a computer service bureau, I. P. Sharp Associates, Ltd., in Toronto, introduced a system capable of supporting very large files on its computers, DSIS began an experiment with a subset of about 10,000 records from its file. The staff wrote programs to support searching in either command mode for experienced searchers, or a prompted or conversational mode for beginners.

DSIS terminated development of the Simulator in November 1972 after extensive demonstrations at a Defence Research Board Symposium in Ottawa; the company decided to proceed with development of an operational but still experimental system, using the I. P. Sharp computer for access by DRB establishments across Canada. The experimental system with limited capabilities was to be completed by spring 1973, with at least a full year of use before implementation of a fully operational system (Smithers 1973). Digital Methods Ltd. of Ottawa designed and developed the search system for DSIS. It continued both the command mode and tutored search modes. It began operation in May 1973 with a database of about 40,000 citations for users from DSIS laboratories and headquarters offices, and soon thereafter had terminals operating in five establishments across Canada. The intention was to extend access to other defense users. RETRO ran on the service bureau of I. P. Sharp Associates, using IBM 370/145 computers, Bell VUCOM I terminals (keyboard plus CRT), and IBM 2741 terminals over public phone lines (15 cps for the IBM 2741, 20 cps for the VUCOM terminals).

1973 Milestone

RETRO may have been the first online search system to offer a bilingual interface option.

In addition to an option for a novice or experienced user interface, an unusual feature was the inclusion of a bilingual search option for user-system interaction (Irvine 1973). At log-in, the searcher had the choice of using French or English. All questions and system responses were in the chosen language. However, the search terms and output were in the language used in the source records. This may have been the first instance of a multilingual user interface; documentation for the DATUM system described in chapter 7 suggests that such a feature was planned as early as 1971, but we have no evidence that it was implemented. Moreover, the QL/SEARCH system had an interface that gave users the option of receiving messages in either French or English, but we are uncertain when it was first implemented. The first instance of a multilingual search capability (i.e., enter a search term in language A and retrieve records that used the equivalent term in language B) came later with the ILO/ISIS system described earlier.

The system allowed searching only by personal or corporate author, or by assigned subject index terms or codes; no title or text word searching was permitted. Search output was limited to the publication's title, accession number, and microform address. This hybrid approach was a compromise to accommodate cost, access, and security concerns (Currie 1973; Irvine 1973). The use of microfilm with a more complete record at the searcher's location allowed citations associated with classified material to be made available to the end-user even though the index search system employed a public computer utility and normal public telephone facilities.

Library of Congress

SCORPIO

The SCORPIO (Subject-Content-Oriented Retriever for Processing Information Online) computer programs were developed by the LC Computer Applications Office for use by LC staff. As described in chapter 4, SCORPIO had its beginning in 1969 with Bill Display, an in-house system for tracking current legislation. In 1973 a second system added another file for the Congressional Research Service. A third application, the Major Issues system, supported a narrative file of the background and policy analysis of issues of interest to Congress, along with references to current legislation, hearings, and document citations. Each of these separate systems served a different user group with different databases. The consolidation of these three major applications in a single coherent system resulted in SCORPIO (Power et al. 1976).

SCORPIO became available online at LC in February 1974 to access several in-house bibliographic and data files (e.g., Legislative Information File, Bibliographic Citation File, Major Issues File, and National Referral Center File). Additional files were added in 1975 (Computer Applications Office 1975). It ran on a computer at LC, and was made available to members of Congress and their staffs, LC staff, and public users in the LC reading rooms.

In December 1974, after only ten months of operation, there were over 300 users, and the number jumped to 1,000 by the end of 1975, with a volume of 600 searches per day. By the end of 1976, SCORPIO was still an in-house system, but was being accessed from over 400 terminals throughout LC and various legislative offices. Databases available at the end of 1976 included the full LC MARC file as well as the pre-MARC file, Congressional Record Abstracts and several files of related legislative information (Computer Applications Office 1977).

MUMS

LC MARC Development Office staff created an online system known as MUMS (Multiple Use MARC System) for support of LC bibliographic application programs. They designed MUMS to maintain a central pool of programmed services to provide message control, task definition and sequencing, and file storage and retrieval functions for MARC records. MUMS operated as an application under the control of IBM's CICS (Customer Information Control System) database/communications software (Avram, Maruyama, and Rather 1972).

Smithsonian Science Information Exchange

The Smithsonian Science Information Exchange (SSIE) in Washington, D.C., was established and began its work in 1950 as the Medical Sciences Information Exchange under the aegis of the National Academy of Sciences (NAS)/National Research Council (NRC) by agreement among the federal agencies that supported medical sciences research (Fitzpatrick and Freeman 1965). In 1953, it was transferred to the Smithsonian Institution as the Bio-Sciences Information Exchange. Its purpose was to facilitate planning and management of scientific research activities, and to provide timely exchange of information about ongoing and recently completed research. Its scope of coverage and range of services has expanded since its beginning, and in the 1970s SSIE was processing information on more than 100,000 research projects each year, relying for its data on reports submitted regularly by research funding agencies. Data about current research projects formed the basis for a computer-readable file created and maintained by SSIE since 1958 and made available for use by outside organizations. A subset of this file, the R&D project descriptions relating to information science, was used as the basis for the COSATI file on that topic, and as the basis for COSATI's 1969 benchmark testing of five online search systems (chapter 4).

To facilitate its own use of this data, SSIE implemented a series of batch programs to do searches on their tape file records, using a series of in-house computers (Burroughs B-205, IBM 1401, IBM 1460, IBM 360/30) from 1958 to 1973 (Marron and Foster 1966). In 1969–1970, SSIE compared their subject code indexing to free text searching of their database records by means of a test using Data Corporation's online system (chapter 7) at their Arlington service bureau (Hersey et al. 1970, 1971).

SSIE implemented an online search system in 1973 to allow its scientists to search its file of more than 170,000 project descriptions to identify material relevant to specific user requests. SSIE also acted as a broker, to search the files, generate special reports, or provide other services to the public on a fee-for-service basis (Hersey et al. 1973). Major participants in the system development included David Hersey, as president, and Martin Snyderman.

The online system began regular production using an IBM 370/135GF at SSIE's own computer facility. It continued until October 1981 when SSIE was terminated as a result of federal budget cuts, and its activities dispersed to other federal agencies such as NTIS.

MEDDOC

MEDDOC was a medical documentation service established by Eli Lilly and Company for in-house current awareness and retrospective searching of published literature about Lilly products. In 1973 the system operated on an in-house IBM 370, with a remote Sanders 720 display terminal along with a microfilm reader-printer. MEDDOC operated with less than 25,000 bibliographic records (Markowitz, Brown, and Leslie, 1973).

IRIS

After several years of experience with an in-house large-scale SDI service with several major bibliographic databases, the central information services unit of ICI Ltd. in the United Kingdom determined to become more involved with online search systems. The unit decided to do this by developing its own interactive system based on an existing in-house file of business information relating to the chemical industry. The name given to this in-house system was IRIS (Information Retrieval by Interactive Search), and it was fully operational by the end of 1974. Even though it had weighted term searching, IRIS was rather primitive—it was restricted to index terms, terminal speeds of 10cps, and service for only one hour per day.

After experience with the initial system, ICI Ltd. decided to become familiar with external online systems and services. It started using the DIALOG service in mid-1975, and based on that experience it modified its internal system to have the equivalent look and feel of DIALOG so that in-house users needed to learn only one search protocol in order to be able to search IRIS or DIALOG. The modification included the ability to do text searching and

Boolean logic. The rewrite of IRIS was complete for its IBM 370/158 by the end of 1975 and was fully operational at the beginning of 1976 (Flynn and Wild 1977).

ASPENSEARCH

As described in chapter 7, Aspen Systems of Rockville, Maryland, expanded on Horty's work on full-text legal information searching at the University of Pittsburgh, and then developed and marketed the ASPENSEARCH IV full-text system. In 1974, Aspen produced an online version and installed it on the NIH computer in Bethesda, for use by the Health Resources Administration. Key Aspen staff during this development period were Jeff Pemberton, director of communications, and Lawrence Berul, executive vice president.

With their text processing experience, Aspen, together with Westat Research, Inc., also worked in 1974 on an NSF-sponsored study of the technical and economic feasibility of a centralized computer-based processing center for journal publications. Berul and Don King were coprincipal investigators (Berul et al. 1974; Berul and Krevitt 1974). Aspensearch V was made available for online use in late 1977.

INIS

The International Nuclear Information System (INIS) in Vienna, Austria, is a bibliographic information system operating under the aegis of the IAEA. INIS activities include developing a major international bibliographic product, Atomindex, first distributed in April 1970, and covering the peaceful applications of nuclear science. Facilities for online interrogation of the INIS database of about 400,000 citations by in-house staff became available in 1975, using IBM STAIRS software with modifications by INIS staff.

A predecessor of the INIS online system was GIPSY (Generalized Information Processing System[9]), developed by Giampaolo Del Bigio at IAEA, to meet the documentation needs of IAEA staff and IAEA member states. GIPSY was a batch search system for a small IBM 1401 computer and became operational in 1965. By late 1967, over 50,000 citations had been entered and stored on magnetic tape (Scott and Lang 1967; Del Bigio 1968). GIPSY was later installed and operated on IBM 1401s at other locations. GIPSY was used to produce a bibliography on nuclear energy, which later evolved into the INIS. GIPSY included a sophisticated duplicate citation checking routine, as well as routines to produce subject and author indexes. GIPSY was replaced by a system for the IBM 360, MYPSY, which developed into INIS (Maxon-Dadd 1994). Remote terminal searching of the INIS database by users at other IAEA-authorized institutions was established in 1977 (Romanenko and Todeschini 1980).

TITUS

J. M. Ducrot developed TITUS (Traitement de Textile Universelle et Selective, or Textile Information Treatment User's Service) at the Institut Textile de France in the early 1970s to reduce duplication and overcome the language barrier by making all textile information available in four languages. About 30,000 documents were entered annually, with a controlled indexing thesaurus of about 11,000 words in English, French, German, and Spanish. Users could ask questions in any of these languages, but TITUS furnished abstracts only in French. TITUS had a multilingual thesaurus and the automatic translation of all stored information, including abstracts, into four languages became possible in 1974 (Tocatlian 1975).

Continuing Experimentation

MEDUSA/RETROMEDUSA

As described in chapter 3, computing lab staff developed MEDUSA at the University of Newcastle-upon-Tyne in the early 1970s and used it primarily for experimentation. In 1974–1975 the

British Library used MEDUSA as an experimental online service for U.K. users in a project to assess the operational and economic aspects of online searching. MEDUSA ran on the university's IBM 360/67 computer, and for online retrospective search purposes it came to be known as RETROMEDUSA. For online searching during the British Library project, it used inverted files with a subset of fifteen months of the MEDLARS file that corresponded to the records for 1,150 biomedical journals of particular interest. The service was aimed toward the end user and was available for five to six hours per day via the BPO telephone network. Users ran five to ten searches per week during the British Library project (Holmes 1977b, 1978).

Library Technical Processing, Bibliographic Utilities, OPACs

Library Technical Processing

Several online library systems were established in the 1970s to serve a focused support role to technical processing services (acquisition, authority control, cataloging, catalog card production) rather than to provide reference service. Some of these systems used large databases—most frequently the LC MARC catalog record file, or variations of it, with a capability to search on the attributes (descriptive or subject cataloging) of the records. These systems were implemented to be used primarily by library technical processing staffs, in the back rooms away from library users. This back room confinement was motivated in part by a desire to focus on one problem at a time, but also was dictated by system constraints, such as the high cost of online memory, and insufficient processing capacity to handle large numbers of simultaneous tasks and users. Representative examples of these early online library technical processing systems are those of Ohio State University (OSU), the University of Chicago, Stanford University, and IBM (ELMS/DOBIS).

The OSU libraries initiated an automated circulation system project in early 1968 to serve their main library and twenty-one departmental libraries. Software development was done under contract with IBM Federal Systems Division in 1969–1970. Conversion of the shelf list of 850,000 titles and 2.4 million volumes was done in 1970. By December 1970, catalog records for all department libraries had been converted and the automated circulation system was fully operational. An online capability, using a campus IBM 360/50 was also implemented to permit searching of the catalog by an author-title search key, using dial-up typewriter and CRT terminals. It was a limited search capability, but it was a pioneering effort for access to an online campus catalog (Guthrie 1971).

In the mid-1960s, library automation staff of the University of Chicago, with NSF support, started developing a comprehensive data processing system to support the library's technical processing and reference activities. With Herman Fussler and Charles Payne as major participants, the work took place over a long period of time and in an orderly manner, with particular emphasis given to the bibliographic database as the core element. Payne (1971, 5) stated, "It was never 'total system' in scope, rather it was a plan for the development of an integrated-file, bibliographic data processing system and was so described." Some of the first modules went into operation in a batch mode in the late 1960s (Payne and Hecht 1971). Online segments started to be developed in 1966, using software developed elsewhere (Fussler and Payne 1967).

McAllister, a participant in the ELMS project (chapter 4), completed her Ph.D. dissertation at the UC-Berkeley in 1971 while she was working at the IBM Advanced Systems Development Division in Los Gatos. While continuing to work for IBM, she moved to Germany to join a project group in 1971 at the University of Dortmund. There she helped to establish an online library system called Dortmund Bibliothek System (DOBIS) for a group of universities and colleges in Dortmund (*Dortmund: Executive guide* 1975). The IBM ELMS software was the basis for the system, but messages and other system communication were in German. IBM gave the system considerable support and publicity (*Dortmund: Application guide* 1975). It ran on an IBM 370 and used IBM 3270 terminals for technical processing and reference functions. In 1976, the system was still being developed for in-house use in technical processing for libraries, and was expected to become operational at the end of 1976 (Jedwabski 1977).

At least four different versions of the software known as DOBIS, DOBIS/LIBIS, or DOBIS/Leuven were installed in libraries in several countries. The searching, cataloging, and maintenance programs were developed at Dortmund and were called DOBIS. Circulation, acquisition, and much of the background processing and batch programs were developed at Leuven and were called LIBIS (McAllister and McAllister 1979). The University of Dortmund contracted for the DOBIS software development to support online cataloging and catalog searching. It later made DOBIS available to major libraries around the world (Deemer 1983).

Bibliographic Utilities

Some of the library technical processing systems grew in scope and capability to be able to provide online processing services to other libraries; some offered a wide range of features and services. Thus, they began to be considered as utilities to be used by other interested libraries. As the name "utility" implies (as in "public utilities"), all of the systems described here were intended to provide a support service to other libraries. Although these systems used relevant technology, they were not central to development of the online search service industry. Therefore only a few of them are described briefly in this text. As these types of systems expanded their functions to include reference searching and included a capacity to handle more users and more search activity, some took on the functions of online public access catalogs (OPACs), described later.

SPIRES/BALLOTS

The BALLOTS system (chapter 3) became operational in the Stanford libraries in 1969. An outside consultant evaluated BALLOTS-I and found that it did not meet the original objectives and was not cost-effective. That triggered the development of BALLOTS-II. The resulting scope definition document was published in February 1970, and in November 1970, Hank Epstein arrived from North American Rockwell to head BALLOTS-II. The SPIRES-2 file maintenance and search software (also in chapter 3) went into service in October 1972. For years not only did it serve as the underlying software for BALLOTS, but Stanford also widely distributed the software by itself and it ran on university computers throughout the United States.

BALLOTS development continued throughout the early 1970s (Epstein et al. 1972; *The BALLOTS project* 1975). BALLOTS II went into production operation at Stanford in November 1972, providing comprehensive online technical processing services to 54 branch libraries since that time ("Project BALLOTS" 1975). Martin (1974) described the status and features of the system as of April 1973. The libraries put online display terminals in the public areas for patron direct use in late 1974.

BALLOTS initially provided technical processing support to the Stanford University libraries, while exploring ways after 1971 for other organizations to use BALLOTS as part of a cooperative network. In 1974, the California State University and College (CSUC) system of nineteen campuses (separate from the UC system of nine campuses) considered running the BALLOTS software on the CSUC facilities (*Survey of library automation* 1974). In 1975, BALLOTS was expanded to permit searching and cataloging by other libraries, and Stanford made it available for use by any organization on a service bureau basis via TYMNET or TELENET, with services ranging from a Level-1 (online search and display only) to Level-3 (including most major services such as record modification capability and catalog card production). BALLOTS completed its initial development phase in 1975 (*The BALLOTS project* 1975; "*Guide to BALLOTS*" 1976). With LSCA support from the California State Library, a BALLOTS terminal was put into trial operation in June 1975 at each of seven California public libraries, forming PLAN (Public Library Automation Network); this was the first non-Stanford use of BALLOTS.

In 1976, new terminals (Zentec 9003s) were installed that had the capability to display the full MARC graphic character set, including diacritical marks and special characters that are important for working with many European and Asian languages (Veaner 1977). This character set was far advanced compared to most of the terminals used with the earliest online systems that were restricted to twenty-six uppercase English letters, numerals 0–9, and a small number of special characters. In 1976, the BALLOTS computer was upgraded to an IBM 360/168, and SPIRES was changed to SPIRES/370.

By the end of 1976, SPIRES was being used in Canada and at other non-California locations; libraries at several UC and CSUC system campuses were using BALLOTS on a trial basis. BALLOTS eventually became the system behind the Research Libraries Group (RLG), which provided technical processing and reference support service to a large group of major research libraries, including the New York Public Library. BALLOTS changed its name to RLIN (Research Libraries Information Network).

OCLC

OCLC, initially the acronym for Ohio College Library Center, but changed in 1977 to OCLC, Inc., and then later to Online Computer Library Center, Inc., to reflect its expanded role and service to institutions outside of Ohio, was incorporated in July 1967 in Ohio by a group of officers and librarians of several Ohio universities (Maciuszko 1984). The incorporation was the culmination of cooperative efforts that had begun several years earlier between the librarians and several of their institutions, working through the Ohio Library Association and the Ohio College Association. At the time of its incorporation as a not-for-profit organization, the principal purpose of the center was to increase resources for the research and educational programs in colleges and universities, and the center's staff was expected to be engaged in R&D activity. The development activity was to be in the direction of nonconventional computerized systems, and the first major operation was to be a computer-based shared cataloging system.

By summer 1967, OCLC was a reality, and Kilgour, who with Ralph Parker had worked as a consultant to help plan the venture, was hired as its first executive director (Kilgour 1987). He came to the position from his Yale University post as associate librarian for research and development, and he guided OCLC development until he retired in 1980. Before he moved to Yale in 1965 he had helped to start the Columbia-Harvard-Yale Medical Libraries Computerization Project. A goal of that early project was swift and thorough computerized retrieval of bibliographic data. His proposals for online library catalogs for the Columbia-Harvard-Yale project were widely known by library automation professionals (including the Lockheed staff) in the early 1960s. Kilgour received the ASIS Annual Award of Merit in 1979 and the ALA Life Membership Award in 1982 for his contributions to library automation. Other major contributors to the early OCLC efforts included James Rush (director of the Research and Development Division), John Wyckoff (senior programmer), and Philip Long (associate director) who joined OCLC in January 1969 with the primary responsibility of developing the hardware/software complement for the online system. Long left at the end of 1973 to go to SUNY (coincidentally, SUNY signed an agreement with OCLC in January 1974 for OCLC service to the SUNY institutions).

During the early years, OCLC staff focused on ways to build and maintain a computer-based union catalog for many libraries, and provide sets of catalog cards on demand for participating libraries. In 1969, OCLC began offline catalog data conversion and card production using a comprehensive program developed earlier at the Yale Medical Library, and modified to run on a standalone IBM 7094 at OSU.

The design of the initial system used a Rockville, Maryland, contractor, COMRESS, Inc., in 1969 to perform computer simulations and evaluations of proposals by ten equipment manufacturers. In the analysis, COMRESS assumed that projects such as remote catalog access and bibliographic IR would consume a far greater amount of the central processor's time than would the cataloging-processing tasks. That concern was later reinforced by actual operating experience, and was reflected in the relatively low priority given by OCLC management in the next decades to a general file searching capability in the OCLC system. On the first simulation runs, all ten computers failed because of inefficiencies in their operating systems. After changes in the operating systems characteristics in the model, some of the systems still failed the second simulation. The results of these simulations convinced one manufacturer to withdraw its proposal, and five others modified their proposed equipment configuration. A decision was finally made to purchase a Xerox Sigma 5 computer for the first OCLC system (Kilgour 1975; Long 1973). This was likely the first instance in which a computer simulation was used to design or evaluate proposed systems for library networks.

The computer arrived in September 1970. It began providing online data entry and cataloging service in October 1971. The LC MARC file was a key part of OCLC's data processing activities; OCLC's decision to use the MARC II record format made it easier to acquire machine-readable data from LC as well as to furnish data to LC and other libraries in return.

By fall 1972, OCLC was supporting the cataloging of forty-nine participating Ohio libraries, and several out-of-state cooperatives, for about 28,000 titles cataloged per month, and printing over 190,000 catalog cards per month. It was doing this over 4,000 miles of telephone lines that linked a private network of eighty terminals. Its resources were devoted primarily to library institutions and their technical processing activities; OCLC gave much less attention the issues of reference retrieval and document delivery that were being addressed by other computer-based information services at that time. That was understandable, given the large scale of OCLC production and service activities; its computer facilities and other resources were completely taken up in meeting its technical processing support commitment to its participating libraries.

In May 1972 OCLC amended its articles of incorporation to relax its membership rules to permit nonprofit nonacademic, public, and other nonprofit libraries of Ohio to join as full members. In March 1973, OCLC membership voted to extend OCLC to regional library groups (i.e., consortia) outside Ohio. In May 1974 they modified the articles of incorporation to expand the membership eligibility to worldwide inclusion of any nonprofit library or groups of libraries. OCLC's primary interests were with academic, public, and other nonprofit libraries, and its management was reluctant to let other types of libraries participate in its cooperative services. Koenig (1995) recalled the difficulty Pfizer had in trying to join OCLC in 1972, because it was a commercial organization. Pfizer was finally accepted in late 1973 or early 1974, becoming the first commercial organization allowed to join OCLC. The arrangement required months of negotiations among Pfizer, NELINET (New England Library Information Network), and OCLC. It was resolved by setting up what amounted to a dummy library network corporation that included Connecticut College (in New London) and Pfizer as the members; this dummy network then became a member of NELINET, which was an institutional member of OCLC.

OCLC first demonstrated a rudimentary online search capability in May 1971 and began its first regular online operation on August 26, 1971, with about forty participating libraries. Its online searching was limited to the LC Card Number (LCCN). Nonetheless, from the beginning, Kilgour (1969, 86) signaled his intention to provide a subject search capability: "Soon after the shared-cataloging project goes into operation, there will be activated a bibliographic information retrieval system which will allow users of Ohio libraries to obtain rapid and complete searches under subjects. An effort will be made to increase amounts of subject indexing, which are presently inadequate in all libraries." However, because of high costs of online storage, and the greater computer capability that would be required, OCLC management chose to defer building indexes to subject headings and chose not to build indexes to title words that would allow users to search on specific words in a book title. Instead, OCLC required users to do title searching on codes constructed on the basis of characters selected from each of several specific words in a book title. In late 1971, OCLC demonstrated a capability for online searching by brief codes that were built by a searcher from selected parts of an author's name or words in a book title. For example, in looking for publications by the author Louisa May Alcott, a searcher entered the search code "alco,lou,m." In looking for the catalog record for the book *For Whom the Bell Tolls*, a searcher keyed in the code "for,w,t,b." This was extremely primitive searching compared to the features available on other online search systems at that time. In January 1972, the OCLC system offered searching on the OCLC Record Number.

Kilgour was the person most responsible for design and implementation of the code searching technique used in the OCLC search system. While at the Yale Library he did his initial study of coding techniques, making use of work by others (Kilgour 1968; Bourne and Ford 1961; Ruecking 1968; Stangl, Lipetz, and Taylor 1969; Lipetz, Stangl, and Taylor 1969). Kilgour continued this work when he moved to OCLC, and in late 1970 he favored a 3,3 search key (3 characters chosen from the name field, and 3 characters chosen from the title field) for use as a search key for a "known item" search of a name-title catalog (Kilgour, Long, and Leiderman 1970). Kilgour (1995) recalled that he had favored the 3,3 key because the fourth position of a search term or name had a demonstratively higher percentage of spelling errors. Kilgour and others continued working on search codes for retrieval through the seventies (Kilgour et al. 1971; Long and Kilgour 1971; Long and Kilgour 1972; Guthrie and Slifko 1972; Landgraf and Kilgour 1973; Landgraf, Rastogi, and Long 1973; Legard and Bourne 1976).

The OCLC designers apparently assumed that catalogers and technical processing staffs would be looking for records for specific known publications ("book-in-hand" cataloging), and thus a search key corresponding to a specific publication would return only a few records. It soon became apparent, however, that certain search keys were returning hundreds of records (e.g., Annual Report). That had not been expected and the initial system unfortunately was not designed to store and display such large answer sets. The November 1, 1972, *OCLC Newsletter* described an attempt to address that problem: "It is now possible to retrieve as many as nine screens of entries in response to a single search key, thereby making available to the user many entries that previously could not be retrieved through the search keys." The designers continued to work on the problem of large answer sets; the February 27, 1973, *OCLC Newsletter* noted that on February 12, the center had activated the extended search function: "Extended search currently handles up to 256 entries per [search] key; the Center will be increasing the number of entries per reply to 1024 so that it will be possible to retrieve all entries for all keys." In late 1973, about 10 percent of the searches were extended term searches. While a DIALOG or ORBIT search in that period could have handled the output of thousands of records, the OCLC search system could not.[10]

As early as 1973, OCLC planned to provide an online capability that would permit direct searching by subject, title, author, and editor. It did not happen, however, during the period covered by this text. OCLC was still doing code searching of a few fields of its LC MARC records in 1974, while, in contrast, SDC in 1974 was providing online searching of all major fields in the corresponding LC MARC records that it made available online in its IDC LIBCON database. In February 1975, OCLC added an online index to permit searching by searcher-derived personal author codes. In March 1975, OCLC added indexes to permit direct online searching by ISBN, ISSN, and CODEN. Kilgour

(1975, 167) acknowledged, "At the present time the most extensive access to an online, monograph data base is that of the BALLOTS system."

OCLC's headquarters and computer facility have always been located in the Columbus, Ohio area. OCLC made extensive use of Xerox Sigma computers, working with a single Sigma 5 from late 1971 to January 1975, then adding four Sigma 9 computers in the following year. OCLC implemented its own data communications network with dedicated lines to each terminal. Dial-up access to OCLC was made available in 1974 through TYMNET as part of a U.S. Federal Library Committee experiment, and by the end of 1976 OCLC was offering a dial-up capability to any interested user. In 1973 all network participants used a terminal customized for OCLC. Kilgour (1995) recalled that he had been partial to the use of special-purpose terminals because they could include hard-wired programs that removed a processing load from the mainframes. At a meeting on the user-terminal interface, Kilgour (1971, 278) noted: "We tried to eliminate as much command language as possible by using function buttons on the terminal. This was because we had an opportunity to participate in a redesign of the terminal to be used. We were successful in getting rid of command language, except for a button, in 90% of the activity. English is great but nobody wants to use it."

In early 1972, CLR gave a grant to NELINET to test the transferability of OCLC to other groups of libraries. A contractor, COMRESS, Inc., used its proprietary computer simulation software using parameters that described the NELINET operating environment, as well as a six-month demonstration at Dartmouth College. Dartmouth finished the study as a subscriber to OCLC, and the OCLC system was not copied. At a December 1973 meeting, OCLC's Board of Trustees unanimously voted to discourage replication of the OCLC system.

Response time was a problem for a large part of the early OCLC history. In the last months of 1974 and early 1975, response time increased due to growth in the volume of use along with a delay in the arrival of the first Sigma 9 upgrade. By February 1975 the average response time was over twenty seconds—considered to be an unacceptably long period. After the installation of the Sigma 9 computer in late February, response time was reduced to less than seven seconds—deemed to be acceptable—and maintained at that level for the next several months. During the last half of 1975, response time again degraded due to delays in linking the two computers together and the August 1975 implementation of the full MARC record display. In October, OCLC was forced to initiate a Saturday service. Although the response time improved in February 1976, the *OCLC Newsletter* for September 30, 1975, reported that OCLC decided to keep the Saturday operations as regular service hours. Even with scheduled cutbacks in service availability (called "feathering" by OCLC; the power companies call them "rolling brownouts") and technical improvements, response time was still over 15 seconds during certain periods in November 1975. In the November 28, 1975, *OCLC Newsletter*, Kilgour noted, "Response time is rising and my credibility is falling." The continued poor response time performance forced a temporary freeze on both the addition of new terminals and new features. Response times returned to their "acceptable" levels (8 seconds) in February 1976, but then increased significantly again (to about 30 seconds) in May 1976 for anyone who used the search enhancements (author/title, title, author searching) installed at that time. This forced OCLC again to institute a freeze on new terminals and to restrict author searching, and searching by personal and corporate name search keys, to non-prime-time hours until a third Sigma 9 was added in late 1976.

By October 1974, OCLC had identified three online search systems that could provide a subject search capability—Lockheed's DIALOG, SDC's ORBIT, and Battelle's BASIS. Kilgour obtained approval from his board of trustees to establish an agreement with Battelle for use of the BASIS software. By March 1975, the contract was signed, and work began on a project that was expected to permit online testing of subject searches in the first part of

1976. OCLC explored the feasibility of using BASIS software for this purpose. The development of an experimental subject search capability with BASIS continued in 1975 and 1976 under the combined efforts of the OCLC and BMI staffs. BMI, under contract to OCLC, worked to construct an index to the OCLC database (Kilgour 1975). The project did not go well (*Ohio College Library* 1976, 15–16):

> The project was plagued with equipment difficulties and indecision as to which operating system the Battelle BASIS program should operate under. Nevertheless, in February [1976] the BASIS program was installed ... and the staff of the National Center on Educational Media and Materials for the Handicapped began to use the subsystem at that time. Subsequently, additional features and various corrections and refinements were added. As yet, there has not been sufficient utilization ... to determine the amount of computer resources required to operate the system for the entire network. However, computer resources that would be necessary appear to be discouragingly large.

At the end of 1976, OCLC was still experimenting with online subject searching on the Sigma 7 but leaning toward a consideration of code rather than term or word searching. As noted earlier, this was at a time when OCLC was experiencing severe computer performance problems in the provision of even their simple search capability. Also during 1976, OCLC staff attended a demonstration of the IBM STAIRS software and tested it at OCLC. By year-end, IBM presented a proposal to OCLC, unsuccessfully, to use the STAIRS software at OCLC.

By the end of 1976, OCLC had more than eighty participating libraries, supported about 1,400 online terminals operating at 240 cps on their private telecommunications network for a scheduled eighty-seven hours per week. It provided rudimentary online search service to its catalog of 2.6 million titles and location symbols for over 12 million volumes held by the participating libraries, which now included many outside Ohio. System availability for the last half of 1976 ranged from 90 to 99 percent. It did this while supporting a major online data entry system (about 28,000 catalog records entered by participating libraries each day) and a major offline printing facility—about 200,000 catalogs cards daily, or 4.0 million cards printed and shipped monthly during 1976, compared to 0.4 million cards printed during its first full year of operation in 1970 (Kilgour 1977). Kilgour had often argued the benefits of economies of scale and this experience upheld his view. OCLC had become the dominant cataloging support utility in the world.

OCLC's online search capability at the end of 1976, however, other than a capability to handle a very large file, was still extremely primitive in comparison with other systems and services operating then such as the SPIRES/BALLOTS cataloging utility or the Washington Library Network; it was still restricted to searching by LCCN, ISBN, ISSN, CODEN, OCLC Record Number, and search codes (author, author-title, and title codes). A direct author search capability had been available, but was suspended for the last third of 1976 because it consumed so much of the computer resources (it represented 3 percent of the queries, but used 35 percent of the computer processing) that it dragged the response time down to unacceptable levels. Nonetheless, even with its limitations, OCLC was the leader in online support to library technical processing activities, particularly in the provision of cataloging data to libraries and the maintenance of a huge online union catalog.

Although OCLC was not a pioneer in the technology of online search systems and the online industry, it was a major contributor to library technical processing, standards, online union catalogs, telecommunications networks, and governance issues of cooperative library activities. The high visibility, potential utility, and cost-effectiveness of OCLC for participating libraries spawned many evaluation studies during the period covered by this text (Hewitt 1974, 1976; *IUC/OCLC* 1975; Nitecki 1976).

UTLAS

UTLAS (University of Toronto Library Automation Systems) is a Canadian bibliographic utility that has provided shared cataloging information services in both English and French to Canadian libraries since 1973. As noted in chapter 3, the library's experience in automation dated from 1963 when it began participating in ONULP, which led to the production of a union catalog in book form of the initial library collections of five Ontario colleges. In 1967, a separate Systems Department within the library was established, along with a dedicated computer facility, including a Sigma 7. It was stipulated that any systems to be developed should be done so for the general library community in addition to the university library. During this period, the library began the conversion of its catalog to machine-readable form, a project that was complete for 1.2 million records in 1975, and was marked by the closing of the card catalog in 1976.

The library recognized the Systems Department as a separate administrative unit in 1971 and renamed it UTLAS. In September 1973, UTLAS inaugurated the catalog support system, with online searching of the main catalog database, initially serving the University of Toronto Library and several other Canadian libraries, but later expanding its service to other Canadian organizations. The online system was implemented on a second UTLAS computer (Sigma 6) configured for online service, with search programs that provided access to all significant parts of the catalog records. The system in early 1974 was still in development. The final report of the Monograph Demonstration Project, an experiment in cooperative library development conducted by the Council of Ontario Universities from July 1973 through April 1975, noted that only two out of nineteen of the planned features existed at the desired level of development when the participating libraries began to use the system in February 1974. By the end of the demonstration project, however, thirteen of the nineteen features had been developed. The report (Council of Ontario Universities 1975) also noted that certain goals were not reached because of "the system's unreliability, resulting from its developmental state and severe technical difficulties" (4) and "performance and reliability of the computer-based system was inadequate to permit the libraries to discontinue traditional technical processing operations" (6).

In 1975, UTLAS began creating a Library Collection Management System that could function as a stand-alone facility in other organizations, or as an integral part of the UTLAS centralized network. Network activity had grown to a point that it was necessary to upgrade the existing computer equipment to obtain a capacity to support 256 remote terminals (Velazquez 1979). By the end of 1976, UTLAS was a major online catalog support service in Canada. However, its online search capability was still limited to searching an online index of LC Card Number, ISBN, ISSN, and forty characters of the title—sufficient for the intended cataloging support, but too awkward for reference search activity (Velazquez and Attila 1979). From 1979 on, UTLAS was classified by the university as an "auxiliary enterprise" and, as such, had its own separate budget, operating as a separate nonprofit organization. International Thomson Organization acquired UTLAS, Inc., in 1985 for an undisclosed sum.

BIBNET

Information Dynamics Corporation. (IDC) of Reading, Massachusetts, introduced a commercial online bibliographic utility to U.S. librarians in January 1974. David Waite, president of IDC, developed the system, called BIBNET, which stored all the available LC MARC catalog records at the IDC facility. BIBNET permitted local catalog record entry or searching to be done remotely at 30 cps from a Datapoint 2200 terminal, coupled with a GE Terminet printer modified to accept catalog card stock for the local printing of catalog cards. Waite noted (1975, 138), "Prior to BIBNET, no nationwide service existed to provide libraries on-line means to access the national bibliographic data base." This was true; the earlier SDC LISTS activity had stopped in 1970, WLN and RLIN were not operating in a national network mode, OCLC was just beginning to offer its services to libraries outside of Ohio, and none of the commercial online services had the LC file online. The BIBNET search software was intended to cover all attributes of the

LC and local catalog records, including library holdings codes. BIBNET also provided for gateway access to other online services. The LC MARC file contained 450,000 records then.

Like OCLC, BIBNET used a programmable terminal rather than a dumb terminal. The terminal was a microcomputer with core memory and two tape cassettes. Catalog records retrieved from online searching were written onto a cassette tape at the terminal. Then the catalog records could be processed in local mode for editing, saving, or printing as catalog cards.

IDC was the successor to an engineering partnership, Forbes & Waite (Edward Forbes and David Waite), incorporated in 1962. Forbes & Waite had been in the business of developing technological solutions to library problems since the mid-1960s. In 1972 they introduced a small minicomputer (General Purpose BIBNET On-Line/Off-Line Network Terminal), later referred to as Bibnet 1000, for prompted catalog record data entry and online terminal applications ("Information Dynamics" 1973).

In 1974, IDC made its database (LIBCON) available for public online access through SDC Search Service. At that time, LIBCON consisted of records prepared by IDC in the course of its work and was separate from the file that later became available from LC as LC MARC. LIBCON contained about 1.2 million records (including all MARC records available at that time), representing most of the material in the LC catalogs from 1965.

In April 1976, IDC filed for reorganization under Chapter 11 bankruptcy.

Washington Library Network

In 1974, after several years of planning and development, the Washington Library Network (WLN) was operating a batch mode bibliographic system on behalf of the state library and 120 public libraries, to create and maintain a machine-readable union catalog database with over 600,000 records to represent the state's library holdings, maintain authority files, and produce book catalogs, catalog cards, and other products on behalf of its member libraries. A contractor, Boeing Computer Services, did most of the technical development. WLN, with the continuing effort of the Washington State Library and Boeing Computer Services, changed the bibliographic and acquisitions systems from batch mode to online mode in 1975, to permit online searching of author, title, subject heading, and other access points (Reed 1975a, b). In 1976, WLN was legally recognized as a Washington state agency, responsible to the State Library Commission.

OPACs

Several academic institutions during the 1970s developed or installed OPACs, primarily for use by their own campus populations. While initially these OPACs were intended to be replacements for the existing card catalogs of the campus libraries, their scope often grew to include an online searching capability for databases (e.g., MEDLARS) produced by external organizations and installed on a local institution's computer. The earlier systems were all homegrown, but some libraries eventually used search software (e.g., BRS/SEARCH) that was available from external organizations. Some academic institutions even began to offer their search systems for use by people outside the campus.

As we noted with the bibliographic utilities, these OPAC systems used technology similar to that of the major online search systems but were not central to development of the online search service industry in the 1970s. Consequently, they are only mentioned briefly in this text. Hildreth (1982) provided a helpful review of OPAC activities during the 1970s.

Hardware and Communications of the Seventies

The launching of the online searching services industry in the seventies was fostered both by enhancements in hardware to improve reliability and performance, enhancements in software to permit time-shared use of computers, and cheaper, more accessible long-distance communications that allowed a much wider audience to use online service. We have discussed the software developments with the related systems; we describe here the general hardware developments as well as the implementation of the telecommunications networks. We defer most of the discussion of telecommunications to the next chapter, since most of the developments were "behind the scenes" or barely noticed by most users of online services.

Hardware

The IBM 360 and 370 series of mainframe computers played a key role in development of large-scale online retrieval systems with multiple databases. The majority of systems in this chapter ran on models of the IBM 360. Most were upgraded during the 1970s to the even larger IBM 370. The few exceptions to the IBM mainframes were the CDC 6400 and 6600, UNIVAC 1108 and 1100, Sigma 6, 7, and 9, DEC PDP-10, and various models of Hitachi HITAC.

The larger mainframes with their economies of scale, and with lower-cost memory capacity, permitted longer service hours, with fewer limitations on hours of access (called time windows) to large files. In January 1974, DIALOG started operating on a full daily schedule, Monday through Friday, for 10.5 hours a day (except for Tuesday, when the computers shut down an hour early for preventative maintenance work) time windows. Alternate Saturdays were added in 1975. At SDC Search Service, all time windows to accommodate large ORBIT files were discontinued by August 1976; service was provided for all files on a 14.5 hour per day basis. For all online services throughout this period, however, service hours were much shorter than are typical today because of the demands made on the computers to do file maintenance and preventative maintenance on the equipment (especially the electromechanical equipment), and because of occasional downtime for replacement or addition of new equipment.

Upgraded terminals also became available. Although most of the larger commercial services supported a variety of types of terminals operating at various transmission rates, many users were moving from typewriter terminals to CRTs, and from slower to faster terminals. Oddly, though, the shift to faster CRTs began to reverse in mid-decade with the introduction of inexpensive, portable, and durable 30 cps typewriter terminals, and as people wanted to access systems such as the Information Bank that were only accessible with expensive high-speed leased lines. The first of a series of portable terminals started to appear in 1970; the first model to gain moderate acceptance was a heavy (but still portable) unit from CCI that used a small modified commercial TV set as the CRT. It was followed over the next ten years by a series of lighter terminals from TI that used rolls of thermal paper as the printing display device. The CRTs were still considered desirable for more permanent installations, but users appreciated the flexibility and economy of the lightweight portables. Throughout this period some leased-line systems continued in operation for high speed terminals; the trend, however, was mainly toward dial-up access from slower-speed terminals using the telecommunications networks. Not until the early 1980s did this trend in terminal equipment change, with the adoption of microcomputers as terminals and the availability of higher-speed lines and modems on the data communication networks.

Another development that appealed to some services and user groups was terminals that were customized to a single search service. MDC introduced customized terminals in the commercial world for the use of lawyers. The Information Bank offered customized terminals even earlier, but they were not received as well as the MDC equipment, perhaps because the Information Bank users tended to search other systems as well; LEXIS searchers were likely to search only LEXIS. Some leased-line systems (e.g., DIALOG private network, Mead, OCLC) were in operation for high speed terminals during most of the time covered in this text.

Long-Distance Communications Networks

A 1971 cost study (Powers 1973) showed that it would be less expensive to have a large number of users share an online service than to have a more limited number of users use a batch service. The costs tipped in favor of online over batch, however, only when a critical mass of searchers was available to share the costs of the giant mainframe computers and realize the economies of scale. Other than for a few organizations with large numbers of in-house users, the large numbers needed would not have been possible without a major technological breakthrough in long-distance networked communications between users' terminals and the remote mainframes.

The first public use of data communications networks by an online search service was in February 1972 when NLM adopted TYMNET service for MEDLINE. As other search services signed onto the network, TYMNET users in about fifty major cities could place a local call or at least one in a nearby city, to get to the network node, and access to the chosen computer center, at a communications cost of about $10 per hour versus $30 per hour for direct dialing (Radwin 1973). Users could be connected to NLM's computer in Maryland, SDC's computer in California, the BASIS computer in Ohio, or by 1973, the SUNY BCN computer in New York that was serving as a backup for NLM. Lockheed was also connected to TYMNET as of mid-1973.

The TELENET network, owned by Telenet Communications Corporation, began service in competition with TYMNET in 1975, at slightly lower hourly rates. Telenet Corporation was founded by the contractors who built ARPANET—Bolt, Beranek and Newman, consulting engineers in Cambridge, Massachusetts. Larry Roberts, who served as ARPA's former director of information processing, was chairman of Telenet Corporation during its initial years. At the urging of Mark Radwin, DIALOG became TELENET's first customer (Provenzano 1987). SDC Search Service added TELENET access in February 1976.

In the 1970s, most of the DIALOG traffic was via TYMNET or TELENET. However, as a continuation of its early NASA and ERIC contracts, DIALOG operated its own 480 cps network for selected users (e.g., the NAL) that provided faster transmission speeds than were possible with the commercial data transmission networks.

The number of TYMNET and TELENET nodes grew steadily through the seventies. By the end of 1976, according to DIALOG's newsletter (*Chronolog*, 32, 34) a total of seventy-seven U.S. cities, six Canadian cities, and four European cities had access to either a TYMNET or TELENET node, and some cities had a choice. All of these public dial-up nodes provided service at thirty characters per second; higher speeds from other than direct dial or leased lines were to come later. Both networks had nodes in major European cities such as Brussels, Frankfurt, Geneva, The Hague, London, Paris, Rome, and Vienna, as well as in other parts of the world such as Hong Kong, Manila, San Juan, and Singapore. North American searchers, however, seldom used these networks to access online services outside North America.

In Canada, CAN/OLE used Dataroute, a nationwide digital dial-up network designed by the Trans-Canada Telephone System. It had nodes at major cities and a capability for speeds up to 30 cps. SCANNET, a data communications network for all Scandinavian countries, was scheduled to become operational in late 1976. EURONET, another intra-European data communication system, did not become operational until late 1978.

Summary

From the public's point of view, the first few years of the online industry were a stimulating period of constant changes and expansion in hardware, software, and services. When we look behind the scenes in the next chapter, we will feel the same sense of excitement about being in the vanguard of developments, but with the added dimensions of competition, overwork, and stress on the major players.

10 Building the Online Industry: Behind the Scenes

Introduction

The emergence of the online enterprises just described had another side—one that was not generally visible. Let us step behind the scenes now to probe that other reality, a story that often varied from the public image. As the leaders of the fledgling industry hammered out policies and strategies, they presented to the public the outcome, but not the process. Actually, "hammered" may be too strong a term to describe pioneer operations and marketing that were characterized more by trial-and-error and seat-of-the-pants risk taking than by methodical planning. In many ways the search service operations were not what the public imagined them to be, including the management decisions about setting prices, acquiring databases, establishing telecommunications links, hiring personnel, grappling with balky hardware that was nearly always lagging in capacity to serve the burgeoning user population, and designing marketing, promotion, and user education programs. In the 1970s, industry insiders discussed only among themselves the fierce competition among search services, including legal battles within the industry that had to be resolved in the courts.

Much material for this behind-the-scenes account came from interviews with the second group of pioneers—the search service managers, trainers, marketing professionals, and customer service staffs (recall that the first group of pioneers chronologically was the programmers, systems designers, and researchers of the 1960s). The pioneers of the seventies were highly visible industry emblems. They were driven with a sense of mission, competition, and excellence. They traveled extensively for marketing demonstrations and training sessions, were seen at conferences in the exhibit booths, and their voices comforted distraught searchers on the 1-800 lines. These industry insiders shared with us their perspectives on selling the idea of online and selling subscriptions for the first commercial systems. They told us war stories and their personal opinions about industry developments, as well as their feelings of exhilaration and exhaustion about their work.

We heard also from the third group of pioneers, the online users, who told us what it was like to be sitting at the terminal end. They, like the other pioneers, had experiences and opinions that they shared at the time only with their colleagues. Enough years have passed that individuals from all of these groups were willing to discuss this personal or proprietary history.

Most pioneers' experiences were similar in general terms—only specific illustrations varied. Consequently, we have collapsed much of the interview material. Unique events or direct quotations from interviews are individually attributed.

Wheeling and Dealing Behind the Scenes

Launching Public Search Services

The developers of prototype systems of the sixties faced a huge hurdle in converting to a profitable, or at least self-sustaining operation. Most pioneers did not make the passage. For those that did, the transition often was harrowing. The stories of SDC Search Service and BRS, among the many that could be told, are illustrative of organizational, financial, and personal obstacles faced and overcome. We have already seen some of the challenges faced and overcome by DIALOG and ESA/IRS, along with obstacles that defeated BASIS and LEADERMART, as well as other interesting start-up stories. We focus on these two here, mainly for the personal element that our sources revealed.

The Struggles of SDC Search Service

In December 1972, SDC management still had not made a final decision about whether to commit to entering the commercial online search service business. There were few examples of successful computer search services of any kind then, and no shining examples of profitable online services. Nevertheless, at Cuadra's urging, the senior managers did give conditional approval for the start of such a service. They set two critical conditions: (1) the service had to be profitable or give solid evidence of profitability within a few months; and (2) it had to use existing SDC computer center resources.

The second condition turned out to be a constraint that crippled SDC Search Service in obtaining computing resources at competitive and cost-effective rates. Although SDC's computer center had a large collection of powerful state-of-the-art equipment and extensive staff resources, it all had been obtained and configured to support the particular R&D interests of their U.S. defense contracts. The costs associated with their computer resources were charged to contracts, and in the climate of the times, this facility perhaps did not feel the same cost performance pressure that a commercial facility would have felt. Hence, its rates for in-house usage were higher than those quoted by most outside service bureaus. SDC's internal charging policy meant that Cuadra was unable to shop for the most cost-effective computer resources for development or operations. Another possible explanation for why SDC charged its own divisions such high rates for computer use was that SDC wanted to establish a profitable "commercial price schedule." Government contracts could then be charged for computer services at that "regular commercial rate." Furthermore, revenues from this "commercial" work would add up to a large enough fraction of total computer center revenues to deny U.S. government auditors access to the computer center's books. We can only speculate on these points.

For whatever reason, SDC senior managers dictated that the Search Service could not acquire its own equipment or use an outside computer center—the Search Senice had to use SDC's facilities. The net result was that the SDC Search Service was prevented from choosing an equipment mix that was optimal for its activities. Thus the base costs for its computer services (file conversion and updating, storage, program development and testing, online searching, output processing, and customer accounting/billing) were significantly higher than the costs its competitors experienced. For example, Lockheed allowed the DIALOG service to obtain its own computer equipment, as long as the equipment was paid for out of DIALOG service earnings. Thus DIALOG managers attempted to obtain the most cost-effective equipment, and its computer supported only the search service. NLM was providing MEDLINE on its own facility then, and charging users only a few dollars per hour, which recovered only a small fraction of the total computer costs. This resulted in extreme price pressure on SDC—which had a more realistic cost recovery structure—when it tried to compete with NLM in offering MEDLINE to the public.

The first challenge that Cuadra faced was loading the first database for his commercial service. He had selected CA Condensates, which had about a half million records then, as the first commercial file (that is, in addition to already loaded ERIC and MEDLINE, which were U.S. government files). SDC's online version was to be called CHEMCON, and it would prove to be a major headache for Cuadra and his development team.

One problem was that CHEMCON was the first database that required a royalty payment, which required new usage accounting and reporting programs. A second problem was that SDC's first two databases (MEDLARS, ERIC) were well-edited products with tightly controlled assigned subject headings, but CHEMCON indexing was not controlled. Even though CHEMCON had a list of standard abbreviations and subject terms for use in the brief summaries, the indexers did not always use them. SDC had not previously encountered such a "dirty" file. This was their largest file to date, and because of initial problems with the file processing, it had to be reloaded two or three times, and at a terrible cost. Neil Cuadra (Carlos Cuadra's son) wrote a conversion program, as well as the accounting and billing programs. Carlos made an "unofficial incentive agreement" that earned Neil a car if his conversion program improved the speed of the existing program. Cuadra (1990) recalled the story:

I borrowed a journeyman programmer from another division to write a conversion program. He spent a month and cost me a few thousand for a program that would load about 4,000 records an hour. I calculated that with 500,000 records to go, I would be wiped out. I was sitting at home one night at the dinner table with my head in my hands and explaining this hideous problem. I'd been given the go-ahead to try out this business that I wanted us to get into, and the programmer had delivered this thing after a whole month. It was so slow it was going to cost $150,000 to load the file. I didn't have that money. My 19-year-old son Neil said, "Maybe I can try it." I said, "But you have to do it fast, because we have burned up all this time and we have nothing." I worked out a chart for him—a reward matrix. It had a number of days to finish the program. It started with 3 days and went to about 30. It had a Matchbox car at 30 days and a Mercedes Benz at 3 days. He started from scratch. He took ten days. The program loaded about 40,000 records an hour and we were able to load the file and keep it on the air. I had to buy him a Toyota! I paid for it myself. Anyhow, we dodged a bullet by the narrowest of escapes and Search Service survived its loading.

The fledgling service faced another trial that also was attributable partly to SDC's policy of charging its own divisions for computer services. Chemical Abstracts Service (CAS) produced CHEMCON. On the advice of CAS staff, the senior Cuadra decided not to index words from titles, but to index only the "keyword strings"—CAS indexing. Within a month after the file was loaded, he knew that the decision had been a blunder, that the title words also should have been indexed for online searching. Cuadra (1990) said later, "That was the only time I ever made the mistake of assuming that these guys [database producers] know how to load their data." Not until several months later did the Search Service bring in enough money that Cuadra could afford to pay the costs of reloading:

Because of the pricing machinery, I could not do it when I wanted to do it. I could not do anything about it until some point in time when enough money became available to blow it on reloading the file. We had to be exceptionally careful. If I had had my own computer and did not have to pay myself money for it, we would have loaded files faster, looked at them, tested them, fixed our mistakes and made a wonderful file. As it was, we had to guess at what was in the file and take our best shot and do it once. I was unable to convince SDC that we were not going to make money taking in each other's washing—that we were in a competitive world and the price of this service was going to be set by the marketplace. If the computer center got rich on me, it meant that Search Service was going to lose money; it was making money in one pocket but losing it out of the other.

This simple fact, then, that SDC Search Service did not have its own computer, as DIALOG Information Retrieval Service did, handicapped it from the beginning in the intense competition between the two services that continued through the 1970s. Cuadra (1990) reflected: "With hindsight, if SDC had bought a small computer and said this is a computer we bought to run this enterprise instead of making it part of a gigantic enterprise that relied on commercial rates to government and commercial folks, our history at SDC would have been very different."

In spite of the restraints imposed on SDC Search Service by its own parent organization, as well as the usual challenges of starting a new business in an untried market, the venture was launched. Most of the first thirty customers were pharmaceutical companies who were members of PMA. But the relationship between SDC, PMA, and NLM became complicated within a short time.

From BCN to BRS

As support from New York state sagged in the mid-seventies, SUNY BCN's loyal users increasingly were dissatisfied with the quality of service, but were unwilling to give it up entirely. By 1976, the users were actively looking for an online system to provide low cost retrieval service similar to what they had been getting from SUNY BCN. Ann Van Camp (1995), a former SUNY BCN Board member, provided an insider's perspective on the start-up story. Pizer, along with Egeland, Quake, and Palmer, got the non-SUNY members together in January 1976 to explore the possibility of starting a new company, patterned after SUNY BCN (with user boards for user input), that would offer a similar system but with faster response time. Snyder (1981) provided further details of the turmoil within the SUNY organization. Smith (1984, 21) quoted Egeland: "As our service grew, it put a larger and larger strain on the computer system which we shared with the university. We were attracting more users than anyone expected. When SUNY began having budget problems and was looking for ways to save money, it became apparent that our network was in jeopardy. At that point [January 1976, according to Van Camp] (1995), our user advisory board came to us to propose that we make the network a private enterprise in order to keep it running." Smith said that when the BCN users approached Egeland with the idea of starting a commercial retrieval system, the suggestion came as a jolt. She had not intended to launch a commercial business. Nonetheless, she was receptive to the idea, and enlisted an ally and former boss, Ron Quake (he had been director of the SUNY Central Office Computer Center from 1970 to 1973). In 1976, when Egeland first asked him to head a new commercial online operation, he refused; he was not keen to gamble on a high-risk technology company and he knew that getting funding capital would be hard. Eventually, Egeland did persuade him, and also Lloyd Palmer, manager of system programming for SUNY Central, to join in the startup of this new enterprise. Egeland, Quake, and Palmer banded together to attempt to launch BRS.

User relations with SUNY took another hit with Pizer's (1976) BCN-2 letter of June 25 that revealed that a consultant's report on SUNY computer operations stated that SUNY intended to continue providing the same (unacceptable) level of service to the network. Improvement in response time could be obtained only by signing up an additional twenty-five subscribers (at $7,500 each) in order to buy additional computer capacity. Pizer's final point was that *all* SUNY applications had a higher priority for service than the BCN! That surely was enough to motivate many users to seek an alternative. Pizer (1976) asserted in his letter: "The BCN has reviewed the offerings of all four vendors [BRS, Lockheed, SDC, SUNY] in this field, and can unhesitatingly recommend to our members that BRS provides the greatest mix of databases, the lowest costs, the best chance for reliable service, the most user-oriented training programs, and the only management which is truly responsive to user needs and desires." In the minds of the staffs of the Lockheed, SDC, and Informatics services then, Pizer's statement was pure conjecture and not founded on any actual formal review. We found no evidence that any other online service was ever asked to submit a proposal as an alternative to the existing SUNY service. However, with Pizer's solid endorsement, the stage was set to hand over the entire package to BRS.

Getting capital for start-up proved to be as difficult as Quake had feared. Their bank did not understand what a commercial online search service was and had no good way to establish a risk associated with the loan. Fortunately, the bank officers thought of an analogy: giving a loan to a publisher. Their concerns about the risk would be eased if this potential borrower could bring to them a prescribed number of prepaid subscriptions. Therefore, in lieu of collateral (which Egeland, Quake, and Palmer did not have anyway), the bank insisted that they collect at least forty institutional users willing to pay $7,500 up front for a year's subscription (Egeland 1979; Provenzano 1987). Each organization had to sign the subscription agreement contingent on BRS being in operation on January 1, 1977. Egeland approached and signed up as many SUNY BCN users as she could, and then she hit the road for many months to drum up the remaining subscriptions. But the exhausting effort paid off; armed with a business prospectus, seventy signed subscribers, and Quake's Chevrolet as collateral, Egeland and Quake convinced Schenectady Trust Company to issue them a line of credit (Smith 1984). With the line of credit and $25,000 in advance commitments from prospective customers, they launched the business (Gupta 1981).

The BCN group took its interest a step further to market for BRS. It might seem extraordinary for a nonprofit educational entity to market a commercial service to other institutions, but that is what was done here. Lucretia McClure, at the University of Rochester Medical School Library, was an early non-SUNY participant who was on the SUNY User Board. McClure (1995) verified that SUNY BCN and its users did help sell the new commercial service. BCN representatives McClure and Van Camp made presentations to non-BCN users to encourage them to sign up for the forthcoming BRS service. Van Camp also helped with the SLA annual meeting exhibit in June 1976 in Denver, where Egeland and Linda Palmer did the first commercial exhibiting for BRS. The BCN volunteers helped BRS also at the MLA annual meeting exhibit in July 1976, working a hotel suite to explain what BRS wanted to do. Concurrent with the MLA meeting, a BCN-2 user meeting was held; BRS and an oral explanation of the prospectus was the primary topic. Commercial involvement by BCN members continued quite openly. A BCN mailing in November 1976, for example, was headlined "BCN Biomedical Communication Network Proudly Presents BRS Search Services." The BCN participants did not perceive it as a significant conflict of interest; they rationalized their activities by a conviction that, "the SUNY system was far superior to NLM" (McClure 1995). There was even a BCN officer with the title of BCN/BRS service manager, although no other official positions were established for representation of other relevant commercial services.

Some might view the BRS start-up as a clear conflict of interest, in which a director of an in-house service was working, at least part of the time, on the in-house payroll, not to continue pursuing the best possible support for the in-house system but to switch usage to an outside commercial service in which she had a significant proprietary interest. On the other hand, we have seen that the death knell apparently had been sounded for BCN; we could argue that Egeland and her partners were looking to rescue the passengers and jump ship before it sank.

The bank's "subscription" thinking established the pricing pattern for the initial BRS service. The commercial service was launched at the beginning of 1977 with a subscription payment structure radically different from that of other search services. To the public, BRS staff promoted the subscription pricing as a benefit to libraries, as part of an overall appeal to market segments not well served by SDC or Lockheed, without mentioning that a bank had imposed it on BRS. Interestingly, SDC and Lockheed moved promptly to offer a similar pricing option. Anne Caputo (1987) recalled that in the DIALOG office in Palo Alto, she and Fran Spigai (DIALOG's marketing manager) responded as soon as they heard about the BRS pricing structure: "Fran and I were up all night on the eve of Thanksgiving and Thanksgiving weekend, figuring out a similar subscription pricing policy for DIALOG, getting it typed, reproduced, and stuffed into envelopes so that we could hit the streets right away."

Establishing physical facilities was perhaps more difficult for BRS than it was for SDC or DIALOG. The May 1976 final prospectus called for the system to run on a dedicated IBM 360/50 at BRS headquarters in Schenectady, New York. However, when the service actually began, BRS did not have its own computer, but instead planned to use some extra capacity on a computer operating in upstate New York at Carrier Corporation. However, six months into the venture, Carrier told BRS that its computers could no longer support the service. So in fall 1977, BRS was given just three months to set up its own computer facility. This required capital that BRS did not have, but fortunately the company worked out a seven-year deal with Memorex to provide the computers in return for monthly payments (Provenzano 1987). BRS then installed its own equipment (an IBM 370/155) at its new headquarters in Scotia, New York. Quake was quoted by Provenzano (1987, 38–39) as follows: "No one in the online industry believed we could keep BRS afloat. We were weakly financed, serving highly specialized customers, and charged very low prices compared to the rest of the industry."

Pricing

Pricing Factors

All of the online services and database producers, whether for-profit or not-for-profit, wrestled with pricing policies (Martin 1976). Some services set their prices on a file-by-file basis. In setting public prices for specific files, many cost factors needed to be considered, some associated with start-up and some with continuing costs. The calculation of start-up costs required consideration of the size and nature of a source file (and the resulting conversion and online file building) and preparation of user documentation. Continuing costs included online storage, and specific costs associated with file maintenance (updates, deletes, periodic reloads), documentation updating associated with changes to the file, royalty payments, and general overhead costs associated with any file (e.g., customer support, accounting, and billing). Setting prices was not only dependent on costs; other aspects of marketing had to be considered. Given the complexities in building, updating, and operating a search service, as well as the uncertainties in a market of users who had almost no knowledge of what online was, it is not surprising that many search services modified their pricing structure several times in the early years.

As an aircraft manufacturer and R&D organization, Lockheed had been used to billing a few big customers for very large sums. Now, with their online service, they were faced with billing a large number of customers for relatively small amounts of money and with doing the necessary accounts payable tasks. Furthermore, Lockheed had not been required up to this point to account for and make royalty payments for using the databases it offered. Compensation for online use of a file was a policy surprise for both online services and database producers.

Black (1987) recalled that SDC's pricing policy for the public service was driven primarily by what their computer center could do, and about all they could do then was collect information on connect hours of use of each file by each password. Consequently, initial SDC pricing was based on connect time. This same computer center limitation also delayed SDC's implementation of a per-record output charge to cover a per-record royalty charge. In early dealings between SDC and CAS, CAS was oriented to output royalty charges, starting with a penny per SDI system output record even before the online service days. Neither SDC nor CAS staffs had any idea then of the average number of output records per hour of connect time, so Cuadra wanted a compromise on a connect hour equivalent to a royalty fee, because he did not want to have to develop the accounting software for counting and billing for online output records. Cuadra (1990) recalled: "We wanted to do things on an hourly basis. Since they thought in terms of a penny a hit, we had to agree on an hour equivalent. I said, 'How about a dollar an hour?' And they said, 'Okay.' They didn't know any better at the time. Now it seems ludicrous." CHEMCON went public on SDC Search Service in February 1973. While this was the first time that SDC encountered the possibility of an output royalty charge, it was not the first online file with a connect hour royalty; that distinction goes to PANDEX on DIALOG in 1971.

Reflecting on his experience as the Information Bank's first marketing manager, Pemberton (1984, 6) commented:

Pricing was extremely difficult . . . we operated in almost total darkness. We had no direct competitors . . . so there was no guidance to be had from that source. Our potential customers had no experience whatever with online services, so they had no feel for what kind of value this new service would offer; hence they had no opinion on what they would be willing to pay. Since we didn't have any customers, we didn't really know how many the computer could handle at the same time, so we didn't know what our true data processing costs were. In the end, we took a deep breath and guessed at a connect hour charge.

Some database producers insisted on a marketing connection to their print products, in an attempt to enhance their value or to protect their print product subscriptions. Subscribers asked why—when they could get the information online—they should continue to subscribe to an expensive print product. Some producers exercised control by means of their license agreements with the online services. The result was that some online databases (e.g., APILIT and APIPAT from the American Petroleum Institute) were only accessible by password to current subscribers of the print products; some online databases were to be made available (again by password) to current print subscribers at a lower connect-hour cost than that charged to nonsubscribers.

The new industry had to address the following pricing questions:

• How would the number of subscribers and the type of charging relate to the costs of running an operation? Bob Landau, in an attempt to establish a pricing structure for Battelle's BASIS, prepared cost figures for running it. His charts, reproduced in Lancaster and Fayen (1973, 384–390) showed the effect on costs of varying the number of terminals, access time, connect time, and size of databases. All of the search services had to conduct some sort of simulation or analysis if they hoped at least to offset their operating costs with usage fees.

• Should service charges be based on actual computer resources used or other direct costs? Most services adopted this cost-based approach for part of their pricing (e.g., for offline prints, for which the costs of computer resources, paper, and postage were directly proportional to the number of prints delivered). Few, if any, however, took this approach for all of their pricing.

• Should searching services be charged as a flat monthly or yearly subscription fee? In addition to a fixed fee for searching, some services added a modest annual fee to cover the distribution costs of newsletters and other documentation. Or should users pay for only as much connect time as they actually used or for as many offline prints as they requested? Between 1973 and 1976, Lockheed and SDC relied exclusively on charging for connect time and offline prints, with great success. Potential users seemed to be more willing to sign up if they did not have to pay start-up fees, meet monthly minimums, or pay annual subscription fees. The "pay only for what you use" approach appealed to potential users in the 1970s who were uncertain of the value of online searching or the extent to which they would use it. Not until BRS introduced a lower-cost annual subscription fee structure for specified numbers of connect hours in 1977 did DIALOG and SDC modify their pricing structures to offer discounts for high-volume users. By the late 1970s, increasing numbers of users were pressing the online services to offer a "fixed price–all you can eat" plan.

• Should a one-time start-up charge be imposed? This seemed to be a good idea initially to the commercial services, in order to guarantee working capital. For example, in 1974, Battelle charged an initial fee of $300 for use of commercial databases. Start-up fees for other services were generally a modest amount and were intended to recover only initial administrative costs. DIALOG, SDC Search Service, Informatics, and the Information Bank all had start-up charges during their first year or so. However, they realized quickly that even these modest fees were depressing the market because many librarians were unsure whether their clients truly needed this unfamiliar service. Most start-up fees were abandoned soon after they were established.

• Should users be required to use or subscribe to a minimum number of hours a month? In 1974, the Informatics TOXLINE service was made available at a minimum of $120 per month (for 2 hours of connect and data communications time at $1 per minute, with a minimum charge of $12 per session). In 1974, MDC required that a firm that subscribed to LEXIS pay for a certain minimum number of hours per month; the required monthly commitment was substantial ($2,500 per month in 1974), and this resulted in only the larger firms finding the installation to be economically feasible. The initial BRS pricing in 1976 was for several levels of fixed dollar amounts for a corresponding number of hours of connect time (e.g., a minimum subscription of $7,500 per year for up to 70 hours per month); this amounts to a user commitment to a minimum dollar amount. Not requiring a monthly minimum fee eventually became a point of differentiation for marketing by the services that did not charge a minimum.

• Should users get discounts, and if so, on what basis (volume of connect hours or total billings, type of institution, geography)? In the early 1970s, some users already were pressing the commercial services for volume discounts or blanket fixed-price agreements. Most users seemed to feel that differential pricing based on volume of usage was fair, and consequently some services developed strategies for inducing customers to use their online service more. In 1976, by means of their different pricing for various subscription levels, BRS introduced a volume use discount. DIALOG had avoided discounts up to then but countered immediately with a more direct volume use discount plan, when they felt that they had to, in order to compete with BRS. SDC introduced its first volume discount plan in December 1976, based on connect hour usage.

• Should the services be offered for no charge, or be at least partially subsidized by tax revenues? For government-based services such as NLM's MEDLINE, DOE's and NASA's RECON, or the ESA/IRS, DIMDI, FIZ, Technik or ECHO services in Europe, this pricing alternative seemed to make sense to the supporting agencies, in order to encourage use that ultimately would be in the agency's or public's interest. During the period covered by this text, U.S. government agencies such as the NAL or the Office of Education were willing to offer their databases (AGRICOLA, ERIC) to the public for no or a low royalty charge in order to encourage wide use. As we saw with NLM's MEDLINE, however, government-sponsored free online services did not survive long in the U.S.—at least not until the arrival of the World Wide Web in the 1990s, which provided a platform for free or inexpensive public access to some databases and online library catalogs.

• Should user charges be based on information actually taken from the database (e.g., output records or posting counts)? Most search services had a charge associated with offline printing and delivery of records, mostly as a means of direct cost recovery (paper, printing, envelopes, postage) and to discourage abuse of a free feature. The first instance of a charge for a record provided online may have been DIALOG's charge per output record in 1975 on the EIS Plants database, in response to a corresponding database royalty charge. CAS followed shortly after with a similar royalty charge for online output records.

• Should higher charges be levied on users who searched at faster communications speeds? This was not much of a consideration in the early online days with slow data transmission speeds, but it received more attention in the late 1970s when users had a greater choice of communication options and when much higher communication speeds (and corresponding reductions in connect time per search) started to have a net negative effect on search service and database producer revenues. The higher communication speeds also increased searching quality, because a searcher could use online EXPANDs or lookups in authority files more, and review more records online in order to improve the search formulation. This pushed search services and producers to find and adopt other charging mechanisms that were less dependant on communications speed used (e.g., a log-in charge to access a specific file, a charge for specific commands, a higher data communication or connect hour price associated with higher data rates).

• Should charging be done on a per search basis? Lawford's plan for QUIC/LAW at Queen's University in late 1972 called for a charge of $1 each time a user signed on to a database, and $1 for each search conducted within that database.

• Should charging be done on a per search term or per index term posting basis? This approach rewarded the search service for the added value of building and searching all the index entries, and it compensated them for the computer resources used to store and process all the entries. As practiced by Mead, it involved charging for the number of occurrences of a term in the database. Users considered it to be unfair because it was unpredictable, particularly with truncated terms; they could not estimate the cost before doing a search. CAS pursued the same approach several years later, followed by NTIS attempts to negotiate royalty schedules with its online search service partners for its databases on the same basis as CAS.

The pricing of online services can be viewed differently from the point of view of the search services, database producers, and searchers. All parties engaged in considerable discussion of this topic during the period covered by this text. Elias (1982) provided a particularly useful overview and Pemberton (1984) gave a concise commentary from a later perspective.

Charging for Telecommunications

Also in the pricing equation was the variable of communications costs, which depended on a user's location relative to the computer site or to a major U.S. city, and on the type of communications link used. Users had the options of leased lines (relatively expensive), regular telephone lines (at $22–$35 per hour within the U.S., also expensive), or data communications networks (at $8–$10 per hour, by far the cheapest alternative). Therefore, in spite of occasional interruptions in service, communications networks were the choice for many users, especially those located in cities with a local telecommunications node for a major network such as TYMNET or TELENET. Costs of data communications services influenced searcher behavior. Cuadra (1975, 83) noted, "Government organizations use dedicated lines; because their telecommunications charges are zero, they have been known to get an online printout of 1,000 citations and leave the terminal unattended while they go home to dinner!"

Telecommunications decisions behind the scenes were not always made in a rational way. Having missed the opportunity to have an outside contract cover the $2,150 monthly cost of a nodal connection to TYMNET, for nearly two years Summit was unable to obtain Lockheed management's budgetary approval for this. The competing online services (except Mead who had its own proprietary terminals and network) had connected, leaving DIALOG at a disadvantage. Finally, Radwin suggested that Summit present the network access device as another peripheral, like a tape drive, that would greatly increase utilization of the computer (Radwin 1997). The approach worked, and in May 1973, Lockheed Information Systems added a TYMNET node, to permit dial-up access at speeds of 10, 15, or 30 cps from forty-one U.S. cities, and the three overseas cities (Paris, Brussels, London) that had TYMNET nodes.

As mentioned earlier, the TYMNET and TELENET organizations did not bill online users directly for data communications. TYMNET and TELENET based the charges to the search services on the total number of characters transmitted and factors other than connect time. The search services converted these costs to a rate representing an equivalent cost per connect hour, and then rebilled users at something above this rate for data communications. The price lists of the services for this period showed different connect hour prices for the same data communications service (e.g., TYMNET) because the search services set the price not only on the basis of cost, but also on marketing and competitive considerations. In Europe and other parts of the world, telecommunications costs were considerably higher. In early 1975, for example, European users were paying high costs for domestic or cross-border European lines, and $22 per hour for the TYMNET link to U.S. computer services.

Negotiating Database Royalties

In setting prices for searching particular databases, search services had to consider not only how much users were willing to pay and what the competition was charging for access, but also how much producers were charging in royalties. For Lockheed, no royalties had been associated with online use of the NASA, AEC, ERIC, NTIS, or any other databases. Once Lockheed decided to offer public online service, however, it wanted to obtain additional machine-readable databases in order to have a stronger package to offer to prospective customers.

> **1971 Milestone**
>
> DIALOG and CCM Information Corporation were the first organizations to establish a license agreement and royalty payments for use of a database on an online search service.

One file considered was PANDEX, a sci-tech bibliographic database developed by Richard Kollin as a commercial venture of PANDEX, Inc. In June 1968, CCM Information Corporation, a subsidiary of Crowell Collier Macmillan, purchased PANDEX. Summit and Kollin had several discussions in 1970–1971 about adding PANDEX to the Lockheed service but could not agree on a method of compensation related to file use. Summit's first royalty discussion with Kollin took place at a conference, on a hotel fire escape outside a cocktail party. Summit, representing Lockheed, and Kollin, representing Macmillan, discussed the proper way to divide revenues associated with adding PANDEX to DIALOG. They settled on a fixed connect hour and offline print royalty (roughly a 50-50 split of earned revenues). They decided not to have a front-end charge or a monthly minimum, because the system was unknown to users. To make potential users aware of PANDEX on DIALOG and start using it would require many live demonstrations. So, as an alternative to expensive and time-consuming demonstrations, Summit and Kollin tried to make it extremely easy for new users to subscribe. In addition to no front-end charges or monthly minimum, they offered $100 worth of free time on PANDEX to new subscribers—a fairly new idea then. Summit (1981) recalled: "I remember the negotiation—Kollin ... wanted considerable up-front money and a percentage of gross for any use of PANDEX online, probably a result of his role as a New York publisher. We finally settled for royalties of something on the order of $10 per hour and $.05 per offline print. Little would either of us know we were setting an industry contracting and pricing standard." The licensing discussions between Summit and Kollin, and the resulting usage royalty model of a specified fee per connect hour and per output record, appear to have been the first instance of a license agreement and royalty payment as part of a relationship between an online search service and a database producer. The agreement set precedents and became a model for many database licenses in the online industry for years to come.

> **1971 Milestone**
>
> PANDEX was the first database produced as a commercial venture that was made publicly available by an online search service.

PANDEX became publicly available online with Lockheed in September 1971. In April 1972, it contained about 500,000 records. This was the first commercially produced database that an online search service made publicly available.

Royalties to database producers were not usually negotiated at cocktail parties. Producers were nervous about losing print subscription revenues to online searching, and therefore considered royalties for online use a weighty issue. Most producers naturally insisted on some sharing in the online revenues, and sometimes they had quite different notions from search services about what was a fair split. In his memoirs of being a database producer and creator of the Enviroline, Energyline, and other databases, James Kollegger (1988, 34) recalled that in fall 1975: "Jeff [Pemberton] and I lunched in Georgetown [Washington, DC] with Roger Summit of Lockheed to hammer out our first online agreement. At that time we were one of the first for-profit databases to deal with Lockheed's DIALOG, and Roger was taken aback by our demands. We wanted 50% of revenues. The lunch almost ended in blows."

With the "sweetener" of an exclusive, and the database producer's agreement to promote heavily, a deal was struck. Pemberton created a marketing campaign that included an hour of free online usage as a promotion device. Later that year, Kollegger (1988, 34) offered a second database, Energyline, in a similar exclusive manner, but this time with the SDC Search Service: "This gave us an excellent vantage point from which to compare the two strongest online services. It also provided a strong negotiating position, because the following year we swapped databases, mounting Energyline on DIALOG and Enviroline on SDC, without sacrificing our royalty percentage. . . . In the next years, we struck similar deals with the European Space Agency (ESRIN) and other specialty networks such as DIMDI (the German Medical Network)."

Richard Harris recalled (1988, 42), when he was at the Institute for Scientific Information (ISI), another database producer, ISI played a similar game, pitting DIALOG and SDC against each other: "We had two files going up. We said, 'We'd like SDC to have one, and we'd like DIALOG to have one.' The market was so small that it seemed unfair to put two 'giant' organizations (that were relatively small at the time) against each other in an embryonic market, and give nobody a chance for success."

Kollegger (1988, 34) was flabbergasted that some online search services "wanted you to *pay them* to mount your data." This was often the case when the search service believed that the proposed file would receive insufficient usage and revenues to offset the costs of loading and maintaining it online. Some producers had goals other than just making their file available online. In some cases there were parallels with "vanity publishing" as it is called in the print publishing industry. On the other hand, when competition was strong for a particular database, search services were willing to give a break to the producer. For example, in response to a request-for-proposal from NTIS for the provision of online service to the NTIS database, Summit offered to mount it for free, which gave Lockheed the edge over Battelle in winning that service contract, since Battelle could not match the bid (Murdock 1990). Once DIALOG had the NTIS service contract, it was able to make the database publicly available with little additional effort.

The private negotiations between search services and producers had been going on for several years before BRS published a chart in 1976 that detailed the amount for each database it was paying to the producer as a royalty (e.g., $4 per connect hour plus $.02 per citation for CA Condensates; $20 per connect hour for Psychological Abstracts; for NTIS it was 10% of user's connect hour rate). This was the first time that the general public understood that the wide variations in online rates were largely dependent on database producer royalties. The data also came as a surprise to many producers. In the late 1970s, royalties constituted roughly 40 percent of the total operating expenses of search services and were increasing; they were a significant part of the cost of online database access.

Pricing Strategies and Structures

As we have seen, pricing issues were murky and complicated. Pemberton (1997) described the situation from inside the Information Bank:

Pricing was highly unscientific. An early management consultant's survey of potential commercial customers had queried people about their willingness to buy unlimited service for $2,000/mo. Of course, people were just answering a survey, not laying out cash, so many respondents said they would spend that. That was the basis on which we eventually charged $1,350 a month. Connect time would have been a better charging basis, but the *Times* was afraid to go out on a limb and risk low usage. A *Times* VP remarked that, 'We may not have so many customers (at $1,350), but at least we'll know how much money we're getting from the ones we have.'

Thus when the Information Bank began in 1973, it was offered to users outside the Times on a subscription basis, at prices of $675 to $1,350 per month, exclusive of terminal, communications, and the full-text microfiche service. The lowest rate bought either unlimited morning access or up to twenty-five hours per month at any time of day; the highest rate bought unlimited access at any time the system was operating (Walsh 1973). Subscribers had to acquire a special terminal and printer; this hardware could be leased for $350 a month or purchased for about $5,000. Communication costs depended on the type of telephone line used and a subscriber's distance from New York (Greengrass 1974). A lower-cost plan was being developed for academic and public libraries, including consideration of a plan to lease the file and search software to run on the subscriber's own computer, with weekly or semiweekly file updates (Rothman 1973). In 1974, the Information Bank offered heavy users a fixed price option of $875 per month. By 1975, the Information Bank was available on a fee-per-use basis, but still with a minimum service level of four hours per month (Bachelder 1976).

The first SDC pricing structure in 1972 included a one-time start-up charge and monthly file maintenance fee, with a minimum use charge of ten hours per month. The basic rates for dial-up access were $38 per hour through SDC's California number and $42 per hour through its Washington number. For extended use, a user or group of users in the same area could take advantage of special flat rates of $2,000 per month (California) or $2,500 per month (Washington) for a full four hours of service each day—or a flat rate of only $23 per hour (LEASCO 1972). So few customers responded to this pricing structure that SDC revised it drastically at the end of 1972. For example, SDC made "special provision" for interested educators to test the ERIC database by becoming "trial users" for a sixty-day period, with no minimum level of use required. Users were to be billed only for their actual terminal time (at the rate of $22–$35 per hour), and offline printouts (which were mailed the same day of search). Users who dialed the nearest "special number" (i.e., telecommunications network node) that connected to the Santa Monica computer, were billed $10 per hour for communications ("SDC offers" 1972). Although this pricing scheme was introduced as a special offer to an exclusive group, SDC kept it for most of its clients. In 1974, Informatics also used a combination pricing structure—$350 annual subscription fee and $45 per hour for access to TOXLINE.

In 1970, SIA charged an annual membership fee of $100–$200 for access to BASIS. When Landau began the SIA marketing for BASIS in 1972, he offered the service on a subscription basis, with a minimum annual fee per database. This was several years before the start of BRS service in 1976 when it sold annual subscriptions of $7,500 to obtain the bulk of the start-up funding needed to begin operations.

MDC offered LEXIS on a subscription basis to law and accounting firms, government agencies, local bar associations, corporate tax and legal departments, law libraries, and law schools. Harrington (1984–1985, 553) reported: "LEXIS was introduced to the world at a news conference held at the Overseas Press Club in New York in April 1973. Introduction was followed immediately by a concerted drive to sell subscriptions, principally to major New York law firms. The drive was successful, and by the fall of 1973 a few major New York firms—plus, of course, the Ohio firms that had hung in through thick and thin—were doing legal research with LEXIS."

Rubin (1998) provided a different perspective on the Ohio usage:

Hardly any Ohio firms were subscribers to LEXIS at the outset. Those who 'had hung in through thick and thin' had paid almost nothing for OBAR. We imposed a significant minimum subscription fee ($36,000 a year) for LEXIS, and most firms, soured by the OBAR experience, were not prepared to pay. Large New York firms, who knew me personally and had not suffered through OBAR, were willing to roll the dice on the new service. Until word got out that major New York firms were making good use of LEXIS, the bad odor of OBAR was our principal marketing obstacle.

The pricing strategy had been carefully formulated as part of a business and marketing plan designed to ensure success for LEXIS. According to Rubin (qtd. in Provenzano 1987, 41): "A price package was set up with the objective of making a profit in three to four years. For the immediate future, there would be losses. However, as the volume of use went up, the computer costs would also be going down and profits would increase. In fact, MDC's business plan was right on target. In 1977, LEXIS turned a profit four years after its birth." The LEXIS strategy, which ultimately proved wise, unfortunately necessitated short-term losses that created tension between the search service and the parent company. Rubin said further, "It was one battle after another to get money from them [Mead] . . . The money was spooned out and the sword of Damocles hung over our heads. Mead threatened to fold MDC at practically every MDC board meeting" (qtd. in Provenzano 1987, 41). The LEXIS managers would have felt a strong kinship with Summit at Lockheed and Cuadra at SDC, if they had known that they also were fighting for autonomy from their parent organizations.

Another part of MDC's early marketing strategy, as we saw in chapter 7, was to limit its customer base to the larger firms, which was accomplished by requiring each LEXIS subscriber to use a certain minimum number of hours per month. The hourly rate was not that high, but the commitment was for a substantial number of hours monthly, which meant that only larger firms would find the installation economically feasible. William Harrington (1974), who by this time was back in private law practice but still serving as a consultant to MDC, said that he hoped that in the future MDC would have more attractive pricing packages for smaller firms.

NLM's pricing strategy was designed to attract as many potential users from the medical community as possible while not overloading the system and degrading performance for everyone. Accordingly, MEDLINE services were provided free of charge to subscribing institutions in the first half of 1973. By summer, however, usage was "going through the roof" ("NLM's MEDLINE" 1973, 1). So, by midyear, "In order to establish a reasonable control in the growth of the services and to maintain financial stability in the operation, NLM established a marginal service charge of $6 per connect hour and $0.10 per computer page printout during the latter part of 1973" ("Report of the National Library" 1974, 147). This was in addition to the TYMNET cost of $6 to $8 per hour for those users that were not in the cities that had toll-free access to the NLM computers. The cost issues were reviewed in a report generated for the Paperwork Reduction Act of 1980 ("National Library" 1983, 14):

In the case of on-line access, charges were introduced for management purposes. The number of users had increased so rapidly that the Board of Regents and NLM staff feared that the growth of services would exceed the appropriation process supporting those services, leaving the Library in the paradoxical position of having to discourage the use of the system it was trying to develop. In addition, the efficiency of the services was being compromised by long queues and the cost of delivering the services was rising because of the inability to regulate the demands on resources.

The public announcement ("NLM user" 1973, 187) read: "NLM, in accord with general library traditions and practices, and in order to maintain a reasonable and equitable access to its resources, has instituted user charges for a number of its services and products . . . Collected fees will be used, in part, to pay line charges for users remote from network nodes so that services will cost the same no matter where a using institution is located." The charging plan was well thought out except for one detail: The Nixon administration imposed a nation-wide wage and price freeze. Discussions between NLM and the Price Control Board confirmed that online user charges would constitute a price increase. Not until the price freeze was lifted did the new charge take effect, on August 20, 1973.

After the user charges were imposed, a professional journal ("NLM's MEDLINE" 1973, 1) reported that the "initial reaction was surprise, disappointment, and a prediction that MEDLINE usage would decline." Usage decline was just the response that NLM wanted; without a budget increase in fiscal 1974, which was unlikely, "given the current budgetary mood of the Nixon administration," MEDLINE directors were deliberately trying to discourage growth. In spite of user charges, however, demand for MEDLINE was not dampened, and so additional rate increases were levied in the next few years, including a differential rate for prime time (10:00 a.m.–5:00 p.m.) and non–prime time. Nonetheless, NLM rates continued to be much lower than the commercial search services, and NLM promised its users, "Any charges that exceed costs would be returned to the U.S. Treasury" ("New user charges" 1975, 1).

As we saw in chapter 9, Pizer was promoting in early 1976 the as yet unnamed service that would replace SUNY BCN via a series of letters to current BCN participants. His March 11 letter carried statements about database royalties that would have to be paid (Chemical Abstracts: $0.01 per citation; BIOSIS: $15 per connect hour; Psychological Abstracts: $20 per connect hour). This appears to have been the first time that users of any online service had seen these figures. Up to that point the other services had bundled royalty costs into a single price for use of a particular file. When BRS actually began, it continued the practice of unbundling the royalties from the base costs for each file. This caused consternation for other online services, and surprises for database suppliers who had no intelligence about royalties charged by other suppliers. This was done, according to William Marovitz, BRS president in the 1980s, for marketing purposes, to highlight one difference between BRS and competing online services.

Acquiring Databases

Several early online systems and services (e.g., MEDLINE, NASA/RECON, Information Bank) were developed to provide access to one or more of an organization's own files already being produced on a continuing basis. Some online services (e.g., Lockheed DIALOG, SDC Search Service, BASIS-70) did not produce a database of their own, because it was an expensive investment and their database producers might have construed it as direct competition. Other services (e.g., Mead, WESTLAW) made a large investment in file building to create their own proprietary files. Most files available online, however, were created by independent producers as a by-product of producing their traditional printed abstracting and indexing publications.

The first experimental online systems had a limited choice of machine-readable files, and many developers had to produce their own. By 1970, the number of files for online searching was roughly fifty. A more exact number is impossible to glean from the written documentation because of ambiguities and inconsistencies in defining and describing different types of databases (bibliographic or nonbibliographic) or availability (only used in-house or available for lease or sale) (Neufeld and Cornog 1986). The number of computerized databases multiplied throughout the 1970s (roughly 300 by the mid-1970s and 600 by 1980). As of this writing, close to 10,000 are available from online search services worldwide.

In the early 1970s, however, few in the online industry imagined this tremendous growth or even considered a large increase to be a desirable goal. Summit, for example, knew of fewer than ten files, and he considered that number to be plenty enough. In fact, the early DIALOG software allowed for the possibility of only ten files, with one-digit file numbers. In a 1988 in-house presentation, Summit recalled that he had been asked by Ken Lew, a senior DIALOG programmer, "What's the maximum number of databases that a user will ever remember? 16? or 32?" Summit had replied: "Better make it 128. I can't imagine we'll ever do more than 128." They both seriously underestimated the number of separate files that would be installed. But when the DIALOG file number capacity eventually was extended beyond ten, it was increased to only ninety-nine. Later it was increased to 999, and only in the 1980s was it expanded beyond that. The system operators had trouble believing that any system would need to be able to handle that many different files. The comment was heard often: "We already have all the important databases; there aren't any more important ones out there that we don't have."

However, many services felt that it was important from a competitive viewpoint to load additional files, including ones already available on other services. By the mid-1970s, analogous to major publishers, the major search services had many more proposals from producers (real and potential) than they could accommodate. The search services learned the hard way that most new databases were "dirty"—that is, full of errors and inexplicable variations in structure and content. Such files were expensive and time-consuming to load and debug. Many proposed files could not pass the search service's screening review (e.g., market potential, return on investment, and degree of fit with existing customers and databases) and were rejected. The rejected files were usually too limited in scope or had too small a target online audience (e.g., Bibliography of Australian Aborigines, 220 Historical Items on Dredging); insiders referred to these as "Shoeshine Daily" or "Quilting Abstracts" publications.

An example of a database from a source other than an established abstracting or indexing service that proved to be extremely successful was ABI/INFORM (Abstracted Business Information, Inc.). Created by two MBA students from the University of Oregon, Dennis Auld and Gregory Payne, it was the first business bibliographic (plus abstracts) database to become publicly available online. ABI was a classic start-from-scratch effort, and for the first year or two of operation, the supplier address given in the user documentation was a post office box. In 1974 Data Courier acquired the database operation.

Most online users did not know of any or many more databases they wanted to access. By 1976, in fact, subscribers were complaining about the bother in learning the scope and structure of all the new databases and about overlap in content. Martha Williams and Sandra Rouse compiled a directory of machine-readable databases that was published at the end of 1976. The directory listed a total of 277 actively updated machine-readable databases in Europe and the United States containing bibliographic or bibliographic-related information, of which 107 were known to be available online (Williams 1976).

The producers held yet another view. For revenues and other reasons, many were anxious to have their databases on as many services as possible. Some made life difficult for the search services in other ways. For example, before the director of the London-based Institution of Electrical Engineers would allow Lockheed to load INSPEC in 1973, he set the condition that Lockheed had to demonstrate that it had 100 users. Summit (1987) admitted, "To get 100, we scraped them from in-house." From the database producers' side, search services could be trying too. For example, Kollegger (1988, 35–36) complained that search services did not disclose basic marketing data about his own files: "Several of the services, DIALOG being the chief offender, would not reveal who your customers were or how they were using your product." The Information Bank also irked Kollegger; it had been the first commercial service to offer him a deal on his Enviroline database (1988, 34): "But their data acquisitions budget was soon eaten up by hardware overruns, and Jeff Pemberton, their marketing manager, left." Kollegger's complaint, though, was not personal; he quickly hired Pemberton as an online advisor.

Databases such as ERIC were available for unlimited and unconditional use on a low-cost purchase or annual subscription basis. This was an effective way to maximize the availability of that information and was often held up by the search services as a model contract if the objective was to get the widest possible distribution of the data. A few databases (e.g., LEXIS) were built by the search services themselves, but this was rare. Most files for the commercial services were acquired by means of license agreements.

License agreements generally called for a specified use of a particular file over a specified number of years. Agreements covered issues such as the duration of the agreement, method of accounting for payments owed to the database producer (e.g., annual fee, royalty on connect hours used or output records provided, or combinations thereof), content of reporting to the producer (e.g., number of hours and output records provided, details of which record numbers were retrieved during the current reporting period, users' demographic characteristics, institutional identification, and full mailing addresses), geographic constraints on file use (e.g., U.S. users only, or worldwide except for Canada), and exclusivity (e.g., online exclusivity in the United States, nonexclusive worldwide).

Commercial U.S. online services were prohibited by law ("restraint of trade") from working together in their mutual interests regarding database licensing. However, database suppliers (at least nonprofits) and users felt less obliged by these conditions, and often worked together to discuss their issues and problems in licensing databases to the batch and online services. Much of the information that we have today about licensing practices is from the printed proceedings of database supplier affinity groups. For example, as early as 1971, the proceedings (*Summary of proceedings*) of ASIDIC meetings included a record of working sessions on: (1) interactions between database producers and processing centers; and (2) recommendations to tape suppliers on pricing structures for files, and data rights and copyright statements. NFAIS had meetings on these topics in the 1970s and 1980s, even publishing handbooks and sample contracts (Bremner and Miller 1987). European database suppliers had the same kinds of discussions at meetings of their counterpart organizations such as EUSIDIC. The ICSU/AB (International Conference on Scientific Unions/Abstracting Board) even published guidelines for cooperation between database producers and online services (Poyen 1976).

As part of the input processing to load a file online during the 1970s, a search service usually took records from a magnetic tape supplied in the producer's format and converted the records to a standard internal ("intermediate") format used by that search service for its processing programs (e.g., index building, output display formatting). Later, more use was made of direct data transmission instead of tape shipments. The producer's source tape and the resulting search service intermediate format tape were then sent to offsite storage after the initial file loading and all later update processing. This resulted in a significant amount of offsite archive storage, but it was needed as backup in the event that a file had to be reloaded because of a system crash or other problem.

Most database producers were reluctant to change their tape formats. Sometimes a producer, however, made unannounced changes to its format, which caused much consternation to a search service. It necessitated diverting programmers away from other projects in order to modify quickly the input conversion program in time to make a regularly scheduled file update run for that database. As a producer changed record and tape formats over the years, the search service was required to make corresponding changes to its conversion program and the resulting intermediate format tape. Thus the search service had a normalized database on tape that was independent of the producer format changes over time.

In the case of the archived DIALOG intermediate files, they became the archive database of choice for many producers. Surprising as it may seem, many producers did not have good archive copies of their own databases. Some lost or even threw away their archive copies. Bourne recalled several times at DIALOG when producers asked for tape copies of parts or all of their database because they could not find them, or when they could not read their own records. One particularly galling instance was a producer's request for a copy of the DIALOG archive intermediate file tapes to use to load the file on a competitor's online service.

Personnel Hiring

Each search service has interesting stories about how they hired and trained their first customer service and marketing staffs. All of them started with virtually no one experienced in these functions; the developers themselves typically performed the first customer service and marketing tasks. Most of those who survived, however, did so because they quickly realized the value of having staff specifically hired and trained for these functions.

For the first few years, DIALOG marketing was done by Bob Donati in New York and Richard

("Rick") Caputo in Washington, DC, both of whom worked with no secretarial support. Caputo especially complained that he could not keep up with all the inquiries being made, and Summit was receiving complaints that calls to the Washington office were not being returned. To illustrate his predicament, Caputo festooned an entire office wall with pink call slips, taping each one to the next. Finally aware of Caputo's overload, Lockheed hired Fran Spigai in 1976 to do full-time marketing for DIALOG. She did not report to Summit; she worked under Lockheed's marketing manager. Still, she had no secretarial support.

The first staff members performed all the customer service and marketing functions of writing database documentation and user manuals, answering telephones, and giving demonstrations, without specific job classifications or job titles. For example, from 1973 to 1975 at Lockheed, all customer support in Palo Alto was provided by one person, Francis Grant, whose generic title, "technical information specialist," was the same as other Research Lab staff members. Most online searching was done by a few individuals who required little training or support. Summit (1980b, 62) noted, "I remember the shock I felt when she indicated she needed an assistant." In mid-1975, Grant left and was replaced by Thomas Crawford, who was hired partly because of his background in physics and chemistry, partly for experience as a trainer at NAL, and also because he had a degree in library science, which was seen as increasingly important in providing appropriate customer services for the many subscribers who were librarians.

Although DIALOG had only about 250 subscribers at the time that Crawford was hired, the workload in answering questions, providing demonstrations and training, and writing documentation was enormous. In his first month on the job, the backlog for training sessions required Crawford to be on the road, out of the Palo Alto office, all but three days. He needed help, and within a year he was able to hire two assistants. He wanted staff with degrees in biology, physics, chemistry, engineering, and business, so they would be knowledgeable about the content of databases in those areas. Over the next few years, he hired staff with just those backgrounds. However, Crawford also insisted that his staff have a certain "look in their eye," a look that meant intelligence, enthusiasm, and resourcefulness. Thus, even though her background was in art history and library science, the first person he hired was Anne Hubbard (later, Caputo)[1] because she had the right sort of "look."

As she worked on her degree in library science, Caputo envisioned a career in an art museum library. Her only exposure to information technology was in a class taught by Eleanor Montague, who in addition to teaching worked at Stanford on the BALLOTS project. Montague arranged for a live in-class demonstration of DIALOG by Barbara West, who worked for the Lockheed marketing staff (not for Summit's operation). When West arrived with her portable terminal, she tried to log in but discovered that the system was down to permit the loading of new files. Caputo (1987) remembered:

So West called Kim Graham, the DIALOG computer operator, and said, 'I need ten minutes of access time, can you bring it up for at least ten minutes?' He did, and at the end of the ten minutes it went down again and that was the end of that. I thought, what incredible power she must have, to be able to call in and say, 'Turn this on for ten minutes for this class demonstration.' There were no other demonstrations in class. Online was considered a future thing; it was not presented as something you need to know when you get out there and have a job, or something you need to have application for right now.

Other than a field trip to view BALLOTS at Stanford, that exposure in Montague's class was the only computer experience Caputo had in library school.

When she was getting close to graduating in late 1975, Caputo's professor, Marty West, asked her if she had a job lined up. She answered that no one in the class did. Asked if she were interested in an advertised opening at Lockheed Retrieval Service, she replied that she was not. West told her not to be stupid; this was an opportunity to get in on the ground floor of something big. At the very least an interview required her to write a résumé, think about the interview process, and practice for future interviews. West insisted on calling Tom Crawford and setting up an interview, whether Caputo wanted it or not. So Caputo reluctantly went along with the plan. In 1987 she described the day of her interview:

I got in my little VW Beetle and drove up to Palo Alto. As it happened, on the day of my interview the Stanford students were picketing outside the gates of the facility, shouting 'Merchants of death!' They were marching back and forth and heckling people who were driving in. This was traumatic to say the least. I parked in the lower parking lot, walked through the hecklers, and when I tried to enter the building, the security staff grilled me like I was going into a military defense facility. Finally Tom [Crawford] came out to meet me. It appeared that he was interested in hiring a librarian, someone who could say 'ready reference' and understand what that meant, and who could talk in reassuring civilian terms about online, someone who was not a techie type who used jargon that customers would not understand. He wanted a computer virgin—someone without any preconceived habits—bad or otherwise. He did not want me to have any skills formed at all; he wanted me to learn these on site. He was also looking for a woman, because they did not have any other than Barbara West, who was not a direct employee anyway. He was looking for someone who had teaching experience, and I had been a high school teacher at some point in my career, and someone who had public speaking skills. I had put on my résumé that I had been on the high school debate championship team in Oregon. He told me later, that clinched it—that was the single most important skill to be had. The fact that I knew nothing from a *use* point of view was not important. Roger [Summit] came in during the interview and asked if I minded travel, and whether I could drive a car, where did I live, how far was my commute, did I mind traveling on an airplane, and did I have children—things you are not supposed to ask anymore. They were logistical questions, really pertinent questions, as it turned out, but nothing to do with my subject knowledge or background. It lasted about five minutes and then he left. Tom told me I would be making 10K on this job. I did not know what a 'K' was! I had no idea and I was not going to ask him. That night I called Eleanor Montague and she told me it meant $10,000.

Years later, Crawford confirmed that her debating team championship was indeed critical in making the job offer. When she graduated from San Jose State University library school, Caputo was one of only three in her class who had positions lined up (the other jobs were in Cutbank, Montana, and Weeping Willow, Alaska). Her classmates were envious of her exciting opportunity at Lockheed, as if she were "being elected to go to the moon with NASA!" Crawford (1987) relayed that the other person that he hired about the same time was Linda Erickson, who was much quieter than Caputo, but "with a really nitpicky mind," well suited to writing documentation and to "picking a database apart and seeing if, in fact, it was up on the system the way it was supposed to be." Caputo was hired because of her debating skills, which transformed into an ability to perform in training and marketing sessions. Erickson was hired for her "nitpicky" mind. Yet another reason cited for hiring was attractive appearance. When the Information Bank hired Sally Bachelder as a marketing representative, a senior-level Times executive, who had not yet met her, "had but a single question concerning her qualifications. 'Is she pretty?'" (Pemberton 1983, 10).

Lockheed was not the only online service looking for staff with special qualities; during the period of rapid expansion in the mid-seventies, all the search services were looking for excellent staff. Many of them were spotted in the audience at training sessions. They had to be quick, enthusiastic, and willing to commit to a grueling work pace.

Marketing the New Services

Surveying Potential Users

When everything—software, hardware, databases, communications networks, staff—was in place (sometimes even *before* it was all in place), the systems and services needed to be sold to potential users. Both for-profit and not-for-profit online searching services had to spread the message of the value of online retrieval as well as to educate users about how to take advantage of it. Marketing the online search services involved different activities and decisions, including advertising, designing logos, developing subscriber lists, giving demonstrations, signing customer contracts, and distributing brochures. A basic marketing tool, however, was to survey the potential for online before the service was established. Recall how Isotta had sent a team to ten European countries to speak to potential users of the ESRO/RECON service in ten different languages. Witness Cuadra's questionnaire fiasco when he tried to assess the potential for his SDC Search Service. A similar testing of the waters was done at Battelle before BASIS was fully developed. John Murdock formed a marketing group to travel around the United States, conducting interviews in the hopes of discovering whether anyone needed online retrieval. The group discovered that few potential users had terminals and, further, that few could imagine needing such a service. The group concluded that no market for online services existed. However, Murdock, like Cuadra when he received little response from his survey, refused to accept the results. Like Cuadra, he decided people do not know whether they will want something until after it is available. Murdock recalled (1990): "What I learned is that when you are going with something that is completely new, that people have never been exposed to, you cannot, even in a lengthy interview, get an intelligent answer with respect to marketing questions. You cannot measure whether there will be a market based on interviews."

Mark Bayer also discovered resistance from potential users of LEXIS; he found it hard to convince the public that online was going to be much better than print indexes. He encountered few people who were receptive initially to the idea of online searching. A lot of marketing was in fact accomplished not by marketing representatives, but by word-of-mouth persuasion from the few pioneer users to their colleagues.

Even some library school faculty felt that online had limited promise. Not all shared the vision of Marty West as she coaxed her student into a job interview at Lockheed. For example, Rutgers University professor Susan Artandi spoke at a conference about the small growth potential of online: "After all," she asked, "How many bibliographies can the world absorb?" Sitting in the audience, Tom Crawford instantly regretted his recent decision to join Lockheed Retrieval Service. Perhaps he would have been reassured if he had known that Lord Kelvin, president of London's Royal Society, said in 1904, "Radio has no future." Or that closer to home, Thomas Watson, an IBM executive, predicted in 1958: "I think there is a world market for about five computers." Soothsaying is chancy, even for the experts.

As the services became established, the two most commonly used marketing tools were printed documentation and personal communication.

Documentation and Promotional Materials

One form of reaching potential users was through printed advertisements in professional journals. We have seen already examples of how Lockheed and SDC used these media, beginning about 1973. The actual number of ads that appeared was small and likely did not have much impact on readers who were not otherwise exposed to online services.

On the other hand, printed materials, in the form of manuals, newsletters, and database descriptions, aimed at those who already were subscribers, had a large educational impact. Even these, though, got off to a rough start. For example, in the first issue of DIALOG's newsletter, *Chronolog* (May 1973), the prose was clumsy: "Keep in mind that a hierarchy of laxity prevails in full testing qualifications." In addition, the quality of advice proffered was questionable. For example, "Is truncating good practice? No. Truncating slows down response time and often does not benefit the user." In a late 1973 issue of *Chronolog*, the searching tip was still simplistic:

COMMAND STRIPS

Some of our users are not using command strips and committing the command symbols to memory. It is highly recommended, if you are one of these searchers, that you contact our office for a command strip and mount it on your terminal.

You will probably find that you can save time by being able to refer to the strip, especially after being away from your terminal for a few days.

Sometimes user documentation was written to develop or maintain an advantage for the search service rather than provide a service to users. In the previous *Chronolog* example, the truncation command consumed a great deal more computer resources (CPU and working memory) than a single-term lookup or logical operation, and could have the effect of dragging down response time for all searchers. It was this kind of resource constraint that inhibited some services from initially providing a truncation feature and also required some systems to impose a limit on the number of word stems included in a truncation search. The same problem happened when searchers selected large sets, such as all records within a range of publication years. Whereas it might be conceptually simpler for a searcher to formulate a search and restrict a subject search by directly specifying a range of publication years or language, some search services discouraged this practice in their documentation and instruction because of the resource demands it placed on the system.

The search service newsletter was an effective means to keep users informed and interested in continuing developments, from both a technical and a proprietary self-interest point of view. Newsletters were the channels by which most users received notice of new features and databases. However, the newsletters were also a marketing tool for both the search service and database producers, with the marketing staffs of both types of organizations trying to get their messages into the newsletters. Some producers worked diligently, like good publicists for public figures, to get positive messages in as many newsletter issues as possible. The editors played a continuing balancing act to keep the producers' "press releases" in line. The newsletters were also used as a platform for annual reports, promises of things to come, and missionary statements by search service managers.

Direct mailing by the search services and the database producers was another means of connecting with customers. This involved inserting printed material with a newsletter mailing, but sometimes it entailed a separate mailing. During the 1970s, direct mailing became a contentious issue between the search services and producers. The issue can be stated succinctly as "Whose customers are they?" Some producers wanted to know who their customers were, including details of institution name, full mailing address, and personal name of the person receiving the bill or the person most responsible for online searching, as well as the volume of use of the producer's database during each month of usage. Most commercial search services were reluctant to disclose these data, based on previous bad experiences when they had released the identity of specific database users to those producers. Examples of real problems that occurred were (1) a database supplier (e.g., ISI, INSPEC) switching to become a competing online search service; (2) a mailing by a producer to users to promote use of their database on competing online services; (3) a follow-up mailing of marketing materials for print products or other products unrelated to online use, which the online customers considered junk mail; and (4) privacy issues for a customer—"I just got a call from this database supplier who noted that I used their file for twelve hours last month. How did they know that? I thought my searching was a privileged communication between myself and the search service." BRS capitulated to the producers on this issue, as a means of distinguishing themselves from other search services, but most commercial services worked out a compromise approach in which the search service prescreened and approved the material to be mailed, then sent the mailing label data to an independent labeling/mailing institution for the actual mailing.

Database guides were another form of documentation prepared for users by search services, usually in cooperation with the producers. Some of these were simple one- or two-page guides, but the ones for more complex databases could be one hundred pages or more. Some producers prepared and issued their own guides, but this got complicated when a database was loaded in different ways on many different online services.

User guides were another major point of contact with users. The manuals needed constant attention by good writers to keep them up-to-date. As systems and services got larger and more experienced, user manuals started to take on an encyclopedic appearance. Sometimes authors of manuals were accused of having written the text in legal jargon to support the rejection of user credit requests: for example, "We can't give you a credit for that charge because the manual says on page _ that simply turning off your terminal will not disconnect you from the service."

Some search services developed general aids to assist in searching databases. Some of these went beyond what individual database producers provided. For example, in the mid-1970s, DIALOG periodically issued a product called DIALIST that was almost the offline equivalent of an EXPAND command, with an alphabetical listing of terms (including the misspelled terms) and their posting counts. Instead of listing the terms in a single database, however, DIALIST provided terms for four different groups of related files, such as the following from the Engineering and Technology group:

INDEX TERM	NTIS	COMPENDEX	INSPEC	ISMEC
AUTOMOBILE	14			
AUTOMOBILBAU	22	2		
AUTOMOBILE	1436	4489	372	335
AUTOMOBILE ACCIDENTS	9			
AUTOMOBILE ALTERNATOR			2	
AUTOMOBILE BODIES	108	2	2	2
AUTOMOBILE BODY		3	3	

The product was bulky and thus available only in microfiche form. The intent was to provide a tool to identify databases of interest and to choose appropriate search terms. It was also a helpful tool for database producers. Considering the effort that went into producing this product, and the possible improvements in searching efficiency, it was not particularly expensive ($250 for the Engineering and Technology set). It was cumbersome to use, however, requiring 204 microfiche for the full Engineering and Technology set, and another 294 microfiche for the full Sciences set; thus it was not used much. More flexible online equivalents replaced it in later years.

Another marketing challenge was promotional materials, including details such as appropriate logos. At SDC, not everyone was thrilled with the logo chosen; the customer services staff secretly nicknamed it "Flying Diaper"(see figure 10.1). SDC staff were not the only ones concerned about the image a logo conveyed; the first logo used by the Lockheed Retrieval Service was the object of derision by its own staff. Conceived by Summit, who called it "thinking head" (see figure 10.2), the logo was dubbed "Roger's man" or "Alka Seltzer man" behind his back—the staff thought that the silhouette of a head with a magnetic tape superimposed and a few dots was silly and unappealing. After Fran Spigai joined Lockheed's marketing staff, she arranged for an outside company to design a new logo, one that expressed the spirit of a forward-looking computer company. The new design was a

Figure 10.1
"Flying Diaper": SDC's corporate logo. Reproduced from cover of *SDC Magazine*, March 1965.

Figure 10.2
"Thinking Head": early logo for DIALOG. Reproduced from May 1976 issue of *Chronolog*.

mathematical infinity sign, except that it had open ends, to suggest an open-ended future. DIALOG staff liked it no better than "thinking head." Some were outraged that several thousand dollars had been spent on the design; they thought the money could have been much better spent elsewhere. Crawford (1987) recalled: "Everybody sat around looking at it and finally I said, 'Well, if you turned it around a little bit, it might look like the stylized L that Lockheed uses and a modern script D that DIALOG uses.' So everybody agreed we should turn it 45 degrees, and that was what we ended up with, with the L and D in blue and brown, to stand out more clearly."

Lockheed management hampered marketing for the DIALOG service during its early years by insisting that the venture use the same advertising firm that did the display advertising work for Lockheed ("if it's good enough for the L-1011, it's good enough for DIALOG") rather than an advertising firm that was more familiar with the DIALOG marketplace and technology. DIALOG senior managers were in a quandary in the mid-1970s regarding how or whether DIALOG's subsidiary relationship with Lockheed should be described. Should the Lockheed connection be *emphasized* (to ride the coattails of leading-edge technology and vision, and broad corporate experience and support), or *deemphasized* (because of some librarian customers' animosity to the Vietnam war and any implied Lockheed role as a "merchant of death")? After the Lockheed scandal of 1975–1976, DIALOG staff wanted to deemphasize the Lockheed name and emphasize DIALOG instead. A combination of approaches was used on a case-by-case basis. Lockheed upper management forced them, however, to continue to print the "ugly" (Summit's characterization) Lockheed logo on all documentation.

DIALOG marketing was hampered also by Summit's insistence that customers or potential customers pay for such basic marketing materials as the first DIALOG database catalog. The charge was only a dime apiece, but it was a nuisance for both staff and customers. Spigai was further frustrated in trying to sell subscriptions to the rapidly growing service because Lockheed kept running out of passwords. The system had been designed to work with a specified maximum number of user accounts, and this number was (as with file numbers) underestimated and required reprogramming to accommodate larger numbers of customer accounts. On at least one occasion, all allowable customer account numbers were used up, and no new customer accounts and passwords could be issued for several months until the reprogramming was completed. Events like these were marketing nightmares.

Personal Communication

Search service staffs spent a considerable amount of time in communicating with current subscribers and potential users. The representatives maintained exhibit booths at professional conferences, made presentations to professional groups, organized user meetings, and traveled to user sites to provide training. Whenever possible, they gave live demonstrations of the operating systems in order to show that online retrieval was indeed rapid, flexible, and thorough. One participant, Edward Housman, testified to the usefulness of the demonstrations in his introduction to a 1973 ARIST chapter (221): "This reviewer cannot... claim to be exhaustive in covering the 1972 literature. The reviewer has, however, sifted through hundreds of references, discovered by use of the Lockheed DIALOG and IBM STAIRS... online literature search systems during their demonstration at the 1972 ASIS Annual Meeting."

> **1974 Milestone**
>
> DIALOG was the first online search service to establish a 1-800 toll-free telephone number for customer service.

Toll-free numbers quickly became an extremely important personal connection between search services and their clientele. Lockheed established the first 1-800 number in 1974; SDC Search Service made a toll-free number available in June 1975. Virtually all the search services followed suit.

> **1975 Milestone**
>
> LEXIS was the first online search service to establish discounts for online access that was part of an academic institution's instructional activities.

Many search services identified students as an important target audience. One of Mead's pioneering marketing activities was its support of LEXIS terminals and subscriptions for law school students and faculty—for use of the entire system and databases, not just with practice or training files. Mead also offered free training to law school students while they were summer interns. It was the first online service to provide such an extensive subsidy to academic use and the training of professionals entering the labor market. This had been done earlier for the OBAR system, but not on such a regular basis and large scale. This not only resulted in more people entering the profession with LEXIS searching skills, but it also was an implied product endorsement by a large number of law schools—which helped win its acceptance by practicing lawyers. Although Lockheed did not follow Mead's free academic service approach, it instituted a Classroom Instruction Program that gave discounts for online access that was part of classroom instruction in a library school, as well as training manuals designed for graduate students. Examples produced by Bourne (1976a, 1977) were described in chapter 9.

Pemberton (1982) reported that he used a different marketing approach in the early days of the Information Bank. He experimented with a strategy of high-level executive presentations involving senior *Times* executives and their counterparts from selected Fortune 500 companies. Mead marketed primarily to attorneys and senior partners at large law firms, not to librarians.

Marketing included signing up customers. The latter often meant waiting until an organization's billing cycle came around or until the librarians could get their terminals. The emphasis was on reaching librarians, not the subject specialists served by the librarians, although that approach was later modified to try to reach the subject specialists who were a good match with the search service's strengths. Marketing was made more challenging for some representatives by the fact that upper management did not inform them about key financial data, such as whether or not the online service was earning any money. For example, no one at SDC Search Service knew about profits or losses, not even the manager, Carlos Cuadra. SDC upper management continually harassed Search Service staff members about needing to increase their efforts in order to make a profit, when in reality the company had been making a profit ever since the second year of operation. At DIALOG, Summit kept basic marketing, revenue, and cost statistics a guarded secret, not just from the database producers, as Kollegger had complained, but from the DIALOG staff as well.

Another potentially valuable marketing secret was lists of subscribers, but not everyone was eager to acquire the lists of other search services. For example, when SIA terminated its online operation in 1974, Landau offered to sell its subscriber list of fifty names to Lockheed. Summit declined to buy; he wanted to develop his own. SDC, however, bought the list.

As with training, producers did some marketing of online services, usually extolling the general virtues of online searching, but discussing and demonstrating their database in particular. Some producers devoted as much time and money on marketing online service as some search services did, and some were sophisticated about their marketing strategies (Elias 1979). One activity that search services and database producers shared, and that was both marketing and training/customer services, was the annual online users meeting. These started as opportunities to tell customers about new features and databases and obtain some feedback, and expanded to be opportunities for database producers to describe their products and new features on that search service, and to obtain useful contacts and feedback. It also grew to accommodate a range of issues of interest to searchers (e.g., how to market and promote online service within their own organizations, fee vs. free services and cost-recovery). Lawrence (1997) remembered the 1974 DIALOG users meeting well, not because of anything associated with DIALOG, but because it was the time of President Nixon's resignation: "Some of us rushed back from dinner to hear the speech in the evening, while looking out the window at the Capitol. The next day, the hotel set up a TV in the hall so we could watch his departure."

The TYMNET telecommunications service also had users meetings. The first TYMNET user group meeting was held in Davis McCarn's backyard, about 1973, with five people in attendance. As described in chapter 6, McCarn was the person at NLM responsible for getting the TYMNET service started with the online bibliographic search services. The user group's informal name was THUG, which had a variable meaning—TYMNET Happy/Harassed/Hostile User Group—depending on the circumstances and mood at the time. The TYMNET host nonetheless always saw to it that group members enjoyed great food at the meetings.

One objective of users meetings was to establish a bonding or brand loyalty. An additional way to do this was to involve users in the review, planning, and operations of the service. This proved to be a good mechanism to learn of user needs and gripes. SUNY BCN and its spin-off, BRS, did this particularly well with their formal user advisory groups. BRS had two groups from its beginning, a Database Subcommittee (concerned with the handling of existing databases and recommendations for new ones), and a Technical Subcommittee (concerned with search enhancements and software features) (Gupta 1981; Van Camp 1992). Members of the BRS Advisory Group seemed to be especially strong and loyal advocates for BRS.

Competition

Between 1972 and 1976, most of the search services that were emerging as industry leaders naturally were competing with each other for customers. The exceptions were services targeted to unique clientele such as LEXIS, which was aimed at lawyers. For the rest, the level of competition was intense but not unfriendly—it was based on price, features, number of files, response time, quality of documentation, training, and customer service. Lockheed DIALOG and SDC Search Service staffs had a strong sense of competition with each other, but they viewed it as a fair fight with a worthy opponent. They encountered each other at conferences and training sites, especially in Europe where training sites were few. Occasionally, they even attended each other's training sessions, and they respected each other's talents. We saw earlier how database producers talked to each other about how they collectively dealt with search services. However, in order to avoid any possible suggestion of search service cooperation or collusion on market matters, DIALOG senior staff were counseled not to meet with any SDC staff unless it was in the presence of a third party. This was a burdensome requirement that hindered the development of what might have been some good personal relationships. In any case, the pioneers believed that the market was so large, so unsaturated, and so unenlightened about the potential for online systems that everyone in the industry had a chance to build a clientele, and everyone needed to contribute to the enormous task of educating the public about online.

In contrast with the high mobility of professional workers between Web-based and e-commerce companies of today, there was an unequivocal practice in the 1970s of not hiring staff from competitors. This attitude grew out of the competitive environment, a preference for "loyal" employees, and concerns that a prospective employee who would leave one online service had already demonstrated a possible inclination to leave your service, along with some of your proprietary information. The practice continued until the early 1980s.

Caputo (1987) recalled that by 1975, many in the industry, including DIALOG staff, viewed SDC Search Service as the leader, with DIALOG scrambling to catch up. At SDC, Cuadra (1978, 8) viewed the competition among commercial search services as a positive way to advance the quality of service for everyone: "Whenever one system offers a new feature or service condition that is attractive to users, the other systems must provide comparable features or services or risk losing some of their clientele to their competitors. The result of such competition has been the rapid growth of a number of important features or services."

This affirmative public stance belied, however, the bitterness that both SDC and Lockheed staffs felt toward the new competition from BRS beginning in late 1976. Lockheed and SDC were enraged by what they considered to be BRS price misrepresentation; BRS was not just claiming to be a little cheaper, BRS was arguing that Lockheed and SDC were charging $50 an hour, whereas BRS was charging "only $25 an hour, plus royalties." Many customers did not pay much attention to the "plus royalties" to see what the true cost comparison was. The BRS marketing strategy included generating and maintaining a feeling among BRS subscribers of belonging to a special club, whose members who were against the "big guys" of the huge corporations such as Lockheed and SDC. From the beginning, BRS positioned themselves as "the good guys in the white hats"—a genuine alternative to the existing for-profit services. They were careful to give the impression that they were something other than an ordinary commercial service; in fact, many people in the early days did not realize that they were a for-profit commercial venture. BRS fostered the impression that only BRS was an advocate for users. Crawford called it a "very clever marketing plan, very well carried out, but fundamentally unfair." *Library Journal* picked up on the competition and reported it as a "price war" ("Database vendors" 1977).

BRS claims of "big guys" against "little guys" was especially stinging for Lockheed staff, who were still defensive about the scandals of 1975–1976, and sensitive to the claim that they represented "merchants of death," and who in fact *were* "little guys"—the DIALOG search service went through the same difficult start-up process as many other small companies. Receiving no initial capitalization, it started and grew with a small and overworked staff, it paid its own way out of earned revenues, and it worked hard for every bit of growth it realized. SDC Search Service similarly went through its own difficult start-up phase with little support from its own institution.

SDC vs. NLM

Another form of intense competition was between the commercial and government sectors. The conflict is best illustrated by a case that ended up in May 1975 as a suit in the U.S. Court of Claims, petition no. 164-75. The story received little if any attention in the public media; we have synthesized the various versions relayed to us in interviews and communications with Cuadra (1990, 1997), Black (1996), McCarn (1987), Koenig (1987), and Cummings (1997).

One root of the tale sprouted in fall 1971, when NLM awarded to SDC a multi-million-dollar contract to create the entire MEDLARS II system (see chapter 6). As part of the total system to be delivered, the contract specified online retrieval, which SDC was able to fulfill almost immediately by modifying its ORBIT software to create ELHILL. ELHILL supported the NLM database, called MEDLINE in its online incarnation. NLM adopted ELHILL and began online service in 1972. We have seen already how the popularity of the service snowballed, even after NLM introduced modest user fees in 1973 in a futile attempt to dampen users' enthusiasm. Another strategy to manage the allocation of limited computer resources was to be selective in allowing access: NLM initially refused to allow for-profit organizations (e.g., pharmaceutical companies) to become subscribers. Also, NLM at this time did not permit individual physicians or researchers to obtain their own accounts and passwords. MEDLINE access was restricted to hospitals and academic institutions. Because SDC continued to offer MEDLINE service in parallel with NLM, PMA members went to SDC for MEDLINE access. Judith Wanger of SDC spent much time on the road during this period, conducting on-site MEDLINE training for pharmaceutical companies.

Unlike NLM, however, SDC had to charge for online access in order to at least recover the costs of making the file available.[2] A barter had been arranged in which NLM determined SDC's charges to PMA users. NLM used the credited SDC revenues to reduce SDC's charges to NLM for the services (AIM-TWX, MEDLARS) that SDC performed for NLM (Cuadra 1990). Thus SDC charged PMA members $45 per hour during 1974 for access to the most current two to three years of MEDLINE. To complement the online service, SDC ran backfile searches in a batch mode. A PMA librarian sent search formulations to Black at SDC in Santa Monica who rekeyed them after prime time and ran them against the backfile tapes.

SDC acquired its copy of MEDLINE not from NLM, but from PMA. To understand this arrangement, we must trace another root of the story back to the mid-sixties, when PMA's central library staff began indexing the drug literature for NLM. In return, NLM gave PMA a copy of the entire database on tape. Since PMA was not prepared to use the magnetic tape to provide online searching, PMA approached SDC, volunteering the tape for unrestricted public use in exchange for online access by PMA's membership at a reduced rate. SDC was happy to comply and was able to load the tape without delay, since SDC had experience in running MEDLINE for NLM. Other SDC users accessed MEDLINE, but the PMA companies enjoyed a lower searching rate because of the donation of the tape and because they committed to a certain minimum number of hours of online use each month.

At SDC, the first indication of trouble was NLM's request to SDC for a list of names and addresses of users of SDC's MEDLINE, for the purpose of facilitating their transition to NLM's own system. As interpreted with alarm by SDC, this meant: "Tell us who your customers are, so we can offer service to them for free." As the date for the end of SDC's service bureau support for NLM loomed, SDC had to decide whether to continue offering PMA companies access to MEDLINE, by means of the MEDLINE files to which PMA was entitled. Another sign of something amiss came at the end of 1974 while SDC was negotiating a contract with PMA to continue the service for PMA members through 1975. PMA delayed sending the contract back. What SDC did not know then was that the large pharmaceutical companies were incensed that NLM, although purporting to allow major biomedical research institutions access to its online service, did not consider for-profit companies to be in that group. Koenig (1987), who was at Pfizer at the time and also the vice chair of the PMA Science Information Section, recalled, "NLM called us the 'fat cats' of the pharmaceutical industry, but we regarded ourselves as major biomedical research institutions." Consequently, when MEDLINE was first announced, he made a phone call to NLM and asked how to sign up. It became clear that no one at NLM had any idea how to handle his question. After being passed to seven or eight different staff, Koenig reached a senior NLM official. He was told that the pharmaceutical industry would get access only after NLM had fulfilled its obligation to serve all public institutions first. Koenig's desire to obtain online access to the database was based on his own experience in batch searching the copy of MEDLARS that Pfizer received from PMA: "We had the biggest computer in a billion-dollar company, and MEDLARS was run every other Thursday night. If you blew it, there was no way you could get another 12 hours of computer time. You rewrote that search and waited two weeks for it to run again."

Koenig, Robert Cuddihy, and others from the Science Information section of PMA were particularly annoyed over what they perceived to be a competitive disadvantage for American companies versus foreign-owned pharmaceutical companies in the Netherlands, the United Kingdom, and West Germany. The medical associations in those countries had the same arrangement with NLM that PMA did: to exchange indexing for a copy of the database. In those countries, however, the pharmaceutical industry was given preferential, government-subsidized MEDLARS access, ahead of academic research institutions, thus creating the situation in which the British part of Pfizer had cheaper access to NLM tapes than the American division did. Further, PMA risked being denied access altogether if SDC could not afford to continue offering MEDLINE. So the Science Information group asked PMA lawyers to telephone the staffs of U.S. Congress members, who in turn called Cummings at NLM and asked why it was that taxpaying American pharmaceutical companies were not receiving the same kind of subsidies that their British, German, and Dutch competitors were. Apparently the telephoning strategy worked; Cummings allowed pharmaceutical companies to become NLM MEDLINE subscribers. In return, NLM received from Congress more funding to increase the number of ports in order to accommodate more subscribers—which lent some relief to NLM's struggles with frequent equipment upgrades in response to growing demands and degraded system performance.

NLM's announcement that it was now willing to offer unrestricted MEDLINE service (at $6 per hour) to all PMA members (compared to SDC's higher commercial price of $45 per hour that was set by NLM) meant that PMA member companies no longer had to use the SDC service. They also no longer had to abstract and index the drug literature for NLM in return for the tapes, and PMA canceled that arrangement with NLM. This unexpected and damaging NLM action plucked a large customer and revenue base away from the fledgling commercial service.

In spite of losing the PMA users, SDC decided that it wanted to continue to offer service with NLM's file. SDC asked NLM to continue providing it, which NLM refused to do. Suddenly, SDC no longer could get MEDLINE update tapes from NLM or PMA. Not only was SDC trying to compete against NLM's subsidized service, it now faced the prospect of not being able to obtain copies of that government database.

Left out in the cold, SDC tried to obtain the tapes under FOIA (Freedom of Information Act) by offering to pay the incremental costs of copying them. NLM refused. At that point, the president of SDC decided to sue NLM. SDC programmers and managers who had labored on the MEDLARS II development contract were alarmed and outraged at the prospect of alienating their major customer and close colleagues. Nevertheless, SDC's president insisted on the suit, which covered two points. The first allegation charged NLM with breach of contract for contract NIH 71-4724. This was the MEDLARS II development contract, which had a clause giving NLM a copy of the ELHILL software but prohibited NLM from operating their system as a service bureau, in competition with SDC. The second complaint was that under FOIA, NLM should give SDC the tapes for only the costs of copying.

The first part of the lawsuit failed because NLM lawyers successfully argued that NLM had a specific charter from Congress to provide access to the biomedical literature, and MEDLINE was a means to fulfill their charter—and that is what they were doing, not running a "service bureau." The second part was thrown out of court when the judge ruled that a magnetic tape was not a record as designated by Congress in the FOIA. Cummings (1997) expanded on NLM's stance in the lawsuits: "NLM's position was based on the fact that it paid SDC to develop ELHILL, and that it paid for the creation and maintenance of its own database, MEDLINE; therefore, SDC should not use both without NLM authorization." At that point SDC management realized that it could not win and the suit was only generating ill will at NLM. SDC quit the entire case and was forced to drop MEDLINE from its service. Almost overnight it lost about 40 percent of its business when the PMA users of MEDLINE moved to NLM. The outcome was a serious blow for SDC, and nearly caused its demise.

About a year later, Martha Williams alluded to the case of SDC versus NLM in a published analysis of the competition between commercial and government-subsidized online services. She concluded that government subsidization was dangerous because it gave an unfair competitive advantage that might lead to the curtailment of desirable data bases being offered by the private sector.[3] Further, even though the U.S. government had funded most of the research and development that fostered the growth of the commercial online industry, it was in danger of destroying those commercial organizations. In characterizing the government as the "goose," Williams (1977, 106) said, "Just as no one wants to kill the goose that laid the golden egg, it also seems unreasonable for the goose to kill its offspring." For its part, SDC Search Service took its lumps but did not die. The offspring moved quickly to fill the void left by the loss of MEDLINE with other databases.

All of NLM's bilateral national agreements (chapter 9), and similar agreements by NASA and the DOE/AEC for their databases and regional partners, gave exclusive search service rights in exchange for indexing support in specific geographic regions, and had an adverse impact on the commercial online services. NLM, for example, prohibited any commercial U.S. online service from offering access to MEDLINE to users in any countries covered by NLM's national agreements (this was most of the world, including Europe). With these geographic licensing constraints and the severe price competition generated by its own subsidized online service, NLM controlled and protected its own market until 1982, when the geographic constraints were removed from the commercial services.

Providing Service Operations Behind the Scenes

Tiny "Giants"

From the public's point of view, the first few years of the online industry were an exciting time of constant changes and expansion in hardware, software, and services. When we look behind the scenes, we feel the same sense of excitement, but with the added dimensions of competition, overwork, and stress on the major players. For example, at DIALOG in the early days were few employees, and these were stretched thin. Everyone participated in all kinds of activities. At off-peak times the computer operators answered customer service calls, and, once a month, everyone formed an assembly line to stuff invoices into envelopes for mailing.

By the mid-seventies, a few of the search services, such as DIALOG, SDC Search Service, and LEXIS, had emerged as larger and more influential in the online industry; they were referred to as the "giants" (Harris 1988). In reality, however, none of them were very big. Because the staffs were so small, all duties were shared and even the top managers took an active role in the day-to-day operations. Caputo remembered being on the telephone responding to a customer complaint when Summit came in, listened for a while to her side, then yanked the telephone out of her hand and said, "I'm Roger Summit and I'm in charge here." When out-of-town trips were planned, schedules were so tight that staff had to be willing to stay and work until 2:00 or 3:00 a.m., getting materials ready to go. Caputo remembered it being "almost a religion."

Not only were staff budgets tight, staff offices were inadequate as well. Crawford was crammed into an office so small that he had to crawl through the kneehole of someone else's desk to get to his own. Computer rooms were relatively small too: before she went to work for Lockheed, Caputo imagined the computer operation to be "a gigantic thing," but actually it was a "dinky little computer room." However, the same was not true of SDC's computer facility. It was a large operation to support its government contract work, and a security clearance was required even to get in the building that housed the computer center.

The 1-800 Numbers

The toll-free 1-800 numbers were immensely popular with users. Inside the search services, however, the picture was different. When Caputo began working at Lockheed in 1976, the 1-800 number had already been established and her first call came right away. Inauspiciously, the caller was trying to reach a venereal disease hotline. Fortunately, this call was *not* the harbinger of things to come. The calls trickled in at first, allowing staff to work on documentation and training programs between calls. Quickly, though, the 1-800 idea at all the search services took off and soon the phones were ringing constantly, including calls to one service from the users of another service—Caputo at DIALOG, for example, received calls for SDC Search Service.[4] Staff expected to field routine questions again and again but could not help feeling peeved when users called in with stupid questions. At such times, overworked staff found it hard to resist countering with a smart remark. Caputo recalled a woman who called on the day before the Thanksgiving holiday and asked, "Can I use DIALOG in New Jersey the day after Thanksgiving?" Caputo retorted, "No, you cannot do it in New Jersey. Everywhere else, but not New Jersey!"

Hapless staff obliged to answer the toll-free numbers were plagued by online "groupies," who called in just for somebody sympathetic to talk to, sometimes several times a week. Groupies often felt isolated and misunderstood at their own workplaces, and trusted that the online services staff were sympathetic. These calls were not necessarily disagreeable, but the sheer volume was tiring and they peaked over the lunch hour so that staff could never go to lunch together, even for special occasions.

Customer Service Support

Search services provided a range of expected customer support such as training, question-answering, problem resolving, user documentation, account administration, and password control. Some producers likewise established service departments to assist online users of their databases. Support services extended to bits of unexpected assistance such as terminal messages from NLM to MEDLINE users about adverse weather conditions and subway construction problems in the Washington and Bethesda areas. Pauline Angione (1999a) recalled that while she was giving a live demonstration to an SDC training class, she received an online message from her boss (an early example of e-mail interruption); the class was amazed and kept asking how they did that.

Stories heard by customer service staff, and associated with password control problems and searcher mistakes circulated among the staffs as bits of pathos or laughter for the day. In the 1970s and later, as the costs of online searching escalated, particularly for the business and pharmaceutical files that had high royalty charges and sometimes large (e.g., $100 per record) output charges, it was increasingly possible to run up huge bills during the course of a single terminal session. Sometimes these large charges were inadvertent mistakes, and no doubt terrorized searchers when they logged off and saw the estimated total cost displayed on the terminal screen. The DIALOG Customer Services department received many phone calls from anguished searchers who, having just realized what they had done, wanted to stop the mailing of thousands of offline printouts and to request a credit. Early examples included:

• A searcher mistakenly gave a large offline print command, and then turned off the terminal, thinking that would cancel the printing.

• A searcher gave a TYPE ALL command to the wrong set number, realized the mistake, hit the BREAK key on the terminal and got no response, and so just shut off the terminal. Unfortunately, the terminal had recently been converted to an internal LAN, and it did not signal a disconnect. The result was a $3,000 bill for eleven hours of connect time and 3,200 output records.

• A searcher was using a terminal that went through her computer center's main frame when she realized she had issued an online TYPE command for the wrong set number and a large number of records. She called DIALOG and was told to turn off the modem. Her supervisor and the MIS staff member, however, were both on vacation and nobody could be found who knew how to turn off the mainframe modem. She turned off her terminal, but the original TYPE command had been received and processed; DIALOG continued to send the output to the user's computer center for *twenty-seven hours*. A *very* large bill resulted.

• An end user asked to have his password changed. He had written an article about the benefits of online searching, and had used some terminal output as an illustration. Unfortunately, his illustration included his password. He found out that he indeed had interested readers—they went out and used his password.

• Angione (1999a) recalled a situation she faced as manager of SDC's Field and Support section in Los Angeles. She took a call from a terrified customer in France—who had to wait through the time zones until the SDC office opened—and asked to have about 2,000 offline prints thrown out that she had requested by mistake.

Most online services issued goodwill credits for situations such as these. One of the major online services, however, did have a tough refund policy, which its president often stated succinctly: "We don't pay for dumbness."

Some customer service problems could be handled easily when the business and staff were small. For example, in early 1973 SDC was serving about sixty or seventy customers and had to adopt a new log-in procedure on short notice. It was possible then for the staff to divide up the customer list and begin calling at 5:00 a.m. PST to tell each of them about the new procedure (Cuadra 1976). That approach would have been impossible by the late 1970s.

Preparing Newsletters and Documentation

We have seen already that newsletters were not written skillfully in the beginning. The desktop publishing tools widely used today were not available then and staffs were learning writing and presentation skills on the job. A further complication was that copy for the newsletters had to be cleared with the legal departments of parent organizations. In addition to writing the copy, all staff members had to pitch in to prepare issues for mailing, which included addressing, stuffing, and sealing envelopes.

Another writing responsibility that had to be shared among all the customer service staff was database user documentation. Often staff members did not have enough time during the day to write documentation, so they worked on it at night. Even if they had time earlier in the day, they could not work at a terminal retrieving examples and illustrations because that would have impacted response time for customers. So they waited until evening when everyone else had logged off. For the first few years, no portable terminals were available for staff to take home for working evenings or weekends. When the first few portables became available, staff signed up to reserve them for overnight and weekend use. Telecommuting would have been useful here, but the technology did not yet support it. However, the portable terminals that training staffs had in the field were used to good advantage to send messages to the main office in a rudimentary e-mail fashion.

In addition to writing documentation for specific databases, search service staffs wrote and maintained various user manuals and quick reference guides and search aids. We saw earlier the example of Lockheed's DIALIST, a reference list of term posting counts for the subject index terms in each of several major files.

Hardware Problems and Solutions

Most online users today give hardware—computers and terminals—little thought. For users and search services in the seventies, however, equipment was a constant worry. The rapid growth of customers and databases meant that the demands on computer resources were always outpacing the capacity. For example, the DIALOG computer had to be upgraded every year, when the response time had degraded to an intolerable level. Because the total volume of online usage dropped to a much lower level during the Christmas holidays, this was the usual time chosen to close down the service for several days to replace, reinstall, and test new equipment and its operation with the existing DIALOG software. After the New Year, with the new computer, everyone was much happier.

SDC's experience in changing computers was not so pleasant. In the early seventies the Search Service used a Q-32, a military computer that was built to be extra reliable and that almost never crashed. When SDC changed to an IBM system, the new machines crashed much more often. Black (1987) commented on the Q-32:

> The equipment was unparalleled. It was built for the military. The Q-32 almost never crashed—it had redundant hardware all over the place. It would sometimes go in a HALT state which you might say was a semi-crash but it would last maybe 30 seconds and come back to life and you hadn't lost anything. But then the [IBM] 360 came along—constant crashes and things like that which had been almost unheard of previously.

Van Camp (1971) recorded what happened one morning when she tried to access AIM-TWX on the SDC computer in California from her terminal in Indiana. The log-in message said, "We may go down at any moment. We're having an earthquake." The earthquake did wipe out a hospital in Los Angeles, but did not interrupt online service.

In 1973, even with expanded computer facilities and increased online storage capacity, DIALOG could not afford to store all the data associated with all the records. When Psychological Abstracts was loaded in 1973, a stop list of 170 words was used, in an attempt to reduce the amount of storage required for the indexes (most major online systems now use a stop word list of 10 words or less). When SciSearch was first loaded in 1975, DIALOG management made the design decision in loading and updating the files to build online indexes to the cited references (i.e., the references cited in the source articles) but not to store the cited references for display purposes; furthermore, it limited the number of cited records indexed for each source citation, to a maximum of 256. This practice was not changed until years later. ISI's own concern for reducing the number of input keystrokes and printed index pages was manifest in its own practice before 1976 of truncating author surnames to fifteen characters; making it tough to search on certain authors' names (e.g., a searcher had to know that H. G. Vonfrankensteinmetz was searchable only as Vonfrankenstein.HG).

Large answer sets also caused online storage space problems. The design of most online search systems specifies that a certain amount of space be set aside and assigned for use as working online storage for individual searchers when they log in, to be used to store at least the final answer sets of retrieved record numbers, and maybe even the answer sets for the partial products of each intermediate search step. There may also be a restriction on the total number of record numbers that can be retrieved by a single search command. For example, in early 1976, the BIOSIS file with 1 million citations had eleven index terms or codes with so many postings (more than 85,000 records) that they could not be searched directly, and had to be searched indirectly by year-subsets. This limit on working storage usually went unnoticed until a searcher generated a larger answer set than could be contained in the assigned working space. In such cases, the system was likely to respond with an error message (e.g., "disk storage overflow") and require the searcher to start again. The amount of working storage space assigned to each searcher should be small (according to the managers responsible for paying the computer storage bills) or large (according to searchers wanting more flexibility in their search procedures—for example, retrieve all 50,000 records with a publication date of 1973, then AND it with a particular search topic in order to impose a date limit on the retrieved items, or as another example, select all records indexed by Language=English, to impose an English-language limit on the retrieved items). Pressure continued to build on the system operators to provide expanded working storage for each searcher as the file sizes were increased by their updates, and as the total number of simultaneous users continued to grow. The disk storage overflow problem continued to be a problem for users of all online search systems until the cost of storage decreased significantly. After October 1976, when the working space per searcher was increased to 600,000 postings, the disk overflow problem was seldom encountered.

A separate but related storage problem had to do with working space needed to accommodate truncation searching. A particular word or term stem (e.g., Author=Brown*) might be associated with hundreds of index entries (e.g., Brown, A., Brown, B.... Browning, A., Browning, B.... Brownslon, A.... and so on) and require extensive working space to store the answers. In 1975, DIALOG addressed this issue for truncation searching by limiting searchers to 100 matching terms; if more than 100 index terms matched the search term, a searcher received an error message ">100 TERMS; RESPECIFY." In January 1976, the limit was increased to 400 terms that began with the specified stem, and in September 1976 it was increased to 800 terms.

Just as DIALOG management underestimated how many file numbers would be required, it seriously underestimated the number of passwords and user accounts needed. Initial DIALOG customer administration software allowed up to 100 different users, and soon had to be changed to a larger number. Management's continuing underestimation of the potential market was evidenced by the decision then to upgrade to accommodate 1,000 users—which also proved to be far too low. Because the user number—and the number of bytes set aside to represent it—were hard coded in many administrative, accounting, and billing programs, it was an extensive and time-consuming chore to change them. Moreover, only a small number of programmers were familiar with these programs, and they had other pressing demands on their time for maintaining and making necessary changes to other DIALOG software, as well as developing new features and support programs. Thus a time came in 1976–1977 when hundreds of requests for new accounts had to be put on hold for several months because the system had run out of customer numbers, and no more could be assigned until all the necessary programming changes were made and tested.[5] Lawrence (1997) recalled another problem of password administration with early DIALOG service—existing customers had to request access to each additional database, and then wait until their password was coded for access to that file. These were only a few of the operational problems faced by a service that went from providing service to a small number of large customers (e.g., NASA, DOE) to a large number of retail customers.

Bob Mitchell remembered his most memorable day in the 1970s was when DIALOG lost all the data at the same time. The single disk drive controller had a failure that caused it to wipe out data on all sixteen of the IBM 3330 disk drives. This happened on a Friday afternoon, and Mitchell, who had come in early Friday morning, stayed until Saturday noon, when the IBM customer engineer found and corrected the fault. Then all the DIALOG files had to be restored, most with complete reloads, which took another twenty-four hours.

Even though the systems of the seventies were intended to accommodate simultaneous users, the reality was that more users generated a reduction in response time and total search speeds. While planning a workshop at UC-Santa Cruz on computer searching in May 1975, Bourne invited Tom Crawford of Lockheed to bring a portable terminal (a Digilog keyboard with 25-inch video monitor) to give a demonstration of DIALOG, and to arrange for demonstration passwords for two other terminals that students were going to use for practice searching. Crawford called back to say that DIALOG had a big training session scheduled in New York for the same day as the Santa Cruz workshop, with as many as four terminals in use. Furthermore, using three terminals at the same time as the four terminals in the New York session might make a heavy load on the computer and they were worried about the impact. Crawford wanted to know if the workshop participants could do with less than three terminals, or practice some other day, or do without live demonstrations.

As mentioned in chapter 7, the OBAR experiment had convinced the developers that the target market for LEXIS (lawyers, government agency staff, and accountants) would be best served with terminals customized to the program, with special function keys and a large color video screen capable of displaying 1920 characters at once, and a hardcopy printer. The customized terminals that Mead touted as the first in the commercial world were a response to trainers' frustrations in trying to teach lawyers to search. The terminals were designed to reduce the amount of time required to learn LEXIS and help users to overcome their initial fears of something new (Rubin 1974). While the terminals were designed to be "attorney-proof" (a variation on the term "idiot-proof") they were not usable for anything but LEXIS searching. Harrington (1984–1985, 552) defended Mead's decision:

Why proprietary terminals, incidentally? The company barely broke even on terminals, so there was no economic motive for insisting on proprietary terminals. Rather, it was because, at first, lawyers approached the terminals with fear and awkwardness, protesting that they had no idea how to type, much less how to control a computer. They called themselves technological illiterates, and MDC personnel were glad to join them in applying the appellation. Ten years would pass before MDC deemed it safe to turn lawyers loose on LEXIS with multipurpose terminals.

Representatives of other search services had argued that another reason for the decision to use a special terminal was strictly the marketing objective of making it more difficult for a LEXIS user to search any other existing or future services that might be competitive. Carl Fisher (1997), a former Mead officer, countered this notion: He said that such a rationale did not exist when they launched the special terminal; the real issue was ease of use as provided by the special function keys. Rubin (1998) reinforced Fisher's view: "The only reason for the special terminal was ease of use. Moreover, there were few computer terminals in law offices in 1973. The suggestion that we wanted to exclude the use of other services is ridiculous."

The 1970s saw a proliferation of various types of terminals, serving a wide variety of needs. The variety of terminals available to choose from in the 1960s had been severely limited by the reluctance of AT&T and the Bell Telephone companies to permit any equipment that was not manufactured by them or their affiliates, or approved by them to be connected to their lines. Using language that they had included in tariffs that they had filed with various regulatory agencies in the 1950s, they simply refused to install or permit the installation of "foreign" equipment; this had a chilling effect on entrepreneurs or manufacturers with ideas for better terminals. This issue was resolved in 1968 with the Carterfone decision by the U.S. Federal Communications Commission that allowed non-carrier-provided terminals to be attached to U.S. telephone lines (Cox 1969).

Telecommunications Problems and Solutions

Before the advent of the digital data communications networks of the 1970s, the direct use of dial-up or leased lines from a local telephone service carried a high risk of poor service. All lines were not equal. Arrangements often had to be made, sometimes on a regular basis (e.g., every Monday), with the local phone service to check or "condition" a line that was going to be used. For example, a 1966 study (*On-line intelligence*, 7–8) noted: "During the early phase of the data-link installation, considerable trouble was encountered in establishing a satisfactory long-distance line ... An interim solution was worked out with Pacific Bell Telephone Company whereby they force our dataphone calls to go out on long-line trunks which are satisfactory. The telephone company engineers are working on a permanent solution to this problem." With regard to error rates: "Currently all transmissions are made in bursts of eight or fewer data words. In about every 25 bursts, one or two errors may be expected. At one time, a burst of 2,000 words was attempted. This was tried for about eight minutes and was never successful in getting the complete transmission error-free."

NLM's experiment with AIM-TWX in 1970 had highlighted the problem of obtaining inexpensive and reliable data transmission for a networked bibliographic retrieval system. The prevailing cost then for long-distance telephone calls was about $25 per hour. What was wanted was data transmission at $10 or less per hour. In early 1971, therefore, NLM contracted with NBS to study available communications options. NBS identified several telephone networks that served specific user populations such as the Federal Telephone Service and the Defense Department's ARPA Multi-Computer Network—otherwise known as ARPANET, the first packet-switched data communications network, which began test operation in 1969, and was the precursor to the Internet. NLM considered ARPANET but found that the institutions it was trying to serve did not have access. This was more than a simple issue of obtaining permission; extensive communications interface equipment was necessary at each network node for a connection. NBS also studied more general network capabilities such as the Inward Wide Area Telephone Service (INWATS), multiplexor networks, commercial networks, and leased lines. The NBS study results indicated that the least expensive alternative for NLM was to request bids from commercially available data communications services such as the existing nationwide computer time-sharing service of Tymshare (McCarn 1973a).

From the responses to the resulting RFP, NLM selected TYMNET, owned by Tymshare, to provide a national data communications network to connect users to the NLM computer via nodes in major U.S. metropolitan areas. TYMNET supported most terminals that could be connected to a telephone. TYMNET service began public operation in February 1972 with NLM's MEDLINE. Tymshare Inc. was then in the business of selling time-shared computer services. It had its own private data communications network with 40,000 miles of leased lines in a network of twenty-one computers with local dial-up service in fifty-five cities. NLM's computer was the first outside computer it accepted in its network; SDC's in Santa Monica was the second. Tymshare had the first fifty system host numbers reserved for its own in-house computer centers, to permit communications between all its centers as part of its existing nationwide computer service bureau business. SDC was assigned System Number 51, the first node outside Tymshare's in-house network. Within a couple of years, the network was being used by several other online search services. This was the start of what was to become a major data communications service and an important element in online industry development.

During the experimental and small-scale operational DIALOG service contracts of the 1960s, a single multidropped polled transcontinental leased line connected all highspeed terminal users. All the terminals shared the 240 to 480 cps capacity, and twenty terminals was the practical limit. Some users also dialed the Palo Alto computer from the Washington area and other areas around the country, first at 10 cps, then 30 cps, and eventually 120 cps. The cost of a long-distance call in this period was about $30 an hour for distances beyond fifty miles.

Internationally, rates of $3 to $6 per minute ($180 to $360 per hour) for 5 cps Telex and 10 cps TWX service (where available) were typical. Thus, communications costs were equal to or greater than online search costs, which were typically $25 to $35 per hour.

Lockheed Missiles & Space Co. was a significant customer of Tymshare. Thus, early in 1970 when Tymshare was considering offering its packet network services to third parties, Mark Radwin (whose responsibilities at Lockheed included data communications network development) was among the first to hear of it. At about this time, the American Institute for Certified Public Accountants (AICPA) had published an RFP for online retrieval of all financial sections of annual reports. In response to the RFP, Radwin was appointed the AICPA technical proposal manager for DIALOG, with Donati designated the overall proposal manager. For use in the proposed system, Radwin obtained the first formal proposal for TYMNET support to an online service. Another novel aspect of the proposal was use of a random access microform cassette device to display text or original images of the relevant report pages at an equivalent transfer rate of over 1,200 cps while actually being driven through a 10–30 cps terminal connection. DIALOG's closest competitor was LEXIS. AICPA was located in New York City, and Radwin recalled that Summit had to use two of five annually budgeted East Coast trips to present the DIALOG proposal. However, the New York–based Mead team was able to "live with the customer" and was able to draw a strong analogy to its legal profession customer base and consequently won the procurement. Because it lost this bid, DIALOG was not able to become Tymshare's first online service customer (as we saw, the MEDLINE service was the first to achieve that distinction).

In early 1975, when Telenet Corporation was about to launch the TELENET network, Radwin signed up DIALOG as its first customer. TELENET access was added in December 1975, at a time when DIALOG was Tymshare's largest customer. In this competitive situation, TELENET drove down the price of access from the existing TYMNET rate of approximately $10 per hour to about $1.60 per hour.

SDC computer center staff did not want to deal with the TYMNET hardware installed in the center, so Black of SDC Search Service was assigned the responsibility to fix problems whenever they happened. Black recalled getting calls in the middle of the night when the network went down; he had to get up and drive to SDC-Santa Monica, boot the communications equipment by means of binary switch settings, and then load the application program by means of a punched paper tape. If everything went smoothly, the process took about fifteen minutes. Blocks of code were stored on the punched paper tape, and if there was a fault with the machine reading of the paper tape, he had to visually read the rows of holes on the tape to see where the blocks were, and start again from there. Database producers also struggled with TYMNET access; Paul Ashton of INSPEC often called SDC from London to say, "We can't get in!"

In spite of these difficulties, the search services recognized how vital a telecommunications capability was to their own success. They pressured the networks to expand their coverage and capacity by establishing nodes in states and cities that did not have them. Looking at a series of geographic maps of network nodes as their tentacles spread out over time was like viewing the earlier growth patterns of railroads and highways. Search services regularly provided TELENET and TYMNET with rank-ordered lists of target cities, along with evidence of the current volume of online traffic they were realizing, as justification for adding more nodes.

Communications in Europe generally were hampered by the incompatible multiple networks that made transmission across country lines difficult and expensive, and by the wide differences in tariff schedules and regulations on line splitting or reselling of the various national systems. European searchers did have access to American online search services via TYMNET or TELENET, through agreements with their national telecommunications authority, usually a PTT agency. Nonetheless, they had difficulty getting reliable and error-free access in the mid-1970s. In some countries, the PTT was slow to move, or had other reasons to delay the implementation of effective data communications into and within their country. For example, the British Library's study of online bibliographic searching by U.K. libraries during the period October 1974–February 1975 revealed that 43 percent of a total of 357 attempts to use the Lockheed service via four TYMNET centers were totally unsuccessful. Of the 466 attempts from March 1975 to June 1975, 21 percent were unsuccessful (Holmes 1977c). In 1975 Cuadra (1976, 83) noted at a European conference: "I've also been startled by comments concerning a restriction in telecommunications areas. There has been more use made of on-line services in Finland than in the United Kingdom. I believe that the United Kingdom has deprived itself of a technology that is freely available in other countries. What is needed most right now, is Tymshare nodes in many more countries."

U.S. users of U.S. search services had an extra convenience over European users of European services because the U.S. phone services permitted U.S. search services to include the telecommunications charges on the bills sent to customers (i.e., to rebill). The communication networks did not charge the search services by the hour; they charged monthly by a combination of fixed monthly charge and a charge for total number of characters transmitted. For rebilling to their customers, the search services chose to convert that total data communication cost to a connect-hour cost figure that was approximately equivalent, and independent of the distance covered by a call, and then set their own per hour price accordingly. Each user of a European search service had to get a separate password and monthly bill from their local PTT.

Even with the rapid growth of online and telecommunications technology, and the establishment of an online industry in other countries, many countries still had never seen an online retrieval search performed locally by the end of 1976. In 1976, for example, Bourne conducted the first online search in the United Arab Republic (Egypt), using a slow (15 cps) Telex terminal to connect to the Lockheed computer in California. It took almost twenty-four hours of repeated dialing just to grab access to one of the four busy data communication lines leaving that city. Similarly, the first online bibliographic search in India was not made until 1976, with a leased-line demonstration from the ESA/IRS computer in Europe to Bombay and then to Bangalore.

Thus we have seen that inexpensive communications was a key to commercial online success, at least for most online services. MDC was an exception to the general adoption of commercial communication networks. The customized LEXIS CRT terminals were connected through leased lines that operated at 120 cps, faster than the maximum 30 cps available from the networks in the seventies (Rubin 1974). MDC knew what it wanted, and it spent the money that was needed to get there; it was no accident that MDC became the most successful professional online service in the 1970s. This approach also worked well for OCLC and RLIN, but not for the Information Bank.

TYMNET staff toyed with the idea of getting into the search service business itself. In 1974, Larry Stevens at TYMNET, working with Derwent, put a test file up on TYMNET's computer, using the RECON software. Stevens was familiar with RECON from his earlier work with it at Informatics, and he probably obtained a copy of it for TYMNET from COSMIC (chapter 5). Stevens saw from the test that it was going to tie up the whole TYMNET system. TYMNET knew that it was in the data communication business, not the online database business, and that the Derwent file would require massive storage capacity and update processing because it had a complex file structure with indexing data coming into individual records at three different times. Stevens and Allen Heintz (vice president of international sales) asked SDC if it would be able to put the Derwent file online, which would require updating on a record-by-record and field-by-field basis. SDC's ORBIT software fortunately had an update capability to facilitate file maintenance work. Derwent also needed a means to restrict access to only those users who were subscribers to various sections of the Derwent printed products. SDC said they could do it, and in 1974 started developing the online file for the World Patent Index (WPI). WPI later had the biggest usage of the SDC databases and produced good revenues for SDC. With an exclusive deal for the file, this was the project that saved the SDC Search Service after it lost MEDLINE. TYMNET staff were doing all of this dealing with SDC *without* the prior knowledge and consent of Derwent. Eventually, Derwent managers were apprised of the situation and agreed to transfer the potential search service activity to SDC (Black 1996).

Database Problems and Solutions

Just as they experienced problems with hardware and telecommunications, online services had difficulty with databases. In fact, database problems were perhaps the most frequent. Search service policy usually dictated that a major problem resulted in taking a file offline for hours or days until it was fixed. If its problems were not serious (e.g., the loss of an index for a lesser attribute such as the language index), a flawed database usually remained online while being fixed.

A search service's file updating practices or software caused some of the problems. The kinds of things that could and did go wrong include adding an update tape to the wrong file, having the index entries point to the wrong records, and failing to process all of the records on an update tape. Even today, major databases (e.g., INSPEC, COMPENDEX, AGRICOLA) that are loaded on several online services rarely have the same total record count across all the services that have the database.

The database producers also caused problems. Examples included sending update tapes with less than the correct number of records, sending update tapes with missing data fields (e.g., journal names missing from all citations) and sending tapes with new—undefined and undocumented—data fields or no tape labels. On several occasions, to their great embarrassment, producers sent their tapes to the wrong search service. During the early part of 1977, no search service updated INSPEC because a labor dispute at the center where the tapes were produced stalled all production and distribution. A newsletter article ("INSPEC file" 1977) commented on the Space Documentation Services' experience with the INSPEC strike: "Once the dispute was over in February, tapes were shipped but were received at SDS with the data distorted and thus could not be used. Consequently new tapes had to be created . . . and this was again subject to delays. This chain of events happened no less than three times! New tapes arrived during the first week in September. Only one appears to be unreadable—so we should have them on-line very shortly." A producer of an unindexed business database took an expensive gamble by supporting the development and implementation of an automatic indexing program that processed text from the titles and abstracts of each of its records to generate and assign indexing terms for those records. It processed its entire file, which DIALOG then reloaded as an "improved version" of it. Unfortunately, this automatic indexing introduced so many searching problems (e.g., no way to distinguish between President Ford, Ford Motor Co., and "ford" as in "ford the river") that the file had to be withdrawn and replaced by its former version.

Some database problems were administrative— caused by a special issue raised by a producer. For example, some producers insisted that users individually acknowledge the producer's terms and conditions for use of their database (e.g., no resale or machine-processing of any records retrieved from it). Some producers limited online access to just their current print edition subscribers, and that required a validation and customer file maintenance procedure, as well as a procedure for enabling customer passwords on a file-by-file basis—a sometimes burdensome and time-consuming task for customers as well as the online service. The online services also felt obliged to send multipage printed brochures of the legal language of the database producers' terms and conditions to all their customers.

On the Road

Demonstrations

The major marketing tool of the online services in the seventies was the live demonstration, which was exciting for an audience, but chancy and stressful for the demonstrators. Their portable terminals used unreliable acoustic couplers, meaning that the connection might not work. One trainer noticed considerable line noise that was traced to a nearby noisy IBM Selectric typewriter that was "talking" to the acoustic coupler. In hotels or large organizations, the telephones used for data communications often went through a central switchboard operator. A demonstrator had to ask an operator to place a call and then immediately key off the line, because the caller was going to be talking to a computer and needed a sustained signal without interruption. Operators who did not understand became curious when the line stayed busy for a long time, so they keyed in to check on the connection. They were even more concerned when they did not hear voices, just some strange noises. Operator interruption caused the connection to be dropped, and the demonstrator had to log in again, sometimes again and again. As mentioned later, to solve the telephone line problem in the hotels it used regularly for demonstrations, Lockheed had its own lines installed with plug-in jacks. The hosts of local training sessions did not always realize the data communication needs of the visiting trainer. Angione (1999a) recounted her arrival at a U.S. naval base to give a scheduled SDC training session. To her surprise she found that the host did not realize that the phone she requested needed to be able to get an *outside* line. She ended up using a pay phone in the auditorium.

Pemberton (1983, 8) told an amusing story of responding to a request for a demonstration at the Soviet Embassy in Washington, D.C. Nearly the entire staff, even Ambassador Dobrynin, turned out in the anteroom for the event (Pemberton was not allowed in the embassy proper). While demonstrating, he encountered static on the telephone line and innocently suggested that the line was experiencing interference. His hosts responded with a large collective guffaw, explaining that the interference was caused by the listening bugs on the line—the CIA, the NSA, the DIA, "plus the KGB. When the laughter died down, I gave them some nice little Boolean searches, linking Henry Kissinger to just about every world leader he had met."

Telephone operators were not the only culprits interrupting demonstrations. Murdock (1990) recalled that another source of interruption was from Battelle's computer staff: "It took a long time to train the computer people not to take down the system during a marketing call. They generally were not used to being an online service with a customer out there." Lawrence (1987) remembered calling the computer operators whenever she was about to conduct a demo for an important person, begging them to try not to let the system crash.

As a backup when the online connection failed or the system went down, Landau prepared an audiotape to emulate the signals coming from Battelle's BASIS. Although it did not work well, he used it a few times: "We just plugged the thing in the back end of the terminal and said, 'Here's the way it looks—when it works.'" In Spigai's first six months on the job, every one of her live DIALOG demonstrations went down. In exasperation, she also resorted to using audiotapes. When demonstrating for Mead, Bayer used a videotape or even searches written out on paper, saying to the audience, "Look, if you did this and this, you would get that and that." Bayer had discovered that getting in the doors of large firms was not hard, because his bosses, Rubin and Bennett, were persuasive and credible. However, when the computer crashed or telecommunications "bombed," Bayer and LEXIS lost credibility. The backup tapes and materials helped only a bit. Fortunately, by the end of the decade, downtime and crashes were no longer a major problem.

Another problem of demonstrations was slow response time that belied claims of online speed and bored an audience. Bayer admitted later that it was common practice to fake "representative" service—to kick users off to improve response time for a demonstration before an important potential LEXIS customer. For the period covered by this text, DIALOG staff members were instructed to defer all of their online use (file testing, preparation of examples, and documentation for training, and documentation purposes) until after 4:00 p.m. Pacific Time in order not to compete for computer resources and communications ports with paying customers or demonstrations. At a 1971 meeting about interactive bibliographic systems, Rosen commented that the U.S. State Department had implemented an effective feedback mechanism: "If somebody in the Secretariat is getting poor response time, he calls down and says, 'Hey, get everybody off the system'" (Katter 1973, 182).

Pemberton (1997) relayed another story that illustrated the impact of demonstrations. While he was working for the Information Bank, the company had high hopes of getting terminals in the offices of U.S. senators and representatives on Capitol Hill:

> I got a call at home on Saturday from a senator (himself, not an aide) who wanted to get some background on a political rival that he could use against him politically. As I recall, I found it for him. The Information Bank had a champion on the Hill named Charlie Rose who was a freshman congressman with a liking for technology who was looking for a cause that could bring him the favorable notice of his colleagues. I gave lots of demos to congressmen and women and their staffs. But in the end, they sent their searches to LC instead of searching themselves.

DIALOG marketing staff had similar hopes for, and a lack of success with, Capitol Hill in those days.

Landau (1997) recalled staffing the Battelle BASIS booth at the 1972 ASIS conference in Washington, D.C. While he was giving demonstrations on the NTIS database he was approached by an official from the Soviet Embassy. Landau demonstrated remote searching of the BASIS files in Columbus, Ohio. The visitor refused to believe what Landau told him was happening. As an ex-CIA employee, Landau was quite familiar with the circumstances and possible outcome of that discussion, and so he offered to sign up the official for the BASIS service for $100. But the visitor refused. It would have been an interesting situation in East-West relations if a deal had been struck.

Another anecdote that illustrates the stresses associated with live demonstrations involved Helen Kolbe of George Washington University, who worked with Mark Bayer and other Informatics staff to create the POPINFORM database (Kolbe 1975). In June 1974 Kolbe traveled to the Philippines to demonstrate POPINFORM on the occasion of the opening of the new Population Center Foundation. Bayer gave Kolbe his home telephone number and assured her that, even though the time difference between Manila and Washington, D.C., was eleven hours, she could call anytime if she were having a problem. The Comnet computer was to be kept running during the night so Kolbe could demonstrate live—the first online retrieval demonstration between the Philippines and the United States. At 1:00 a.m., Bayer was routed out of bed by Kolbe's call. Stuck in the middle of a demonstration, her problem was to design a workable search strategy. He helped her and was rewarded later with a souvenir monkeywood statue.

Demonstrators received an education, sometimes rapidly and painfully, in the complexities of the system and databases they were showing. A common pitfall in live demonstrations was what Crawford called the database "warts and uglies"—the errors and inconsistencies that were revealed, especially when the online index was displayed. Sometimes demonstrators learned by being embarrassed when a demonstration search failed to retrieve what was expected. Landau (1990) recalled a demonstration at CAS:

> Ben Weil came by when we were giving a demonstration of BASIS. I said to him, 'Name a word and we will show how many references there are in this file.' He said, because he was from Exxon, 'oil.' So I typed in 'oil.' And nothing came back! Ben said, 'Hey Bob, something is

wrong with your system. I know damn well I have written 20 articles on oil and I know they are in there someplace!' We learned afterward that there was a stop list of all words of three characters or less. We sure learned that fast!

To save storage space, Battelle programmers had eliminated all three-letter words from the indexes. Ben Weil was later quoted by Everett Brenner at the National Online Meeting in May 1989 as commenting drily that oil and gas were *quite* important to Exxon. In a live demonstration of ORBIT, Wanger experienced the same problem in a demonstration in which no records could be found for NOW—the National Organization for Women. Apparently the SDC programmers had also thought that all words of three characters or less were trivial.

Wanger was the topic of another story told by Black (1995), a fellow SDC customer service representative then:

When they loaded ERIC initially, they were still using an early version of the file generator program that had a quirk to it—you couldn't update an empty file. You always had to have something in a file before you could load it. Burket and Blankenship were rushing to bring up ERIC for a demo, and were faced with this program quirk. So they made up three fictitious records from scratch. They keyed these records into the database, and then used the file generator program to complete the rest of the ERIC file loading. At one of the first public demonstrations of the online ERIC database, somebody asked Judy Wanger a question. She searched the file, and the first record displayed was a fictitious and perhaps scatological record. Reportedly, there was an immediate reaction, and an animated phone call back to the California office.

Wanger confirmed the story, saying that she was scrolling the index and was first puzzled when she encountered the term "ennui"—a term she did not expect to find in ERIC—and she knew the ERIC database well. As she continued scrolling the index and ran into "horse," she knew something was definitely amiss. An examination of the records disclosed additional homemade ones with titles such as "A glorious and comprehensive design for the automation of drinking fountains, with suggested applications in the field of existential philosophy

(applied)" and "Non-sentential sententiousness in sentence form, Part II." The offending records were removed, but this story remains as a reflection of the spirit of the times.

In spite of the frustrations and anxieties for the demonstrators, the live displays still excited audiences and were an effective way to sell the online services. As Anne Caputo had in 1974, Ann Van Camp watched a demonstration in library school in 1968. Van Camp's reaction was enthusiastic, even as she remembered it years later (1988, 38): "Typically, the system went down during the demo, but it was still pretty impressive." Another testimonial to the effectiveness of live demonstrations came from Bayer (1995), who recalled an instance when he was working for Informatics in 1974. ARCO, a major oil company and client of a law firm in Washington, D.C., asked the law firm to provide a demonstration of the Informatics online service. ARCO wanted the demo in Los Angeles the next day. Bayer hopped on a plane, with his Execuport portable terminal as baggage, and made the presentation. ARCO became Informatics' first major customer for litigation support services.

Not only were the demonstrations effective, some of the demonstrators genuinely enjoyed the activity and being on the road. Tally (1995) recalled "fond memories of traveling around Wisconsin, giving demonstrations of the system using a portable terminal and pay phone" when he was promoting WISE-ONE.

Librarians also conducted demonstrations to staff and users within their own institutions. Sometimes these pioneers faced a hostile internal environment. One librarian later recalled that the first reaction of the university librarian to an online search of their own catalog was not one of optimism about the good things that would flow from this technology, but instead the question, "What happens if you can't type?"

Training

Training new users was a major part of the job for most search service staff in the seventies. At least one search service had a quota of "training days" for each customer service staff. In half-day, one-day, or two-day sessions, the online services were training more people every year in database and online searching fundamentals than were being graduated from all of the world's library schools in that year. Some commercial search services were training at least 10,000 people a year by the end of 1976. Bayer alone trained 3,000 people in three years. With all that experience, Bayer still recalled how embarrassing his first DIALOG training session was. His new boss, Tom Crawford, came with him to observe. When Bayer tried in mid-morning to get the attendees to sit at terminals and conduct a simple search, one man simply froze in front of a terminal, paralyzed with fear. No amount of coaxing induced him to move a muscle. Even though it was only 10:30 a.m., Bayer broke for lunch. Crawford watched with amusement.

Trainers, like demonstrators, had to be prepared for the unexpected and to be armed with extra lecture notes, worksheets, or other backup devices, because they could not count on a system to be up and running. Nonetheless, even with the best preparation, disasters happened. At one of Crawford's first training sessions, in Corvallis, Oregon, the attendees were extremely keen—*too* enthusiastic. About twenty-five of them jammed into a training room designed for ten people. The earliest to arrive grabbed one of the few terminals and would not let go. With the noise, heat, and congestion, an exasperated and sweaty Crawford could not make himself heard or understood. Afterward, the Corvallis organizers complained that the training did not go well.

Like Bayer, Crawford faced audiences that refused to participate in the training. Crawford (1987) recalled:

At the first DIALOG training session I did in Germany I could get only three people to come—even with no charge. I could not get anybody to sit down at a terminal. They were all high-level. They looked over my shoulder, saying 'Yes, yes'—it was obvious that they were well informed. But none of them was going to sit down in front of the others and reveal whether he could use a terminal or not. They just would not do that. So I had to sit and 'play piano' for them for half the afternoon. They had excellent questions, they were really interested in the system, but they would not sit at a terminal.

Cuadra had a trick to involve the participants in demonstrations. He would sit at the terminal and type so slowly that the group standing around him became impatient. Eventually, somebody would volunteer to take over the typing while he described what was happening with the system and what should be keyed in next.

Sick animals and natural disasters also challenged the trainers. Joyce Camp taught a DIALOG course at a new host training site in Dallas. A blind person was in attendance and her Seeing Eye dog got sick on the new carpet. Camp also conducted a class in Denver in which a tornado touched down about six blocks from the training site, discouraging all but five people from showing up. Camp drove through the swirling debris of the tornado to teach the session, but she had to question the old adage "the show must go on."

Tampa, Florida, was the site of a memorable DIALOG training session for Bill Mercier. The established host training site at a public utility headquarters building recently had moved its computer lab to a different building in downtown Tampa. Because of the move the computer equipment had been disconnected. Although the utility's information center staff promised that all would be in working order for the training, such was not the case. Mercier and the local host struggled frantically for an hour to get only two of five workstations hooked up. This was just the beginning of a disastrous DIALOG training day. While Mercier and the host were working on the computers, members of the class flooded a bathroom on that floor, and people at another meeting pilfered the coffee and refreshments set out for the class. Then the final two blows: Going down to lunch from the seventh floor to get to the street level, Mercier and all the attendees got stuck in the elevator—and one attendee was in a wheelchair. After twenty minutes the building maintenance staff came and was able to open the doors to get the victims some fresh air. Later, they all were able to climb out except for one person with a bad back who had to be lifted out. Mercier sent the attendees off to lunch and stayed with the man in the wheelchair to wait for the elevator maintenance company. The attendees returned after a while, and he tried to resume the session, only to find that the training room was locked and the master key did not open the door. The host located a conference room in another building and a few terminals in the library (two blocks away) and Mercier managed to get the attendees online. The host finally found the key to the original room; she and Mercier collected briefcases and training materials and somehow got through a few more pages of the seminar. Postscript: The attendees were not charged for the training.

In spite of his own rough experiences with difficult groups, Crawford was highly demanding of his own staff about quality of training. Caputo (1987) remembered, "When we got back from training sessions, Tom would read our evaluations out loud, to the amusement of everyone." Wanting to motivate his trainers to improve their presentation skills, Crawford made them compete against one another for ratings.

All the search service trainers have anecdotes that are amusing now, but that made them anxious at the time. In spite of the strain, however, trainers tried to coordinate the online training times so they did not impact on one other and regular customers. One reward for their commitment was the admiration and respect accorded them by ardent librarians in the exhibits at conferences. Crawford (1987) recalled that staff were "covered like a banana by ants," but they were delighted with the attention.

As the search services grew, some of them established regional offices to support training and marketing. In most cases it was more cost-effective to bring users to a dedicated training room in the search service's own offices than to rent or borrow space at some hotel or other facility. Lockheed, SDC, Data Corporation, and Mead all had field offices in 1973; BRS used regional field representatives who generally operated out of their own homes and conducted training in hotel meeting rooms.

DIALOG did not have sufficient office space of its own in the early 1970s to hold classes at its own headquarters in the San Francisco Bay area, so it regularly used a room at a nearby Holiday Inn in Palo Alto. Such a training facility had to have several telephone lines coming into the room in order to permit simultaneous use of several terminals. In cooperation with the hotel, DIALOG solved this logistics problem by having the telephone company install several permanent phone lines, terminating in several wall jacks around that room, and charged them to a DIALOG account. On a training day, the DIALOG trainer brought the required number of phones to the location and plugged them in; these were ordinary desktop telephones, to be used with portable terminals that had built-in acoustic couplers to connect with the phones.

1974 Milestones

Mead was the first online search service to designate and equip a room at one of its offices to be a dedicated training facility.

Mead was the first online search service to use a videotape for training.

MDC was the first, in 1974, to designate and equip a room at one of its offices to be a dedicated training facility and to establish permanent training rooms (Mead called them "learning centers") in offices around the country. Mead also was the first to use a videotape for training, both to give a quick overview of the service and to fill in when a live demonstration could not be given (Bayer 1987).

By the end of 1976, search services, database producers, and academic institutions were discussing among themselves the nature and extent of training for online searching that was, and should be, provided by each of those groups (*Training methods*

1977). Producers were providing sessions to instruct people—as many as 1,500 per year by some producers—on how to search their database online. These trainers often had their job complicated by having to develop materials and teach classes for a database as provided online by each of several different online services—with different file loading, indexing, and search features. In 1977, BIOSIS, for example, was available on seven different systems.

Living Out of a Suitcase

Training and marketing staff traveled frequently—some almost constantly. Crawford characterized his first few months at DIALOG as a "baptism by fire"; he was on the road day after day. At the end of each day, he was fatigued and sometimes jet lagged. Nonetheless, he sat up late in the evenings in his motel room writing documentation because "databases were being added faster than staff." Most trainers spent many days on the road, giving training sessions and marketing demonstrations away from their home office. This might have been interesting at first, but as one trainer said, "The excitement kind of runs out after your third trip to Duluth or Des Moines." Some staff spent so much time on the road that they had no time for personal chores. For example, Egeland confided to Caputo that she was on the road so much that she could not go home often enough to do her laundry. She learned to discard all her dirty underwear every time she arrived in a new town and to buy a new supply at a local department store.

Angione (1999b) described a typical day on the road for an SDC trainer: Get doughnuts for the class. Take customer/host to breakfast. Train the trainees. Take trainees to lunch. Train the trainees. Take customer/host out to dinner and/or speak to a local user group. Then the first day back at the office was spent on expense reports and planning the next trip.

The travelers occasionally faced budget-conscious hosts who tried to reduce training costs by economizing on trainers' expenses. A frugal host picked up a trainer at the airport to save on car rental. Dinner after an all-day session was a home-cooked meal at the host's home—never a gourmet meal—and not much appreciated by a weary trainer who mostly wanted to be left alone. Overnight accommodations were at the cheapest motel in town.

Another challenge of the road was lugging heavy terminals (40–45 lbs.) that were too fragile to ship, and toting training materials that cost too much to ship and that might not arrive in time if shipped. The women especially were vulnerable to tendinitis in their arms (they called it "terminal elbow") because they carried the terminals out from their bodies to avoid bruising their legs and ripping their stockings. Crawford recalled carrying an early TI terminal with him on an airplane. It had to be placed in the seat next to him, and required a seat belt extension to go around it and hold it in place. Compare that with today's laptops!

Regardless of the tribulations, most of the travelers refused to be daunted or to let fatigue and jet lag slow them down, especially when the trips were to interesting cities or foreign countries. Spigai (1987) recalled, "You would get there and you would have so much adrenaline that the fatigue came after the training rather than before. I think that was how it was for most of us, because we felt like we were at the forefront of something big." Caputo (1987) echoed the feeling: "We were pioneers doing great things, really, really exciting things that were going to change the world—change the world of information anyway. We were out there blazing trails." Being pumped full of coffee and sugar doughnuts probably had an effect also on both trainers and students.

These hardy pioneers had to be prepared for almost anything. When Black went to London for SDC, his host had set up the terminal in a closet, which made it almost impossible for the observers to see anything. On the same trip, the PTTs were an obstacle to connecting online, so Black skirted the issue by dialing from London illegally. When Angione (1999a) went to the U.S. naval base mentioned earlier, to show ORBIT to a group of students, she found that the monitor in the auditorium was not working. While her associate tried to train the group, Angione upstaged her by repairing the terminal. She always carried a set of TV repairman screwdrivers on her training trips, and when she "whipped out a screwdriver" to fix the machine, the young cadets were dumbfounded to see a woman being so facile with high technology.

An additional stressor for the Lockheed training staff was the aircraft bribery scandals described in chapter 9. Crawford was in Tokyo for training sessions in February 1976 when the scandal was revealed there. He remembered (1987) ruefully:

You were not DIALOG, regardless of what you wanted to think you were. You were Lockheed. Those were tough times—not pleasant. Mostly, I got snide comments that the people thought I would not understand. However, when you spend a lot of time abroad, you may not be able to speak the language, but you get to a point where you can understand, and certainly can get the gist. Comments were made that were personally embarrassing. I was there to talk about a bibliographic information retrieval system, and they wanted to know, 'If I sign up for a training course, will I get some graft?' It was an unpleasant time.

Anne Caputo, who had just been hired, was especially vulnerable to the criticisms leveled at Lockheed. She recalled (1987):

I was shocked when the Dean of the library school at Arizona came to one of my training sessions and said sarcastically that the profits that DIALOG was making would be plowed back into Lockheed corporate profits. I remember how angry that made me feel. No! We're not working for those jerks who are killing people with missiles! We are working for this wonderful information thing! When I told Fran Spigai, she said, 'Well, you know, she is right.' I was really disheartened and shocked that we were piling money back into a corporation that had very different goals and ideas about things than we had. To me, working for DIALOG was like working for a library in a sense; your job was to provide a service to people without much thought to profit.

On the Other Side of the Terminal: Online Users

Most users of online services of the seventies were information professionals—mainly special librarians in government and industry. Most had credentials in library and information science and sometimes in a subject area—for example, all staff of the literature searching service at Bell Telephone Labs had doctoral degrees in a technical field (Hawkins and Stevens 1976). The typical information professionals of this era were familiar with literature searching, but they had no programming background and were not sophisticated in using computers or terminal equipment. They therefore had high expectations of system performance and were critical of deficiencies in the operations, but they did not question how or why the systems were structured the way they were. Some were fearful of automated retrieval because they assumed that their jobs would no longer be needed if a computer could do the work they were doing. On the other hand, according to Riddle (1997), "There were several others who belonged to organizations anxious to automate, thus reinforcing the security of their jobs."

This earliest group of users amounted to less than a thousand among all the search services and no more than a few hundred each even for the largest services. A large percentage were known by name to the search service staffs. We have already seen how some isolated users maintained regular telephone contact with the search services staffs—probably more than was really needed just to search successfully. Other users were perhaps not so desperate for friendship, but they still enjoyed the sense of clubbiness, of belonging to an invisible community of fellow users. The early users were not only delighted to stay in contact with the search services through the telephone and the online messages but eager to attend users meetings and to view the newest developments at professional conferences.

End Users

Even though most searchers of the early era were librarians, from the beginning a few end users were willing and even eager to learn to conduct their own searches (Del Frate and Riddle 1973). The designers of the first online systems had presumed that searching would be done by end users; that assumption undergirded system design. MEDLINE was intended to be used by medical researchers and clinicians, NASA/RECON was designed for aerospace engineers and scientists, LEADERMART was designed for engineers and users in industry and business, and LEXIS was marketed directly to individual attorneys. For many reasons, however, most users through the seventies were librarians and trained intermediaries working on behalf of end users. In fact, some professional searchers worried that even *allowing* eager end users to get at the terminals was a bad idea. Koenig (1987) recalled the concerns: "When I went to professional meetings in the early seventies, we had lots of discussions about end-user searching, including heated arguments about whether end users should be searching. There was a great deal of concern that some end users would insist on doing their own searches, but would not remember how to do it and would spend gobs of money and time doing crummy searches." At Pfizer, a small percentage of the library users were interested in online searching. Koenig characterized them as being of two types. The first were those who were intrigued at the notion of online, but once they discovered how it was done, were content to let someone else do it, or to sit with the intermediary, making comments and suggesting terms, while the search was run. The other group were those who did their own searching regularly and became good searchers. A group of end-user searchers who insisted on doing it, but did it so infrequently that they did it dreadfully and wastefully did not exist, at least not at Pfizer.

Not everyone shared Koenig's positive attitude toward end users. In her marketing capacity, Spigai did not think much about end users: "At that time the library market was seen as *the* market. The end users were never a major consideration." Spigai (1987) recalled that not only did she not give end users much thought, she viewed the presence of end users at a training session as a bother:

> There were a few end users at training sessions, but not like today, where it is a major portion of the training seminar group. Then they were considered nuisances because there would be one or two users who were end users and there would be 25 librarians, and the librarians would be so far ahead in terms of understanding what was going on, and the end users would come in and ask really basic questions that showed no understanding. So in the sessions I gave, I tried to have separate groups, rather than a mix of librarians and end users, because it really was a problem.

Lawrence (1997) recalled that her demonstrations for Exxon were scary: "Would the system stay up? Would a user ask a question that retrieved zero hits? But in the end, there were more successes than not." She recalled training end users in 1976, and found that few of them continued searching by themselves, although they did develop an appreciation for the service, and asked for complex searches to be done for them.

Another perspective on end users came from Rogers (1974, 83), who earlier had been director of NLM. Rogers supposed that learning to search online was not difficult: "The ease of operating a terminal in an interactive system is simplicity itself compared to the complex rigmarole required for inputting a search into a tape system. Anyone can learn to operate a terminal, under the general rules of a particular system, in half an hour." Rogers came to believe, however, that end users did not want to conduct their own searches. He cited his own taste of searching for one day—afterward he was "worn out" and "fatigue [caused] me to make a number of input errors, which then required repeated corrections" (86). Rogers argued (83) against the view espoused by Lancaster and others that end users really wanted to search on their own:

> This writer remains profoundly skeptical of the validity of such a position. There are too many inarticulate clients, too many clients with only the vaguest notion of what they

are after, too many clients with too much impatience and greater exasperation when confronted with a system conceived as having magical properties, but which cannot respond to 'you know what I mean.' There is also the fact that a majority of clients prefer not to be involved in the actual searching process, as well as the fact that queuing problems inevitably develop when there is free access to the terminal, and this is accentuated by the slow speeds of search formulation and modification characteristic of persons who, unlike the librarian search-analyst, do not have daily practice and familiarity with the system.

Dan Wilde (1997) recalled a situation he observed in the early days when NASA decided to put a RECON terminal in the reading room at Goddard Space Flight Center in Maryland: "It sat there for 60 days and no one wanted to use it. So, they moved the terminal into the back room so the librarians could use it. No one wanted to learn their job and learn to search at the same time."

Searchers as Trainees

Some new users, whether librarians or end users, were either overly assertive—at a training session they grabbed a terminal and tried to hang onto it for the entire time—or were timorous, afraid even to approach the terminal. If coaxed to sit down, some in the second group froze in fear, as at Bayer's first training session. Fortunately, most attendees at training sessions were open to learning and quickly conquered their consternation.

Some novices' fears were grounded in the notion that they would be expected to know or have to learn computer programming. Even after discovering that programming was not a requirement, some found the commands, protocols, and search strategies to be complicated and confusing. They then worried that they would be left behind when other librarians who had mastered online moved ahead. This concern was strong especially among public librarians, who generally were more timid than others, especially about the equipment. The DIALIB project (chapter 9) that tested DIALOG in California public libraries helped to ease the misgivings among this group about the future of online

in public libraries. Some were terrified because they had been designated as the person to come back to train the other staff; but they usually lost their terror when they learned about on-site customer training.

At the opposite end of the spectrum were those with a background in computer programming or systems analysis. They were impatient with the presentations because they imagined that they knew it all already. Some lied on their training application to get in an advanced class because they did not want to waste time with the basics. One restless attendee at a seminar taught by Caputo kept saying, "I know how that works . . . I know how this works . . . I know this . . . I know that . . . well, *I* invented Boolean logic you see!" Perhaps he was not aware that the English mathematician George Boole had died 110 years earlier. Or, maybe he was Mr. Boole, returned from the netherworld to brush up on the latest applications of his algebraic system by attending a DIALOG training seminar.[6]

The audiences were mixed also in the sense that some attendees were present only because their bosses had sent them, and these reluctant recruits tended to be skeptical of technological change. Others, however, made great sacrifices to get there—including two young women from Coos Bay, Oregon, who drove down to Palo Alto at Christmastime to attend an online training session. They spent their own money for the registration and travel expenses and gave up part of their holiday from library school at the University of Oregon because they wanted to be information brokers—although the term had not yet been coined for those who wanted to conduct searches for others as an independent commercial enterprise. Some signed up for an advanced training class, because they did not quite get it during the beginning class and their employers would not pay for the same class twice. The addition of a quick review of the basics in the advanced classes helped with this problem.

The Searcher's Job

Back at home after being trained, new users learned to cope with the unreliability of online search service performance. As Philip Rosenstein, director of libraries at the College of Medicine & Dentistry of New Jersey expressed it: "Our searchers . . . have their highs and lows manning the terminal." He cautioned, "If you are an administrator, stay far away on the low days when the terminal is down" (Spiegel and Crager 1971, 3). In spite of the stresses, however, most librarians learned to cope with the unpredictable, troublesome, and slow online computers (see figure 10.3). Van Camp, who worked as a reference librarian at Indiana University School of Medicine Library, and was a heavy user of online systems, structured her hectic schedule so she could complete all the searches. She recalled (1988, 39): "I learned how to take advantage of slowness and downtime. It seemed we had a constant daily flow of 10 to 25 or more searches. I designed search strategies for the easy questions first, input them into the terminal, started printing, and then had time to concentrate on the more difficult questions. Using this efficient technique, most questions were processed within 24 hours."

In Van Camp's library, librarians could search MEDLINE on both the NLM and SUNY BCN systems. Unfortunately, the dedicated SUNY IBM terminal could not be used for NLM, so to save money they decided to search NLM on their interlibrary loan TWX terminal. Search response time on both systems ran to minutes rather than seconds, but that delay allowed the librarians to run back and forth between the two machines, which were in separate rooms. Van Camp (1988, 39) recalled:

SUNY was programmed to process the entire search strategy and print the first ten citations. Then the search had to be repeated to retrieve more than ten citations. Search time sometimes took four to five minutes. When we were extremely busy, I would start a search on the SUNY terminal, run to the TWX in another room, start a MEDLINE search on NLM, and then go back to recycle the SUNY search. While these two systems were slow by today's standards, the whole procedure was magnificent because we were now able to process as many online bibliographies in a month as we used to be able to do in a whole year.

Van Camp (1988, 39) was not typical of those users then and now who have difficulty moving from one online system to another and who confuse the commands and features: "I never had problems getting SUNY commands mixed up with NLM commands as some other searchers reported. In 1977, we acquired a TI Silent 700 terminal to use on BRS, NLM, and other systems. At first I got NLM commands confused with BRS. Apparently my lack of prior confusion was related to terminal usage: for example, TWX meant NLM, IBM meant SUNY commands."

Users were not only ingenious in figuring out ways to optimize their search productivity in spite of slow systems but clever in getting access to systems for which they did not qualify. We have seen already how librarians at the PMA companies used congressional pressure to influence the director of NLM to allow their libraries to subscribe to NLM MEDLINE. Several years before that event, even before MEDLINE was available from SDC, Koenig's library at Pfizer was interested in obtaining access to the database from SUNY BCN. BCN was interested in selling services, but could not because of New York state and SUNY regulations. Koenig discussed the frustrating situation with Egeland and Quake, who visited the Pfizer library in Groton, Connecticut, and Koenig visited Albany to see its operation. In chapter 8 we saw that they plotted a complex solution whereby Pfizer would contribute money to SUNY BCN to support a research study comparing NLM's *MeSH* and Excerpta Medica's *MALIMET* for online retrieval. SUNY BCN would mount a subset of Excerpta Medica for the study (available from Pfizer, who had the tapes) and MEDLARS online. The real purpose, of course, was for Pfizer to get day-to-day access to the online medical databases and for SUNY BCN to receive money. When SDC's MEDLINE appeared, the plan was abandoned. Even though it was not implemented, the elaborate proposal nonetheless demonstrates the lengths to which some users were willing to go to get access to an online system.

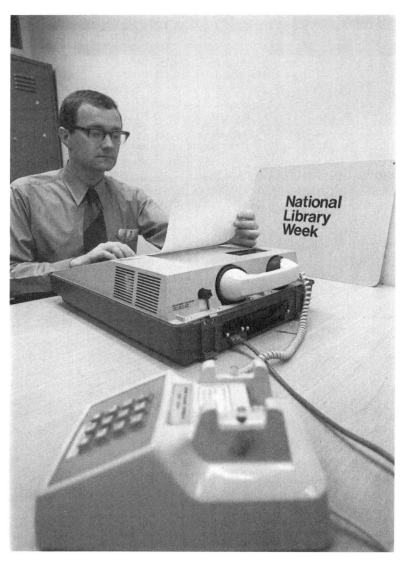

Figure 10.3
Donald Hawkins, online user at Bell Laboratories, Whippany, New Jersey, is seated at a teletypewriter terminal hooked via acoustic coupler to a desk telephone. April 8, 1976. Photo from private archive of Donald Hawkins.

Users' Perceptions of Costs

From searchers' perspective, the variety of search service pricing mechanisms in effect was bewildering. Calculating charges was further complicated by the variations associated with skill and speed of individual searchers, type of terminal and printer used, time of day, and number of concurrent users. Murdock and Opello's article in 1973 was just one of several that appeared that attempted to explicate for librarians the comparable costs for online searching though different databases and search services and to compare these costs with manual literature searching. Brown, Yeates, and Van Hoesen (1975) were of the opinion that the value and economy of a database offered by more than one search service could not be measured solely in connect rates, but was dependent also on updating and availability considerations. Furthermore, rapid changes in features available and the difficulty in running exactly the same search on different systems made it nearly impossible to draw conclusions as to whether one search system was more economical than another.

Another important cost issue for some users, especially those who had paid an annual subscription fee, was how to maximize their use of the service to which they had committed. For example, subscribers to SUNY BCN in 1970–1971 were faced with the dilemma of choosing between online SUNY BCN and batch-processed MEDLARS searches, or even of opting to conduct free, but time-consuming manual searches. Because they enjoyed operating the terminal and formulating the online searches, and because they had paid a subscription up front, they tended to choose SUNY BCN: "Since we have paid the money for it we sometimes think we'd better do a SUNY search in order to get our money's worth since its value is enhanced the more searches we do" (Spiegel and Crager 1971, 8). Even so, they worried that this was not the best criteria for choosing.

Librarian customers of the search services paid considerable attention within their profession to the cost issues (e.g., fee versus free service, methods of charging and cost recovery) (Lynch 1981). They also looked for ways to obtain online services at reduced costs. Maier (1974, 183), for example, considered the idea of a consortium: "It is unlikely we will be able to afford the complete service [DIALOG] as demonstrated unless we can enter into a compact with other local libraries for joint support of it."

Searchers in the 1970s, mindful of and ever alert to the costs, system performance problems, frailties, and quirks of the online services, prepared their own internal ground rules for use. An example of such a set of rules proposed in 1974 by a U.S. government agency—which we shall mercifully keep anonymous—included the following admonitions:

1. All online terminal searching should be done between 8:00 a.m. and 11:00 a.m.

2. Routine searches should be completed in 15 minutes, other searches should not exceed 45 minutes.

3. Typeouts, other than accession numbers, are not an economical use of computer connect time and so should be avoided.

4. Scanning titles or abstracts on the terminal is also very costly and should be done sparingly.

5. Always use short cuts in selecting terms, combining sets and printing items in order to save time and money.

6. Online terminal operators should avoid answering the telephone or receiving telephone calls while at the terminal.

7. Except for brief demonstrations, requesters or observers should not be permitted to interface with or interrupt terminal operators.

N.B. Remember that each minute at the terminal costs approximately $1.00.

These rules remind us that many users of that era viewed online searching as being extremely costly, in spite of published studies on careful cost comparisons that revealed that online searching was much more cost-effective than manual literature searching. Angione (1999a) recalled giving a demonstration to a room full of librarians at a university library and being asked for information about a specific company. She did a search and found one article, at which point several librarians said, "We had already found that one." A voice in the back of the room said, "But it took us several days to find it." Users apparently were bothered more by the direct, out-of-pocket costs associated with an online search than they were with the indirect costs associated with days of staff research to accomplish the same task. They valued the speed of online retrieval, but continued to be nervous about the charges.

User Initiatives in Online Searching

In many ways, the professional searchers of the early period were the best allies the search services and database producers could have wished for. Librarians surveyed potential users, experimented with promotional and educational materials, devised various pricing and recharging schemes, and in other ways enhanced the industry's marketing efforts. For example, in January 1973 at Calspan Corporation Library in Buffalo, New York, librarians Barbara Kunkel and Betty Miller (1975, 129) named their new literature searching service COINS (Calspan On-Line Information Service). Although they understood the value of word-of-mouth marketing from satisfied users in attracting new users, they also sent announcements to department heads, placed advertisements in the company newsletter and on the company bulletin board whenever a new database became available, prepared a descriptive brochure and placed it in strategic spots in the company for maximum exposure, and prepared handouts for researchers that described the major databases in specific fields. When all of these efforts proved inadequate in reaching Calspan scientists and engineers, Kunkel and Miller tried harder. They held departmental seminars and lugged a terminal to departments to give demonstrations to staff who refused to come to the library. They prepared a large display to show the databases pictorially and set it up in the company cafeteria during lunch hour. They produced an eight-minute movie for use in a portable Technicolor showcase. Although they could not measure precisely the effects of their private marketing campaign, they were pleased that the number of search requests increased over a two-year period from 19 to 125 per month. Kunkel and Miller should have received a bonus from the beneficiaries in the online industry of this increased business!

Librarians provided the impetus for the first users meetings. For example, the idea for a joint conference, sponsored by SLA's Government Information Services Committee, the Federation of Information Users, and Lockheed Information Systems, was suggested by Joan Sweeney, Research Librarian at the Institute for Defense Analysis (IDA) in Arlington, Virginia. She and several other IDA librarians coordinated the planning between all the sponsoring groups and her library, the site of the two-day users meeting. The meeting format was a workshop to exchange ideas among users, Lockheed staff and representatives from nine database producers: CAS, Engineering Index, USOE, Institution of Electrical Engineers, NAL, Macmillan Information Company, Predicasts, American Psychological Association, and NTIS. Sessions were structured to be short enough so that users could meet with various industry representatives and personally exchange information and problems. The most common problems cited were the need for thesauri and other search aids, and the need to learn search techniques specific for individual databases. It should be noted that at this early users meeting, even though it was organized by and for librarians, six attendees were end users (Federation of Information Users 1974).

Users also took the initiative in research. Independent of the search services, some users banded together to study the online phenomenon. In 1971, the ASIS Council chartered a new Special Interest Group (SIG) called User On-Line Interaction (UOI), chaired by Thomas Martin of Stanford University. As reported in an article ("ASIS forms" 1972), SIG/UOI was founded with the following mission: "To encourage the development, investigation, and refinement of on-line interaction models as they relate to various user, computer system, and information environments; the utilization of the model for highlighting common features and function differences in existing or proposed user/system information interfaces; and the adoption of compatible interfaces in response to common environments."

In retrospect, the online searchers of the early era do not seem much different from those today. It is no longer true that librarians worry about losing their jobs, or sit in front of terminals frozen in fear, or run back and forth from one room to another to conduct searches on two systems simultaneously. Students in schools of library and information science today, however, still are excited about learning online searching. Librarians have been joined by many thousands of end-user subscribers, and librarians are still worrying about the quality of end-user searches. Users still fret about costs and complain about having to learn more than one system. Nonetheless, all online users today exhibit the same eagerness, enthusiasm, and sense of adventure in accessing the thousands of databases available on CD-ROM and via the Internet. None would wish to return to the pre-online era.

11 Summing Up the Story

In chapter 1, we outlined the major themes and motifs of this book. These represented the research questions that guided the investigation. Those questions are repeated below, with a summary of the major findings.

What role did hardware, software, telecommunications, and database developments play in driving the progress of online systems?

During the sixties, third-generation online computers, by today's standards, had extremely small core memories, direct access memories, and processing capability. The earliest terminals were either slow, clumsy teletypewriters, or astonishingly sophisticated CRTs, some with embellishments such as light pens, color monitors, and interactive video displays. None, however, were really portable or inexpensive. For both computers and terminals, a great deal of variety in storage capacities, speeds, reliability, and various "bells and whistles" distinguished the hardware of one project or experiment from another. In all of the projects of this period, the designers were conceiving systems that were ahead of the technology, with the expectation that the hardware would catch up.

While the equipment did expand rapidly in speed and storage capabilities, the pioneers invented remarkable mechanisms to cope with the existing equipment and cost limitations. Collections of databases that were too large to be loaded online at the same time were split into "time windows." If printers were slow, searchers were encouraged to narrow their strategies until they had only a few records to print out, or to use offline printing, which meant a delay in receiving the output. When the computers or communications hardware went down (an everyday occurrence), users were persuaded to wait patiently. Researchers who wanted to experiment with novel searching algorithms that used more computer processing capability than was available limited themselves to tiny databases. Overall, the pioneers seemed optimistic that the hardware eventually would match their expectations, and in the meantime they wanted to get on with the research, demonstration, and implementation. It was not the available hardware, but the pioneers' visions of possibilities that pushed the frontier.

The changing character and size of "stop lists" provided another measure of relief from hardware constraints over the history of online searching. Very common words (e.g., a, an, in, now, the) were excluded from the online indexes in the early systems because they took up too much storage space and consumed lots of computer resources when included in search formulations. The other rationale given at that time was that these words were not significant to searchers—although that turned out to be not true in every case. Designers who built stop lists of every string of three characters or less found their systems useless for some types of databases and records (e.g., gas, oil, IBM, ATT, B-36, CO_2, Vitamin A). As storage costs continued to decline, systems designers reduced the size of their stop lists, to eventually become ten words or less, or even zero, as appropriate for specific files. Another example of how search capabilities were improved as computer mainframes became more powerful and ran more cheaply was the implementation of various word proximity search options as soon as it was feasible.

Like the hardware, the software exhibited remarkable variability. Most interfaces were designed for end users; a few were deliberately not. Some were menu-based, others command-based, and others based on natural language. Some, but not all, were recursive, that is, the intermediate results of a search could be used to modify the strategy to improve the quality of the retrieval.

The searching features built into the software were remarkably sophisticated. Boolean operators, right-hand and left-hand truncation, cited reference searching, natural language free-text searching, saved output for later searching, "wild" characters, online thesauri, relevance-ranked output, automatic incorporation of synonyms and hierarchically related terms into search statements, search term weighting, and novice vs. experiencd search interfaces all appeared in the milestones before 1967. These were not new features; they had been implemented or demonstrated years earlier with batch retrieval systems. It was, however, a challenging implementation feat to make these same features work in real time, with simultaneous users and systems operating with practical hardware constraints—such as, for example, the amount of working memory that could be set aside for multiple users to do truncation searching that generated large posting counts.

It also became apparent early on that some of these features were beyond the capacity of the intended users to understand or appreciate. It takes a sophisticated searcher, for example, to appreciate the ways in which the left-truncation or cited reference feature can be used. The systems that survived did so by streamlining their feature list to concentrate on those that were cost-effective and made the most difference to users. Their success, in fact, can be attributed largely to the developers' responsiveness to user feedback. From thousands of user comments, reviews of the competition, and in-house reviews, every search service always had a list of desirable features that it would like to add to its system. While a feature might appear on a list of desiderata for ten years, it might never reach a priority level and development payback potential to justify implementing it. For example, DIALOG had requests for and knew about the potential utility of text searching of abstracts in its files but could not justify the extra computer processing time for file building or the extra storage required until computer capacities increased and direct access storage costs dropped significantly. Some systems chose not to implement title word searching, even though it was a standard feature on other systems at the time. SDC knew that its customers wanted to do word adjacency or proximity searching on its databases, but it had to implement that feature file-by-file over a period of several years, because it lacked the resources to do it all at once. Because of budget and other resource constraints, the spin-off NASA/RECON, DOE/RECON, and JURIS systems could not implement all the new features added to the evolving DIALOG system. There were always more known features that could be added, but that the search services could not afford for one reason or another.

The databases of the early online era were few and generally small. Because of the paucity of publicly available machine-readable databases, most of the developers of the earliest systems constructed their own in order to build prototype systems. Most of the earliest databases were bibliographic, but a few were based on other types of data such as text of encyclopedia articles, chemical nomenclature, or inventory lists. The stored data were usually represented in restricted character sets (e.g., uppercase only) and output devices displayed the data in the same restricted form. Only a few of the earliest online bibliographic databases included abstracts along with the bibliographic description. By the late sixties, collaboration between the system builders and outside database producers to offer online access to large files was becoming common.

A key component in the growth of online retrieval systems was the development of inexpensive, reliable, long-distance data transmission. The major time-shared communications systems, however, did not appear until the early seventies. As in the case of the hardware limitations, the developers in the sixties did not allow this missing element to slow their experimentation. They either hard-wired the terminals to the computers; used the existing telephone lines, the extremely slow Teletypewriter Exchange Network of AT&T, the Teletype network of Western Union; or leased lines. These mechanisms were either not entirely satisfactory or else could not be implemented on a large scale, but again, the dreams were not deterred by the existing handicaps.

What were the characteristics of the early online services? What were their purposes and functions, and how well did they accomplish them?

While the earliest online services were of two distinct types, by the end of the sixties the activities and functions of each overlapped. The first type was the research systems, that existed primarily for the purpose of learning about computerizing linguistic phenomena, evaluating human-computer interfaces, demonstrating proof of concept, observing human searching behavior, and observing how scientists use the literature. These systems were typically small, but their activities were well documented. A few years later the production systems appeared that existed primarily to provide a useful service, such as accessing library records faster and more cost efficiently. Typically much larger than the research systems, they had larger databases (sometimes a variety of them) and more users, and they required large computers. Some were public and others were proprietary or limited to a restricted clientele. From the beginning, the production services offered telephone assistance to users, training programs, user manuals, online help messages, and other forms of customer support.

Even the most successful of the production systems, which grew eventually to become major well-known systems in common use, struggled in their early days with obstacles and limitations. For example, not only were service hours short, but in some cases scheduling was inconveniently timed in order to accommodate other projects on the computer that had higher priority. Slow response times were only a little less exasperating than the system failures, the "down time," which happened often. The output that could be printed online was sometimes limited, and even if it was not, the slow speed and noise of the printers made long printouts impractical. Users complained about all of these problems but they continued to access the services anyway, probably because, even with irritating service problems, online was still superior to the manual or batch-searching alternatives.

Almost none of the early systems had online provision of source documents, or even abstracts of documents. Limitations in storage capacity dictated brief records. However, the developers were acutely aware that users needed information from the original source—not just a bibliographic description. To get around the computer limitations they created auxiliary storage and retrieval devices, usually based on microform technology. It was an imperfect solution, but it demonstrated that they well understood users' basic needs and preferences.

Between 1967 and 1970, more search functions were initiated. Searchers could specify proximity between search terms. Interesting variations on database access were tried such as searching by classification codes or in-depth index terms to books. CRT displays became a lot fancier and more colorful—with highlighting and KWIC displays of search terms in retrieved text. Most of the milestones of this period, however, were oriented less to innovations in functions and more to expansion of services and databases. During this period, for example, a national online search service network was established. Search systems were used from terminals outside the country in which the computer operated. Online search services became available in Europe. Very large full-text and bibliographic databases were accessible (albeit sometimes only in "time windows"). Multiple files could be searched simultaneously. Abstracts were available online for both searching and output. Library holdings and availability information were incorporated into output records. Full-text statutory and case law could be searched online. Online tutorials and help capability were instituted. Online searching was introduced into the curricula of graduate programs of library and information science. Search services began holding users' meetings.

In the period 1971–1976, many milestones were generated having to do with aspects of establishing public online search services, open to any interested user. Licensing agreements and royalty payments for database use, pricing policies, bilingual interface options, elimination of time windows, online document ordering, and marketing and customer service such as advertising, newsletters, 1-800 toll-free numbers, large training programs, and dedicated training facilities were all instituted. Innovations in public data communications networks brought the search services closer to the desktops of many more users, and allowed the online industry to flourish.

What role did formal evaluation play in the progress of online systems and services?

Most of what is known now about how users reacted to the first operational systems was collected carefully by researchers or systems operators, using various methods of data gathering and analysis. Users answered questionnaires, participated in individual and focus group interviews, and submitted complaints on the telephone, in writing, and online. In a few cases, online transactions were systematically logged and analyzed; elaborate automatic data collection programs were employed to monitor usage patterns, success rates, and satisfaction.

Analyses of users' reactions were complemented by studies of the performance characteristics of the system themselves. All of these studies, whether practical in orientation or done for basic science research, contributed to advancing the systems and services.

What was the role of government and private funding?

Another critical element in the confluence of hardware, software, databases, and services, without which little of the developmental work or evaluation studies could have been done, was the enormous (relative to today) funding contributions from public and private agencies. The rapid developments of the 1960s were a direct result of the plenitude of government support for information storage and retrieval research, experimentation, and development. This support was critical because these systems were expensive, requiring access to big, state-of-the-art computers and professionals with a variety of high-level programming, systems analysis, database design, and management skills. Because of the variety of funding opportunities available to willing and capable researchers, independent projects sprouted at numerous sites. Federal and private funding was available to universities and private research laboratories; thus both were involved in experimentation and building of prototypes.

Funding agencies that required grantees to write progress reports and final reports on their systems, activities, and findings contributed greatly to documenting the research and development. If we had to rely now on what was captured by the formal journal literature, our account of events would be far less detailed and robust. Then (and now), some hard-working R&D researchers and developers were averse to stopping and taking time to publish their work. Having to generate a report for a funding agency in order to keep the money flowing, however, was a strong incentive to document one's work. Further, the journal literature frequently lagged far behind the quarterly reports written for the funding agencies, and so were not as reliable or as complete a source of data for our timeline of milestone developments.

It was thanks to imaginative funders such as the U.S. Department of Health, Education, and Welfare, UNIVAC, the Council on Library Resources, Rome Air Development Center, and others that the general public had an opportunity to experience firsthand at a World's Fair the sensationally speedy information retrieval that they had seen dramatized in the movie *Desk Set* a few years earlier.

What were the characteristics, behavior, and attitudes of the online pioneers?

Nearly all of the research and development work in the sixties was conducted in the United States; with a few exceptions, the genesis was an American phenomenon. Quite a few of the key pioneers, however, were not American-born. The United States was the fortunate recipient of a significant brain drain from other countries such as Russia, Poland, Germany, England, Canada, and New Zealand. Since apparently none of these individuals was permitted to work directly on classified U.S. government research contracts, such as those awarded to SDC or LMSC, they exercised their talents by initiating projects in American universities.

The pioneering designers and developers had a wide variety of educational backgrounds. As was true of information science generally, the innovators in online retrieval came from a variety of disciplines such as psychology, computer science, engineering, physics, philosophy, social science, mathematics, and library science. While in most cases they mutated into information scientists of some sort, a few of the early drivers propelling online developments were lawyers or physicians.

Many designers and developers were remarkable for achievements and leadership outside the specific area of online IR. A surprising number held the office of president of the American Society for Information Science, earned the ASIS Award of Merit, the ASIS Best Information Book Award, the ASIS Outstanding Teacher Award, or significant awards of other professional associations. The characteristics that contributed to their success as online pioneers—intelligence, creativity, energy, ambition, and charisma—led to their achieving distinction and high status in the field overall. They did not hide behind the closed doors of their labs.

The second group of pioneers—the managers, promoters, trainers, and customer service representatives—were the ones who set service policies, sold potential users on the idea of online searching, convinced librarians, scientists, lawyers, and others to use the services themselves, and showed them how. This group was visible, highly energized, zealous, and competitive. If necessary to sell the product, they faked online demonstrations. They endured physical hardships and personal indignities traveling and training across the United States and around the world.

Very few of the second group of pioneers published in the professional literature; their contributions were made through writing system documentation, training manuals, and promotional materials, by conducting training sessions and demonstrations, and through one-on-one customer services. To endure their rigorous jobs they had to be persuasive, clever, resourceful, and unfailingly charming—and it did not hurt to be attractive as well. To accomplish the task of turning a nascent online system that had all sorts of operational problems and limitations into a commercial success, they had to believe in online.

The users themselves constituted the third group. They too were pioneers who were willing to endure unreliable equipment, capricious response times, and restrictive service policies. They tested training programs and documentation and found both to be deficient. They searched small databases, using interface programs that they could not fully understand. They allowed themselves to be interviewed and monitored online. They gamely answered questionnaires, participated in experiments, and watched systems change even before they had mastered the existing versions. Much of the eventual successes of the interfaces, manuals, and training programs can be attributed to the constructive feedback supplied by users, who also played an important role in determining pricing and service policies.

Users were both end-users and intermediaries, many more of the latter than the former. This was in spite of the fact that a large percentage of the pioneering systems were designed for direct access by a specific target group of end users. The designers, however, seemed to have a blind spot in believing that their systems were easy to use. A few even imagined that virtually no training at all was required. Their intuition about a deep-rooted preference among end users to do their own searching has been proven correct by the phenomenal success in the 1990s of World Wide Web search engines. In the 1960s, 1970s, and 1980s, however, most designers did not seem to grasp the many impediments that inhibited end user searching.

The early adopters among the intermediaries were primarily librarians in defense and NASA information centers, medical libraries, and pharmaceutical companies. Many of these librarians likewise wished for end users to be able to conduct their own searches. They expended a great deal of time and effort in demonstration, training, and evaluation trying to make it happen. But in case after case, the end users backed off. They resisted expending the amount of learning time needed to master the search interaction, or they did not search frequently enough to maintain their skills, or they never grasped the fine points of logical operations, search languages, or indexing vocabularies. Even a system such as LEADERMART that was based on natural language interaction was adopted, not by the intended end users, but by librarians. The librarians then complained about the lack of explicit Boolean operators to structure search strategies.

Librarians nonetheless were loyal allies to the search services, assisting with marketing, documentation, training, and other online service tasks. A few of them were nervous about the impact of online retrieval on their own job security, but most recognized that it would in fact enhance their status and improve the quality of their professional work. Mr. Sumner's comments in *Desk Set*—"EMERAC is not going to take over. It was never intended to take over. It was never intended to replace you. It is here merely to free your time for research. It is just here to help you"—resonated with these librarians.

Within all three groups of pioneers were three subgroups, divided on the issue of subject access to records. One group was convinced that searching based on subject indexing from a controlled vocabulary yielded the best results. Designers and users of *MeSH* and the MEDLINE database exemplified this group. The second group believed that "full-text" searching (usually of titles and abstracts, rarely the full documents) was superior, the easiest to learn, and the wave of the future. LEADER-MART and LEXIS and many other systems were based on this philosophy. A third group was comprised of individuals who experimented with subject access via some sort of classification codes or other indirect means, such as cited references. All these years later, none of the three modes of subject access has won out and eliminated the others. Today, the three modes coexist in thousands of online indexes and catalogs.

A Final Quick Summary

This is a big story to sum up succinctly. It has hundred of actors in many different roles, inventing and using a wide variety of systems, software, and services. The online pioneers were embarking on an adventure that has burgeoned into a multi-billion-dollar business that impacts on all of our everyday lives—professionally and personally. In retrospect, the online story may be boiled down to these few steps:

- In modern times people needed more information than was available from their immediate colleagues, friends, and family. They relied on various printed indexes, catalogs, and bibliographies to keep track of information sources so they could search them manually when they needed information.

- When the number of information sources became extremely large, they got impatient with manual searching. They wanted computers to search painstakingly through huge stores of information for them.

- Then they became impatient with batch computer searching because the turnaround was measured in days and weeks. They wanted online searching because it was extremely fast.

- They were not satisfied with online searching that was available only at mainframe computer sites, at limited times, and without direct interaction to modify a search in progress. They wanted to be able to search interactively anywhere, at any time.

- Then they wanted more enhancements—faster and faster speeds, larger files, full text, images, and more.

"Everything's up to date in Kansas City; they've gone about as far as they can go!" This lyric from the popular stage and movie musical of the 1940s, "Oklahoma!" was not true then and it is not true now. In the time since our story closed at about the end of 1976, information wants have continued to grow insatiably and search systems and services have continued to respond. It would be futile to try to sum up here just where we are as of this writing—the world of computer-based information storage and retrieval and broadband communications technology is changing too fast and heading in unimaginable directions. Every day a new story is just around the corner.

Notes

2 Early Research and Development Activities

1. Engelbart created the mouse in 1965, as an employee of SRI, which assumed full rights to the patent. Engelbart has been lauded by various professional associations and societies for his important contributions to computer windows, online help systems, networking, word processing, electronic mail, and popular use of the Internet.

2. The Protosynthex work was not the first to process or analyze text with computers. Computer processing of full-text material had been demonstrated as early as 1955 with a concordance to the Bible. Extensive computer-based analysis of legal text material had been done in 1960 with batch systems to analyze legal statutes and break them down into schematic logic diagrams to show their basic meaning.

3. Sutherland today is remembered best as a prominent pioneer in virtual reality, the technology that gives users the impression of being in a lifelike environment that is actually computer generated. In the 1960s, while a computer scientist at MIT, Harvard University, and the University of Utah, Sutherland hooked up a computer to a small television screen, built his own head-mounted display, and wrote the software that allowed a viewer to have the sensation of moving among simple geometric shapes projected on screens directly in front of a viewer's eyes. He also gained fame for Sketchpad and the earliest 3-D CRT graphics.

4. In February 1965, Firschein and Drew proposed how the *Engineers Joint Council Thesaurus* could be used online to formulate a search, but they did not implement it in any early Lockheed systems (see chapter 5). The TIRP project (chapter 3) also implemented an online thesaurus in 1966, using the *Thesaurus of Textile Terms*.

5. Wolfe (1970) observed: "Expanding literature search depth by checking reference commonality is a venerable information retrieval technique, heavily used in manual literature searches" (40).

6. This is now a standard search approach for databases such as Science Citation Index and Social Science Citation Index, both produced by ISI.

7. An inverted file is created when all the records that have in common a particular value in a specific field are partitioned and grouped together. Thus an inverted file is broken into collections of records, called subfiles, all of which have some common value, for example, "heart disease" used as a subject indexing term or "Johnson, A. J." used as an author name.

8. As an aside, it is interesting to speculate why H. W. Wilson, one of the first commercial indexing services to obtain experience using their information in machine-readable form, did so little in that area during the next twenty years.

3 Further Experimentation and Prototypes in Universities, Mid-1960s to Early 1970s

1. The acronym first appeared as INTREX but later appeared generally as Intrex, so we have adopted that form.

2. Allderidge also appears as Alderidge in certain documents.

3. The Barnhart Dictionary Companion (1983), *Prentice-Hall Standard Glossary of Computer Terminology* (1985), and *Oxford English Dictionary*, 2d ed. (1989) date the general adoption of "user friendly" to the early 1980s, replacing the pejorative term "idiot-proof."

4. See chapter 7 for a discussion of the possible confusion of BIDAP with another batch processing system called BIRS, developed at Michigan State University.

5 Lockheed DIALOG and Related Systems, 1961–1972

1. RECON, as used here, is not an abbreviation for reconnaissance, nor for the LC REtrospective CONversion project.

2. However, a precedent for storing multiple sources of data for online (but not interactive) access was set with the 1964 World's Fair exhibit (chapter 2). In that demonstration, librarians could access essays written by research assistants, annotated reading lists on a variety of topics, and bibliographic entries from *Reader's Guide to Periodical Literature*. In March 1967, a demonstration of Data Corporation's online system took place, involving three separate files (see chapter 7).

3. Jo Robinson—later Jo Maxon-Dadd, then Jo Dadd, and currently Jo Maxon—worked for Bourne as a research assistant and lab instructor at UC-Berkeley, and later as a product manager for sci-tech databases at DIALOG.

6 SDC ORBIT and Related Systems, 1963–1972

1. Cuadra (1997) recalled that SDC lent an early copy of its TDMS/CDMS to the University of Texas. When SDC tried to get it back, the University said that it could not return it because it was in the possession of their vendor, a company called EDS. The University made no effort to reclaim it from EDS. As far as Cuadra knows, SDC never got it back. EDS grew to become a major computer services firm.

2. Many investigations in the years since the CIRCOL studies of cost/benefit trade-offs between controlled vocabulary indexing and natural language retrieval have demonstrated that some combination of natural and controlled vocabularies is optimum.

3. A more extensive history of NLM is available in Miles 1982.

4. Medlars is also a fruit resembling a crab apple that is used in preserves. In very early times, it was used for medical purposes.

5. American online search services and CD-ROM publishers were later required to pay millions of dollars in royalty payments for limited rights to use the MEDLARS files.

6. The individuals during this period who created computer search formulations and retrieved search results had functional job titles of "documentalists," "search specialists," or "information specialists." Stiller (1970) noted that a particular SUNY feature was useful to "computer oriented information specialists (hereafter referred to as 'searchers')." Early publications also referred to SDI profilers as "search strategists," "strategy designers," and "search editors."

7. Cuadra was in charge of recruiting and training other training specialists who would be stationed at SAGE Air Defense Sites throughout the United States. During interviews he used Minot, North Dakota, as the acid test for an applicant's willingness to relocate. (Only one team ever picked Minot as their site.)

7 Computer Searching for the Legal Profession, 1964–1972

1. This "Recon Central" is not the same as the RECON systems of NASA or AEC (chapter 5) or LC's RECON (REtrospective CONversion) project.

2. Giering, who relayed much of the detail in this section via correspondence and interviews, specified BIDAP in this context. However, BIDAP seems to have been only KWIC programs. Another batch processing system developed about the same time that *was* applied to indexing and searching of bibliographic data or textual material was called BIRS (Basic Indexing and Retrieval System). John Vinsonhaler (1967) developed BIRS at Michigan State University. Perhaps Giering meant the combination of BIDAP and BIRS.

3. A precedent for storing multiple sources of information for online access (but not interactive) was set with the 1964 World's Fair exhibit (chapter 2). Later, in October 1968, with the addition of a second NASA file, RECON operated for the first time in an online multifile mode (chapter 5).

4. A great amount of research and development was being conducted in the Dayton area during this period. Paul Evans Peters (1993) dubbed it a "hotbed of invention." He remarked that he was an undergraduate computer science major at the University of Dayton then, when the UD computer science program was one of only a handful in the country—using mostly adjunct faculty from WPAFB, NCR, and other local organizations.

5. Stop lists had been used previously in batch search systems, and in the 1963 SRI system (chapter 2).

6. These costs were far greater than those associated with some of the technological options available today, for example, PC servers and terminals on the Internet, publication and issuance of CD-ROM file updates for local PC systems.

7. Psychological Abstracts was also used in the 1969–1971 SUPARS project at Syracuse University (chapter 3).

8. Lancaster and Fayen (1973, 393–398) included tables and plots of costs for a projected NINDS online retrieval system for neurology.

9. If Lockheed and SDC had known of these study results, they might have stopped right then, but instead they became the dominant commercial online services over the next ten years.

8 State University of New York Biomedical Communications Network, 1965–1976

1. In 1964, as part of the planning with IBM for an online bibliographic retrieval system, Fred Kilgour of the

Columbia-Harvard-Yale project had the Yale Medical Library catalogers increase the depth of their subject indexing to an average of 10.4 *MeSH* terms for each monograph title. A cooperative online system was planned, but not implemented (Kilgour 1966). Starting in 1965 the Intrex project also worked with enhanced indexes to book records.

2. Bourne recalled hearing in conversation years ago: "Poor response time is defined as any response time slower than the fastest response time I've seen somewhere."

3. An explanation for BCN's funding constraints may be that New York City and the state were falling on hard times. In the early 1970s, New York City was suffering a serious financial crisis and was nearly bankrupt, which affected all state funding activities, including funding of the SUNY Central Office Computer Center.

4. Koenig (1987) said that NLM denied Pfizer and all other pharmaceutical companies access to MEDLINE at that time. NLM did not agree to make MEDLINE access available to U.S. pharmaceutical companies until much later.

9 The Online Industry: The Public View

1. An exception was MDC LEXIS, which went commercial with a big press conference in New York in April 1973; there is no uncertainty about that date.

2. Lest a reader jump to the erroneous conclusion that services provided by a government agency are always less costly than are the equivalent services provided by the private sector, the reduction here of costs *to the user*, going from $45 to $15 per hour, was the result of NLM's decision to provide the service without charging the full cost of providing it—thus subsidizing the service to provide lower *user* charges, but not lower total costs. For example, users of the Informatics system were paying a fee intended to cover the costs of the computer equipment and staff, office space and overhead, training and customer services support, and billing operations; NLM did not try to recover such costs in its pricing. Its charging policy was to recover distribution costs, but not file building and maintenance costs.

3. Online services today claim availability rates on the order of 99.96 percent.

4. Technically, the AEC changed its name in January 1975 to ERDA (U.S. Energy Research and Development Administration), and changed it again in October 1977 to DOE. For simplicity, the current name, DOE, is used throughout this chapter.

5. By the end of 1973 three online services began offering access to CAC records: SDC Search Service, SIA/BASIS, and Informatics with a subset of CAC for NLM's TOXLINE service.

6. This pattern is the opposite of current user demands for *faster* speeds than the search system normally provides.

7. This is in great contrast to most systems of today that permit output record sets and output processing of hundreds of thousands of records if desired.

8. The forms "WESTLAW" and "Westlaw" both appear in the descriptive reports and the literature of information sciences. We have adopted WESTLAW here.

9. This GIPSY should not be confused with GIPSY at the University of Oklahoma (chapter 3).

10. As a point of further contrast, the May/June 2000 newsletter for the STN search service (vol. 16, no. 3: 21) announced the STN system had doubled its answer set size limit of 4 million answers per file to 8 million answers per file.

10 Building the Online Industry: Behind the Scenes

1. Anne Hubbard met Rick Caputo at a DIALOG Update and they courted for a year over the telephone between the East and West Coasts before marrying.

2. As a separate issue, we have already seen how NLM issued an RFP for backup online MEDLINE services. In response, SDC Search Service submitted a bid, but lost, with the contract going to SUNY BCN who then got the NLM database and contract funding directly from NLM in March 1973, and started to provide online service to SUNY and other institutions.

3. In 1982, when NLM finally permitted a commercial organization (BRS) to offer public MEDLINE service, it continued to impose severe restrictions (e.g., prohibiting BRS from offering service to users overseas in countries that were being served already by NLM's international partners; and requiring significant royalty payments for MEDLINE use). NLM was in effect controlling and protecting its own monopoly and marketplace.

4. Along the same line, DIALOG and SDC both received file update tapes that had been mistakenly sent to the

wrong service, which usually forwarded them promptly to the other service.

5. Twenty years later, this type of problem reappeared with some Internet service providers.

6. Smith (1993) described how George Boole's theoretical contributions were applied in the twentieth century to computerized information storage and retrieval.

Summary of Online Milestones

1963

SATIRE was the first bibliographic retrieval system (but probably not an online system) in which microform storage at a searcher's workstation provided expanded versions (e.g., abstracts, extracts, tables of contents, source publications) of the information available online. (See parallel milestone for MICRO.)

SRI demonstrated the first online bibliographic search system.

SRI demonstrated the first online full-text search system.

SRI provided the first demonstration of *remote* online bibliographic and full-text searching.

SRI provided the first long-distance demonstration of an online search system.

SRI provided the first demonstration of an online search system with a CRT terminal for interaction between humans and machines.

SRI provided the first demonstration of an online search system with CRT display of search output.

SRI was the first to demonstrate an online search system that retrieved records on the basis of bibliographic citation elements such as author, publication date, title words, or abstracts.

SRI provided the first demonstration of a user-specified output display format option.

SRI provided the first demonstration of online search and output display of abstracts with bibliographic or full-text records.

SRI provided the first demonstration of a stop list in an online search system.

1964

GE-Valley Forge was among the first online search systems to use Boolean logic to combine terms in searching for bibliographic records. (See parallel milestone for TIP.)

Law Research Service was the first computer-based bibliographic search service provided on a regular basis by a commercial organization.

The Library/USA demonstration was the first time that the general public witnessed and participated in retrieving bibliographic information using online technology.

The Library/USA demonstration may have been the first online search system to demonstrate inverted file searching.

Library/USA may have been the first demonstration of an online search system providing a searcher with a choice of multiple online databases.

The Library/USA demonstration was the first instance of an update as frequently as weekly to an operational online bibliographic retrieval system.

Library/USA was the first online search system to demonstrate simultaneous multiple-terminal access to the same database and search software.

Library/USA provided the first possibility for interactive communication through a computer with reference librarians remotely located from the computer facility and the requesters.

Library/USA provided the first access for the general public to an online retrieval system from long-distance, using teletypewriters or standard telephone lines.

TEXTIR was the first online search system to accept search questions in natural language form.

TEXTIR was the first online search system to demonstrate a search approach that selected the source text material that most closely represented the question text.

TEXTIR was the first online search system to demonstrate an output relevance ranking algorithm, and the first to provide search output in rank order by a query relevance score.

TIP was the first online search system to retrieve citations on the basis of cited references or bibliographic coupling.

TIP was the first online search system to allow a searcher to save search output for later searching or use.

TIP was the first online search system to provide a searcher the option of online output or later offline printing.

TIP was the first online search system to implement stem searching.

TIP was the first online search system to implement left-truncation searching.

TIP was among the first online search systems to use Boolean logic to combine terms in searching for bibliographic records. (See parallel milestone for GE-Valley Forge.)

TIP was the first online search system to use a database of more than 25,000 records.

Summary of Online Milestones

1965

BOLD was the first online search system to use an existing machine-readable file of bibliographic records (a sample from the DDC database) created by another organization.

BOLD was the first online search system to demonstrate retrieval by subject classification codes rather than text words.

BOLD was the first online search system to provide posting counts of the number of records associated with each search term.

CIDS was the first system to demonstrate online searching of chemical structures.

The DDC database was the first machine-readable file of bibliographic records to be used in an online search system created by another organization (SDC's BOLD).

LUCID was the first search system to permit a searcher to modify the database online.

MICRO was the first online search system to allow searchers the option to work in either a novice or experienced searcher interface mode.

MICRO was the first online search system to allow searchers the option of receiving a user-specified number of long or short output records.

MICRO was the first online search system to provide at the terminal site microform storage of expanded versions (e.g., abstracts, extracts, tables of contents, source publications) of the information available online. (See parallel milestone for SATIRE.)

TEXTIR was the first online search system to incorporate synonyms automatically into the search formulation.

TEXTIR was the first online search system to prompt a searcher for information about search specifications.

TEXTIR was the first online search system to demonstrate search term weighting.

TIP was the first online search system to implement "wild card" character searching.

TIP was the first online search system to permit a searcher to store a search formulation to be recalled and incorporated into another query or used for later runs on updated files.

1966

BOLD may have been the first online bibliographic search system that enabled users to display an online thesaurus as a search aid. (See parallel milestone for TIRP.)

Bunker-Ramo's version of RECON was the first online search system to use a file of more than 200,000 records (the NASA database).

Bunker-Ramo's version of RECON was the first online search system with a capability for online ordering of source documents.

DIALOG was the first online search system to provide set numbers to intermediate search products, along with a means to make use of those sets in later operations.

Law Research Service may have been the first online search service provided on a regular basis by a commercial organization.

Multilist was the first online search system to permit a searcher to retrieve automatically all the records that were either hierarchically subordinate to or hierarchically superior to a given search term.

TIRP may have been the first online bibliographic search system that allowed users to display an online thesaurus as a search aid. (See parallel milestone for BOLD.)

TIRP was the first online bibliographic search system to offer a way to distinguish major and minor descriptors in searching.

TIRP was the first online bibliographic search system to display automatically alternate search terms and their posting counts when a query found no records for a term.

TIRP was the first online bibliographic system to provide a means of identification and removal of duplicate records from search output.

1967

BOLD was the first online search system to be searched from a terminal outside the country in which the computer operated.

Data Central was the first online bibliographic search system to incorporate an arithmetic search capability.

Data Corporation's online system was among the first online bibliographic search systems to operate in a multifile access mode.

1968

AUDACIOUS was the first online search system to demonstrate an online decimal classification authority file as an online search aid.

COLEX was the first online search system to use time windows to handle large or multiple databases.

COLEX was the first operational national online search service network.

COLEX provided the first large-scale use of an online search system.

LEADER was the first online search system to store, provide access to, and display a significant amount (10,000 source documents) of full-text information online.

NASA/RECON was among the first online bibliographic search systems to operate in a multifile access mode.

SUNY BCN was the first online search system to provide service on a regularly scheduled basis to a geographically dispersed network of users, with the intention of continuing to operate as a regular service rather than just running as an experiment.

SUNY BCN was the first online search system to use an online bibliographic database of more than 500,000 records.

SUNY BCN was the first online search system to offer a database with in-depth indexing to books and other monographs.

SUNY BCN was the first online search system to incorporate library holdings and availability information in specific output records.

SUNY BCN was the first online search service to hold an annual users conference.

1969

Data Central was among the first online search systems to demonstrate word proximity searching (i.e., allowing word sequence and proximity to be part of the search formulation).

DIALOG, with the ERIC database, provided the first instance of extensive availability of abstracts online for search output.

DIALOG was the first online search system to provide an on-demand online display of the current search formulation and associated posting counts.

ESRO/RECON was the first online search service to run in Europe and provide online search service in Europe.

Using Data Central, OBAR was the first large-scale use of online full-text searching.

Using Data Central, OBAR was the first large-scale online system to operate with full-text statutory and case law.

STAIRS may have been the first online search system to provide a significant online tutorial/help capability.

Syracuse University School of Library Science was the first academic institution to introduce and integrate online searching into regular classroom instruction.

Terminal TEXT-PAC was among the first online search systems to demonstrate word proximity searching (i.e., allowing word sequence and proximity to be part of the search formulation).

Terminal TEXT-PAC was the first online search system to allow the inclusion, and meaningful use, of upper/lower case information in the search formulation.

1970

CIMARON was the first online search system to demonstrate phonetic searching.

Data Central was the first online search system to highlight the terms in the retrieved records that caused a record to be retrieved.

Data Central was the first online search system to allow users to generate a KWIC display of a specified number of text words on either side of a search term in the retrieved text.

Data Central was the first online search system to use a color CRT output device.

Data Central was the first online search system to use color contrast in search output displays to highlight the search term in the retrieved record.

Data Central was the first online search system to allow searchers to page backward to reexamine previously displayed records.

ELMS may have been the first OPAC.

Intrex was the first online search system in which a terminal could display on the same viewing screen input-output communication and microform images of source documents.

Summary of Online Milestones

SUPARS, with Psychological Abstracts, was the first instance of extensive availability of abstracts online for both searching and output.

SUPARS, with Psychological Abstracts, was the first instance of a widely known database made available online on a regular basis to an entire campus community.

SUPARS was the first online search system to allow users to search for and examine search strategies created by other searchers.

1971

DIALOG and CCM Information Corporation were the first organizations to establish a license agreement and royalty payments for use of a database on an online search service.

LEADERMART was the first fully operational public online search service, providing service to any interested user.

LEADERMART was the first online search service to institute connect-hour charging.

PANDEX was the first database produced as a commercial venture that was made publicly available by an online search service.

1972

NLM and SDC MEDLINE, with TYMNET, provided the first instance of use of a public data communication network with an online search service.

1973

BASIS was the first online search service to provide access at any time to an online collection of more than 1 million records.

CAN/OLE may have been the first online search system to offer a bilingual interface option.

DIALOG was the first online search service to advertise in journal publications.

DIALOG was the first online search service to produce a regular newsletter for its customers.

RETRO may have been the first online search system to offer a bilingual interface option.

1974

DIALOG was the first online search service to establish a 1–800 toll-free telephone number for customer service.

Mead was the first online search service to designate and equip a room at one of its offices to be a dedicated training facility.

Mead was the first online search service to use a videotape for training.

SDC Search Service was the first online search service to provide publicly available online document ordering service.

1975

Dow Jones News/Retrieval may have been the first online bibliographic or full-text retrieval system to provide file updates on a real-time basis.

LEXIS was the first online search service to establish discounts for online access that was part of an academic institution's instructional activities.

1976

ILO/ISIS may have been the first online search system to allow search terms entered in one language to retrieve records indexed by corresponding terms in another language.

Bibliography

Aagaard, J. S. 1967. BIDAP: A bibliographic data processing program for keyword indexing. *American Behavioral Scientist* 10 (6), 24–27. Feb.

Aagaard, J. S. 1997. Personal communication to C. P. Bourne. Aug. 28.

Abramowitz, D. 1975. At last, a user-oriented system: LEXIS. *Proceedings of the American Society for Information Science* 12, 125–126. Aug. 28.

Adams, S. 1964. MEDLARS and the library community. *Bulletin of the Medical Library Association* 52 (1), 171–177. Jan.

Adams, S. 1965a. MEDLARS: Performance, problems, possibilities. *Bulletin of the Medical Library Association* 53 (2), 139–151. Apr.

Adams, S. 1965b. MEDLARS: Progress and prospects. In M. Rubinoff (ed.), *Toward a National Information System,* 77–85. Washington, DC: Spartan Books. (Proceedings of the Second Annual National Colloquium on Information Retrieval, Philadelphia, PA, Apr. 23–24.)

Adams, S. 1972. The way of the innovator: Notes toward a prehistory of MEDLARS. *Bulletin of the Medical Library Association* 60 (4), 523–533. Oct.

Adams, S., and S. Taine. 1964. The National Library of Medicine and MEDLARS. *Revue Internationale de la Documentation* 31 (3), 107–110. Aug.

Addis, L. 1970. Stanford Linear Accelerator Center participation in SPIRES. In *System scope for library automation and generalized information storage and retrieval at Stanford University,* 122–134. Stanford, CA: Stanford University. Feb.

Adkinson, B. W. 1978. *Two centuries of federal information.* Stroudsberg, PA: Dowden, Hutchinson & Ross.

Ahlgren, A. E. 1975. Factors affecting the adoption of on-line search services by the public library. *Proceedings of the 4th Mid-Year Meeting of the American Society for Information Science,* 123–132.

Aiyer, A. K. 1971. *The CIMARON system: Modular programs for the organization and search of large files.* (ERIC No. ED 061 978.) Berkeley: University of California, Institute of Library Research. Sept. 57 pp.

Alber, F., and D. M. Heaps. 1971. Classifying, indexing, and searching resources management information via an on-line thesaurus. In *Proceedings of the Third Annual Meeting of the Western Canada Chapter of ASIS, Banff, Canada,* 107–116.

Alexander, R. W. 1967. Toward the future integrated library system. In *33rd Conference of FID and International Congress on Documentation.* (Abstract No. III64.) Tokyo: International Federation for Documentation.

Alexander, R. W. 1968. *Library Management System (LMS): Descriptive specifications for an on-line, real-time integrated library system.* (Report No. 16.196.) Los Gatos, CA: IBM Advanced Systems Development Division. Sept. 20. 181 pp.

Alexander, R. W., and R. W. Harvey. 1970. *An overview of the Experimental Library Management System (ELMS).* (Report No. 16.197.) Los Gatos, CA: IBM Advanced Systems Development Division. May 25.

Allderidge, J. M., and P. J. Knoke. 1966. *Design considerations for an on-line management system; Final report.* (Report No. SURC TR 20; RADC-TR-65-424; NTIS No. AD 488 455.) Syracuse, NY: Syracuse University Research Corporation. July.

Alley, D., H. Lawford, and P. Wolters. 1978. Canadian online use: Trends, implications, policies. *Proceedings of the Sixth Canadian Conference on Information Science,* 61–90.

Allison, A. M., and A. Allan. 1979. *OCLC: A national library network.* Short Hills, NJ: Enslow. Allocation of MEDLINE terminals in Canada. 1972. *Information; Part 1/News; Sources; Profiles* 4 (6), 315. Nov.–Dec.

Allocation of MEDLINE terminals in Canada. 1972. *Information; Part 1/News; Sources; Profiles* 4 (6), 315. Nov.–Dec.

Alt, F. L., and R. A. Kirsch. 1968. Citation searching and bibliographic coupling with remote on-line computer access. *Journal of Research of the National Bureau of Standards: B. Mathematical Sciences* 72 (B1), 61–78. Jan.–Feb.

American Library Association. 1963. *The library and information network of the future.* (Report No. RADC TDR-62-614; NTIS No. AD 401 347.) Chicago: ALA. Apr. 8.

Anderson, R. R., A. J. Kasarda, and D. M. Reed. 1967. *Experimental retrieval systems studies; Report no. 3.* (NTIS No. AD 653 280.) Bethlehem, PA: Lehigh University, Center for the Information Sciences. Apr. 15. 88 pp.

Angione, P. 1999a. Interview. June 30.

Angione, P. 1999b. Personal communication to C. P. Bourne. Oct. 25.

Annual Review Staff. 1966. New hardware developments. *Annual Review of Information Science and Technology* 1, 191–220.

Anthony, L. J., D. H. Carpenter, and A.G. Cheney. 1968. Selective dissemination of information using a KDF9 computer. *Aslib Proceedings* 20 (1), 40–64. Jan.

Anthony, L. J., A. G. Cheney, and E. K. Whelan. 1968. Some experiments in the selective dissemination of information in the field of plasma physics. *Information Storage & Retrieval* 4, 187–200. June.

Armstrong, A. A. 1982. Battelle's battle for science. *Bulletin of the American Society for Information Science* 8 (6), 25–26. Aug.

Arnett, E. M., and A. Kent. 1973. *Computer-based chemical information.* New York: Dekker.

Artandi, S., and L. Struminger. 1971. *TEXT-PAC for teaching information science: A library manual.* (NTIS No. PB 198 493.) New Brunswick, NJ: Rutgers University, Graduate School of Library Science. 42 pp.

ASIS Forms New SIG's. 1972. *Information; Part I/News; Sources; Profiles* 4 (1), 15. Jan.–Feb.

Asleson, R. 1987. Interview. Apr. 22.

Asman, R. J. 1973. OBAR: Ohio State Bar Automated Research. In R. A. May (ed.), *Automated law research; A collection of presentations delivered at the First National Conference on Automated Law Research,* 43–47. American Bar Association, Standing Committee on Law and Technology.

Atherton, P. 1970. *Development of a computer-based laboratory for library science students using LC/MARC tapes.* (ERIC No. ED 037 224.) Syracuse, NY: Syracuse University, School of Library Science. Jan. 47 pp.

Atherton, P. 1971, July. *SUPARS; Syracuse University Psychological Abstracts Retrieval Service; Final report to the Rome Air Development Center; Large scale information processing systems; Section IV-A: The user component of the system-A.* Syracuse, NY: Syracuse University, School of Library Science. 59 pp. (Other contributing authors include S. Browning, K. H. Cook, E. Frierson, and C. Morse.)

Atherton, P. 1977. Improved subject access to books in on-line library catalogs. In *Proceedings of the First International Online Information Meeting,* 131–138. Oxford, England: Learned Information.

Atherton, P. 1978a. Books are for use—Evaluation of MARC records in online subject retrieval systems. *Proceedings of American Society for Information Science* 15, 17–20.

Atherton, P. 1978b. *Books are for use: Final report of the subject access project to the Council on Library Resources.* (Report No. IST-10; ERIC No. ED 156 131.) Syracuse, NY: Syracuse University, School of Information Studies. Feb. 172 pp.

Atherton, P., and K. B. Miller. 1970. LC/MARC on MOLDS; An experiment in computer-based, interactive bibliographic storage, search, retrieval, and processing. *Journal of Library Automation* 3 (2), 142–165. June.

Atherton, P., K. B. Miller, D. Aurrichio, and H. Schwarzlander. 1970. *Large scale information processing systems, v. II: Investigations in data management; Final technical report, 15 July 1967–15 Jan. 1970.* (Report No. RADC-TR-70-80-Vol. 2; NTIS No. AD 708 726.) Syracuse, NY: Syracuse University Research Corporation. May. 74 pp.

Atherton, P., and J. Tessier. 1970. Teaching with MARC tapes. *Journal of Library Automation* 3 (1), 24–35. Mar.

Atherton, P., and J. Wyman. 1969. Searching MARC project tapes using IBM/Document Processing System. *Proceedings of the American Society for Information Science* 6, 83–88.

Atherton, P. A., K. H. Cook, and J. Katzer. 1972. *Free text retrieval evaluation; Final report, 1 Feb. 1971–31 Jan. 1972.* (Report No. RADC-TR-72-159; NTIS No. AD 748 218.) Syracuse, NY: Syracuse University, School of Library Science. July. 219 pp.

Atherton, P. A., D. W. King, and R. R. Freeman. 1968. *Evaluation of the retrieval of nuclear science document references using the Universal Decimal Classification as the indexing language for a computer-based system.* (Report No. AIP/UDC-8; NTIS No. PB 179 679.) New York: American Institute of Physics. May 1.

Austin, C. J. 1966. Transmission of bibliographic information. In J. Harrison and P. Laslett (eds.), *The Brasnose Conference on the Automation of Libraries,* 143–150. Chicago: Mansell. (Proceedings of Anglo-American Conference on the Mechanization of Library Services, Oxford, June 30–July 3.)

Austin, C. J. 1968. *MEDLARS 1963–1967.* Bethesda, MD: NLM. 76 pp.

Avram, H. D., L. S. Maruyama, and J. C. Rather. 1972. Automation activities in the processing department of the Library of Congress. *Library Resources & Technical Services* 16 (2), 195–239. Spring.

Bachelder, S. 1976. The New York Times Information Bank: A user's perspective. In F. W. Lancaster (ed.), *The use of computers in literature searching and related reference activities in libraries,* 17–30. Urbana-Champaign:

University of Illinois, Graduate School of Library Science. (Proceedings of the 1975 Clinic on Library Applications of Data Processing.)

Backer, S. 1967. The thesaurus as a first step in an information retrieval system. *Textile Institute and Industry* 5 (4), 91–96. Apr.

Backer, S. 1997. Personal communication to C. P. Bourne. Dec. 12.

Backer, S., E. I. Valko, and M. Liang. 1967. The problems of textile information retrieval. *Textile Research Journal* 37, 880–894. Oct.

Bagley, P. R. 1951. Electronic digital machines for high-speed information searching. Master's thesis, MIT, Cambridge, MA.

Baker, A. W., and J. L. Smith. 1968a. *COLEX (CIRC On-Line Experimentation); Final report, 1 Oct. 1966–31 Oct. 1967, Vol. 1.* (Report No. TM-DA-L-15, Vol. 1; RADC-TR-68-12-Vol. 1; NTIS No. AD 390 887.) Santa Monica, CA: SDC. May. 97 pp.

Baker, A. W., and J. L. Smith. 1968b. *COLEX (CIRC On-Line Experimentation); Final report; 1 Oct. 1966–31 Oct. 1967. Vol. 2.* (Report No. TM-DA-1-15, Vol. 2; RADC-TR-68-12-Vol-2; NTIS No. AD 834 236.) Santa Monica, CA: SDC. May. 60 pp. (Vol. 2 also includes L. Cegala and E. Waller, *COLEX user's manual.* Falls Church, VA: SDC. Report No. TM-WD-405/000/00. Undated.)

Baker, F. T. 1972. Chief programmer team management of production programming. *IBM Systems Journal* 11 (1), 56–73.

The BALLOTS project: Final report to the National Endowment for the Humanities; Sep. 1, 1972–Jan. 31, 1975. 1975. (ERIC No. ED 121 333.) Stanford, CA: Stanford University, Stanford Center for Information Processing. Oct. 80 pp.

Barber, A. S., E. D. Barraclough, and W. A. Gray. 1972. Closing the gap between the medical researcher and the literature. *British Medical Journal* 1 (Feb.), 368–370.

Barber, A. S., E. D. Barraclough, and W. A. Gray. 1973. On-line information retrieval as a scientist's tool. *Information Storage & Retrieval* 9 (Aug.), 429–440.

Barden, W.A. 1965. Part II: Request processing. In J. J. Maher (ed.), *Proceedings of the Workshop on Working with Semi-Automatic Documentation Systems, Warrenton, VA, May 2–5, 1965,* 79–84. Santa Monica, CA: SDC. (NTIS No. 620 360.)

Barden, W. A., W. Hammond, and J. H. Heald. 1959. *Automation of ASTIA: A preliminary report.* (NTIS No. AD 227 000.) Arlington, VA: Armed Services Technical Information Agency. Dec. 50 pp.

Barnholdt, B., and M. Hein. 1973. *ELMS Experimental Library Management System (IBM's integrated data base system for libraries): A special study of the possible applications and performance of the system in Danish libraries.* Lyngby, Denmark: Danish Technical University Library. 59 pp. (Partial English translation.)

Barraclough, E. 1970. Efficiency in British MEDLARS. *Catalogue & Index, no. 18,* 4–6. Apr.

Barrett, G. V., C. L. Thornton, and P. A. Cabe. 1968. Human factors evaluation of a computer based information storage and retrieval system. *Human Factors* 10 (Aug.), 431–436.

Barrett, R. P. 1965. CIRC-Centralized Information Reference and Control. In J. J. Maher (ed.), *Proceedings of the Workshop on Working with Semi-Automatic Documentation Systems, Warrenton, VA, May 2–5, 1965,* 15–31. Santa Monica, CA: SDC. (Report No. AFOSR-65-1699; NTIS No. AD 620 360.)

Basheer, B. W. 1973. JURIS: Justice Retrieval and Inquiry System. R.A. May (ed.), *Automated law research: A collection of presentations delivered at the First National Conference on Automated Law Research,* 55–65. American Bar Association, Standing Committee on Law and Technology.

Bateman, B. B., and E. H. Farris. 1968. Operating a multilibrary system using long-distance communications to an on-line computer. *Proceedings of the American Society for Information Science* 5, 155–162.

Baum, C. 1981. *The system builders; The story of SDC.* Santa Monica, CA: SDC.

Baxamoosa, S. 1970. A study of SDC's Time-Shared Data Management System: Research project. M.S. thesis in Electrical Engineering and Computer Science, University of California at Berkeley. 27 pp.

Bayer, M. 1980. Personal communication to C. P. Bourne. May 1.

Bayer, M. 1987. Interview. May 6.

Bayer, M. 1995. Personal communication to C. P. Bourne. Oct. 4.

Beard, J. J. 1969. Computers and the law: Caveats, prognostications and other desiderata. *Suffolk University Law Review* 3 (2), 366–379. Spring.

Beard, J. J. 1971. Information systems applications in law. *Annual Review of Information Science and Technology,* 369–396.

Beckelhimer, M. A., J. W. Cox, J. W. Hutchins, and D. L. Kenton. 1978. The MEDLINE hardware and software. *Medical Informatics* 3 (3), 197–209.

Becker, J. 1964. Demonstrating remote retrieval by computer at Library/USA. *American Library Association Bulletin* 58 (Oct.), 822–824.

Becker, J. 1975. A brief history of online bibliographic systems. In J. Sherrod (ed.), *Information systems and networks,* 3–13. Westport, CT: Greenwood Press. (Proceedings of the Eleventh Annual Symposium in Information Processing, Los Angeles, CA, Mar. 27–29, 1974.)

Becker, J. 1984, An information scientist's view on evolving information technology. *Journal of the American Society for Information Science* 35 (May), 164–165.

Becker, J. 1987. Interview. Oct. 6.

Becker, J., and R. M. Hayes.1963. *Information storage and retrieval: Tools, elements, theories.* New York: John Wiley & Sons.

Becker, J., and R. M. Hayes. 1970. *A plan for a Wisconsin library and information network; Knowledge network of Wisconsin.* (ERIC No. ED 111 430.) Madison, WI: Wisconsin Department of Public Instruction, Division of Library Sciences. Oct.

Bell, J. M., and C. McAllister. 1970. *User needs in the Experimental Library Management System (ELMS).* (Report No. 16.189.) Los Gatos, CA: IBM Advanced Systems Development Division. Feb. 16. 23 pp.

Bellardo, T. 1984. Some attributes of online search intermediaries that relate to search outcome. Unpublished doctoral diss., Drexel University, Philadelphia, PA.

Bellardo, T. 1985. An investigation of online searcher traits and their relationship to search outcome. *Journal of the American Society for Information Science* 36, 241–250.

Benbow, J. A. 1972. On-line automation of a UDC based library. In A. B. Piternick (ed.), *Proceedings of the Fourth Annual Meeting of the American Society for Information Science, Western Canada Chapter,* 113–121. Winnipeg, Canada: University of British Columbia, School of Librarianship. Sept.

Benenfeld, A. R. 1969. Generation and encoding of the Project INTREX augmented catalog data base. In D. E. Carroll (ed.), *Proceedings of the 1968 Clinic on Library Applications of Data Processing,* 155–198. Urbana-Champaign: University of Illinois, Graduate School of Library Science.

Bennertz, R. K. 1971. *Development of the Defense Documentation Center remote on-line retrieval system: Past, present and future.* (Report No. DDC-TR-71-2; NTIS No. AD 720 900.) Alexandria, VA: DDC. Mar. 51 pp.

Bennett, E., E. C. Haines, and J. K. Summers. 1965. AESOP: A prototype for on-line user control of organizational data storage, retrieval and processing. *Proceedings of the AFIPS Fall Joint Computer Conference* 27 (pt. 1), 435–455.

Bennett, J. L. 1969. On-line access to information: NSF as an aid to the indexer/cataloger. *American Documentation* 20 (July), 213–220.

Bennett, R. E. 1997. Personal communication to C. P. Bourne. July 14.

Bennett, R. E., and S. J. Frycki. 1971. Internal processing of external reference services. *Journal of Chemical Documentation* 11, 76–83.

Bering, E. A. 1967. The Neurological Information Network of the National Institute of Neurological Diseases and Blindness. *Bulletin of the Medical Library Association* 55 (2), 135–140. Apr.

Berul, L. H. 1969. Document retrieval. *Annual Review of Information Science and Technology* 4, 203–227.

Berul, L. H., D. W. King, and J. G. Yates. 1974. *Editorial processing centers: A study to determine economic and technical feasibility.* (NTIS No. PB 234 959.) Rockville, MD: Westat; Aspen Systems Corporation. July. 107 pp.

Berul, L. H., and B. I. Krevitt. 1974. Innovative editorial procedure: The Editorial processing center concept. *Proceedings of the American Society for Information Science* 11, 98–102.

Bichel, R. L., and J. L. Smith.1965. *List processing project final report.* (Report No. TM-DA-4/001.) Santa Monica, CA: SDC. Aug. 61 pp.

Bielsker, R. 1969. *SPIRES reference manual.* Stanford, CA: Stanford University, Institute for Communications Research. Jan.

Biomedical Communication Network dedication proceedings. 1969. *Library Bulletin* (*SUNY Upstate Medical Center Library*) 9 (Feb.) (suppl. 1).

Biomedical Communication Network to be dedicated Oct. 18. 1968. *Upstate Medical Center Newsletter* 8 (2), 1–3. Oct. 9.

Bivans, M. M. 1974. A comparison of manual and machine literature searches. *Special Libraries* 65 (5/6), 216–222. May–June.

Bixby, W. E. 1962. Applications of microxerographic techniques to information recording. In V. D. Tate (ed.), *Pro-*

ceedings of the eleventh annual meeting and convention, 228–247. Annapolis, MD: National Microfilm Assn.

Black, D. V. 1969. Library information system time-sharing on a large, general-purpose computer. In D. E. Carroll (ed.), *Proceedings of the 1968 Clinic on Library Applications of Data Processing,* 139–154. Urbana-Champaign: University of Illinois.

Black, D. V. 1970. *Library Information System Time-Sharing (LISTS) project; Final report.* (Report No. TM-4547; ERIC No. ED 039 009.) Santa Monica, CA: SDC. May 1.

Black, D. V. 1987. Interview. Mar. 13.

Black, D. V. 1995. Interview. Aug. 2.

Black, D. V. 1996. Interview. Oct. 18.

Black, D. V., and D. M. Bethe. 1969. Library serials control using a general purpose data management system. *Proceedings of the American Society for Information Science* 6, 5–11.

Black, D. V., G. M. Cady, and R. V. Katter. 1971. *ELHILL II–MEDLARS II; Interface study: Final report.* (Report No. TM-(L)-4732/000/01.) Santa Monica, CA: SDC. May 12. 24 pp.

Black, D. V., and A. W. Luke. 1971. A comprehensive automated materials handling system for school districts. *Proceedings of the American Society for Information Science* 8, 279–285.

Blair, D. C. 1996. STAIRS redux: Thoughts on the STAIRS evaluation, ten years after. *Journal of the American Society for Information Science* 47 (1), 4–22. Jan.

Blair, D. C., and M. E. Maron. 1985. An evaluation of retrieval effectiveness for a full-text document retrieval system. *Communications of the ACM* 28 (3), 289–299. Mar.

Blanken, R. R., and B. T. Stern. 1975. Planning and design of on-line systems for the ultimate users of biomedical information. *Information Processing & Management* 11 (8/12), 207–227.

Bleier, R. E. 1967. Treating hierarchical data structures in the SDC Time-shared Data Management System (TAMS.) *Proceedings of the 22nd National Conference of the Association for Computing Machinery,* 41–49. (Report No. SP-2750.) Santa Monica, CA: SDC. Aug. 29. 23 pp. Published earlier as Report No. SP-2750, SDC, Santa Monica, CA. Aug. 29. 23 pp.

Bleier, R. E., and A. H. Vorhaus. 1969. File organization in the SDC Time-Shared Data Management System (TSMS.) In A. J. H. Morrell (ed.), *Information processing 1968,* vol. 2, 1245–1252. (Proceedings of the IFIP Congress 68, Edinburgh, Aug. 5–10, 1968.) Amsterdam: North-Holland.

Bloemeke, M. J., and S. Treu. 1969. Searching chemical titles in the Pittsburgh time-sharing system. *Journal of Chemical Documentation* 9 (3), 155–157.

The BOLD librarian. 1966. *Electronics* 39 (Oct. 17).

Borgman, C. L., and J. Trapani. Novice user training on PIRETS (Pittsburgh Information Retrieval System). *Proceedings of the American Society for Information Science* 12, 149–150.

Borko, H. 1965a. *BOLD–Bibliographic on-line display.* (Report No. TM-2295/024.) Santa Monica, CA: SDC. June 23.

Borko, H. 1965b. *Man-machine communication via on-line bibliographic displays.* (SDC Report No. SP-2164.) Paper presented at International Conference on General Semantics, San Francisco State College, Aug. 9. 4 pp.

Borko, H. 1967. Utilization of on-line interactive displays. In D. E. Walker (ed.), *Information system science and technology,* 327–334. (Proceedings of the Third Congress on Information System Science and Technology, 1966.) Washington, DC: Thompson Book Co. Published originally as Report No. SP-2575; NTIS No. AD 640 652, SDC, Santa Monica, CA. Aug. 22, 1966. 31 pp.

Borko, H. 1968. Interactive document storage and retrieval system—Design concepts. In K. Samuelson (ed.), *Mechanized information storage, retrieval and dissemination,* 591–599. (Proceedings of the FID/IFIP Joint Conference, Rome, June 14–17, 1967.) Amsterdam: North-Holland.

Borko, H. 1985. Interview. Oct. 23.

Borko, H. 1994. Personal communication to C. P. Bourne. Oct. 10.

Borko, H., and H. P. Burnaugh. 1966. Interactive displays for document retrieval. *Information Display* 3 (5), 47–48, 52–53, 90. Sept. Published originally as Report No. SP-2557; NTIS No. PB 173 477; NTIS No. AD 661 657, SDC, Santa Monica, CA. Aug. 4. 28 pp.

Borman, L., R. Hay, and B. Mittman. 1973. Information retrieval, statistical analysis and graphics: An integrated approach. *Information Storage & Retrieval* 9 (June), 309–319.

Borman, L., and B. Mittman. 1972. Interactive search of bibliographic data bases in an academic environment. *Journal of the American Society for Information Science* 23 (3), 164–171. May–June.

Bourne, C. P. 1963, Nov. *Research on computer augmented information management.* (Report No. ESD-TDR-64-177; NTIS No. AD 432 098.) Menlo Park, CA: SRI.

Bourne, C. P. 1969. *COSATI inventory of information sciences technology; Reports of federally funded research and development projects in the information sciences, FY 1968.* (Report No. COSATI 70-6; NTIS No. PB 188 880.) Palo Alto, CA: Information General Corporation. 2200 pp. (A shorter edition with same title and date, 671 pp., was issued as COSATI Report No. 70-2-FO; NTIS No. AD 877 496. May.)

Bourne, C. P. 1976a. *DIALOG laboratory workbook; Training exercises for the Lockheed DIALOG Information Retrieval Service.* Berkeley: University of California, Institute of Library Research. Oct. 110 pp.

Bourne, C. P. 1976b. Improvements in the coupling of SDI system output with document delivery systems. *Journal of Chemical Information and Computer Sciences* 16 (1), 27–30. Feb.

Bourne, C. P. 1977. *ORBIT laboratory workbook; Training exercises for the System Development Corporation ORBIT system.* Berkeley: University of California, Institute of Library Research. June. 50 pp.

Bourne, C. P. 1980a. On-line systems: History, technology, and economics. *Journal of the American Society for Information Science* 31 (3), 155–160. May.

Bourne, C. P. 1980b. Overlapping coverage and other points of comparison with the Excerpta Medica and MEDLINE online search files. In *Technology in support of library science and Information Service: With particular emphasis on computer-assisted reference service,* 62–76. Bangalore, India: Sarada Ranganathan Endowment for Library Science. (Sarada Ranganathan Lectures 12, 1978.)

Bourne, C. P. 1999. 40 years of database distribution and use: An overview and observation. *NFAIS Newsletter.* (1999 Miles Conrad Memorial Lecture at the NFAIS Annual Conference, Philadelphia, Feb. 23.) Apr.–May.

Bourne, C. P., and D. F. Ford. 1961. A study of methods for systematically abbreviating English words and names. *Journal of the Association for Computing Machinery* 8 (4), 538–552. Oct.

Bourne, C. P., J. B. North, and M. S. Kasson. 1969. *Preparation of 3rd COSATI inventory of current R&D in the information sciences; Final technical report.* (Report No. IGC-PA-69-42.) Palo Alto, CA: Information General Corporation. Nov. 17. 45 pp.

Bourne, C. P., J. Robinson, and J. Todd. 1974. *Analysis of ERIC on-line file searching procedures and guidelines for searching.* (Report No. ILR-74-005; ERIC No. ED 101 757.) Berkeley: University of California, Institute of Library Research. Nov. 148 pp.

Bower, C. A. 1971. MEDLARS: What the user thinks. *NLL Review* 1 (1), 10–13. Jan.

Bowman, S. 1965. General Purpose Display System (GPDS.) In C. Baum and L. Gorsuch (eds.), *Proceedings of the Second Symposium on Computer-Centered Data Base Systems,* 4–7. Santa Monica, CA: SDC. Dec. 1. (Report No. TM-2624/100; NTIS No. AD 625 417.)

Bowman, S., and R. A. Lickhalter. 1968. Graphical data management in a time-shared environment. *Proceedings of the AFIPS Spring Joint Computer Conference* 32, 353–362.

Brady, J. 1976. *The craft of interviewing.* Cincinnati, OH: Writer's Digest. Brain Information Service. 1971. In *Inventory of major information systems and services in science and technology,* 83–84. Paris: Organization for Economic Co-operation and Development.

Brandhorst, W. T. 1993. *The Educational Resources Information Center (ERIC): An annotated bibliography of documents and journal articles about ERIC (covering the period 1960–92).* (Report No. ED 355 974.) Rockville, MD: ERIC Processing and Reference Facility. Jan. 154 pp.

Brandhorst, W. T. 1995. Personal communication to C. P. Bourne. Mar. 9; Aug. 9.

Brandhorst, W. T. 1997. Personal communication to C. P. Bourne. July 18.

Brandhorst, W. T., and P. F. Eckert. 1972. Document retrieval and dissemination systems. *Annual Review of Information Science and Technology* 7, 379–437.

Bregzis, R. 1965. The Ontario new universities library project—An automated bibliographic data control system. *College & Research Libraries* 26 (Nov.), 495–508.

Bregzis, R. 1966. The ONULP bibliographic control system: An evaluation. In F. B. Jenkins (ed.), *Proceedings of the 1965 Clinic on Library Applications of Data Processing,* 112–140. Urbana-Champaign: University of Illinois.

Bregzis, R. 1967. Query language for the reactive catalogue. In A. B. Tonik (ed.), *Information retrieval: The user's viewpoint; An aid to design,* 77–91. (Fourth Annual National Colloquium on Information Retrieval, Philadelphia, May 3–4.) Philadelphia: International Information.

Bremner, J., and P. Miller. 1987. *Guide to database distribution: Legal aspects and model contracts.* Philadelphia: NFAIS. 93 pp.

Bribe overruns. 1976. *Nation* 222 (194). Feb. 21.

Bridegam, W. E., and E. Meyerhoff. 1970. Library participation in a biomedical communication and information network. *Bulletin of the Medical Library Association* 58 (2), 103–111. Apr.

Bridges, D. B. J. 1967. Executive programs for the LACONIQ time-shared retrieval monitor. *Proceedings of the AFIPS Fall Joint Computer Conference* 31, 231–242. Published originally as Report No. LMSC-TIC-2024, LMSC, Palo Alto, CA. Apr. 29 pp.

Briner, L. L. 1973. Cost benefits of automatic back-of-book indexing. *Proceedings of the American Society for Information Science* 10, 26.

Brodman, E., and M. Ohta. 1967. Medicine. *Library Trends* 15 (Apr.), 896–908.

Brown, C. P., E. J. Yeates, and M. J. Van Hoesen. 1975. Use and cost of on-line systems at the National Bureau of Standards library. *Proceedings of the American Society for Information Science* 12, 132–133.

Brown, R. R., and P. Nordyke. 1968. ICS; An information control system. In K. Samuelson (ed.), *Mechanized information storage, retrieval and dissemination.* Amsterdam: North-Holland. (Proceedings of the FID/IFIP Joint Conference, Rome, June 14–17, 1967.)

Brown, S. C. 1966. A bibliographic search by computer. *Physics Today* 19 (5), 59–64. May.

BRS: Bibliographic Retrieval Services, Inc.; Final prospectus. 1976. Schenectady, NY: Bibliographic Retrieval Services. May. 17 pp.

Brugioni, D. A. 1996. The art and science of photoreconnaissance. *Scientific American* 274 (3), 78–85. Mar.

Bryant, J. H., and P. Semple. 1966. GIS and file management. *Proceedings of 21st National Conference of the Association for Computing Machinery*, 97–107.

Buchanan, J. R., and E. M. Kidd. 1969. Development of a computer system with console capability for the Nuclear Safety Information Center. *Proceedings of the American Society for Information Science* 6, 151–158.

Buginas, S. J., and N. B. Crow. 1973. The computerized file management system: A tool for the reference librarian. *Special Libraries* 64 (1), 12–17. Jan.

Burchinal, L. G. 1970. The Educational Resources Information Center: An emergent national system. *Journal of Educational Data Processing* 7 (2), 55–67. Apr.

Burchinal, L. G. 1975. Notes from OSIS. *Bulletin of the American Society for Information Science* 1 (6), 7. Jan.

Burchinal, L. G. 1983. ERIC—The international education information system. In W. J. Paisley and M. Butler (eds.), *Knowledge utilization systems in education: Dissemination, technical assistance, networking*, 43–64. Beverly Hills, CA: Sage Publications.

Burchinal, L. G. 1995. Personal communication to C. P. Bourne. Sept. 4.

Burke, C. 1996. A rough road to the information superhighway; Project INTREX: A view from the CLR archives. *Information Processing & Management* 32 (1), 19–32.

Burnaugh, H. P. 1966a. *The BOLD user's manual for retrieval.* (Report No. TM-2306/004.) Santa Monica, CA: SDC. Sept. 6. A later version was published as *The BOLD user's manual* (Report No. TM-2306/004/02), Santa Monica, CA: SDC. 27 pp. Jan. 16, 1967.

Burnaugh, H. P. 1966b. *Data base generator for the BOLD system.* (Report No. TM-2306/001/02.) Santa Monica, CA: SDC. Aug. 31. 16 pp.

Burnaugh, H. P. 1966c. *Retrieval program for the BOLD system.* (Report No. TM-2306/002.) Santa Monica, CA: SDC. Jan. 10. 12 pp.

Burnaugh, H. P. 1967. The BOLD (Bibliographic On-Line Display) system. In G. Schecter (ed.), *Information retrieval: A critical review*, 53–66. (Proceedings of the Third Annual National Colloquium on Information Retrieval, Philadelphia, May 12–13, 1966.) Washington, DC: Thompson Book Co. Published originally as Report No. SP-2338/000/01; NTIS No. AD 632 473, SDC, Santa Monica, CA. Apr. 6. 23 pp.

Burrows, J. H. 1964. Automated data management (ADAM.) In A. Walker (ed.), *Proceedings of the symposium on development and management of a computer-centered data base*, 63–86. (SDC Corporate Communications No. BRT-41.) Santa Monica, CA: SDC. Jan. 6.

Bush, V. 1945. As we may think. *Atlantic Monthly* 176 (July), 101–108.

Byrne, J. R. 1975. Relative effectiveness of titles, abstracts, and subject headings for machine retrieval from the COMPENDEX services. *Journal of the American Society for Information Science* 26 (4), 223–229. July–Aug.

Cain, A. M. 1967. Steps towards a computer-based library network: A survey of three medical libraries. *Bulletin of the Medical Library Association* 55 (3), 279–289. July.

Cain, A. M. 1969. Thesaural problems in an on-line system. *Bulletin of the Medical Library Association* 57 (3), 250–259.

Cain, A. M., and I. H. Pizer. 1967. The SUNY Biomedical Communication Network: Implementation of an on-line, real-time, user-oriented system. *Proceedings of the American Documentation Institute* 4, 258–262.

Canfield, J. H. 1973. Comparison of retrieval using controlled-vocabulary indexing and machine-indexed text. In M. B. Henderson (ed.), *Interactive bibliographic systems*, 23–25. Washington, DC: U.S. Atomic Energy Commission. AEC Report No. CONF-711010. Apr. (Proceedings of a forum, Gaithersburg, MD, Oct. 4–5, 1971.)

Caputo, A. 1987. Interview. June 29.

Carroll, D. E., R. T. Chien, K. C. Kelley, F. P. Preparata, P. Reynolds, S. R. Ray, and F. A. Stahl. 1968. *An interactive document retrieval system.* (Report No. R-398; NTIS No. AD 679 915.) Urbana-Champaign: University of Illinois, Coordinated Science Lab. Dec. 30 pp.

Carroll, K. D., and R. K. Summit. 1962. *MATICO; Machine Applications to Technical Information Center Operations.* (Report No. LMSC-5-13-62-1.) Sunnyvale, CA: LMSC. Sept. 24 pp.

Carter, B., B. Shaffer, and D. DeWitt. 1965. A computer-generated index publishing system. In *Abstracts of the International Federation for Documentation (FID) Congress*, 63. Washington, DC: FID Congress, Secretariat.

Carter, L. F., F. N. Marzocco, and D. L. Drukey. 1965. *Research & technology division report for 1964.* (Report No. TM-530/008; NTIS No. AD 612 614.) Santa Monica, CA: SDC. Jan.

Caruso, D. E. 1970. Tutorial programs for operation of on-line retrieval systems. *Journal of Chemical Documentation* 10 (2), 98–105.

Carville, M., L. D. Higgins, and F. J. Smith. 1971. Interactive reference retrieval in large files. *Information Storage & Retrieval* 7, 205–210.

Cataldo, F. 1965. Three COLINGO-like approaches to the data base problem. In C. Baum and L. Gorsuch (eds.), *Proceedings of the second symposium on computer-centered data base systems*, 3-31–3-122. (Report No. TM-2624/100; NTIS No. AD 625 417.) Santa Monica, CA: SDC. Dec. 1.

Cautin, H. 1969. Real English: A translator to English natural language man-machine conversation. Unpublished doctoral diss., University of Pennsylvania, Philadelphia. Published as *Real English: A translator to enable natural language man-machine conversation; Interim report.* (NTIS No. AD 689 280.) Philadelphia: University of Pennsylvania, Moore School of Electrical Engineering. May. 175 pp.

Cautin, H., T. C. Lowe, F. Rapp, and M. Rubinoff. 1967. *An experimental on-line information retrieval system.* (NTIS No. AD 671 962.) Philadelphia: University of Pennsylvania, Moore School of Electrical Engineering, Information Systems Lab. Apr. 107 pp.; May. 20 pp.

Central Information Reference and Control System (CIRC II). 1971. Jan.

Chai, D. T. 1968, Aug. Chinese-English machine translation. *Law and Computer Technology* 1 (8), 10–16.

Chartrand, R. 1994. Personal communications to C. P. Bourne. Oct. 21.

Chasen, L. I. 1967. The development of random access information retrieval in the GE/MSD library and user interactions. In A. B. Tonik (ed.), *Information retrieval; The user's viewpoint; An aid to design*, 93–101. Philadelphia: International Information. (Fourth Annual National Colloquium on Information Retrieval, Philadelphia, May 3–4.)

Chen, S. P. J. 1973. Automated cataloging and reclassification by ATS. *Special Libraries* 64 (4), 193–197. Apr.

Chronolog; Monthly Newsletter of the DIALOG Information Retrieval Service. 1973–1976.

Clark, H. L. 1973a. Interactive information systems: Selection and performance evaluation. In M. B. Henderson (ed.), *Interactive bibliographic systems*, 105–114. Washington, DC: U.S. Atomic Energy Commission. AEC Report No. CONF-711 010. Apr. (Proceedings of a forum, Gaithersburg, MD, Oct. 4–5, 1971.)

Clark, H. L. 1973b. Legal research systems and the Congress. In R. A. May (ed.), *Automated law research; A collection of presentations delivered at the First National Conference on Automated Law Research*, 135–138. American Bar Association Standing Committee on Law and Technology.

Clarke, D. C. 1970. Query formulation for on-line reference retrieval: Design considerations from the indexer/searcher viewpoint. *Proceedings of the American Society for Information Science* 7, 83–86.

Cobbs, S. 1971, May. *AIM-TWX users' guide.* (Report No. RHSL-38.) Seattle, WA: University of Washington, Pacific Northwest Regional Health Sciences Library.

Cochrane Atherton, P. 1989. Interview. Jan.

Cochrane Atherton, P. 1990. Interview. May 21.

Cochrane Atherton, P. 1991. Personal communication to C. P. Bourne. June 20.

Cochrane Atherton, P. 1997. Personal communication to C. P. Bourne. June.

Coles, V. L. 1973. Remote evaluation of a remote console information-retrieval system (NASA/RECON.) In M. B. Henderson (ed.), *Interactive bibliographic systems*, 133–142. Washington, DC: U.S. Atomic Energy Commission. Apr. AEC Report No. CONF-711-010. (Proceedings of a forum, Gaithersburg, MD, Oct. 4–5, 1971.)

Collins, G. O. 1967, Jan. *Final report on a study of the remote use of computers.* (Report No. TR-67-679-1; NTIS No. PB 175 666.) Bethesda, MD: Informatics. 108 pp.

The combined file search system; Operating instructions for an information storage and retrieval system. 1968a. (Report No. APTD-1152; NTIS No. PB 211 069.) New York: Service Bureau Corporation. July. 28 pp.

The combined file search system; Program manual for an information storage and retrieval system. 1968b. (Report No. APTD-1153; NTIS No. PB 211 070.) New York: Service Bureau Corporation. July. 315 pp.

The combined file search system; User's manual for an information storage and retrieval system. 1968c. (Report No. APTD-1151; NTIS No. PB 211 068.) New York: Service Bureau Corporation. July. 130 pp.

Computer Applications Office. 1975. *Reference guide to SCORPIO; Subject-Content-Oriented Retriever for Processing Information Online.* Washington, DC: Library of Congress. 49 pp. + appendix.

Computer Applications Office. 1977. *Reference guide; SCORPIO; Subject-Content-Oriented Retriever for Processing Information On-Line.* Washington, DC: Library of Congress. 85 pp. + appendix.

Computer is researcher's best friend. 1970. *Ohio State University College of Medicine Journal* (Winter), 7–8.

Computer retrieval of the law: A challenge to the concept of unauthorized practice? 1968. June. *University of Pennsylvania Law* Review 116 (8), 1261–1284.

Computerized legal research; FLITE. 1981. *The Army Lawyer* (Feb.), 41.

COMSEARCH—Computer search of habeas corpus opinions. 1966. *Jurimetrics Journal* 8 (2), 110–112. Dec.

Connors, T. L. 1966. ADAM: A generalized data management system. *Proceedings of the AFIPS Spring Joint Computer Conference* 28, 193–203.

Cook, K. H. 1970. An experimental on-line system for Psychological Abstracts. *Proceedings of the American Society for Information Science* 7, 111–114.

Cook, K. H. 1971. Section I: Introduction and overview. *SUPARS: Syracuse University Psychological Abstracts Retrieval Service; Final report to the Rome Air Development Center; Large scale information processing systems.* Syracuse, NY: Syracuse University, School of Library Science. June. 11 pp.

Cook, K. H., L. H. Trump, P. A. Atherton, and J. Katzer. 1971. *SUPARS: Syracuse University Psychological Abstracts Retrieval Service; Final report to the Rome Air Development Center; Large scale information processing systems.* Syracuse, NY: Syracuse University, School of Library Science. (6 sections in 7 vols.) July.

Cooper, M. D. 1977. May. Input-output relationships in on-line bibliographic searching. *Journal of the American Society for Information Science* 28 (3), 153–160.

Cooper, M. D., and N. A. DeWath. 1976. The cost of on-line bibliographic searching. *Journal of Library Automation* 9 (3), 195–209. Sept.

Corbató, F. J., M. Merwin-Daggett, and R. C. Daley. 1962. An experimental time-sharing system. *Proceedings of the AFIPS Spring Joint Computer Conference* 21, 335–344.

Corbett, L. 1968. Using commercially available literature tapes for a current awareness service. *The Information Scientist* 2 (3), 83–102. Nov.

Corbin, H. S., and W. L. Frank. 1966. Display oriented computer usage system. *Proceedings of 21st National Conference of Association for Computing Machinery*, 515–526.

Cordaro, J. T., and R. T. Chien. 1970, *Design considerations of on-line document retrieval systems.* (Report No. R-456; NTIS No. AD 701 972.) Urbana-Champaign: University of Illinois, Coordinated Science Lab. Feb. 28 pp.

Corning, M. E. 1972. The U.S. National Library of Medicine and international MEDLARS cooperation. *Information Storage & Retrieval* 8 (6), 255–264. Dec.

The COSATI data base. 1969. Black & white motion picture. Columbus, OH: Battelle Memorial Institute.

Cottrell, N. 1974. Personal communication to C. P. Bourne. Apr. 22.

Council of Ontario Universities. 1975. *UNICAT/ TELECAT: A report of the cooperative use of a computer-based cataloging support system.* Toronto: Council of Ontario Universities, Office of Library Coordination. Oct. 111 pp. + appendix.

Council on Library Resources. 1993. *Thirty-seventh annual report (special insert.)* Washington, DC: CLR.

Covington, M. W. 1969. The Copper Data Center: A worldwide network. In L. Schultz (ed.), *The information bazaar*, 151–154. Philadelphia, PA: College of Physicians of Philadelphia. (Proceedings of the Sixth Annual National Colloquium on Information Retrieval, May 8–9.)

Cox, K. A. 1969. Carterphone and the computer utility concept. *Law and Computer Technology* 2 (4), 2–8. Apr.

Craig, J. A., S. C. Berezner, H. C. Carney, and C. R. Longyear. 1966. DEACON: Direct English and control. *Proceedings of the AFIPS Fall Joint Computer Conference* 29, 365–380.

Crawford, T. 1987. Interview. June 27.

Crossley, W. O. 1965. *The MADAM system.* (Report No. TM-2198/001; NTIS No. AD 620 661.) Santa Monica, CA: SDC. Aug. 57 pp.

Crow, N. B., and D. R. Elchesen. 1971. Monitoring and retrieving literature searches using a generalized file management system. *Proceedings of the American Society for Information Science* 8, 169–178.

Crowe, J. 1967. Retrospective searching; RSIC users and the DDC searches. In *Automation in Libraries, 15–17 Nov. 1966*, 129–134. (Report No. RSIC-625; NTIS No. AD 654 766.) Redstone Arsenal, AL: Redstone Scientific Information Center. June.

Cuadra, C. A. 1971a. Are computer service agencies responding to the needs of libraries? *Law Library Journal* 64 (2), 126–132. May.

Cuadra, C. A. 1971b. The commercial service approach to library automation. In P. J. Fasana and A. Veaner (eds.), *Collaborative library systems development*, 110–117. Cambridge, MA: The MIT Press.

Cuadra, C. A. 1971c. Online systems: Promise and pitfalls. *Journal of the American Society for Information Science* 22 (2), 107–114. Mar.–Apr.

Cuadra, C. A. 1975. SDC experiences with large data bases. *Journal of Chemical Information and Computer Sciences* 15 (1), 48–51. Feb.

Cuadra, C. A. 1976. Problems of growth in on-line information services. In G. Pratt and S. Harvey (eds.), *The on-line age: Plans and needs for on-line information retrieval*, 53–62. London: Aslib/EUSIDIC. (Proceedings of the Eusidic Conference, Oslo, Dec. 4–5, 1975.)

Cuadra, C. A. 1978. Commercially funded on-line retrieval services—Past, present, future. *Aslib Proceedings* 30 (1), 2–15. Jan.

Cuadra, C. A. 1980. Surviving the eighties: New roles for publishers, information service organizations, and users. *NFAIS Newsletter* 22, 23–39.

Cuadra, C. A. 1990. Interview. June 12.

Cuadra, C. A. 1997. Personal communication to C. P. Bourne. Aug. 29.

Cummings, M. M. 1965a. Health sciences (MEDLARS.) In K. Kent and O. E. Taulbee (eds.), *Electronic information handling*, 111–119. Washington, DC: Spartan Books.

Cummings, M. M. 1965b. MEDLARS in operation. *Library Journal* 90 (5), 1218. Mar. 15.

Cummings, M. M. 1965c. Modern bibliographic control of the biomedical literature as an aid to teaching, research, and practice. In *Proceedings of the 7th IBM Medical Symposium, Oct. 25–28, 1965*, 17–25. Poughkeepsie, NY: IBM.

Cummings, M. M. 1966. Plans for the development of a medical library network. In W. Simonton and C. Mason (eds.), *Information retrieval with special reference to the biomedical sciences*, 175–187. Minneapolis, MN: University of Minnesota, Nolte Center for Continuing Education. (Papers presented at the Second Institute on Information Retrieval, Nov. 10–13, 1965.)

Cummings, M. M. 1967a. Needs of the health sciences. In A. Kent, O. E. Taulbee, and G. D. Goldstein (eds.), *Electronic handling of information: Testing & evaluation*, 13–23. Washington, DC: Thompson Book Co.

Cummings, M. M. 1967b. The role of the National Library of Medicine in the national biomedical library network. *Annals of the New York Academy of Sciences* 142, 503–512. Mar. 31.

Cummings, M. M. 1976a. *The fate of the dinosaur.* (ERIC No. ED 127 961.) Paper presented at 95th ALA annual conference, Chicago, IL, July 18.

Cummings, M. M. 1976b. Message from the director. *National Library of Medicine News* 31 (12): 1. Dec.

Cummings, M. M. 1985. Senator Lister Hill, 1894–1984. *Bulletin of the Medical Library Association* 73 (3), 317–318. July.

Cummings, M. M. 1997. Personal communication to C. P. Bourne. Oct. 17; Nov. 1.

Cummings, M. M., and M. E. Corning. 1971. The Medical Library Assistance Act: An analysis of the NLM extramural programs, 1965–1970. *Bulletin of the Medical Library Association* 59, 375–391. July.

Cunningham, J. L., W. D. Schieber, and R. M. Shoffner. 1969. *A study of the organization and search of biblio-*

graphic holdings records in on-line computer systems: Phase I; Final report. (ERIC No. ED 029 679; NTIS No. PB 185 655.) Berkeley: University of California, Institute of Library Research. Mar. 277 pp.

Curran, W. J. 1977. The National Medical Library's MEDLARS: Freedom of information or protected systems? *American Journal of Public Health* 67 (2), 188–189. Feb.

Currie, J. D. 1973. A hybrid interactive search system. In G. R. Mauerhoff (ed.), *First Open Conference on Information Science in Canada*, 90–96. Chalk River, Ontario: Atomic Energy of Canada Ltd.

Damerau, F. J. 1997. Personal communication to C. P. Bourne. June 23.

Darling, L. 1966. MEDLARS: A regional search center. In W. Simonton, and C. Mason (eds.), *Information retrieval with special reference to the biomedical sciences*, 49–62. Minneapolis, MN: University of Minnesota, Nolte Center for Continuing Education. (Paper presented at the Second Institute on Information Retrieval, Nov. 10–13, 1965.)

Darling, L. 1970. SUNY-MEDLARS Letter to the editor. *Bulletin of the Medical Library Association* 58 (4), 603–604. Oct.

Database vendors in a price war? 1977. *Library Journal* 102 (6), 665. Mar. 15.

DATUM project (Jurimetrics). 1970. *Law and Computer Technology* 310, 236–237.

Davis, R. M. 1966. Man-machine communication. *Annual Review of Information Science and Technology* 1, 221–254.

Davis, R. M. 1969. The relationship of regional networks to the National Library of Medicine's Biomedical Communications Network. *The Bookmark* 28 (4), 109–113. Jan. Published also in *Library Bulletin (SUNY Upstate Medical Center Library)* 9 (Feb.) (suppl.1: Biomedical Communication Network dedication proceedings), 49–55.

Davis, R. P. 1965. LITE: Legal Information Through Electronics. *Modern Uses of Logic in Law (M.U.L.L.)* (Sept.), 138–140.

Davis, R. P. 1966a. Let there be LITE (Legal Information Through Electronics.) *Jurimetrics Journal* 8 (2), 118–124. Dec.

Davis, R. P. 1966b. The LITE system. *Judge Advocate General Law Review* 8 (6), 6–10. Nov.–Dec.

Deemer, S. S. 1983. Public access searching through DOBIS. *Software Review* 2 (3), 148–157. Sept.

Del Bigio, G. 1968. GIPSY: A Generalized Information Processing System. *Proceedings of the AFIPS Spring Joint Computer Conference* 32, 183–191.

Del Frate, A. A. 1973. Use of RECON: A report from the front lines. In M. B. Henderson (ed.), *Interactive bibliographic systems*, 1–8. Washington, DC: U.S. Atomic Energy Commission. AEC Report No. CONF-711 010. Apr. (Proceedings of a forum, Gaithersburg, MD, Oct. 4–5, 1971.)

Del Frate, A. A., and J .T. Riddle, 1973. Computer-user interaction: Does it exist? *Proceedings of the American Society for Information Science* 10, 45–46.

Dennis, S. F. 1965a. The construction of a thesaurus automatically from a sample of text. In M. E. Stevens, V. E. Giuliano, and L. B. Heilprin (eds.), *Statistical association methods for mechanized documentation*, 61–73. Washington, DC: National Bureau of Standards. (NBS Miscellaneous Publication No. 269.) Dec. 15. (Proceedings of a Symposium, Washington, DC, 1964.)

Dennis, S. F. 1965b. Status of American Bar Foundation research on automatic indexing-searching computer system. *Modern Uses of Logic in Law (M.U.L.L.)* (Sept.), 131–132.

Dennis, S. F. 1967. The design and testing of a fully automatic indexing-searching system for documents consisting of expository text. In G. Schecter (ed.), *Information retrieval; A critical view*, 67–94. Washington, DC: Thompson Book Co. (Proceedings of the Third Annual National Colloquium on Information Retrieval, Philadelphia, May 12–13, 1966.)

DIALOG users manual. 1966. (Report No. LMSC-N-07-66-1.) Palo Alto, CA: LMSC. Nov.

DiFondi, N. M., C. A. Mangio, and R. N. Roberti. 1973. Benefits and costs of free-text searching on the FTD CIRC reference retrieval system. *Proceedings of the American Society for Information Science* 10, 47–48.

Dimsdale, J. J. 1973. File structure for an on-line catalog of one million titles. *Journal of Library Automation* 6 (1), 37–55. Mar.

Dixon, P. J., and J. Sable. 1967. DM-1—A generalized data management system. *Proceedings of the AFIPS Spring Joint Computer Conference* 30, 185–198.

Dolby, J. L. 1970. An algorithm for variable-length proper-name compression. *Journal of Library Automation* 3 (4), 257–275. Dec.

Dominick, W. D. 1975. System performance evaluation of interactive retrieval. In B. Mittman, and L. Borman (eds.),

Personalized data base systems, 216–227. Los Angeles, CA: Melville.

Dominick, W. D., and Mittman, B. 1973. Information retrieval system cost/performance analysis via interactive graphics. *Proceedings of the American Society for Information Science* 10, 49.

Donati, R. 1973. Information center profile: Lockheed Information Sciences. *Information; Part I/News; Sources; Profiles* 5 (2), 114–117. Mar.–Apr.

Dortmund library system—DOBIS: Application guide. 1975. (Report No. GE15-6069.) Feltham, England: IBM United Kingdom Ltd. Oct. 79 pp.

Dortmund library system—DOBIS; Executive guide. 1975. (Report No. GE15-6068.) Feltham, England: IBM United Kingdom Ltd. Oct. 11 pp.

Dovel, J. A. 1969. *Compilation of DOD scientific and technical intelligence thesaurus; Final report, Mar. 68–Jul 69.* (Report No. TM-WD-(L)–321; RADC-TR-69-308; NTIS No. AD 861 129.) Falls Church, VA: SDC. Oct. 35 pp.

Doyle, L. B. 1975. *Information retrieval and processing.* Los Angeles, CA: Melville.

Drew, D. L. c1964a. *Comments on man-machine system design.* (Information Retrieval Note No. 40.) Palo Alto, CA: LMSC. Oct. 3 pp.

Drew, D. L. c1964b. *Development of on-line reference retrieval system.* (Information Retrieval Note No. 39.) Palo Alto, CA: LMSC. Oct. 9 pp.

Drew, D. L. 1964c, *MATICO.* (Report No. LMSC-IRN-3; Information Retrieval Note No. 3.) Palo Alto, CA: LMSC. May 8. 2 pp.

Drew, D. L. 1964d, *On-line reference retrieval—Pilot—System design.* (Technical Note No. 33.) Palo Alto, CA: LMSC. Oct. 8. 25 pp.

Drew, D. L. 1965a. *General remarks: On-line information retrieval systems.* (Information Retrieval Note No. 74.) Palo Alto, CA: LMSC. June 15. 27 pp.

Drew, D. L. 1965b. *Notes on the problem of word stems and endings.* (Information Retrieval Note No. 65.) Palo Alto, CA: LMSC. Mar. 12. 4 pp.

Drew, D. L. 1965c. *Preliminary outline: Time-sharing software for reference retrieval.* (Information Retrieval Note No. 80.) Palo Alto, CA: LMSC. Sept. 29. 8 pp.

Drew, D. L. 1965d. *Reference retrieval dialogue—III.* (Information Retrieval Note No. 64.) Palo Alto, CA: LMSC. Mar. 12. 17 pp.

Drew, D. L. 1965e. *Time-sharing software—II.* (Information Retrieval Note No. 81.) Palo Alto, CA: LMSC. Oct. 23. 14 pp.

Drew, D. L. 1965f. *Two reference-retrieval dialogues.* (Information Retrieval Note No. 78.) Palo Alto, CA: LMSC. Aug. 11. 43 pp.

Drew, D. L. 1967. The LACONIQ Monitor: Time sharing for online dialogues. *Communications of the ACM*, *10*, 765–771. Dec.

Drew, D. L. 1996. Personal communication to C. P. Bourne. Mar. 15

Drew, D. L. 1997. Personal communication to C. P. Bourne. July 13.

Drew, D. L., E. Graziano, C. Satterfield., and R. K. Summit. 1964. *Proposed on-line information retrieval system.* (Information Retrieval Note No. 31.) Palo Alto, CA: LMSC. Sept. 9. 16 pp.

Drew, D. L., and R. D. Merrill. 1965. *A memory tube IR console system.* (Information Retrieval Note No. 67.) Palo Alto, CA: LMSC. Mar. 29. 6 pp.

Drew, D. L., R. K. Summit, R. I. Tanaka, and R. B. Whiteley. 1965. May. *An on-line technical library reference retrieval system.* (Report No. 6-75-65-17.) Palo Alto, CA: LMSC, Electronic Sciences Lab. 13 pp. A short version was published in *Information processing 1965*, vol. 2, ed. W. A. Kalenich, 341–342. Washington, DC: Spartan Books, 1966. (Proceedings of the IFIP Congress 65, New York, NY, May 24–29, 1965.)

Drew, D. L., R. K. Summit, R. I. Tanaka, and R. B. Whiteley. 1966. An on-line technical library reference retrieval system. *American Documentation* 17 (Jan.), 3–7.

Durkin, K., and J. Egeland. 1974. An experiment to evaluate the use of BA Previews in an on-line interactive mode. *Proceedings of the American Society for Information Science* 11, 141–144.

Earl, L. L., and H. R Robison. 1969. Mar. *Annual report: Automatic informative abstracting and extracting.* (Report No. M-21-69-1.) Palo Alto, CA: LMSC, Research Lab.

Egeland, J. 1971. User-interaction in the State University of New York (SUNY) Biomedical Communication Network. In D. E. Walker (ed.), *Interactive bibliographic search; The user/computer interface*, 105–120. Montvale, NJ: AFIPS Press. (Proceedings of The User Interface for Interactive Search of Bibliographic Data Bases, Palo Alto, CA, Jan. 14–15.)

Egeland, J. 1972. In-depth indexing of monograph literature for an on-line retrieval system: A pilot project.

Bulletin of the Medical Library Association 60 (3), 432–438. July.

Egeland, J. 1974. The importance of user education and training in a multi-data base online information network. *Proceedings of the American Society for Information Science* 11, 137–140.

Egeland, J. 1975a. Biomedical network brings SUNY international recognition. *Data Division Computer Center Newsletter (SUNY)* 1 (Summer), 3.

Egeland, J. 1975b. The SUNY Biomedical Communication Network: Six years of progress in on-line bibliographic retrieval. *Bulletin of the Medical Library Association* 63 (2), 189–194. Apr.

Egeland, J. 1979. Speech presented to San Francisco Chapter of ASIS. Mar. 16.

Egeland, J., and G. Foreman. 1973. *Coordination of two on-line information retrieval services at the University of Minnesota Bio-Medical Library.* (ERIC No. ED 088 434.) Minneapolis: University of Minnesota Libraries. 7 pp.

El-Hadidy, B. 1995. Personal communication to C. P. Bourne. Aug. 15.

Eldridge, W. B. 1965. The American Bar Foundation project. *Modern Uses of Logic in Law (M.U.L.L.)* (Sept.), 129–131.

Eldridge, W. B., and S. F. Dennis. 1963a. The computer as a tool for legal research. *Law and Contemporary Problems* 28 (Winter), 78–99.

Eldridge, W. B., and S. F. Dennis. 1963b. Report of status of the Joint American Bar Foundation—IBM study of electronic methods applied to legal information retrieval. *Modern Uses of Logic in Law (M.U.L.L.)* (Mar.), 27–34.

Electronic legal retrieval. 1974. *Law and Computer Technology* 7 (2), 50–54. Mar.–Apr.

Elias, A. W. 1979. Marketing for online bibliographic services. *Online Review* 3 (1), 107–117. Mar.

Elias, A. W. 1982. Pricing strategies and impacts on producers, vendors and users. *Information Services & Use* 1 (6), 351–357. May.

Elmaleh, J. S. 1968. Project CALM (Computer Application to Legal Methodology.) *Jurimetrics Journal* 9, 23–30.

End of an era. 1975. *National Library of Medicine News* 30 (4), 1. Apr.

Engelbart, D. C. 1962. *Augmenting human intellect: A conceptual framework; Summary report.* (Report No. AFOSR-3223, NTIS No. AD 289 565.) Menlo, CA: SRI. Oct.

Epstein, A. H. 1973. An overview of operational BALLOTS. *Proceedings of the American Society for Information Science* 10, 56–57.

Epstein, A. H., W. Davison, E. Montague, M. Stovel, and A. B. Veaner. 1972. *Bibliographic automation of large library operations using a time-sharing system.* (ERIC No. ED 060 883.) Stanford. CA: Stanford University Libraries. Feb. 206 pp.

ERDA/RECON Newsletter. 1977. No. 22. June.

ERIC on-line. 1972. *Special Libraries* 63 (1), 45. Jan.

Eriksson, A. M., and D. A. Johnston. 1967. Ohio's computer code retrieval system. *Information Retrieval Letter* 2 (9), 1–3. Jan.

Esposito, A. V., R. Fleischer, S. D. Friedman, S. Kaufman, S. Rogers, S. Skye, and M. Shotkin. 1968. *TEXT-PAC S/360 normal text information processing, retrieval, and current information selection system.* (Report No. Program order no. 360D-06.7.020.) Hawthorne, NY: IBM Program Information Department. 474 pp. Dec. 24.

European MEDLARS co-operation. 1971. *NLL Review* 1 (4), 139. Oct.

Experimental Library Management System (ELMS): Librarian's user manual. 1972. (Report No. 16.211.) Los Gatos, CA: IBM Advanced Systems Development Division. Sept. 172 pp.

Falkenberg, G. 1975. Medline at BMDC, Karolinska Institutet. In S. Schwarz (ed.), *The interactive library; Computerized processes in library and information networks.* Stockholm: Swedish Society for Technical Documentation (TLS.) (Proceedings of seminar, Stockholm, Nov. 25–28, 1974.)

Fano, R. M. 1965a. The MAC system: A progress report. In M. A. Sass, and W. D. Willison (eds.), *Symposium on Computer Augmentation of Human Reasoning, June 16–17, 1964,* 131–150. Washington, DC: Spartan Books.

Fano, R. M. 1965b, The MAC system: The computer utility approach. *IEEE Spectrum* 2 (Jan.), 56–64.

Farell, J. 1965, May 5. *TEXTIR: A natural language information retrieval system.* (Report No. TM-2392; NTIS No. AD 615 763.) Santa Monica, CA: SDC. 37 pp.

Fay, R. J. 1971, May. Full-text information retrieval. *Law Library Journal* 64 (2), 167–175.

Federation of Information Users. 1974. *DIALOG users workshop, Arlington, VA, Aug. 8–9, 1974.* (ERIC No. ED 104 377.) Pittsburgh: Author. Aug.

Feinman, H. B. 1973. Aspen: Organization of litigation files. In R. A. May (ed.), *Automated law research; A collection of presentations delivered at the First National Conference on Automated Law Research,* 143–145. American Bar Association, Standing Committee on Law and Technology.

Fife, D. W., K. Rankin, E. Fong E., J. C. Walker, and B. A. Marron. 1974. Mar. *A technical index of interactive information systems.* (ERIC No. ED 092 163.) Washington, DC: National Bureau of Standards. 73 pp.

Final technical report for MEDLARS preliminary design. 1962. Washington, DC: General Electric, Information Systems Operation. Jan. 31. 143 pp.

Firschein, O. 1987. Personal communication to C. P. Bourne. Apr. 17.

Firschein, O. 1993. Personal communication to C. P. Bourne. June 23.

Firschein, O., and D. L. Drew. 1965. *Reference retrieval dialogue.* (Information Retrieval Note No. 58.) Palo Alto, CA: LMSC. Feb. 4. 11 pp.

Firschein, O., and R. K. Summit. 1977. Online search in the public library: Results of a three-year study. *Proceedings of the American Society for Information Science* 9.

Firschein, O., R. K. Summit, and C. K. Mick. 1978. Use of on-line bibliographic search in public libraries: A retrospective evaluation. *Online Review* 2 (1), 41–55. Mar.

Firth, F. E. 1958a. *An experiment in literature searching.* (Report No. RJ142.) San Jose, CA: IBM. Sept. 11.

Firth, F. E. 1958b. *An experiment in literature searching with the IBM 305 RAMAC.* San Jose, CA: IBM. Nov. 17.

Fischer, P. 1995. Personal communication to C. P. Bourne. Aug. 17.

Fisher, C. P. 1997. Personal communication to C. P. Bourne. Aug. 15.

Fisher, F. M., J. W. McKie, and R. B. Manke. 1983. *IBM and the U.S. data processing industry: An economic history.* (Praeger Studies in Select Basic Industries.) New York: Praeger.

Fitzpatrick, W. H., and M. E. Freeman. 1965. The Science Information Exchange: The evolution of a unique information storage and retrieval system. *Libri* 15 (2), 127–137.

Flavin, J. M. 1973. Computerized legal retrieval in New York. In R. A. May (ed.), *Automated law research; A collection of presentations delivered at the first National Conference on Automated Law Research,* 49–53. American Bar Association, Standing Committee on Law and Technology.

Flynn, T., and A. E. Wild. 1977. Integrated on-line information systems in a large multinational company. In *Proceedings of the First International Online Information Meeting,* 45–52. Oxford, England: Learned Information.

Fong, E. 1971. *A survey of selected document processing systems.* (Report No. NBS-TN-599; ERIC No. ED 058 892.) Washington, DC: National Bureau of Standards. Oct. 67 pp.

Fossum, E. G., and G. Kaskey. 1966. *Optimization and standardization of information retrieval languages and systems; Final report.* (Report No. AFOSR-66-0628; NTIS No. AD 630 797.) Blue Bell, PA: Sperry Rand, UNIVAC Division. Jan. 28. 87 pp.

Franks, E. W. 1963. *Development and management of a computer-centered database.* (Report No. TM-1456/007; NTIS No. AD 662 957.) Santa Monica, CA: SDC. (Proceedings of the symposium, June 10–11; Part 7: LUCID.) Sept. 6. 9 pp.

Franks, E. W., and P. S. DeSimone. 1965. LUCID: Language used to communicate information system design. In *Research & technology division report for 1964,* 36–37. (Report No. TM-530/008; NTIS No. AD 612 614.) Santa Monica, CA: SDC. Jan.

Frazier, J. P. I. 1978. An introduction to DOE/RECON and NASA/RECON. *Sci-Tech News* 32 (4), 85–87. Oct.

Freeman Heyworth, J. 1995. Personal communication to C. P. Bourne.

Freeman Heyworth, J. 1997. Personal communication to C. P. Bourne. July 11; Feb. 3.

Freeman, R. R. 1964. Computer and classification systems. *Journal of Documentation* 20 (3), 137–145. Sept.

Freeman, R. R. 1966. *Research project for the evaluation of the UDC as the indexing language for a mechanized reference retrieval system: Progress report for the period July 1, 1965–Jan. 31, 1966.* (Report No. AIP/DRP UDC-2.) New York: American Institute of Physics. Feb. 1.

Freeman, R. R. 1968. *Evaluation of the retrieval of metallurgical document reference using the Universal Decimal Classification in a computer-based system.* (Report No. AIP/UDC-6.) New York: American Institute of Physics. Apr. 1.

Freeman, R. R. 1995. Personal communication to C. P. Bourne. Jan. 22.

Freeman, R. R., and P. A. Atherton. 1968a. *AUDACIOUS—An experiment with an on-line interactive reference retrieval system using the Universal Decimal*

Classification as the index language in the field of nuclear science. (Report No. AIP/UDC-7.) New York: American Institute of Physics. A short version with same title was published in *Proceedings of the American Society for Information Science* 5 (Apr. 25), 193–199.

Freeman, R. R., and P. A. Atherton. 1968b. File organization and search strategy using UDC in mechanized reference retrieval systems. In K. Samuelson (ed.), *Mechanized information storage, retrieval, and dissemination,* 122–152. Amsterdam: North-Holland. (Proceedings of the FID/IFIP Joint Conference, Rome, June 14–17, 1967.) Reprinted by American Institute of Physics, Sept. 15, 1967. (Report No. AIP/UDC-5; NTIS No. PB 176 152.) 37 pp.

Fried, J. B. 1971. BASIS-70 user interface. In D. E. Walker (ed.), *Interactive bibliographic search: The user/computer interface,* 143–158. Montvale, NJ: AFIPS Press. (Proceedings of The User Interface for Interactive Search of Bibliographic Data Bases, Palo Alto, CA, Jan. 14–15.)

Frierson, E., and P. A. Atherton. 1971. Survey of attitudes towards SUPARS. *Proceedings of the American Society for Information Science* 8, 65–69.

Frycki, S. J. 1970. Information transfer from source to user utilizing a pharmaceutical data base. In A. D. Berton (ed.), *The social impact of information retrieval,* 306–333. Philadelphia: College of Physicians of Philadelphia. (Proceedings of the 7th Annual National Colloquium on Information Retrieval.)

Full texts of state statutes and U.S. Code available in computerized information system. 1970. *Jurimetrics Journal* 10 (3), 112. Mar.

Fuller, T. 1974. Textron-Lockheed deal. *Newsweek* 83 (83). June 17.

Fuller, W. D. 1965. *El Camino Community Hospital information system analysis report.* (Report No. LMSC-671062.) Palo Alto, CA: LMSC. 20 pp.

Furth, S. E. 1972. STAIRS—A user-oriented full text retrieval system. *Law and Computer Technology* 5 (5), 114–119. Sept.–Oct. Reprinted from *Computer Weekly,* June 8, 1972.

Furth, S. E. 1968. Automated retrieval of legal information: State of the art. *Computers and Automation* 17 (12), 25–38. Dec.

Furth, S. E. 1973. STAIRS: An interactive full-text retrieval system. In R. A. May (ed.), *Automated law research; A collection of presentations delivered at the First National Conference on Automated Law Research,* 19–34. American Bar Association, Standing Committee on Law and Technology.

Fussler, H. H., and C. T. Payne. 1967. *Development of an integrated, computer-based, bibliographical data system for a large university library: Annual report 1966/67.* (NTIS No. PB 176 469.) Chicago, IL: University of Chicago. 48 pp.

Gabrini, P. J. 1966. Automatic introduction of information into a remote-access system: A physics library catalog. Unpublished master's thesis, University of Pennsylvania, Philadelphia, Mar. 25 pp.

Garrard, R. F. 1965. Misleading and unfounded (Comment on letter by R. R. Shaw.) *Library Journal* 90 (7), 1580. Apr. 1.

Garvis, F. J. 1966. The UCLA MEDLARS computer system. *Bulletin of the Medical Library Association* 54 (1), 14–15. Jan.

Gechman, M. C. 1972. Machine-readable bibliographic data bases. *Annual Review of Information Science and Technology* 7, 328–378.

Gielow, K. R. 1964. *An on-line real estate listing service using QUIKTRAN.* (Information Retrieval Note No. 51.) Palo Alto, CA: LMSC. Dec. 21. 5 pp.

Giering, R. H. 1967a. *Analysis of existing and proposed data handling systems.* (Report No. DTN-67-9.) Arlington, VA: Data Corporation. Oct. 23. 32 pp.

Giering, R. H. 1967b. *Information processing and the data spectrum.* (Report No. DTN-68-2.) Arlington, VA: Data Corporation. Oct. 18 pp.

Giering, R. H. 1972. *This is Data Central 1972 technical specifications* (Report No. DTN-72-2.) Dayton, OH: Data Corporation. Mar. 34 pp.

Giering, R. H. 1980. Personal communication to C. P. Bourne. May 9.

Giering, R. H. 1983. Personal communication to C. P. Bourne. June 11.

Giering, R. H. 1995. Personal communication to C. P. Bourne. Sept. 25; Oct. 20.

Gillcrist, J. A. 1974. *AEC/RECON user's manual.* (Report No. ORNL-4943.) Oak Ridge, TN. May.

Ginnow, A. O. 1975. The West computer-assisted legal retrieval system. *Law and Computer Technology* 8 (4), 82–86. July–Aug.

Goldfarb, C. F., E. J. Mosher, and T. I. Peterson. 1970. An online system for integrated text processing. *Proceedings of the American Society for Information Science* 7, 147–150.

Goldstein, C. 1973. Discussion comments. In M. B. Henderson (ed.), *Interactive bibliographic systems,* 131. Washington, DC: U.S. Atomic Energy Commission. AEC Report No. CONF-711 010. Apr. (Proceedings of a forum, Gaithersburg, MD, Oct. 4–5, 1971.)

Gordon, R. L. 1969. *Interviewing: Strategy, techniques and tactics.* Homewood, IL: The Dorsey Press.

Gorog, W. 1997. Personal communication to C. P. Bourne. June 11.

Gray, H. J., W. I. Landauer, D. Lefkowitz, S. Litwin, and N. S. Prywes. 1961. *The Multi-List system; Technical report no. 1.* (NTIS No. AD 270 573.) Philadelphia: University of Pennsylvania, Moore School of Electrical Engineering. 3 parts in 2 vols. Nov. 30. 239 pp.

Graziano, E. E. 1964. Automated library. *New Reports* 5 (11), cover. Oct. 15.

Graziano, E. E. 1965. *The California Public Library Development Act of 1963.* (Information Retrieval Note No. 54.) Palo Alto, CA: LMSC. Jan. 20. 7 pp.

Greengrass, A. 1974. Information center profile: The New York Times Information Bank. *Information; Part 1/News; Sources; Profiles* 6 (1), 29–30. Jan.

Grunstra, N. S., and K. J. Johnson. 1970. Implementation and evaluation of two computerized information retrieval systems at the University of Pittsburgh. *Journal of Chemical Documentation* 10 (4), 272–277.

Guide to BALLOTS network services. 1976. Stanford, CA: Stanford University. Apr. 199 pp.

Guide to MEDLARS services. 1968. (Report No. Public Health Services Publication No. 1694.) Bethesda, MD: NLM.

Gull, C. D. 1997. Personal communication to C. P. Bourne. Sept. 2.

Gupta, U. 1981. Inviting customers to speak their minds. *Venture* 3 (10), 54–55. Oct.

Guthrie, G. D. 1971. An on-line remote catalog access and circulation control system. *Proceedings of the American Society for Information Science* 34, 305–309.

Guthrie, G. D., and S. D. Slifko. 1972. Analysis of search key retrieval on a large bibliographic file. *Journal of Library Automation* 5 (2), 96–100.

Haeuslein, G. K., and A. H. Culkowski. 1975. *The Oak Ridge modular RECON program.* (Report No. UCCND-CSD-9.) Oak Ridge, TN: Union Carbide Corporation. Apr. 106 pp.

Hahn, T. B. 1994. Pioneers of the online age. Paper presented at pre-conference workshop on History of Information Science at ASIS annual meeting, Washington, DC, Oct.

Hahn, T. B. 1996. Pioneers of the online age. *Information Processing & Management* 32 (1), 33–48.

Hahn, T. B. 1997. Online information retrieval: How far have we come?" Paper presented at ASIS annual meeting, Washington, DC, Oct.

Hahn, T. B. 1998. Text retrieval online: Historical perspectives on Web search engines. *ASIS Bulletin* 24 (4), 7–10.

Hahn, T. B. 1999. Hindsight on interface designs of the early online era. Paper presented at ASIS mid-year meeting, Pasadena, CA, May.

Haibt, L., M. Fischer, M. Kastner, R. Ketelhut, J. Ogg, and J. H. Wooley. 1967. Retrieving 4000 references without indexing. In A. B. Tonik (ed.), *Information retrieval; The user's viewpoint; An aid to design,* 127–133. Philadelphia: International Information. (Fourth Annual National Colloquium on Information Retrieval, Philadelphia, May 3–4.)

Hall, J. L. 1977. *On-line information retrieval 1965–1976; A bibliography with a guide to on-line data bases and systems.* London: Aslib.

Hall, J. L., A. E. Negus, and D. J. Dancy. 1971. Towards instant information. *New Scientist and Science Journal* 51 (July 22), 210–212.

Hall, J. L., A. E. Negus, and D. J. Dancy. 1972. On-line information retrieval: A method of query formulation using a video terminal. *Program* 6 (July), 175–186.

Halpin, R. F. 1967. An on-line information retrieval system with an application to Western Canadian history. Unpublished M.S. thesis, University of Alberta, Edmonton, Alberta. 111 pp.

Hambleton, J. E. 1976. JURIS: Legal information in the Department of Justice. *Law Library Journal* 69 (2), 199–202. May.

Hamilton, L. C. 1973. Interactive information systems: Selection and performance evaluation. In M. B. Henderson (ed.), *Interactive bibliographic systems,* 105–114. Washington, DC: U.S. Atomic Energy Commission. AEC Report No. CONF-711 010. Apr. (Proceedings of a forum, Gaithersburg, MD, Oct. 4–5, 1971.)

Hamilton, V. V. 1987. *Lister Hill; Statesman from the South.* Chapel Hill: University of North Carolina Press.

Hammond, W. 1960. Preparing for automation. In *Controlling literature by automation, Proceedings of the 4th annual military librarians' workshop,* 1–9. Washington, DC: Armed Services Technical Information Agency. (NTIS No. AD 243 000.)

Hampel, V. E., and J. A. Wade. 1969. MASTER CONTROL—A unifying free-form data storage and data retrieval system for dissimilar data bases. *Proceedings of the American Society for Information Science* 6, 159–174.

Haring, D. R. 1968a. Computer-driven display facilities for an experimental computer-based library. *Proceedings of the AFIPS Fall Joint Computer Conference* 33 (pt. 1), 255–265.

Haring, D. R. 1968b. A display console for an experimental computer-based augmented library catalog. *Proceedings of the 23rd National Conference of the Association for Computing Machinery,* 35–43.

Haring, D. R., and J. K. Roberge. 1969. A combined display for computer-generated data and scanned photographic images. *Proceedings of the AFIPS Spring Joint Computer Conference* 34, 483–490.

Harley, A. J. 1971a. Computer terminal at the NLL. *NLL Review* 1 (2), 59–60. Apr.

Harley, A. J. 1971b. Dialogue with a computer. *NLL Review* 1 (4), 123–136. Oct.

Harley, A. J. 1975. The U.K. MEDLARS service. *Bulletin of the American Society for Information Science* 2 (4), 16–17, 23. Nov.

Harley, A. J. 1977. The UK MEDLARS service: A personal view of its first decade. *Aslib Proceedings* 29 (9), 320–325. Sept.

Harrington, W. G. 1970. Computers and legal research. *American Bar Association Journal* 56, 1145–1148. Dec.

Harrington, W. G. 1974. What's happening in computer-assisted legal research? *American Bar Association Journal* 60 (2), 924–931. Aug.

Harrington, W. G. 1984–1985. A brief history of computer-assisted legal research. *Law Library Journal* 77 (3), 543–556.

Harrington, W. G., H. D. Wilson, and R. L. Bennett. 1971. The Mead Data Central system of computerized legal research. *Law Library Journal* 64 (2), 184–189. May.

Harris, R. 1988. The database industry: Looking into the future. *Database* 11 (5), 42–46. Oct.

Hartner, E. P. 1973. *Instructions for coding strategies; PIRETS; Pitt Information Retrieval System.* Pittsburgh, PA: University of Pittsburgh. Apr. 19. 18 pp.

Hawkins, D. T. 1980. *Online information retrieval bibliography, 1964–1979.* Marlton, NJ: Learned Information.

Hawkins, D. T., and B. A. Stevens. 1976. Computer-aided information retrieval in a large industrial library. In F. W. Lancaster (ed.), *The use of computers in literature searching and related reference activities in libraries,* 31–55. Urbana-Champaign: University of Illinois, Graduate School of Library Science. (Proceedings of the 1975 Clinic on Library Applications of Data Processing.)

Hayes, R. M. 1967. *Mechanized library procedures for the IBM Advanced Systems Development Division Library, Los Gatos, California.* White Plains, NY: IBM. 82 pp.

Hayes, R. M. 1995. Joseph Becker: A lifetime of service to the profession of library and information science. *Bulletin of the American Society for Information Science* 22 (1), 24–26. Oct.–Nov. Reprinted as In memoriam; Joseph Becker, Apr. 15, 1923–July 23, 1995, *Journal of the American Society for Information Science* 47 (6), 412–414, June 1996.

Hayes, R. M., and J. Becker. 1970. *Handbook of data processing for libraries.* Bethesda, MD: Becker & Hayes.

Healy, M. J. 1964. *SATIRE: A user's system of information retrieval.* (Report No. SP-1432; NTIS No. AD 630 150.) Santa Monica, CA: SDC. Apr. 1.

Heaps, D. M., and P. Sorenson. 1968. An online personal documentation system. *Proceedings of the American Society for Information Science* 5, 201–207.

Heilik, J. 1976a. CAN/OLE: A technical description. *Proceedings of the Fourth Canadian Conference on Information Science,* 47–55.

Heilik, J. 1976b. Canadian on-line enquiry: Making the information explosion more manageable. *Canadian Library Journal* 33 (6), 505–507. Dec.

Henderson, M. B. (ed.). 1973. *Interactive bibliographic systems.* Washington, DC: U.S. Atomic Energy Commission. AEC Report No. CONF-711 010. Apr. (Proceedings of a forum, Gaithersburg, MD, Oct. 4–5, 1971.)

Herner, S., M. J. Weinstock, R. L. Sisson, M. Herner, E. Leyman, and R. B. Schneider. 1966. *A recommended design for the United States medical library and information system.* Vol. 1: *System design, implementation, and costs.* Rev. ed. (NTIS No. PB 172 923.) Washington, DC: Herner and Co. July. 110 pp.

Herrmann, W. W., and H. H. Isaacs. 1964. *Natural language computer processing of Los Angeles Police Department crime information, Progress report no. 1.* (Report No. TM-1793.) Santa Monica, CA: SDC. Apr. 1. 66 pp.

Herron, A. 1979. Sharing resources—Sharing costs through the Shared Information Service. *Proceedings of the Seventh Canadian Conference on Information Science,* 81–93.

Hersey, D. F., W. R. Foster, E. W. Stalder, and W. T. Carlson. 1970. Comparison of on-line retrieval using free text words and scientist indexing. *Proceedings of the American Society for Information Science* 7, 265–268.

Hersey, D. F., W. R. Foster, E. W. Stalder, and W. T. Carlson. 1971. Free text word retrieval and scientist indexing: Performance profiles and costs. *Journal of Documentation* 27 (3), 167–183. Sept.

Hersey, D. F., M. Snyderman, W. R. Foster, B. Hunt, and P. Morgan. 1973. On-line retrieval and machine-aided indexing in a large data base of ongoing research information. *Proceedings of the American Society for Information Science* 10, 89–90.

Hewitt, J. A. 1974. *The Ohio College Library Center: Impact and evaluation; A report to the Board of Trustees of the Bibliographic Center for Research.* Rocky Mountain Region, Inc. Sept. 67 pp.

Hewitt, J. A. 1976. The impact of OCLC. *American Libraries* 7 (5), 268–275. May.

Higgins, L. D., and F. J. Smith. 1969. On-line subject indexing and retrieval. *Program* 3 (Nov.), 147–156.

Higgins, L. D., and F. J. Smith. 1971. Disc access algorithms. *Computer Journal* 14, 243–253.

Hildreth, C. R. 1982. *Online public access catalogs: The user interface.* OCLC Library, Information, and Computer Science Series. Dublin, OH: OCLC, Inc.

Hillman, D. J. 1964a. The notion of relevance (I.) *American Documentation* 15 (Jan.), 26–34.

Hillman, D. J. 1964b. On concept-formation and relevance. *Proceedings of the American Documentation Institute* 1, 23–29.

Hillman, D. J. 1964c. Two models for retrieval system design. *American Documentation* 15 (July), 217–225.

Hillman, D. J. 1965. Mathematical classification techniques for non-static document collections, with particular reference to the problem of relevance. In P. Atherton (ed.), *Classification research,* 177–209. Copenhagen: Munksgaard. (Proceedings of the Second International Study Conference on Classification Research, Elsinore, Denmark, Sept. 14–18, 1964.)

Hillman, D. J. 1968. Negotiation of inquiries in an on-line retrieval system. *Information Storage & Retrieval* 4 (June), 219–223. (Presented earlier at First Canfield International Conference on Mechanized Information Storage and Retrieval Systems, Canfield, England, Aug. 29–31, 1967.)

Hillman, D. J. 1970. The future of information provision. In C. M. Lincoln (ed.), *Educating the library user,* M-1–M-15. Loughborough University of Technology: ADELE. (Proceedings of the Fourth Triennial Meeting.)

Hillman, D. J. 1973. Customized user services via interactions with LEADERMART. *Information torage & Retrieval* 9 (Nov.), 587–596.

Hillman, D. J. 1974a. An operational experiment for the marketing of scientific and technical information. In *Twelfth Annual Allerton Conference on Circuit and System Theory, Allerton House, Monticello, IL, Oct. 2–4, 1974,* 495–501. Sponsored by the Department of Electrical Engineering and the Coordinated Science Laboratory of the University of Illinois, Urbana-Champaign.

Hillman, D. J. 1974b. A system approach to data base sales management. *Proceedings of the American Society for Information Science* 11, 24–27.

Hillman, D. J. 1977. Model for the on-line management of knowledge transfer. *On-Line Review* 1 (1), 23–30. Mar.

Hillman, D. J. 1996. Personal communication to C. P. Bourne. Feb. 7.

Hillman, D. J., and A. J. Kasarda. 1969. The LEADER retrieval system. *Proceedings of the AFIPS Spring Joint Computer Conference* 34, 447–455.

Hines, D. L. 1975. Computerized literature search services in an engineering library. *Special Libraries* 66 (4), 197–204. Apr.

Hirschfield, L. G. 1972. *University of Michigan Medical Center Library: MEDLARS cumulative report 1966–1972.* (ERIC No. ED 069 297.) Ann Arbor, MI: University of Michigan Medical Center Library. 9 pp.

Hjerppe, R. 1975. Experiences of an interactive retrieval system: ESRO/RECON. In S. Schwarz (ed.), *The interactive library: Computerized processes in library and information networks,* 113–129. Stockholm: Swedish Society for Technical Documentation. (Proceedings of seminar, Stockholm, Nov. 25–28, 1974.)

Hlava, M. K. 1978. The NASA information system. *Proceedings of the Second International Online Information Meeting,* 251–256. Oxford, England: Learned Information.

Hodgson, P. 1972. MEDLARS in Australasia. *New Zealand Libraries* 35 (5), 288–294. Oct.

Hogan, R. 1966. An evaluation of MEDLARS output: Demand and recurring bibliographies. *Bulletin of the Medical Library Association* 54 (4), 321–324. Oct.

Holmes, P. L. 1977a. The British Library automated information service. *Aslib Proceedings* 29 (6), 214–220. June.

Holmes, P. L. 1977b. A description of the British Library's short-term experimental information network project. In *Proceedings of the First International Online Information Meeting*, 231–237. Oxford, England: Learned Information.

Holmes, P. L. 1977c. *On-line information retrieval; An introduction and guide to the British Library's short-term experimental information network project; Volume one; Experimental use of non-medical information services.* (Report No. 5360 HC.) London: British Library, Research & Development Department. May. 61 pp.

Holmes, P. L. 1978. *On-line information retrieval; An introduction and guide to the British Library's short-term experimental information network project; Volume two: Experimental use of medical information services.* (Report No. 5397.) London: British Library, Research & Development Department. Aug. 66 pp.

Holzbauer, F. W., and E. H. Farris. 1966. *Library information processing using an on-line, real-time computer system.* (Report No. TR 00.1548; ERIC No. ED 019 970.) Poughkeepsie, NY: IBM Systems Development Division. Dec. 7.

Hoopes, J. 1979. *Oral history: An introduction for students.* Chapel Hill, NC: The University of North Carolina Press.

Hoppenfeld, E. C. 1966. Law Research Service/Inc. *Modern Uses of Logic in Law (M.U.L.L.)* (Mar.), 46–52.

Horty, J. F. 1960a. *Application of information retrieval techniques to legal research.* (NTIS No. PB 169 597.) Pittsburgh, PA: University of Pittsburgh. Nov. 1.

Horty, J. F. 1960b. Experience with the application of electronic data processing systems in general law. *Modern Uses of Logic in Law (M.U.L.L.)* (Dec.), 60D, 158–168.

Horty, J. F. 1962. The "key words in combination" approach. *Modern Uses of Logic in Law (M.U.L.L.)* (Mar.), 54–64.

Horty, J. F. 1965. A look at research in legal information retrieval. In P. A. Atherton (ed), *Classification research: Proceedings of the 2nd International Study Conference, Elsinore, Denmark, 14–18 Sept. 1964*, 382–396. Copenhagen: Munksgaard.

Horty, J. F. 1966. Use of the computer in statutory research and the legislative process. In R. P. Bigelow (ed.), *Computers and the law; An introductory handbook*, 48–55. New York: Commerce Clearing House.

Horty, J. F., and T. B. Walsh. 1963. Use of Flexowriters to prepare large amounts of alphabetic legal data for computer retrieval. *Proceedings of the 26th Annual Meeting of the American Documentation Institute, Pt. 2*, 259–260.

Houghton, B., and J. Convey. 1977. *On-line information retrieval systems.* Hamden, CT: Linnet Books.

Houghton, B., V. A. D. Webster, and J. Smith. 1982. A comparison of Excerpta Medica and MEDLINE for the provision of drug information to health care professionals. In *Proceedings of the Sixth International Online Information Meeting*, 115–127. Oxford, England: Learned Information.

Housman, E. M. 1973. Selective dissemination of information. *Annual Review of Information Science and Technology* 8, 221–241.

Hsaio, D. K., and F. Manola. 1972. Data management with variable structure and rapid access. In *First USA-Japan Computer Conference Proceedings*, 624–631. Montvale, NJ: AFIPS. Co-sponsored by AFIPS and IPSJ.

Hsiao, D. K., and N. S. Prywes. 1968. A system to manage an information system. In K. Samuelson (ed.), *Mechanized information storage, retrieval and dissemination*, 637–660. Amsterdam: North-Holland. (Proceedings of the FID/IFIP Joint Conference, Rome, June 14–17, 1967.)

Hudson, J. A. 1970. Searching MARC/DPS records for area studies: Comparative results using keywords, LC, and DC class numbers. *Library Resources & Technical Services* 14 (Fall), 530–545.

Hughes, T. E. 1973. Open discussion. In M. B. Henderson (ed.), *Interactive bibliographic systems*, 13–22. AEC Report No. CONF-711 010. Washington, DC: U.S. Atomic Energy Commission. Apr. (Proceedings of a forum, Gaithersburg, MD, Oct. 4–5, 1971.)

Hughes, T. E., and A. A. Brooks. 1975. The AEC/RECON system: A case study. *Information systems: Their interconnection and compatibility; Proceedings of a symposium*, 189–195. Vienna: International Atomic Energy Agency.

Hummel, D. J. 1975. A comparative report on an on-line retrieval service employing two distinct software systems. *Journal of Chemical Information and Computer Sciences* 15 (1), 24–27. Feb.

Humphrey, A. 1995. Personal communication to C. P. Bourne. Jan. 7.

Humphrey, A. 1997. Personal communication to C. P. Bourne. July 15.

Humphrey, S. M. 1974. Searching the MEDLARS citation file on-line using ELHILL 2 and STAIRS: A comparison. *Information Storage & Retrieval* 10 (9–10), 321–329. Sept.–Oct.

Humphrey, S. M. 1976. Searching the MEDLARS citation file on-line using ELHILL and STAIRS: An updated comparison. *Information Processing & Management* 12 (1), 63–70.

Hutton, F. C. 1968. RESPONSA–A computer search of a subject index. *Proceedings of the American Society for Information Science* 5, 121–124.

Hyslop, M. R. 1966. Joint development of a common information system by two organizations working in different disciplines. *Proceedings of the American Documentation Institute* 3, 207–216.

IBM System/360 Document Processing System (360A-CX-12X) program description and operations manual. 1967. (Report No. H20-0477-0.) White Plains, NY: IBM. 282 pp.

Information activities of major international organizations. 1971. Paris: Organisation for Economic Co-operation and Development, Directorate for Scientific Affairs.

The Information Bank picture story. 1980. *Online* 4 (3), 49–54. July.

Information Dynamics unveils Bibnet for on-site processing. 1973. *Advanced Technology Libraries* 2 (2), 1–2. Feb.

Information retrieval at DTIE using RECON III system. 1970. Apr. *Technical Information Bulletin* 21 (Apr.), 6. Published at Brookhaven National Laboratory for AEC's Technical Information Panel.

Information retrieval demonstration and research project; Final report. 1974. (ERIC No. ED 098 306.) Madison: University of Wisconsin, Center for Studies in Vocational and Technical Education. 59 pp. June.

INSPEC file. 1977. *Space Documentation Service News and Views.* Dec.

Irvine, J. J. 1973. A remote-terminal retrospective search facility using a hybrid of microform and computer storage. *Information Storage & Retrieval* 9 (11), 597–606. Nov.

Irwin Howard Pizer, 1934–1991 [Obituary]. 1992. *Bulletin of the Medical Library Association* 80 (1), 63–65. Jan.

Isaacs, H. H. 1966. Crime pattern recognition in natural language. In W. A. Kalenich (ed.), *Information processing 1965*, vol. 2, 548–550. Washington, DC: Spartan Books. (Proceedings of the IFIP Congress 65, New York, NY, May 24–29, 1965.) Published originally as SDC Report No. SP-2077; NTIS No. AD 615 720. May 1965.

Isotta, N. E. C. 1970a. Europe's first information retrieval network. *ESRO/ELDO Space Document Service Bulletin* 9, 9–17.

Isotta, N. E. C. 1970b. The user and the automated system in a European environment. In *Problems in mechanization of small information centers*, 27–34. Neuilly-sur-Seine, France: North Atlantic Treaty Organization, Advisory Group for Aerospace Research and Development. (Papers presented at Specialist Meeting of the AGARD Technical Information Panel, Ottowa, Canada, Sept. 16–17, 1969.)

Isotta, N. E. C. 1972a. International information networks; I. The ESRO system. *Aslib Proceedings* 24 (1), 33–34. Jan.

Isotta, N. E. C. 1972b. Space Documentation Service of the European Space Research Organization and the European Vehicle Launcher Development Organization. *Proceedings of the American Society for Information Science* 9, 189–196.

Isotta, N. E. C. 1975. ESRO's interactive System: An aid for development. In S. Schwarz (ed.), *The Interactive Library: Computerized Processes in Library and Information Networks*, 93–112. Stockholm: Swedish Society for Technical Documentation. (Proceedings of seminar, Stockholm, Nov. 25–28, 1974.)

Isotta, N. E. C. 1976. On-line technological opportunity in the European Space Agency. In G. Pratt, and S. Harvey (eds.), *The on-line age: Plans and needs for on-line information retrieval*, 21–33. London: Aslib/EUSIDIC. (Proceedings of the Eusidic conference, Oslo, Dec. 4–5, 1975.)

IUC/OCLC network evaluation; Final report. 1975. (ERIC No. ED 115 288.) Rockville, MD: Westat Research. Aug. 31. 229 pp.

Ives, E. D. 1980. *The tape-recorded interview; A manual for field workers in folklore and oral history.* Knoxville: The University of Tennessee Press.

Ivie, E. L. 1966. *Search procedures based on measures of relatedness between documents.* (Report No. MAC-TR-29; NTIS No. AD 636 275.) Cambridge, MA: MIT. May. 243 pp.

Jack, R. F. 1982. The NASA/RECON search system: A file-by-file description of a major—but little known—collection of scientific information. *Online* 6 (Nov.), 40–54.

Jedwabski, B. 1977. The on-line system DOBIS. In E. Edelhoff, and K.-D. Lehmann (eds.), *On-line library* and network systems, 141–157. Frankfurt: Vittorio Klostermann. (Proceedings of a symposium held at Dortmund University, Mar. 22–24, 1976.)

Jenkins, G. T. 1972. The MEDLARS demand search quality control program. *Bulletin of the Medical Library Association* 60 (3), 423–426. July.

Jenkins, L. H. 1997. Personal communication to C. P. Bourne. Oct. 17.

Jenkins, L. H. 1998. Personal communication to C. P. Bourne. May 8.

Jurimetrics: The electronic digital computer and its application in legal research. 1965. *Iowa Law Review* 50, 1114–1134.

Kallenbach, P. A. 1972. Towards a European information utility network. *Proceedings of the American Society for Information Science* 9, 197–204.

Kasarda, A. J., and D. J. Hillman. 1972. The Leadermart system and service. *Proceedings of the 27th National Conference of the Association for Computing Machinery*, 469–477.

Katajapuro, L. 1971. Finnish experience from SDI-Service based on Nuclear Science Abstracts (NSA). In *Library occasional paper #4*, 8–12. Otaniemi, Finland: Helsinki University of Technology.

Katter, R. V. 1970. *On the on-line users of remote-access citation retrieval services.* (Report No. TM-(L)-4494.) Santa Monica, CA: SDC. Jan. 8. 30 pp.

Katter, R. V. 1973. Insights in implementing the redesign cycle. In M. B. Henderson (ed.), *Interactive bibliographic systems*, 175–189. Washington, DC: U.S. Atomic Energy Commission. AEC Report No. CONF-711 010. Apr. (Proceedings of a forum, Gaithersburg, MD, Oct. 4–5, 1971.)

Katter, R. V. 1998. Personal communication to C. P. Bourne. Feb. 2.

Katter, R. V., and D. A. Blankenship. 1969a. *On-line interfaces for document information systems; Considerations for the Biomedical Communications Network.* (Report No. TM-(L)-4320.) Santa Monica, CA: SDC. June 3. 59 pp.

Katter, R. V., and D. A. Blankenship. 1969b. *Plan for empirical studies of on-line interface problems for NLM.* (Report No. TM-L-4321.) Santa Monica, CA: SDC. 15 pp. June 3.

Katter, R. V., and D. B. McCarn. 1971. AIM/TWX: An experimental on-line bibliographic retrieval system. In D. E. Walker (ed.), *Interactive bibliographic search; The user/computer interface*, 121–142. Montvale, NJ: AFIPS Press. (Proceedings of The User Interface for Interactive Search of Bibliographic Data Bases, Palo Alto, CA, Jan. 14–15.)

Katter, R. V., and K. M. Pearson. 1975. MEDLARS II: A third generation bibliographic production system. *Journal of Library Automation* 8 (2), 87–97. June.

Katzer, J. 1971. SUPARS letter to the editor. *Journal of the American Society for Information Science* 22 (6), 411. Nov.–Dec.

Katzer, J. 1972. The development of a semantic differential to assess users' attitudes towards an on-line interactive reference retrieval system. *Journal of the American Society for Information Science* 23 (2), 122–127. Mar.–Apr.

Katzer, J. 1973. The cost-performance of an on-line, free-text bibliographic retrieval system. *Information Storage & Retrieval* 9 (June), 321–329.

Katzer, J., and P. Moell. 1973. On the dimensionality of users' attitudes toward on-line systems—A replication? *Journal of the American Society for Information Science* 24 (4), 307–308. July–Aug.

Kaufman, S. 1966. The IBM information retrieval center—(ITIRC) system techniques and applications. *Proceedings of the 21st National Conference of the Association for Computing Machinery*, 505–512. Published originally as Report No. ITIRC-008, IBM Technical Information Retrieval Center, Yorktown Heights, NY. Aug. 12 pp. + appendix.

Kaufman, S. 1969. TEXT-PAC design considerations. *Proceedings of the American Society for Information Science* 6, 77–81. Published originally as report no. ITIRC-024, IBM Technical Information Retrieval Center, Yorktown Heights, NY.

Kaufman, S. 1970. ITIRC today. IBM *International Quarterly* (Apr.), 83–89.

Kaufman, S. 1997. Personal communication to C. P. Bourne. Oct. 14; Dec. 8.

Kaufman, S. 1998. Personal communication to C. P. Bourne. Feb. 20; Apr. 27.

Kaufman, S., and W. E. Brooks. 1965. *7090–1401 current information selection (dissemination) and retrospective search system; Type III program release to the SHARE general program library.* Dec. 20. 115 pp.

Kaufman, S., T. F. Lindsley, and J. J. Magnino. 1963. Storage and retrieval of technical data using PRIME; A normal text information retrieval system. Paper presented at 145th meeting of the ACS, Division of Chemical Literature, New York, Sept. 11.

Kaufman, S., and J. J. Magnino. (Inventors.) 1967. *Information retrieval system and method.* (U.S. Patent No. 3,350,695.) Oct. 31.

Kays, O. 1995. Personal communication to C. P. Bourne. Jan. 3.

Kayton, I. 1966. Retrieving case law by computer: Fact, fiction, and future. *George Washington Law Review* 35 (1), 1–49. Oct.

Keenan, S., and E. Terry. 1968. *Retrieval of the 1964 laser literature using MIT's Project TIP.* (Report No. ID 68-2.) New York: American Institute of Physics, Information Division. 13 pp. Mar.

Kehl, W. B., J. F. Horty, C. R. T. Bacon, and D. S. Mitchell. 1961. An information retrieval language for legal studies. *Communications of the ACM* 4 (9), 380–389. Sept.

Kellogg, C. H. 1968a. CONVERSE—A system for the on-line description and retrieval of structured data using natural language. In K. Samuelson (ed.), *Mechanized information storage, retrieval and dissemination*, 608–621. Amsterdam: North-Holland. (Proceedings of the FID/IFIP Joint Conference, Rome, June 14–17, 1967.) Published originally as Report No. SP-2635, SDC, Santa Monica, CA. May 26, 1967. 15 pp.

Kellogg, C. H. 1968b. A natural language compiler for on-line data management. *Proceedings of the AFIPS Fall Joint Computer Conference* 33 (pt. 1), 473–492.

Kellogg, C. H. 1968c. On-line translation of natural language questions into artificial language queries. *Information Storage & Retrieval* 4 (Aug.), 287–307. Published originally as Report No. SP-2827, SDC, Santa Monica, CA. Apr. 28, 1967. 47 pp.

Kershaw, G. A., D. Crowder, J. E. Davis, E. G. Loges, and E. Merendini. 1966. *Mechanization study of the Foreign Technology Division, Wright-Patterson AFB, Ohio.* (Report No. BAARINC 914-1-3; NTIS No. AD 489 996.) Bethesda, MD: Booz, Allen Applied Research. Sept.

Kershaw, G. A., D. Crowder, J. E. Davis, E. G. Loges, E. Merendini, and S. M. Thomas. 1966. *Mechanization study of the RECON CENTRAL, Reconnaissance Division, Air Force Avionics Lab., Wright-Patterson AFB, Ohio.* (Report No. BAARINC 914-1-20; NTIS No. AD 640 115.) Bethesda, MD: Booz-Allen Applied Research. Sept. 37 pp.

Kessler, M. M. 1960. *An experimental communication center for scientific and technical information.* (Report No. 4G-0002; NTIS No. AD 255 656; NTIS No. PB 171 833.) Lexington, MA: MIT, Lincoln Lab. Mar. 31. 35 pp.

Kessler, M. M. 1964. *The M.I.T. Technical Information Project; I. system description.* (NTIS No. AD 608 502.) Cambridge, MA: MIT. Nov. 2.

Kessler, M. M. 1965a. The M.I.T. Technical Information Project. In *1965 Congress of the International Federation for Documentation (FID)* (Abstracts), 39. Washington, DC: FID Secretariat.

Kessler, M. M. 1965b. The MIT technical information project. *Physics Today* 18 (3), 28–36. Mar.

Kessler, M. M. 1965c. *TIP user's manual: A guide for on-line search and retrieval of the current literature in physics.* (Report No. TIP-TM-010.) Cambridge, MA: Technical Information Program and Project MAC. Dec. 1. 26 pp. A second printing was issued in Dec. 1966 as NTIS No. AD 635 163, 77 pp.

Kessler, M. M. 1966. Search strategies of the M.I.T. Technical Information Program. In W. Simonton, and C. Mason (eds.), *Information retrieval with special reference to the biomedical sciences*, 23–33. Minneapolis: University of Minnesota, Nolte Center for Continuing Education. (Papers presented at the Second Institute on Information Retrieval, Nov. 10–13, 1965.)

Kessler, M. M. 1967a. The 'on-line' technical information system at M.I.T. (Project TIP.) *IEEE International Convention Record*, Part 10, 40–43. New York: Institute of Electrical and Electronics Engineers.

Kessler, M. M. 1967b. *TIP library maintenance; A description of the methods and operating procedures used by TIP personnel in the production of a machine-usable library of journal articles, its maintenance and up-dating.* Cambridge, MA: MIT. Oct. 14 pp.

Kessler, M. M. 1967c. *TIP programs: A functional description of the programs available to users of the TIP system.* Cambridge, MA: MIT. Oct. 21 pp.

Kessler, M. M. 1967d. *TIP system applications; A description of TIP operations and a preliminary analysis of system experience.* Cambridge, MA: MIT, Technical Information Program. Oct. 27 pp.

Kessler, M. M. 1967e. *TIP system report.* (NTIS No. AD 671 269.) Cambridge, MA: MIT. Oct. (A collection of reports and published articles, assembled under one cover.)

Kessler, M. M. 1967f. *TIP user's manual; A guide for on-line search and retrieval of the current literature in physics.* Cambridge, MA: MIT, Technical Information Project and Project MAC. Oct.

Kessler, M. M., E. L. Ivie, and W. D. Mathews. 1964. The M.I.T. technical information project—A prototype system. *Proceedings of the American Documentation Institute* 1, 263–268.

Kessler, R. 1964. New computer system to locate scientific articles by contents. *Boston Sunday Herald*, Oct. 4, p. A55.

Kidd, E. M., C. E. Price, and S. L. Yount 1969. *Study of the Data Central system for information retrieval applied to NSA data.* (Report No. CTC-INF-942; NTIS No. PB 183–450.) Oak Ridge, TN: Union Carbide Corporation, Nuclear Division, Computer Technology Center. Feb. 26. 30 pp.

Kilgour, F. G. 1966. Computer applications in biomedical libraries. In *Proceedings of the IBM Scientific Computing Symposium on Man-Machine Communication*, 101–110. White Plains, NY: IBM, Data Processing Division.

Kilgour, F. G. 1968. Retrieval of single entries from a computerized library catalog file. *Proceedings of the American Society for Information Science* 5, 133–136.

Kilgour, F. G. 1969. Initial system design for the Ohio College Library Center: A case history. In D. E. Carroll (ed.), *Proceedings of the 1968 Clinic on Library Applications of Data Processing*, 79–88. Urbana-Champaign: University of Illinois, Graduate School of Library Science.

Kilgour, F. G. 1971. User needs, feedback, and training. In D. E. Walker (ed.), *Interactive bibliographic search: The user/computer interface*, 278. Montvale, NJ: AFIPS Press. (Proceedings of a workshop held in Palo Alto, CA, Jan. 14–15.)

Kilgour, F. G. 1975. Computerized library networks. In *2nd USA-Japan computer conference proceedings*, 166–171. Montvale, NJ: AFIPS.

Kilgour, F. G. 1977. New concepts in librarianship. In E. Edelhoff, and K.-D. Lehman (eds.), *On-line library and network systems*, 84–93. Frankfurt: Vittorio Klostermann. (Proceedings of a symposium held at Dortmund University, Mar. 22–24, 1976.)

Kilgour, F. G. 1987. Historical note: A personalized prehistory of OCLC. *Journal of the American Society for Information Science* 38 (5), 381–384. Sept.

Kilgour, F. G. 1995. Personal communication to C. P. Bourne. July 27.

Kilgour, F. G., P. L. Long, and E. B. Leiderman. 1970. Retrieval of bibliographic entries from a name-title catalog by use of truncated search keys. *Proceedings of the American Society for Information Science* 7, 79–82.

Kilgour, F. G., P. L. Long, E. B. Leiderman, and A. L. Landgraf. 1971. Title-only entries retrieved by use of truncated search keys. *Journal of Library Automation* 4 (4), 207–210.

King, D. W., and N. W. Caldwell. 1970. *Study of the cost-effectiveness of retrospective search systems.* (ERIC No. ED 046 446.) Rockville, MD: Westat Research. June. 44 pp.

King, D. W., P. W. Neel, and B. L. Wood. 1972. *Comparative evaluation of the retrieval effectiveness of descriptor and free-text search systems using CIRCOL (Central Information Reference and Control On-Line); Final technical report 1 Apr. 70–1 Jul. 71.* (Report No. RADC-TR-71–311; NTIS No. AD 738 299.) Rockville, MD: Westat Research. Jan. 126 pp.

King, G. W. 1963. *Automation and the Library of Congress.* Washington, DC: Library of Congress.

King, G. W., G. W. Brown, and L. N. Ridenour. 1953. Photographic techniques for information storage. *Proceedings of the I.R.E.* 41 (Oct.), 1421–1428.

Kissman, H. M. 1973. The Toxicology Information Conversational On-Line Network (TOXICON): A status report. Paper presented at 8th Middle Atlantic Regional Meeting of the American Chemical Society, Washington, DC, Jan. 17.

Kissman, H. M. 1974. Conversational access to toxicological information. Paris: UNESCO. Paper presented at First World Congress of Environmental Medicine and Biology; Section on Environmental Data Banks, July 1–5.

Kissman, H. M. 1975a. Building an on-line data retrieval system. *Bulletin of the American Society for Information Science* 1 (7), 16, 36–37. Feb.

Kissman, H. M. 1975b. An online information retrieval system for toxicology. In J. Sherrod (ed.), Information systems and networks. Westport, CT: Greenwood Press. (Proceedings of the Eleventh Annual Symposium in Information Processing, Los Angeles, Mar. 27–29, 1974.)

Kissman, H. M. 1995. Personal communication to C. P. Bourne. Oct. 18.

Kissman, H. M., and D. J. Hummel. 1972a. *The Toxicology Information Conversational On-Line Network Service (TOXICON).* Paper presented at the 164th Annual Meeting of the American Chemical Society, New York, Aug. 28–31.

Kissman, H. M., and D. J. Hummel. 1972b. TOXICON—An on-line toxicology information service. *Chemical Technolog* 2 (12), 727, 729–770.

Kissman, H. M., and P. Wexler. 1985. Aug. Toxicology information systems: A historical perspective. *Journal of Chemical Information and Computer Science* 25 (3), 212–217.

Klass, P. J. 1995. CIA reveals details of early spy satellites. *Aviation Week & Space Technology* 142 (24), 167–173. June 12.

Klingbiel, P. H., and C. R. Jacobs. 1966. *DDC descriptor frequencies*. Alexandria, VA: DDC. May. 53 pp.

Knapp, S. D. 1983. Online searching: Past, present, and future. In *Online searching technique and management*, 3–15. Chicago: ALA.

Knudson, D. R., and S. N. Teicher. 1969. Remote text access in a computerized library information retrieval system. *Proceedings of the AFIPS Spring Joint Computer Conference* 34, 475–481.

Koenig, M. E. D. 1987. Interview. May 18.

Koenig, M. E. D. 1992. How close we came. *Information Processing & Management* 28 (3), 433–436.

Koenig, M. E. D. 1995. Personal communication to C. P. Bourne. July 20.

Kolbe, H. K. 1975. Networks. *Bulletin of the American Society for Information Science* 1 (8), 23–24. Mar. (Guest column for C. H. Stevens.)

Kollegger, J. G. 1988. An online database producer's memoirs. *Database* 11 (5), 33–36. Oct.

Komoto, D. T. 1970. WESRAC system. *Datamation* 16 (9), 45–47. Aug. 15.

Kondos, G. S. 1968. DIALOG: Computer-assisted legal research, on-line. *Law and Computer Technology* 1 (11), 8–14. Nov.

Kondos, G. S. 1971. JURIS: Remote terminal legal information retrieval at the United States Department of Justice. *Law and Computer Technology* 4 (6), 147–155. Nov.–Dec.

Kondos, G. S. 1974. JURIS and LITE: A progress report. *Law and Computer Technology* 7 (Jan.–Feb.), 11–16.

Kozumplik, W. A., and R. T. Lange. 1966. *Computer-produced microfilm library catalog*. (Report No. LMSC 50-10-66-6; NTIS No. AD 647 174.) Sunnyvale, CA: LMSC. Oct. 21 pp.

Krulee, G., and B. Mittman. 1969. Computer-based information systems for university research and teaching. In L. Schultz (ed.), *The information bazaar*, 237–253. Philadelphia: College of Physicians of Philadelphia. (Proceedings of the Sixth Annual National Colloquium on Information Retrieval, Philadelphia, May 8–9, 1969.)

Kuhn, T. S. 1970. *The structure of scientific revolutions*, 2d ed. Chicago, IL: University of Chicago Press.

Kunkel, B., and B. Miller. 1975. In-house promotion of on-line retrieval in a technical library. *Proceedings of the American Society for Information Science* 12, 129.

Lambert, R. H., and C. R. Grady. 1975. *Wisconsin's ERIC on-line information retrieval demonstration and research (Information retrieval and research project): Final report.* (Report No. P-19-031-151-225; ERIC No. ED 111 430.) Madison: University of Wisconsin, Center for Studies in Vocational and Technical Education. June 30. 77 pp.

Lancaster, F. W. 1967. Evaluating the performance of a large operating retrieval system. In A. Kent, O. E. Taulbee, J. Belzer, and G. D. Goldstein (eds.), *Electronic handling of information: Testing & evaluation*, 199–216. Washington, DC: Thompson Book Co.

Lancaster, F. W. 1968a. *Evaluation of the operating efficiency of MEDLARS; Final report.* (NTIS No. PB 178 660.) Bethesda, MD: NLM. 276 pp. Jan. Also published under the title *Evaluation of the MEDLARS demand search service.*

Lancaster, F. W. 1968b. Interaction between requesters and a large mechanized retrieval system. *Information Storage & Retrieval* 4 (2), 239–252. June.

Lancaster, F. W. 1969a. Evaluating the performance of a large computerized information system. *Journal of the American Medical Association* 207 (1), 114–120. Jan. 6.

Lancaster, F. W. 1969b. MEDLARS: Report on the evaluation of its operating efficiency. *American Documentation* 20 (2), 119–142. Apr.

Lancaster, F. W. 1971a. Aftermath of an evaluation. *Journal of Documentation* 27 (1), 1–10. Mar.

Lancaster, F. W. 1971b. *An evaluation of EARS (Epilepsy Abstracts Retrieval System) and factors governing its effectiveness.* (NTIS No. PB 218 654.) Urbana-Champaign: University of Illinois, Graduate School of Library Science. Oct. 58 pp.

Lancaster, F. W. 1972. *Evaluation of on-line searching in MEDLARS (AIM-TWX) by biomedical practitioners.* (ERIC No. ED 062 989.) Urbana-Champaign: University of Illinois, Graduate School of Library Science. Occasional paper no. 101. Feb. 19 pp.

Lancaster, F. W. 1979. *Information retrieval systems: Characteristics, testing and evaluation*, 2d ed. New York: Wiley.

Lancaster, F. W., and E. G. Fayen. 1973. *Information retrieval on-line*. Los Angeles: Melville.

Lancaster, F. W., and G. T. Jenkins. 1970. "Quality control" applied to the operation of a large information system. *Journal of the American Society for Information Service* 21 (5), 370–371. Sept.–Oct.

Lancaster, F. W., and J. M. Owen. 1976. Information retrieval by computer. In D. P. Hammer (ed.), *The information age; Its development and impact*, 1–33. Metuchen, NJ: Scarecrow Press.

Lancaster, F. W., R. L. Rapport, and J. K. Penry. 1972. Evaluating the effectiveness of an on-line natural language retrieval system. *Information Storage & Retrieval* 8 (5), 223–245. Oct.

Landau, R. M. 1969a. The federal information research science and technology network. *Proceedings of the American Society for Information Science* 6, 439–440.

Landau, R. M. 1969b. On-line interactive systems. In L. Schultz (ed.), *The information bazaar*, 359–372. Philadelphia: College of Physicians of Philadelphia. (Proceedings of Sixth Annual National Colloquium on Information Retrieval, Philadelphia, May 8–9.)

Landau, R. M. 1990. Interview. July 27.

Landau, R. M. 1997. Personal communication to C. P. Bourne. Nov. 19.

Landgraf, A. L., and F. G. Kilgour. 1973. Catalog records retrieved by personal author using derived search keys. *Journal of Library Automation* 6 (2), 103–108.

Landgraf, A. L., K. B. Rastogi, and P. L. Long. 1973. Corporate author entry records retrieved by use of derived truncated search keys. *Journal of Library Automation* 6 (3), 156–161.

Larson, S. 1977. Online systems for legal research. *Online* 1 (3), 10–14. July.

Lawford, H. 1973. QUIC/LAW: Project of Queen's University. In R. A. May (ed.), *Automated law research; A collection of presentations delivered at the First National Conference on Automated Law Research*, 67–93. American Bar Association, Standing Committee on Law and Technology.

Lawrence, B. 1987. Interview. Sept. 24.

Lawrence, B. 1997. Personal communication to C. P. Bourne. Sept. 9.

Lawrence, B., B. H. Weil, and M. H. Graham. 1974. Making on-line search available in an industrial research environment. *Journal of the American Society for Information Science* 25 (6), 364–369. Nov.–Dec.

Lazorick, G. J. 1969. Computer/communications system at SUNY Buffalo. *EDUCOM: Bulletin of the Interuniversity Communications Council* 4 (1), 1–4. Feb.

LEASCO and SDC offer new services from ERIC data base. 1972. *Information; Part 1/News; Sources; Profiles* 4 (1), 12. Jan.–Feb.

Leasing of LITE materials. 1968. *Law and Computer Technology* 1 (7), 20. July.

Leblanc, E. S. 1978. CAN/OLE's on-line document ordering facility. *Proceedings of the Sixth Canadian Conference on Information Science*, 168–177.

Lefkowitz, D. 1969. *File structures for on-line systems*. New York: Spartan Books.

Lefkowitz, D. 1975. The large data base file structure dilemma. *Journal of Chemical Information and Computer Sciences* 15 (Feb.), 14–15.

Lefkowitz, D., and R. V. Powers. 1967. A list-structured chemical information retrieval system. In G. Schecter (ed.), *Information retrieval: A critical review*, 109–129. Washington, DC: Thompson Book Co. (Proceedings of the Third Annual National Colloquium on Information Retrieval, Philadelphia, May 12–13, 1966.)

Lefkowitz, D., and C. T. Van Meter. 1966. An experimental real time chemical information system. *Journal of Chemical Documentation* 6 (Aug.), 173–183.

Legard, L. K., and C. P. Bourne. 1976. An improved title word search key for large catalog files. *Journal of Library Automation* 9 (4), 318–327. Dec.

Lehigh's LEADERMART linked with U of Georgia. 1972. *Information; Part 1/News; Sources; Profiles* 4 (4), 183, 185–186. July–Aug.

Leiter, J., and C. D. Gull. 1968. The MEDLARS system in 1968. *Proceedings of the American Society for Information Science* 5, 255–262.

Leiter, J., and R. Mehnert. 1972. Medical Literature and Analysis Retrieval System (MEDLARS). In S. Herner and M. J. vellucci (eds.), *Selected federal computer-based information systems*, 94–102. Washington, DC: Information Resources Press.

Lesk, M. E. 1996. Gerald Salton, Mar. 8, 1927 to Aug. 28, 1995—In memoriam. *Journal of the American Society for Information Science* 47 (Feb.), 110–111.

Lesk, M. E., and G. Salton. 1969. Interactive search and retrieval methods using automatic information displays. *Proceedings of the AFIPS Spring Joint Computer Conference* 34, 435–446. Published originally as *Information storage and retrieval* (Report No. ISR-14, Section IX;

NTIS No. PB 180 931.) Ithaca, NY: Cornell University, Department of Computer Science. Oct. 1968.

Lesser, M. L., and J. W. Haanstra. 1957. The random-access memory accounting machine; I. System organization of the IBM 305. *IBM Journal of Research and Development* 1 (2), 62–75. Jan.

Levinson, L. H. 1967. Automated legal research at the University of Florida College of Law: Development of a new service for Florida lawyers. *Florida Bar Journal* 41 (2), 81–90. Feb.

Lewis, R. F. 1966, The MEDLARS project at the UCLA Biomedical Library. *Bulletin of the Medical Library Association* 54 (1), 11–13. Jan.

Library/USA; A bibliographic and descriptive report. 1967. Chicago: ALA.

Licklider, J. C. R. 1964. Information in decision making. *Proceedings of the American Documentation Institute* 1, 9–21.

Licklider, J. C. R. 1965a. *Libraries of the future.* Cambridge, MA: The MIT Press.

Licklider, J. C. R. 1965b. Man-computer interaction in information systems. In M. Rubinoff (ed.), *Toward a national information system*, 63–75. Washington, DC: Spartan Books. (Proceedings of the Second Annual National Colloquium on Information Retrieval, Philadelphia, Apr. 23–24.)

Licklider, J. C. R. 1968. Interactive information processing, retrieval, and transfer. In *Storage and retrieval of information: A user-supplier dialogue*, XIV/1–XIV/4.) Neuilly-Sur-Seine, France: NATO, Advisory Group for Aerospace Research & Development (AGARD.)

Licklider, J. C. R. 1968. Man-computer communication. *Annual Review of Information Science and Technology* 3, 201–240.

Link, D. T. 1973. Law searching by computer. In R. A. May (ed.), *Automated law research; A collection of presentations delivered at the First National Conference on Automated Law Research*, 3–9. American Bar Association, Standing Committee on Law and Technology.

Lipetz, B., P. Stangl, and K. F. Taylor. 1969. Performance of Ruecking's word-compression method when applied to machine retrieval from a library catalog. *Journal of Library Automation* 2 (4), 266–271. Dec.

LITE research capabilities. 1968. *Jurimetrics Journal* 9 (1), 39. Sept.

LITE source data automation. 1968. *Jurimetrics Journal* 8 (4), 106. June.

Lockheed Missiles & Space Company. 1972. *Proposal to provide an online bibliographic information search and retrieval system.* (Report No. LMSC-D082220.) Palo Alto, CA: LMSC, Palo Alto Research Lab. Apr.

Long, P. L. 1973. OCLC: From concept to functioning network. In F. W. Lancaster (ed.), *Proceedings of the 1973 Clinic on Library Applications of Data Processing*, 165–170. Urbana-Champaign: University of Illinois, Graduate School of Library Science.

Long, P. L., and F. G. Kilgour. 1971. Name-title entry retrieval from a MARC file. *Journal of Library Automation* 4 (4), 211–212.

Long, P. L., and F. G. Kilgour. 1972. A truncated search by title index. *Journal of Library Automation* 4 (1), 17–20.

Long, R. J. 1964. *Evidence retrieval and correlation (An automated system.)* Silver Spring, MD: Datatrol Corporation. June 15. 32 pp.

Longgood, W. 1973. The New York Times; Terminals come to the newsroom. *Think* (Aug.), 20–24.

Losee, M. W. 1971. May. The NASA information system: Citations in seconds. *Law Library Journal* 64 (2), 198–202. A condensed version published as On-line access: Multidisciplinary information retrieval, *Law and Computer Technology* 4 (6): 142–146. Nov./Dec.

Lowe, T. C. 1966. Design principles for an on-line information retrieval system. Unpublished doctoral diss., University of Pennsylvania, Philadelphia. Published also by University of Pennsylvania, Moore School of Electrical Engineering (Technical Report No. 67-14; AFOSR 67-0423; NTIS No. AD 647 196). Dec. 136 pp.

Lowe, T. C., and D. C. Roberts. 1969. *On-line retrieval.* (Report No. RADC-TR-69-304; NTIS No. AD 863 796.) Bethesda, MD: Informatics. Nov. 212 pp.

Lynch, M. J. 1981. *Financing online search services in publicly supported libraries: The report of an ALA survey.* Chicago: ALA. 55 pp.

Lyons, J. C. 1962. New frontiers of the legal technique. *Modern Uses of Logic in Law (M.U.L.L.)* (Dec.), 256–267.

Maciuszko, K. L. 1984. *OCLC: A decade of development, 1967–1977.* Littleton, CO: Libraries Unlimited.

Mackay, E. 1973. DATUM: Documentation automatique des textes juridiques de l'Universite de Montreal. In R. A. May (ed.), *Automated law research*; *A collection of presentations delivered at the First National Conference on Automated Law Research*, 103–109. American Bar Association, Standing Committee on Law and Technology.

Mader, I. 1981. The Information Retrieval Service of the European Space Agency, its network and the FSTA file. In U. Schutzsack, and E. J. Mann (eds.), *Proceedings of the Symposium on Food Science and Technology Abstracts (FSTA), Berlin, Oct. 21st–23rd, 1980*, 57–68. Frankfurt: International Food Information Service.

Magnino, J. J. 1962a. *Computer searching of normal text for information retrieval.* IBM Corporation, Thomas J. Watson Research Center. Unpublished handout for Patent Engineering Managers' Conference, June.

Magnino, J. J. 1962b. An operating information retrieval system utilizing a computer to search normal text. Paper presented at the Fourth Annual IBM Librarians' Conference, Poughkeepsie, NY, Nov.

Magnino, J. J. 1964. *PRIME—A computer searching system using normal text.* Yorktown Heights, NY: IBM, Thomas J. Watson Research Center, Technical Information Retrieval Center. Oct.

Magnino, J. J. 1965a. IBM Technical Information Retrieval Center–Normal text techniques. In M. Rubinoff (ed.), *Toward a national information system*, 199–216. Washington, DC: Spartan Books. (Proceedings of the Second Annual National Colloquium on Information Retrieval, Philadelphia, PA, Apr. 23–24.)

Magnino, J. J. 1965b. Textual information retrieval and the IBM suggestion plan. Yorktown Heights, NY: IBM. (Paper presented at Congress of the International Federation for Documentation (FID), Oct. Only abstract of paper was published in *Abstracts*, p. 76.)

Magnino, J. J. 1966. IBM Technical Information Retrieval Center progress and plans. *Proceedings of the American Documentation Institute* 3, 467–481.

Magnino, J. J. 1967a. Information technology and management science. Paper presented at Institute of Management Sciences, 14th International Meeting, Mexico City, Aug. 26.

Magnino, J. J. 1967b. Normal text information retrieval—management and line use within IBM. Paper presented at 31st national meeting of the Operations Research Society of America, May–June.

Magnino, J. J. 1997. Personal communication to C. P. Bourne. July.

Maier, J. M. 1974. The scientist versus machine search services: We are the missing link. *Special Libraries* 65 (4), 180–188. Apr.

Mallow, C. S. 1973. LITE: Legal Information Through Electronics. In R. A. May (ed.), *Automated law research: A collection of presentations delivered at the First National Conference on Automated Law Research*, 97–102. American Bar Association, Standing Committee on Law and Technology.

Man/machine; a contemporary dialogue. 1967. *SDC Magazine* 10 (9), 13–19. Sept.

Mann, A. R. 1974. *RETROSPEC-1; information retrieval from a computerised data base.* (Report No. GS/EX/51/73/C; NTIS No. PB 234 295/4GA.) Sheffield, England: British Steel Corporation, Information Services. June. 10 pp.

Marcus, R. S. 1991. Personal communication to C. P. Bourne. Mar. 28.

Marcus, R. S. 1997. Project Intrex and the information superhighway: Information science issues from an historical perspective. Manuscript in preparation. Sept.

Marcus, R. S. 1997. Personal communication to C. P. Bourne. Sept. 20.

Marcus, R. S., A. R. Benenfeld, and P. Kugel. 1971. The user interface for the Intrex retrieval system. In D. E. Walker (ed.), *Interactive bibliographic search; The user/computer interface*, 159–201. Montvale, NJ: AFIPS Press. (Proceedings of The User Interface for Interactive Search of Bibliographic Data Bases, Palo Alto, CA, Jan. 14–15.)

Marcus, R. S., P. Kugel, and A. R. Benenfeld. 1978. Catalog information and text as indicators of relevance. *Journal of the American Society for Information Science* 29 (Jan.), 15–30.

Marcus, R. S., P. Kugel, and R. L. Kusik. 1969. An experimental computer-stored, augmented catalog of professional literature. *Proceedings of the AFIPS Spring Joint Computer Conference* 34, 461–473.

Markey, K., and P. A. Atherton. 1978. *ONTAP: Online training and practice manual for ERIC data base searchers.* (ERIC No. ED 160 109.) Syracuse, NY: Syracuse University, ERIC Clearinghouse on Information Resources. June. 182 pp. (Based on earlier unpublished work of C. P. Bourne, B. Anderson, and J. Robinson.)

Markey, K., and P. A. Cochrane. 1981. Oct. *Online training and practice manual for ERIC data base searchers;* 2d ed. (ERIC No. ED 212 296.) Syracuse, NY: Syracuse University, ERIC Clearinghouse on Information Resources. 181 pp. (Based on earlier unpublished work of C. P. Bourne, B. Anderson, and J. Robinson.)

Markowitz, T., W. F. Brown, and C. Leslie. 1973. MEDDOC; A medical documentation service for published information on Lilly Pharmaceutical. *Proceedings of the American Society for Information Science* 10, 135–136.

Markuson, B. E., J. Wanger, S. Schatz, and D. V. Black. 1971. *Handbook on Federal library automation.* Falls Church, VA: SDC. July.

Maron, M. E., A. J. Humphrey, and J. C. Meredith. 1969. *An information processing laboratory for education and research in library science: Phase I.* Berkeley, CA: University of California, Institute of Library Research. 150 pp. July.

Maron, M. E., and D. Sherman. 1971. Sept. *An information processing laboratory for education and research in library science; Phase II.* (ERIC No. ED 060 916.) Berkeley, CA: University of California, Institute of Library Research.

Marron, B., E. Fong, D. W. Fife, and K. Rankin. 1973. *A study of six university-based information systems.* (Report No. NBS-TN-781; COM-74-50139/6, GPO No. C13.46: 781.) Washington, DC: National Bureau of Standards, Institute for Computer Science and Technology. 98 pp. June.

Marron, H. 1995. Personal communication to C. P. Bourne. May 8.

Marron, H., and W. R. Foster. 1966. Subject searches on current research information of parallel computer and manual files. *Proceedings of the American Documentation Institute* 3, 123–135.

Martin, G. P., R. M. Hayes, and I. Lieberman. 1963. *Recruitment and training of staff and support of staff dissemination activities at the American Library Association LIBRARY 21 exhibit Seattle World's Fair (B-252.)* Seattle: University of Washington, School of Librarianship. 118 pp.

Martin, M. D. 1976. Pricing and service policies: A supplier's point of view. In G. Pratt, and S. Harvey (eds.), *The on-line age: Plans and needs for on-line information retrieval,* 86–91. London: Aslib/EUSIDIC. (Proceedings of the Eusidic Conference, Oslo, Dec. 4–5, 1975.)

Martin, T. H. 1974. *A feature analysis of interactive retrieval systems.* (Report No. SU-COMM-ICR-74-1; NTIS No. PB 235 952.) Stanford, CA: Stanford University Institute for Communications Research. Sept. 86 pp.

Martin, T. H. 1975. Reflections upon the state-of-the-art in interactive information retrieval. In J. Sherrod (ed.), *Information systems and networks,* 77–83. Westport, CT: Greenwood Press. (Proceedings of the Eleventh Annual Symposium in Information Processing, Los Angeles, CA, Mar. 27–29, 1974.)

Martin, T. H., and E. B. Parker. 1971. Designing for user acceptance of an interactive bibliographic search facility. In D. E. Walker (ed.), *Interactive bibliographic search: The user/computer interface,* 45–52. Montvale, NJ: AFIPS Press. (Proceedings of The User Interface for Interactive Search of Bibliographic Data Bases, Palo Alto, CA, Jan. 14–15.)

Martin, W. A. 1969. ESRO/ELDO Space Documentation Service. *Aslib Proceedings* 21 (9), 353–359. Sept.

Martin, W. A. 1973. A comparative study of terminal user techniques in four European countries on a large common on-line interactive information retrieval system. In *First European Congress on Documentation Systems and Networks,* 107–167, 201–203. Luxembourg: Commission of the European Communities.

Martinez, S. J. 1973. A cooperative information storage and retrieval system for the petroleum industry. *Journal of Chemical Documentation* 13 (2), 59–65. May.

Mathews, W. D. 1970. Using the TIP system in the ASIS file management exercise. *Journal of the American Society for Information Science* 21 (3), 204–208. May–June.

Mathews, W. D. 1966. *TIP program description.* (NTIS No. AD 635 164.) Cambridge, MA: MIT. Jan. 1.

Mathews, W. D. 1967. The TIP retrieval system at MIT. In G. Schecter (ed.), *Information retrieval: A critical view,* 95–108. Washington, DC: Thompson Book Co. (Proceedings of the Third Annual National Colloquium on Information Retrieval, Philadelphia, May 12–13, 1966.)

Mathews, W. D. 1968. *TIP reference manual.* (Report No. TIP-TM-104.) Cambridge, MA: MIT, Technical Information Program. Aug. 5. 43 pp.

Mathews, W. D. 1995. Personal communication to C. P. Bourne. Dec. 5.

Mattison, E. M. 1969. *Library catalog card production using TIP subsystems.* (Report No. TIP-AN-106.) Cambridge, MA: MIT. Mar. 7. 34 pp.

Maxon-Dadd, J. 1994. Personal communication to C. P. Bourne. Dec. 15.

McAllister, C. 1971. On-line library housekeeping systems. *Special Libraries* 62 (11), 457–468. Nov.

McAllister, C., and J. M. Bell. 1971. Human factors in the design of an interactive library system. *Journal of the American Society for Information Science* 22 (2), 96–104. Mar.–Apr.

McAllister, C., and A. S. McAllister. 1979. DOBIS/LIBIS: An integrated, on-line library management system. *Journal of Library Automation* 12 (4), 300–313. Dec.

McCabe, D. F. 1971. Automated legal research—A discussion of current effectiveness and future development. *Judicature* 54 (7), 283–289. Feb. Reprinted in *Law and Computer Technology* 4 (2): 30–37, Mar.–Apr.

McCabe, D. F. 1973. Automated research: The Ohio experience. *Computers and the Legal Profession (Special Issue)*, 15–16. Chicago, IL: American Bar Association. June.

McCabe, L. B., and L. Farr. 1966. An information system for law enforcement. *Proceedings of the AFIPS Fall Joint Computer Conference* 29, 513–522.

McCarn, D. B. 1970a. Getting ready. *Datamation* (Aug. 1), 22–26.

McCarn, D. B. 1970b. Planning for on-line bibliographic access by the Lister Hill National Center for Biomedical Communications. *Bulletin of the Medical Library Association* 58 (3), 303–310. July.

McCarn, D. B. 1971. Networks with emphasis on planning an on-line bibliographic access system. *Information Storage & Retrieval* 7 (6), 271–279. Dec. (Appears to be the same as a presentation with same title made at the Canfield Conference on Information Retrieval, Nov. 10. Franklin F. Kuo wrote summaries of the presentations and they were made available as an Office of Naval Research, London, England Branch Office Conference Report, NTIS No. AD 734 388.)

McCarn, D. B. 1973. Communications for on-line bibliographic systems. In M. B. Henderson (ed.), *Interactive bibliographic systems* 97–99. Washington, DC: U.S. Atomic Energy Commission. AEC Report No. CONF-711 010. Apr. (Proceedings of a forum, Gaithersburg, MD, Oct. 4–5, 1971.)

McCarn, D. B. 1974. Trends in information. *Proceedings of the American Society for Information Science* 11, 145–150.

McCarn, D. B. 1987. Interview. Mar. 3.

McCarn, D. B. 1995. Personal communication to C. P. Bourne. Oct. 17.

McCarn, D. B., and J. Leiter. 1973. On-line services in medicine and beyond. *Science* 181 (4097), 318–324. July 27.

McCarthy, J., S. Boilen, E. Fredkin, and J. C. R. Licklider. 1963. A time-sharing debugging system for a small computer. *Proceedings of the AFIPS Spring Joint Computer Conference* 23, 51–57.

McCarthy, W. E. 1971. LITE (Legal Information Through Electronics): A progress report. *Law Library Journal* 64 (2), 193–197. May.

McCauley, E. V. 1972. *Natural language data base; Technical progress report for period Jan. 1969-Mar. 1972.* (Report No. DDC-TR-72-1; NTIS No. AD 743 600.) Alexandria, VA: DDC. May.

McClure, L. 1972. Library patrons do their own searching at Rochester. *Network Newsletter (SUNY BCN)* 5 (3), 1. July–Aug.

McClure, L. 1973. Ad hoc committee reports on network operations. *Network Newsletter (SUNY BCN)* 6 (1), 2. Jan.–Mar.

McClure, L. 1995. Personal communication to C. P. Bourne. July.

McConlogue, K., and R. F. Simmons. 1965. Analyzing English syntax with a pattern-learning parser. *Communications of the ACM* 8 (Nov.), 687–698. Published originally as Report No. SP-1950; NTIS No. AD 612 941, SDC, Santa Monica, CA. Feb. 5. 42 pp.

McEwin, B. W. 1971. A brief note on the use of MEDLARS at the Australian National University. *Australian Academic and Research Libraries* 2 (3), 83–85. July.

McGinnis, L. L. 1997. Personal communication to C. P. Bourne. Oct. 22.

McIsaac, D. N., and T. Olson. 1973. *Retrieval of ERIC files; An on-line approach.* (ERIC No. ED 087 454.) Madison, WI: University of Wisconsin. Apr. 10 pp. (Presented at the Association for Educational Data Systems annual convention, New Orleans, LA.)

McNamara, A. B. 1969. Textile information storage and retrieval in the 1970's—The role of the professional societies. *Textile Institute and Industry*, 209–212. Aug.

Meadow, C. T. 1973. Discussion notes. In M. B. Henderson (ed.), *Interactive bibliographic systems*, 130. Washington, DC: U.S. Atomic Energy Commission. AEC Report No. CONF-711010. Apr. (Proceedings of a forum, Gaithersburg, MD, Oct. 4–5, 1971.)

Meadow, C. T. 1987. Letter to the editor. *Journal of the Americana Society for Information Science* 38 (4), 309. July.

Meadow, C. T. 1988a. Back to the future: Making and interpreting the database industry timeline. *Database* 11 (5), 14–22. Oct.

Meadow, C. T. 1988b. Online database industry timeline. *Database* 11 (5), 23–31. Oct.

Meanwhile, in Italy. 1976. *Time* 108 (Dec. 20), 33.

Mechanization study of the library; U.S. Naval Postgraduate School, Monterey, California. 1966. (Report No. BAARINC 914-1-15; NTIS No. AD 640 110.) Bethesda, MD: Booz, Allen Applied Research. Sept. 37 pp.

MEDLARS and health information policy: A technical memorandum. 1982, Sept. Washington, DC: U.S. Congress, Office of Technology Assessment.

MEDLARS decentralization subject of UCLA study. 1965. *Scientific Information Notes* 7 (1), 14. Feb.–Mar.

MEDLARS II for National Library of Medicine. 1968. *Law and Computer Technology* 1 (11), 24. Nov.

MEDLARS: Searches processed. 1972. *NLL Review* 2(2), 42–43. Apr.

MEDLINE service . . . Evaluated and expanded. 1973. *Information; Part 1/News; Sources; Profiles* 5 (2), 77. Mar.–Apr.

MEDLINE: Where it's at. 1976, Mar. *National Library of Medicine News* 31 (3), 2–3.

Meister, D., and D. J. Sullivan. 1967. *Evaluation of user reactions to a prototype on-line information retrieval system*, appendix, 31–58. (Report No. NASA CR 918.) Canoga Park, CA: Bunker-Ramo Corporation. Oct.

Melton, J. S. 1962. The "semantic coded abstract" approach. *Modern Uses of Logic in Law (M.U.L.L.)* (Mar.), 48–54.

Melton, J. S., and R. C. Bensing. 1960. Searching legal literature electronically: Results of a test program. *Minnesota Law Review* 45 (2), 229–248. Dec.

Members in the news. 1975. *Bulletin of the American Society for Information Science* 2 (1), 57. June–July.

Meredith, J. C. 1971a. Machine-assisted approach to general reference material. *Journal of the American Society for Information Science* 22 (3), 176–186. May–June.

Meredith, J. C. 1971b. *Reference search system (REFSEARCH) users' manual.* Berkeley, CA: University of California, Institute of Library Research. Apr. 124 pp.

Mermin, S. 1967. Winter. Computers, law, and justice: An introductory lecture. *Wisconsin Law Review* 1, 43–87.

Merrill, R. D. 1964. *A new input/output approach for information retrieval applications.* (Information Retrieval Note No. 48.) Sunnyvale, CA: LMSC. Dec. 14. 8 pp.

Mick, C. K. 1977. *Investigation of the public library as a linking agent to major scientific, educational, social, and environmental data bases; Final evaluation report, June 74–June 77.* (NTIS No. PB 276 727/5ST.) Stanford, CA: Stanford University, Applied Communication Research. Sept.

Middleton, M. 1977. Developments in the Australasian MEDLARS service. *LASIE* 7 (5), 4–15. Mar.–Apr.

Mignon, E., and I. Travis. 1971. *LABSEARCH: ILR associative search system terminal users' manual.* (ERIC No. 060 917.) Berkeley, CA: University of California, Institute of Library Research. 83 pp. Sept.

Miles, W. D. 1982. *A history of the National Library of Medicine; The nation's treasury of medical knowledge.* (Report No. NIH Publication No. 82-1904.) Bethesda, MD: NLM. 531 pp.

Miller, K. C., H. B. Gerstner, and R. O. Beauchamp. 1974. Toxicology information retrieval and dissemination at the Toxicology Information Response Center. *Journal of Chemical Documentation* 14 (1), 32–36. Feb.

Mills, R. G. 1967. Man-machine communication and problem-solving. *Annual Review of Information Science and Technology*, 2, 223–254.

Minker, J., and J. Sable. 1967. File organization and data management. *Annual Review of Information Science and Technology* 2, 123–160.

Minor, W. H. 1969. A practical approach to information retrieval. *Datamation* 15 (9), 109–110, 115, 117, 119, 121, 124. Sept.

Mitchell, H. F. 1965. Bunker-Ramo direct electronic library. Canoga Park, CA: Bunker-Ramo Corporation. 18 pp.

Mitchell, H. F. 1964. Direct electronic library: A study of the use of electronic library reference centers for the National Aeronautics and Space Administration. Unsolicited proposal, Bunker-Ramo Corporation, Canoga Park, CA, Eastern Technical Center. 14 pp.

Mitchell, H. F. 1990. *My biography.* Cape Coral, FL: Author.

Mitchell, P. C. 1971. The design of an on-line interactive document retrieval system and the general utility of the design techniques. Unpublished doctoral diss., Washington State University.

Mitchell, P. C., J. T. Rickman, and W. E. Walden. 1973. SOLAR: A storage and on-line automatic retrieval system. *Journal of the American Society for Information Science* 24 (5), 347–358. Sept.–Oct.

Mitchell, W. 2001. The genesis of NASA RECON. (Notes from presentation at an unnamed workshop at the University of California, Berkeley, Sept.)

Mittman, B., R. Chalice, and D. Dillaman. 1973. Mixed data structures in a multi-purpose retrieval system. *Journal of the American Society for Information Science* 24 (2), 135–141. Mar.–Apr.

Mittman, B., and W. D. Dominick. 1973. Developing monitoring techniques for an on-line information retrieval system. *Information Storage & Retrieval* 9, 297–307. June. (Presented earlier at ACM Special Interest Group on Information Retrieval, Fall Joint Computer Conference, Anaheim, CA, Dec. 5–7, 1972.)

Mittman, B., and Krulee, G. 1966. Development of a remote information management system—RIMS. *Proceedings of the American Society for Information Science* 6, 199–206.

Moghdam, D. 1974. The New York Times Information Bank in an academic environment and a computer-assisted tutorial for its non-specialist users. Unpublished doctoral diss., University of Pittsburgh, Pittsburgh, PA.

Molholm, K. N. 1995. Personal communication to C. P. Bourne. May 12.

Moll, W. 1971. AIM-TWX service at the University of Virginia: A review and evaluation. *Bulletin of the Medical Library Association* 59 (3), 458–462. July.

Moll, W. 1972. Observation on the AIM-TWX service at the University of Virginia Medical Library. *Bulletin of the Medical Library Association* 60 (4), 571–574. Oct.

Moll, W. 1974. MEDLINE evaluation study. *Bulletin of the Medical Library Association* 62 (1), 1–5. Jan.

Moody, D. W., and O. Kays. 1972. Development of the U.S. Geological Survey bibliographic system using GIPSY. *Journal of the American Society for Information Science* 23 (1), 39–49. Jan.–Feb.

Morgan, R. T. 1962. The "point of law" approach. *Modern Uses of Logic in Law (M.U.L.L.)* (Mar.), 44–48.

Morrill, C. S., N. C. Goodwin, and S. L. Smith. 1968. User input mode and computer-aided instruction. *Human Factors* 10 (June), 225–232.

Morrissey, J. H. 1965. The Quicktran system. In E. Burgess (ed.), *On-line computing systems*, 116–126. Detroit, MI: American Data Processing. (Proceedings of the Symposium Sponsored by UCLA and Informatics, Feb. 2–4.)

Morrissey, M. 1970. Federal Library Committee. *LC Information Bulletin* 29 (30), 377–378. July 30.

Motobayashi, S., T. Masuda, and N. Takahashi. 1969. The HITAC 5020 time sharing system. *Proceedings of the 24th National Conference of the Association of Computing Machinery*, 419–429.

Murdock, J. 1990. Interview. July 27.

Murdock, L., and O. Opello. 1973. Computer literature searches in the physical sciences. *Special Libraries* 64 (10), 442–445. Oct.

Nance, J. W., and J. W. Lathrop. 1968. *System design specifications: General Purpose ORBIT.* (Report No. TM-20.) Santa Monica, CA: SDC. Sept. 15. 31 pp.

NASA-RECON. 1969. *Information Storage & Retrieval* 5 (2), 82. July.

NASA/RECON—Computer Library at Your Desk. 1966. May. Canoga Park, CA: Bunker-Ramo Corporation. 19 pp.

Nash, M. M. 1979. Dec. The Globe and Mail database—A Canadian first. *Online Review* 3 (4), 367–371.

National Library of Medicine: Cost recovery and competition with the private sector. 1983. In *Information system review under the provisions of the Paperwork Reduction Act of 1980, P.L. 96-511*, 14. Washington, DC: U.S. Department of Health and Human Services. Dec. 23.

The National Library of Medicine Index Mechanization Project; July 1, 1958–June 30, 1960. 1961. *Bulletin of the Medical Library Association*, 49 (1), 1–96. Part 2 of 2 parts. Jan.

National Library of Medicine programs and services; Fiscal year 1973. 1974. (Report No. DHEW Publication No. (NIH) 74-286.) Bethesda: MD NLM.

National Library of Medicine programs and services; Fiscal year 1974. 1975. Bethesda, MD: NLM.

Nees, M., and H. O. Green. 1977. *The BIOSIS data base: Evaluation of its indexes and the STRATBLDR, CHEMFILE, STAIRS, and DIALOG systems for on-line searching.* (Report No. STR-508, NASA-CR-2893.) Washington, DC: National Aeronautics and Space Administration. Sept. 65 pp.

Negus, A. E. 1971. A real time interactive reference retrieval system. *The Information Scientist* 5 (1), 29–44. Mar.

Negus, A. E. 1979. Development of the EURONET—DIANE Common Command Language. In *Proceedings of the Third International Online Information Meeting*, 95–98. Oxford, England: Learned Information.

Negus, A. E. 1980. Personal communication to C. B. Bourne. May 6.

Negus, A. E., and J. L. Hall. 1971. Towards an effective on-line reference retrieval system. *Information Storage & Retrieval* 7 (Dec.), 249–270.

Network adds four new users. 1972. *Network Newsletter (SUNY BCN)* 5 (1), 1. Apr.

Network statistics. 1972. *Network Newsletter (SUNY BCN)* 5 (1), 4–5. Apr.

Neufeld, M. L., and M. Cornog. 1986. Database history: From dinosaurs to compact discs. *Journal of the American Society for Information Science* 37 (4), 183–190.

New film on DDC bibliographic services. 1973, *Information; Part 1/News; Sources; Profiles* 5 (1), 13–14. Jan.–Feb.

New MEDLARS Center at Colorado. 1965. *Bulletin of the Medical Library Association* 53 (3), 473–474. July.

New network software. 1972. *Network Newsletter (SUNY BCN)*, 5 (2), 1. May–June.

New storage/retrieval system uses commands in plain English. 1969. *Computerworld* 16, 16. Apr. 9.

New user charges for NLM on-line services. 1975. *National Library of Medicine News* 23 (5), 1. May.

New user terminals. 1973. *Network Newsletter (SUNY BCN)* 6 (3 + 4), 2. July–Dec.

New York Times Co. to give up marketing of information service. 1983. *Wall Street Journal*, Feb. 7, p. 8.

New York Times Index to go on computer. 1968, *Publishers' Weekly* 193 (2), 46. Jan. 8.

The New York Times Information Bank; Seventy years of news goes online. 1973. *Modern Data* 6 (9), 70–71. Sept.

Nichols, A. J., and A. Reiter. 1967. *ALLSTAR: Programmer-oriented software for information storage and retrieval.* (Information Retrieval Note No. 92.) Palo Alto, CA: LMSC. Apr. 13. 23 pp.

Nitecki, J. Z. 1976. *OCLC in retrospect: A review of the impact of the OCLC system on the administration of a large university technical services operations*. Occasional paper no. 123. Urbana-Champaign: University of Illinois, Graduate School of Library Science. 35 pp. (A paper with same title was presented at the ALA midwinter meeting, Chicago, Jan. 1974: ERIC No. ED 087 482.)

NLM contract awarded. 1973. *Network Newsletter (SUNY BCN)* 6 (1), 1. Jan.–Mar.

NLM contracts with UCLA for pilot study to decentralize MEDLARS. 1964. *National Library of Medicine News* 19 (11), 1–2. Nov.

NLM introduces MEDLINE service. 1972. *Information; Part 1/News; Sources; Profiles* 4 (1), 6. Jan.–Feb.

NLM offers on-line chemical dictionary. 1974. *Chemical and Engineering News* 52 (4), 22–23. Jan. 28.

NLM's MEDLINE to charge users starting in July. 1973. *Advanced Technology Libraries* 2 (2), 1–3. Feb.

NLM Toxicology Info Program develops TOXICON. 1972. *Information; Part 1/News; Sources; Profiles*, 4 (6), 315–316. Nov.–Dec.

NLM 'user charges' policy. 1973. *Information; Part 1/News; Sources; Profiles*, 5 (4), 187. July–Aug.

Nolan, J. J. 1958. *Principles of information storage and retrieval using a large scale random access memory*. San Jose, CA: IBM. Nov. 17.

Novell, M. 1967. An information retrieval system for the inexperienced-experienced user: How a user would view the system. In A. B. Tonik (ed.), *Information retrieval: The user's viewpoint; An aid to design*, 61–76. Philadelphia, PA: International Information. (Fourth Annual National Colloquium on Information Retrieval, Philadelphia, PA, May 3–4.)

NTIS search. 1973. *Special Libraries*, 64 (1), 58. Jan.

NY Times Info Bank to be on-line late 1972. 1972. *Information; Part 1/News; Sources; Profiles* 4 (2), 65–66. Mar.–Apr.

Ohio College Library Center annual report 1975/1976. 1976. Columbus, OH: OCLC, Inc.

Ojala, M. 1987. First there was the Information Bank. *Online* 11 (1), 112–117. Jan.

Olson, T., D. N. McIsaac, D. W. Spuck, and R. D. Tally. 1975. Wisconsin Information Systems for Education (WISE); User documentation; WISE-ONE. In R. H. Lambert, and C. R. Grady (eds.), *Wisconsin's ERIC on-line information retrieval demonstration and research; Final report*, 41–68; appendix G. (ERIC No. ED 111 430.) Madison, WI: University of Wisconsin, Center for Studies in Vocational and Technical Education. June 30. 77 pp.

On-line intelligence processing system. 1966. (Report No. RADC-TR-66-2; NTIS No. AD 489 386.) Canoga Park, CA: Bunker-Ramo. July. 82 pp.

Online performance test. 1972. Sept.–Dec. *Network Newsletter (SUNY BCN)* 5 (4), 1.

Onsi, P. W., and S. J. Pelosi. 1970 Apr. Cooperative cataloging from the participants' point of view: A record of SUNY's and Countway's experience. *Bulletin of the Medical Library Association* 58 (2), 126–133.

Operating history and network administration. 1972. Apr. *Network Newsletter (SUNY BCN)* 5 (1), 1–2.

Opler, A., and T. R. Norton. 1966. New speed to structural searches. *Chemical and Engineering News* 34 (June 4), 2812–2816.

ORBIT for bibliographic access and project documentation files. 1971. Mar.–Apr. *Information* 3 (2), 80.

ORBIT III on-line retrieval system. 1974. (Report No. TM-5294.) Santa Monica, CA: SDC. 41 pp. Apr.

OSIRIS—On-line Search Information Retrieval Information Storage. 1968. *Digital Computer Newsletter/ONR* 20 (1), 20–25.

Overhage, C. F. J. 1966. Plans for project Intrex. *Science* 152 (3725), 1032–1037. May 20.

Overhage, C. F. J. 1972. *Project Intrex; A brief description.* Cambridge, MA: MIT. 37 pp.

Overhage, C. F. J., and R. J. Harman. 1965. *INTREX: Report of a planning conference on information transfer experiments.* Cambridge, MA: The MIT Press.

Overhage, C. F. J., and J. F. Reintjes. 1969. Information transfer experiments at M.I.T. In A. J. H. Morrell (ed.), *Information processing 1968*, vol. 2, 1321–1325. Amsterdam: North-Holland. (Proceedings of the IFIP Congress 68, Edinburgh, Aug. 5–10, 1968.)

Overhage, C. F. J., and J. F. Reintjes. 1974. Project Intrex: A general review. *Information Storage & Retrieval* 10 (May–June), 157–188.

Paisley, W. J. 1995. Apr. 3. Personal communication to C. P. Bourne.

Parker, E. B. 1967. *SPIRES (Stanford Physics Information Retrieval System); 1967 annual report.* Stanford, CA: Stanford University, Institute for Communications Research. Dec.

Parker, E. B. 1969. Jan. *SPIRES (Stanford Public Information Retrieval System); 1968 annual report.* (NTIS No. PB 184 960.) Stanford University, Institute for Communication Research.

Parker, E. B. 1971a. Developing a campus information retrieval system. In P. J. Fasana, and A. Veaner (eds.), *Collaborative library systems development,* 215–225. Cambridge, MA: The MIT Press.

Parker, E. B. 1971b. *SPIRES (Stanford Public Information Retrieval System); 1970–71 annual report.* Stanford University, Institute for Communication Research. Dec.

Parker, E. B. 1988. Interview. Feb. 28.

Pauly, D. 1975. Hearings: "I prefer not to answer" *Newsweek* 86 (54), Sept. 8.

Payne, C. T. 1971. The Chicago experience. In P.J. Fasana, and A. Veaner (eds.), *Collaborative library systems development,* 5–10. Cambridge, MA: The MIT Press.

Payne, C. T., and K. Hecht. 1971. The University of Chicago's book processing system. In P. J. Fasana, and A. Veaner (eds.), *Collaborative library systems development,* 183–192. Cambridge, MA: The MIT Press.

Peel, B. B. 1977. Canadian university libraries. In L. S. Garry, and C. Garry (eds.), *Canadian libraries and their changing environment,* 182–200. Downsview, Ontario: York University, Centre for Continuing Education.

Pemberton, J. K. 1971. Retrieval. In A. B. Morrison (ed.), *Microform utilization: The academic library environment,* 107–122. Denver, CO: University of Denver. (Report of conference held at Denver, CO, Dec. 7–9, 1970.)

Pemberton, J. K. 1981. The inverted file. *Online* 5 (2), 29–31. Apr.

Pemberton, J. K. 1982. Monitor round table. *Monitor* 21 (Nov.), 4–7.

Pemberton, J. K. 1983. A backward and forward look at the New York Times Information Bank; A tale of ironies compounded . . . and an analysis of the Mead deal. *Online* 7 (4), 7–17.

Pemberton, J. K. 1984. Some observations on the pricing of online services The inverted file column. *Online* 8 (4), 6–7. July.

Pemberton, J. K. 1988 DIALOG for sale. A watershed in the online world. *Online* 12 (3), 6–7. July.

Pemberton, J. K. 1994. July. Who will buy Mead Data Central . . . how much will they pay? The New York Times holds the key: A news analysis of the Mead Data Central sale. *Online* 18 (4), 13–14.

Pemberton, J. K. 1995, July 12. Personal communication to C. P. Bourne.

Pemberton, J. K. 1996, Mar.–Apr. The online business is new, right? How about a quarter-century old? *Online User* 2 (2), 5.

Pemberton, J. K. 1997. Personal communication to C. P. Bourne. Sept. 10.

Penniman, W. D. 1971a. *BASIS-70: Design, implementation, and operation.* Columbus, OH: Battelle Memorial Institute. Jan. 13. 19 pp. Paper first presented at joint meeting of Central Ohio Chapters of ASIS and ACM, Jan. 13, 1971, and then at 7th Annual Symposium on On-Line

Systems sponsored by New York Chapter of ASIS, Oct. 9.

Penniman, W. D. 1975b. A stochastic process analysis of on-line user behavior. *Proceedings of the American Society for Information Science* 12, 147–148.

Penniman, W. D. 1975. Rhythms of dialogue in human-computer conversation. Unpublished doctoral diss., Ohio State University, Columbus. 281 pp.

Penniman, W. D. 1994. Personal communication to C. P. Bourne. May 23.

Penry, J. K., and J. F. Caponio. 1969. On-line full text retrieval of *Epilepsy Abstracts*. *Electroencephalography and Clinical Neurophysiology* 27 (7), 734.

Peters, P. E. 1993. Interview.

Phillips, T. D. 1966. On-line processing of library materials with the IBM Administrative Terminal System. In W. A. Kalenich (ed.), *Information processing 1965,* vol. 2, 343–344. Washington, DC: Spartan Books. (Proceedings of the IFIP Congress 65, New York, NY, May 24–29, 1965.)

Pizer, I. H. 1966. The State University of New York computerized biomedical information resource. In J. Harrison, and P. Laslett (eds.), *The Brasenose Conference on the Automation of Libraries,* 151–162. Chicago: Mansell. (Proceedings of Anglo-American Conference on the Mechanization of Library Services, Oxford, England, June 30–July 3.)

Pizer, I. H. 1967. The application of computers in the State University of New York Biomedical Communication Network. In *Proceedings of the 8th IBM Medical Symposium, Apr. 3–6, 1967,* 57–65. Poughkeepsie, NY: IBM.

Pizer, I. H. 1969. A regional medical library network. *Bulletin of the Medical Library Association* 57 (2), 101–115. Apr.

Pizer, I. H. 1971. Why we are where we are. In P. J. Fasana, and A. Veaner (eds.), *Collaborative library systems development,* 119–120. Cambridge, MA: The MIT Press.

Pizer, I. H. 1972a. How does the network serve the researcher? In D. P. Hammer, and G. Levis (comps.), *Indiana Seminar on Information Networks (ISIN),* 61–91. West Lafayette, IN: Purdue University Libraries. (ERIC No. ED 070 459.)

Pizer, I. H. 1972b. On-line technology in a library network; Advantages of on-line systems. In F. W. Lancaster (ed.), *Proceedings of the 1972 Clinic on Library Applications of Data Processing,* 54–68. Urbana-Champaign: University of Illinois, Graduate School of Library Science.

Pizer, I. H. 1976. Letters to BCN members. Feb. 19; Mar. 2; Mar. 11; June 25.

Pizer, I. H. 1984. Looking backward, 1984–1959: Twenty-five years of library automation—A personal view. *Bulletin of the Medical Library Association* 72 (4), 335–348. Oct.

Pizer, I. H., I. T. Anderson, and E. Brodman. 1964. Apr. Mechanization of library procedures in the medium-sized medical library, II; Circulation records. *Bulletin of the Medical Library Association* 52 (2), 370–385.

Pizer, I. H., D. R. Franz, and E. Brodman. 1963. July. Mechanization of library procedures in the medium-sized medical library, I; The serial record. *Bulletin of the Medical Library Association* 51 (3), 313–338.

A plan for a library processing center for the State University of New York. 1967. (Report No. C-69541.) Cambridge, MA: Arthur D. Little. Nov. 134 pp.

Plowden-Wardlaw, T. C. 1968. The Lawyers' Center for Electronic Legal Research. *Law and Computer Technology* 1 (10), 9–12. Oct.

Porter, R. J., J. K. Penry, and J. F. Caponio. 1971. Epilepsy Abstracts Retrieval System (EARS): A new concept for medical literature storage and retrieval. *Bulletin of the Medical Library Association* 59 (3), 430–432. July. A slightly shorter version was published in 1970 *Proceedings of the American Society for Information Science* 7, 171–172.

A potentially huge database operation takes shape as Mead technology readies network access to newspaper and magazine files. 1978. *Database* 1 (1), 7–8, 68–69. Sept. (Written by J. K. Pemberton, whose name does not appear in byline.)

Powell, J. R. 1976. Evaluation of Excerpta Medica on-line. *Special Libraries* 67 (3), 153–157. Mar.

Power, D. L., C. A. Woody, F. Scott, and M. Fitzgerald. 1976. SCORPIO, a Subject Content Oriented Retriever for Processing Information On-Line. *Special Libraries* 67 (7): 285–288. July.

Powers, J. M. 1973. The defense RDTE on-line system retrieval. In M. B. Henderson (ed.), *Interactive bibliographic systems,* 69–86. Washington, DC: U.S. Atomic Energy Commission. AEC Report No. CONF-711 010. Apr. (Proceedings of a forum, Gaithersburg, MD, Oct. 4–5, 1971.)

Powers, R. V., and H. N. Hill. 1971. Designing CIDS—The U.S. Army Chemical Information and Data System. *Journal of Chemical Documentation,* 11 (1), 30–38. Feb.

Poyen, J. 1976. *Guidelines for cooperation between data base suppliers and host organizations.* Paris: ICSU AB. 6 pp.

Pratt, G., and S. Harvey (eds.). 1976. *The on-line age; Plans and needs for on-line information retrieval.* London: Aslib/EUSIDIC. Reprint. (Proceedings of the Eusidic conference, Oslo, Dec. 4–5, 1975.)

The President's Commission on Heart Disease, Cancer and Stroke. 1964. Dec. (v. 1); 1965, Feb. (v. 2). Washington, DC: U.S. Government Printing Office.

Preston, J. F. 1971. OBAR and Mead Data Central System. *Law Library Journal* 64 (2), 190–192. May.

Prewitt, B. G. 1974, Aug. On-line searching of computer data bases. *Journal of Chemical Documentation* 14 (3), 115–117.

The principles of MEDLARS. n.d. Bethesda, MD: NLM.

Program Assisted Console Evaluation and Review (PACER) system description, v. I. 1972, Apr. (Report No. RADC-TR-72-89.) Griffiss Air Force Base, NY: RADC, Air Force Systems Command.

Progress in scientific & technical communications; COSATI 1969 annual report. 1970. (Report No. COSATI 70-3; NTIS No. PB 193 386.) Washington, DC: Committee on Scientific and Technical Information of the Federal Council for Science and Technology.

Progress in scientific & technical communications; COSATI 1970 annual report. 1971. (Report No. COSATI 71-1; NTIS No. PB 202 448.) Washington, DC: Federal Council for Science and Technology, Committee on Scientific and Technical Information.

Progress in scientific & technical communications; COSATI annual report 1971. 1972. (Report No. COSATI 72-2; NTIS No. PB 212 500.) Washington, DC: Committee on Scientific and Technical Information of the Federal Council for Science and Technology.

Progress of the United States government in scientific & technical communication; 1965 COSATI annual report. 1966. (NTIS No. PB 173 510.) Washington, DC: Executive Office of the President, Committee on Scientific and Technical Information of the Federal Council for Science and Technology.

Progress of the United States government in scientific & technical communications; COSATI 1967 annual report. 1967. (NTIS No. PB 180 867.) Washington, DC: Executive Office of the President, Committee on Scientific and Technical Information of the Federal Council for Science and Technology.

Project BALLOTS, and Stanford University Libraries. 1975. Stanford University's BALLOTS system. *Journal of Library Automation* 8 (1), 31–50. Mar.

Project INTREX: Semiannual activity report no. 1 (20 Sep. 65–15 Mar. 66.) 1966. (NTIS No. PB 197 134.) Cambridge, MA: MIT. Mar. 15. 17 pp.

Project Intrex: Semi-annual activity report, 15 Mar. 1968 to 15 Sep. 1968. 1968. (Report No. PR-6; NTIS No. AD 680 547.) Cambridge, MA: MIT. Sept. 15. 71 pp.

Project INTREX: Semiannual activity report 15 Sep. 1968 to Mar. 1969. 1969a. (Report No. PR-7; NTIS No. PB 183 295.) Cambridge, MA: MIT. Mar. 15. 36 pp.

Project Intrex Semiannual activity report no. 8, 15 Mar. 1969 to 15 Sep. 1969. 1969b. (NTIS No. PB 183 138.) Cambridge, MA: MIT. Sept. 15. 39 pp.

Provenzano, D. 1987. Where are they now? *Online* 11 (1), 28–44. Jan.

Pryor, H. E. 1975a. An evaluation of the NASA scientific and technical information system. *Special Libraries* 66 (11), 515–519. Nov.

Pryor, H. E. 1975b. Managing aerospace information. In J. Sherrod (ed.), *Information systems and networks,* 85–92. Westport, CT: Greenwood Press. (Proceedings of the Eleventh Annual Symposium in Information Processing, Los Angeles, CA, Mar. 27–29, 1974.)

Prywes, N. S. 1964. *The organization of files for command and control; Interim technical report.* (Report No. 64-12; NTIS No. AD 600 980.) Philadelphia: University of Pennsylvania, Moore School of Electrical Engineering. Mar. 25. 33 pp.

Prywes, N. S. 1965a. Browsing in an automated library through remote access. In M. A. Sass, and W. D. Willison (eds.), *Symposium on computer augmentation of human reasoning, June 16–17, 1964,* 105–130. Washington, DC: Spartan Books.

Prywes, N. S. 1965b. *A storage and retrieval system for real-time problem solving.* (Report No. 66-05, NTIS No. AD 467 454.) Philadelphia: University of Pennsylvania, Moore School of Electrical Engineering. June 1. 52 pp.

Prywes, N. S. 1966. Man-computer problem solving with Multilist. *Proceedings of the IEEE* 54 (12), 1788–1801. Dec.

Prywes, N. S. 1968. On-line information storage and retrieval. In H. F. Vessey, and I. J. Gabelman (eds.), *Storage and retrieval of information: A user-supplier dialogue,* 77–88. (Proceedings of the June 18–30, 1968, meeting of the North Atlantic Treaty Organization, Advisory Group for Aerospace Research & Development, Munich; AGARD Conference Proceedings No. 39.)

Prywes, N. S., and H. J. Gray. 1963. The Multi-List system for real-time storage and retrieval. In C. M. Popplewell (ed.), *Information processing 1962,* 273–278. Amsterdam: North-Holland. (Proceedings of the IFIP Congress 62, Munich, Aug.)

Prywes, N. S., and B. Litofsky. 1970. All-automatic processing for a large library. *Proceedings of the AFIPS Spring Joint Computer Conference* 36, 323–331.

Prywes, N. S., S. Litwin, and H. J. Gray (inventors). 1968. *Data processing means.* (U.S. 3,388,381.) Filed Dec. 31, 1962. June 11.

Pugh, E. W. 1995. *Building IBM: Shaping an industry and its technology.* Cambridge, MA: The MIT Press.

QUIKTRAN User's Guide. 1966. (Report No. IBM E20-0240-0.) White Plains, NY: IBM. 90 pp.

Radwin, M. S. 1973. The new era of online information retrieval: Evaluation of its costs and benefits—A professional imperative. *Proceedings of the American Society for Information Science* 10, 191–192.

Radwin, M. S. 1997. Personal communication to C. P. Bourne. Aug. 28.

Rae, P. D. J. 1970. On-line information retrieval systems; Experience of the Parkinson Information Center using the SUNY Biomedical Communication Network. *Proceedings of the American Society for Information Science* 7, 173–176.

Raitt, D. I. 1970. The European Space Documentation Service. *Library Association Record* 72 (3), 97–99. Mar.

Raizada, A. S. 1977. The Rabat workshop—A pointer for resource mobilization. *UNESCO Bulletin for Libraries* 31 (1), 35–39, 60. Jan.–Feb.

Rapport, R. L. I., F. W. Lancaster, and J. K. Penry. 1972. Critical evaluation of a computer-based medical literature search and retrieval system. *Postgraduate Medicine* 51 (5), 47–50. May.

Rea, R. H. 1967. *Annual historical summary: 1 July 1966 to 30 June 1967.* (NTIS No. AD 662 600.) Alexandria, VA: DDC. Oct. 1. 50 pp.

RECON CENTRAL; Keyword book. 1964. (NTIS No. AD 452 118.) Dayton, OH: Technology, Inc. Sept. 143 pp.

Reed, M. J. P. 1975a. Cost figures: Washington Library Network. *Proceedings of the 4th Mid-Year Meeting of the American Society for Information Science,* 62–66.

Reed, M. J. P. 1975b. The Washington Library Network's computerized bibliographic system. *Journal of Library Automation* 8 (3), 174–179. Sept.

Rees, A. M. 1967. Evaluation of information systems and services. *Annual Review of Information Science and Technology* 2, 63–86.

Reintjes, J. F. 1969. System characteristics of Intrex. *Proceedings of the AFIPS Spring Joint Computer Conference* 34, 457–459.

Reiter, A. 1967. A resource-allocation scheme for multiuser on-line operation of a small computer. *Proceedings of the AFIPS Spring Joint Computer Conference* 30, 1–7.

Reitman, W., R. B. Roberts, R. W. Sauvain, D. D. Wheeler, and W. Linn. 1969. AUTONOTE: A personal information storage and retrieval system. *Proceedings of the 24th National Conference of the Association of Computing Machinery,* 67–76.

Report of the National Library of Medicine. 1974. *Minutes of the 83rd meeting of the Association of Research Libraries,* p. 147 (appendix). Chicago: ARL. Jan. 19.

Report on information retrieval and library automation studies. 1972. University of Alberta, Department of Computing Science. July 1.

Resnick, M., and J. Sable. 1968. INSCAN: A syntax-directed language processor. *Proceedings of 23rd National Conference of the Association for Computing Machinery,* 423–432.

Rhydwen, D. A. 1977, Feb. Computerized storage and retrieval of newspaper stories at the Globe and Mail Library, Toronto, Canada. *Special Libraries* 68 (2), 57–61.

Richmond, P. A. 1972. Document description and representation. *Annual Review of Information Science and Technology* 7, 73–102.

Rickman, J. T., A. E. Harvey, and C. G. Shaw. 1972. SOLAR: An on-line information retrieval system for plant pathology. *Washington Agriculture Experiment Station Bulletin, No. 758* (June), 1–8.

Riddle, J. T. 1997. Personal communication to C. P. Bourne. Aug. 28.

Riddles, A. J. 1969. Computer based concept searching of United States patent claims. *Law and Computer Technology* 2 (3), 15–25. Mar.

Roach, J. P. 1961. Dec. 28. SATIRE—The technical librarian's EAM application of semi-automatic technical information retrieval. (Report No. SP-595, NTIS No. AD 666 300.) Paramus, NJ: SDC.

Roach, J. P. 1962. *SATIRE—Computer applications of semi-automatic technical information retrieval.* (Report No. SP-857; NTIS No. AD 666 299.) Paramus, NJ: SDC. July 26. (Presented earlier at the SLA conference, Washington, DC, May 27–31.)

Roach, J. P. 1963a. SATIRE display subsystem. *Proceedings of the 26th Annual Meeting of the American Documentation Institute* (pt. 2, short papers), 165–166.

Roach, J. P. 1963b. *SATIRE—Remote communications subsystem: A feasibility study.* Santa Monica, CA: SDC. Mar. 18.

Roach, R. A. 1997. Personal communication to C. P. Bourne. Nov. 24.

Robins, W. R. 1968. Automated legal information retrieval. *Houston Law Review* 5 (4), 691–716. Mar.

Rocchio, J. J., and G. Salton. 1965. Information search optimization and interactive retrieval techniques. *Proceedings of the AFIPS Fall Joint Computer Conference* 27 (pt. 1), 293–305.

Rogers, F. B. 1963. *The MEDLARS story at the National Library of Medicine.* Washington, DC: U.S. Department of Health, Education and Welfare, Public Health Service.

Rogers, F. B. 1964. The development of MEDLARS. *Bulletin of the Medical Library Association* 52 (1), 150–151. Jan.

Rogers, F. B. 1966a. MEDLARS operating experience: Addendum. *Bulletin of the Medical Library Association* 54 (4), 316–320. Oct.

Rogers, F. B. 1966b. MEDLARS operating experience at the University of Colorado. *Bulletin of the Medical Library Association* 54 (1), 1–10. Jan.

Rogers, F. B. 1968. Costs of operating an information retrieval service. *Drexel Library Quarterly* 4 (4), 271–278. Oct.

Rogers, F. B. 1974. Computerized bibliographic retrieval services. *Library Trends,* 23 (1), 73–88. July.

Rogers, F. B. 1982. The origins of MEDLARS. *Bulletin of the History of Medicine (Henry E. Sigerist Supplements)* 6, 77–84.

Rogers, H. 1978. High speed online searching at the National Library of Canada. *Proceedings of the Sixth Canadian Conference on Information Science,* 189-1–189-4.

Romanenko, A. G., and C. Todeschini. 1980. The International Nuclear Information System online services. In *Proceedings of Fourth International Online Information Meeting,* 355–361. Oxford, England: Learned Information.

Romerio, G. F. 1973. A teledocumentation network for Europe. *Euro Spectra* 12 (1), 12–25. Mar.

Rothman, J. 1968. Automated information processing at the New York Times. *Proceedings of the American Society for Information Science* 5, 85–87.

Rothman, J. 1969. *Statement to the 91st Congress, House of Representatives, General Subcommittee on Education of the Committee on Education and Labor.* Washington, DC: GPO. Hearings held Apr. 29–30.

Rothman, J. 1972. The New York Times Information Bank. *Special Libraries* 63 (3), 111–115. Mar.

Rothman, J. 1973. The Times Information Bank on campus. *Educom* 8 (3), 14–19. Fall.

Rubin, J. S. 1973. LEXIS: An automated research system. In R. A. May (ed.), *Automated law research; A collection of presentations delivered at the First National Conference on Automated Law Research,* 35–42. American Bar Association.

Rubin, J. S. 1974. LEXIS has made computer-assisted legal research in the United States a practical reality. *Law & Computer Technology* 7 (2), 34–50. Mar.–Apr.

Rubin, J. S. 1998. Personal communication to C. P. Bourne. Feb. 4.

Rubin, J. S., and R. L. Woodard. 1974a. LEXIS: A new tool for tax research. *Journal of Corporate Taxation* 1 (Spring), 42–55.

Rubin, J. S., and R. L. Woodard. 1974b. LEXIS: A progress report. *Jurimetrics Journal* 15 (2), 86–89. Winter.

Rubinoff, M. 1966. A rapid procedure for launching a microthesaurus. *IEEE Transactions on Engineering Writing and Speech* 9 (1), 8–14. July.

Rubinoff, M. 1973. *Man-machine communication through a teletypewriter; Final report, 23 Mar. 1965–30 Nov. 1971.* (NTIS No. AD 763 926.) Philadelphia: University of Pennsylvania, Moore School of Electrical Engineering. May. 276 pp.

Rubinoff, M., S. Bergman, H. Cautin, and F. Rapp. 1968a. Easy English, a language for information retrieval through a remote typewrite console. *Communications of the ACM* 11 (Oct.), 693–696. Published originally as NTIS No. AD 660 081, University of Pennsylvania, Moore School of Electrical Engineering, in cooperation with Pennsylvania Research Associates. Apr. 1967. 15 pp.

Rubinoff, M., S. Bergman, W. Franks, and E. R. Rubinoff. 1968b. Experimental evaluation of information retrieval through a teletypewriter. *Communications of the ACM* 11 (Sept.), 598–604. Published originally by University of Pennsylvania, Moore School of Electrical Engineering. June 1967.

Rubinoff, M., W. Franks, and D. C. Stone. 1967. *Description of an experiment investigating term relationships as interpreted by humans.* (Report No. AFOSR-68-1599; NTIS No. AD 671 906.) University of Pennsylvania, Moore School of Electrical Engineering, Philadelphia. June. 29 pp.

Rubinoff, M., and D. C. Stone. 1967. Semantic tools in information retrieval. *Proceedings of the Annual Meeting of the American Documentation Institute* 4, 169–174. Published originally as NTIS No. AD 660 087, University of Pennsylvania, Moore School of Electrical Engineering, Philadelphia. May.

Rubinoff, M., and J. F. White. 1965a. *Description of cataloging and indexing system for the ACM repository.* (Report No. AFOSR-65-0424; NTIS No. AD 612 277.) University of Pennsylvania, Moore School of Electrical Engineering, Philadelphia. Jan. 25. 2 pp.

Rubinoff, M., and J. F. White. 1965b. Establishment of the ACM repository and principles of the IR system applied to its operation. *Communications of the ACM* 8 (Oct.), 595–601. Published originally as Report No. AFOSR-66-0011; NTIS No. AD 632 185, University of Pennsylvania, Philadelphia, Moore School of Electrical Engineering. July.

Ruecking, F. H. 1968. Bibliographic retrieval from bibliographic input: The hypothesis and construction of a test. *Journal of Library Automation* 1 (4), 227–238. Dec.

Rules for Lockheed. 1975. *Time 106* (Sept. 8), 60.

Rushbrook, A. E., and H. Lawford. 1976. World Aluminum Abstracts computer retrieval using QL Systems: User commentary and demonstration. *Proceedings of the Fourth Canadian Conference on Information Science*, 221–231.

Salton, G. 1964. A document retrieval system for man-machine interaction. *Proceedings of the 19th National Conference of the Association for Computing Machinery*, L2.3-1–L2.3-20.

Salton, G. 1965. The evaluation of automatic retrieval procedures—Selected test results using the SMART system. *American Documentation* 16 (July), 209–222.

Salton, G. 1968. *Automatic information organization and retrieval.* New York: McGraw-Hill.

Salton, G. 1969. Search and retrieval experiments in real-time information retrieval. In A. J. H. Morrell (ed.), *Information processing 1968*, vol. 2, 1082–1093. Amsterdam: North-Holland. (Proceedings of the IFIP Congress 68, Edinburgh, Aug. 5–10, 1968.)

Salton, G. 1971a. The performance of interactive information retrieval. *Information Processing Letters* 1 (2), 35–41. July.

Salton, G. 1971b. *The SMART retrieval system—Experiments in automatic document processing.* Englewood Cliffs, NJ: Prentice-Hall.

Scandals: Lockheed's Kuro Maku. 1976. *Time* 107 (Feb. 16), 56.

Schafer, M. E., and M. Brandreth. 1976. The International Development Research Centre and computerized retrieval services. *Proceedings of the Fourth Canadian Conference on Information Science*, 17–24.

Scheffler, F. L. 1974. *Optimization of retrieval techniques and file structures for the CIRCOL (Central Information Reference and Control On-Line) system.* (Report No. UDRI-TR-73-53; RADC-TR-73-420; NTIS No. AD 776 299.) Dayton, OH: University of Dayton Research Institute. Feb. 151 pp.

Schieber, W. D. 1971. *ISIS; A general description of an approach to computerized bibliographic control.* Geneva: International Labour Office. 115 pp.

Schieber, W. D. 1972. *Technical manual on ISIS (A generalized information storage and retrieval system designed at the International Labor Office).* Stockholm: Statskontoret (Swedish Agency for Administrative Development). 74 pp.

Schmidt, C. T. 1970. A dictionary structure for use with an English language preprocessor to a computerized information retrieval system. (NTIS No. AD 710 363.) Monterey, CA: Naval Postgraduate School. Unpublished master's thesis. June. 52 pp.

Schmidt, K. A. 1994. ALA's attic: Curiosities from the archives. *American Libraries* 25 (May), 470.

Schon, D. A. 1965. The clearinghouse for federal scientific and technical information. In M. Rubinoff (ed.), *Toward a national information system*, 27–34. Washington, DC: Spartan Books. (Proceedings of the Second Annual National Colloquium on Information Retrieval, Philadelphia, PA, Apr. 23–24.)

Schreur, H. K. 1963. "Dual-inverted"" file method for computer retrieval under study at Southwestern Legal Center. *Modern Uses of Logic in Law (M.U.L.L.)* (Dec.), 162–164.

Schultheisz, R. J. 1981. TOXLINE: Evolution of an online interactive bibliographic database. *Journal of the American Society for Information Science* 32 (6), 421–429. Nov.

Schultheisz, R. J., D. F. Walker, and K. L. Kannan. 1978. Design and implementation of an on-line chemical dictionary (CHEMLINE). *Journal of the American Society for Information Science* 29 (4), 173–179. July.

Schultz, C. K. 1997. Personal communication to C. P. Bourne. Sept.; Oct. 1.

Schwarcz, R. M., J. F. Burger, and R. F. Simmons. 1970. A deductive question-answerer for natural language inference. *Communications of the ACM* 13 (Mar.), 167–183. Published originally as Report No. SP-3272; NTIS No. AD 681 531, SDC, Santa Monica, CA. 53 pp.

Schwartz, J. I. 1968. Interactive systems; Promises, present and future. *Proceedings of the AFIPS Fall Joint Computer Conference* 33 (pt. 1), 89–173.

Schwartz, J. I., E. G. Coffman, and C. Weissman. 1964. A general-purpose time-sharing system. *Proceedings of the AFIPS Spring Joint Computer Conference* 25, 397–411. Published originally as Report SP-1499, SDC, Santa Monica, CA. Apr.

Schwartz, J. I., and C. Weissman. 1967. The SDC time-sharing system revisited. *Proceedings of the 22nd National Conference of the Association for Computing Machinery*, 263–271.

Scott, T. W., and F. Lang. 1967. Coding and structuring input data for the GIPSY system. *Proceedings of the American Documentation Institute* 4, 114–118.

Scroggins, J. L. 1968. *NLM/ORBIT; Final report.* (Report No. TM-WD-733.) Falls Church, VA: SDC. Nov. 18.

SDC offers "trial use" on ERIC search service. 1972. *Information; Part 1/News; Sources; Profiles* 4 (6), 312–313. Nov.–Dec.

A search: 1967 style. 1967. *SDC Magazine* 10 (9), 15–19. Sept.

Searching normal text for information retrieval. 1970. May. (IBM Data Processing Application Report No. GE20-0335-1.) White Plains, NY: IBM. 18 pp.

Seastrom, D. E., and D. A. Thompson. 1972. Adaptive document retrieval displays to accommodate system learning. *Proceedings of the American Society for Information Science* 9, paper no. 18.

Seastrom, D. E., and D. A. Thompson. 1973. ADMIRE; A study of an adaptable document retrieval system with assistive displays. *Proceedings of the American Society for Information Science* 10, 207–208.

Second Canfield international conference on information storage and retrieval. 1970. *Program* 4 (Jan.), 42–47.

See, R. 1967. Machine-aided translation and information retrieval. In K. Allen Kent, O. E. Taulbee, J. Belzer, and G. D. Goldstein (eds.), *Electronic handling of information: Testing and evaluation,* 89–108. Washington, DC: Thompson Book Co.

Seiden, H. R. 1970. *A comparative analysis of interactive information storage and retrieval systems with implications for BCN design.* (Report No. TM-4421; ERIC No. ED 039 893.) Santa Monica, CA: SDC. Jan. 12.

Semturs, F. 1978. STAIRS/TLS; A system for "free text" and "descriptor" searching. *Proceedings of the American Society for Information Science* 15, 295–298.

Session IV—User needs, feedback, and training. 1971. In D. E. Walker (ed.), *Interactive bibliographic search: The user/computer interface,* 279. Montvale, NJ: AFIPS Press. (Proceedings of The User Interface for Interactive Searching of Bibliographic Data Bases, Palo Alto, CA, Jan. 14–15.)

Sessions, V. S., and L. W. Sloan. 1971. *Urbandoc/A bibliographic information system demonstration report.* New York: City University of New York, Graduate Division. 3 vols. Vol. 1: *Demonstration report.* (ERIC No. ED 051 821.) 166 pp. Vol. 2: *Technical supplement 1/General manual.* (ERIC No. ED 051 822.) 208 pp. Vol. 3: *Technical supplement 2/Operations manual.* (ERIC No. ED 051 823.)

Settles, W. P., and W. T. Black. 1978. The copper industry and scientific and technical information. *Proceedings of the American Society for Information Science* 15, 299–302.

Sewell, W. 1997. Personal communication to C. P. Bourne. Aug. 16.

Shaffer, S. S. 1965. Jan. List processing languages. In *Research & technology division report for 1964,* 25–26. Santa Monica, CA: SDC. (Report No. TM-530/008; NTIS No. AD 612 614.)

Shaw, R. R. 1965a. The form and the substance. *Library Journal* 90 (3), 567–571. Feb. 1.

Shaw, R. R. 1965b. Social disorder. *Library Journal* 90 (7), 1580, 1582–1583. Apr. 1.

Sheehan, P. M. 1971. A cost-responsive acquisitions systems. *Proceedings of the American Society for Information Science* 8, 311–319.

Sheldon, R. C. 1998. Personal communication to C. P. Bourne. July 31.

Sheldon, R. C., and S. Backer. 1967. *Design of information storage and retrieval system; Part 3: Development of a time-shared storage and retrieval system.* (NTIS No. PB 176 551.) Cambridge, MA: MIT, Department of Mechanical Engineering. Jan. (Report to National Bureau of Standards, Textile and Apparel Technology Center. Based on Sheldon's MIT master's thesis: Development of a time-shared storage and retrieval system.)

Sheldon, R. C., R. A. Roach, and S. Backer. 1968. Design of an on-line computer-based textile information retrieval system. *Textile Research Journal* 38 (1), 81–100. Jan. (Presented earlier at the 37th annual meeting of Textile Research Institute, New York, Apr. 5–7, 1967.)

Shepard, R. F. 1996. *The paper's papers: A reporter's journey through the archives of the New York Times.* New York: Times Books.

Shepherd, C. A. 1965. Progress in the development of a generalized information retrieval system at ASM. In M. Rubinoff (ed.), *Toward a national information system,* 157–162. Washington, DC: Spartan Books. (Proceedings of the Second Annual National Colloquium on Information Retrieval, Philadelphia, PA, Apr. 23–24.)

Shiban, J. R. 1967. *QUUP user's manual.* (Report No. TM-2711/000/02.) Santa Monica, CA: SDC. 147 pp. Sept. 29.

Shiner, G. 1958. The USAF automatic language translator, MARK I. In *1958 IRE National Convention Record* (pt. 4), 296–304. New York: Institute of Radio Engineers.

Shoffner, R. M., and J. L. Cunningham. 1971. *The organization and search of bibliographic records: Component studies.* Berkeley: University of California, Institute of Library Research. Sept.

Showalter, A. K. 1968. Test OSIRIS (On-line Search Information Retrieval Information Storage.) In K. Samuelson (ed.), *Mechanized information storage, retrieval and dissemination,* 683–691. Amsterdam: North-Holland. (Proceedings of the FID/IFIP Joint Conference, Rome, June 14–17, 1967.)

Shumway, N. 1966. MEDLARS: Vocabulary construction and medical subject headings. In W. Simonton, and C. Mason (eds.), *Information retrieval with special reference to the biomedical sciences,* 35–47. Minneapolis, MN: University of Minnesota, Nolte Center for Continuing Education. (Papers presented at the Second Institute on Information Retrieval, Nov. 10–13, 1965.)

Sieburg, J. 1972, Computer applications of the LITE system. *JAG Law Review* 14 (1), 14–24. Winter.

Silver, S. S. 1971. *The organization and search of bibliographic records in on-line computer systems, FMS: Users' guide to the format manipulation system for natural language documents.* (ERIC No. ED 061 976.) Berkeley: University of California, Institute of Library Research. Sept. 46 pp.

Silver, S. S., and J. C. Meredith. 1971. *The DISCUS interactive system users' manual.* (ERIC No. ED 060 919.) Berkeley: University of California, Institute of Library Research. Sept. 170 pp.

Simmons, R. A. 1969. Management of the design and development of the Biomedical Communications Network. In A. B. Veaner and P. J. Fasana (eds.), *Stanford Conference on Collaborative Library Systems Development,* 75–118. Stanford, CA: Stanford University Libraries. (Proceedings of a conference held at Stanford University Libraries, Oct. 4–5, 1968.)

Simmons, R. F. 1960a. *Anticipated developments in machine literature processing in the next decade.* (Report No. SP-129; NTIS No. PB 166 458.) Santa Monica, CA: SDC. 18 pp. Mar. 10. (Also presented at Western Psychological Association Symposium, Machine Literature Search in Human Factors, San Jose, CA, Apr.)

Simmons, R. F. 1960b. *A conceptual framework for language data processing in Synthex.* (Report No. TM-560; NTIS No. PB 166 525.) Santa Monica, CA: SDC. Nov. 28. 16 pp.

Simmons, R. F. 1962. Synthex: Toward computer synthesis of human language behavior. In H. Borko (ed.), *Computer applications in the behavioral sciences,* 360–393. Englewood Cliffs, NJ: Prentice-Hall.

Simmons, R. F. 1964. *Synthex 64: A progress report and a research plan.* (Report No. TM-1807.) Santa Monica, CA: SDC. May 6. 33 pp.

Simmons, R. F. 1965a. Answering English questions by computer: A survey. *Communications of the ACM* 8, 53–70. Jan. Published originally as Report No. SP-1556, SDC, Santa Monica, CA. Apr. 2, 1964.

Simmons, R. F. 1965b. Natural language processing and information retrieval research program at SDC. *SDC Magazine* 8 (3), 1–11. Mar.

Simmons, R. F. 1966a. Automated language processing. *Annual Review of Information Science and Technology* 1, 137–169.

Simmons, R. F. 1966b. *On-line interactive displays in application to linguistics analysis and information processing and retrieval.* (Report No. SP-2432/001; NTIS No. AD 640 647.) Santa Monica, CA: SDC. Sept. 6. 19 pp. (Also presented at Symposium on Man/Machine Interaction, Paris, Oct. 10–17.)

Simmons, R. F. 1966c. Storage and retrieval aspects of meaning in directed graph structures. *Communications of the ACM* 9, 211–215. Mar. Published originally as Report No. SP-1975/001/02; NTIS No. AD 622 017, SDC, Santa Monica, CA. Sept. 23, 1965. 21 pp.

Simmons, R. F. 1967. Answering English questions by computer. In H. Borko (ed.), *Automated language processing*, 253–289. New York: Wiley.

Simmons, R. F., and H. Borko. 1965. Language processing and retrieval. In L. F. Carter, F. N. Marzocco, and D. L. Drukey, *Research & technology division report for 1964*, 51–59. Santa Monica, CA: SDC. Jan. (Report No. TM-530/008; NTIS No. AD 612 614.)

Simmons, R. F., and H. Borko. 1966. Language processing and retrieval. In *Research & technology report for 1965*, 5-1–5-11. Santa Monica, CA: SDC. Jan. (Report No. TM-530/010/009.)

Simmons, R. F., and H. Borko. 1967. Language processing and retrieval. In *Research & technology report for 1966*, 5-1–5-25. Santa Monica, CA: SDC, Jan. (Report No. TM-530/010.)

Simmons, R. F., J. F. Burger, and R. E. Long. 1966. An approach toward answering English questions from text. *Proceedings of the AFIPS Fall Joint Computer Conference* 29, 357–363. Published originally as Report No. SP-2445, SDC, Santa Monica, CA. Apr. 27.

Simmons, R. F., J. F Burger, H. Manelowitz, and R. E. Long. 1967. Syntex: The computer synthesis of language behavior. In *Research & technology report for 1966*, 5-7–5-11. Santa Monica, CA: SDC. Jan. (Report No. TM-530/010.)

Simmons, R. F., J. F. Burger, and R. M. Schwarcz. 1968. A computational model of verbal understanding. *Proceedings of the AFIPS Fall Joint Computer Conference* 33 (pt. 1), 441–456. Published originally as Report No. SP-3132, NTIS No. AD 672 782, SDC, Santa Monica, CA. Apr. 30. 54 pp.

Simmons, R. F., L. Doyle, and D. Estavan. 1960. *A proposal for research toward the design of a general purpose cognitive language processing system.* (Report No. TM-493.) Santa Monica, CA: SDC. May 14.

Simmons, R. F., J. Farell, D. L. Londe, H. Manelowitz, and K. L. McConlogue. 1964. Syntex: The computer synthesis of language behavior. In C. Baum (ed.), *Research directorate report*, 7–8. Santa Monica, CA: SDC. Jan. (Report No. TM-530/007.)

Simmons, R. F., S. Klein, and K. McConlogue. 1962. Toward the synthesis of human language behavior. *Computers in Behavioral Science* 7, 402–407.

Simmons, R. F., S. Klein, and K. McConlogue. 1964. Indexing and dependency logic for answering English questions. *American Documentation* 15 (July), 196–204.

Simmons, R. F., and K. L. McConlogue. 1963. Maximum-depth indexing for computer retrieval of English language data. *American Documentation* 14 (Jan.), 68–73.

Sinopoli A. B. 1969. COSTAR—A conversational on-line storage and retrieval system. In L. Schultz (ed.), *The information bazaar*, 173–189. Philadelphia, PA: College of Physicians of Philadelphia. (Proceedings of Sixth Annual National Colloquium on Information Retrieval, Philadelphia, PA, May 8–9.)

Skelly, S. J. 1968a. Computerization of Canadian statute law. *Law and Computer Technology* 1 (2), 10–14. Feb.

Skelly, S. J. 1968b. Computers and the law. *Saskatchewan Law Review* 33 (3), 167–178. Fall.

Skye, S. 1990. STAIRS. In S. Kaufman (ed.), *A history of textual information retrieval at IBM*. Unpublished draft, undated, but est. 1990. 7 pp.

Smith, B. 1984. BRS—Prepped for progress. *Information Today* 1 (8), 21–23. Sept.

Smith, B. 1985. Inforonics—"Can do" outlook guides small entrepreneur. *Information Today* 17 (Nov.), 19.

Smith, E. S. 1993. On the shoulders of giants: From Boole to Shannon to Taube: The origins and development of computerized information from the mid-19th century to the present. *Information Technology and Libraries* 12 (2), 217–226. June.

Smith, J. L. 1966. *MICRO: A strategy for retrieving, ranking, and qualifying document references.* (Report No. SP-2289.) Santa Monica, CA: SDC. Jan. 15. 17 pp.

Smith, J. L., J. D. Hofmann, and J. C. Cornelli. 1968. *COLEX (CIRC-On-Line Experiment); Final report: Phase II of COLEX operation, 1 Dec 67–30 June 68.* (Report No.

TM-80006/000; RADC-TR-68-332; NTIS No. AD 844 594.) Dayton, OH: SDC. Nov. 35 pp.

Smith, K. A., and R. B. Mehnert. 1986. The National Library of Medicine: From MEDLARS to the sesquicentennial and beyond. *Bulletin of the Medical Library Association* 74 (4), 325–332. Oct.

Smith, W. B. 1965. Computers wide government role. *New York Times*, Nov. 7, pp. 1, 14.

Smithers, P. R. 1973. *The current status of computer-aided retrospective searching in DSIS.* (DSIS Technical Note No. 14; NTIS No. AD 779 526.) Ottawa, Ontario: Defence Scientific Information Service. June 20. 46 pp.

Snyder, L. S. 1981. *A study of the State University of New York Biomedical Communication Network (SUNY/BCN) from 1968 to 1977.* (ERIC No. ED 235 830.) 12 pp.

Sophar, G. J., and D. E. Berninger. 1972. ASIS-72 international information retrieval network. *ASIS Newsletter* (Nov.–Dec.), 9–10.

Spiegel, I. 1972. CMDNJ uses two information systems in comprehensive retrieval program. *Network Newsletter (SUNY BCN)* 5 (4), 3. Sept.–Dec.

Spiegel, I., and J. Crager. 1971. *SUNY Biomedical Communication Network; Work session, Apr. 20, 1971.* (ERIC No. ED 059 743.) Newark, NJ: New Jersey College of Medicine & Dentistry. 79 pp.

Spiegel, I., and J. Crager. 1973. Comparison of SUNY and MEDLINE searches. *Bulletin of the Medical Library Association* 61 (2), 205–209. Apr.

Spiegel, J., J. K. Summers, and E. M. Bennett. 1966. *AESOP: A general purpose approach to real-time, direct access management information systems.* (Report No. MTP-33; Air Force Report No. ESD-TR-66-289; NTIS No. AD 634 371.) Bedford, MA: Mitre. June. 31 pp.

Spierer, M. M., and R. B. Wills. 1968. *Applications of a large-scale time-sharing system.* (Report No. SP-3062.) Santa Monica, CA: SDC. Aug. 30. 31 pp. (Presented earlier at the IEEE International Convention, New York, NY, Mar. 18.)

Spierer, M. M., and R. B. Wills. 1969. How a powerful time sharing system became indispensable. *Computers and Automation*, 18 (11), 22–33. Oct.

Spigai, F. 1986. Displays in database search systems. In J. F. Williams (ed.), *Online catalog screen displays; A series of discussions*, 63–115. Washington, DC: Council on Library Resources. June.

Spigai, F. 1987. Interview. Mar. 12.

Sprowl, J. A. 1976a. Computer-assisted legal research: An analysis of full-text document retrieval systems, particularly the LEXIS system. *American Bar Foundation Research Journal* 1, 175–226.

Sprowl, J. A. 1976b. The WESTLAW system: A different approach to computer-assisted legal research. *Jurimetrics Journal* 16 (3), 142–148. Spring.

Spuck, D. W., D. N. McIsaac, T. Olson, and R. Tally. 1974. *Information retrieval: Presentation and documentation of an interactive computer-based search program.* (ERIC No. ED 090 920.) Apr. 19. 46 pp. (A symposium presented at 59th annual meeting of the American Educational Research Association, Chicago, IL.)

Standera, O. 1970. *COMPENDEX/TEXT-PAC: CIS.* (ERIC No. ED 044 120.) Calgary, Alberta, Canada: Calgary University, Data Centre. Aug. 94 pp.

Standera, O. 1971. *COMPENDEX/TEXT-PAC: Retrospective search.* (ERIC No. ED 051 862.) Calgary, Alberta, Canada: Calgary University. May. 65 pp.

Stangl, P., B. Lipetz, and K. F. Taylor. 1969. Performance of Kilgour's truncation algorithm when applied to bibliographic retrieval from library catalogs. *Proceedings of the American Society for Information Science* 6, 125–127.

Starke, A. C., F. R. Whaley, E. C. Carlson, and W. B. Thompson. 1968. GAF document storage and retrieval system. *American Documentation* 19 (Apr.), 173–180.

Starker, L. N., K. C. Owen, and J. W. Martin. 1971. Multilevel retrieval systems: IV; Large systems. *Journal of Chemical Documentation* 11 (Aug.), 238–242. Presented at the meeting of the American Chemical Society, Los Angeles, CA, Mar. 30.

Steil, G. 1967. File management on a small computer; The C-10 system. *Proceedings of the AFIPS Spring Joint Computer Conference* 30, 199–212.

Stein, J. D., F. M. Delaney, S. D. Peluso, and L. N. Starker. 1973. A computer-based comprehensive bio-data information retrieval system. *Journal of Chemical Documentation* 13 (Aug.), 145–152.

Stentzel, J. 1976. Fallout of bribery: Lockheed aids Japan's militarists. *Nation* 222 (262). Mar. 6.

Stevens, N. D. 1970. MEDLARS: A summary review and evaluation of three reports. *Library Resources and Technical Services* 14 (1), 109–121. Winter.

Stevens, R. L. 1973. Economics of on-line information retrieval. In M. B. Henderson (ed.), *Interactive bibliographic systems*, 115–118, 128–129. Washington, DC:

U.S. Atomic Energy Commission. AEC Report No. CONF-711 010. (Proceedings of a forum, Gaithersburg, MD, Oct. 4–5, 1971.)

Stiller, J. D. 1970. Use of on-line remote access information retrieval systems. *Proceedings of the American Society for Information Science* 7, 107–109.

Stone, D., M. Rubinoff, S. Bergman, H. Cautin, and T. Johnson. 1966. Aug. *Word association experiments—basic considerations.* (NTIS No. AD 660 087.) Philadelphia: University of Pennsylvania, Moore School of Electrical Engineering. 19 pp.

Storie, J. M. 1971. *An interactive key word information retrieval system for the IBM 1130 computer.* (Report No. 8; NTIS No. PB 201 591.) Seattle: University of Washington, Urban Data Center.

Stromer, P. R. 1964. *Market analysis LMSC information retrieval project—Preliminary edition prepared for use on the LMSC information storage and retrieval program.* (Information Retrieval Note No. 10.) Sunnyvale, CA: LMSC. June. 23 pp.

Sullivan, D. J., and D. Meister. 1967. Evaluation of user reactions to a prototype on-line information retrieval system. *Proceedings of the American Documentation Institute* 4, 90–94.

Summary of proceedings of ASIDIC meeting, Arlington Heights, IL, Sept. 26–28, 1971. 1971. (ERIC No. ED 060 879.) ASIDIC. 28 pp.

Summers, J. K., and E. Bennett. 1967. AESOP—A final report: A prototype on-line interactive information control system. In D. E. Walker (ed.), *Information system science and technology*, 69–86. Washington, DC: Thompson Book Co. (Also available as NTIS No. PB 178 792.)

Summit and Gore among featured honorees at ASIS annual meeting. 1991. *Bulletin of the American Society for Information Science* 18 (Oct.–Nov.), 4.

Summit, R. K. 1962. MATICO—A computer-based reference retrieval system. Paper presented at IBM Information Retrieval Workshop, San Jose, CA.

Summit, R. K. 1965. *Conversational information retrieval.* (Information Retrieval Note No. 61.) Palo Alto, CA: LMSC. Feb. 11. 5 pp.

Summit, R. K. 1966a. *DIALOG: An operational on-line reference retrieval system.* (Information Retrieval Note No. 88.) Palo Alto, CA: LMSC. 21 pp. Nov. 7. Published later in *Proceedings of the 22nd National Conference of the Association for Computer Machinery*, 51–56. Washington, DC: Thompson Book Co., 1967.

Summit, R. K. 1966b. *On the establishment of a Hawaiian Oceanographic Information Center.* Palo Alto, CA: LMSC. Appendix: CONVERSE II; System description. Mar. 29. 11 pp.

Summit, R. K. 1966c. *Project DIALOG; A real time information retrieval system.* (Information Retrieval Note No. 85.) Palo Alto, CA: LMSC, Research Lab. June. 25 pp.

Summit, R. K. 1967a. *DIALOG II user's manual.* (Report No. LMSC Report No. 6-77–67-14.) Palo Alto, CA: LMSC. Mar.

Summit, R. K. 1967b. *Remote information retrieval facility—Ames Research Center; Final report.* (Report No. NASA Report No. CR-1318.) Palo Alto, CA: LMSC. 21 pp. Sept. Republished as *Remote information retrieval; Ames Research Center; Experimental findings*, Information Retrieval Note No. 96, Apr. 1, 1968.

Summit, R. K. 1968a. *Lunar/earth data bank study.* (Report No. LMSC–71-68-1-Vol. 3; NASA Report No. N69-28022.) Palo Alto, CA: LMSC, Research Lab. Jan. 48 pp.

Summit, R. K. 1968b. On-line information retrieval comes of age. In *Computer impact on engineering management*, 49–51. Pittsburgh, PA: Instrument Society of America. (Proceedings of the Joint Engineering Management Conference, Philadelphia, PA, Sept. 30–Oct. 1.)

Summit, R. K. 1969a. Information retrieval and marine technology. In *Proceedings of the International Marine Information Symposium, 31 Oct.–1 Nov. 1968*, 65–70. Washington, DC: Marine Technology Society.

Summit, R. K. 1969b. *Remote information retrieval facility.* (Report No. NASA CR-1318.) Palo Alto, CA: LMSC. Apr. 44 pp.

Summit, R. K. 1970a. *ERIC online retrieval system—Use of the DIALOG online information retrieval system with ERIC Research in Education files; Final report.* (Report No. LMSC–6R-70-1; ERIC No. ED 040 592.) Palo Alto, CA: LMSC, Research Lab. Apr. 58 pp.

Summit, R. K. 1970b. *Users manual; AEC/DIALOG online retrieval system.* (Report No. LMSC-N-6R-69-2.) Palo Alto, CA: LMSC, Research Lab. Aug. 32 pp.

Summit, R. K. 1971. DIALOG and the user: An evaluation of the user interface with a major on-line retrieval system. In D. E. Walker (ed.), *Interactive bibliographic search: The user-computer interface.* Montvale, NJ: AFIPS Press. (Proceedings of The User Interface for Interactive Search of Bibliographic Data Bases, Palo Alto, CA, Jan. 14–15.)

Summit, R. K. 1972. Personal communication to C. P. Bourne. Aug. 2.

Summit, R. K. 1973. Evolution and future of information retrieval. In M. B. Henderson (ed.), *Interactive bibliographic systems*, 190–196. Washington, DC: U.S. Atomic Energy Commission. AEC Report No. CONF-711010. Apr. (Proceedings of a forum, Gaithersburg, MD, Oct. 4–5, 1971.)

Summit, R. K. 1975a. Information retrieval—Make vs. buy. In J. Sherrod (ed.), *Information systems and networks*, 101–103. Westport, CT: Greenwood Press. (Proceedings of the Eleventh Annual Symposium in Information Processing, Los Angeles, CA, Mar. 27–29, 1974.)

Summit, R. K. 1975b. Lockheed experience in processing large data bases for its commercial information retrieval service. *Journal of Chemical Documentation* 15 (1), 40–42. Feb.

Summit, R. K. 1980a. Personal communication to C. P. Bourne. Nov. 10.

Summit, R. K. 1980b. The dynamics of costs and finances of on-line computer searching. *RQ* 20 (1), 60–63. Fall.

Summit, R. K. 1980c. Online perspective keynote address. Paper presented at Online Conference Meeting, San Francisco, CA, Nov. 12.

Summit, R. K. 1981. Information retrieval; Past, present and future. Keynote address at the Annual New Mexico Library Association Conference, Albuquerque, Apr. 30.

Summit, R. K. 1987. Interview. Mar. 10.

Summit, R. K., and S. J. Drew. 1976. The public library as an information dissemination center: An experiment in information retrieval services for the general public. In F. W. Lancaster (ed.), *Proceedings of the 1975 Clinic on Library Applications of Data Processing*, 91–102. Urbana-Champaign: University of Illinois, Graduate School of Library Science.

Summit, R. K., and O. Firschein. 1974. Document retrieval systems and techniques. *Annual Review of Information Science and Technology* 9, 285–331.

Summit, R. K., and O. Firschein. 1977a. *Investigation of the public library as linking agent to major scientific, educational, social, and environmental data bases; Final report*. (Report No. LMSC-D560986; NTIS No. PB 276 726.) Palo Alto, CA: LMSC, Palo Alto Research Lab. Oct. 1. 175 pp.

Summit, R. K., and O. Firschein. 1977b. Public library use of online bibliographic retrieval services: Experience in four public libraries in northern California. *Online* 1 (4), 58–64. Oct.

Summit, R. K., and M. S. Radwin. 1969. *Use of an online information retrieval system for preliminary analysis of parole data*. Palo Alto, CA: LMSC, Information Sciences Lab. 12 pp. (Presented at the 16th National Institute on Crime and Delinquency, Boston, June 9–10.)

Summit, R. K., and D. C. Shoultz. 1967. *DIALOG linear and inverted file conversion programs*. (Information Retrieval Note No. 89.) Palo Alto, CA: LMSC. Feb. 2. 36 pp.

Sundeen, D. H. 1968. General purpose software. *Datamation* 14(1), 22–27. Jan.

SUNY/Albany joins NLM to double MEDLINE capacity. 1973. *Information; Part 1/News; Sources; Profiles* 5 (2), 76–77. Mar.–Apr.

SUNY and BIOSIS plan data base project. 1973, July–Dec. *Network Newsletter (SUNY BCN)* 6 (3 + 4), 3.

SUNY operates computer ports for NLM's MEDLINE system. 1973. *Library Journal* 98 (7), 1074. Apr. 1.

Survey of library automation systems; Phase 2 final report; v. 2: Stanford University BALLOTS. 1974. Maynard, MA: Inforonics; Stanford, CA: Butler Associates. May. 154 pp.

Suwa S. 1980. JOIS-II: JICST's new online information retrieval system. In *Proceedings of the Fourth International Online Information Meeting*, 363–375. Oxford, England: Learned Information.

Swanson, R. W. 1981. *Study of online instruction methodologies for the DTIC training program*. (NTIS No. AD A101 460.) Alexandria, VA: Defense Technical Information Center. Feb.

System development study for the automation program of the Library of Congress. 1966. Santa Monica, CA: SDC. Feb. 126 pp. (Technical Proposal No. 759.)

Taine, S. I. 1963a. The National Library of Medicine Medical Literature Analysis and Retrieval System (MEDLARS.) *Proceedings of the American Documentation Institute, Pt. 1*, 105–106.

Taine, S. I. 1963b. The Medical Literature Analysis and Retrieval System. *Bulletin of the Medical Library Association* 51 (2), 157–167. Apr.

Talbott, G. D. 1966. Hot line to the heart. *Journal of the American Medical Association* 196 (11), 146–148. June 13.

Tally, R. D. 1995. Personal communication to C. P. Bourne. Nov. 1.

Tanaka, R. I. 1964. Interdepartmental Communication Commendation: Personnel on ADA Retrieval System. Oct. 21.

Tancredi, S. A., and W. R. Ryerson. 1972. NTISearch: A National Technical Information Service bibliographic search system. *Proceedings of the American Society for Information Science* 9, paper no. 17. Contributed papers: Author forums.

Taulbee, O. E. 1967a. An approach to comprehensive evaluation. In A. Kent, O. E. Taulbee, J. Belzer, and G. D. Goldstein (eds.), *Electronic handling of information: Testing & evaluation*, 217–229. Washington, DC: Thompson Book Co.

Taulbee, O. E. 1967b. *Testing and evaluation of the FTD CIRC system*. (Report No. GER-13099; NTIS No. AD 816 618.) Akron, OH: Goodyear Aerospace Corporation. Mar. 15. 231 pp.

Taylor, R. W. 1990. *In memoriam, J. C. R. Licklider, 1915–1990*. (Report No. SRC 61.) Digital Equipment Corporation, Systems Research Center. Aug. 7.

Thomas, A. L. 1972. GIPSY: General Information System for Oklahoma. In R. A. May (ed.), *Automated law research: A collection of presentations delivered at the First National Conference on Automated Law Research*, 119–124. Chicago, IL: American Bar Association, Standing Committee on Law and Technology.

Thompson, D. A. 1969. The man-computer system; Toward balanced cooperation in intellectual activities. In *International Symposium on Man-machine Systems* (Sept.), 8–12. Cambridge, England.

Thompson, D. A. 1971. Interface design for an interactive information retrieval system: A literature survey and a research system description. *Journal of the American Society for Information Science* 22 (6), 361–373. Nov.–Dec.

Thompson, D. A., L. A., Bennigson, and D. Whitman. 1967. Structuring information bases to minimize user search time. *Proceedings of the American Documentation Institute* 4, 164–168.

Thompson, D. A., L. A., Bennigson, and D. Whitman. 1968. A proposed structure for displayed information to minimize search time through a data base. *American Documentation* 19 (Jan.), 80–84.

Thompson, F. B. 1966. English for the computer. *Proceedings of the AFIPS Fall Joint Computer Conference* 29, 349–364.

Thompson, G. K. 1968. Computerization of information retrieval and index production in the field of economic and social development. *UNESCO Bulletin for Libraries* 22 (2), 66–72. Mar.–Apr.

Thompson, G. K. 1970. Some cost estimates for bibliographical searching in a large-scale social sciences information system. *Information Storage & Retrieval* 6 (June), 179–186.

Thompson, G. K., and W. D. Schieber. 1970. Computerized information systems and development assistance. *Industrial Research and Development News* 5 (3), 2–5. Autumn.

Timbie, M., and D. Coombs. 1969. *An interactive information retrieval system—Case studies on the use of DIALOG to search the ERIC document file*. (Report No. ED 034 431.) Stanford, CA: Stanford University, ERIC Clearinghouse on Educational Media and Technology. Dec. 90 pp.

Tocatlian, J. 1975. International information systems. In M. J. Voigt (ed.), *Advances in Librarianship*, vol. 5, 1–60. New York: Academic Press.

Tomberg, A. 1979, The development of commercially available databases in Europe. *Online Review* 3 (4), 343–353. Dec.

TOXICON renamed TOXLINE: New data retrieval system announced. 1973. *Information; Part I/News; Sources; Profiles* 5 (4), 184–185. July–Aug.

TOXLINE transferred to NLM computer. 1974. *Information; News and Sources* 6 (7), 202. Sept.

Training methods: The 'how' of teaching. 1977. (Summary of presentations by M. Williams, J. Wanger, A. Elias, L. Eisenberg, P. Atherton, C. Bourne, C. Meadow, and J. Eisele at ASIDIC spring meeting, Mar. 13–15, 1977.) Mar. 16 pp.

Trester, D. J. 1981. *ERIC—The first fifteen years: 1964–1979*. (ERIC No. ED 195 289.) Columbus, OH: Ohio State University, College of Education, SMEAC Information Reference Center. Sept.

Treu, S. 1967. Testing and evaluation: Literature review. In A. Kent, O. E. Taulbee, J. Belzer, and G. D. Goldstein (eds.), *Electronic handling of information: Testing and evaluation*, 71–88. Washington, DC: Thompson Book Co.

Troy, F. J. 1969. Ohio Bar Automated Research; A practical system of computerized legal research. *Jurimetrics Journal* 10 (2), 62–69. Dec.

Trump, L. H. 1971. *Large scale information processing systems; Section III: SUPARS/DPS systems hardware and software.* Syracuse, NY: Syracuse University, School of Library Science. 28 pp. July.

UCLA Brain Information Service (Los Angeles, CA). 1969. *Electroencephalography & Clinical Neurophysiology* 27 (7), 730. (An extra number containing papers presented at the 7th International Congress of Electroencephalography and Clinical Neurophysiology, San Diego, CA, Sept. 13–19.)

UCLA gets contract for pilot study on decentralization of MEDLARS. 1965. *Library Journal* 90 (3), 603–604. Feb. 1.

Univ of Pitt is first computer link with the New York Times. 1973. *Information; Part 1/News; Sources; Profiles* 5 (Jan.–Feb.), 1.

User committee meets in Apr. 1973. *Network Newsletter (SUNY BCN)* 6 (2), 1–2. Apr.–June.

User manual; New index. 1975. *Network Newsletter (SUNY BCN)* 9 (3 & 4), 3. July–Dec.

Vaden, W. M. 1969. Progress report: On-line, direct access experiment. Oak Ridge, TN: AEC, Division of Technical Information. Unpublished notes for presentation. Nov. 5. 4 pp.

Vaden, W. M. 1979. *Remarks for presentation at the 1979 RECON users meeting.* 4 pp. Jan. 23.

Vaden, W. M. 1992. *The Oak Ridge Technical Information Center: A trailblazer in federal documentation.* Oak Ridge, TN: U.S. Department of Energy, Office of Scientific and Technical Information. 361 pp.

Vallee, J. F. 1970. DIRAC: An interactive retrieval language with computational interface. *Information Storage & Retrieval* 6, 387–399. Dec.

Vallee, J. F., and J. A. Hynek. 1966. An automatic question-answering system for stellar astronomy. *Publications of the Astronomical Society of the Pacific* 78 (463), 315–323. Aug.

Vallee, J. F., J. A. Hynek, G. Ray, and P. Wolf. 1971. The organization of research data banks: Experience with DIRAC-based information systems. *Proceedings of the American Society for Information Science* 8, 387–394.

Vallee, J. F., G. K. Krulee, and A. A. Grau. 1968. Retrieval formulae for inquiry systems. *Information Storage & Retrieval* 6 (Mar.), 387–399.

Van Camp, A. J. 1971. On-line retrieval of MEDLARS information at Indiana University School of Medicine Library. In *V-M Library Newsletter.* Attachment to newsletter. May. 2 pp.

Van Camp, A. J. 1973. Comparison of the SUNY and MEDLINE systems. Unpublished paper. Apr. 16.

Van Camp, A. J. 1988. Memories of an online pioneer. *Database* 11 (5), 38–41. Oct.

Van Camp, A. J. 1992. User advisory groups and the online industry. *Online* 16 (Mar.), 40–45.

Van Camp, A. J. 1994. In memoriam: Reflections on the BRS era, 1976–1994. *Online* 18 (5), 66. Sept./Oct.

Van Camp, A. J. 1995. Personal communication to C. P. Bourne. June 20.

Vann, J. O. 1963. Defense Documentation Center (DDC) for scientific and technical information. *Journal of Chemical Documentation* 3 (4), 220–222. Oct.

Veaner, A. B. 1969. Stanford University Libraries Project BALLOTS. In A. B. Veaner, and P. J. Fasana (eds.), *Stanford conference on collaborative library systems development, Oct. 4–5, 1968,* 42–49. Stanford, CA: Stanford University Libraries.

Veaner, A. B. 1977. BALLOTS: Bibliographic Automation of Large Library Operations Using a Time Sharing System. In E. Edelhoff, and K.-D. Lehmann (eds.), *Online library and network systems,* 130–139. Frankfurt: Vittorio Klostermann. (Proceedings of a symposium held at Dortmund University, Mar. 22–24, 1976.)

Velazquez, H. 1979. University of Toronto Library Automation Systems. *Online Review* 3 (3), 253–263. Sept.

Velazquez, H., and E. Anttila. 1979. Inter-library searching through an on-line catalogue. *Proceedings of the Seventh Canadian Conference on Information Science,* 130–134.

Verheijen-Voogd, C., and A. Malhijsen. 1974. A contribution to the comparison of the usefulness of the data bases of Excerpta Medica and MEDLARS in biomedical literature retrieval. *Aslib Proceedings* 26 (4), 136–151. Apr.

Vinsonhaler, J. F. 1967. BIRS: A system of general purpose computer programs for information retrieval in the behavioral sciences. *The American Behavioral Scientist* 10 (6), 12, 21–24. Feb.

Vitagliano, V. J. 1965. Systems concepts for establishing an automated information center. In *Abstracts of the International Federation for Documentation (FID) Congress,* 91. Washington, DC: FID Congress, Secretariat.

Volino, R. L. 1972. LITE in review—Two aspects. *JAG Law Review* 14 (1), 25–34.

Vorhaus, A. H. 1965. General purpose display system. *SDC Magazine* 8 (Aug.), 1–15.

Waite, D. P. 1975. The minicomputer: Its role in a nationwide bibliographic and information network. In *Proceedings of the 1974 Clinic on Library Applications of Data Processing*, 136–157. Urbana-Champaign: University of Illinois, Graduate School of Library Science.

Walker, D. E. 1967. SAFARI; An on-line text processing system. *Proceedings of the American Documentation Institute* 4, 144–147.

Walker, D. E. 1971a. Bibliography on computer-user interface. In D. E. Walker (ed.), *Interactive bibliographic search: The user/computer interface*. Montvale, NJ: AFIPS Press.

Walker, D. E. (ed.) 1971b. *Interactive bibliographic search: The user/computer interface*. Montvale, NJ: AFIPS Press. (Proceedings of The User Interface for Interactive Search of Bibliographic Data Bases, Palo Alto, CA, Jan. 14–15.)

Walker, R. D., and J. R. Luedtke. 1979. DOE/RECON and the energy files. *Database* 2 (4), 54–67. Dec.

Wallace, E. M. 1966a. User requirements, personal indexes, and computer support. *Proceedings of the American Documentation Institute* 3, 73–80.

Wallace, E. M. 1966b. *A user's guide to SURF: Support of user records and files*. (Report No. TM-2913; NTIS No. AD 66 838.) Santa Monica, CA: SDC. June 24. 27 pp.

Wallace, E. M. 1967. SURF: EDP-based support of user records and files. In *Research & technology report for 1966*, 5–25. Santa Monica, CA: SDC. Jan. (Report No. TM-530/010.)

Wallace, E. M., and B. R. Park. 1968. SURF: EDP-based support of users records and files. In *Research & technology report for 1967*, 4-10–4-11. Santa Monica, CA: SDC. Jan. (Report No. TM-530/011.)

Wallace, L. E. 1995. *The story of the Defense Technical Information Center*. Fort Belvoir, VA: DTIC.

Walsh, J. 1973. New York Times: All the news that's fit to printout. *Science* 181 (4100), 640–642. Aug. 17.

Warheit, I. A. 1965. The combined file search system: A case study of system design for information retrieval. In *Abstracts of the International Federation for Documentation (FID) Congress*, 92. Washington, DC: FID Congress, Secretariat.

Warren, P. A., P. J. Vinken, and R. van der Walle. 1969. Design and operation of an advanced computer system for the storage, retrieval and dissemination of the world's biomedical information. *Proceedings of the American Society for Information Science* 6, 423–429.

Washington State University. 1971. *SOLAR; Manual 1: User instructions, 2d ed.; SOLAR; Manual 2: Data base preparation, 1st ed.; SOLAR; Manual 3: System concepts, 1st ed.* Author. June.

Wedgeworth, R. 1997. Personal communication to C. P. Bourne. Nov. 20.

Weil, H. 1975. All the data fit to bank. *Change* 7 (3), 53–54. Apr.

Weinstock, M. J., L. C. Dorney, H. A. Bloomquist, I. H. Pizer, L. F. Lunin, J. L. Martinson, and M. Herner. 1966. *A recommended design for the United States medical library and information system*. Vol. 2: *Background studies*. (NTIS No. PB 172 924.) Washington, DC: Herner and Co. Jan. 374 pp.

Welch, N. O. 1968. *A survey of five on-line retrieval systems*. (Report No. MTP-322; COSATI Report No. 69-4; NTIS No. AD 686 812.) Washington, DC: Mitre. Aug. 55 pp.

Wenk, E. A., D. M. Gottfredson, and M. S. Radwin. 1970. A modern information system for Uniform Parole Reports data. *Journal of Research in Crime and Delinquency* 7 (1), 58–70. Jan.

Wenk, E. A., M. S. Radwin, R. K. Summit, and C. McHugh. 1970. New developments in on-line information retrieval techniques in the United States as applied to the Uniform Parole Reports. *Abstracts on Criminology and Penology* 10 (1), 8–17. Jan.–Feb.

Wente, V. A. 1965. Specificity and accessibility in a system of information centers on space and aeronautics. In B. F. Cheydleur (ed.), *Colloquium on technical preconditions for retrieval center operation*, 55–60. Washington, DC: Spartan Books.

Wente, V. A. 1968. The human interface in lieu of direct interaction by the user with the system. In J.W. Ramey (ed.), *Impact of mechanization on libraries and information Centers*, 183–186. Philadelphia, PA: Information Interscience. (Proceedings of the Fifth Annual National Colloquium on Information Retrieval, Philadelphia, May 3–4.)

Wente, V. A. 1971. NASA/RECON and users interface considerations. In D. E. Walker (ed.), *Interactive bibliographic search: The user/computer interface*, 95–104. Montvale, NJ: AFIPS Press. (Proceedings of The User Interface for Interactive Search of Bibliographic Data Bases, Palo Alto, CA, Jan. 14–15.)

Wente, V. A. 1987. Interview. Sept. 24.

Wente, V. A. 1995. Personal communication to C. P. Bourne. Oct. 20; Nov. 17.

Wente, V. A. 1997. Personal communication to C. P. Bourne. Aug. 8.

West Publishing test marketing new legal data base priced less than LEXIS. 1976. *Applied Technology/Libraries.* Apr.

Whaley, F. R., and E. A. Wainio. 1967. Experimental SDI products and services at Engineering Index. *Proceedings of the American Documentation Institute* 4, 296–300.

White, R. O. 1973. LIS: Legislative Information System for Washington. In R. A. May (ed.), *Automated law research; A collection of presentations delivered at the First National Conference on Automated Law Research,* 113–117. American Bar Association, Standing Committee on Law and Technology.

Wilde, D. U. 1997. Personal communication to C. P. Bourne. July 27; Sept. 3.

Wilkins, T. B. 1972. History of LITE. *JAG Law Review* 14 (1), 7–9. Winter.

Wilkinson, W. D., and G. Martins. 1965. *On-line command and control study; Part I. Annual progress report.* (Report No. D58-5UI; NTIS No. AD 471 492.) Canoga Park, CA: Bunker-Ramo Corporation. Sept. 77 pp.

Williams, J. H. 1969. *BROWSER, An automated indexing on-line text retrieval system; Annual progress report.* (NTIS No. AD 693 143.) Gaithersburg, MD: IBM Federal Systems Division. Sept.

Williams, J. H. 1971a. Functions of a man-machine interactive information retrieval system. *Journal of the American Society for Information Science* 22 (5), 311–317. Sept.–Oct. Published originally as an IBM report, NTIS No. AD 716 954. Oct. 1970. 32 pp.

Williams, J. H. 1971b. *An interactive browsing technique.* (Report No. N71-30815; NTIS No. AD 722 672.) Gaithersburg, MD: IBM Federal Systems Division. Apr.

Williams, J. H., and M. P. Perriens. 1968. *Automatic full text indexing and searching system.* Gaithersburg, MD: IBM Federal Systems Division.

Williams, M. E. 1976. Data bases and data about data bases Data base column. *Bulletin of the American Society for Information Science* 3 (2), 20–21. Dec.

Williams, M. E. 1977. The impact of machine-readable data bases on library and information services. *Information Processing & Management* 13, 95–107.

Wilson, R. A. 1962a. Computer retrieval of case law. *Southwestern Law Journal* 16 (3), 409–438. Sept.

Wilson, R. A. 1962b. Minutes of the annual meeting of the Special Committee on Electronic Data Retrieval of the American Bar Association; Aug. 8, 1962. *Modern Uses of Logic in Law (M.U.L.L.)* (Dec.), 267–269.

Wilson, R. A. 1966. Case law searching by machine. In R. P. Bigelow (ed.), *Computers and the law: An introductory handbook,* 55–59. New York: Commerce Clearing House.

Winik, R. 1972, Reference function with an on-line catalog. *Special Libraries* 63 (5/6), 217–221. May–June.

WISE search program; Reference manual for the 1110. 1977. Sept. Madison, WI: University of Wisconsin, Academic Computing Center. 60 pp. (Supercedes the WISE search program reference manual of Jan., 1976.)

Wixon, D. W., and E. Housman. 1968. *Development and evaluation of a large-scale system for selective dissemination of information (SDI.)* (Report No. ECOM-3001; NTIS No. AD 674 661.) Fort Monmouth, NJ: U.S. Army Electronics Command. Aug. 31 pp.

Wolf, P. L., H. R. Ludwig, and J. F. Vallee. 1971. Progress towards a direct-access hematology data base: Stanford's experience with the DIRAC language. *Archives of Pathology,* 91 (June), 542–549.

Wolfe, T. 1970. *An evaluation of on-line information retrieval system techniques; Final report.* (Report No. NSRDC-3548; NTIS No. AD 723 214.) Washington, DC: U.S. Department of the Navy, Naval Ship Research and Development Center. Dec. 56 pp.

Woods, W. A. 1971. *The Defense Documentation Center natural English preprocessor.* (Report No. BBN-2182; NTIS No. AD 727 992.) Cambridge, MA: Bolt, Beranek, and Newman. July 31. 274 pp.

Woodsmall, R. M. 1991. Personal communication to T. Bellardo. Dec. 18.

Yamamoto, T. Kumai, K. Nakano, C. T. L. Kunii, H. Takahasi, and S. Fugiwara. 1971. Todai scientific information retrieval (TSIR-1) system; I. Generation, updating, and listing of a scientific literature data base by conversational input. *Journal of Chemical Documentation* 11 (Nov.), 228–231.

Yamamoto, T., Kunii, T.L., S. Fujiwara, and H. Takahashi. 1972. An on-line scientific information retrieval system based on a natural language data base. In *First USA-Japan computer conference proceedings,* 632–637. Montvale, NJ: AFIPS.

Yamamoto, T., M. Negishi, M. Ushimaru, Y. Tozawa, K. Okabe, and S. Fujiwara. 1975. TOOL-IR: An on-line information retrieval system at an inter-university computer center. In *2nd USA-Japan computer conference proceedings,* 159–165. Montvale, NJ: AFIPS and IPSJ.

Yamamoto, T., M. Ushimara, T. L. Kunii, H. Takahasi, and S. Fugiwara, 1972. Todai scientific information retrieval (TSIR-1) system; II. Generation of a scientific literature data base in a center-oriented format by a tape-to-tape conversion of CAS SDF data base. *Journal of Chemical Documentation* 12 (May), 113–116.

Zais, H. W. 1974. *Comparison of three on-line information retrieval services.* (ERIC No. ED 090 965.) Berkeley: University of California, Lawrence Berkeley Lab. Apr. 32 pp.

Ziehe T. W. 1967. *Data management: A comparison of system features.* (Report No. TRACOR 67-904-U; NTIS No. AD 661 861.) Austin, TX: TRACOR. Oct. 37 pp.

Zimmerman, B., D. Lefkowitz, and N. S. Prywes. 1964, The Naval Aviation Supply Office inventory retrieval system; A case study in file automation. *Management Science* 10 (Apr.), 421–428.

Zimmerman, W., and R. MacKinnon. 1979. A Canadian online BRS consortium: First impressions. *Proceedings of the Seventh Canadian Conference on Information Science*, 67–80.

Index

Aagard, James S., 93–94
Abramowitz, Diane, 303
ACM (Association for Computing Machinery), 77
ADA (Automated Data Acquisition), 141, 145–149, 160
Adage AGT-30 Graphics Computer, 86
ADAM (Advanced Data Management), 104–105
Adams, Scott, 197–200, 202–204, 209, 212–213
Addis, Louise, 84–85
ADEPT Time-sharing System, 18
ADI (American Documentation Institute), 6, 42, 49
Adkinson, Burton W., 113, 176
ADL. *See* Arthur D. Little
Advanced Research Projects Agency. *See* ARPA
AEC (U.S. Atomic Energy Commission), 101, 110, 141, 168, 175–180
AEC/RECON, 168, 177–180, 252, 307–308
AESOP (An Evolutionary System for On-line Processing), 105
AEWIS (Army Electronic Warfare Information System), 169
AF (U.S. Air Force), 17, 35, 73, 104–105, 187, 239
AF-ESD (Air Force Electronic Systems Division), 13, 59
AFAFC (Air Force Accounting and Finance Center), 230, 232–233
AFIPS, Fall Joint Computer Conference, 13
AFOSR (Air Force Office of Scientific Research), 77–78, 94
AHI (Augmented Human Intellect), 13–15
Ahlgren, A. E., 284
AIM-TWX (*Abridged Index Medicus*-TeletypeWriter Exchange Network), 3, 185, 212–219, 254, 269
Aines, Andrew, 137
AIP (American Institute of Physics), 62, 69–70
Air Force Electronic Systems Division (AF-ESD), 13, 59
Aiyer, Arjun K., 89–90
ALA (American Library Association), 48–52
Alber, F., 88
Alexander, Robert W., 134–136
Allan, A., 277
Allderidge, J. M., 73
Allen-Babcock, 121
Alley, Doreen H., 329
Allison, A. M., 277
ALPS (Automated Library Processing Service), 103, 186–187
Alt, Franz L., 47–48
ALTAIR (Automatic Logical Translation and Information Retrieval), 87
American Bar Foundation (ABF), 230–232
American Documentation Institute (ADI), 6, 42, 49
American Federation of Information Processing Societies (AFIPS), 6
American Institute of Physics (AIP), 62, 69–70
American Library Association (ALA), 48–52
American Psychological Association (APA), 253
American Society for Information Science & Technology (ASIST), 6
American Society for Information Science (ASIS), 6, 13
Anderson, Barbara E., 284
Anderson, R. R., 82
Angell, Thomas, 40
Angione, Pauline B., 287, 381–382, 390, 395–396, 401–402
Annual Review of Information Science and Technology, 6
Anthony, L. D., 108
Anthra, Jane, 194
Anttila, Eric, 349
APA (American Psychological Association), 253
APL programming language, 87
AQUARIUS (A Query and Retrieval Interactive User System), 130–131
ARGUS, 203
Armstrong, Anne A., 319
Arnett, Edward M., 96
ARPA (Advanced Research Projects Agency), 13, 15, 17, 20, 28, 30, 48, 59, 63
Artandi, Susan, 128, 371
Arthur D. Little (ADL), 246, 255–256, 260, 324
Ashton, Paul, 387
ASIDIC (Association for Information Dissemination Centers), 6, 128, 368

Index

Asleson, Robert, 73
ASLIB (Association of Special Libraries and Information Bureaus), 108
Asman, Robert J., 250, 252
Aspen Systems Corporation, 238
ASPENSEARCH, 238, 341
Association for Computing Machinery (ACM), 77
Association for Information Dissemination Centers (ASIDIC), 6, 128, 368
Association of Special Libraries and Information Bureaus (ASLIB), 108
ASTIA (Armed Services Technical Information Agency), 37, 112–113, 118
Atherton, Pauline, 9, 69–73, 74–77, 97, 125, 263, 276, 284–285
Atomic Energy Commission (AEC), 175–180
ATS (Administrative Terminal System), 115–116, 121–122, 263
AUDACIOUS (Automatic Direct Access to Information with the On-Line UDC System), 69–77
Auerbach Corporation, 107–108, 219
Augenstein, Bruno, 220
Augmented Human Intellect (AHI), 13–15
Auld, Dennis, 367
Aurrichio, D., 72
Austin, Charles J., 198, 201–202, 204–206, 208
AUTOLEX (automating lexicographic), 193
Automated Law Searching, Inc., 238
AUTONOTE (Automatic Notebook), 92
Avionics Central, 254
Avram, Henrietta D., 339
Ayala, Norma, 337

Bachelder, Sally, 325–327, 370
Backer, Stanley, 66–69
Bacon, Charles R. T., 230
Bagley, Philip R., 2
Baker, A. W., 189–190, 192
Baker, F. Terry, 325
Baker, Ray, 221
BALLOTS (Bibliographic Automation of Large Libraries Using a Time-Sharing System), 85–86, 343–344

Bandreth, M., 332
Barber, A. Stephanie, 99
Barber, Peggy, 52
Barden, William A., 25, 113, 116
Barnholdt, B., 136
Barraclough, Elizabeth D., 99, 208
Barrett, Gerald V., 188–189
Barrett, Raymond P., 189, 194
Basheer, B. W., 233, 335
BASIS, 315–320, 347–348, 359, 364
Bateman, B. B., 122
Battelle, Gordon, 319
Battelle Memorial Institute (BMI), 137, 315–320
Baum, Claude, 4, 21, 24, 28–29
Baxamoosa, S., 186
Bayer, Mark, 112, 245, 250, 253, 321–322, 371, 390–394
BCN (Biomedical Communications Network), 211–212
BCN-2, 295–296
Beard, Joseph J., 238
Beauchamp, R. O., 298
Beckelheimer, M. A., 293
Becker, Joseph, 2, 5, 21, 29, 48–52, 333
BEER (Biological Effects from Non-Electromagnetic Radiation), 253
Bell, John M., 135
Bellardo, Trudi. See Hahn, Trudi Bellardo
Benbow, J. A., 88
Benenfeld, Alan R., 63–66, 66
Bennertz, Richard K., 114, 116, 118–119
Bennett, Edward M., 105
Bennett, John L., 9, 136
Bennett, Ralph E., 112, 246
Bennett, Robert L., 243, 250–251, 256–257, 300, 303
Bennigson, Lawrence A., 86
Bensing, Robert C., 230
Berezner, Susan C., 57
Bergman, Samuel, 78
Bering, Edgar A., 210
Berninger, D. E., 175
Berul, Lawrence H., 124, 238, 341

Bethe, D. M., 103
Bibliographic coupling, 42–44, 68–69
Bibliographic Retrieval Services, Inc. *See* BRS
Bibliographic utilities, 343–350
BIBNET, 349–350
Bichel, R. L., 35, 188
BIDAP (Bibliographic Data Processing), 93–94, 192–193, 240, 247
Bielsker, Richard, 83–84
Bill Display System, 121
Billings, John Shaw, 187
Biomedical Communication Network. *See* SUNY BCN
Biomedical Communications Network (BCN), 211–212
BIRD, 92
Bivans, Margaret M., 120, 307
Bixby, W. E., 319
Black, Donald V., 100, 102–103, 186–187, 190, 192, 196, 213–215, 219–221, 223, 225, 287–289, 358, 378, 383, 387, 395
Black, William T., 320
Blair, David C., 132
BLAISE (British Library Automated Information Service), 292
Blanken, R. R., 120, 132, 274, 322
Blankenship, Donald A., 185, 190, 195–196, 212, 221, 289
Blasik, Ray, 307
Bleier, Robert E., 28, 186
Bloemeke, Mary Jane, 96
Bloomquist, Harold A., 211, 260
BMI (Battelle Memorial Institute), 137, 315–320
Boilen, S., 17
BOLD, 2–3, 11, 29–35, 115
Bold, Eugene, 244
Bolt, Beranek, and Newman, 119
Booth, Michael, 116
Borgman, Christine L., 338
Borko, Harold, 22–23, 29–35, 96, 192
Borman, Lorraine, 94–95
Boston Globe, 304, 329
Bourne, Charles P., 4–5, 13–17, 88, 97, 137–138, 146, 165, 255, 270, 283–284, 322, 346, 375

Bower, C. A., 207
Bowman, Sally, 28, 30
Brain Information Service, 93
Brandhorst, Wesley Theodore (Ted), 112, 172–174, 286
Bregzis, Ritvars, 61, 79
Bremner, Joseph, 368
Brenner, Everett, 392
Bridegam, Willis E., 204, 260–262, 264–266, 268–270, 272
Bridges, D. B. J., 148, 152
Briner, L. L., 122
British Library, and MEDUSA project, 342
British Library Automated Information Service (BLAISE), 292
British Library Lending Division, 207–208
Brodman, Estelle, 197–198, 207, 259
Brooks, Albert A., 176, 180
Brooks, Wallace E., 54, 124
Brown, Carolyn P., 401
Brown, George W., 53
Brown, Herschel, 145
Brown, Jack E., 292
Brown, R. R., 103
Brown, Sanborn C., 44
Brown, William, 307
Brown, W. F., 340
Browning, Sandra, 75
BROWSER (Browsing On-Line with Selective Retrieval), 133–134
BRS (Bibliographic Retrieval Services, Inc.), 3, 296–297, 355–357, 360, 363–364, 366
Brugioni, Dino A., 239
Brunenkant, Edward, 176, 252
Bryant, J. H., 123
Buchanan, J. R., 252
Buckland, Laurence, 75
Buginas, Scott J., 111
Bunker, George, 56
Bunker-Ramo Corporation, 56–57, 141, 156–159
Burchinal, Lee G., 169–171, 224, 284, 311
Burger, John F., 24
Burke, Colin, 5, 66

Burket, Robert C., 190, 195–196, 221, 224, 289
Burnaugh, Howard P., 29–34
Burr, Stephan, 152
Burrows, J. H., 104–105
Bush, Vannevar, 20, 63
Byrne, Jerry R., 111

Cabe, Patrick A., 188–189
Cady, George M., 220–221
Cahill, Lysle, 245
Cain, Alexander M., 260–261, 263, 265, 273
Caldwell, Nancy W., 253
Camp, Joyce, 393
CAN/OLE (Canadian On-Line Enquiry), 329–330
Canada Institute for Scientific and Technical Information (CISTI), 329
Canfield, James H., 193–194
Caponio, Joseph F., 106, 253–254
Caputo, Anne S., 286, 357, 369–370, 377, 381, 392, 394–396, 398
Caputo, Richard, 369
Carlisle, James, 9, 250
Carlson, Chester, 319
Carlson, E. C., 123
Carlson, William T., 255, 340
Carnegie Corporation, 61, 63, 66
Carney, Homer C., 57
Carpenter, D. H., 108
Carroll, D. E., 79–80
Carroll, Kenneth, 144
Carter, B., 123
Carter, Launor F., 30, 185
Caruso, Dorothy E., 96
Carville, M., 91–92
CASI (Center for Aerospace Information), 307
Cataldo, Frank, 105
Cautin, Harvey, 77–78
CBC (Center for Biomedical Communications), 211
CCA (Computer Corporation of America), 107, 137
CDA (Copper Development Association), 196, 316
CDC computers, 15, 79–80, 82, 94, 100, 104, 110–111, 234, 351

CDMS (Commercial Data Management System), 102, 186
Cegala, L., 190
Center for Aerospace Information (CASI), 307
Center for Biomedical Communications (CBC), 211
Central Media Bureau, Inc., 236, 323
CFSS (Combined File Search System), 122–123
CFSTI (Clearinghouse for Scientific and Technical Information), 114
Chai, D. T., 187
Chaitin, Leonard J., 14
Chalice, Robert, 94
Chamberlin, Donald, 160
Chao, Jennifer, 304
Chartrand, Robert L., 55, 233
Chasen Lawrence I., 58
Chemical information searching, 40–41, 95–96, 289, 299–300
Chen, Simon P. J., 122
Cheney, A. G., 108
Chien, R. T., 79–80
Chomsky, Noam, 43
CICS (Customer Information Control System), 121, 130
CIDS (Chemical Information and Data System), 40
CIMARON, 90–91
CIRC (Centralized Information Reference and Control), 187–189
CIRCOL (CIRC-On-Line), 193–195
CISTI (Canada Institute for Scientific and Technical Information), 329
Citation analysis, 42
Cited reference searching, 43–44, 68–69
Clabby, William, 331
Clark, H. L., 122
Clarke, D. C., 136
Classification authority file, 71
Classification research, 29–33, 35, 69–71
Classroom instruction, 74, 77, 285. *See also* Training
Clearinghouse for Scientific and Technical Information (CFSTI), 114
Cleverdon, Cyril, 97, 203

CLR (Council on Library Resources), 48, 59, 61, 63–64, 66, 85, 102, 198, 230–231, 347
Cobbs, Sharon, 213
COBOL, 77, 203
Cochrane, Pauline A. *See* Atherton, Pauline
Coffman, Edward G., 6, 18
Cohen, Donald, 220–221, 222
Cohen, Morris L., 40
Coleman, Howard, 320–321
Coles, Victor L., 163, 167, 215
COLEX (CIRC On-Line Experiment), 3, 185, 189–193, 195, 209–210, 241–242, 259
COLINGO (Compile On-Line and Go), 105–106
Collins, George O., 104, 304
Color terminal displays, 243, 247
Columbo, David, 315
Communications networks. *See* Telecommunications networks
COMNET (Computer Network Corporation), 298
Computer Corporation of America (CCA), 107, 137
Computer Sciences Corporation (CSC), 219–221
COMRESS, Inc., 345, 347
COMSEARCH, 238
Conferences about online, 11, 101, 104, 163, 279
Connors, Thomas L., 105
Control Data Corporation, 127–128
CONVERSE, 28, 101–102, 148, 160
Convey, John, 3
Cook, Kenneth H., 75–77, 125
Coombs, Don, 171–173
Cooper, M. D., 284
Copper Development Association (CDA), 196, 316
Corbató, Fernando J., 17
Corbett, L., 108
Corbin, Harold S., 104
Cordaro, J. T., 80
Corey, Barbara, 180
Cornell University, Computer Science Department, 96–97
Cornelli, J. C., 190–191
Corning, Mary E., 204, 207
Cornog, Martha, 4, 366

COSATI (Committee on Scientific and Technical Information)
conferences, 101
demonstrations, 107, 136–139, 255, 340
film, 28, 137
Inventory, 28, 136–137
COSMIC (Computer Software Management and Information Center), 168
COSMIS (Computer Systems for Medical Information Services), 220
COSTAR, 108
Cottrell, Norman E., 318, 319
Council on Library Resources. *See* CLR
Covington, Mary W., 196, 316
Cox, J. W., 293
Cox, Kenneth A., 385
Cox Coronary Heart Institute, 106
Crager, Janet, 269, 271, 276, 294, 399, 401
Craig, James A., 57
Craveth, Swain, and Moore (CS&M), 127
Crawford, Thomas M., 369–371, 374, 377, 385, 391, 393–396
Crossley, William O., 18, 25
Crouch, Len, 239
Crow, Neil B., 110–111
Crowder, D., 239
Crowder, J. E., 186–189
Crowe, Jane, 116
CS&M (Craveth, Swain, and Moore), 127, 132
CSC (Computer Sciences Corporation), 219–221
CTC (Computer Technology Center, Union Carbide), 252
CTSS (Compatible Time-Sharing System), 41–42, 67
Cuadra, Carlos A., 3, 17–18, 102–103, 112, 181, 183, 185–190, 195–196, 212–215, 219–226, 287–289, 353–355, 358, 361, 371, 377–378, 382, 388, 393
Cuadra, Neil, 289, 354–355
Cuddihy, Robert, 379
Culkowski, A. H., 180, 307
Cummings, Martin M., 197–198, 201–204, 206–207, 211, 217, 291, 378–380
Cunningham, Jay L., 89
Curran, William J., 294

Currie, John D., 339
Customer support services
  personnel hiring, 368
  toll-free numbers, 375, 381
  troubleshooting, 381–382
  user guides and documentation, 372–373, 382–383
Cybernet Timesharing Ltd., 331

Daley, Robert C., 17
Damerau, Frederick J., 55, 123
Dancy, David J., 108–110
Darling, Louise, 203–204, 210, 269–270
Data Central, 3, 14, 137, 176, 240–248, 251–256, 304
Data Corporation, 129, 137–138, 176, 192, 236, 239–253, 255–257
Data Retrieval Corporation of America, 238
Database, 4, 279
Databases
  acquisition of, 366–368
  development of, 4
  licensing for, 367–368
  problems of, 389
  royalties for using, 361–363
DATACOM, 320
Dataroute, 352
DATATEXT, 82, 138, 263
Datatrol Corporation, 231
DATRIX (Direct Access to Reference Information: A Xerox Service), 70, 73, 112
DATUM (documentation automatique des textes juridiques de l'Université de Montreal), 234
Davis, J. E., 186–189, 239
Davis, Richard P., 232
Davis, Ruth M., 185, 209, 261–262
Davison, Wayne, 86, 343
Day, Melvin S., 156–157, 198
DDC (Defense Documentation Center), 31, 33–34, 112–120, 137, 336–337
DEACON (Direct English Access and Control), 57–58, 200
DeBakey, Michael E., 204
DEC computers, 351
Deemer, Selden, 43

Defence Scientific Information Service (DSIS), 338
Defense Documentation Center. *See* DDC
Defense Intelligence Agency (DIA), 241–242
Defense Technical Information Center (DTIC), 112–113
Del Bigio, Giampaolo, 341
Del Frate, Adelaide A., 165–167, 397
Delaney, Frances M., 112
DeLanoy, Diana, 84, 224
Dempsey, T. F., 48
Dennis, Bernard, 315
Dennis, Sally F., 231–232
Department of Justice. *See* DOJ
DeSimone, P. A., 28
Deutsche Institute für Medizinische Dokumentation und Information (DIMDI), 208
DeWath, Nancy A., 284
DeWitt, D., 123
DIA (Defense Intelligence Agency), 241–242
DIALIB (DIALOG in Libraries), 283, 398
DIALOG, 3, 34, 46, 137, 141–183, 226, 280–286, 354
DiFondi, Nicholas M., 188, 194
Digital Equipment computers, 41
Dilliman, Donald, 94
DIMDI (Deutsche Institute für Medizinische Dokumentation und Information), 208
Dimsdale, J. J., 88
DIRAC (Direct Access), 87
Dixon, P. J., 108
Dixon, Wilfred, 203
DM-1 (Data Manager-1), 107–108
DOBIS (Dortmund Bibliothek System), 342
DOC PROC. *See* DPS
Document Processing System (DPS), 74
Documentation, Inc., 163
DOCUS (Display Oriented Computer Usage System), 104
DOD (U.S. Department of Defense), 13, 112–114
DOE/RECON, 177–180, 180, 308
DOJ (U.S. Department of Justice), 127–129, 132, 141, 168, 181, 334–336
Dolby, James L., 91, 142–143, 148
Dominick, Wayne D., 94–95

Don, Peggy, 160
Donati, Robert, 182, 282, 368, 387
Dorney, Lindsay C., 211, 260
Dorr, James, 262
DOSIR (Department of State Information Retrieval), 223
Dovel, John A., 188, 193
Dow Jones News/Retrieval, 331
Doyle, Lauren B., 1–2, 11, 20, 22–24, 29, 185
DPS (Document Processing System), 74–75, 124–125, 193, 262–263, 267–268, 273–274
Drew, Daniel L., 46, 142–153, 162
Drew, Sally J., 284
DROLS (Defense RDT&E On-Line System), 116, 336–337
Drukey, Donald L., 30
DSIS (Defence Scientific Information Service), 338
DTIC (Defense Technical Information Center), 112–113
Ducrot J. M., 341
Duncan, C. Eugene, 142, 182
Duncan, Libby, 337
Durkin, Kay, 132, 275

Earl, Lois L., 142–143, 169
EARS (Epilepsy Abstracts Retrieval Service), 253–254
Easy English, 78
Eckert, Philip F., 112
Eckhardt, Keith, 160
Edmundson, H. P., 56
Egeland, Janet, 132, 261–263, 268–269, 271, 273–277, 294–297, 355–357, 395, 399
El-Hadidy, Bahaa, 337
El-Hadidy, Libby, 337
Elchesen, D. R., 110
ELDO (European Launcher Development Organization), 174
Eldridge, William B., 231–232
ELHILL, 213–217, 221–223, 289–293
Eli Lilly and Company, 340
Elias, Arthur W., 361, 376
Elmaleh, Joseph S., 40
ELMS (Experimental Library Management System), 134–136, 342–343

EMF. *See* Excerpta Medica Foundation
End users, 155, 167, 217–218, 302–303, 310–311, 316–317, 327, 397–398
Energy Research and Development Administration (ERDA), 180
Engelbart, Douglas C., 13–14
English Electric KDF9 computer, 108–109, 207–208
ENVIRON (Environmental Information Retrieval Online), 253
EPA (Environmental Protection Agency), 253
Epstein, A. H. (Hank), 86, 343
ERDA (Energy Research and Development Administration), 180
ERDA/RECON, 180, 308
ERIC (Educational Resources Information Center), 169–174, 224, 333
Erickson, Linda J., 370
Eriksson, A. M., 244
ESA/IRS, 306
ESRIN (European Space Research Institute), 305
ESRO (European Space Research Organization), 141, 174–175
ESRO/RECON, 174–175, 304–306
Estavan, D. P., 20
Estes, Ed, 152
EURONET, 305, 352
European Association of Scientific Information Dissemination Centers (EUSIDIC), 6, 368
European Launcher Development Organization (ELDO), 174
European Space Research Institute (ESRIN), 305
European Space Research Organization (ESRO), 141, 174–175
EUSIDIC (European Association of Scientific Information Dissemination Centers), 6, 368
Evaluation studies
  AIM-TWX, 16–218
  AUDACIOUS, 70–72
  COLEX, 192–194
  DDC Remote On-Line Retrieval System, 118–119
  DIALOG, 283
  DIALOG/ERIC, 172–173
  Intrex, 64–65

Evaluation studies (cont.)
    MEDLARS, 203, 322
    RECON, 158–159, 164–165, 167
    RIQS, 95
    SMART, 96–97
    SPIRES, 85
    SSIE, 255
    SUPARS, 76–77
Excerpta Medica Foundation (EMF), 120, 274–275, 322
EXPLICIT, 150–151

Falkenberg, Gören, 207
Fano, R. M., 42, 48
Farell, Jules, 22, 25, 27
Farr, Leonard, 27
Farris, Eugene H., 122
Fastrand Drum Memory, 50, 116, 158
Fay, Robert J., 126, 133, 313
Fayen, Emily, 2, 76, 78, 194, 215, 247, 249, 253, 318, 359
Federal Information Research Science and Technology (FIRST) Network, 136
Feinman, H. B., 238
Ferguson, Douglas, 86
FFS (Formatted File System), 123, 241
Fick, Len, 152
FID (International Federation for Documentation), 46–47
Fife, Dennis W., 83, 95, 110, 112, 288, 304, 310, 316, 337
Filleman, Walter, 231
Finserv Computer Corporation, 296
Firschein, Oscar, 142–143, 147, 283–284, 312
FIRST (Federal Information Research Science and Technology), 136
Firth, F. E., 11, 53
Fischer, Margaret T. (Peggy), 123, 325, 328
Fischler, M., 142
Fisher, Carl P., 238, 301, 303, 385
Fisher, Franklin M., 53
Fitzgerald, Michael P., 339
Fitzpatrick, W. H., 340
Flavin, James M., 122, 235, 238, 251

FLITE (Federal Legal Information through Electronics), 233, 336
Flynn, T., 341
Fong, Elizabeth, 83, 95, 110, 112, 119, 165, 193, 247, 279, 288, 304, 310, 316, 337
Forbes, Edward J., 350
Ford, D. F., 346
Ford Foundation, 230
Foreign Technology Division (FTD), 35
Foreman, Gertrude, 276, 294
Formatted File System (FFS), 241
FORTRAN programming language, 73–74, 82, 94, 109, 317, 338
Fossum, Earl G., 115
Foster, Willis R., 255, 340
Frank, Werner L., 104
Franks, Emory, 28
Franks, Winifred, 78
Franz, D. R., 259
Frazier, John P. I., 177
Fredkin, E., 17
Freeman, Janice Heyworth, 72, 88
Freeman, M. E., 340
Freeman, Robert R., 20, 34, 69, 70–73, 123, 180
FREESEARCH, 331
Fried, John, 9, 315, 317
Friedman, Stan, 126, 130
Frierson, E., 76
Frojmovic, Vivian, 89
Fry, Bernard M., 114
Frycki, Stephen J., 112
FTD (Foreign Technology Division), 35
Fujiwara, Shizuo, 100, 337
Fuller, T., 285
Fuller, W. D., 143
Funding for online research, 3–4, 8–9, 155–156, 408
Funding of project monitors, 11
Furman, Ronald, 73, 112
Furtado, Victor, 337
Furth, Steven E., 123–124, 127, 130–131, 211, 231, 233
Fussler, Herman H., 63, 342

Gabrini, Philippe J., 39
Galidos, Panos, 200
Garland, John L. (Jack), 233
Garrard, Richard F., 200, 202
Garvis, F. J., 204
GE. *See* General Electric Company
Gechman, Marvin C., 253
General Electric Company (GE), 46, 57–58, 137, 199–201, 203
General Purpose ORBIT, 35, 185, 195–196
George Washington University Graduate School of Public Law, 231
Gertsner, H. B., 298
Gielow, Kenneth R., 142, 147, 150, 152
Giering, Richard H., 123–124, 186, 192–193, 239–249, 251, 256–257, 300, 302, 304, 329
Giles, Shelly, 160, 280
Gillcrist, J. A., 308
Ginnow, Arnold O., 330
GIPSY (Generalized Information Processing System), 92–93, 341
GIS (Generalized Information System), 123, 241
Glass, R. D., 210
Globe and Mail, The (Toronto), 314
GNIS (Geographic Names Information System), 93
Gold, Dan, 144
Goldfarb, C. F., 125
Goldstein, Charles M., 119, 333
Goodwin, Nancy C., 105
Gorog, William F., 138, 236, 239, 242–244, 256
Gottfredson, Don M., 168
Gottschalk, Charles, 308
Gottsman, Edward J., 255, 257, 300, 303
Gove, N. B. (Woody), 178, 180, 308
Government funding. *See* Funding for online research
GPDS (General Purpose Display System), 30–34
GRACE (Graphic Arts Composing Equipment), 201–202
Grady, Carl R., 334
Graham, Kim, 369
Graham, Margaret H., 287
Grant, Francis L., 369

Grau, Albert A., 87
Gray, Harry J., 37–40
Gray, W. Alexander, 99
Graziano, Eugene E., 145–147, 146
Green, Hannah O., 132
Green, R. A., 329
Greengrass, Alan, 327, 364
Grunstra, Neale S., 96, 127–128
Gull, Cloyd Dake, 200, 201, 205, 219
Gupta, Udayan, 376
Guthrie, G. D., 342, 346

H. W. Wilson Company, 51
Haanstra, J. W., 53
Haber, Richard, 40
Haeuslein, G. Karl, 180, 307–308
Hahn, Trudi Bellardo, 5, 285
Haibt, Luther, 123
Haines, Edward C., 105
Haire, Gloria, 179
Hall, James L., 3, 108–110
Halpin, Roger F., 87–88
Hambleton, James E., 336
Hamilton, L. Clark, 121
Hamilton, V. V., 197
Hammerlin, Frank, 180
Hammond, William, 113, 231
Hammons, Charles, 180
Hampel, Viktor E., 9, 110–111
Harcharik, J. Robert, 299, 320–321
Haring, Donald R., 65
Harley, Anthony J., 98–99, 207–208
Harlin, Cathy, 130
Harm, Dwight, 195
Harman, R. Joyce, 63, 83
Harrington, William G., 4, 230, 235–236, 244–251, 256, 300–301, 330, 365
Harris, Richard, 4, 186, 363, 380
Hartner, E. P., 337
Harvard University Computation Laboratory, 96–97
Harvey, A. E., 98

Index 478

Harvey, R. W., 135
Hawkins, Donald T., 3, 396, 400
Hay, Richard, 94
Hayes, Robert M., 5, 49–51, 88, 134, 333
Heald, J. Heston, 113
Healy, M., 20
Heaps, Doreen M., 72, 88
Heaps, H. S., 88
Hecht, Kenney, 342
Heilik, James, 329–330
Hein, Morton, 136
Henderson, Madeline M. (Berry), 101, 253
Herner, Mary, 211, 260, 264
Herner, Saul M., 211, 264
Herrmann, William W., 25
Herron, A., 313–314
Hersey, David F., 255, 340
HEW (U.S. Department of Health, Education and Welfare), 49, 254
Hewitt, J. A., 348
Heyworth, Janice. *See* Freeman, Janice Heyworth
Higgins, L. D., 91–92
Hildreth, Charles R., 350
Hill, Helen N., 40–41
Hill, Lister, 197
Hillman, Donald J., 61, 80–82, 308–312
Hines, David L., 129
Hirschfeld, Lorraine G., 207
Hitachi HITAC computers, 100, 351
Hjerrpe, Roland, 175, 305
Hlava, Marjorie M. K., 156
Hodgson, Paul, 207
Hoffman, J. P., 190–191
Hogan, Rose, 206
Holmes, P. L., 292, 331, 342, 388
Holzbauer, Frederick W., 122
Honeywell computers, 107, 200–201, 204
Hoppenfeld, Elias C., 236
Horty, John F., 40, 229–233, 235, 238, 244
Houghton, Bernard, 3, 322
House of Commons Library, 108

Housman, Edward, 115, 375
Hsaio, David K., 39–40, 73
Hubbard, Anne. *See* Caputo, Anne S.
Hudson, J. A., 74
Hughes, Thomas E., 165–166, 176, 180
Hull, Cynthia, 187
Hummel, Donald J., 293, 298–299, 321
Humphrey, Allan, 89–90, 91
Humphrey, Suzanne, 132, 276, 294
Hunt, B., 340
Hutchins, J. W., 293
Hutton, F. C., 176
Hynek, J. Allen, 87
Hyslop, M. R., 123

IBM Corporation (International Business Machines)
 American Bar Foundation Project, 231–232
 computers, 11, 13–16, 18–19, 21, 24–26, 28–30, 35–36, 40–43, 59, 64–67, 70, 75, 78–79, 82–83, 87–88, 95–96, 98–99, 101–103, 105–107, 111–112, 115, 131–134, 142, 151–152, 162, 174, 178, 186, 194–196, 204, 207, 220–223, 229, 342–343, 351
 contract programming, 55
 contributions to SUNY BCN, 262, 267
 IR equipment and research, 52–55
 ITIRC (Technical Information Retrieval Center), 54–55, 126–127
 software development, 121–136
ICL Ltd. Computers, 91, 109–110, 208, 340
ICS (Information Control System), 103
ICSU/AB (International Conference on Scientific Unions/Abstracting Board), 368
IDC (Information Dynamics Corporation), 349–350
IDRC (International Development Research Centre), 332
ILO (International Labour Office), 111–112, 332
ILR (Institute of Library Research), 88–91
IMPLICIT, 150–151
Independence Foundation of Philadelphia, 63, 66
Info Globe, 331–332
InfoData Systems, Inc., 112
INFORM/360, 125–126
Informatics, Inc., 103, 108, 120, 163, 168, 253, 298–299, 307, 320–322, 333, 359, 364

Index   479

Information Bank, 3, 4, 322–329, 358, 363–364
Information Dynamics Corporation (IDC), 349–350
Information Retrieval System (IRS), 306
INIS (International Nuclear Information System), 341
INQUIRE, 73, 112
International Business Machines. *See* IBM Corporation
International Development Research Centre (IDRC), 332
International Federation for Documentation (FID), 46–47
International Labour Office (ILO), 111–112, 332
International Nuclear Information System (INIS), 341
International online access, 34–35, 64, 68, 165, 175, 177–178, 180
Intrex (Information Transfer Experiments), 48, 63–66
IP Sharp Associates, Ltd., 338
IPL-V programming language, 35
IRIS (Information Retrieval by Interactive Search), 340–341
IRS (Information Retrieval System), 306
Irvine, J. J., 338
Isaacs, Herbert H., 25
ISIS (Integrated Scientific Information System), 111–112, 332
Isner, Dale, 337
Isotta, Noel E. C., 174–175, 177, 305–306, 371
ITIRC (IBM Technical Information Retrieval Center), 54–55, 129
Ivie, Evan L., 42, 63, 146

Jack, Robert F., 307
Jackson, Eugene B., 123
Jacobs, C. R., 118
Janda, Kenneth, 93–94
Japan Information Center of Science and Technology (JICST), 332
Japanese Ministry of Education, 337
Jedwabski, Barbara, 343
Jenkins, Grace T., 203, 206
Jenkins, Lawrence H., 115, 118, 337
JICST (Japan Information Center of Science and Technology), 332
Johnson, K. Jeffrey, 96, 127–128
Johnson, Robert, 307

Johnson, T., 78
Johnston, D. A., 244
JOIS (JICST Online System), 332
Jones, Clara, 52
JOVIAL programming language, 21, 24, 31, 35, 190
JURIS (Justice Retrieval and Inquiry System), 168, 181, 233, 334–336

Kallenbach, Peter A., 174–175, 305
Kalo, Carl, 200
Kannan, Kay L., 298, 300, 321
Kapowitz, Harry, 73, 112
Kappler, Melvin O., 17
Karolinska Institutet, 207, 292–293
Kasarda, Andrew J., 82, 310
Kaskey, Gilbert, 115
Kasson, Madeline S., 138, 255
Kastner, Margaret, 123
Katajapuro, L., 128
Katter, Robert V., 9, 19, 29, 185–186, 190, 196, 211–214, 216, 220–223, 289, 293, 391
Katzer, Jeffrey, 75–77, 125
Kaufman, Samuel, 53–55, 126–129, 130
Kays, Olaf, 92–93
Kayton, Irving, 232
Keen, E. M., 97
Keenan, Stella, 62
Kehl, William B., 230
Kelley, K. C., 79–80
Kellogg, Charles H., 101–102
Kelly, Michael, 321
Kennedy, John F., 197
Kent, Allen, 96, 326, 337
Kenton, David L., 195–196, 221, 293
Kerr, Breen, 158
Kershaw, G. A., 186–189, 239
Kessler, Myer M., 2, 42–48, 62–63, 69, 146
Kessler, Ronald, 42, 46
Ketelhut, Robert, 123
Kidd, E. M., 176, 252
Kilgour, Frederick G., 4, 146, 201, 211, 260, 267, 344–348

Index   480

King, Donald W., 71, 72, 75, 193–194, 253, 341
King, Gilbert W., 53, 142, 145, 260
Kirsch, Russell A., 47–48
Kissman, Henry M., 289, 297–300
Klass, Philip J., 239
Klein, Sheldon, 20–21, 23
Klingbiel, Paul H., 118
Knapp, Sara D., 4
Knoke, P. J., 73
Knox, J. Douglas, 199
Knudson, Donald R., 63, 65
Koenig, Michael E. D., 272, 275, 286–287, 309, 312, 345, 378–379, 397, 399
Kolbe, Helen K., 391
Kollegger, James G., 4, 362–363, 367
Kollin, Richard, 362
Komoto, David T., 320
Kondos, George S., 155, 335–336
Kovacs, Helen, 260
Kozumplik, William A., 144, 146, 152
Krevitt, Beth I., 341
Kripalani, Naresh, 89
Krulee, Gilbert K., 87, 94
Kugel, Peter, 63–66
Kuhn, Thomas, 6
Kunii, Tosiyasu L., 100, 337
Kunkel, Barbara, 280, 402
Kurtz, Peter, 333
Kusik, Robert L., 63, 66
KWIC (keyword-in-context), 44, 93, 135, 243, 247
KWOC (keyword-out-of-context), 93

LABSEARCH, 90
LACONIQ (Laboratory Computer Online Inquiry), 143, 151–153
LaMar, D. M., 73
Lambert, Roger H., 334
Lancaster, F. Wilfrid, 2–3, 76, 78, 194, 202–203, 206, 215–218, 247, 249, 253–254, 318, 359, 397
Landau, Robert M., 136, 138, 255, 318–319, 359, 390–391
Landauer, W., 38
Landgraf, A. L., 346
Lang, F., 341
Lange, R. T., 152
LAPD (Los Angeles Police Department), 25–27
Larson, S., 330
Lathrop, J. W., 195–196
Law Research Service, 236–238
Lawford, Hugh, 122, 126, 313–314, 329, 332, 360
Lawrence, Barbara, 287, 309, 376, 384, 390, 397
Lawrence Livermore Laboratory (LLL), 110–111
LAWSEARCH, 40, 234
Lawyer's Center for Electronic Legal Research (LCELR), 235
Lazorick, Gerald J., 122, 263
LC (Library of Congress), 73, 103, 121–122, 168, 339
LCELR (Lawyer's Center for Electronic Legal Research), 235
LEADER (Lehigh Automatic Device for Efficient Retrieval), 80–82
LEADERMART, 82, 308–312
Leblanc, Eric S., 329
Lederberg, Joshua, 171
LEEP (Library Education Experimental Project), 74
Lefkowitz, David, 37–39, 40, 41
Legard, Lawrence K., 346
Leggett, John, 40
Lehigh University, 308–312
Lehigh University Center for Information Sciences, 80–82
Leiderman, Eugene B., 346
Leiter, Joseph, 198, 205, 207, 212, 219, 222, 261–262, 291, 295
Lemasters, Clinton, 116
Lemon, Richard, 321
Lesk, Michael E., 5, 97
Leslie, C., 340
Lesser, M. L., 53
Levinson, Leslie H., 234
Lew, Kenneth M., 160, 162–163, 280, 366
Lewis, Chester, 325
Lewis, Robert F., 203
LEXIS, 3, 94, 236, 257, 300–304, 336, 364–365

Index 481

Leyman, Edward, 211, 264
Liang, M., 68
Libbey, Miriam, 260
Library 21 exhibit, 48–49
Library of Congress. *See* LC
Library technical processing, 102, 342–343
Library/USA, 42, 49–52, 158
Lickhalter, Richard A., 28
Licklider, Joseph C. R., 5, 15, 17, 48, 62–63, 105
Lieberman, Irving, 49
Light pen, 15, 28, 30–33, 80, 86, 105–106
Lincoln Laboratory (MIT), 42
Link, David T., 230
Linn, William, 92
Lipetz, Ben-Ami, 346
LISP programming language, 23
LISR (Line Information Storage and Retrieval), 333
Lister Hill Center for Biomedical Communications, 209, 211
LISTS (Library Information System Time-Sharing), 102, 186
LITE (Legal Information through Electronics), 230, 232–233, 335
Litofsky, B., 40
Litwin, Samuel, 37
LLL (Lawrence Livermore Laboratory), 110–111
Loan, Robert, 73, 112
Lockheed Missiles and Space Company, 3, 137–139, 141–183, 252, 285–286
Lockheed Retrieval Service, 173, 181–183, 226, 280–286, 354, 358–359
Logan, Timothy, 86
Loges, E. G., 186–189, 239
Long, Philip L., 344–346
Long, R. E., 24
Long, Raymond J., 231
Long-distance demonstration of online searching, 15
Longgood, William, 323, 326
Longyear, Christopher R., 57
Los Angeles Police Department (LAPD), 25–27
Losee, Madeline W., 163, 165, 335
Lowe, Thomas C., 77–78, 104, 107, 333

LUCID, 28–29, 101, 137
Ludwig, Herbert R., 87
Luedtke, John R., 308
Luhn, Hans Peter, 30, 144
Luke, Ann W., 103
Lunin, Lois F., 211, 260
Lynch, Mary Jo, 401
Lyons, John C., 231

McAllister, A. Stratton, 343
McAllister, Caryl K., 135–136, 342–343
McCabe, Diana Fitch, 251
McCabe, LeRoy B., 25, 27
McCarn, Davis B., 9, 124, 185, 193, 205, 209–216, 218–225, 261, 272, 291, 376, 378, 386
McCarthy, J., 17
McCarthy, William E., 233
McCauley, Ellen V., 119, 337
McClure, Lucretia, 264, 268, 274, 277, 356–357
McConlogue, Keren L., 20–23
McEwin, B. W., 207
McGinnis, Linda L., 114
McHugh, Conal, 168
McIsaac, Donald N., 334
Maciuszko, K. L., 344
Mackay, E., 234
MacKinnon, Ron, 297
McKie, James W., 53
McNamara, A. B., 67–68
McNamara, John, 75
McSweeney, James, 245
MADAM (Moderately Advanced Data Management), 18
Mader, Irene, 306
Madnick, Stuart E., 152
Magnino, Joseph J., 53–55, 124, 126–130, 229
Maier, Joan M., 401
Main, W. F., 142, 145
Malhijsen, A., 322
MALIMET (Master List of Medical Indexing Terms), 120
Mallow, C. S., 233

Mangio, Charles A., 188, 194
Manke, Richard B., 53
Mann, A. R., 331
Manola, Frank, 40, 73
MARC (Machine-Readable Cataloging), 73–74, 79, 103, 261, 345–346, 349–350
Marcus, Richard S., 5, 9, 44, 63–66
Marketing online services
  advertising, 282–283
  competition, 376–380
  demonstrations, 390–392
  documentation and promotional materials, 371–374
  personal communication, 374–376
  pricing, 249, 251–252, 266–267, 284, 291, 294, 296, 299, 310, 357–361
  surveying potential users, 282, 370–376
Markey, Karen, 285
Markowitz, T., 340
Markuson, B. E., 100
Maron, M. E. (Bill), 88–91, 132
Marovitz, William F., 366
Marron, Beatrice A., 83, 95, 110, 112, 288, 304, 310, 316, 337
Marron, Harvey, 139, 170, 340
Marshek, James, 84
Martel, Franklin, 73
Marthaler, Marc, 111
Martin, Gordon P., 48, 49
Martin, J. W., 112
Martin, M. D., 357
Martin, Thomas H., 13–14, 66, 83, 94, 132, 224, 279, 305, 308, 316, 326, 333, 343, 402
Martin, W. A., 174
Martinez, Samuel J., 338
Martins, G., 56
Martinson, John L., 211, 260
Maruyama, L. S., 339
Marzocco, F. N., 30
Massachusetts Institute of Technology. *See* MIT
MASTER CONTROL, 110–111
Masuda, Takashi, 100
Mathews, William D., 9, 42–48, 63, 69, 146

MATICO (Machine-Aided Technical Information Center Operations), 141, 144–145, 148
Mattison, E. M., 62
Maxon-Dadd, Jo, 341
MDC (Mead Data Central), 235, 249–252, 256–257, 365
Mead Corporation, 245–246, 251, 254–255, 303–304
Mead Data Central (MDC), 235, 249–252, 254, 256–257, 300–304, 365
Mead Technology Laboratories (MTL), 257, 303–304
Meadow, Charles T., 4–5, 55, 138
MEDDOC, 340
Medical Library Assistance Act, 204–205, 211
MEDLARS (Medical Literature Analysis and Retrieval System), 198–201, 208–209, 219–223
  regional centers, 261
MEDLINE, 3, 222–223, 276, 289–295, 354, 360, 365
MEDUSA, 98–99, 341
Mehnert, Robert B., 207, 293
Meinhardt, David J., 178
Meister, David, 158–159, 162, 164
Melton, Jessica S., 230
Mercier, Marcel, 72
Mercier, William, 393–394
Meredith, Joseph C., 89–90
Merendini, E., 186–189, 239
Mermin, Samuel, 232, 236, 238
Merrill, Roy D., 143, 147
Merritt, C. Allen, 124
Mersel, Jules, 187
Merwin-Daggett, Marjorie, 17
META/LISPX programming language, 101
Meyerhoff, Erich, 204, 260–262, 264–266, 268–270, 272
Miche Company, 238
Mick, C. K., 284
MICRO (Multiple Indexing with Console Retrieval Options), 35–37
Microform storage, 19, 36–37, 62, 106, 158, 161, 187, 231, 281, 325–326, 339
Middleton, Mike, 293
Mignon, Edmond, 90
Miles, Wyndham D., 203, 209, 219–220, 222
Miller, Betty, 280, 402

Miller, K. B., 72–73
Miller, K. C., 298
Miller, Peggy, 368
Milligan, Karen, 161
Mills, R. G., 44
Milne, Mary, 40
Minker, J., 123
Minor, William H., 121
MIT (Massachusetts Institute of Technology), 41–48, 62–69
  James M. Barker Engineering Library, 63–64
  Lincoln Laboratory, 42
  Mechanical Engineering Department, 66–69
  School of Engineering, 63
Mitchell, David S., 230
Mitchell, Herbert F., 49, 57, 156–159, 162
Mitchell, P. C., 98
Mitchell, Robert, 160, 384
Mitchell, William, 159
Mitre Corporation, 104–106, 137
Mittman, Benjamin, 9, 94–95
Mizoue, J. K., 210
Moell, Patricia, 76
Moghdam, Dineh, 326
MOLDS (Managerial On-Line Data System), 73
Molholm, Kurt N., 337
Moll, Wilhelm, 216, 295
Montague, Eleanor, 84, 343, 369
Moody, D. W., 92
Moore, William H., 29, 30
Morgan, P., 340
Morgan, Robert T., 29, 232
Morrill, Charles S., 105
Morrissey, John H., 150
Morrissey, Marlene, 150, 334
Mortell, Hilma, 84
Morton, L. H., 48
Mosher, E. J., 125
Motobayashi, Shigeru, 100
MTL (Mead Technology Laboratories), 257, 303–304
Mulhauser, Gerd, 174
Multhouse, William, 180

MULTICS (Multiplexed Information and Computing Service), 41
Multilist, 36–41, 70, 78, 112, 118, 234
MUMS (Multiple Use MARC System), 339
Murdock, John, 315–318, 363, 371, 390
Murdock, Lindsay, 401
Musson, W., 136

NAL (National Agriculture Library), 282
Nance, John William, 194–196
NASA (National Aeronautics and Space Administration), 58, 141, 153, 156–168, 174, 185, 333
NASA/RECON, 3, 57, 104, 156–168, 191, 306–307, 335
Nash, Mary M., 314
National Aeronautics and Space Administration. *See* NASA
National Agriculture Library (NAL), 282
National Bureau of Standards (NBS), 47, 101
National Cancer Institute, 41
National Center for Automated Information Retrieval (NCAIR), 301
National Council on Crime and Delinquency (NCCD), 168
National Federation for Abstracting and Indexing Services (NFAIS), 6, 368
National Heart Institute (NHI), 199
National Institute of Neurological Diseases and Blindness (NINDB), 93
National Institute of Neurological Diseases and Stroke (NINDS), 254
National Lending Library (NLL), 207–208
National Library of Australia, 293
National Library of Medicine. *See* NLM
National Research Council Computation Centre, 329
National Science Foundation. *See* NSF
National Science Library (NSL), 291–292
National Technical Information Service (NTIS), 115, 182, 281
Naval Postgraduate School, 100
NBS (National Bureau of Standards), 47, 101
NCAIR (National Center for Automated Information Retrieval), 301

NCCD (National Council on Crime and Delinquency), 168
NCR (National Cash Register), 120, 315–501
Neel, Peggy W., 193–194
Nees, Monica, 132
Negishi, Masamitsu, 100, 337
Negotiated Search Facility (NSF), 136
Negus, Alan E., 92, 99, 108–110
NELINET (New England Library Information Network), 345, 347
Neufeld, M. Lynne, 4, 366
Neurology database experiment, 210–211
New England Library Information Network (NELINET), 345
New York State Bar Association (NYSBA), 235, 251
New York Times Information Bank, 322–329
NFAIS (National Federation for Abstracting and Indexing Services), 6, 368
NHI (National Heart Institute), 199
Niblet, G. B. F., 109
Nichols, A. J., 142, 149, 152
NIH (National Institutes of Health), 106, 230
NINDB (National Institute of Neurological Diseases and Blindness), 93
NINDS (National Institute of Neurological Diseases and Stroke), 254
Nissen, W. I., 48
Nitecki, J. Z., 348
NLL (National Lending Library), 207–208
NLM (National Library of Medicine)
  BCN, 211–212
  competition with, SDC, 377–380
  contributions to, SUNY BCN, 261–262
  funding agency, 86, 185, 276
  international partners, 207–208, 292–293
  MEDLARS development, 197–199, 208–209, 219–222
  MEDLINE, 289–295
  regional search centers, 203–207
  user charges, 365
Nolan, J. J., 11, 53
Nordyke, P., 103
North, Jeanne B., 138, 255
North American Rockwell Corporation, 103

Northern Colorado Educational Board of Cooperative Services, 333
Northwestern University, 93–95
Norton, T. R., 40
Nottingham University, 208
Novell, Monroe, 163
November, Robert, 325
NSF (National Science Foundation), 29, 42, 47, 59, 61–63, 66, 69, 80, 82–83, 85, 95–96, 175, 211, 283–284, 310–311, 326
NSF (Negotiated Search Facility), 136
NSL (National Science Library), 291–292
NTIS (National Technical Information Service), 115, 182, 281
NYSBA (New York State Bar Association), 235, 251

OBAR (Ohio Bar Automated Research), 3, 235–236, 244–245, 248–252, 255–256, 300
OCLC, 4, 320, 344–348
Oettinger, Anthony, 300
Office of Naval Research. *See* ONR
Office of Scientific and Technical Information. *See* OSTI
Office of Technical Services (OTS), 113
Ogg, Jay, 123
OGRE (Oil and Gas Reports, Electronic), 231
Ohio Bar Automated Research (OBAR), 235–236
Ohio State Bar Association, 235–236, 244–245, 251
Ohio State University, 342
Ohta, Miwa, 197, 207
Ojala, Marydee, 328
Okabe, Kenji, 100, 337
Oklahoma State University, 229
Olney, John C., 22
Olson, Thomas, 334
On-Line Review, 279
Online, 4, 279
Online public access catalogs. *See* OPACs
Online searching techniques
  adjacency, 54, 131
  Boolean operators, 46, 58, 71, 78, 82, 92, 146, 154–155, 217, 268
  cited reference searching, 43–44, 68–69
  full-text searching, 16, 236, 243, 248–249, 301

Index 485

major/minor descriptors, 68, 112, 118
phonetic searching, 91
stem searching, 44–45
stringsearching, 288, 293
term weighting, 27, 98, 118
truncation, 44–45, 214, 246, 289
wild card characters, 45, 246
word proximity searching, 128–129, 230, 230–231, 246, 302
word root searching, 44–45
Online system features
  abstracts available, 170–171
  bilingual access, 234, 314–315, 330, 332, 338–339
  classification number display, 213
  document ordering, 158, 214, 288
  duplicate record removal, 68
  help, 131
  hierarchical displays, 31–32, 39, 71, 86–87, 99, 105, 118, 213
  highlighting of terms, 247, 298
  multi-file access, 163, 241
  multilingual access, 234, 314–315, 330, 332, 338–339, 341
  natural language processing, 20–25, 57–58, 71, 78, 80–82, 96, 101–102, 134, 309–310, 313–314
  ordering source documents, 158
  output display format, 16
  posting counts, 32–33, 98
  question-answering, 20–24, 28, 57–58, 87, 101, 104–105, 150–151
  relevance ranking of output, 26–27, 34, 37, 98, 131, 191, 195, 214
  remote searching, 15
  saved searches, 44–45, 76, 131, 150, 284
  status report message, 26
  stop word lists, 16, 288, 317, 405
  stored searches, 306
  synonym processing, 26, 32, 68, 99, 246
  thesaurus display, 32–34, 67–68, 98, 99, 269
  time windows, 190–191, 224, 287–288, 289, 329, 351
  uppercase and lowercase letters, 129, 170, 238, 311
ONR (Office of Naval Research), 29, 38–39, 56, 59
Onsi, P. W., 261
ONTAP (Online Training and Practice), 285
ONULP (Ontario New Universities Library Project), 79
OPACs (online public access catalogs), 79, 135–136, 350

Opello, Olivia, 401
Opler, A., 40
Oral history techniques, 5
ORBIT, 3, 185, 196–197, 210–217, 221–224, 269, 288
ORBIT Search Service. *See* SDC Search Service
ORVYL, 83
OSIRIS (On-line Search Information Retrieval Information Storage), 106–107
OSTI (Office of Scientific and Technical Information), 61, 91, 99, 108, 207–208
OTS (Office of Technical Services), 113
Overhage, Carl F. J., 61, 63, 66, 69, 83
Owen, Jeanne M., 2, 3
Owen, K. C., 112

PACER (Program Assisted Console Evaluation and Review), 57, 108
PADAT (Psychological Abstracts-Direct Access Terminal), 253
Paisley, William J., 170–171, 173–174
Palmer, Linda, 357
Palmer, Lloyd G., 132, 267, 275, 277, 296–297, 355–356
Park, B. R., 18
Parker, Edwin B., 9, 23, 61, 82–86, 149
Parker, John, 56–57
Parker, Ralph, 344
PASS (Petroleum Abstracts Search System), 338
Patent Office In-House System, 107
Patent searching, 133–134
Pauly, David, 285
Payne, Charles T., 342
Payne, Gregory, 367
Pearson, Karl M., 186, 213, 221–222, 289, 293
Peel, Bruce B., 329
Pelosi, S. J., 261
Peluso, Sal D., 12
Pemberton, Jeffrey K., 4–5, 238, 245, 270, 286, 303, 323–326, 328, 331, 341, 358, 361–363, 367, 375, 390–391
Penniman, William David (Dave), 315, 319
Penry, J. Kiffin, 106, 253–254

Perriens, Matthew P., 133
Personal Documentation System, 87
Peterson, T. I., 125
Pfizer Pharmaceuticals, Inc., 272–273, 275, 286–287, 345, 399
Pharmaceutical Manufacturers Association. *See* PMA
Philco 2000 computer, 35
Phillips, David, 86
Phillips, Theodore D., 122
Photon Company, 201–202
PIRETS (Pittsburgh Information Retrieval System), 337–338
Pitts, William, 169
Pittsburgh Chemical Information Center, 96
Pizer, Irwin H., 4–5, 75, 122–123, 125, 204, 211, 218, 259–270, 272–273, 276–277, 295–297, 355–356, 366
PL 360 computer, 86
Pl/1 programming language, 83, 112, 160, 196, 288
Planning Research Corporation (PRC), 108
Plemens, Ray, 180
Pletzke, Chester, 293
Plowden-Wardlaw, Thomas C., 235
PMA (Pharmaceutical Manufacturers Association), 215, 225, 275, 286, 355, 378–380
POLLS (Parliamentary On-Line Library Study), 109
Pool, Ithiel de Sola, 63
Porter, Roger J., 106, 253–254
Powell, James R., 322
Powell, Robert F., 253
Power, D. Lee, 339
Powers, Joseph M., 118, 119, 352
Powers, Ruth V., 40–41
Poyen, J., 368
PRC (Planning Research Corporation), 108
Preparata, F. P., 79–80
Preston, James F., 235–236, 244–245, 247–248
Prevel, James, 170, 173
Prewitt, Barbara, 309, 312
Price, Charles E., 176, 180, 252
Pricing. *See* Marketing online services
PRIME (Planning through Retrieval of Information for Management Extrapolation), 54, 127, 133

Programmatics, 137
Project MAC, 41–42, 47–48, 62
Project OGRE (Oil and Gas Reports, Electronic), 231
Project POTOMAC (Patent Office Techniques of Mechanized Access and Classification), 107
Protosynthex, 11, 20–24
Provenzano, Dominic, 4, 256, 323, 326, 352, 356–357
Pryor, Harold E., 156, 307
Prywes, Noah S., 37–40, 70, 188
Pugh, Emerson W., 11

QL Systems, 72, 313–315, 332
QL/Search, 314–315
Quake, Ronald P., 273, 275, 277, 295–297, 355–357, 399
Queen's University, 313–314
Queen's University of Belfast Department of Computer Science, 91–92
QUIC/LAW, 125–126, 313–314, 360
Quigley, Donald, 194
QUIKTRAN, 55, 82, 150
QUOBIRD (Queen's University On-line Bibliographic Information Retrieval and Dissemination System), 91–92
QUUP (Query and Update), 101, 186

RADC (Rome Air Development Center), 35, 38, 48, 53, 56–57, 59, 73–75, 77, 104, 107–108, 189
RADC System, 104
RADCOL (RADC Automatic Document Classification On-Line), 333
Radwin, Mark S., 152–153, 160, 168–169, 173, 182, 280, 352, 361, 387
Rae, Patrick D. J., 125, 267, 270
Raitt, David I., 174–175
Raizada, A. S., 306
RAMAC (Random Access Method of Accounting and Control), 11
Ramo, Simon, 56, 156–157
Ramo Wooldridge, 56
RAND Corporation, 17, 29, 220, 226
Rankin, Kirk, 83, 95, 110, 112, 288, 304, 310, 316, 337

Rapid Search Machine, 137
Rapp, Fredericka, 77–78, 78
Rapport, Richard L., 254
Rastogi, K. B., 346
Rather, J. C., 339
Raucher, V. L., 186
Ravi, C., 90
Rawson, Richard, 56
Ray, G., 87
Ray, S. R., 79–80
RCA computers, 78, 106, 145
RDT&E (research, development, test, and evaluation), 114
Rea, R. H., 116
Reactive Catalogue, 79
Real English, 78
Recon Central, 239–242, 253, 254
RECON (Remote Console), 3, 141, 156–159, 156–168
Reed, D. M., 82
Reed, Mary Jane P., 350
Rees, Alan M., 97
REFSEARCH, 90
Regan, Peter H., 260
Reintjes, J. Francis, 63, 65
Reiter, Allen, 149, 152
Reitman, Walter, 92
Remote On-Line Retrieval System, 116–120
REQUEST, 79–80
Resnick, Mark, 107
Resnikoff, Howard L., 142–143, 148
RETRO, 338–339
RETROMEDUSA, 342
RETROSPEC, 331
Reynolds, P., 79–80
Rhydwen, David A., 314
Richmond, Phyllis, 133
Rickman, Jon T., 98
Riddle, Jane T., 166–167, 396–397
Riddle, William, 84
Riddles, A. J., 133
Ridenour, Louis N., 53

Rigby, Malcolm, 70
RIMS (Remote Information Management System), 94
RIOT (Retrieval of Information by On-line Terminal), 108–110
RIQS (Remote Information Query System), 94
RIQSONLINE, 95
RISC (Remote Information Systems Center), 209
Roach, John P., 18–20
Roach, Roger A., 66–69
Roalof, Robert, 239
Roberge, James K., 65
Roberts, David C., 104, 107, 333
Roberts, Larry, 352
Roberts, R. Bruce, 92
Robins, W. Ronald, 229–230, 232, 238
Robinson, Jo, 180, 283–284
Robison, H. R., 142, 169
Rocchio, Joseph J., 96–97
Rogers, Frank B., 2, 197–200, 202–206, 212, 289, 291, 397
Romanenko, A. G., 132, 341
Rome Air Development Center. *See* RADC
Romerio, Giovanni F., 175
Root, Eugene, 145
Rosen, Sheldon A., 223, 391
Rosenstein, Philip, 399
Rosenthal, Abraham M., 323, 328
Rothman, John, 322–329, 364
Rouse, Sandra, 367
RTIS (Remote Terminal Input System), 115–116
Rubens, Linda, 287
Ruberti, Robert N., 188, 194
Rubin, Jerome S., 235, 239, 246–250, 256–257, 300–303, 335, 364, 385
Rubinoff, Elayne R., 78
Rubinoff, Morris, 61, 77–78
Ruecking, F. H., 346
Ruhl, Mary Jane, 287
Rush, James, 344
Rushbrook, Audrey E., 314, 332
Ryerson, William R., 182, 281

SABIRS (Selected Automatic Bibliographic Information Retrieval System), 100
Sable, Jerome, 107, 123
SAFARI, 106
SAGE (Semi-Automated Ground Environment), 11, 17, 20, 30, 42, 226
Salford University, 208
Saline, Lindon, 200
Salton, Gerard, 5, 62, 96–97, 151, 206
SARA (Storage and Retrieval Alberta), 87–88
SATIRE (Semi-Automatic Information Retrieval), 11, 18–20, 240
Satterfield, C. D., 145–146, 148
Sauvain, Richard W., 92
Savage, Terry, 144
SCANNET, 352
Schafer, Marilyn E., 332
Schatz, S., 100
Scheffler, Frederic L., 132, 194
Scheidecker, Paul, 233
Schick, Gordon, 280
Schieber, William D., 89, 111, 332
Schmidt, Charles T., 100
Schmidt, Karen A., 50
Schneider, Richard B., 211, 264
Schoene, William J., 24
Schon, Donald A., 113–114
Schreur, Harm K., 231
Schrier, Robert, 73, 112
Schultheisz, Robert J., 298, 300, 321
Schultz, Claire K., 113, 199–200
Schwarcz, Robert M., 24
Schwartz, Jules I., 16, 18, 21
Schwarzlander, H., 72
Schwimmer, H. S., 186
Science Information Association (SIA), 317–320
Scientific Resources Corporation, 108
Scientific and Technical Information Facility (STIF), 104, 162–163, 307
SCORPIO (Subject-Content-Oriented Retriever for Processing Information Online), 339
Scott, Francis, 339

Scott, T. W., 341
Scroggins, John L., 194–195, 210–211
SDC Search Service, 4, 224–227, 286–289, 353–355, 358–359, 364, 378–380
SDC (System Development Corporation), 3, 11, 17–37, 101–103, 137–138, 181, 185–227, 294, 353–355
SDI (selective dissemination of information), 44–45, 88, 95–96, 108, 124, 194
SDS computers, 79, 108
SDS (Space Documentation Service), 174–175, 305–306
Seastrom, Dale E., 86–87
See, Richard, 187
Seiden, Herbert R., 108, 125, 196, 212
Semple, Parlan, 123
Semturs, Friedrich, 132
Sessions, Vivian S., 122, 123
Settles, Warren P., 320
Sewell, Winifred, 198–199, 206
Shaffer, B., 123
Shaffer, S. S., 36
Shaw, C. G., 98
Shaw, Ralph R., 202
Shawley, James, 194
Shayer, Sidney, 152
Sheehan, P. M., 62
Sheldon, Robert C., 66–69
Shepard, Richard F., 329
Shepherd, Clayton A., 113, 123
Sherman, Donald, 90–91
Sherman, Neil, 224
Sherr, Bonnie, 40
Shiban, J. R., 186
Shiner, George, 53
Shoffner, Ralph M., 88–89
Shoultz, Dexter C., 160, 280
Showalter, A. K., 106
Shumway, Norman, 202
SIA (Science Information Association), 317–321, 364
Sieburg, Jack, 233
Sigma computers, 79, 351
Silver, S. S., 89–90

Simmons, Ralph A., 209, 211, 220
Simmons, Robert F., 20–24, 28–30, 34–35, 43, 57, 80, 185
Sinopoli, Albert B., 108
Sisson, Roger L., 211, 264
Skelly, Stephen J., 234
Skye, Steve, 126, 130
SLA (Special Libraries Association), 49
SLAC (Stanford Linear Accelerator Center), 83–84
Slifko, S. D., 346
Sloan, Lynda W., 122, 123
SMART, 80, 96–97
Smith, Bev, 75, 355–356
Smith, Elizabeth S., 414
Smith, Francis J., 91–92
Smith, James L., 35–37, 188–192
Smith, John, 322
Smith, Kent A., 293
Smith, Sidney L., 105
Smith, William D., 27
Smithers, Peter R., 338
Smithsonian Science Information Exchange (SSIE), 255, 339–340
Snyder, Linda S., 272, 355
Snyderman, Martin, 340
SOLAR, 45, 98
SOLER (System for On-Line Entry and Retrieval), 77–78
Sophar, G. J., 175
Sorenson, Paul, 87
Southwestern Legal Foundation, 230–231
Space Documentation Service (SDS), 174–175, 305–306
Special Libraries Association (SLA), 49
Spiegel, Isabel, 269, 271, 276, 294, 399, 401
Spiegel, J., 105
Spierer, Monroe M., 18, 25, 29, 35, 101, 193
Spigai, Frances D., 29, 66, 357, 369, 374, 390, 395–397
SPIRES (Stanford Public Information Retrieval System), 82–86, 343–344
Sprowl, James A., 303, 330
Spuck, Dennis W., 334

SRI (Stanford Research Institute), 11–17, 129, 170, 246
SSIE (Smithsonian Science Information Exchange), 255, 339–340
Stahl, F. A., 79–80
STAIRS (Storage and Information Retrieval System), 127–132, 194, 268–269, 273–275
Stalder, Ernest W., 255, 340
Standera, Oldrich, 128
Stanford Linear Accelerator Center (SLAC), 83–84
Stanford Research Institute. See SRI
Stanford Research System, 86–87
Stanford University Institute for Communication and Research, 82–87
Stanford University libraries, 343–344
Stangl, P., 346
Stark, M. R., 148
Starke, A. C., 123
Starker, Lee N., 112
Steenblock, Nancy, 81
Steil, Gilbert, 106
Stein, Jerome D., 112
Stentzel, James, 286
Stern, B. T., 120, 132, 274, 322
Stevens, B. A., 396
Stevens, Charles H., 66
Stevens, N. D., 206
Stevens, R. Lawrence, 162, 233, 320, 335
STIF (Scientific and Technical Information Facility), 104, 162–163, 307
Stiles, H. Edmund, 231
Stiller, Joy D., 269
STIMS (Scientific and Technical Information Modular System), 163
Stone, Duane, 78, 189
Storie, J. Michael, 95
Stovel, Madeline (Leny), 86, 343
Stratakos, S. M., 73
Stromer, P. R., 143
Struminger, Leny, 128
Sullivan, Dennis J., 158–159, 162, 164
Sulzberber, Punch, 325
Summers, John K., 105

Index

Summit, Roger K., 9, 20, 137, 139, 141–182, 224–225, 280–286, 312, 320, 361–362, 366–367, 369, 374
Sundeen, Donald H., 123
SUNY BCN (State University of New York Biomedical Communication System), 3–4, 26, 77, 191, 210, 218, 259–277, 291, 355–357
SUPARS (Syracuse University Psychological Abstracts Retrieval Service), 45, 74–77, 170
SURC (Syracuse University Research Corporation), 73
SURF (Support of User Records and Files), 14, 18
Sussenguth, E. H., 97
Sutherland, Ivan E., 28
Suwa, Shusaku, 332
Swank, Raynard, 88
Swanson, Donald, 56
Swanson, Rowena W., 195
Sweeney, James, 92–93
Sweeney, Joan, 402
SYMBIOSIS (System for Medical and Biological Sciences Information Searching), 262
Synthex, 20, 22, 25–26, 80
Syracuse University, 69–77
Syracuse University Research Corporation (SURC), 73
Syracuse University School of Library Science, 70, 73–74
System Development Corporation. *See* SDC

Taine, Seymour I., 198–200, 202, 209
Takahashi, Nobumasa, 100
Takahasi, Hidetosi, 100, 337
Talbott, G. Douglas, 106
Tally, Roy D., 333–334, 392
Tanaka, Richard I., 142, 145–148
Tancredi, Samuel A., 182, 281
Taube, Mortimer, 217
Taulbee, Orrin E., 187–188
Taylor, Betty, 234
Taylor, K. F., 346
Taylor, Robert W., 5, 48
TDIS (Terminal Data Input System), 115–116, 119
TDMS (Time-Shared Data Management System), 29, 102–103, 105, 137, 186–187

Teicher, S. N., 65
Telecommunications networks, 4, 282, 385–389
TELENET, 289, 297, 352, 361, 387
Teletypewriter terminals, 15, 18, 25–26, 30–32, 40–41, 43–44, 57–58, 83
Telex network, 43, 67, 68
Terminal TEXT-PAC, 130
Terry, Edward, 62
Tessier, Judith, 74, 125
TEXT-PAC, 54–55, 96, 126–130
TEXTIR, 24–27
Thomas, Alvin L., 92
Thomas, S. M., 188, 239
Thompson, David A., 9, 86–87
Thompson, Frederick B., 57–58
Thompson, George K., 111
Thompson, W. B., 123
Thompson Ramo Wooldridge (TRW), 56–57
Thornton, Carl L., 188–189
Timbie, Michele, 171–173
Time, Inc., 123–124
TIMPS (Technical Information Management and Planning System), 253
TIP (Technical Information Project), 2–3, 11, 39, 42–48, 51, 62–63
TIP (Toxicology Information Program), 297–300
TIPS (Tulane Information Processing System), 92
TIRP (Textile Information Retrieval Project), 66
TITUS (Traitement de Textile Universelle et Selective), 341
Tocatlian, Jacques, 332, 341
Todd, Judy, 283
Todeschini, C., 132, 341
Tomberg, Alex, 4
TOOL-IR (University of Tokyo On-Line Information Retrieval System), 337
TORQUE, 137
Toxicology Information Program (TIP), 297–300
TOXICON (Toxicology Information On-line Conversational Network), 168, 298–299
TOXLINE, 299, 321
Tozawa, Yoshio, 100, 337

Index   491

Training, 65, 76, 250, 284–285, 287, 291, 302, 375, 392–395, 398
Transaction log analysis, 76
Trapani, J., 338
Travis, Irene, 90
Tressel, George, 137
Trester, D. J., 170
Treu, Siegfried, 96, 188
Trezza, Alphonse F., 48, 50
Troy, Frank J., 244–245
Trump, Lynn H., 77, 125
TRW (Thompson Ramo Wooldridge), 56–57
TSIR-1 (TODAI Scientific Information Retrieval System, 1st version), 100, 337
TSS (Time-Sharing System), 15, 17–18, 36, 101, 190–191
TWX (TeletypeWriter Exchange Network), 41, 43, 67, 212–219
TYMNET, 223, 286, 289, 292, 298, 319, 352, 361, 386–387

U.K. Atomic Energy Authority. *See* UKAEA
U.S. Air Force (USAF). *See* AF
U.S. Army Edgewood Arsenal, 40–41
U.S. Army Research Office, 77–78
U.S. Atomic Energy Commission. *See* AEC
U.S. Census database, 28
U.S. Department of Commerce, 69
U.S. Department of Defense (DOD), 13, 112–144
U.S. Department of Health, Education and Welfare (HEW), 49, 254
U.S. Department of Justice. *See* DOJ
U.S. Department of State, 223–224
U.S. Department of Transportation, 95
U.S. Forest Service, 98
U.S. Naval Material Command, 106–107
U.S. Office of Education. *See* USOE
U.S. Patent Office, 107
Uber, Gordon, 142, 152
UDC (Universal Decimal Classification), 69–72, 88
UKAEA (United Kingdom Atomic Energy Authority), 71, 108–110

UKCIS (United Kingdom Chemical Information Service), 208
UNESCO, 306
Union Carbide, 252
United Kingdom Atomic Energy Authority. *See* UKAEA
United Kingdom Chemical Information Service (UKCIS), 208
UNIVAC Corporation, computers, 41, 48, 50, 113, 116, 116–117, 119, 199, 237, 351
Universal Decimal Classification (UDC), 69–72, 88
University of Alberta, Department of Computing Science, 87–88
University of California-Berkeley, Institute of Library Research, 88–91
University of California-Los Angeles, 93
University of Chicago, 342
University of Dortmund, 342
University of Florida, College of Law, 234
University of Illinois, Coordinated Science Laboratory, 79–80
University of Iowa, College of Law, 233–234
University of Manitoba, Faculty of Law, 234
University of Michigan, 92
University of Montreal, 234
University of Newcastle upon Tyne, 98–99, 208
University of Oklahoma, 92–93
University of Pennsylvania, 77–78
University of Pennsylvania Law School, 40, 234
University of Pennsylvania Moore School of Electrical Engineering, 37–41, 77–78
University of Pittsburgh
  Computation and Data Processing Center, 230
  Health Law Center, 229–230, 232–233
  Knowledge Availability Systems Center (KASC), 337
University of Pittsburgh, Department of Chemistry, 95–96
University of Pittsburgh, Hillman Library, 326
University of Tokyo, 100, 337
University of Toronto, 79, 348–349
University of Tulsa, 338
University of Virginia, Medical Library, 216
University of Washington, Urban Data Center, 95

University of Wisconsin, School of Education, 334
USAF (U.S. Air Force). *See* AF
User groups, 166, 280, 284, 288, 293–294
Users of online services, 396–403. *See also* End users
Ushimaru, Mamoru, 100, 337
USOE (U.S. Office of Education), 61, 74, 83, 85–86, 89, 141, 170, 173, 224, 230
UTLAS (University of Toronto Library Automation Systems), 79, 348–349

Vaden, William M., 176–177, 180, 252, 308
Vagianos, Louis, 52
Valko, E. I., 68
Vallee, Jacques F., 87
Valley Forge Library, 58
Van Camp, Ann J., 4–5, 218, 261, 266, 269, 275, 277, 295, 297, 355–357, 376, 383, 392, 399
van der Walle, Frans, 274
van der Walle, R., 120
Van Hoesen, Mary J., 401
Van Meter, Clarence T., 40, 41
Vann, James O., 113
Vann, Peter J., 256–257
VARDIS (Variable Display), 30
Veaner, Allen B., 86, 343–344
Veit, Ivan, 325
Velazquez, Harriet, 349
VEREAD (Value Engineering Retrieval of Esoteric Administrative Data), 121
Verheijen-Voogd, Christine, 322
Vestal, Allan D., 233
Vinken, Pierre J., 120, 274
Vinsonhaler, John F., 412
Vitagliano, V. J., 123
Vlahopoulis, Kathy, 337
Volino, R. L., 232
von Briesen, Richard, 313–314
Vorhaus, Alfred H., 30, 186
Vredenberg, Robert, 200

Wade, John A., 110–111
Wainio, E. A., 123
Waite, David P., 349–350
Walden, W. E., 98
Walker, C., 288, 316
Walker, Donald E., 3, 101, 106
Walker, Donald F., 298, 300, 321
Walker, Justin C., 95, 110, 112
Walker, Richard D., 308
Wallace, Everett M., 18
Wallace, Lane E., 113
Waller, E., 190
Walsh, John, 364
Walsh, T. B., 230
Wanger, Judith, 100, 186, 189, 224–225, 287, 392
Warheit, Israel Albert, 63, 122–123
Warren, Peter A., 120, 274
Washington Library Network (WLN), 350
Washington State University, 98
WATDOC, 72
Watt, James, 199
Webster, Victoria A. D., 322
Wedgeworth, Robert, 48, 52
Weil, Ben H., 287, 392
Weil, Henry, 324, 326–327
Weinberg, Paul, 40
Weinstock, Melvin, J., 211, 260, 264
Weissman, Clark, 16, 18
Welch, John T., 188
Welch, Noreen O., 28, 107, 137, 169, 186, 255
Wenk, Ernest A., 168
Wente, Van A., 154, 156–158, 161–164, 166, 176, 252, 307
WESRAC (Western Research Application Center), 320
West, Barbara, 369
West, Marty, 369–370
West Publishing Company, 248, 301, 303, 330
Westat Research, Inc., 341
Western Kentucky University Library, 122
Western Research Application Center (WESRAC), 320
Western Reserve University, 230
WESTLAW, 303, 313, 315, 330–331
Wexler, Philip, 300

Whaley, F. R., 123
Wheeler, Daniel D., 92
Whelan, E. K., 108
White, John F., 77–78
White, R. O., 129
Whitely, Robert B., 142, 146–148
Whitman, David, 86
Wild, A. E., 341
Wilde, Daniel U., 161, 398
Wiley, R. G., 73
Wilkins, Thomas B., 233
Wilkinson, W. D., 56
Williams, John H., 133–134
Williams, Martha E., 367, 380
Williamson, Robert E., 97
Wills, Robert D., 18, 25, 29, 35, 101, 186, 193
Wilson, H. Donald, 250, 255–257, 300–301
Wilson, Robert A., 229–231
Winik, Ruth, 135–136
WIRE (Wisconsin Information Retrieval for Education), 333–334
Wisconsin Department of Public Instruction, 334
WISE (Wisconsin Information System for Education), 333–334
Wixon, D. W., 115
WLN (Washington Library Network), 350
Wolf, Paul L., 87
Wolfe, Theodore, 63, 116, 118–119, 165–167
Wolters, Peter, 329
Wood, Barbara L., 193–194
Woodard, Robin L., 302–303
Woods, W. A., 118
Woodsmall, Rose Marie, 214–215
Woody, Charlene A., 339
Wooley, Jon H., 123
Wooster, Harold, 137
World's Fair (1962 Seattle), 48–49
World's Fair (1964 New York), 49–52
WPAFB (Wright-Patterson Air Force Base), 94, 187–195
WUIS (Work Unit Information System), 114, 116

Wyckoff, John A., 344
Wyman, John, 74

Xerox Corporation, 70, 73

Yamamoto, Takeo, 100, 337
Yates, John G., 341
Yeates, Elizabeth J., 401
Yount, S. Leon, 176, 252, 308

Zais, H. W., 320
Zappert, Fred, 280
Ziehe, T. W., 108, 123, 186
Zimmerman, Barry, 38
Zimmerman, Walter, 297
Zipf, Alfred, 220